Law and Society

The International Library of Essays in Law and Legal Theory
Series Editor: Tom D. Campbell

Schools

Natural Law, Vols I & II *John Finnis*
Justice *Thomas Morawetz*
Law and Economics, Vols I & II *Jules Coleman and Jeffrey Lange*
Critical Legal Studies *James Boyle*
Marxian Legal Theory *Csaba Varga*
Legal Reasoning, Vols I & II *Aulis Aarnio and D. Neil MacCormick*
Legal Positivism *Mario Jori*
American Legal Theory *Robert Samuel Summers*
Postmodernism and Law *Dennis Patterson*

Law and History *David Sugarman*
Law and Language *Fred Schauer*
Sociological Theories of Law *Kahei Rokumoto*
Rights *Carlos Nino*
Law and Psychology *Martin Lyon Levine*
Feminist Legal Theory, Vols I & II *Frances Olsen*
Law and Society *Roger Cotterrell*
Contemporary Criminological Theory *Francis T. Cullen and Velmer S. Burton Jr.*

Areas

Criminal Law *Thomas Morawetz*
Tort Law *Ernest J. Weinrib*
Contract Law, Vols I & II *Larry Alexander*
Anti-Discrimination Law *Christopher McCrudden*
Consumer Law *Iain Ramsay*
International Law *Martti Koskenniemi*
Property Law, Vols I & II *Elizabeth Mensch and Alan Freeman*
Constitutional Law *Mark V. Tushnet*
Procedure *D.J. Galligan*
Evidence and Proof *William Twining and Alex Stein*
Company Law *Sally Wheeler*
Privacy, Vols I & II *Raymond Wacks*
Lawyers' Ethics *David J. Luban*
Administrative Law *D.J. Galligan*

Child Law *Harry D. Krause*
Family Law, Vols I & II *Harry D. Krause*
Welfare Law *Peter Robson*
Medicine and the Law *Bernard M. Dickens*
Commercial Law *Ross Cranston*
Environmental Law *Michael C. Blumm*
Conflict of Laws *Richard Fentiman*
Law and Religion *Wojciech Sadurski*
Human Rights Law *Philip Alston*
European Community Law, Vols I & II *Francis Snyder*
Tax Law, Vols I & II *Patricia D. White*
Media Law *Eric Barendt*
Labour Law *David L. Gregory*
Alternative Dispute Resolution *Michael D.A. Freeman*

Legal Cultures

Comparative Legal Cultures *Csaba Varga*
Law and Anthropology *Peter Sack*
Hindu Law and Legal Theory *Ved Nanda*
Islamic Law and Legal Theory *Ian Edge*
Chinese Law and Legal Theory *Michael Palmer*
Socialist Law *W. Butler*
Common Law *Michael Arnheim*

Japanese Law and Legal Theory *Koichiro Fujikura*
Law and Development *Anthony Carty*
Jewish Law and Legal Theory *Martin P. Golding*
Legal Education *Martin Lyon Levine*
Civil Law *Ralf Rogowski*

Future Volumes
African Law and Legal Theory and Cumulative index.

Law and Society

Edited by

Roger Cotterrell

Professor of Legal Theory and Dean of the Faculty of Laws,
Queen Mary and Westfield College, University of London

Dartmouth
Aldershot · Singapore · Sydney

Published by
Dartmouth Publishing Company Limited
Gower House
Croft Road
Aldershot
Hants GU11 3HR
England

British Library Cataloguing in Publication Data
Law and Society. – (International Library
of Essays in Law & Legal Theory)
  I. Cotterrell, Roger II. Series
  340.115

ISBN 1 85521 496 2

Printed in Great Britain by Galliard (Printers) Ltd, Great Yarmouth

Contents

PART III LAW AND THE PRODUCTION OF SOCIAL UNDERSTANDINGS

PART IV LAW AND THE STRUCTURING OF COMMUNITIES

Acknowledgements

The editor and publishers wish to thank the following for permission to use copyright material.

Academic Press Limited for the essay: Richard L. Abel (1981), 'Conservative Conflict and the Reproduction of Capitalism: The Role of Informal Justice', *International Journal of the Sociology of Law*, **9**, pp. 245–67.

American Anthropological Association for the essay: Sally Engle Merry (1986), 'Everyday Understandings of the Law in Working-Class America', *American Ethnologist*, **13**, pp. 253–70.

American Sociological Association for the essays: E. Bittner (1967), 'The Police on Skid-Row: A Study of Peace Keeping', *American Sociological Review*, **32**, pp. 699–715; Stewart Macaulay (1963), 'Non-Contractual Relations in Business: A Preliminary Study', *American Sociological Review*, **28**, pp. 55–67.

Blackwell Publishers for the essays: Doreen McBarnet (1981), 'Magistrates' Courts and the Ideology of Justice', *British Journal of Law & Society*, **8**, pp. 181–97; Alan Norrie and Sammy Adelman (1989), '"Consensual Authoritarianism" and Criminal Justice in Thatcher's Britain', *Journal of Law and Society*, **16**, pp. 112–28.

The Journal of Legal Studies for the essay: Donald J. Black (1973), 'The Mobilization of Law', *Journal of Legal Studies*, **2**, pp. 125–49.

Law and Society Association for the essays: William L.F. Felstiner (1974), 'Influences of Social Organization on Dispute Processing', *Law & Society Review*, **9**, pp. 63–94; William L.F. Felstiner, Richard L. Abel and Austin Sarat (1980–81), 'The Emergence and Transformation of Disputes: Naming, Blaming, Claiming...', *Law & Society Review*, **15**, pp. 631–54; Lawrence M. Friedman and Robert V. Percival (1976), 'A Tale of Two Courts: Litigation in Alameda and San Benito Counties', *Law & Society Review*, **10**, pp. 267–301; Abraham S. Blumberg (1967), 'The Practice of Law as Confidence Game: Organizational Cooptation of a Profession', *Law & Society Review*, **1**, pp. 15–39; Marc Galanter (1974), 'Why the "Haves" Come Out Ahead: Speculations on the Limits of Legal Change', *Law & Society Review*, **9**, pp. 95–160; William M. O'Barr and John M. Conley (1988), 'Lay Expectations of the Civil Justice System', *Law & Society Review*, **22**, pp. 137–61; Tom R. Tyler (1988), 'What is Procedural Justice?: Criteria Used by Citizens to Assess the Fairness of Legal Procedures', *Law & Society Review*, **22**, pp. 103–35; David M. Engel (1984), 'The Oven Bird's Song: Insiders, Outsiders and Personal Injuries in an American Community', *Law & Society Review*, **18**, pp. 551–82. Reprinted by permission of the Law and Society Association.

Series Preface

The International Library of Law and Legal Theory is designed to provide important research materials in an accessible form. Each volume contains essays of central theoretical importance in its subject area. The series as a whole makes available an extensive range of valuable material which will be of considerable interest to those involved in the research, teaching and study of law.

The series has been divided into three sections. The Schools section is intended to represent the main distinctive approaches and topics of special concern to groups of scholars. The Areas section takes in the main branches of law with an emphasis on essays which present analytical and theoretical insights of broad application. The section on Legal Cultures makes available the distinctive legal theories of different legal traditions and takes up topics of general comparative and developmental concern.

I have been delighted and impressed by the way in which the editors of the individual volumes have set about the difficult task of selecting, ordering and presenting essays from the immense quantity of academic legal writing published in journals throughout the world. Editors were asked to pick out those essays from law, philosophy and social science journals which they consider to be fundamental for the understanding of law, as seen from the perspective of a particular approach or sphere of legal interest. This is not an easy task and many difficult decisions have had to be made in order to ensure that a representative sample of the best journal essays available takes account of the scope of each topic or school.

I should like to express my thanks to all the volume editors for their willing participation and scholarly judgement. The interest and enthusiasm which the project has generated is well illustrated by the fact that an original projection of 12 volumes drawn up in 1989 has now become a list of some 60 volumes. I must also acknowledge the vision, persistence and constant cheerfulness of John Irwin of the Dartmouth Publishing Company and the marvellous work done in the Dartmouth office by Mrs Margaret O'Reilly and Sonia Hubbard.

TOM D. CAMPBELL
Series Editor
The Faculty of Law
The Australian National University

Introduction: The Law and Society Tradition

Roger Cotterrell

I

In legal studies in the English-speaking world 'law and society' does not designate a unified field of scholarship, a distinct subject or an academic discipline. It is a label for very varied researches which need to be categorized in this special way only because of pervasive failures of imagination in traditional legal scholarship. 'Law and society' is a special category because, typically, legal studies have analytically separated law *from* society, treating it in isolation from the systematic study of its social settings. 'Law and society' encompasses rather unfocused claims influenced by many different theoretical and disciplinary traditions in the social sciences. The claims are that the social significance of professionalized law – the doctrine, institutions and practices with which lawyers work – cannot be assumed without further inquiry; and that the extent to which law is significant must be judged using the empirical methods of social science.

Nowadays this label is attached to many kinds of social research on law. Finding a central core of meaning in 'law and society' involves identifying basic assumptions that have influenced the development of law and society research (even if these assumptions have often been explicitly or implicitly repudiated by particular authors). We need to think initially in terms of formative outlooks which established the law and society tradition but which many contemporary researchers might be anxious to disown, or at least de-emphasize.

Law and society research developed from demands for systematic information about modern law's actual or potential impact on social conditions. Coupled with this was the need for a clearer, more explicit analysis of law's role and capacities as an instrument of social control, direction or guidance. Insofar as law has been increasingly seen by lawyers and legislators as a policy instrument, much law and society research was originally encouraged and inspired by the dilemmas and responsibilities of modern law's policy-setting and policy-implementing roles. 'Law and society' initially found its niche in the world of funded research by holding out the prospect of reliable policy-relevant findings in a legal environment in which policy argument might otherwise seem at risk of getting out of control – at least, out of the control of lawyers' professional legal knowledge. 'Law and society' offered useful knowledge for a legal world increasingly dominated by policy concerns. The price of this help was that legal specialists (legal advisers, lawmakers, law interpreters and law enforcers) should accept that knowledge of positive legal doctrine was incomplete and inadequate without supplementation by empirical research on the social conditions which law presupposes or purports to address.

Thus, 'law and society' refers, in its original core meaning, to a reaction against narrow legal orthodoxies. It does not propose a specific theoretical or practical agenda to *supersede* traditional legal scholarship. Although it has many antecedents in various kinds of social studies of law, it is the product of a particular time and place in which law's key role as a policy instrument became widely recognized. 'Law and society' emerged as a specific movement in research in the United States on the foundations of pioneer work during the 1950s and became clearly institutionalized with the Law and Society Association, founded in 1964, and the *Law and Society Review*, published on behalf of the Association continuously since 1966. From its beginnings, the movement and its specific institutions were explicitly multi-disciplinary. Although most of those who founded the Law and Society Association were sociologists, no effective claim was made as the movement established itself that any particular social science discipline was uniquely suited to remedy the inadequacies of lawyers' legal understandings (Levine 1990, pp. 9ff). The law and society enterprise, from its modern origins until now, has provided a meeting place for all disciplines within the human and social sciences. Membership in this open club required nothing more than an empirical 'social' focus of some kind on some legal matter, usually interpreting the concept of law in a sense familiar to lawyers, for example as judicial decisions and doctrine, legislation or the practices of legal professionals. But, as will be seen, researchers in law and society have often also adopted characterizations of law that do not privilege the practices, knowledges and institutions of lawyers' law or state law, but extend the concept of law to embrace other normative systems.

In Britain, and in some other countries, the term 'socio-legal studies', current since the late 1960s, is an almost exact equivalent of 'law and society', similarly implying multi-disciplinarity. Important law and society research has also been done in many Western countries within the ambit of criminology, which has almost always operated as a loose coalition of contrasting disciplinary approaches. But in Europe the term 'law and society' has been less often used to categorize social research on law than terms importing specific disciplinary or theoretical commitments. For example, much of what has been done in the way of empirical inquiry about the social character and impact of contemporary law has been labelled 'sociology of law' outside the United States.

Sociology of law does not need to be (and should not be) considered a subdiscipline of academic sociology, tied in its destiny to the dominant concerns of its parent discipline and parasitic on theoretical developments in academic sociology (Cotterrell 1986). Nevertheless, the term 'sociology' in sociology of law firmly couples this area of legal scholarship to a broad, long-established intellectual tradition of sociological inquiry; a tradition with complex, rich and ambiguous theoretical resources and an extensive historical accumulation of debates on method and on epistemological questions relating to social research. The sociological tradition, in this very broad sense, is not the tradition of a distinct, professionally defined, specialized academic discipline of sociology. The idea of a 'sociology of law' invokes sociology, not as a discrete intellectual discipline, but as a tradition of thought and a storehouse of theory, data and methods. It declares it to be, in this sense, of *special* importance to legal inquiries. The uncompromising assertion is that legal study *requires* the intellectual resources of the sociological tradition, and is inadequate and limited in its vision without them.

In general, through most of its modern development, the law and society movement has not competed directly with lawyers and legal philosophers in explaining the character of legal knowledge, ideas or doctrine. It has often accepted as 'the legal' only what legal professionals themselves typically recognize as the practices or institutions of law. It has not usually tried to displace lawyers' conceptions of law. By contrast, sociology of law as an enterprise always contains these kinds of imperialistic ambitions, at least potentially. This is so even though they must be pursued with a determination to understand, appreciate and reinterpret legal participants' legal knowledge and experience. Broadly speaking, 'law and society' has opted for theoretical eclecticism and catholicity of methods and has avoided ranking intellectual disciplines in terms of their explanatory power. Its concern has been to supplement lawyers' interpretations of the world in ways that could be considered useful by legal professionals, legislators and law enforcers, as well as by citizens needing to orient themselves towards this professional world of law. The predominant emphasis has been on producing empirical social research to serve this need.

Law and society research has proliferated as funding for this research has grown. That in turn has been a consequence of the successful claim by those involved in law and society studies that their inquiries are potentially practically useful; practical, that is, in the sense of helping to make legal processes more efficient, to make their effects more predictable, or to link them better with the problems, interests and experiences of citizens and agencies that are seen as their targets or special concerns.

The word 'and' in 'law and society' is therefore no insignificant conjunction. It implies a fundamental, taken-for-granted analytical *distinction* between law and the society it regulates. The original slogan of the movement was not 'law *in* society', which might presuppose eventually a rethinking of the very nature of law in social terms. 'Law and society' enshrined, in the architecture of the original concept, the idea of law impacting on a social world outside itself and receiving inputs from this social world (Silbey and Sarat 1987, p. 172). The concept of law itself was usually left to be defined by lawyers as specialists in legal ideas, or else based on common sense assumptions about existing structures of government. 'Law' was treated as a professional or political 'given'.

II

If 'law and society' has a core, it is still probably in the exploration of relationships between the practices, institutions and doctrine of law, as lawyers and lawmakers understand these, and the social contexts to which these are intended (again by lawyers and lawmakers) to relate. For this reason, a too definite divide has been maintained between doctrinal legal research, pursued by legal scholars according to lawyers' criteria of legal relevance, and social scientific law and society research. Lawyers in advanced Western societies have tried, with increasing difficulty during the 20th century, to maintain an analytical separation between what they see as issues of policy on the one hand, and issues of legal principle on the other, the latter involving rationalization of the unifying, stabilizing value structures of legal doctrine. Insofar as this policy–principle dichotomy has been maintained, it has been possible to marginalize much law and society work as only indirectly relevant to legal debates, insofar as these are understood as lawyers' debates on matters of principle.

Nevertheless, as research on law's social functions, social origins and social effects has become more ambitious and sophisticated, law and society research has increasingly suggested the inadequacy of orthodox juristic conceptions. Relatively recently, the law and society movement has developed a sustained attack across a broad front on lawyers' most central assumptions about the nature and scope of law.

For example, it has done this by recovering and developing pluralist conceptions of law from anthropology and early sociology of law which assert that normative systems unrecognized by lawyers as legal systems must in fact be given the name 'law', and hence that lawyers' typical assumptions about the doctrinal essence or limits of law are problematic. It has done so also by linking law and society concerns with those of critical, feminist and ethnic minority legal scholarship to reveal that legal principles, and even the most basic components of legal rationality, are often founded on the shifting sands of social or political contingency. With these developments 'law and society' is finally shedding the limitations of the 'and' in its name. Its concern is with law *in* society. It has become, in its most central fields of research activity, part of the long international tradition of theoretically ambitious sociology of law.

To claim that the expansion of the law and society movement's horizons has been gradual is certainly not to suggest that law and society work in general, even in its earliest phases, adopted an atheoretical outlook. 'Law and society' has established itself academically because its predominantly empirical work has had significant theoretical implications which have inspired the interest of later researchers. Good empirical work was assumed, in the most influential practices of the American law and society movement from its beginnings, to be capable of yielding (and required to yield) theoretical insights. But the emphasis on detailed empirical study, reflecting the dominant outlook of American social science, has meant that the broad perspectives of classic social theory, which are typically a major foundation of the less empirical tradition of European sociology of law, have been more peripheral to the American law and society tradition as it has developed through the second half of the 20th century.

The situation is changing rapidly. Recent engagements with macro-theory have forced a reconsideration of the empirical traditions of the law and society movement, spurring intense debate about the conditions of validity of empirical socio-legal research (Trubek 1984; Trubek and Esser 1989; Sarat 1990; Esser and Trubek 1990), about the limitations and achievements of the law and society movement itself (Levine 1990; Friedman 1986; Macaulay 1984) and about appropriate relationships between socio-legal researchers' aims and the demands of policy-makers and policy-implementers (Sarat and Silbey 1988).

The title of this book suggests, then, a somewhat nebulous area, but it also indicates what has been and remains a vibrant, exciting, enriching and illuminating enterprise of very diverse social research. 'Law and society' should be understood today as a project of demystifying law in action and, in a sense, recapturing it from the professional monopoly of lawyers, judges, legislators and administrators so as to return it to public view, revealing law in a new light in the many social settings where ordinary citizens encounter its professionalized doctrine and practices.

Sometimes the self-conscious professionalization of social science imported into law and society researches has obscured this public view, encouraging an esoteric technicality that prevents these researches from reaching a wide, non-professional audience. Nevertheless, the potential for overcoming such constraints exists and derives primarily from the law and society movement's multidisciplinary character. Being the preserve of no single recognized academic discipline and drawing its strength from the communication of research ideas between scholars representing widely contrasting intellectual traditions, 'law and society' demands, and has been built on, the effort to communicate ideas beyond particular professional communities. It exemplifies the possibilities of productive interdisciplinary research. It suggests, at least in its aspirations, a radical, stimulating and necessary weakening of disciplinary prerogatives as part of the continual broadening of perspectives on social experience.

III

Within this diversity, fundamental shared characteristics unify the best work in the law and society tradition. First is a respect for *rigour in empirical enquiry*. The greatest strength of law and society research has been its capacity to produce pictures of the social world of law whose plausibility depends in large measure on their depth and detail of observation. Outstanding law and society scholarship uses rigorous research methods in unobtrusive ways. Like good social research in other fields, it follows a finely judged path in matters of method. It shows a careful concern with methodology that inspires confidence in the systematic character of the observations of experience presented. At the same time, it ensures that a concern with research methods and their justification does not obscure the power and immediacy of findings through the manner of their presentation. Proper methodological caution should not cramp the scholar's imagination in pursuing the kind of insights and ideas for which no research manual can prescribe a means of discovery.

Method is also a matter of local appropriateness rather than universal correctness. The essays included in this book show many different approaches to empirical inquiry. They range from the explicit use of elaborate quantitative methods, through reliance on ethnographic accounts and the systematic presentation of observational data, to more generalized references to history and social experience. A recognition of the possible validity of many different approaches to the production and presentation of knowledge of the social world of law implies much about what 'science' in law and society studies must be taken to mean. Social science has often been considered to have, as its essential methodological hallmark, the aim of *testing* – the testing of hypotheses to determine in some way their truth or (more modestly) their falsity. But much important inquiry has been largely and perhaps arbitrarily excluded from the scope of this positivistic social science. Certainly, social science in law, as in other research fields, can conduct tests of experience in certain ways. But in law and society work, no uniform and detailed protocols of scientific method are properly applicable to all kinds of research.

Much that is included in this book is not concerned with testing hypotheses about law and society. Much of it is concerned with representing certain experiences of 'the legal' that are no more 'true' or 'false' than is the colour of the landscape seen from a certain vantage point and at a certain time of day. Yet the portrayal of these 'colours' of law enables us to see as though we looked through the observer's eyes, and thus to appreciate new perspectives on the legal landscape. Methodological positions in social science are the basis of particular perspectives on the social world and of particular ways of confronting and interacting with it. The diversity of these positions is a reflection of the radical diversity of possible perspectives on social life. The plausibility of methods of empirical inquiry and interpretation is mainly established through the confrontation and comparison of these perspectives.

A second unifying characteristic of the best law and society work is a sceptical, persistent *intellectual curiosity*. This curiosity may direct attention to aspects of modern law that appear almost trivial to lawyers but turn out to be pivotal when the social consequences of regulation are in focus. With such characteristics, outstanding law and society work often shocks to some degree, revealing a sometimes disturbingly disordered or problematic social reality which demands recognition alongside what lawyers may portray as orderly patterns of systematized legal professional knowledge. The subject-matter of empirical research is often the common-places of professional legal experience. The power of research is in its capacity to reveal the commonplace as uncommon, or the legally trivial as socially important; to show that the 'common sense' of legal practices actually requires explanation and, often, justification or reform. Equally the power of research may lie in its capacity to show that what to lawyers or lawmakers are the uncommon, even pathological, features of legal processes or practices are socially commonplace; that what legal professionals see as aberrations are actually the everyday practices and experiences of many citizens.

Thirdly, the best law and society work acquires *theoretical power* and suggestiveness by distilling theoretical insights out of close attention to the practicalities of law as professionals and lay citizens experience them. Ideally it deduces theoretical implications with the same tight rigour that it applies in shaping empirical conclusions. If law and society work has not, in general and on a wide scale, directly confronted the most abstract social theory, the best contributions have nevertheless helped to illuminate general issues in social theory through analyses of specific legal contexts.

Another way of expressing this point is to say that the best law and society research is inherently comparative. This is not necessarily in the sense that more than one legal system or society is being studied empirically, or even that analysis is deliberately extended beyond a concern for local settings of legal experience. It is in the sense that the conclusions of research have a resonance far beyond the particularities studied and have theoretical implications for an indefinite range of legal and social contexts.

How far this resonance extends varies with different kinds of research. Some essays included here make comparisons between legal situations in Western and non-Western societies. Modern anthropological and ethnographic studies of Western legal processes and of the legal experiences of citizens in contemporary Western societies often employ methods clearly related to those that anthropologists have long used in the study of non-Western systems. In the 1960s and 1970s, studies of law and development in non-Western societies attempted to extend the reach of 'law and society' on a large scale beyond a relatively localized concern for advanced Western societies and their law. More generally, the broadening perspectives of sociology of law continually press towards ideas that link experience in societies and legal systems of radically different character.

Nevertheless, most law and society research, which derives its funding from advanced Western societies and can be assumed to be supported financially mainly for the benefits it might provide in those societies, has focused on contemporary Western law. 'Society' in 'law and society' has often remained undefined and merely been assumed to be the particular society in which the empirical research is located. Implicitly, however, 'society' has usually meant the advanced industrialized societies of Western Europe and North America, the successor societies to those that classic 19th-century social theory tended to identify as exemplifying 'modern society'.

IV

The work of the American law and society movement has not been unique. Much research done under the banners of socio-legal studies and sociology of law in Europe and elsewhere has shared similar aspirations and possesses the qualities suggested above as characteristic of the best law and society research. The selections included in this volume derive from various

Western countries. Nevertheless, the great proliferation and sophisticated development of law and society research in the United States since the middle of the 20th century, aided by relatively generous and often farsighted funding policies, ensures that American contributions predominate among the most important literature so far produced.

Various principles – some specific to this volume and its subject matter, some general across the series of volumes of which this is part – govern the selection of papers. In conformity with the general plan of the series, only journal articles are included; moreover, where possible and reasonable, a preference for shorter rather than longer essays has been followed. Selections are restricted to pieces that are, in some way, empirically based in terms of orthodox understandings of the nature of empirical research in social science. Some are more explicitly empirical in focus than others, but none is an essay in general legal or social theory. They refer to and evoke relatively specific empirical contexts either directly or indirectly. They appeal to particular contexts of law, particular regions of legal practice or experience, and they build their insights from the local towards the general. My aim, above all, in choosing these varied pieces is to reflect the rich imagery of different social realities of law which empirical socio-legal research can evoke.

Ultimately, however, each essay stakes its claim to enduring significance on the basis of theoretical relevance. Each paper has contributed in some important way to a refashioning of general theoretical knowledge of law. In this sense each takes its place within the integrated body of theoretical ideas and empirical analyses that makes up the patchwork of sociology of law, the theoretical science of law in society. Most of the papers have been widely cited. Many are classics in that they have forced a rethinking of law's social character and consequences, sometimes in radical ways, and have inspired or influenced much subsequent commentary and further empirical research.

In a single volume no attempt can be made to provide a representative selection from the whole range of law and society research. Concern here is with studies of the confrontation of state law (legislation and judicial decisions, as well as practices of state legal agencies) with other social norm systems or systems of action and belief. To that extent the selection reflects the traditional significance of the 'and' in 'law and society': the encounter between law as understood by the lawyer or government official and the social settings of its development, interpretation, application or enforcement. The selections are not chosen specifically to demonstrate empirical analyses of the organization and structure of state legal institutions (for example, courts, legal professions or law enforcement agencies), although many pieces do involve this kind of analysis. In conformity with the main tradition of law and society research, the focus is on state law's various impacts on, conditions of existence in, and significance for social environments beyond the institutions and agencies of state law themselves.

Nevertheless, the research of this character that is of most enduring significance is mainly that which has freed itself from some fundamental assumptions underpinning much early law and society work. This is especially so in the case of studies of legal impact or legal effectiveness and of the potential of law as an instrument of social change. These kinds of studies have occupied a prominent position in law and society literature. Legal impact research – concerned with identifying empirically the social effects of particular laws, legal institutions or legal strategies – is often directly relevant to policy debates. Studies of this kind have typically considered the impact or potential impact of particular changes in legal policy or in specific law enforcement practices on the behaviour of legal actors such as ordinary citizens. Correspondingly, law and social change studies have typically plotted general relationships between legal changes (especially those in legal doctrine, processes or agencies) and wider social change. They have asked how far law can be an instrument of planned social change and what are the limits of this role and the optimal techniques for fulfilling it.

Much valuable literature has been produced on legal effectiveness and on law as an instrument of social change. But these closely related areas of research highlight difficult problems of the inherited 'and' in the tradition of 'law and society'. Both kinds of research have tended to treat law as acting (as a kind of external force) on society and have sought in some way to measure law's social impact; alternatively, they have tended to suggest means of extending that impact, as well as inherent limitations created by the character- istics of legal institutions and practices, or the unforeseen social effects of legal strategies. Empirical law and social change studies have often seemed least problematic when they have restricted themselves to relatively specific technical issues about the appropriate means of maximizing law's influence in particular contexts (e.g. Evan 1965). When they go beyond this, they are usually forced to confront very general fundamental theoretical questions about the nature of social change, questions that lead quickly to the heart of social theory, especially where they concern the very possibility of theorizing about determinants of social development.

These matters can certainly be addressed in socio-legal research. The problem is that they tend to become unmanageable when the research focus remains on law as, in some way, a discrete or distinctive agent of social change. Systematic analysis of processes of social change requires social theory – that is, theory seeking to explain systematically the structure of societies or the nature of social relationships in general, as well as the conditions of social order, stability and change. A serious engagement with social theory requires that the very idea of law acting in some independent or relatively autonomous way on society should itself be put at issue theoretically. In what way, specifically, can law be conceptualized as socially autonomous? Where are the sources of its independent effectivity? The project becomes very substantial (e.g. Norrie 1993); it also becomes difficult to address systematically within a particular tradition of empirical law and society research in which theory is intended to build out from, or be closely focused on, particular empirical studies. The theory required even to conceptualize the research is part of the most general core of social theory.

Legal impact or effectiveness studies often closely limit their concerns to small-scale legal developments and seek to identify only specific, relatively *localized* changes in, for example, the behaviour of regulated citizens or organizations. There may be no attempt to offer any long-run perspective on change or any overall view of the character of legal institutions and practices in general which would require theoretical justification. However, studies following this kind of strategy run the risk of being criticized for narrow, atheoretical, policy-focused aims.

The difficulty of producing satisfying theoretical insights from empirical studies is acute in both legal impact studies and in law and social change literature. The root problem is the same in both cases. Both types of research largely work within the formative tradition of 'law and society', which treats law as acting upon a society considered as its external environment. Insofar as these types of studies try to conceptualize the nature of the change or impact which they see law producing or implicated in, they demand a perspective on social change that confronts central questions of social theory. The pull towards social theory is, however, also a demand for a fully elaborated theoretical justification for treating law as an autonomous, or even semi-autonomous, agent of change.

These theoretical questions are largely unavoidable. But the empirical tradition of law and society research to some extent deters direct and sustained engagement with them. The best writing on legal and social change usually discards the idea of law as an independent causal factor in social change and instead considers legal practices, institutions and ideas as elements or aspects of a changing field of social experience. The best writing recognizes the complexity of the interactions in which these legal elements both influence and are influenced by a wide range of social, cultural, economic or political forces. These forces envelop the elements we choose to call 'legal' without necessarily reducing to insignificance the more or less distinctive features by which we identify them. Insofar as both legal impact studies and law and social change studies grapple effectively with the theoretical issues entailed in their projects, they move decisively towards an explicit conceptualization of law *in* society. This is the case with writings in this volume that address, in one way or another, questions concerning the social impact of particular laws or questions about legal and social change.

V

As it has expanded its scope, law and society research has raised critical issues for legal and social theory. One aim of this volume is to highlight work that, remaining firmly grounded in the tradition of empirical research (the most valuable aspect of the law and society movement), may help towards rethinking the very idea of law as an aspect or field of social experience.

Why might such new conceptualizations be important? I have suggested that, despite many countercurrents, law and society research remains dominated by the concerns of legal policy; that is, by the demand that law be made a more efficient instrument to deliver the results – in terms of desired social, economic, political or cultural conditions – that policy-makers seek. Given that much research funding comes either from government agencies or from grant-awarding foundations necessarily concerned with communicable judgments of utility and value-for-money, this situation is hardly surprising. Yet a significant amount of law and society research, avoiding the 'pull of the policy audience' (cf. Sarat and Silbey 1988), has set agendas which, while far from irrelevant to policy matters, have been concerned with imagining new possibilities for law and with identifying problems of law that are unlikely to impinge directly on lawmakers' policy agendas.

Some of these agenda items have been questions about law's moral place in society and about its contribution (positive or negative) to the shaping of the moral climate of social life. In societies of intense individualism, driven by powerful ideologies of independence, freedom and personal choice, questions concerning the nature of community and its moral basis are often marginalized. Yet the difficult questions of law's role in, or even its compatibility with, moral structures of human interdependence, solidarity and community in contemporary Western societies are asked with increasing urgency. Richard Schwartz's essay on the structure of kibbutz societies (included here as Chapter 19) is a relatively unusual early attempt in American law and society work to approach empirically the issue of the place of law in structures of community.

Concerns with law's relations with structures of community life imply the need for some restructuring of thinking about regulation, so that it is seen not only as a 'top-down' policy instrument of often relatively centralized governmental control and direction, but also as an expression of relatively local, diverse and specific needs. It is necessary to ask, with the aid of empirical research, a largely neglected question in relation to legal theory. Under what circumstances can the organization of people in cohesive but non-repressive and essentially voluntary communities produce, through participatory democratic processes, appropriate regulation for these communities? That is to say, under what circumstances can regulation be produced that is morally meaningful to the members of such communities because it derives from and in some ways reflects and expresses directly their everyday lived experience, rather than being imposed by what may seem relatively remote legislative processes?

Given its systematic empirical focus, law and society research is likely to adopt a refreshingly tough-minded and practically-oriented approach to such broad issues about the place of law in society. Large questions about law's moral destiny and responsibility are hard to operationalize as the basis of empirical research projects. Nevertheless, an important trajectory of law and society work does seem to carry research priorities towards a focus on law's place in the moral milieux of communities.

Research adopting this focus has been carried out in recent years by anthropologists and other scholars relying mainly on ethnographic methods. It has shifted the emphasis away from asking how law, 'officially' conceived within the state legal system, impacts on or is affected by particular contexts of its application. It has introduced, more directly and insistently than in earlier literature, questions about how legal ideas are shaped, used, reinterpreted and negotiated in local social settings. In some of this work the claim is that 'official' interpretations of law and understandings of the nature of its institutions and practices co-exist with many contrasting 'popular' understandings of law, which are adopted or formed in everyday social interaction. The patterns of this interaction may be relatively uncontrolled by law in the lawyer's sense. Often they remain invisible to – never brought to the attention of – lawyers or officials of the state legal system.

These kinds of researches (reflected mainly in some essays in Part IV of this volume) suggest new horizons for law and society scholarship. They pose questions about the multiple meanings of 'the legal' as understood in relation to various moral frameworks of social interaction. Revealing, as they sometimes do, numerous socially significant, non-professional inter-pretations or appropriations of law, they may prepare the ground for a sociological rethinking of the nature of law in Western societies – as a continuum of regulation representing far more than a directive instrument of government. Examining the interaction of state law and community structures encourages a reconsideration of the kinds of regulation that can relate most appropriately and responsively to local conditions of social interaction.

Ironically, it may be that the effort to see legal doctrine and legal processes *in* society – invoked, reinterpreted, confronted, avoided, ignored or appropriated in patterns of everyday community life – finally makes clear the real significance of the idea of 'law *and* society': that is, law *separated from* society. The need radically to rethink and replan legal regulation and the means of its production and use arises primarily in order to confront tendencies that seem to make the professional world of state law dangerously remote both from the moral conditions of life of many citizens and from their everyday projects and aspirations, burdens and dangers, misfortunes and crises.

VI

For reasons of space, the selections included here are restricted to sociologically oriented studies, including within this category anthropological and social psychological researches. In particular, this volume does not seek to represent economic analysis of law. The focus is on law as a field of social experience, not necessarily structured around economically rational action, nor indeed rational action at all. The general assumption underlying the diverse essays presented here is that, as a focus of social research, law can be understood to some significant degree in terms of patterns of social action and experience which allow theoretical generalization and comparative study.

As has been noted earlier in relation to questions of research method, law and society research, in accordance with its dominant empirical traditions, commits itself implicitly or explicitly to the possibility of 'science' – social science – as applied to law. Fundamental debate and disagreement exist as to what constitutes valid empirical or theoretical knowledge of social phenomena, but law and society research must accept by the nature of its projects that such knowledge is possible, communicable and capable of reliable assessment.

To this extent the law and society movement stands resolutely on a terrain of 'modern' preconceptions about knowledge and the modes of its production (cf. Cotterrell 1992, p. 309). The advent of postmodernist ideas in philosophy and social theory throws doubt on the once confident protocols of social scientific research. Law and society research now confronts fundamental questions about the significance of its researches in an era in which appeals to all metadiscourses of scientific validity and truth are challenged (see e.g. Lyotard 1984). The demand in recent times has increasingly been for social research on law to be guided by the aim of critique or by the search for ethical principle. This provokes important debates. Is a *critical* empiricism possible (Trubek and Esser 1989; Sarat 1990), and would the explicit aim of critique somehow substitute for the claim to value-freedom once considered possible and necessary in social research? Can law and society research serve demands for a rethinking of the meaning and requirements of justice in a patently unjust world, or in a world in which the very coherence of the idea of justice seems problematic?

These questions pose some of the greatest challenges that 'law and society' faces at the level of fundamental theoretical underpinnings of the research enterprise as a whole. Yet the general validity of this enterprise seems to me to be illustrated by the pieces that follow. They often speak of and through experiences of law with which the reader can empathize. These essays are no more value-free than any other kinds of writings on social life can be yet they ask that their vision of the legal world be taken seriously in its scholarly presentation, whatever the reader's and researcher's values. They express a rigour demonstrated in familiar forms of theoretical logic applied to new purposes, and in the sensitivity, detail and systematic organization of their observation and recording. Their accounts of particular social experiences of law are not repositories of truth, but diverse perspectives on a multi-faceted and elusive reality. Like all social observations, those collected here are mediated by ideological preconceptions. Nevertheless, these studies extend our experience of the legal world vicariously by taking the reader into aspects of it that lie beyond his or her personal knowledge. They help to crack the prisms of ideological thought through the sharp, untidy detail of the empirical record that they help to present. And, in the main, they offer theory only as a way of making provisional sense of what these researches have registered as legal experience.

We may not have travelled as far as we wished towards a richer empirical understanding of law. But a recognition that ultimate truth about law in society is unobtainable should not lead to any undervaluing of the partial insights and perspectives that law and society literature offers. The task of theory is to try ceaselessly to understand, interpret and reconcile these partial perspectives; to fit them into some wider, and ever-widening, perspective without distorting, trivializing or discarding the narrower, particular views of legal experience that they offer. The task of empirical study is always to prevent theory from turning into dogma; to present it continuously with new disconcerting evidences, new reports from experience and new challenges to its orderly images of society. In this way empirical research serves theory – strengthening and enriching it – not only by providing the material to be theorized, but by discouraging theoretical analysis from supposing that it can offer true and complete pictures of the infinite complexity of the social world.

References

Cotterrell, R.B.M. (1986), 'Law and Sociology: Notes on the Constitution and Confrontations of Disciplines', *Journal of Law and Society*, **13**, 9–34.

Cotterrell, R.B.M. (1992), *The Sociology of Law: An Introduction*, 2nd edn, London: Butterworth.

Esser, J. and Trubek, D.M. (1990), 'From "Scientism Without Determinism" to "Interpretation Without Politics": A Reply to Sarat, Harrington and Yngvesson', *Law and Social Inquiry*, **15**, 171–80.

Evan, W.M. (1965), 'Law as an Instrument of Social Change' reprinted in W.M. Evan (ed.) (1980), *The Sociology of Law: A Social-Structural Perspective*, New York: Free Press, 554–62.

Friedman, L.M. (1986), 'The Law and Society Movement', *Stanford Law Review*, **38**, 763–80.

Levine, F.J. (1990), 'Goose Bumps and "The Search for Signs of Intelligent Life" in Sociolegal Studies: After Twenty-Five Years', *Law and Society Review*, **24**, 7–33.

Lyotard, J.-F. (1984), *The Postmodern Condition: A Report on Knowledge*, transl. by G. Bennington and B. Massumi, Manchester: Manchester University Press.

Macaulay, S. (1984), 'Law and the Behavioral Sciences: Is There Any There There?', *Law and Policy*, **6**, 149–87.

Norrie, A. (ed.) (1993), *Closure or Critique? New Directions in Legal Theory*, Edinburgh: Edinburgh University Press.

Sarat, A. (1990), 'Off to Meet the Wizard: Beyond Validity and Reliability in the Search for a Post-Empiricist Sociology of Law', *Law and Social Inquiry*, **15**, 155–70.

Sarat, A. and Silbey, S.S. (1988), 'The Pull of the Policy Audience', *Law and Policy*, **10**, 97–166.

Silbey, S.S. and Sarat, A. (1987), 'Critical Traditions in Law and Society Research', *Law and Society Review*, **21**, 165–74.

Trubek, D.M. (1984), 'Where the Action Is: Critical Legal Studies and Empiricism', *Stanford Law Review*, **36**, 575–622.

Trubek, D.M. and Esser, J. (1989), '"Critical Empiricism" in American Legal Studies: Paradox, Program, or Pandora's Box', *Law and Social Inquiry*, **14**, 3–52.

Part I
Law and the Management
of Disputes

[1]

THE MOBILIZATION OF LAW

DONALD J. BLACK*

INTRODUCTION

A theory of social control seeks to understand patterns of social control and their relation to other aspects of social organization. Little theory of this type can be found in social science, although over the years occasional, self-conscious efforts in this direction have been made in sociology and social anthropology.[1] Sociological thought about social control has been too broad for some purposes, too narrow for others. The subject matter has been defined as the conditions for social order—a subject matter some would give to sociology as a whole—while the detailed study of social control has centered on how official reactions to deviant behavior affect individual motivation.[2] Focussing thus upon the relationship between control and individual adaptation, sociology has neglected the character and integrity of social control as a natural system.[3] In the anthropological work on social control more emphasis has been placed upon systems of social control and dispute settlement than upon the influence of these systems at the level of individual motivation. Un-

* Assistant Professor of Sociology and Lecturer in Law, Yale University. For comments on an earlier draft the author is grateful to John Griffiths, Jerrold Guben, Robert Kagan, Richard Lempert, Michael E. Libonati, Maureen Mileski, Albert J. Reiss, Jr., David M. Trubek, and Stanton Wheeler. Support was provided by the Russell Sage Program in Law and Social Science and by the Law and Modernization Program, both of Yale Law School.

[1] For examples of the earlier works, see Edward Alsworth Ross, Social Control: A Survey of the Foundations of Order (1901); Bronislaw Malinowski, Crime and Custom in Savage Society (1926); Karl Mannheim, Man and Society in an Age of Reconstruction: Studies in Modern Social Structure (1940); Karl N. Llewellyn & E. Adamson Hoebel, The Cheyenne Way: Conflict and Case Law in Primitive Jurisprudence (1941); August B. Hollingshead, The Concept of Social Control, 6 Am. Soc. Rev. 217 (1941).

[2] E.g., Erving Goffman, Asylums: Essays on the Social Situation of Mental Patients and Other Inmates (1961); Thomas J. Scheff, Being Mentally Ill: A Sociological Theory (1966); Johannes Andenaes, The General Preventive Effects of Punishment, 114 U. Pa. L. Rev. 949 (1966); William J. Chambliss, Types of Deviance and the Effectiveness of Legal Sanctions, 1967 Wis. L. Rev. 703.

[3] But see, e.g., Richard D. Schwartz, Social Factors in the Development of Legal Control: A Case Study of Two Israeli Settlements, 63 Yale L.J. 471 (1954); Irving Piliavin & Scott Briar, Police Encounters with Juveniles, 70 Am. J. Soc. 206 (1964); Donald J. Black, Production of Crime Rates, 35 Am. Soc. Rev. 733 (1970), and The Social Organization of Arrest, 23 Stan. L. Rev. 1087 (1971).

125

fortunately, however, anthropologists stress concrete description and have shown little interest in the development of general theory.[4]

The sociology of law is in the long term preliminary to a general theory of social control. Theoretical tools for understanding social control systems of all kinds will undoubtedly be fashioned in the study of law. Although its social characteristics are highly complicated, writ large in law are properties and processes that inhere in all systems of social control but that escape our notice in systems lacking its scale, formalization, and intrusiveness.

Law may be defined, very simply, as *governmental social control*.[5] In this essay I discuss a single dimension of legal systems: the *mobilization of law*,[6] the process by which a legal system acquires its cases.[7] The day-by-day entry of cases into any legal system cannot be taken for granted. Cases of alleged illegality and disputes do not move automatically to legal agencies for disposition or settlement. Without mobilization of the law, a legal control system lies out of touch with the human problems it is designed to oversee. Mobilization is the link between the law and the people served or controlled by the law.

[4] But see, *e.g.*, Paul Bohannan, The Differing Realms of the Law, 67 Am. Anthro., Special Publication, No. 6, pt. 2, at 33 (Dec. 1965); Leopold Pospisil, Anthropology of Law: A Comparative Theory (1971).

[5] Donald J. Black, The Boundaries of Legal Sociology, 81 Yale L. J. 1086 (1972). My approach to law is uncompromisingly positivist and therefore departs fundamentally from much recent work by sociologists. Cf. Philip Selznick, Law, Society and Industrial Justice (1969), and Sociology and Natural Law, 6 Natural L. Forum. 84 (1961); Jerome H. Skolnick, Justice Without Trial: Law Enforcement in Democratic Society (1966).

[6] While this use of the word "mobilization" is hardly standard, it is not utterly unknown. For instance, Bronislaw Malinowski speaks of the "juridical machinery" being "mobilized." A New Instrument for the Interpretation of Law—Especially Primitive, 51 Yale L. J. 1237, 1250 (1942). Nevertheless, I have misgivings about the appropriateness of the word mobilization in this context. Colleagues have commented that it has a militaristic flavor and that it is too heavy for these purposes. I agree with these criticisms and would add that mobilization is a word ordinarily used in the analysis of larger-scale social phenomena, as in the mobilization of a society for war or the mobilization of dissent for a political movement. Still, I have been unable to find an adequate substitute. "Invocation" is too narrow, for instance, while "activation" seems even more awkward than mobilization. It is to be hoped that someone will eventually improve upon my choice. In the meantime I console myself with the thought that the problem with words reflects the lack of scholarly attention to the analytic problem itself.

[7] Perhaps more specification is required: By "legal system" I mean any governmental organization involved in defining or enforcing normative order. Thus, I speak of a total governmental apparatus as a legal system—the American legal system—but I also refer to a specific legal agency such as the police as a legal system. By "case" I mean any dispute or instance of alleged illegality that enters a legal system. A breach of contract, for example, becomes a case only when a suit is filed; a burglary becomes a case when it is reported to the police. A mobilization of law, then, is a complaint made to or by a legal agency. Mobilization occurs at several stages in some legal processes, *e.g.*, at a detection stage, an evidentiary or prosecutorial stage, and an adjudicatory stage.

The literature of jurisprudence shows little interest in the problem of mobilization, although here and there an exception is encountered. A century ago, for instance, Jhering appealed to the citizenry to call the law to action in every case of infringement of their legal rights. He argued that without continual mobilization the law would lose its deterrent power and claimed that legal mobilization is the moral obligation of every citizen whose rights are offended.[8] Roscoe Pound, too, warned that the effective power of the law requires a citizenry ready and willing to activate the legal process.[9] Pound's point is occasionally repeated by contemporary legal critics and scholars,[10] but the problem of mobilization more often is ignored.

Likewise, legal sociology rarely deals with the problem of mobilization. Usually the study of law as a social control system concerns the process of legal prescription or policy-making, such as legislation, or of legal disposition or dispute settlement, such as we see in judicial decision-making or police encounters. Legal mobilization mediates between the prescriptions of law and the disposition of cases, between rules and their application. Although the usual focus of legal sociology is either rules or their application, a few theoretical references to the problem of mobilization can be found.[11] Also, there is a valuable body of empirical research relevant to a theory of mobilization, revolving primarily around the questions of when and why people go to the law to solve their problems.[12]

In the present discussion I slight the social conditions under which the law is mobilized. My concern is *how* the law is set into motion. I try to show that whether or not the state selects the legal cases it handles makes a critical difference in the character of law as a social control system. I examine the organization of legal mobilization as it relates to other aspects of legal control, including a) legal intelligence, b) the availability of law, c) the organization of discretion, and d) legal change. In so doing, I show how mobilization systems influence diverse aspects of legal life, such as the kinds of cases a legal

---

[8] Rudolph von Jhering, The Struggle for Law (1879).

[9] The Limits of Effective Legal Action, 27 Int'l J. Ethics 150 (1917).

[10] *E.g.*, Harry W. Jones, The Efficacy of Law 21-26 (1969).

[11] Leon H. Mayhew, Law and Equal Opportunity: A Study of the Massachusetts Commission Against Discrimination 15-16 (1968); Paul Bohannan, *supra* note 4; Vilhelm Aubert, Courts and Conflict Resolution, 11 J. Conflict Resolution 40 (1967).

[12] *E.g.*, P. H. Gulliver, Social Control in an African Society: A Study of the Arusha, Agricultural Masai of Northern Tanganyika (1963); Alan Macfarlane, Witchcraft in Tudor and Stuart England: A Regional and Comparative Study (1970); Stewart Macaulay, Non-Contractual Relations in Business: A Preliminary Study, 28 Am. Soc. Rev. 55 (1963); Laura Nader & Duane Metzger, Conflict Resolution in Two Mexican Communities, 65 Am. Anthro. 584 (1963); Takeyoshi Kawashima, Dispute Resolution in Contemporary Japan, in Law in Japan: The Legal Order of a Changing Society 41 (Arthur Taylor von Mehren ed. 1963).

system handles, the accessibility of the population to the law, the degree of particularism in law enforcement, and the responsiveness of the law to moral change in the citizenry.

THE STRUCTURE OF LEGAL MOBILIZATION

A case can enter a legal system from two possible directions. A citizen may set the legal process in motion by bringing a complaint; or the state may initiate a complaint upon its own authority, with no participation of a citizen complainant. In the first sequence a legal agency reacts to a citizen, so we refer to it as a *reactive* mobilization process. In the second sequence, where a legal official acts with no prompting from a citizen, we may speak of a *proactive* mobilization process.[13]

Across societies, history, and substantive areas of law there is enormous variability in how the law is mobilized, whether by means of citizens, the state, or both. Some legal processes are organized to allow the government to take action on its own; in others no such route is provided. In the United States, for example, the government has no responsibility for mobilizing what is traditionally called "private law," such as contract law, torts, and property law. There are no government organizations or officers empowered to bring a private-law case on behalf of a private citizen. There are only the courts, where citizens, assisted by attorneys, can make their own claims on their own behalf.[14] American public law presents an entirely different appearance. Here the government is authorized to initiate cases independently of the grievances of private citizens.[15] The major examples are criminal law and the regulatory

[13] In psychology the concepts "reactive" and "proactive" have been used to classify individual actions in terms of their origins, the former referring to actions originating in the environment, the latter to those originating within the actor. See Henry A. Murray, Toward a Classification of Interactions, in Toward a General Theory of Action 434 (Talcott Parsons & Edward A. Shils eds. 1951).

Instead of reactive and proactive legal systems we could speak, respectively, of passive and active legal systems. See Philip Selznick, Law, Society, and Industrial Justice, *supra* note 5, at 225-28.

[14] Of course, the state can and often does initiate private-law cases on its own behalf as a private party such as when the government is the victim of a breach of contract. The point is that the government cannot bring a private-law case on behalf of a private individual as it does, in effect, in many criminal cases. The participation of a legal-aid lawyer in a private action does not constitute government initiative analogous to a criminal prosecution, since legal aid implies no partisanship on the part of the state itself.

[15] In fact, mobilization provides a useful way to distinguish between public law and private law, although it corresponds only roughly to traditional usage. We can define public law as law that the state is authorized to enforce upon its own initiative, private law as law in which the initiative is granted exclusively to private citizens. By this definition a legal process formally is part of public law whether or not in practice the state acts upon the authority vested in it.

This distinction is very close to one advanced by A. R. Radcliffe-Brown: "In the law of private delicts a dispute between persons or groups of persons is brought before the

laws establishing and enforced by federal and local government agencies such as the Federal Trade Commission, the Internal Revenue Service, city health departments, and local licensing agencies. The government is organizationally as well as legally equipped to initiate public law cases since there is a network of government agencies that routinely carry out investigations concerned with detecting illegality. Most visible are the federal, state, county, and city police forces, but numerous government agencies outside the operational jurisdiction of the police are also engaged in proactive enforcement of public law. In the Soviet Union, owing in good part to the office of procurator, considerably more state-initiated legal cases arise than in the United States. The Soviet procuracy is the prosecuting arm in criminal cases but also watches over all civil proceedings and may initiate or enter any lawsuit at any stage on either side of the dispute.[16] In earlier historical periods, the proactive capacity of the state in the American system was considerably less than it is now, but never was the American government so passive in the mobilization of law as was, for example, the government of republican Rome, to cite an extreme case where proactive enforcement was almost wholly absent.[17]

But legal agencies with the capacity to initiate cases do not necessarily use that capacity to its limits, if they use it at all. For instance, in legal theory and in the popular mind, American criminal justice is a process in which the government is highly aggressive in ferreting out illegality and bringing actions in court, but in fact the criminal justice system resembles a private-law system far more than is generally recognized. The typical criminal case comes to the attention of the authorities not on account of police initiative but through the initiative of a private citizen acting in the role of complainant.[18] Among the uniformed patrol force of a large police department, where the heaviest part of the police workload is carried, the vast majority of citizen contacts arise at the instigation of citizens who mobilize the police.[19] The police do initiate most cases of vice and narcotics enforcement and are very aggressive in traffic and crowd control. These patterns disproportionately influence the police image in the community, but, again, they are exceptional. Recent studies of other public-law systems, such as antidiscrimination commissions

---

judicial tribunal for settlement; in the law of public delicts the central authority itself and on its own initiative takes action against an offender." Structure and Function in Primitive Society 219 (1965).

[16] A description is provided by Harold J. Berman, Justice in the U.S.S.R.: An Interpretation of Soviet Law 239 (rev. ed. 1963).

[17] See generally A. W. Lintott, Violence in Republican Rome (1968).

[18] See Albert J. Reiss, Jr., & David J. Bordua, Environment and Organization: A Perspective on the Police, in The Police: Six Sociological Essays 25, 29-32 (D. J. Bordua ed. 1967).

[19] See Donald J. Black, The Social Organization of Arrest, *supra* note 3, at 1090-92.

and housing-code enforcement agencies, reveal a similar dependence upon citizen complainants for their influx of cases.[20]

Like any analytic distinction, the reactive-proactive distinction encounters occasional difficulties when it confronts the empirical world. One marginal situation, for example, is when legal cases are brought to court by paid citizen informers. In England the use of common informers who make money from the misdeeds of their fellow citizens has a long history. These informers were a primary source of cases in some areas of English law—notably economic regulation—in the 16th and 17th centuries.[21] Informers also were frequently put to use in the early American legal process.[22] They are still widely employed by the police in narcotics work, vice enforcement, and political surveillance. The Internal Revenue Service offers financial incentives to informers against tax evaders. As an actor in the legal control process, the informer mixes the roles of citizen complainant and public official. Another marginal pattern is voluntary surrender and confession by a law-violator. In most areas of early Chinese law a citizen was rewarded with complete immunity if he confessed to an offense before it had been detected.[23] Voluntary confession still holds an important place in Chinese legal practice, and it is by no means unknown or unrewarded in Western legal systems.

I move now to several aspects of law for which the structure of legal mobilization carries significant implications, each being an important topic in its own right in the study of legal control. The first is legal intelligence.

LEGAL INTELLIGENCE

By legal intelligence I mean the knowledge that a legal system has about law violations in its jurisdiction. How the mobilization of law is organized has profound consequences for the discovery of illegality. A reactive system lodges the responsibility for detection of violations in citizens, thereby blinding the control process to whatever law violations citizens are unable to see, fail to notice, or choose to ignore. Thus, private law systems, such as the law of contracts or torts, remain ignorant of that vast number of breaches of law

---

[20] Morroe Berger, Equality by Statute: The Revolution in Civil Rights (rev. ed. 1967); Leon H. Mayhew, *supra* note 11; Maureen Mileski, Policing Slum Landlords: An Observation Study of Administrative Control, 1971, at 60-65 (unpublished dissertation in Dep't of Sociology, Yale Univ.).

[21] M. W. Beresford, The Common Informer, the Penal Statutes and Economic Regulation, 10 Econ. Hist. Rev. 221 (2d ser. 1957).

[22] Selden D. Bacon, The Early Development of American Municipal Police: A Study of the Evolution of Formal Controls in a Changing Society, 1939 (unpublished dissertation in Dep't of Pol. Sci. Yale Univ.).

[23] W. Allyn Rickett, Voluntary Surrender and Confession in Chinese Law: The Problem of Continuity, 30 J. Asian Studies 797 (1971).

about which the citizenry is silent.[24] On the other hand, a citizen-based system of legal intelligence receives much information about legal cases that would otherwise elude its attention. From a sociological standpoint, however, there is no "proper" or even "effective" system of legal intelligence. The adequacy of any aspect of legal control is not a scientific question.[25]

Access to Cases. The proactive strategy of mobilization often appears in legal systems where a reactive strategy would fail to uncover illegality of a particular kind. A reactive strategy would be almost useless in traffic control and impracticable in vice or "morals" control. Frequently those few among the citizens who would make vice complaints do not have access to the violative situations, so they cannot inform the police, and most of those with access do not complain. Detection and enforcement in these cases require a government-initiated mobilization system. Apart from crimes under the authority of the police, numerous forms of illegality, such as income tax evasion and violations of health and safety standards by businesses, are unlikely to be known or recognized by ordinary citizens; enforcement in these cases necessitates a system of inspection carried out by government agencies. To facilitate its enforcement program the government may, for instance, require self-reports from citizens and organizations, as is seen in tax enforcement, antidiscrimination surveys, and price and wage control. Registration and licensing systems similarly assist the government in learning about the population and its activities. Totalitarian regimes employ self-report systems extensively. It might be added that the more differentiated a society becomes, the more illegality tends to arise in specialized domains of social life where the offenders are encapsulated beyond the reach of a citizen detection system. Accordingly, as the process of social differentiation continues, notably in the economic sphere, we see an ever-enlarging battery of administrative agencies involved in proactive enforcement.[26]

---

[24] Perhaps it is apparent that my concept of illegality is considerably broader than an American lawyer might deem proper. I treat an act as illegal if it falls within a *class* of acts for which there is a *probability* of official sanction, resistance, or redress after the fact of detection. Put another way, an act is illegal if it is *vulnerable* to legal action. A concept of this kind is required if a breach of private law not responded to as such is to be understood as illegality. By contrast, the American lawyer tends to view a breach of private law as illegality only if a complaint is made or if it is defined as such in a court of law. From this legalistic view it is impossible to consider the mobilization of private law as a problem for investigation, since where there is no mobilization there is by definition no illegality. From a sociological standpoint, however, unenforced private law is perfectly analogous to unenforced public law; in both cases the mobilization of law is problematic.

[25] For a critique of studies on legal effectiveness, see Donald J. Black, The Boundaries of Legal Sociology, *supra* note 5.

[26] See Emile Durkheim, The Division of Labor in Society 221-22 (George Simpson transl. 1964).

The location of law violations is another factor conditioning the access of a legal process to its cases. Most illegality arises in private rather than public settings, making access to much illegality difficult for a government enforcement system. In part this is because of legal restrictions protecting private places from government intrusion.[27] Yet the impact of the law of privacy on legal intelligence can easily be exaggerated. Even if privacy law were totally eliminated, opening every private place to government intrusion at any time, still the sheer unpredictability of illegal behavior would bar the government from knowledge of most illegality. Unless it were to go to the technological lengths fictionalized in George Orwell's *1984*, a government could not possibly achieve the surveillance necessary to detect even a minute proportion of all the illegal conduct. This applies to many kinds of law violations. Policemen on patrol in public settings, for instance, rarely discover any but the relatively trivial varieties of criminal behavior. The more serious violations, such as homicide, burglary, and grand larceny, take place behind closed doors. The police therefore depend upon ordinary citizens to provide them with information about crimes that have been committed. Of course much illegality escapes the knowledge of citizens as well. Nevertheless, the latent power of a hostile or alienated citizenry to undermine the capacity of the government to locate violations is undeniable and is amply demonstrated in the history of colonial, revolutionary, and other kinds of authoritarian legal systems.[28] Unpopular law-enforcement programs such as these often use paid informers.

The power of the citizenry is all the greater in private law, where enforcement without the initiative of citizens is impossible. Here the location of illegality is a moot question. People can entirely ignore domestic law or the law of negligence, for example, and the government can do nothing short of redefining these areas as public law. It is popularly believed that laws fall into disuse on account of government indifference or indolence. But in fact the demise of laws is more likely to result from citizens who fail to mobilize courts or other legal agencies. One by one, citizens may lose interest in a law, and, in private, the law may die a slow death.

Limits on Legal Intelligence. Any legal system relying upon the active participation of ordinary citizens must absorb whatever naiveté and ignorance is found among the citizenry. The common man makes occasional errors when he applies what he takes to be legal standards to his everyday life, not only because of his lack of legal training but also because many social situations have a legally ambiguous character. In complex legal systems miscalculations

---

[27] See Arthur L. Stinchcombe, Institutions of Privacy in the Determination of Police Administrative Practice, 69 Am. J. Soc. 150 (1963).

[28] *E.g.*, Gregory J. Massell, Law as an Instrument of Revolutionary Change in a Traditional Milieu: the Case of Soviet Central Asia, 2 L. & Soc. Rev. 179 (1968).

by citizens are continually routed away from the courts by legal gatekeepers of various kinds. In private law, a major gatekeeping burden is carried by the private attorney.[29] In the process of advising their clients, attorneys serve the larger legal process as intelligence agents, sorting through and narrowing the raw input of cases moving toward the courts from day to day. In public law, other gatekeepers screen out the legal dross: government prosecutors, police, and the many enforcement officers attached to administrative agencies, such as health officers, food and drug inspectors, and internal revenue agents. Without these gatekeepers all the intelligence gaps in the citizenry would reappear in the legal system.

Other intelligence losses greatly overshadow those resulting from citizen error. Much illegality is unknown because so many citizens fail to call upon the law when they experience law violations. The reluctance of citizens to mobilize the law is so widespread, indeed, that it may be appropriate to view legal inaction as the dominant pattern in empirical legal life. The number of unknown law violations probably is greater in private law than in public law, although only speculation is possible. The outline of legal inaction is just now beginning to be known through surveys of the citizen population.[30] Other relevant research is afoot. A recent study of dispute settlement in a Swedish fishing village, for instance, indicates that communities can passively absorb an enormous amount of illegal behavior, even when it continues for many years and includes numerous well-defined victimizations.[31] In fact, legal mobilization sometimes is more socially disruptive than the illegal behavior that gives rise to it. Gradually a research literature is collecting around the question of when people mobilize the law, given illegality. The nature of the social relationship enveloping a legal dispute or violation emerges as an especially powerful predictor of legal mobilization. Thus, we know from East African and Japanese materials, among others, that resort to a government court occurs primarily in legal conflicts between relative strangers or persons who live in different communities.[32] Persons in intimate relationships tend to use extralegal mechanisms of dispute settlement when quarrels arise. However, they do not hesitate to call upon the law to settle their disputes when extralegal social control is unavailable to persons in intimate social relationships, a pattern seen, for example, in the loosely structured barrios of Vene-

[29] See Talcott Parsons, A Sociologist Looks at the Legal Profession, in Essays in Sociological Theory 370 (rev. ed. 1964).

[30] See U.S. President's Comm'n on Law Enforcement & Admin. of Justice, Crime and Its Impact—An Assessment 17-19 (Task Force Report, 1967).

[31] Barbara Yngvesson, Decision-Making and Dispute Settlement in a Swedish Fishing Village: An Ethnography of Law, 1970 (unpublished dissertation in Dep't of Anthropology, Univ. of Calif., Berkeley).

[32] P. H. Gulliver, *supra* note 12, at 204, 263-66; Takeyoshi Kawashima, *supra* note 12.

zuela.[33] Usually, the likelihood that extralegal control will be available in a social relationship is a function of the intimacy of the relationship as measured by such indicators as its duration, the frequency of interaction, the intensity of interaction, the degree of interdependence between the parties, and the number of dimensions along which interaction between the parties occurs. Accordingly, we expect that mobilization of the law will be infrequent in what Gluckman in his classic study of the Barotse of Zambia calls "multiplex" relationships.[34]

Much of this may be summarized in the following proposition: the greater the relational distance between the parties to a dispute, the more likely is law to be used to settle the dispute.[35] With social predictors of this sort we can easily anticipate many empirical patterns, such as the finding that breach of contract rarely leads to a court case when it takes place between businessmen who have a continuing relationship with recurrent transactions.[36] We may observe, then, that a reactive legal system acts to reinforce the tendency of citizens to use law only as a last resort, since it allows citizens to establish their own priorities. Because citizens use the law reluctantly, they help to make the law a conservative enterprise that for the most part leaves the *status quo* to its own designs. Social research on law eventually will reveal the extent and social context of legal inaction in numerous areas of law and across societies, thereby making possible a comprehensive theory of the mobilization of law.[37]

A legal intelligence system resting upon the initiative of citizens involves another kind of limitation, one that occurs regardless of the rate at which citizens mobilize the law. This limitation inheres in the simple fact that reactive systems operate on a case-by-case basis.[38] Cases enter the system one by one, and they are processed one by one. This creates an intelligence

---

[33] Lisa Redfield Peattie, The View from the Barrio 57-59 (1968).

[34] Max Gluckman, The Judicial Process among the Barotse of Northern Rhodesia 18-19 (rev. ed. 1967).

[35] See Donald J. Black, Production of Crime Rates, *supra* note 3, at 740-42; The Social Organization of Arrest, *supra* note 3, at 1107-08.

[36] Stewart Macaulay, *supra* note 12.

[37] As noted earlier, I make no effort here to survey the social factors that predict the mobilization of law. My discussion of relational distance above is intended only to allude to this issue and to illustrate how it may be approached with general theory. A more comprehensive treatment would include, for example: the seriousness of the dispute or illegality, measured by the nature of the sanction or restitution or by its effects upon the on-going social order; the organization and integration of the community context; the resources required for the mobilization of law; the social status of the parties; the cultural context, including the degree of normative integration between the parties; and the organization of the dispute-settlement process itself, whether adversarial or conciliatory, formal or informal. The concern of this essay—the organization of mobilization—also relates to the probability of mobilization.

[38] Leon H. Mayhew, *supra* note 11, at 159.

gap about the relations among and between cases. It is difficult to link patterns of illegal behavior to single or similar violators and thus to deal with the sources rather than merely the symptoms of these patterns. To discover these patterns a systematic search for factual similarities across cases is needed.

Police systems do some pattern-oriented analysis of the cases coming to their attention through citizen complaints, but most patterns of illegality escape their detection net. One consequence may be a higher chance of survival for professional criminals,[39] although some patterned criminality is uncovered through *modus operandi* files. In other areas where the government does its own investigations, strategies for finding patterns of violation can likewise be used, although illegality varies in its amenability to pattern detection. Proactive enforcement campaigns often originate from single complaints. One case of processed food contamination, for instance, can lead to an inspection effort covering all businesses producing and distributing that particular variety of food. The inspection may expose one business routinely violating health standards or a number of businesses involved in the same category of violative behavior. Frequently one case of illegality by a business enterprise implies a pattern of illegality, since much business activity is by its nature programmed and repetitious. One violation of safety requirements by an automobile manufacturer, for example, usually means that numerous cases are at large in the community, and government inspections may unveil similar violations by other manufacturers. Similarly, in some cities housing-code enforcement officers inspect the whole of an apartment building when they learn, by complaint, of one violation in the building; they assume that the landlord may fail to meet code specifications in all of his units.[40] In the criminal justice system single complaints about narcotics or vice can provide the police with opportunities to penetrate offense networks and markets and discover large numbers of interrelated violations.

The enforcement of private law sharply contrasts with these illustrations from public law. A good case in point is contract law, where it is not unusual to find patterns of breach emanating from a single individual or business or from members of a broader category of legal actors, such as real estate agents, mail order businesses, or insurance companies. Apart from patterns involving a recurrent breach, one act by a single business may involve numerous breaches of contract with individuals dispersed in the population, as when a holiday tour or an entertainment event is ended prematurely and the promoters do not make a monetary refund to the many victims. Private-law

---

[39] Egon Bittner & Sheldon L. Messinger, Some Reflections on the Police and "Professional Crime" in West City, Sept. 1966 (unpublished paper, Center for the Study of Law & Society, Univ. of Calif., Berkeley).

[40] Maureen Mileski, *supra* note 20.

violations such as these can be remedied through "class actions," single legal suits covering a number of complaints of the same kind, but their frequency is far behind the rate at which patterns of private-law violation apparently occur and would be much greater if the government were involved in enforcement. The government would learn of more patterns of illegality, if only because information about all known violations would pass through one central processing system similar to a police system. At present the only official information on private-law cases is generally to be found in court records. Since no record is made of the private-law cases that do not reach the court, there can be no legal intelligence about them analogous to police records in the criminal realm. And even the court records on file are presently irrelevant to the on-going process of legal control.[41]

Also eluding any case-by-case legal process is the larger pattern by which legal problems are distributed in the population of citizens. Owing to social conditions beyond the reach of any case-oriented mobilization system, legal trouble is differentially visited upon the citizenry. Crimes of violence and interpersonal conflicts of all kinds disproportionately afflict the lower social strata (family-related violence, for example, is particularly common among poor blacks) and property matters often create a need for law among the higher status segments of the population. These structurally embedded patterns cannot be a direct concern of reactive control systems, although case records can be useful to social engineering efforts of other kinds. Because these patterns of misery cannot be confronted by single legal officials dealing with single cases of so many isolated victims and violators, their job is very much a matter of picking up the social debris deposited by larger social forces. Apart from its deterrence effect, the extent of which is unknown, a reactive legal system ever listens to the troubles of the citizenry, while the larger principles and mechanisms by which these troubles come into being escape it. In this sense, a case-oriented legal process always begins too late.[42] While a proactive system also is unable to attack the broader social conditions underlying law violations, it does have an ability to intervene in social arrangements that reactive systems lack. It can, for instance, destroy an illegal business operation, such as a gambling enterprise or crime syndicate, that may be the source of thousands of violations a week. Police control of auto-

---

[41] I make no effort in this essay to review the extra-governmental controls operating in response to illegal behavior. Some pattern-oriented control of private-law violations, for instance, occurs through credit bureaus and informal reputational networks and black-listing systems.

[42] This is not to deny that a legal agency can respond to pressures built up in a reactive mobilization process. For instance, a high rate of purse-snatching complaints may lead the police to institute patrol or undercover operations to deal more effectively with the problem. In this way, the caseload of a citizen-based mobilization system can be an important source of intelligence to legal administrators and policy-makers.

mobile traffic, too, involves prevention through social engineering of a kind impossible in a legal process relying solely upon citizen complaints.

The proactive system also has the power to prevent illegality in specific situations. While it cannot reach the many forms of illegality occurring in private places, a proactive system can prevent some violations in public places. The degree of prevention is difficult to assess, however, and in any case the forms of illegal behavior subject to situational prevention are likely to be minor. In a reactive process, prevention of this kind occurs only in the rare case when a citizen contacts a legal agency concerning an illegal act that is imminent or in progress and the agency intercedes. The heavy reliance of legal systems upon citizens thus assures that prevention will not be a major accomplishment. This is a more concrete sense in which a reactive system begins too late. To this inherent sluggishness of any citizen-based system, private law adds the delay involved in gaining a hearing in court. No civil police are available for immediate aid and advice to people involved in private-law problems. This will probably come with further legal evolution and differentiation, but in the meantime private-law systems lag far behind in the wake of the problems they are established to control.

In sum, a mobilization system implies a particular organization of knowledge about law violations. A reactive system places responsibility in the citizenry and thereby brings law to the private place, with its numerous and serious forms of illegality. A proactive system can discover violations that citizens are unable or unwilling to report but misses much private illegality. In a reactive system the kinds and rates of cases are a function of the kinds and rates of complaints by private citizens. In a proactive system the kinds and rates of cases result from the distribution of official resources by the control system itself. Because of the reactive system's reliance upon citizens and its case-by-case schedule of operation, it involves certain intelligence weaknesses, such as a near incapacity to identify patterns of illegality necessary to prevention. The proactive system can deal with patterns rather than mere instances of illegality, which gives it a strong preventive capacity, but it is limited largely to marginal and minor forms of illegality. The legally more important problems, then, are the responsibility of a mobilization system that cannot prevent them.

THE AVAILABILITY OF LAW

The previous section concerned the access of a legal system to the cases within its jurisdiction. Now we reverse our viewpoint and consider the access of citizens to the law. We must view legal life from below as well as from above,[43] since every instance of legal control is also an instance of legal

[43] Laura Nader & Barbara Yngvesson, On Studying the Ethnography of Law and Its

service. The availability of law to citizens varies markedly across and within legal systems and cannot be taken for granted in a sociological theory of law. Access to law is a function of empirical legal organization.

Two Models of Law. The reactive mobilization system portrays an *entrepreneurial model of law.* It assumes that each citizen will voluntarily and rationally pursue his own interests, with the greatest legal good of the greatest number presumptively arising from the selfish enterprise of the atomized mass. It is the legal analogue of a market economy.

Indeed, it has been argued that the organization of private law as a reactive system is not merely the analogue of a market economy; it is also the legal substructure essential to a market economy. Historically the system of "private rights" in contract, property, and tort law emerged and flourished with capitalism.[44] Here, however, I am suggesting only that a citizen-based system of mobilization—whatever the type of law—operates according to the same behavioral principles as a market system of economic life.[45] In their primordial forms, both are self-help systems. The proactive system, by contrast, is a *social-welfare model of law,* with the legal good of the citizenry being defined and then imposed by government administrators, albeit with some influence by interest groups in the citizen population. In the pure type of the social-welfare model of law, however, no role is provided for members of the citizenry in the determination of legal policy, just as in the pure type of welfare economy the will of the population need not be systematically introduced into the decision process. We might say, then, that a proactive system does not merely make the law available; it imposes the law.

Consequences, in Handbook of Social and Cultural Anthropology (John J. Honigmann ed. forthcoming).

[44] David M. Trubek, Law, Planning, and Economic Development, 1971, at 65-70 (unpublished paper, Yale Law School).

[45] This claim has also been made for the common law system in general, since, like an economic market, it is highly decentralized, competitive, largely private, and generates strong pressures for efficient performance among individuals. Richard A. Posner, A Theory of Negligence, 1 J. Legal Studies, 29, 49 (1972). Posner also notes that the mobilization of negligence law is literally an economic market system:

The motive force of the system is supplied by the economic self-interest of the participants in accidents. If the victim of an accident has a colorable legal claim to damages, it pays him to take steps to investigate the circumstances surrounding the accident; if the investigation suggests liability, to submit a claim to the party who injured him or the party's insurance company; if an amicable settlement cannot be reached, to press his claim in a lawsuit, if necessary to the highest appellate level. The other party has a similar incentive to discover the circumstances of the accident, to attempt a reasonable settlement, and, failing that, to defend the action in court. By creating economic incentives for private individuals and firms to investigate accidents and bring them to the attention of the courts, the system enables society to dispense with the elaborate governmental apparatus that would be necessary for gathering information about the extent and causes of accidents had the parties no incentive to report and investigate them exhaustively. *Supra,* at 48.

Legal systems that operate with a reactive strategy often employ mechanisms assuring that mobilization will be truly voluntary and entrepreneurial, although this may not be the motive behind their implementation. One American illustration is the prohibition against solicitation by attorneys. Were attorneys authorized to gather legal cases through solicitation, the input of legal business surely would change, since many otherwise passive victims of illegality undoubtedly would be persuaded to mobilize the law.[46] The already great influence that lawyers exert on the input of cases would also be increased. In the American system, where attorneys stand to profit from some cases, the same incentives that entice private citizens to bring suits, such as treble damages in private antitrust actions, might entice attorneys to solicit business. Insofar as attorneys create their own business through solicitation, they in effect become private prosecutors, diluting the purity of the legal market. The legal doctrine of "standing" is another device that buttresses the entrepreneurial organization of law. This doctrine holds that before a party may complain in a lawsuit, he must show that his interests are directly affected in the case at issue. Here it is uninvolved citizens rather than attorneys who are barred from influencing the mobilization of law, again protecting the purity of the legal market.

There are few corresponding mechanisms to accommodate citizens who have occasion to mobilize the law. This is not surprising, since, like any entrepreneurial process, a reactive legal system assumes that those wanting to pursue their interests are able to do so.

Limits on Legal Availability. The cost of litigation is a widely recognized limitation on the availability of private law. While services such as legal aid programs and small-claims courts have been established to reduce the financial burden for low-income citizens, the fact remains that the effectiveness with which citizens can pursue their legal interests often is affected by their wealth. In the criminal-law domain, on the other hand, the quality of legal representation does not depend upon a complainant's wealth. This is not to deny that wealthy and socially prominent complainants may receive better service from the public authorities, a form of discrimination in their behalf. But criminal justice is not organized so that wealthy complainants can secure better attorneys in court, since all complainants are represented by a public prosecutor.

---

[46] It may be useful to distinguish between mere advertising and active solicitation, although both are ethical breaches in the United States. By mere advertising I mean a process by which the legal consumer is simply informed of available legal services, while active soliciting involves an attempt to persuade an already informed consumer. Mere advertising would appear consistent with an entrepreneurial legal process since, unlike solicitation, it does not fly in the face of the assumptions of voluntariness and rationality in the entrepreneurial decision-making model. But then it is also arguable that even active solicitation does not disturb *assumptions* of voluntariness and rationality. Honest advertising and solicitation of all kinds are usually understood as consistent with a market economy.

A variety of other circumstances can lessen the availability of law, whether public or private, for some segments of the community. Sheer physical proximity to legal institutions can be a highly significant factor in pre-modern legal systems, owing to the meager communication and transportation systems in these societies. In nineteenth century China, for example, the farther a complainant lived from a court, the less likely it was that he could pursue his case. This was especially noticeable in civil matters, but it was also true in criminal matters. If the plaintiff resided in a city containing a court, his civil suit would reach a final disposition in 60 per cent of the cases, while the corresponding figure was only 20 per cent for plaintiffs living 71 to 80 *li* away (one *li* is about one-third of a mile).[47] Some modernizing nations now employ so-called "popular tribunals" at the neighborhood level, thereby providing law to the common people and, at the same time, a mechanism of social integration important to the modernization process itself. Other pre-modern societies, however, are characterized by a high degree of legal availability. In seventeenth century Massachusetts, for instance, each town had its own court of general jurisdiction, easily accessible to all. In fact, the ease of access to these courts seemingly tempted the citizenry to great litigiousness, resulting in a high rate of trivial, unfounded, and vexatious suits.[48] Back home in England the law had not been nearly so available to the common man. In tribal societies the availability of law also tends to be quite high.

Another force that sometimes interferes with the operation of a reactive legal process is a countervailing normative system. Informal norms among some pockets of the citizenry prohibit citizens from mobilizing the official control system. Generally it seems that people are discouraged from mobilizing social control systems against their status equals. With respect to the police, for instance, some citizens are subject among their peers to norms against "squealing" or "ratting." This morality appears rather clearly in the American black subculture, a factor reducing an already low rate of police mobilization by blacks. We also see strong antimobilization norms in total institutions such as prisons, concentration camps, mental hospitals, and basic training camps in the military. Similarly, these norms appear among the indigenous population in colonial societies, schools, and factories. Even in the traditional family, children enforce a rule against "tattling." Antimobilization norms seem to be particularly strong among the rank and file wherever there is a fairly clear split in the authority structure of a social system.[49]

[47] David C. Buxbaum, Some Aspects of Civil Procedure and Practice at the Trial Level in Tanshui and Hsinchu from 1789 to 1895, 30 J. Asian Studies 255, 274-75 (1971).

[48] George Lee Haskins, Law and Authority in Early Massachusetts: A Study in Tradition and Design 212-13 (1960).

[49] While I am emphasizing here the role of *informal* norms against the mobilization of law, it might be noted that one of the hallmarks of social oppression is a formal incapacity to mobilize the law. For instance, in early medieval England a woman could

In light of the foregoing, we may propose that whenever there is comparatively open conflict between an authority system and those subject to it, reactive legal systems will tend toward desuetude and there will be pressure for greater use of the proactive control strategy. We should therefore expect to find that governments disproportionately adopt proactive systems of legal mobilization when a social control problem primarily involves the bottom of the social-class system. It appears, for instance, that the emergence of a proactive police in early nineteenth century England reflected the elite's fear of growing class consciousness among the lower orders.[50] In cross-national perspective we see that police authority and political power are generally concentrated at the same points and that every police system is to some extent an instrument of political control. This is especially noticeable in the underdeveloped world; in most of Asia, Africa, and the Middle East the roots of proactive police systems are to be found in earlier colonial policies.[51] Similarly, it appears that proactive control in republican Rome was routinely exercised only upon slaves and that urban throng sometimes known as the "riff-raff."[52] The common forms of legal misconduct in which upper status citizens indulge, such as breach of contract and warranty, civil negligence, and various forms of trust violation and corruption, are usually left to the gentler hand of a reactive mobilization process.

In theory the law is available to all. In fact, the availability of law is in every legal system greater for the citizenry of higher social status, while the imposition of law tends to be reserved for those at the bottom. Thus, the mobilization of law, like every legal process, reflects and perpetuates systems of social stratification. In contemporary Western society the availability of law is nevertheless greater for the mass of citizens than in any previous historical period, and the trend is toward ever-greater availability. And yet it appears that the scope and depth of legal imposition is also greater than ever before.

THE ORGANIZATION OF DISCRETION

Students of law often comment that legal decision-making inevitably allows the legal agent a margin of freedom or discretion. Sometimes this margin

---

not bring a felony complaint unless the crime of which she complained was violence to her own person or the slaughter of her husband. Women were excluded from other aspects of the legal process as well, such as jury service, with the result at that time that they were largely unable to give evidence. Frederick Pollock & Frederic William Maitland, 1 The History of English Law: Before the Time of Edward I 484-85 (2d ed. 1968).

50 See Allan Silver, The Demand for Order in Civil Society: A Review of Some Themes in the History of Urban Crime, Police, and Riot, in The Police: Six Sociological Essays 1 (David J. Bordua ed. 1967).

51 See David H. Bayley, The Police and Political Change in Comparative Perspective, 6 L. & Soc. Rev. 91 (1971).

52 A. W. Lintott, *supra* note 17, at 102, 106.

does not much exceed the degree of ambiguity inherent in the meaning of the law, an ambiguity resulting in uncertainty about how the law will be interpreted under variable factual circumstances. Because of this ambiguity and factual variability, a degree of slippage is unavoidable in legal reasoning.[53] Sometimes the decision-maker's margin of freedom is so great, as in much of administrative law, that more of the man than the law determines the decisions made.[54]

Moral Diversity. The organization of a legal system allocates the discretion to decide when legal intervention is appropriate. A reactive system places this discretion in the ordinary citizen rather than in a legal official. This has far-reaching consequences for legal control. It allows the moral standards of the citizenry to affect the input of cases into the legal system. Much of the citizen's power lies in his ability not to invoke the legal process when he is confronted with illegality; this gives him the capacity to participate, however unwittingly, in a pattern of selective law enforcement. Each citizen determines for himself what within his private world is the law's business and what is not; each becomes a kind of legislator beneath the formal surface of legal life.

The anthropologist Paul Bohannan suggests that law functions to "re-institutionalize" the customary rules of the various social institutions, such as the family, religion, and the polity.[55] According to this view, law is an auxiliary normative mechanism that comes into play to lend needed support to nonlegal rules. This notion of "double institutionalization" is an extension of the older and simpler view that law enforces the common morality. A conception like this may have serious shortcomings as a way of understanding modern legislative and judicial behavior,[56] but it has some relevance to an analysis of legal mobilization. When citizens call the law to action according to their own moral standards, they in effect use the law as supplementary support for those standards. The functional relationship between the individual and the law is an analogue of the relationship proposed by Bohannan at the level of the total society. But this individual pattern cannot be generalized to the level of the total society, since the moral standards of the citizenry are not homogeneous across social classes, ethnic groups, the races, the sexes, generations, and other such aggregates. On the contrary, the reactive system makes it possible for members of these social segments and enclaves to use the law to enforce the rules of their own moral subcultures. From this standpoint, when the law is reactive it does present a pattern of double insti-

[53] Edward H. Levi, An Introduction to Legal Reasoning (1948).

[54] See Kenneth Culp Davis, Discretionary Justice: A Preliminary Inquiry (1969).

[55] *Supra* note 4, at 34-37.

[56] See Stanley Diamond, The Rule of Law Versus the Order of Custom, in The Rule of Law 115 (Robert Paul Wolff ed. 1971).

tutionalization, but it is a doubling of multiple institutions, as multiple as the moral subcultures we find in society. Thus the law perpetuates the moral diversity in the mass of citizens.[57] This may seem a strange role for some government agencies such as the police and for other predominantly reactive control systems, but the law and morality relationship is very complicated and is bound occasionally to disagree with common sense. In societies characterized by moral heterogeneity, it is only through proactive control that one morality can be imposed on all.[58]

Discrimination. Discretionary authority often carries with it the possibility of particularistic law enforcement or, more simply, discrimination. From a sociological standpoint, legal discrimination provides an interesting problem in the relation between law and social stratification. The liberal fear of a proactive legal system has long been part of a fear of discriminatory enforcement. But whether a system of mobilization is reactive or proactive does not determine the probability of discriminatory enforcement; rather, it organizes that probability. A reactive system deprives state officials of the opportunity to invoke the law according to their own prejudices, but it creates that opportunity for the average citizen. When a legal system is brought into operation by citizen demands, its direction follows the whims of the unmonitored population, whether they are universalistic or not. Each citizen has the discretionary power to decide which people, of those who are legally vulnerable, deserve official attention. The white citizen has the power to be more lenient toward the white than the black, and vice versa; the bourgeois can discriminate against the bohemian, the older against the younger, the rich against the poor. Even if we assume, *arguendo,* that each citizen does what his conscience dictates, what he thinks is right, the aggregative result of all these individual decisions surely distributes legal jeopardy unequally across the population of law violators, especially when we consider decisions *not* to mobilize the law.[59] The possibilities of government surveillance over this kind of discrimination seem minimal. Reactive mobilization is no more accessible to surveillance than many of the illegal acts in private settings that a reactive system uncovers. The amenability of a proactive legal system to

[57] For a comment on this pattern in police work, see Donald J. Black, The Social Organization of Arrest, *supra* note 3, at 1105.

[58] Proactive control sometimes emerges under conditions of moral diversity in a population and serves to integrate the larger system. The same may be said of law itself. See M. Fortas & E. E. Evans-Pritchard, Introduction, in African Political Systems 9 (M. Fortas & E. E. Evans-Pritchard eds. 1940). Proactive law seems particularly likely to arise when moral diversity in a population includes a high degree of normative conflict among the diverse elements, as we see, for instance, among tribal and ethnic groups in new nations. We might go further and suggest that normative conflict is an important predictor of authoritarian law in general.

[59] Donald J. Black, Production of Crime Rates, *supra* note 3, at 739.

surveillance and control is far greater, if only because a proactive system by its nature involves an organizational base that can be penetrated. Proactive control is itself subject to proactive control while reactive control is dispersed in the citizen mass and is therefore extraordinarily difficult to reach. In short, patterns of legal discrimination in reactive systems, the more democratic form of legal process, are more elusive, and consequently they are more intransigent than are similar patterns in proactive mobilization systems.[60] And yet it remains likely that a government-initiated mobilization system contributes more to the maintenance of the existing forms of social stratification than does a system geared to the demands of the citizenry. Discriminatory decision-making by citizens to a degree cancels itself out in the citizen mass, while discriminatory behavior by legal officials mirrors their own biases, and these are apt to flow in only one direction.

Besides accommodating discrimination by citizens, a reactive legal system permits individuals to appropriate the law for functions that lawmakers may never have anticipated. People may mobilize the law in order to bankrupt or destroy the reputations of their competitors,[61] to delay transfers of property or payments of debts,[62] or for revenge.[63] Within the limits imposed by law and legal officials, the discretion accorded to every citizen by a reactive control process, then, lets every citizen do with law what he will, with little concern for the long-range social results.[64]

[60] Just as it organizes the possibility of discrimination and its control, a system of mobilization organizes the possibility of legal corruption. We discover corruption, like discrimination, where it is easier to control, namely, in proactive systems of law enforcement. In police work, for example, we hear about corruption in vice control and traffic control rather than at the level of the citizen complainant, where it is probably most frequent.

[61] See, *e.g.*, Bernard S. Cohn, Some Notes on Law and Change in North India, 8 Econ. Devel. & Cultural Change 79 (1959).

[62] *E.g.*, Daniel S. Lev, Judicial Institutions and Legal Change in Indonesia, 1971, at 64 (unpublished paper, Dep't of Pol. Sci., Univ. of Washington).

[63] *E.g.*, Maureen Mileski, *supra* note 20, at 66-68.

[64] The diverse input of requests made upon reactive legal processes can teach much about the internal dynamics of a community. We learn about aspects of male-female interaction, for instance, by looking at who brings whom to court. Laura Nader, An Analysis of Zapotec Law Cases, 3 Ethnology 404 (1964). Likewise, the fact that citizens implicate the police in so many non-criminal disputes suggests that American urban life lacks the battery of extralegal mechanisms of dispute settlement often seen among preliterate peoples. The police find themselves playing conciliatory as well as adversarial roles in dispute settlement. These roles are sometimes wholly differentiated in tribal societies. See, *e.g.*, James L. Gibbs, Jr., The Kpelle Moot: A Therapeutic Model for the Informal Settlement of Disputes, 33 Africa 1 (1963).

Like reactive control, systems of proactive mobilization can be put to a variety of uses. These may be public or private. A proactive enforcement campaign, for example, can augment the government treasury through the collection of fines, such as traffic fines, or it can advance or subvert the interests of political figures or political organizations, as is sometimes seen in vice crackdowns and corruption scandals.

LEGAL CHANGE

Students of legal change have traditionally occupied themselves mainly with changes in the substance of legal rules. Legal scholars have paid particular attention to changes in legal rules occurring by accretion in the judicial decision-making process,[65] whereas recent work in social science has been concerned more with legislative change.[66] There has also been some interest in changes in legal organization.[67] Yet in modern societies nearly every aspect of legal life is in a state of flux. Apart from changes in legal rules and organization, continuous shifts are taking place in the kinds and rates of cases that enter the legal process through mobilization, in modes and patterns of disposition, in legal personnel, and in the relationship between legal control and other aspects of social life, such as status hierarchies, informal control mechanisms, the cultural sphere, political movements, and, as Durkheim noted,[68] the ever increasing scope of social differentiation.

Moral Change. As changes occur in the kinds of legal problems citizens have, and in their definitions of legal problems as such, changes follow in the workload of a legal system organized to respond to the citizenry.[69] A reactive system by its nature absorbs every such change that comes about in the population.[70] The police, for example, who are notorious for their conservatism, will nonetheless change their workload to adapt to moral changes in the citizenry. Because they are organized to respond to citizen calls for service, they are organized for change, just as they are organized to provide different police services to the various segments of the population. Whatever the police attitude toward the *status quo* may be, the citizen-based mobilization process renders them eminently pliable.

The legal work that government officials do through their own initiative

---

[65] *E.g.*, Oliver Wendell Holmes, Jr., The Common Law (1881); Benjamin N. Cardozo, The Nature of the Judicial Process (1921), and The Growth of the Law (1924); Edward H. Levi, *supra* note 53.

[66] *E.g.*, Joseph R. Gusfield, Symbolic Crusade: Status Politics and the American Temperance Movement (1963); Leon H. Mayhew, *supra* note 11; Edwin M. Lemert, Social Action and Legal Change: Revolution within the Juvenile Court (1970).

[67] *E.g.*, Max Weber, Max Weber on Law in Economy and Society (Max Rheinstein ed., Edward Shils & M. Rheinstein transl. 1954); Richard D. Schwartz & James C. Miller, Legal Evolution and Societal Complexity, 70 Am. J. Soc. 159 (1964); Sally Falk Moore, Politics, Procedures, and Norms in Changing Chagga Law, 40 Africa 321 (1970).

[68] Emile Durkheim, *supra* note 26.

[69] I make no assumption that citizens will see their own problems as those problems are defined by law, nor that they will necessarily be willing or able to act upon what they experience as their problems. When they do act upon their grievances, however, the reactive system can listen in a way the proactive system cannot.

[70] It has been suggested that democratic organization in general—of which the reactive system is an instance—is especially suited to accommodate social change. Warren G. Bennis & Philip E. Slater, The Temporary Society 4 (1968).

is not nearly so adaptable to the felt needs of citizens. Although citizens can and often do affect the course of proactive legal work by a kind of lobbying activity, the fact remains that it is possible for attitudes of officials that may not be shared by many or even most citizens to influence the selection of cases. A proactive system therefore displays a potential rigidity under conditions of moral change in the citizen population. Beyond its potential rigidity, a proactive control process can aggressively enforce a legal policy upon a resistant population, as has been strikingly illustrated by the political police of authoritarian regimes. It is just this kind of aggressiveness that may be essential to the implementation of law in a modernizing society, where the population is likely to be legally flaccid or apathetic, if not hostile, toward official innovations. Still, because there is no mechanism by which the sentiments of the citizenry are routinely recorded or sampled, as we find in reactive systems, it is always difficult to ascertain whether a proactive control process is following, repressing, or leading moral change in the mass of citizens.

Planned Change. While a citizen-based system may be more attuned to moral shifts in the population, it may be recalcitrant in the face of attempts at centrally directed planned change. Just as the discretionary authority of citizens in a reactive system creates the possibility of discrimination and provides no sure means of controlling it, so in general the citizenry is beyond the reach of other kinds of intentional legal reform. In a reactive process there is no way to intervene systematically in the selection of incidents for legal disposition; hence, public policy may be redefined and public purpose invisibly attenuated.[71] The proactive system, by comparison, is a willing instrument of planned change, for it is under the authority of the planners themselves.

Questions about legal change again call up the economic analogy. Because the reactive mobilization system is built around an entrepreneurial model, because it operates in accordance with the market for legal services, it registers legal changes just as changes appear in economic markets. The changes do not and cannot arise from a center; they arise by increments throughout the citizen population, following a plan no more tangible than the "invisible hand" of the market. Historical drift can express itself in market behavior, and it can similarly flow through the many channels of a citizen-based mobilization system.[72] Proactive mobilization, resembling as it does a social-welfare system, in its pure form involves a central plan with intentional changes and constancies that may or may not take the expressed wishes of the citizenry into account.

[71] Philip Selznick, *supra* note 5, at 228.
[72] See Laura Nader & Barbara Yngvesson, *supra* note 43, at 46-48.

Even in a proactive system oriented to the felt needs of the population, however, individuals may not come forth to make known their wishes, since only in isolation from their fellows are individuals likely to pursue their interests with positive action.[73] In a mobilization system geared to the initiative of citizens, each individual in fact is isolated and must pursue his interests, or no one will. Where a government system is concerned, on the other hand, aggregates of individuals typically share concerns realizable through law, but for that very reason each individual by himself can assume that someone else will look after the legal policies that benefit him. When others use the same calculus as he, they do not act to influence legal policy, and the outcome is an unknown relation between the changing interests of the citizenry and the selection of cases through the initiative of the state. Where planned legal change is possible, then, there is no mechanism to learn the felt requirements of the population. Where there is such a mechanism, there is no way to plan.

Legal Evolution. Perhaps the clearest trend in legal evolution over the past several centuries has been the increasing role of law as a means of social control, a development closely related to the gradual breakdown of other agencies of control such as the kinship group, the close-knit community, and the religious organization.[74] This trend continues along a number of dimensions of the legal world, including the ever greater volume and scope of legislation and adjudication by the state. There seems to be a historical drift toward a state monopoly of the exercise of social control.[75]

An examination of the role of mobilization systems in legal evolution shows that this trend is proceeding in part at the bidding of the citizenry. With the continuing dissolution of extralegal social control, these atomized citizens more and more frequently go to the state to help them when they have no one else. One by one these individual citizens draw in the law to solve their personal troubles, although one by one they would probably agree that the larger outcome of their many decisions is an historical crisis. And yet to deprive these individuals of the initiative they now possess may do nothing more than to substitute a plan for what is now unplanned, while their fate would remain the same.

CONCLUSION

How deviant behavior and disorder come to meet resistance is a problem for investigation, whatever the social context and form of social control. Some

[73] See Mancur Olson, Jr., The Logic of Collective Action: Public Goods and the Theory of Groups (1965).

[74] Roscoe Pound, Social Control Through Law (1942).

[75] See Stanley Diamond, *supra* note 56, at 124.

societies have managed very well with almost no social control beyond that brought to bear by the complainant and his kinfolk.[76] In others, systems of proactive mobilization emerge and disappear in rhythm with the collectivity's involvement in corporate action; during warfare or a hunt in some earlier societies, proactive control would arise, only to recede during less eventful times.[77] Another pattern occurs in coercive institutions, such as prisons or mental hospitals, where it seems that proactive strategies are used almost exclusively in the everyday maintenance of the official order. At still another extreme are face-to-face encounters among social equals, where social control is more diffuse and there appears a kind of orderly anarchy with no mobilization at all.[78] We see variation expressing the texture of life from one setting to the next, and it is apparent that law makes visible a process found in every system of social control.

One scientific advance consists in raising the level of generality at which the empirical world is understood. A relationship once seen as unique is shown to be one of a set; that set may in turn be revealed as a member of a still more general class. My observations on the mobilization of law are very general, since they cut across substantive areas of law, societies, and history. This is both the strength and weakness of the observations. Any reader can produce exceptions to my generalizations, and perhaps I made some over-generalizations, where the number of exceptions will overturn the initial formulations. Yet even with this tentativeness, it is useful to point the direction of a still more general level to which we aspire in legal sociology. We may generalize about all of law, again without regard to substance, place, or time, but now also without regard to a particular dimension of the legal process.

What consequences follow when law is arranged reactively so that ordinary citizens can direct its course? What should we expect if law is proactive, the responsibility of government officials alone? These questions have guided my analysis of legal mobilization. Yet citizen participation in legal life is a problem for study not only in the mobilization of law, but also in other legal processes such as legal prescription and legal disposition. The ultimate issue is: How democratic is the law? Legal rules and policies may arise at the direction of the citizenry, as by plebiscite or by a representative legislature,

[76] *E.g.*, Rafael Karsten, Blood Revenge, War, and Victory Feasts among the Jibaro Indians of Eastern Equador 1-32 (1923); E. E. Evans-Pritchard, The Nuer: A Description of the Modes of Livelihood and Political Institutions of a Nilotic People 150-91 (1940).

[77] A pattern common among many Indian tribes of North America; see Robert H. Lowie, Some Aspects of Political Organization among the American Aborigines, 78 J. Royal Anthro. Inst. 11 (1948).

[78] See Erving Goffman, Embarrassment and Social Organization, 62 Am. J. Soc. 264 (1956).

or at the direction of state officialdom alone, as by dictum or edict. Like the mobilization of law, the degree to which the prescription of law is democratic, then, varies across legal systems. Likewise, the disposition of law, or dispute settlement, may be more or less democratic, as is clear when we compare, for instance, the popular tribunals of some socialist countries[79] to the lower courts of the United States with their powerful adjudicatory officials.[80] In modern societies the grand jury and the trial jury are well-known mechanisms by which the citizenry is introduced into legal decision-making. A general theory of law should tell us what difference democratic organization makes.

I close with several examples of propositions about democratic law applicable to a variety of legal situations. Patterns in the mobilization of law suggest these more general propositions. As illustrations, consider the following:

1. *The more democratic a legal system, the more it perpetuates the existing morality of the population.* Democratic law perpetuates moral diversity as well as moral homogeneity among the citizenry.
2. *The more democratic a legal system, the more the citizenry perpetuates the existing system of social stratification.* Where law is democratic, legal discrimination is practiced by citizens more than by government officials and is therefore more difficult to detect and eliminate.
3. *The more democratic a legal system, the more the law reflects moral and other social change among the citizenry.* Democratic law accommodates social change by historical drift more than planned change.

These propositions about democratic law are preliminary and in need of much refinement. But even primitive propositions give us a necessary starting place. With each unexplained exception comes the possibility of creative reformulation, the heart of theoretical development. With each successful application we have the satisfaction of explanation, even as uncultured as it may presently be. Surely it is worthwhile to build a vocabulary and to make some statements, however haltingly, in a general theory of law.

---

[79] *E.g.,* Jesse Berman, The Cuban Popular Tribunals, 69 Colum. L. Rev. 1317 (1969).

[80] *E.g.,* Maureen Mileski, Courtroom Encounters: An Observation Study of a Lower Criminal Court, 5 L. & Soc. Rev. 473 (1971).

[2]

THE BRITISH JOURNAL
OF
CRIMINOLOGY

Vol. 17   January 1977   No. 1

CONFLICTS AS PROPERTY*

NILS CHRISTIE (*Oslo*) †

Abstract

CONFLICTS are seen as important elements in society. Highly industrialised societies do not have too much internal conflict, they have too little. We have to organise social systems so that conflicts are both nurtured and made visible and also see to it that professionals do not monopolise the handling of them. Victims of crime have in particular lost their rights to participate. A court procedure that restores the participants' rights to their own conflicts is outlined.

Introduction

Maybe we should not have any criminology. Maybe we should rather abolish institutes, not open them. Maybe the social consequences of criminology are more dubious than we like to think.

I think they are. And I think this relates to my topic—conflicts as property. My suspicion is that criminology to some extent has amplified a process where conflicts have been taken away from the parties directly involved and thereby have either disappeared or become other people's property. In both cases a deplorable outcome. Conflicts ought to be used, not only left in erosion. And they ought to be used, and become useful, for those originally involved in the conflict. Conflicts *might* hurt individuals as well as social systems. That is what we learn in school. That is why we have officials. Without them, private vengeance and vendettas will blossom. We have learned this so solidly that we have lost track of the other side of the coin: our industrialised large-scale society is not one with too many internal conflicts. It is one with too little. Conflicts might kill, but too little of them might paralyse. I will

* Foundation Lecture of the Centre for Criminological Studies, University of Sheffield, delivered March 31, 1976. Valuable comments on preliminary drafts of the manuscript were received from Vigdis Christie, Tove Stang Dahl and Annika Snare.
† Professor of Criminology, University of Oslo.

I

NILS CHRISTIE

use this occasion to give a sketch of this situation. It cannot be more than a sketch. This paper represents the beginning of the development of some ideas, not the polished end-product.

On Happenings and Non-Happenings

Let us take our point of departure far away. Let us move to Tanzania. Let us approach our problem from the sunny hillside of the Arusha province. Here, inside a relatively large house in a very small village, a sort of happening took place. The house was overcrowded. Most grown-ups from the village and several from adjoining ones were there. It was a happy happening, fast talking, jokes, smiles, eager attention, not a sentence was to be lost. It was circus, it was drama. It was a court case.

The conflict this time was between a man and a woman. They had been engaged. He had invested a lot in the relationship through a long period, until she broke it off. Now he wanted it back. Gold and silver and money were easily decided on, but what about utilities already worn, and what about general expenses?

The outcome is of no interest in our context. But the framework for conflict solution is. Five elements ought to be particularly mentioned:

1. The parties, the former lovers, were in *the centre* of the room and in the centre of everyone's attention. They talked often and were eagerly listened to.

2. Close to them were relatives and friends who also took part. But they did not *take over*.

3. There was also participation from the general audience with short questions, information, or jokes.

4. The judges, three local party secretaries, were extremely inactive. They were obviously ignorant with regard to village matters. All the other people in the room were experts. They were experts on norms as well as actions. And they crystallised norms and clarified what had happened through participation in the procedure.

5. No reporters attended. They were all there.

My personal knowledge when it comes to British courts is limited indeed. I have some vague memories of juvenile courts where I counted some 15 or 20 persons present, mostly social workers using the room for preparatory work or small conferences A child or a young person must have attended, but except for the judge, or maybe it was the clerk, nobody seemed to pay any particular attention. The child or young person was most probably utterly confused as to who was who and for what, a fact confirmed in a small study by Peter Scott (1959). In the United States of America, Martha Baum (1968) has made similar observations. Recently, Bottoms and McClean (1976) have added another important observation: "There is one truth which is seldom revealed in the literature of the law or in studies of the administration of criminal justice. It is a truth which was made evident to all those involved in this research project as they sat through the cases which made up our sample. The truth is that, for the most part, the business of the criminal courts is dull, commonplace, ordinary and after a while downright tedious ".

But let me keep quiet about your system, and instead concentrate on my

CONFLICTS AS PROPERTY

own. And let me assure you: what goes on is no happening. It is all a negation of the Tanzanian case. What is striking in nearly all the Scandinavian cases is the greyness, the dullness, and the lack of any important audience. Courts are not central elements in the daily life of our citizens, but peripheral in four major ways:—

1. They are situated in the administrative centres of the towns, outside the territories of ordinary people.

2. Within these centres they are often centralised within one or two large buildings of considerable complexity. Lawyers often complain that they need months to find their way within these buildings It does not demand much fantasy to imagine the situation of parties or public when they are trapped within these structures. A comparative study of court architecture might become equally relevant for the sociology of law as Oscar Newman's (1972) study of defensible space is for criminology. But even without any study, I feel it safe to say that both physical situation and architectural design are strong indicators that courts in Scandinavia belong to the administrators of law.

3. This impression is strengthened when you enter the courtroom itself— if you are lucky enough to find your way to it. Here again, the periphery of the parties is the striking observation. The parties are represented, and it is these representatives and the judge or judges who express the little activity that is activated within these rooms. Honoré Daumier's famous drawings from the courts are as representative for Scandinavia as they are for France.

There are variations. In the small cities, or in the countryside, the courts are more easily reached than in the larger towns. And at the very lowest end of the court system—the so-called arbitration boards—the parties are sometimes less heavily represented through experts in law. But the symbol of the whole system is the Supreme Court where the directly involved parties do not even attend their own court cases.

4. I have not yet made any distinction between civil and criminal conflicts. But it was not by chance that the Tanzania case was a civil one. Full participation in your own conflict presupposes elements of civil law. The key element in a criminal proceeding is that the proceeding is converted from something between the concrete parties into a conflict between one of the parties and the state. So, in a modern criminal trial, two important things have happened. First, the parties are being *represented*. Secondly, the one party that is represented by the state, namely the victim, is so thoroughly represented that she or he for most of the proceedings is pushed completely out of the arena, reduced to the triggerer-off of the whole thing. She or he is a sort of double loser; first, *vis-à-vis* the offender, but secondly and often in a more crippling manner by being denied rights to full participation in what might have been one of the more important ritual encounters in life. The victim has lost the case to the state.

Professional Thieves

As we all know, there are many honourable as well as dishonourable reasons behind this development. The honourable ones have to do with the state's

NILS CHRISTIE

need for conflict reduction and certainly also its wishes for the protection of the victim. It is rather obvious. So is also the less honourable temptation for the state, or Emperor, or whoever is in power, to use the criminal case for personal gain. Offenders might pay for their sins. Authorities have in time past shown considerable willingness, in representing the victim, to act as receivers of the money or other property from the offender. Those days are gone; the crime control system is not run for profit. And yet they are not gone. There are, in all banality, many interests at stake here, most of them related to professionalisation.

Lawyers are particularly good at stealing conflicts. They are trained for it. They are trained to prevent and solve conflicts. They are socialised into a sub-culture with a surprisingly high agreement concerning interpretation of norms, and regarding what sort of information can be accepted as relevant in each case. Many among us have, as laymen, experienced the sad moments of truth when our lawyers tell us that our best arguments in our fight against our neighbour are without any legal relevance whatsoever and that we for God's sake ought to keep quiet about them in court. Instead they pick out arguments we might find irrelevant or even wrong to use. My favourite example took place just after the war. One of my country's absolutely top defenders told with pride how he had just rescued a poor client. The client had collaborated with the Germans. The prosecutor claimed that the client had been one of the key people in the organisation of the Nazi movement. He had been one of the master-minds behind it all. The defender, however, saved his client. He saved him by pointing out to the jury how weak, how lacking in ability, how obviously deficient his client was, socially as well as organisationally. His client could simply not have been one of the organisers among the collaborators; he was without talents. And he won his case. His client got a very minor sentence as a very minor figure. The defender ended his story by telling me—with some indignation—that neither the accused, nor his wife, had ever thanked him, they had not even talked to him afterwards.

Conflicts become the property of lawyers. But lawyers don't hide that it is conflicts they handle. And the organisational framework of the courts underlines this point. The opposing parties, the judge, the ban against privileged communication within the court system, the lack of encouragement for specialisation—specialists cannot be internally controlled—it all underlines that this is an organisation for the handling of conflicts. *Treatment personnel* are in another position. They are more interested in *converting the image of the case from one of conflict into one of non-conflict*. The basic model of healers is not one of opposing parties, but one where one party has to be helped in the direction of one generally accepted goal—the preservation or restoration of health. They are not trained into a system where it is important that parties can control each other. There is, in the ideal case, nothing to control, because there is only one goal. Specialisation is encouraged. It increases the amount of available knowledge, and the loss of internal control is of no relevance. A conflict perspective creates unpleasant doubts with regard to the healer's suitability for the job. A non-conflict perspective is a precondition for defining crime as a legitimate target for treatment.

4

CONFLICTS AS PROPERTY

One way of reducing attention to the conflict is reduced attention given to the victim. Another is concentrated attention given to those attributes in the criminal's background which the healer is particularly trained to handle. Biological defects are perfect. So also are personality defects when they are established far back in time—far away from the recent conflict. And so are also the whole row of explanatory variables that criminology might offer. We have, in criminology, to a large extent functioned as an auxiliary science for the professionals within the crime control system. We have focused on the offender, made her or him into an object for study, manipulation and control. We have added to all those forces that have reduced the victim to a nonentity and the offender to a thing. And this critique is perhaps not only relevant for the old criminology, but also for the new criminology. While the old one explained crime from personal defects or social handicaps, the new criminology explains crime as the result of broad economic conflicts. The old criminology loses the conflicts, the new one converts them from interpersonal conflicts to class conflicts. And they are. They are class conflicts—also. But, by stressing this, the conflicts are again taken away from the directly involved parties. So, as a preliminary statement: Criminal conflicts have either become *other people's property*—primarily the property of lawyers—or it has been in other people's interests to *define conflicts away*.

Structural Thieves

But there is more to it than professional manipulation of conflicts. Changes in the basic social structure have worked in the same way.

What I particularly have in mind are *two types of segmentation* easily observed in highly industrialised societies. First, there is the question of segmentation *in space*. We function each day, as migrants moving between sets of people which do not need to have any link—except through the mover. Often, therefore, we know our work-mates only as work-mates, neighbours only as neighbours, fellow cross-country skiers only as fellow cross-country skiers. We get to know them as *roles*, not as total persons. This situation is accentuated by the extreme degree of division of labour we accept to live with. Only experts can evaluate each other according to individual—personal—competence. Outside the speciality we have to fall back on a general evaluation of the supposed importance of the work. Except between specialists, we cannot evaluate how good anybody is in his work, only how good, in the sense of important, the role is. Through all this, we get limited possibilities for understanding other people's behaviour. Their behaviour will also get limited relevance for us. Role-players are more easily exchanged than persons.

The second type of segmentation has to do with what I would like to call our re-establishment of caste-society. I am not saying class-society, even though there are obvious tendencies also in that direction. In my framework, however, I find the elements of caste even more important. What I have in mind is the segregation based on biological attributes such as sex, colour, physical handicaps or the number of winters that have passed since birth. Age is particularly important. It is an attribute nearly perfectly synchronised to a modern complex industrialised society. It is a continuous variable where

NILS CHRISTIE

we can introduce as many intervals as we might need. We can split the population in two: children and adults. But we also can split it in ten: babies,
pre-school children, school-children, teenagers, older youth, adults, pre-
pensioned, pensioned, old people, the senile. And most important: the cutting
points can be moved up and down according to social needs. The concept
" teenager " was particularly suitable 10 years ago. It would not have caught
on if social realities had not been in accordance with the word. Today the
concept is not often used in my country. The condition of youth is not over at
19. Young people have to wait even longer before they are allowed to enter
the work force. The caste of those outside the work force has been extended
far into the twenties. At the same time departure from the work force—if you
ever were admitted, if you were not kept completely out because of race or
sex-attributes—is brought forward into the early sixties in a person's life.
In my tiny country of four million inhabitants, we have 800,000 persons
segregated within the educational system. Increased scarcity of work has
immediately led authorities to increase the capacity of educational incarceration. Another 600,000 are pensioners.

Segmentation according to space and according to caste attributes has
several consequences. First and foremost it leads into a *depersonalisation* of
social life. Individuals are to a smaller extent linked to each other in close
social networks where they are confronted with *all* the significant roles of the
significant others. This creates a situation with limited amounts of information with regard to each other. We do know less about other people, and get
limited possibilities both for understanding and for prediction of their
behaviour. If a conflict is created, we are less able to cope with this situation.
Not only are professionals there, able and willing to take the conflict away,
but we are also more willing to give it away.

Secondly, segmentation leads to destruction of certain conflicts even before
they get going. The depersonalisation and mobility within industrial society
melt away some essential conditions for living conflicts; those between parties
that mean a lot to each other. What I have particularly in mind is crime
against other people's honour, libel or defamation of character. All the
Scandinavian countries have had a dramatic decrease in this form of crime.
In my interpretation, this is not because honour has become more respected,
but because there is less honour to respect. The various forms of segmentation
mean that human beings are inter-related in ways where they simply mean.
less to each other. When they are hurt, they are only hurt partially. And if
they are troubled, they can easily move away. And after all, who cares?
Nobody knows me. In my evaluation, the decrease in the crimes of infamy
and libel is one of the most interesting and sad symptoms of dangerous
developments within modern industrialised societies. The decrease here is
clearly related to social conditions that lead to increase in other forms of
crime brought to the attention of the authorities. It is an important goal for
crime prevention to re-create social conditions which lead to an increase in
the number of crimes against other people's honour.

A third consequence of segmentation according to space and age is that
certain conflicts are made completely invisible, and thereby don't get any

CONFLICTS AS PROPERTY

decent solution whatsoever. I have here in mind conflicts at the two extremes of a continuum. On the one extreme we have the over-privatised ones, those taking place against individuals captured within one of the segments. Wife beating or child battering represent examples. The more isolated a segment is, the more the weakest among parties is alone, open for abuse. Inghe and Riemer (1943) made the classical study many years ago of a related phenomenon in their book on incest. Their major point was that the social isolation of certain categories of proletarised Swedish farm-workers was the necessary condition for this type of crime. Poverty meant that the parties within the nuclear family became completely dependent on each other. Isolation meant that the weakest parties within the family had no external network where they could appeal for help. The physical strength of the husband got an undue importance. At the other extreme we have crimes done by large economic organisations against individuals too weak and ignorant to be able even to realise they have been victimised. In both cases the goal for crime prevention might be to re-create social conditions which make the conflicts visible and thereafter manageable.

Conflicts as Property

Conflicts are taken away, given away, melt away, or are made invisible. Does it matter, does it really matter?

Most of us would probably agree that we ought to protect the invisible victims just mentioned. Many would also nod approvingly to ideas saying that states, or Governments, or other authorities ought to stop stealing fines, and instead let the poor victim receive this money. I at least would approve such an arragement. But I will not go into that problem area here and now. Material compensation is not what I have in mind with the formulation " conflicts as property ". It is the *conflict itself* that represents the most interesting property taken away, not the goods originally taken away from the victim, or given back to him. In our types of society, conflicts are more scarce than property. And they are immensely more valuable.

They are valuable in several ways. Let me start at the societal level, since here I have already presented the necessary fragments of analysis that might allow us to see what the problem is. Highly industrialised societies face major problems in organising their members in ways such that a decent quota take part in any activity at all. Segmentation according to age and sex can be seen as shrewd methods for segregation. Participation is such a scarcity that insiders create monopolies against outsiders, particularly with regard to work. In this perspective, it will easily be seen that conflicts represent a *potential for activity, for participation*. Modern criminal control systems represent one of the many cases of lost opportunities for involving citizens in tasks that are of immediate importance to them. Ours is a society of task-monopolists.

The victim is a particularly heavy loser in this situation. Not only has he suffered, lost materially or become hurt, physically or otherwise. And not only does the state take the compensation. But above all he has lost participation in his own case. It is the Crown that comes into the spotlight, not the victim. It is the Crown that describes the losses, not the victim. It is the Crown

7

NILS CHRISTIE

that appears in the newspaper, very seldom the victim. It is the Crown that
gets a chance to talk to the offender, and neither the Crown nor the offender
are particularly interested in carrying on that conversation. The prosecutor
is fed-up long since. The victim would not have been. He might have been
scared to death, panic-stricken, or furious. But he would not have been uninvolved. It would have been one of the important days in his life. Something
that belonged to him has been taken away from that victim.[1]

But the big loser is us—to the extent that society is us. This loss is first and
foremost a loss in *opportunities for norm-clarification*. It is a loss of pedagogical
possibilities. It is a loss of opportunities for a continuous discussion of what
represents the law of the land. How wrong was the thief, how right was the
victim? Lawyers are, as we saw, trained into agreement on what is relevant
in a case. But that means a trained incapacity in letting the parties decide
what *they* think is relevant. It means that it is difficult to stage what we might
call a political debate in the court. When the victim is small and the offender
big—in size or power—how blameworthy then is the crime? And what about
the opposite case, the small thief and the big house-owner? If the offender is
well educated, ought he then to suffer more. or maybe less, for his sins? Or if
he is black, or if he is young, or if the other party is an insurance company,
or if his wife has just left him, or if his factory will break down if he has to go
to jail, or if his daughter will lose her fiancé, or if he was drunk, or if he was
sad, or if he was mad? There is no end to it. And maybe there ought to be
none. Maybe Barotse law as described by Max Gluckman (1967) is a better
instrument for norm-clarification, allowing the conflicting parties to bring
in the whole chain of old complaints and arguments each time. Maybe
decisions on relevance and on the weight of what is found relevant ought to
be taken away from legal scholars, the chief ideologists of crime control
systems, and brought back for free decisions in the court-rooms.

A further general loss—both for the victim and for society in general—
has to do with anxiety-level and misconceptions. It is again the possibilities
for personalised encounters I have in mind. The victim is so totally out of the
case that he has no chance, ever, to come to know the offender. We leave
him outside, angry, maybe humiliated through a cross-examination in court,
without any human contact with the offender. He has no alternative. He will
need all the classical stereotypes around " the criminal " to get a grasp on
the whole thing. He has a need for understanding, but is instead a non-person
in a Kafka play. Of course, he will go away more frightened than ever, more
in need than ever of an explanation of criminals as non-human.

The offender represents a more complicated case. Not much introspection
is needed to see that direct victim-participation might be experienced as
painful indeed. Most of us would shy away from a confrontation of this
character. That is the first reaction. But the second one is slightly more positive. Human beings have reasons for their actions. If the situation is staged
so that reasons can be given (reasons as the parties see them, not only the
selection lawyers have decided to classify as relevant), in such a case maybe
the situation would not be all that humiliating. And, particularly, if the situa-

[1] For a preliminary report on victim dissatisfaction, see Vennard (1976).

CONFLICTS AS PROPERTY

tion was staged in such a manner that the central question was not meting out guilt, but a thorough discussion of what could be done to undo the deed, then the situation might change. And this is exactly what ought to happen when the victim is re-introduced in the case. Serious attention will centre on the victim's losses. That leads to a natural attention as to how they can be softened. It leads into a discussion of restitution. The offender gets a possibility to change his position from being a listener to a discussion—often a highly unintelligible one—of how much pain he ought to receive, into a participant in a discussion of how he could make it good again. The offender has lost the opportunity to explain himself to a person whose evaluation of him might have mattered. He has thereby also lost one of the most important possibilities for being forgiven. Compared to the humiliations in an ordinary court—vividly described by Pat Carlen (1976) in a recent issue of the *British Journal of Criminology*—this is not obviously any bad deal for the criminal.

But let me add that I think we should do it quite independently of his wishes. It is not health-control we are discussing. It is crime control. If criminals are shocked by the initial thought of close confrontation with the victim, preferably a confrontation in the very local neighbourhood of one of the parties, what then? I know from recent conversations on these matters that most people sentenced are shocked. After all, they prefer distance from the victim, from neighbours, from listeners and maybe also from their own court case through the vocabulary and the behavioural science experts who might happen to be present. They are perfectly willing to give away their property right to the conflict. So the question is more: are *we* willing to let them give it away? Are we willing to give them this easy way out? [2]

Let me be quite explicit on one point: I am not suggesting these ideas out of any particular interest in the treatment or improvement of criminals. I am not basing my reasoning on a belief that a more personalised meeting between offender and victim would lead to reduced recidivism. Maybe it would. I think it would. As it is now, the offender has lost the opportunity for participation in a personal confrontation of a very serious nature. He has lost the opportunity to receive a type of blame that it would be very difficult to neutralise. However, I would have suggested these arrangements even if it was absolutely certain they had no effects on recidivism, maybe even if they had a negative effect. I would have done that because of the other, more general gains. And let me also add—it is not much to lose. As we all know today, at least nearly all, we have not been able to invent any cure for crime. Except for execution, castration or incarceration for life, no measure has a proven minimum of efficiency compared to any other measure. We might as well react to crime according to what closely involved parties find is just and in accordance with general values in society.

With this last statement, as with most of the others I have made, I raise many more problems than I answer. Statements on criminal politics, particularly from those with the burden of responsibility, are usually filled with

[2] I tend to take the same position with regard to a criminal's property right to his own conflict as John Locke on property rights to one's own life—one has no right to give it away (*cf.* C. B. MacPherson (1962)).

NILS CHRISTIE

answers. It is questions we need. The gravity of our topic makes us much too pedantic and thereby useless as paradigm-changers.

A Victim-Oriented Court

There is clearly a model of neighbourhood courts behind my reasoning. But it is one with some peculiar features, and it is only these I will discuss in what follows.

First and foremost; it is a *victim-oriented* organisation. Not in its initial stage, though. The first stage will be a traditional one where it is established whether it is true that the law has been broken, and whether it was this particular person who broke it.

Then comes the second stage, which in these courts would be of the utmost importance. That would be the stage where the victim's situation was considered, where every detail regarding what had happened—legally relevant or not—was brought to the court's attention. Particularly important here would be detailed consideration regarding what could be done for him, first and foremost by the offender, secondly by the local neighbourhood, thirdly by the state. Could the harm be compensated, the window repaired, the lock replaced, the wall painted, the loss of time because the car was stolen given back through garden work or washing of the car ten Sundays in a row? Or maybe, when this discussion started, the damage was not so important as it looked in documents written to impress insurance companies? Could physical suffering become slightly less painful by any action from the offender, during days, months or years? But, in addition, had the community exhausted all resources that might have offered help? Was it absolutely certain that the local hospital could not do anything? What about a helping hand from the janitor twice a day if the offender took over the cleaning of the basement every Saturday? None of these ideas is unknown or untried, particularly not in England. But we need an organisation for the systematic application of them.

Only after this stage was passed, and it ought to take hours, maybe days, to pass it, only then would come the time for an eventual decision on punishment. Punishment, then, becomes that suffering which the judge found necessary to apply *in addition to* those unintended constructive sufferings the offender would go through in his restitutive actions *vis-à-vis* the victim. Maybe nothing could be done or nothing would be done. But neighbourhoods might find it intolerable that nothing happened. Local courts out of tune with local values are not local courts. That is just the trouble with them, seen from the liberal reformer's point of view.

A fourth stage has to be added. That is the stage for service to the offender. His general social and personal situation is by now well-known to the court. The discussion of his possibilities for restoring the victim's situation cannot be carried out without at the same time giving information about the offender's situation. This might have exposed needs for social, educational, medical or religious action—not to prevent further crime, but because needs ought to be met. Courts are public arenas, needs are made visible. But it is important that this stage comes *after* sentencing. Otherwise we get a re-emergence of

CONFLICTS AS PROPERTY

the whole array of so-called " special measures "—compulsory treatments—very often only euphemisms for indeterminate imprisonment.

Through these four stages, these courts would represent a blend of elements from civil and criminal courts, but with a strong emphasis on the civil side.

A Lay-Oriented Court

The second major peculiarity with the court model I have in mind is that it will be one with an extreme degree of lay-orientation. This is essential when conflicts are seen as property that ought to be shared. It is with conflicts as with so many good things: they are in no unlimited supply. Conflicts can be cared for, protected, nurtured. But there are limits. If some are given more access in the disposal of conflicts, others are getting less. It is as simple as that.

Specialisation in conflict solution is the major enemy; specialisation that in due—or undue—time leads to professionalisation. That is when the specialists get sufficient power to claim that they have acquired special gifts, mostly through education, gifts so powerful that it is obvious that they can only be handled by the certified craftsman.

With a clarification of the enemy, we are also able to specify the goal; let us reduce specialisation and particularly our dependence on the professionals within the crime control system to the utmost.

The ideal is clear; it ought to be a court of equals representing themselves. When they are able to find a solution between themselves, no judges are needed. When they are not, the judges ought also to be their equals.

Maybe the judge would be the easiest to replace, if we made a serious attempt to bring our present courts nearer to this model of lay orientation. We have lay judges already, in principle. But that is a far cry from realities. What we have, both in England and in my own country, is a sort of specialised non-specialist. First, they are used *again and again*. Secondly, some are even *trained*, given special courses or sent on excursions to foreign countries to learn about how to behave as a lay judge. Thirdly, most of them do also represent an extremely *biased sample* of the population with regard to sex, age, education, income, class [3] and personal experience as criminals. With real lay judges, I conceive of a system where nobody was given the right to take part in conflict solution more than a few times, and then had to wait until all other community members had had the same experience.

Should lawyers be admitted to court? We had an old law in Norway that forbids them to enter the rural districts. Maybe they should be admitted in stage one where it is decided if the man is guilty. I am not sure. Experts are as cancer to any lay body. It is exactly as Ivan Illich describes for the educational system in general. Each time you increase the length of compulsory education in a society, each time you also decrease the same population's trust in what they have learned and understood quite by themselves.

Behaviour experts represent the same dilemma. Is there a place for them in this model? Ought there to be any place? In stage 1, decisions on facts, certainly not. In stage 3, decisions on eventual punishment, certainly not. It is too obvious to waste words on. We have the painful row of mistakes from

[3] For the most recent documentation, see Baldwin (1976).

NILS CHRISTIE

Lombroso, through the movement for social defence and up to recent attempts to dispose of supposedly dangerous people through predictions of who they are and when they are not dangerous any more. Let these ideas die, without further comments.

The real problem has to do with the service function of behaviour experts. Social scientists can be perceived as functional answers to a segmented society. Most of us have lost the physical possibility to experience the totality, both on the social system level and on the personality level. Psychologists can be seen as historians for the individual; sociologists have much of the same function for the social system. Social workers are oil in the machinery, a sort of security counsel. Can we function without them, would the victim and the offender be worse off?

Maybe. But it would be immensely difficult to get such a court to function if they were all there. Our theme is social conflict. Who is not at least made slightly uneasy in the handling of her or his own social conflicts if we get to know that there is an expert on this very matter at the same table? I have no clear answer, only strong feelings behind a vague conclusion: let us have as few behaviour experts as we dare to. And if we have any, let us for God's sake not have any that specialise in crime and conflict resolution. Let us have generalised experts with a solid base outside the crime control system. And a last point with relevance for both behaviour experts and lawyers: if we find them unavoidable in certain cases or at certain stages, let us try to get across to them the problems they create for broad social participation. Let us try to get them to perceive themselves as resource-persons, answering when asked, but not domineering, not in the centre. They might help to stage conflicts, not take them over.

Rolling Stones

There are hundreds of blocks against getting such a system to operate within our western culture. Let me only mention three major ones. They are:

1. There is a lack of neighbourhoods.
2. There are too few victims.
3. There are too many professionals around.

With lack of neighbourhoods I have in mind the very same phenomenon I described as a consequence of industrialised living; segmentation according to space and age. Much of our trouble stems from killed neighbourhoods or killed local communities. How can we then thrust towards neighbourhoods a task that presupposes they are highly alive? I have no really good arguments, only two weak ones. First, it is not quite that bad. The death is not complete. Secondly, one of the major ideas behind the formulation ' Conflicts as Property' is that it is neighbourhood-property. It is not private. It belongs to the system. It is intended as a vitaliser for neighbourhoods. The more fainting the neighbourhood is, the more we need neighbourhood courts as one of the many functions any social system needs for not dying through lack of challenge.

Equally bad is the lack of victims. Here I have particularly in mind the lack of personal victims. The problem behind this is again the large units in

CONFLICTS AS PROPERTY

industrialised society. Woolworth or British Rail are not good victims. But again I will say: there is not a complete lack of personal victims, and their needs ought to get priority. But we should not forget the large organisations. They, or their boards, would certainly prefer not to have to appear as victims in 5000 neighbourhood courts all over the country. But maybe they ought to be compelled to appear. If the complaint is serious enough to bring the offender into the ranks of the criminal, then the victim ought to appear. A related problem has to do with insurance companies—the industrialised alternative to friendship or kinship. Again we have a case where the crutches deteriorate the condition. Insurance takes the consequences of crime away. We will therefore have to take insurance away. Or rather: we will have to keep the possibilities for compensation through the insurance companies back until in the procedure I have described it has been proved behond all possible doubt that there are no other alternatives left—particularly that the offender has no possibilities whatsoever. Such a solution will create more paper-work, less predictability, more aggression from customers. And the solution will not necessarily be seen as good from the perspective of the policy-holder. But it will help to protect conflicts as social fuel.

None of these troubles can, however, compete with the third and last I will comment on: the abundance of professionals. We know it all from our own personal biographies or personal observations. And in addition we get it confirmed from all sorts of social science research: the educational system of any society is not necessarily synchronised with any needs for the product of this system. Once upon a time we thought there was a direct causal relation from the number of highly educated persons in a country to the Gross National Product. Today we suspect the relationship to go the other way, if we are at all willing to use GNP as a meaningful indicator. We also know that most educational systems are extremely class-biased. We know that most academic people have had profitable investments in our education, that we fight for the same for our children, and that we also often have vested interests in making our part of the educational system even bigger. More schools for more lawyers, social workers, sociologists, criminologists. While I am *talking* deprofessionalisation, we are increasing the capacity to be able to fill up the whole world with them.

There is no solid base for optimism. On the other hand insights about the situation, and goal formulation, is a pre-condition for action. Of course, the crime control system is not the domineering one in our type of society. But it has some importance. And occurrences here are unusually well suited as pedagogical illustrations of general trends in society. There is also some room for manoeuvre. And when we hit the limits, or are hit by them, this collision represents in itself a renewed argument for more broadly conceived changes.

Another source for hope: ideas formulated here are not quite so isolated or in dissonance with the mainstream of thinking when we leave our crime control area and enter other institutions. I have already mentioned Ivan Illich with his attempts to get learning away from the teachers and back to active human beings. Compulsory learning, compulsory medication and compulsory consummation of conflict solutions have interesting similarities.

13

NILS CHRISTIE

When Ivan Illich and Paulo Freire are listened to, and my impression is that they increasingly are, the crime control system will also become more easily influenced.

Another, but related, major shift in paradigm is about to happen within the whole field of technology. Partly, it is the lessons from the third world that now are more easily seen, partly it is the experience from the ecology debate. The globe is obviously suffering from what we, through our technique, are doing to her. Social systems in the third world are equally obviously suffering. So the suspicion starts. Maybe the first world can't take all this technology either. Maybe some of the old social thinkers were not so dumb after all. Maybe social systems can be perceived as biological ones. And maybe there are certain types of large-scale technology that kill social systems, as they kill globes. Schumacher (1973) with his book *Small is Beautiful* and the related Institute for Intermediate Technology come in here. So do also the numerous attempts, particularly by several outstanding Institutes for Peace Research, to show the dangers in the concept of Gross National Product, and replace it with indicators that take care of dignity, equity and justice. The perspective developed in Johan Galtung's research group on World Indicators might prove extremely useful also within our own field of crime control.

There is also a political phenomenon opening vistas. At least in Scandinavia social democrats and related groupings have considerable power, but are without an explicated ideology regarding the goals for a reconstructed society. This vacuum is being felt by many, and creates a willingness to accept and even expect considerable institutional experimentation.

Then to my very last point: what about the universities in this picture? What about the new Centre in Sheffield? The answer has probably to be the old one: universities have to re-emphasise the old tasks of understanding and of criticising. But the task of training professionals ought to be looked into with renewed scepticism. Let us re-establish the credibility of encounters between critical human beings: low-paid, highly regarded, but with no extra power—outside the weight of their good ideas. That is as it ought to be.

REFERENCES

BALDWIN, J (1976) " The Social Composition of the Magistracy " Brit. J Criminol., **16**, 171–174.

BAUM, M. AND WHEELER, S. (1968). " Becoming an inmate," Ch. 7, pp. 153–187, in Wheeler, S. (ed.), *Controlling Delinquents*. New York: Wiley.

BOTTOMS, A. E. AND McCLEAN, J. D. (1976). *Defendants in the Criminal Process*. London: Routledge and Kegan Paul.

CARLEN, P. (1976). " The Staging of Magistrates' Justice." Brit. J. Criminol., **16**, 48–55.

GLUCKMAN, M. (1967). *The Judicial Process among the Barotse of Northern Rhodesia* Manchester University Press.

KINBERG, O., INGHE, G., AND RIEMER, S. (1943). *Incest-Problemet i Sverige*. Sth.

CONFLICTS AS PROPERTY

MacPherson, C. B. (1962). *The Political Theory of Possessive Individualism: Hobbes to Locke.* London: Oxford University Press.

Newman, O. (1972). *Defensible Space: People and Design in the Violent City.* London: Architectural Press.

Schumacher, E. F. (1973). *Small is Beautiful: A Study of Economics as if People Mattered.* London: Blond and Briggs.

Scott, P. D. (1959). "Juvenile Courts: the Juvenile's Point of View." *Brit. J. Delinq.,* **9,** 200–210.

Vennard, J. (1976). "Justice and Recompense for Victims of Crime." *New Society,* **36,** 378–380.

[3]

INFLUENCES OF SOCIAL ORGANIZATION ON DISPUTE PROCESSING*

WILLIAM L.F. FELSTINER

University of California
Los Angeles

Man is an ingenious social animal. Institutionalized responses to interpersonal conflict, for instance, stretch from song duels and witchcraft to moots and mediation to self-conscious therapy and hierarchical, professionalized courts. The dispute processing practices prevailing in any particular society are a product of its values, its psychological imperatives, its history and its economic, political and social organization.[1] It is unlikely that any general theory encompassing all of these factors will be developed until there have been many piecemeal attempts to understand something of the influence of each.

This paper first outlines several types of social organization and analyzes certain forms of dispute processing. It then suggests that these forms of dispute processing either depend on an availability of resources (such as coercive power or pre-dispute information) which varies with social organization or have different negative consequences in different social contexts. Finally, the paper explores the implications of this linkage be-

* I received substantial encouragement in working through this analysis from Jan Collier, Richard Danzig, Robert Stevens and David Trubek and valuable direction from Richard Abel, Celestine Arndt, Richard Canter, Marc Galanter, Robert Kidder and Mark Peterson.

1. This paper reflects a preference for the term "dispute processing" instead of the more common "dispute settlement." My aversion to "dispute settlement" is based on the conviction that a significant amount of dispute processing is not intended to settle disputes, that a greater amount does not do so and that it is often difficult to know whether a dispute which has been processed has been settled, or even what the dispute was about in the first place (*see* Collier, 1973: 169; Gulliver, 1969: 14-15; Gibbs, 1969: 193). These questions persist even when issues in dispute are sharply defined, as by written pleadings. In many such formal cases one or all of the parties seek something other than a resolution, even an advantageous resolution. of the matter in dispute. Such a phenomenon is recognized in the U.S. (Sykes, 1969: 330; Nader, 1965: 19) and is thought to be endemic in India. Litigation is used as a skirmish or an important maneuver in economic and political warfare: the expense, inconvenience and disgrace of court involvement imposed on one's opponent outweigh one's concern about the end result of the ostensible dispute, if ever an end result is intended (Kidder, 1973: 137; Cohn, 1967: 154; Rudolph and Rudolph, 1967: 262). It does not then seem to make sense to talk about a "settlement" process when frequently it is not demonstrable that settlement is the objective of the process, and when it is often impossible to determine what is to be settled or whether that result has been achieved (*see* Van Velsen, 1969: 147). The term "dispute processing" avoids all of these difficulties.

tween social organization and dispute processing for certain reforms currently advocated in the U.S.

A cautionary word about the proposed level of analysis may
be appropriate. An important theme in legal anthropology has
been the examination of why disputants choose as they do among
several available dispute processing institutions (Pospisil, 1967:
12; Gulliver, 1963: 173-215; Nader and Metzger, 1963; Collier,
1973: 65-74). This paper does not face that question. It attempts the simpler, but generally disregarded (*but see* Nader,
1969: 86-91; 1965: 22), task of describing the social conditions
under which several forms of dispute processing are likely to
occur. Collier implies that these questions are really a single
issue when she suggests that institutions are simply the result
of cumulative individual choices (1973: 251). But if the choice
of institutions that is made by any particular disputants frequently depends on the relationship between them (Collier, 1973:
49), the choices that *can* be made will depend in important respects on the cumulative relationships between people in that
social group. Not all forms of dispute processing exist in all
social groups. Resort to the supernatural, for instance, is rare
in an American suburb. Cumulative relationships (social organization) must therefore be explored if one's aim is to understand
why some institutions do not exist in a particular society as weil
as why others do exist.

I.   IDEAL TYPES OF SOCIAL ORGANIZATION

Social organization in these propositions means any regulari-
ties in geographic, economic, kin or other relationships among
people within a single society. But in any particular society alternative and competing institutions may organize the same relationships. As a consequence, analysis of the effect of social
organization on any social process is extremely complicated. In
the same society, for example, families may either be nuclear
or cohere on extended lines. Vocations may or may not persist
across generations. Neighbors may be friends or strangers. We
know very little about the regularity with which these variables
associate. Since the effect of social organization on forms of
dispute processing cannot be explored using a real empirical base
because the data do not exist, insight must come, if at all,
through the use of ideal types. Weber's (1968: 497) notion of
ideal types includes "one-sided accentuation" of important social
characteristics. It is this dimension of ideal types which distinguishes them from empirical generalizations and which insulates
them from empirical falsification. The ideal types used in this

paper incorporate such accentuation (*e.g.*, in one type of society friendships *are* unstable), but they also include many social characteristics which are less than absolute (*e.g.*, adults *infrequently* live in the same neighborhood as their parents). The Weberian accentuation in this paper is mainly constructed by the inclusion in each type of society of components of social organization all of which cut in one direction, that is toward either an atomistic or integrated pattern.

Two ideal types of social organization will be contrasted: a technologically complex rich society (TCRS) and a technologically simple poor society (TSPS). In a TCRS the family unit is nuclear (conjugal) and biological (*see* Nimkoff & Middleton, 1968: 35). Marriage and its functional equivalents are unstable, are not arranged, and constitute a liaison between individuals rather than between family groups. Relationships between extra-nuclear family members are either unimportant—in that they are not a source of companionship, therapy, economic or political support, education, ceremony or self-definition—or they tend to be grounded not upon kinship but upon the same factors which give rise to relationships outside the family. Adults infrequently live in the same neighborhood as their parents, siblings or adult children. Financial assistance in old age is the responsibility not of the family but of the state. Working members of a family do not share work sites or occupations.[2]

2. The controversy over the degree of isolation of nuclear families in America has been summarized almost as frequently as it has been conducted (*see* Leslie, 1967: 332-38; Winch and Blumberg, 1968: 70-71; Turner, 1970: 419-22; Reiss, 1971: 266-78). For the purposes of this paper it is important to note first that the relative isolation stipulated for families in a TCSR is relative not to families in rural areas in the same society, which is what a significant part of the controversy has been about (Wirth, 1938: 12; Burgess, Locke and Thomas, 1963: 62-63; Winch, 1968: 134), but to the family situation in another type of society altogether (*see* Parsons, 1965: 35; Adams, 1971: 287). Second, those researchers who have identified functional relations between nuclear family and other kin have frequently concentrated on tangential or sporadic functions (Axelrod, 1956:16—getting together; Sharp and Axelrod, 1956: 436-37—babysitting, help when sick, help with housework and financial aid; Bell and Boat, 1957: 396—care when sick; Bell, 1968: 142—emergency help; Winch, 1968: 133—babysitting, borrowing and lending equipment, emergency help). The major difference in kin relations on which this paper focuses is not that of frequency of contact but in the content of contacts, a matter relatively ignored by sociologists of the family in the U.S. Such researchers have also tended to ignore relations other than those between parents and children. Reiss (1962: 335), an exception, reports that less than one-half of siblings interact annually (*see* also Adams, 1971: 291). Young and Willmott, who observed sustained relations between children and parents in East London, found contact with a wider kin network to be generally limited to *rites de passage* (1957: 63-66; *see* Townsend 1957: 115). Third, the proportion of the populations studied who maintain some form of active relations with kin beyond the nuclear family are not unimportant, but they are nevertheless usually in the minority (Winch, 1968: 134—high functionality to familism 40%; one or more family visits

66   LAW AND SOCIETY / FALL 1974

In a TCRS friendships are unstable; long-term interpersonal
relationships are difficult to maintain. Adults do not live where
they have lived as children and are schooled in more than one
locale. They do not live in one house or neighborhood for an
adult life, and they are not employed in one place for a working
life. Friendship is geared to rough equivalence in economic status, and individuals do not proceed up or down the economic
scale at the same pace as any particular acquaintances. Because
of access to convenient transport, social intercourse is little restricted by proximity: friends are not necessarily neighbors and
neighbors are not necessarily friends.[3] Especially in urban areas,
friendships tend to be routine rather than intimate, reflections
of Alexander's autonomy-withdrawal syndrome (1966: 19-33).

Vocational mobility in a TCRS is high, although more from
job to job than from occupation to occupation. If the requirement of specialized skills tends to reduce mobility between occupational strata, the labor market has few other structural impediments; group barriers are progressively ineffective and nepotism is unimportant. Only a small proportion of the labor force
is self or family employed, working in agriculture or in jobs
acutely restricted in locale. Disfavored occupations (manual,
farm and domestic labor, food services, low-level factory employment) account for only a small proportion of total employment,
and consequently relatively few workers with disfavored jobs are
competing for jobs in favored occupations. The work force has
received a substantial general education; many opportunities to
develop the specialized skills required of a technologically advanced industrial apparatus are available.

Residential mobility also is high in a TCSR. Housing availability rarely inhibts moves. Although the trauma and burdens
of moving are worse for women than for men, a move is neither
extremely uncomfortable nor administratively difficult. Jobs
are not fungible because contacts, customers, seniority and local

per week, Reiss, 1962: 334—9-13%; Litwak, 1960a: 15—34-39%;
Axelrod, 1956: 16—49%; Bell and Boat, 1957: 394—30-45%; Greer,
1956: 22—49-55%). For comparative purposes, Townsend (1957:110)
reports that in an established section of London 58% of old people
saw relatives of the two succeeding generations *nearly every day*.
And last, it may be relevant that researchers using survey techniques (and therefore concentrating on frequencies) have tended to
find more middle class kin interaction than those who engaged in
sustained participant observation (and therefore concentrated on the
significance and meaning of rates). Compare Sussman, 1959:333-40
to Seeley, Sim & Loosley, 1956: 160, 183.

3.   Above all, one thought
        Baffled my understanding, how men lived
        Even next-door neighbours, as we say, yet still
        Strangers, and knowing not each other's names.
        (Wordsworth, 1933: 108)

custom make each one somewhat singular, but a move generally
does not require a change of occupation. Few moves are inhibited by the prospect of disturbing close family relationships
because in most instances the family lives somewhere else to begin with. The process of making new familiars out of strangers
is not encumbered by differences in language, eating habits, dress
or notions of acceptable behavior. A move spells no greater cultural than social sacrifice. Climate is valued over history, and
facilities (aesthetic, sport, spectator) over nostalgia. No space-
confined relationship with the dead, immediate or long past,
exists. Whatever artifacts, religious, educational and child-rear-
ing practices, entertainment, dress or manners are left behind
will be found virtually duplicated at the new doorstep. The
anxiety of moves is reduced by the experience of earlier non-
traumatic moves. Local moves do not mandate a change of job,
of friends, of family relations or of cultural context.

A crucial dimension of the social organization of a TCRS is
the range and importance of the interaction of individuals with
large-scale bureaucratic organizations. Such enterprises dominate relationships which involve employment, credit, consumer
purchasing, education, health and welfare services and government.

In a TSPS the family unit is generally extended and frequently includes significant fictive elements. Marriage is either
a relationship of restricted contact reflecting purdah considerations or else tends to be unstable.[4] In either case marriages are
generally arranged by family elders and constitute relationships
between family groups as well as between marriage partners.
Family relations beyond husband and wife dominate social organization. Whether it be a matter of clan, lineage, sib, avuncu-
late, *jati*, co-residence or some other extended family or functionally equivalent (*e.g.*, compadre) arrangement, the enlarged family is the basis for economic, political, ceremonial and therapeutic
sustenance, general education and companionship. Young people, married or not, tend to be subject to significant older generation control until the older generation dies. Since the old have
no savings and no pension, and the state has no resources for
them either, they are, by choice or default, dependent on their
family. Vocational separation between generations is unusual;
farmer begets farmer, weaver begets weaver. In a TSPS, in

---

4. Marital instability is as characteristic of the one ideal type as of the
   other. It is therefore ignored in the intertype comparison of the consequences of various forms of dispute processing.

other words, people tend to be aggregated with their parents, children and other kin in residence, in work and in responsibility.

In a TSPS the geographical range of non-family liaisons is restricted. Friends tend to be neighbors, neighbors tend to rely on each other for economic cooperation and significant public works projects require community cooperation as much as government assistance. Local politics are governed by shifting alignments which reflect personal loyalties and economic opportunities more than ideological or programmatic differences. The full picture of interpersonal relations is a complicated, highly articulated cross-cutting network in which individuals are involved on their own account and as representatives of kin-based groups. It is conventionally contrasted to the nuclear family centered, unconnected, single-stranded organization of societies resembling a TCSR. (P. Cohen, 1968: 152-54; Nader and Yngvesson, 1973: 912).

The contrast in residential mobility between a TCSR and a TSPS is not as stark as the difference in type of family relationships. In a TSPS a move of any distance may be tantamount to exile, an anxious passage to a place where language, food and manners are foreign or distasteful and where cultural artifacts, especially those geared to religious activity (temples, shrines, holy places), may not be easily reproduced. More importantly, moves may eliminate family and extra-family (compadre, age set, faction, clique) support crucial to economic and emotional health. In a TSPS most long distance moves involve country people moving to cities and therefore generally require a change of occupation. On the other hand, a move in a TSPS may be no more than an easy transfer, often made in groups, from a village to an urban neighborhood peopled with acquaintances who have migrated to the city from the same village. Economic and cultural as well as social dislocation may then be tempered by the existence of an island of the familiar and supportive in a sea of the strange and indifferent.[5] Nevertheless, moves in a TSPS are much more dependent upon tying into an existing social network at the destination and involve more economic hardship, social and cultural alienation and emotional trauma than do moves in a TCRS.

Vocational mobility is also lower in a TSPS. Higher unemployment means more competition for jobs when existing employment arrangements are severed. Ascriptive preferences and

---

5. Litwak's (1960b: 386) discussion of how the modified extended family may aid geographical mobility would apply even more strongly to the classical extended family.

nepotism are commonplace. A significant proportion of the labor force is self or family employed and thus involved in work which is restricted in locale. Social contacts tend to precede rather than follow vocational opportunities.

The crucial role of large-scale organizations in a TCRS is not duplicated in a TSPS. Employment may be with major enterprises, but is generally not; credit is extended by individual money lenders and merchants rather than by commercial banks and large stores; consumer purchasing is carried on in small shops; primary education is provided in small local schools; and health services are indigenous and individualized rather than imported and bureaucratic. Only in the administration of welfare (i.e., public works projects, famine relief) and other government activities does the citizenry of a TSPS confront bureaucracies comparable to those which dominate social life in a TCRS.

II. COMPONENTS OF FORMS OF DISPUTE PROCESSING

The basic question underlying this paper is whether the consequences of, and the availability of resources required by, *any* form of dispute processing vary with social organization. This proposition will be explored through analysis of adjudication, mediation and avoidance as they are applicable to disputes in which individuals or small groups are involved.[6]

Adjudication and mediation are distinguishable from negotiation and self-help by the necessary presence of a third party, someone who is neither asserting nor resisting the assertion of a claim in his own behalf nor is acting as the agent of such a party. Conventionally we label as adjudication that process in which the third party is acknowledged to have the power to stipulate an outcome of the dispute, although in many instances such power will be exercised only when the adjudicator is unable to persuade the disputants to agree to an outcome. In mediation, on the other hand, outcomes[7] are produced by the third party only when he can secure disputant consent to proposals of accommodation[8] (Collier, 1973: 26; Fuller, 1971: 308; Kawashima,

---

6. For a telling argument that American legal anthropologists should begin to focus on American institutions, see Nader 1972: 284-88. This paper, by concentrating on forms of dispute processing important in the U.S., attempts to provide an analytic framework for such a focus.

7. Disputes have outcomes rather than resolutions for the same reason that they are processed rather than settled.

8. Abel (1974: 221) believes that we unnecessarily distort reality when we dichotomize behavior which is empirically continuous. It is no doubt frequently difficult to determine whether or not a particular third party can produce outcomes without disputant consent. How, for instance, would one classify the village muxtaar described by Rothenberger (1970: 152)?

Law and Society

1963: 50). By avoidance I mean limiting the relationship with the other disputant sufficiently so that the dispute no longer remains salient. Avoidance resembles Hirschman's (1970) notion of exit. But avoidance, unlike exit behavior, does not necessarily imply a *switch* of relations to a new object, but may simply involve *withdrawal* from or contraction of the dispute-producing relationship.

In adjudication, outcomes may be sensitive to a wide range of extrinsic factors including class membership, political alliances, economic consequences and corruption, but in the main the behavior of the disputants is evaluated by reference to generalized rules of conduct. Most such rules are not immutable, but they are stable. Adjudication as a consequence tends to focus on "what facts" and "which norms" rather than on any need for normative shifts.[9] This concentration on the behavior of the

---

[The muxtaar] does exercise strong executive and particularly judicial influence in the village. He acted as a remedy agent in more disputes than any other remedy agent in or out of the village and was instrumental in settling many disputes. His technique in dispute resolution is to say very little himself, but to be very attentive and noncommittal in hearing all the arguments on all sides and the opinions of others as to how the matter should be solved. Then finally he will usually offer some sort of suggestion which will offer the possibility of solving the question, often with some sort of compromise and usually in line with the consensus of the opinions of the other kibaar who have spoken. The person against whom the combined weight of general opinion and the muxtaar's pressures have gone will usually finally agree by saying, "Whatever you wish," and may invite everyone back to his house for the ceremonial cup of coffee signifying peacemaking.

The key is the behavioral content of "the person . . . will usually finally agree" (*see* Kawashima, 1963: 50-51). If in context he has no practical alternative but to agree, the muxtaar is an adjudicator; if it is feasible for him not to agree, the muxtaar is a powerful mediator, but a mediator nonetheless. But this empirical difficulty should not force us to deny qualitative differences in behavior which, given sufficient information, can be identified. The imposition of a continuum on data which reflect the presence or absence of an observable property would itself distort reality.

But in which mold ought we to consider the adjudicator-mediator distinction? What if a disputant before Rothenberger's muxtaar faces the following situation? If he does not do as the muxtaar suggests he will lose something (*e.g.*, the community's or the muxtaar's esteem or access to some social group), but he is normatively entitled to make that calculation; it is not inappropriate for him to decide to sacrifice those values as he continues to prosecute the dispute. The difficulty in making an operational distinction between adjudication and mediation, then, arises not from an attempt to dichotomize continuous behavior, but because different processes are distinguishable by the attitude of participants to their situation rather than by the behavior in which they engage. Technical considerations of measurement aside, the relevant attitudes are as much empirical data subject to identification as is observable physical behavior.

9. If most adjudication were concerned with the wisdom of rules it would not be nearly as psychologically threatening. A loss then could be rationalized as a difference of opinion about future utilities rather than understood as negative labeling of past behavior.
   Aubert (1963: 36-37) has identified some of the psychological

disputants, rather than on the merits of abstract rules, creates a significant potential for psychological trauma. The effect of losing a dispute is to be told that what you consider as history was either an illusion or a lie, that what you considered normatively appropriate behavior is characterized as anti-social, and that what you consider your property or your prerogative will now, because of your failings, by fiat become your enemy's (Aubert, 1969: 286).[10]

The psychological consequence is frequently to alienate the loser from the adjudicative process. The process is generally endowed with a high degree of legitimacy derived from its ritual and trappings as well as from the participants' prior socialization. The loss of the case puts the loser in an unstable psychological condition. He must change either his attitude toward the process or toward his past behavior. Although some losers may be convinced of their errors by the adjudication, that many will change their attitude toward the process rather than toward their past behavior is suggested by the least effort principle (Abelson, 1968: 115). This "psycho-logical" rule indicates that change will be made in the direction which involves the actor in making the least significant other changes in his cognitive structure. Change in attitude toward past behavior may also involve changes in attitude toward the role and behavior of close associates, toward related behavior, and toward important values and elements of self-definition. It is thus likely to require more effort than a change in attitude toward a rarely encountered and generally alien institution. One would, therefore, expect that loser compliance with adjudicative decisions is produced not by their merits, but by the coercive power which they command. Unconvinced of their original error, losers respond to an adverse decision only because the consequences of not responding would be worse.[11]

---

considerations which push adjudication toward evaluating conduct against rules rather than seeking to identify and change the psychological origins of disputes.

10. Some adjudicative processes may avoid these psychological strains. The therapeutic structure of the Kpelle moot (Gibbs, 1967: 284-89) frequently educates the deviant to reinterpret his past behavior so that he views it in the same vein as does the community. Gibbs (1967: 284) attributes the re-educative effect of the moot to its incorporation "writ large" of all of the crucial elements of individual or group psychotherapy. But most adjudication, certainly that in government courts, does not allow the permissiveness and denial of reciprocity considered important to therapy by Gibbs. In addition, in most adjudication the evaluation of conduct by rules imposes a narrow range of empirical inquiry; it is unproductive to investigate behavior which is unrelated to the rules, although general expression of thoughts, feelings and other behavior are critical in terms of therapy.

11. One of Nader's reports on Zapotec adjudication (1969: 69, 86-88)

72   LAW AND SOCIETY / FALL 1974

The predicted association of adjudication and coercive power
appears to be borne out empirically. Wimberley's Guttman scale
for legal evolution lists twenty-seven societies which use courts
(defined as institutions possessing socially recognized authority
to make binding decisions). Eighteen of those societies maintained a court-directed police force and five of the remainder
used autonomic ordeals (Wimberly, 1973: 81,82), that is compulsion by the will of the gods (Roberts, 1965: 209). And all nine
of the court/no police societies had strong corporate kin groupings suggesting an internal coercive potential which does not
depend upon specialized functionaries.[12] (For a counter-instance
see Schlegel, 1970: 171). The variety of coercive power employ-
able by different adjudicative systems is extensive. Mild social
ostracism or negative public opinion (Gough, 1955: 50; Mayer,
1960: 264-66; Bohannon, 1957: 68), closed access to marriage
partners (Srinivas, 1954: 157), termination of all social intercourse (Hitchcock, 1960: 243; Llewellyn & Hoebel, 1941: 103),
banishment (Canter, 1973: 9; Brandt, 1971: 209-10), protected
self-help (Pospisil, 1964: 147-48) and police action (Collier, 1973:
103; Gluckman, 1955: 222) are common.

---

would critically limit such an analysis to what she considers the
zero-sum decision making of formal government courts. Local Zapotec adjudication she characterizes, on the other hand, as "compromise arrived at by adjudication or in some cases, adjudication based
on compromise." In either case, the consensual element in the outcome should reduce the psychological dilemma of the participants.
The cases Nader presents to illustrate this hybrid process (1969:88)
may not, however, support her characterization. In four of the five
cases there appears to be a definite winner, someone who is paid
money or whose opponent goes to jail or pays a fine. The loser's
only solace is that the money he pays goes to the municipality rather
than to his opponent. It is not surprising then that even in such
a procedure, in which the loser's loss is marginally blunted, the outcome "is backed by coercive force."

12. A sample of adjudication backed by coercive power in the U.S.
would include courts, arbitration enforceable in courts, industry um-
pires, professional sports commissioners, race track stewards, union
disciplinary committees, student conduct committees, civil service review boards and the self-government agencies of trade associations,
stock and commodity exchanges, athletic associations, fraternal organizations, social clubs, ethnic associations, street gangs, professional associations, political parties and religious groups. Some of
these were suggested by and are documented in Galanter, n.d.
The association of coercion and adjudication may not always be
stable. Moore (1970:328) reports that pre-colonial Chagga chiefs did
not always enforce their judgments. "If the loser were a rich man
with a strong lineage that threatened to emigrate as a body if there
were any property confiscated, the chief preferred tactics of persuasion." If the chief would not coerce compliance, the winner could
engage in the "risky business" of self-help or swing the cursing pot.
Neither always worked.
Where community cooperation is disintegrating as in social units
confronting Siegel and Beals' pervasive factionalism (1960), old adjudicative forms may outlive their coercive powers for a while, but
it is doubtful that they would do so indefinitely. Either the community disorganization will be reversed or the adjudication will
cease.

The relationship between social organization and adjudication appears to depend not only on the availability of coercive power, but also on the presence or absence of social groups.[13] Most adjudication systems operate as an aspect of specific groups. Adjudicative entrepreneurs who sell their services to an unassociated set of disputants seeking third party assistance (the American Arbitration Association, for example) are uncommon.[14] Exactly why this is so is not entirely clear. To the extent that dispute processing is politics by another name (Barnes, 1961), it is obvious that political struggles can only have meaning if they take place within the political unit which will feel their consequences. To the extent that adjudication is a process of evaluating behavior in the light of a particular normative system, the norms must originate with and be used by some specific group. To the extent that adverse adjudicated decisions will be ignored unless compliance can be coerced, compliance will depend on the threat of some sanction acceptable to, and generally administered by, a group. To the extent that judicial specialization reflects general social role differentiation (Abel, 1974: 288), many societies are simply not sufficiently differentiated to produce wandering adjudicators. In fact, when one focuses on the normative system used by the AAA and on the coercion available to it, the Association may not really provide any group-unrelated adjudication, but rather may constitute an adjunct to government courts whose substantive rules and police powers it borrows.

Adjudication requires expertise in the social rules governing behavior and, frequently, in the secondary rules governing the conduct of disputes. This expertise is relatively easy to create on a mass basis.[15] The expertise required of a mediator is different. Since successful mediation requires an outcome accept-

13. To paraphrase Nadel (1951: 146), groups are collections of individuals in long-term relationships whose actions toward each other and toward outsiders are importantly influenced by the existence and standards of the group.

14. Even the work of the AAA falls generally into four areas—commercial, labor and international disputes and personal injury claims (Jones, 1964: 676). The inability of the AAA's National Center for Dispute Settlement to develop a program of consumer arbitration in Washington, D.C. (McGonagle, 1972: 72-75) reflects the difficulty of establishing adjudication across groups.

15. The ratio of faculty to students in an American law school tends to be about 1 to 20 (Boyer and Crampton, 1974: 289). Aubert (1969: 301) notes that "in Norway during the last century, three or four professors sufficed to train all the lawyers, and they needed no equipment and no laboratories—only a few books." A tale popular in law and development circles is that President Nasser once told the Dean of the Cairo law school to double the size of the student body virtually overnight by buying a microphone and hiring a bigger hall.

able to the parties, the mediator cannot rely primarily on rules but must construct an outcome in the light of the social and cultural context of the dispute, the full scope of the relations between the disputants and the perspectives from which they view the dispute. Mediation, then, flourishes where mediators share the social and cultural experience of the disputants they serve, and where they bring to the processing of disputes an intimate and detailed knowledge of the perspectives of the disputants.[16] In the absence of such shared experience and such pre-processing knowledge, the effort a mediator would have to make to fill the gaps would be disproportionate to the social stakes involved in the dispute. Because of these characteristics of mediation, deliberate mass production of mediators is generally infeasible.[17] On the other hand, since the outcomes it produces are consensual and are generally compromises, mediation need not be backed by coercive power.

Why is it important for a mediator who does not know the disputants to acquire insight into their priorities and feelings as a part of the mediation process? Let us assume that mediated outcomes are of two kinds. They may be personality independ-

---

16. That mediation depends upon understanding the particular perspectives of particular disputants as well as on understanding the context in which they act is an example of the importance of the influence of symbolic interactionism on role theory. Rather than emphasizing the deterministic effect of role expectations (Parsons, 1951: 190-97), symbolic interactionists stress the importance of the interpretation process used by individuals in human encounters (Blumer, 1969: 56). To them a dispute cannot be analyzed as a set confrontation between conflicting role expectations, but rather involves individuals who continually redefine themselves and their situations and realign their behavior accordingly. Thus an understanding of the disputants' perspectives as well as the biography of a dispute is crucial in mediation.

  Does the Japanese experience indicate that the text overstates the case? In the early 1920s, the Japanese instituted compulsory mediation by laymen and judge prior to litigation of landlord and tenant, and some debt and domestic relations, cases. This state-provided mediation is considered by Kawashima (1963: 54-55) to have successfully disposed of a significant proportion of such cases. One can quibble with his conclusion. Since the mediation was compulsory it is not surprising that there was quite a bit of it. Since the number of lawsuits in these substantive areas did not decrease (1963: 55), one could say that his aggregate data indicate that the mediation was rather ineffective. Without sampling individual cases it might be difficult to tell what the effect of mediation actually was. In any event, it is also possible that this success in mediation which is not based on anterior knowledge of disputant perspectives arises from the respect owed mediators in Japanese culture in general, so that Japanese mediation takes on some of the coercive attributes of adjudication (*see* Kawashima, 1963: 50-51).

17. Note, for instance, the extent of the efforts made by the Maoist mediator described by Lubman (1967: 1321-22). That such efforts are regularly made in a socialist society is probably a reflection of the degree to which political education has been introduced into ordinary dispute processing. Lubman (1967: 1323) also notes that the Party expects "mediators to know well the people among whom they dwell."

ent in the sense that the mediator is able to suggest a result which adequately meets the interests of each disputant as those interests would be identified by any persons in their positions. In such situations the mediator's ingenuity is affected only by his understanding of the disputants' manifest interests. It may well be feasible to acquire such information adequately during the mediation.

On the other hand, an outcome may be personality dependent in the sense that an acceptable scheme which sufficiently meets the demands of both disputants must reflect these demands as they idiosyncratically view them. In this case the feelings of the disputants are crucial and the possibility that a mediator will acquire sufficient insight during mediation is more doubtful. The difficulty may arise in part because the disputants are not particularly self-conscious about their own feelings and therefore fail to give the mediator adequate information so that he may understand them. Even when the disputants are conscious of their feelings, they may nevertheless restrict their communications to the mediator to matters they believe will promote their cause on an instrumental, rather than an affective, level or according to motives which they believe it is acceptable for them to maintain rather than expose their real, but embarrassing, needs. In either case the information presented to the mediator is probably not as rich as the more general information available to a mediator who has widely-shared experience with the disputants. It would be imprudent to set theoretical limits to the successes of mediative geniuses, but for the run-of-the-mill mediators upon whom institutionalized mediation must be based long-term and relatively intimate prior association with the disputants may be highly functional in all settings and necessary for reaching personality dependent outcomes[18] (*see* Gulliver, 1969: 40-48).

---

18. Labor mediation is probably a special case. It tends to involve a limited set of issues most of which have been confronted in principle before. Most of the participants are professionals, and the outcomes are more affected by economic and political considerations than by personalities. As a consequence, a background in other labor disputes may be more useful to a labor mediator than shared experience with particular bargaining agents. Knowles (1958: 780-3), however, suggests that most issues in labor mediation involve both objective and subjective factors, and that effective labor mediation is a close parallel to effective psychotherapy.

To the extent that disputes which ostensibly involve a few individuals are functionally group controversies, the emphasis in the text on the personalities of the disputants may be misplaced. Although I do not assert with any assurance that group concerns do not underlie many individual disputes, there is considerable evidence that the feelings of specific disputants are relevant in mediation even in highly organized societies (*see, e.g.,* Gulliver, 1969: 47, 60, 65; Collier, 1973: 63).

Adjudication and mediation are relatively visible processes. They tend to be public to the group in which they take place, notorious within the group and didactic for the group. Avoidance, on the other hand, is more difficult for an outsider to identify and is less frequently reported.[19] Even a recital of a few characteristic avoidance techniques will, however, demonstrate how common it is. Note, for instance, the unexceptional nature in the U.S. of adolescent children limiting contacts with their parents to perfunctory matters because matters of importance have proved to be too contentious, of friends curtailing their relations because of past quarrels, of consumers switching their trade from one retail merchant to another after a dispute, of casual workers (gas station attendants, waitresses, dishwashers, gardeners, housekeepers) quitting jobs because of problems with employers, of children moving out of their parents' houses because of unreconcilable values and of neighbors who visit less because of offensive pets, obstreperous children, loud parties and unseemly yards.

The most important social characteristic of avoidance for dispute processing theory is its variable costs. To understand that variation one has only to focus on Gluckman's (1955: 19) classic distinction between single-interest linkages and multiplex relationships, those which serve many interests. The cost of avoidance is always a reduction in the content of the relationship which has been truncated or terminated. If the relationship was geared to a single interest, only that interest is affected. If the relationship was multiplex, all the interests are affected, even though the cause of the avoidance grew out of only one. The difference, for example, is between losing a sibling only and losing a sibling who is also a neighbor, a companion, a therapist, a political ally, an economic co-adventurer and a ceremonial confederate (*see* Nader and Metzger, 1963: 590-91).

III. THE EFFECT OF SOCIAL ORGANIZATION ON INSTITUTIONALIZING DIFFERENT FORMS OF DISPUTE PROCESSING

For our purposes, then, the key to adjudication is groups and coercion,[20] to mediation is shared experience, and to avoidance

---

19. Schwartz (1954: 490) provides an early, if marginal, reference to "withdrawal from interaction" as an alternative to legal controls. His provocative analysis of two Israeli communities has been generally overlooked by anthropologists of law, perhaps because it was originally published in a law journal (*see also* Abel, 1974: 229; Fürer-Haimendorf, 1967: 22-23).

20. The asserted correlation between adjudication and coercion should not be understood as an affirmation of Pospisil's notion of "the attribute of authority." To the contrary, I believe that Pospisil can

is its variable costs. Within any society on an institutional basis, we should expect to find less adjudication where groups are infrequent and the coercive power which can be marshalled is weak, less mediation where shared experience is rare and less avoidance where avoidance costs are high. What insights concerning the distribution of forms of dispute processing might these propositions produce in the ideal type societies de-

---

characterize authority as universal only by disregarding empirical evidence at odds with his concepts. Pospisil (1971: 39-40) attempts to define "the attributes of an analytical concept of law . . . that can be applied cross-culturally." One such attribute is the attribute of authority.

A decision, to be legally relevant, or in other words, to effect social control, must either be accepted as a solution by the parties to a dispute or, if they resist, be forced upon them. Such a decision, of necessity, is passed by an individual, or group of individuals, who can either persuade the litigants to comply or who possess power over enforcement agents or the group membership in general to compel them to execute the verdict, judgement, or informal decision even over protests and resistance of either or both parties to the dispute. Individuals who possess the power to induce or force the majority of the members of their social group to conform to their decisions I shall call the legal authority. Whereas this authority is formalized and specialized on the state level in our own and in other civilizations, in tribal societies and in some of the state's subgroups it often coincides with the leadership of various groups that exercises several functions besides the legal one. (1971: 44).

Pospisil's argument (1971: 44-78) that authority is present in all societies takes the form of demonstrating that it is present in several societies where ethnographers have declared it to be absent. The argument has, I think, two failings. First, Pospisil links leadership (supramodal influence on the behavior of others) and authority (the power to coerce the behavior of others). He then identifies leaders in social units which other characterize as leaderless without pinpointing the leaders' or anyone else's, coercive power. This is the logic of his analysis of Gusinde's work on the Yaghar Indians of Tierra del Fuego (1971: 44-45).

Second, and more important, Pospisil overlooks or misconstrues both classic accounts and recent analyses of dispute processing—namely, Miller (1955) on the Fox, Evans-Pritchard (1940) and Howell (1954) on the Nuer of the Sudan and Gulliver (1963, 1969) on the Arusha and Ndendueli of Tanzania. Gulliver reports that "the solution of a dispute between Arusha does not come from authoritative decision, but through agreement resulting from discussion and negotiation between the parties which are in conflict" (1963: 299) and that settlement of intra-community disputes among the Ndendueli "must be an agreed settlement . . . a principal cannot be compelled to accept an imposed settlement, for there is no means of enforcing it" (1969: 69). Both conclusions are supported by extensive case analyses. Gulliver's Arushan summary may be slightly overstated: he does note rare instances of physical and ritual coercion in cases of extreme obduracy or contempt of process (1963: 275-96). But his characterization is fair for the great preponderance of Arushan disputes and for all Ndendueli behavior.

Nor did observers identify such coercion among the Central Algonkian tribes, especially the Fox. Miller, for instance, notes that although the war-chief role is "the most 'powerful' authority role in Fox society . . . war-party members could act on [his suggestions] or not, as they saw fit" (1955: 283-84). Controversies in less critical circumstances were also processed without compulsion: "no course of action was agreed on by the council unless all members were in accord with the final decision"; no coercion was required to implement decisions since "the act of decision-making itself insured the tribal validation of the decision" (1955: 283-84).

Law and Society

scribed earlier?   In a TSPS either adjudication or mediation will occur at the level of face-to-face groups such
as kin units, factions and villages.   The coercion necessary for
adjudication rests ultimately on the group's power to expel con-
tumacious disputants.   Since the group's functions are central
to the members' well-being, participation in group adjudication
and adherence to adjudicated outcomes are self-generating.   The
size of such groups and the intensity of relations within them
make mediation a realistic alternative to adjudication: the requisite knowledge of dispute context and participant perspective
are available without inordinate mediator efforts.   Whether
groups in any particular society will use both institutionalized
adjudication and mediation, or one more than the other, may
then be a function of considerations other than social organization.   Values and their psychological derivatives may in some
contexts be crucial ingredients.[21]   The stress on mediation in
eastern societies has often been attributed to the importance of
Confucian distaste for conflict and self-assertion (J. Cohen, 1967:
60; Hahm, 1969: 20; Kawashima, 1963: 44) while antipathy to
self-arrogation and authoritative control has had the same effect
in hyper-egalitarian western societies (Evans-Pritchard, 1940:
180-84; Emmett, 1964:   47, 80-89; Miller, 1955:   271-72, 283-86;
Yngvesson, 1970:   95-96, 258).   On the other hand, despite the con-

---

Evans-Pritchard and Howell report that the Nuer do not adjudicate.   No one can "compel either party to accept a decision" (Howell, 1954:   255); there was an "absence of any institutionalized body
to enforce payment" (Howell, 1954: 224, 226).   Later in his book,
Pospisil, quoting Evans-Pritchard, notes that "within a village differences between persons are discussed by the elders of the village
and agreement is generally and easily reached" (1971: 101).   What
Pospisil does not point out is that if they could not agree, the only
options available to quarreling Nuer were self-help, emigration and
avoidance (Howell, 1954: 226-27).   Even Greuel (1971:   1120), who
believes that Evans-Pritchard has seriously understated the political
power of the leopard-skin chief, agrees that the chief cannot enforce
his opinions upon disputants.
      Of course, the Nuer, Arusha and Ndendueli all inhabit areas now
subject to the political and judicial jurisdiction of centralized states
and, in that sense, have recourse to compulsive process.   But Pospisil's legal attributes are presumably valid over time as well as space.
      Lowy (1973:   954) has criticized Pospisil on similar grounds.
Pospisil's response (1973:   1170) suggests that the attribute of authority may be satisfied in any society whose leaders' suggestions
as to outcomes of disputes are *sometimes* accepted by the disputants.
Authority defined as loosely as this may be universal.   But so construed it fails to meet the standard set by Pospisil himself for his
attributes—that they define "modes of conduct made obligatory"
(1971:   40).   Nor is such a construction consistent with the language
of Pospisil's definition of authority (1971:   42) which seems to say
that authority is present only where compulsion is available against
those who "resist" persuasion.

21. As other variables which may affect the shape of dispute processing,
Nader has suggested government prescriptions, the type of claims,
and the personalities of third parties (1969:   90-91).   *See also* Aubert, 1963: 33.

ventional notion that mediated compromises better preserve the continuing relationships characteristic of small communities or multiplex groups (Nader, 1969: 87-88; Nader and Yngvesson, 1973: 912),[22] adjudication is quite common in such situations (see Hitchcock, 1960: 261-64; Srinivas, 1954: 155; Cohn, 1965: 83; Gluckman, 1955: 80-81; Moore, 1970: 331; Gibbs, 1962: 345; Collier, 1973: 36-39; Metzger, 1960: 36). Sometimes institutionalized mediation is available as a step preceeding such adjudication (Hitchcock, 1960: 242; Cohn, 1967: 143; Moore, 1970: 327; Collier, 1973: 26-28), sometimes it is not (Srinivas, 1954: 159; Gibbs, 1967: 380-83; Nader and Metzger, 1963: 586-87), and sometimes one cannot tell (*e.g.*, Gluckman, 1955: 26).

As the size of the groups on which one focuses in a TSPS grows, from village to tribe or from extended family to sub-caste, adjudication will become the dominant form of dispute processing. Mediation is no longer feasible because, whatever the shared general social and cultural experience, no specific mediators nor occupants of specific social positions will possess as a matter of existing experience sufficient information about the particular perspectives and histories of the particular disputants to be able efficiently to suggest acceptable outcomes. Adjudicative expertise in rules, on the other hand, is either widely possessed where the rules are not specialized (in the sense that they are readily available only to professionals) or can be generated on a mass basis where specialization is important.

The frequency of avoidance as a form of dispute processing in a TSPS should be affected by its high costs. These costs would be incurred whether avoidance takes place within the kin group, within a non-family multiplex relationship, or in economic activities. Within the family if disputants terminate or decrease their contacts, relations between groups, which may have political and economic as well as social connotations, are jeopardized as well. Where marriages are arranged, decisions about who marries whom are generally made on prudential grounds, in a corporate process and under the influence of past social relations. As a result, disputes which are processed by avoidance will cast a long shadow, interfering with the future marriage prospects of many group members (*see* Beals, 1961: 33). Use of avoidance as a technique where the disputants, such as parent and grown child

---

22. Grossman and Sarat attribute informal dispute processing in "simpler societies" in part to a "framework of trust . . . between the disputing individuals" (1973: 3). A substantial volume of ethnographic data contradicts this hypothesis: high levels of hostility and distrust are very frequently observed in ongoing relationships in simpler societies (Foster, 1960: 175-77; Lewis, 1965: 498; Carstairs, 1967: 40-43; Brandt, 1971: 184).

80   LAW AND SOCIETY / FALL 1974

or siblings or affines, live and work and conduct other important activities together, is logistically difficult and psychologically dangerous—the repressed hostility felt toward the other disputant is likely to be shifted to someone or something else. Even worse, the failure to express or act upon predictable hostility will in many societies lead to accusations of witchcraft against the person who hides his antagonisms (see Collier, 1973: 222). Yet physical separation, by moving residence or work, may be socially infeasible, economically disastrous and emotionally traumatic. Since many relationships beyond the family are multiplex, avoidance as a reaction to dispute impairs not only the interest out of which the dispute arose, but all other interests shared by the disputants (see Van Velsen, 1969: 138). As Moore (1973: 738) points out for the Chagga, "the continuing control exercised by the lineage neighborhood nexus over its members is illustrated by every dispute it settles. No man can hope to keep his head above water if he does not have the approval and support of his neighbors and kinsmen." This analysis should not be construed to imply that avoidance would never or rarely occur in small communities in technologically simple societies. In fact, in nomadic tribes, where avoidance by physical separation is easy, dispute processing by such tactics is commonplace (Furer-Haimendorf, 1967: 22-23). The point is rather that avoidance has high costs in a TSPS and one would as a result expect significant use of other forms of dispute processing which are more likely to aid the maintenance of threatened, but important, social relationships.

In both a TCRS and a TSPS adjudication is predictable at the level of the state which is a group with an important normative system and substantial coercive power. The degree of use of such adjudicative process will depend upon the extent to which it is viewed as expensive, degrading, alien, slow, time-consuming, ineffective and destructive, upon the available alternatives and their characteristics and upon litigant objectives.[23]

In both types of societies adjudication may also be an important form of dispute processing within large-scale organizations.

---

23. These qualities are expressed negatively rather than positively (cheap, ennobling, familiar, quick, effective, time saving and constructive) because it is the negative characterizations which populate the literature. See, e.g., Friedman, 1973: 338 (U.S.); Yale Law Journal, 1970: 1179 (U.S.); Nader, 1972: 290 (U.S.); Stoltz, 1968: f.n. 14 (U.S.); Wiser and Wiser, 1969: 123-24 (India); Barnes, 1961: 188 (Zambia); Hunt and Hunt, 1969: 137 (Mexico); Emmett, 1964: 89 (Wales); Cohen, 1967: 59, 63-65, 67 (China); Stirling, 1957: 25 (Turkey); Rosenn, 1971: 538-41 (Brazil). Of course, even an ostensibly negative characteristic may have positive functions. Rosenberg, for instance, has analyzed the possible gains from court delays (1965) as has Kidder (1973: 128-30).

Such organizations must establish a normative system to govern their operations: coercive power is located both in their power to expel constituents and in their power to vary tasks and rewards. Rules and compulsive power may explain why adjuducation can work if it is established. But they do not entirely explain why it is established. Making decisions in particular cases is inevitable. Where there are rules and power, the people with the power will enforce some rules. Whether that process is controlled by people who are directly affected by their own decisions or by people who are importantly influenced by considerations of neutrality will depend upon locally prevalent values and on the countervailing power, individual or organized, of those subjected to the rules. If organized political opposition (labor vs. management, students vs. administration) exists within organizations, controversies about past behavior are more likely to be adjudicated by a third party than decided by a participant (*see* Weber, 1967: 335-56). And the more a society values procedural fairness over instrumental efficiency, the more likely it is that the same result will occur. Mediation within organizations may be equally feasible since in the operations of an organization extensive shared social, cultural and personal experience is generated. And adjudicative and mediative institutions may co-exist within an organization (at my university decanal adjudication is paralleled by ombudsman mediation).

Between outsiders who have some contact with a large organization and the organization, a significant amount of dispute processing may be a special form of avoidance termed "lumping it." In lumping it the salience of the dispute is reduced not so much by limiting the contacts between the disputants, but by ignoring the dispute, by declining to take any or much action in response to the controversy. The complaint against the retail merchant or the health insurance company is foregone although the complainant's grievance has not been satisfied, or even acknowledged, and although interaction between the individual and the organization is not altered. It would be uncommon for such grievances to be mediated since there is little incentive for the organization to change its posture. Because of the discrepancy in size and power even the threat of withdrawal by the individual is futile to coerce compromise by the organization. And no adjudication short of the government courts may be possible because no other power exists to coerce decisions against the organization[24] (*see* McGonagle, 1972: 72-75).

---

24. Friedmann (1973: 64) has recently documented the determination of a large proportion of samples of the populations of Alberta and

The clearest difference between dispute processing in a TSPS and a TCRS should be located in disputes between individuals or family and social groups. The availability of adjudication and mediation and the high costs of avoidance in a TSPS have been examined. The opposite conditions are predictable for a TCRS: adjudication and mediation of such disputes will be hard to institutionalize and avoidance will carry significantly lower costs. The obstacle to adjudication of interpersonal disputes in a TCRS is the limited coercion available to agencies other than government courts. The forms of coercion available in nongovernment adjudication in a TSPS depend either on membership in groups, especially kin-related groups, or on participation in multiple interest relationships. In a TCRS such groups and associations are either non-existent or weak. One cannot be influenced by public opinion if there is no relevant public, nor exiled from a group to which one does not belong. What sanction in a neighborhood of single interest relationships might a neighborhood adjudicator employ? With what, after childhood, can most parents threaten a child or an uncle a niece? (Turner, 1970: 414).

At the same time structural factors exist in a TCRS which reduce the utility of adjudicating interpersonal disputes in government courts. To the extent that such courts are staffed by specialists, as one would expect them to be in such a society unless it is organized according to a revolutionary socialist ideology, the rules they apply will tend to become specialized, importantly procedural and alien from everyday norms (Abel, 1974: 270-84). Specialized rules will require litigants to hire professional counsel. Professional counsel means added expense, inconvenience and mystification. Government courts frequently process a large volume of routine quasi-administrative matters (foreclosures and evictions, divorce, collections, repossessions and the filing and marshalling of liens). These routine matters, coupled to a high criminal caseload and a sensitivity to the demands of due process and to the autonomy of judges which impedes reforms aimed at efficiency, tax the government courts' capacity to process individual interpersonal cases quickly (Sykes, 1969: 330-37). If court

---

Britain not to complain about perceived maladministration of public authorities. Can one simply assert that in both ideal types similar disputes will be processed similarly if we define disputes in terms of their gravity? Family disputes are serious in a TSPS and will thus infrequently be ignored. Such disputes are much less grave in a TCRS and therefore will frequently be lumped. But despite their undoubted seriousness, individuals' grievances against large organizations in societies resembling a TCRS cannot easily be adjudicated or mediated.

Some large organizations may, however, establish international adjudicators endowed with coercive power independent of the organization's ordinary chain of command.

litigation may be fairly characterized as costly, slow and alienating, we can expect relatively little use to be made of it in situations in which, as in most interpersonal disputing, the economic stakes are low (Danzig, 1973: 44), unless, as in divorce and custody cases, a government imprimatur is an absolute necessity.

This analysis is not entirely compatible with Black's (1973: 53) belief that use of government courts is a stage in an evolutionary process reached when sub-government controls are weak or unavailable. First, considerable data points to high simultaneous use of government and sub-government dispute processing. The best documented instance may be colonial India (Rudolph & Rudolph, 1967: 260-62; Galanter, 1968: 69), but there is no evidence that nineteenth century America witnessed proportionately less interpersonal litigation than mid-twentieth century America despite more cohesive kin and residential systems (see Friedman, 1973: 338). And second, Black entirely ignores the role of avoidance: he does not consider the possibility that as "communities" and their informal controls disappear, the need for any external civil dispute processing between individuals may also substantially fade.

Institutionalized mediation of interpersonal disputes will also be infrequent in a TCRS. Because of the crucial importance of shared experience in mediation, the less role differentiated a social unit, the more mediators will be available for disputes of varying origin. In the technologically simplest societies all adult members, having generally the same experience, are equipped on that dimension to mediate all disputes. But in a TCRS, where role differentiation is intense, few persons are qualified by experience to mediate any disputes: almost everybody's role set is too specialized to be common to a significant number of potential disputants. It is not true, of course, that in no case will anyone with sufficient common experience with any disputants be available to mediate any disputes. But institutionalized mediation—which involves the regular participation of specific third parties, or the occupants of specific social positions—requires more than an occasional person with the requisite background to mediate a particular dispute in a reasonable time. It requires many such persons, each with sufficient background to mediate a variety of disputes. Where interpersonal social organization is dominated by single interest relationships, such people will not exist in requisite numbers.

The relatively weaker bonds of family, of friendship, of job and of place in a TCRS make institutionalizing adjudication and mediation difficult, but they also reduce the negative conse-

84   LAW AND SOCIETY / FALL 1974

quences of avoidance. Avoidance behavior between generations
within a family, for instance, generally will not seriously
threaten either disputants' economic security, political position
or ceremonial or therapeutic opportunities. Reducing as well as
eliminating contact within a continuing social framework is
relatively easy where relations are more formal than functional.
Difficult vocational relationships may be terminated with better
alternatives than unemployment. New friendships may be
struck and old contacts turned sour may be easily avoided. Although the most important cause of voluntary residential moves
is probably changing needs produced by the life cycle (Simmons,
1968: 636-37), many moves may be made because of deteriorating
interpersonal relations (Rossi, 1955: 142; Greer, 1962: 112) or
because of a desire for greater privacy (Lansing and Barth, 1964:
22); that is, to avoid prospective quarrels with neighbors as well
as to avoid neighbors with whom one is presently quarreling.

Where there are pockets within a TCRS where social organization is more like that postulated for a TSPS, then one would
expect that avoidance, having higher costs, would be less important and that adjudication and mediation, being more feasible,
would be more frequently institutionalized.[25] Such pockets are
likely to arise where there are unassimilated ethnic minorities
with a strong tradition of internal government or where a pattern of social discrimination severely limits the economic, residential and social mobility of distinctive minority groups. This
qualification is not meant to imply that every ethnic ghetto will
be organized and use the dispute processing machinery of a Pun-
jabi village, but simply that dispute processing will in important
respects be a function of social organization. And the social organization which exercises that influence will be the local version, however the dominant majority organizes its affairs.

To summarize this section, adjudication and mediation, on
the one hand, and avoidance, on the other, are complementary.
Where adjudication and mediation are feasible, avoidance is

25. The opposite should, of course, be equally true. Estimates of the
utility of the ideal types described in this paper made by testing
any of their constituents against the attributes of real societies, if
indeed such a test is a fair measure of the use of ideal types, must
be careful to insure that reference is made to the modal condition
of the real society, and not to minority instances which are organized
on contrasting lines (e.g., Gans, 1962: 50-51, 72; Bott, 1957: 53-54).
Doo's study of Chinese-American communities, for instance, indicates
that their social organization has until recently been based on Chinese rather than American patterns. He describes dispute processing
within these communities as internal adjudication and mediation
backed by a powerful ability to ostracize members from the community (1973: 634, 645, 652). Despite the fact that he is describing
"American" communities, his analysis supports, rather than challenges, this paper's principal argument.

costly: where avoidance has tolerable costs, adjudication and mediation are difficult to institutionalize. This complementarity has a logical base. The same set of social circumstances which makes one set of processes available frustrates the other and vice-versa.[26] The predicament of unorganized individuals who have a dispute with large organizations of which they are not members may be an exception: adjudication and mediation are generally unavailable and avoidance costly to the individual. It is this social pathology which has probably led to recent calls for ombudsmen in government, in universities and for public utilities (*see* Gellhorn, 1966: 25, 28-29, 215-17).[27]

IV. IMPLICATIONS OF THE ANALYSIS FOR DISPUTE PROCESSING REFORMS IN THE UNITED STATES

One of the frequently criticized aspects of life in America is the failure of the society's institutions to cope adequately with the people's grievances against each other. Ordinary courts cost money and time, are slow and mystifying, and tilted against the poor, the uninitiated and the occasional user (*e.g.*, Galanter, 1974; Wald and Wald, 1968: 34-37; Carlin and Howard, 1965: 381-429). Small claims courts are alleged to have been transformed by sellers of consumer goods and services into taxpayer supported collection agencies (Small Claims Study Group, 1972: 128; *Calif. Law Rev.*, 1964: 884-90; Bruff, 1973: 12, 13). Although there is an occasional note to the effect that "private-informal dispute settlement . . . is significant in complex societies" (Grossman and Sarat, 1973: 14), the references to non-government institutionalized adjudication or mediation in the United States are very sparse except within organizations, within organized commercial activities and within some minority groups.[28]

---

26. Reduced to its simplest form, this paper argues that mediation and adjudication will not be institutionalized where they will not work. But what is "work"? The manifest function of these institutions is to bring disputes to an end. But many social institutions, courts among them, may thrive although they do not fulfill their ostensible purpose. The actual function of dispute processing institutions may not be what they do for disputants, but what they do for the third parties by way, for instance, of reinforcing their prestige or political authority. Whether a dispute processing institution will flourish when nurtured primarily by such a latent function should depend on whether disputants themselves seek to end disputes. Where they do, it is difficult to understand why they would activate a process which rarely produced that result. Kidder notes "that everyone interviewed believed that the courts above those that they directly experienced would be free of the complications they had found in their own experience" (1973: 134). But he does not account for such considerable naiveté.

27. The apparent high regard of automobile manufacturers for customer good will makes the administration of automobile warranties an exception in the U.S. (*see* Whitford, 1968: 1023, 1044).

28. It is not possible to tell whether Grossman and Sarat (1973: 12)

This paper suggests that much of the slack may be absorbed by avoidance. The degree to which avoidance is as much an empirical reality as it is a sociological possibility will need to be determined through field studies. Whatever such studies may reveal, current dissatisfaction is so pervasive that advocacy of consciously engineered reform and creation of dispute processing institutions is hardly likely to abate. The sponsors of neighborhood ghetto courts (Statsky, 1974; Hager, 1972; Cahn and Cahn, 1970: 1019), community moots (Danzig, 1973: 41-48), reoriented small claims courts (Small Claims Study Group 1972: 197-213), clergy dominated dispute processing for religious minorities (Balderman, 1974: 41-42) and mediation systems for public housing, consumer-merchant and private criminal complaints (Abner, 1969: 12-18) will not be convinced by social scientists that avoidance is an adequate substitute for their proposed reforms. But their reforms may perhaps be more effective if they heed the influence of social organization on what they set out to do.[29]

Let us use Danzig's proposed neighborhood moots as an example. He advocates a transplant of the Kpelle (Liberia) moot to American urban neighborhoods. Danzig (1973: 47-48) is alert to the effect of cultural differences and aware that moot success

---

were attempting to provide a complete catalogue of descriptions of private informal dispute processing in the U.S. Whatever their aim, their references consist only of the involvement in marital disputes of one priest in one parish, the activities of marriage counselors, private police in shoplifting cases and two types of commercial arbitration. There are other descriptions (Yaffe: 1972; Doo: 1973; Grace: 1970; Kaufman: 1971), but they are either ethnically specific or unimportant. Presumably there is more private activity than has been documented. Ironically, we have better data about dispute processing in Indian villages, Mexican towns and east African tribes than we have about that process in American communities.

29. Police family crisis intervention units have been omitted from the list on the assumption that they cannot be viewed as instruments of mediation in an orthodox sense. Their primary objective is to prevent immediate violence between citizens and against themselves, rather than to persuade citizens to new and less contentious relationships (Bard, 1973: 416). Arriving while a quarrel is likely to be in an aggravated phase, they rarely know any history of a dispute and will not spend more than 40 minutes in attendance at it (Liebman and Schwartz, 1973: 437, 447-48). Note how the demands of time shape a crisis intervention trained officer in constructing rules of relevance:

> Now, I find that the wife is running rather rampant about a
> great many problems. She's beginning to tell me things
> that happened a week ago, two weeks ago—things that have
> happened the night before, things that are completely irrele-
> vant to the problem at hand (Toch. 1973: 480).

Having tried to reduce the likelihood of violence, crisis intervention trained police rely on referrals to social agencies (on 75% of calls in New York City) for long term dispute processing (Liebman and Schwartz, 1973: 432, 468-69). If orthodox mediation were attempted by police, the importance of shared experience and intimate knowledge suggests that housing authority police would have more success than the ordinary variety (*see* Liebman and Schwartz, 1973: 459-60).

may depend on the level of "primary group interaction." But he does not suggest how frequently sufficient primary group interaction occurs in any American neighborhoods. Moreover, Danzig (1973: 46) seems insensitive to the role of the mediator, suggesting only that he be a "salaried counselor." Gibbs (1967: 288-9), on the other hand, pays considerable attention to the importance of the social position of the Kpelle mediator. Selected by the complainant, he is a kinsman and town chief or quarter elder. He can produce a therapeutic effect because he is "a member of two social systems," that of the disputants (kinsman) and of the wider community (elder). In my terms Danzig's mediator is unlikely to be functional unless he shares significant intimate experience with the disputants. If such a criterion is ignored or cannot be met in counselor selection, the Kpelle experience may be impossible to duplicate.[30] The Kpelle moot, moreover, is not really mediation. It decides who is mainly at fault, it imposes sanctions and requires apologies (Gibbs, 1967: 280, 283). It can exercise such coercion because it is an institution of a group—a village quarter composed of several virilocal polygamous families (1967: 279). Gibbs (1967: 287) highlights the crucial role of group approval. In addition, in an earlier article (1962: 341-42) he reports that the Kpelle have internalized a particularly strong respect for authority. A successful transplant of the Kpelle version of a moot thus may require a psychological set and social organization which parallels the Kpelle's as well as counselors with high quotients of shared experience with their clientele.

Religious courts open to secular disputes are not unknown in the U.S. (*Columbia Journal of Law and Soc. Probs.*, 1970: 56-68; Balderman, 1974: 18-20). Their supposed advantages over civil courts are speed, less expense, less specialized procedures, privacy and adjudication by members of the same minority group as the disputants and according to its value system. (*Columbia Journal of Law and Soc. Probs.*, 1970: 68-70). Balderman's (1974: 30, 34) study of Jewish courts in Los Angeles, however, indicates that they are rarely used as alternatives to civil courts. The religious courts are employed rather to hear claims which the civil courts will not (Jewish divorces, conversions) and to define the nature of Jewish religious life.

Advocates of minority group institutions as an alternative to government courts, such as the Bet Tzedek proposal in Los

---

30. The success of local justice in Britain has been attributed to the fact that magistrates "administer justice amongst people with whom they are acquainted and of whose lives and family history they know something" (Giles, 1949: 34).

Angeles (Balderman, 1974: 41), ought to face the question of why existing religious courts may have failed to fulfill this function. These institutions are adjudicative. They may compel compliance with their decisions either through resort to government courts based on party execution of irrevocable arbitration agreements or through the persuasive effect of community pressure. As one would predict, the existing Jewish courts in Los Angeles are able to mobilize community coercion when the disputants are members of a functioning, closely-knit group and are unable to do so where they are not. Thus, disputes involving synagogues and synagogue personnel are effectively adjudicated while those between Jews who play no special religious role remain troublesome (Balderman, 1974: 20-30). One might expect that the necessity of hiring a lawyer and of invoking civil court process would make the arbitration agreement rather ineffective. Empirically this seems to have been the case in Los Angeles. Despite the fact that the losing party often fails to obey the Jewish court's decision, the rabbis of that court cannot recall a single instance in the past twenty-five years in which the prevailing party has sought government court coercion through enforcing the obligatory arbitration agreement (Balderman, 1974: 19).

New institutions, then, ought to be adjudicative only when they expect to serve a clientele which is socially organized to coerce its members into compliance with decisions without secondary recourse to government courts. Where dispute processing is to be provided for a different kind of social unit, it would be well to recognize at the outset that only mediation may be effective, and to maximize the use of third parties who are likely to share the social and cultural experience of the disputants and who have some pre-processing information about them as personalities—a neighborhood notable is preferable to a trained social worker or lawyer who is an "outsider" (*see* Yaffe, 1972: 58, 266-67).

Innovative neighborhood "courts" have recently begun to operate in New York City and East Palo Alto, California. (Statsky, 1974; Hager, 1972). In New York, mediation is conducted by non-professional neighborhood residents who secure extensive information about the backgrounds and personalities of juveniles referred to the mediators and of the adults with whom they are quarreling. In East Palo Alto neighborhood judges adjudicate complaints against juveniles and penalize offenders with neighborhood work tasks. Although the behavioral theories implicit in these two approaches are obviously different, each of these institutions seems to be more sensitive to the different prerequisites of mediation and adjudication than are the advocates of neighborhood moots and religious arbitration boards.

In any event, the effect of such reforms, even if they were adopted by a single community, is limited. Juvenile problems and problems within families and within religious groups could be processed in a new forum. But neighborhood disputes, work disputes, consumer disputes and citizen-government disputes would be unaffected. For these disputes, either avoidance is adequate or major changes must be made in government courts, particularly in small claims courts. Since the need for such a court reform has been apparent for decades (Smith, 1924: 9; Nelson, 1949: 239; *Stanford Law Review*, 1952: 238), the utility of avoidance must be viewed as a blessing. In a world that is too infrequently symmetrical, our inability to process many disputes by adjudication or mediation may generally be balanced by a lesser need to do so.

REFERENCES

ABEL, Richard L. (1974) "A Comparative Theory of Dispute Institutions in Society," 8 *Law & Society Review* 217.

ABELSON, Robert P. (1968) "Psychological Implications," in Robert P. ABELSON *et al.* (eds.) *Theories of Cognitive Consistency: A Sourcebook.* Chicago: Rand McNally.

ABNER, Willoughby (1969) "Conflict in a Free Society," Presented at the University of Massachusetts in Amherst.

ADAMS, Bert N. (1971) *The American Family: A Sociological Interpretation.* Chicago: Markham.

ALEXANDER, Christopher (1966) *The City as a Mechanism for Sustaining Human Contact.* Berkeley: Institute of Urban & Regional Development, University of California.

AUBERT, Vilhelm (1969) "Law as a Way of Resolving Conflicts: The Case of a Small Industrialized Society," in Laura NADER (ed.) *Law in Culture and Society.* Chicago: Aldine.

——————————— (1963) "Competition and Dissensus: Two Types of Conflict and of Conflict Resolution," 7 *Journal of Conflict Resolution* 26.

AXELROD, Morris (1956) "Urban Structure and Social Participation," 21 *American Sociological Review* 13.

BALDERMAN, Evelyn (1974) "Jewish Courts." Unpublished manuscript in the custody of the U.C.L.A. Law School Library.

BARD, Morton (1973) "The Role of Law Enforcement in the Helping System," in John R. SNIBBE and Homa M. SNIBBE (eds.) *The Urban Policeman in Transition.* Springfield, Ill.: Charles C. Thomas.

BARNES, J.A. (1961) "Law as Politically Active," in Geoffrey SAWYER (ed.) *Studies in the Sociology of Law.* Canberra: Australian National University Press.

BEALS, Alan R. (1961) "Cleavage and Internal Conflict: An Example from India," 5 *Journal of Conflict Resolution* 27.

BELL, Wendell (1968) "The City, the Suburb, and a Theory of Social Choice," in Scott GREER *et al.* (eds.) *The New Urbanization.* New York: St. Martin's Press.

——————————— and Marion D. BOAT (1957) "Urban Neighborhoods and Informal Social Relations," 62 *American Journal of Sociology* 391.

90   LAW AND SOCIETY / FALL 1974

BLACK, Donald (1973) "The Boundaries of Legal Sociology," in Donald BLACK and Maureen MILEWSKI (eds.) *The Social Organization of Law.* New York: Seminar Press.

BLUMER, Herbert (1969) *Symbolic Interaction: Perspective and Method.* Englewood Cliffs: Prentice-Hall.

BOHANNON, Paul (1957) *Justice and Judgement Among the Tiv.* London: Oxford University Press.

BOTT, Elizabeth (1957) *Family and Social Network.* London: Tavistock Publications.

BOYER, Barry B. and Roger C. CRAMPTON (1974) "American Legal Education: An Agenda for Research and Reform," 59 *Cornell Law Review* 221.

BRANDT, Victor S.R. (1971) *A Korean Village between Farm and Sea.* Cambridge: Harvard University Press.

BRUFF, Harold H. (1973) "Arizona's Inferior Courts," [1973] *Law and the Social Order* 1.

BURGESS, Ernest W., Harvey J. LOCKE and Mary Margaret THOMAS (1963) *The Family: From Institution to Companionship* (3rd ed.). New York: American Book Company.

CAHN, Edgar S. and Jean C. CAHN (1970) "Power to the People or the Profession?—The Public Interest in Public Interest Law," 79 *Yale Law Journal* 1005.

CALIFORNIA LAW REVIEW (1964) "The California Small Claims Court," 52 *California Law Review* 876.

CANTER, Richard S. (1973) "Consequences of Legal Engineering: A Case from Zambia." Presented at the 72nd Meeting of the American Anthropological Association in New Orleans.

CARLIN, Jerome and Jan HOWARD (1965) "Legal Representation and Class Justice," 12 *U.C.L.A. Law Review* 381.

CARSTAIRS, G. Morris (1967) *The Twice Born.* Bloomington: Indiana University Press.

COHEN, Jerome Alan (1967) "Chinese Mediation on the Eve of Modernization," 2 *Journal of Asian and African Studies* 54.

COHEN, Percy S. (1968) *Modern Social Theory.* London: Heinemann Educational Books.

COHN, Bernard S. (1967) "Some Notes on Law and Change in North India," in Paul BOHANNON (ed.) *Law and Warfare.* Garden City: The Natural History Press.

——————— (1965) "Anthropological Notes on Disputes and Law in India," 67 *American Anthropologist* (pt. 2) 82.

COLLIER, Jane Fishburne (1973) *Law and Social Change in Zinacantan.* Stanford: Stanford University Press.

COLUMBIA JOURNAL OF LAW AND SOCIAL PROBLEMS (1970) "Rabbinical Courts: Modern Day Solomons," 6 *Columbia Journal of Law and Social Problems* 49.

DANZIG, Richard (1973) "Toward the Creation of a Complementary, Decentralized System of Criminal Justice," 26 *Stanford Law Review* 1.

DOO, Leigh-Woo (1973) "Dispute Settlement in Chinese-American Communities," 21 *American Journal of Comparative Law* 627.

EMMETT, Isabel (1964) *A North Wales Village.* London: Routledge & Kegan Paul.

EVANS-PRITCHARD, E.E. (1940) *The Nuer.* Oxford: Oxford University Press.

FOSTER, George M. (1960) "Interpersonal Relations in Peasant Society," 19 *Human Organization* 174.

FRIEDMAN. Lawrence M. (1973) *A History of American Law.* New York: Simon and Schuster.

FRIEDMANN, Karl A. (1973) "Complaining—Comparative Aspects of Complaint Behavior and Attitudes Towards Complaining in Canada and Britain." Presented at the Annual Meeting of the Canadian Political Science Association in Montreal.

FULLER, Lon L. (1971) "Mediation—Its Forms and Functions," 44 *Southern California Law Review* 305.

FÜRER-HAIMENDORF, Christoph von (1967) *Morals and Merit.* London: Weidenfeld and Nicholson.

GALANTER, Marc (1975) "Why the "Haves" Come Out Ahead: Speculations on the Limits of Legal Change," 9 *Law & Society Review* 95.

——————— (1968) "The Displacement of Traditional Law in Modern India," 24 *Journal of Social Issues* 65.

——————— (n.d.) "Private Alternatives to Official Dispute Processing: Newspaper Source Materials." Buffalo: Faculty of Law and Jurisprudence, SUNY.

GANS, Herbert J. (1962) *The Urban Villagers.* New York: The Free Press of Glencoe.

GELLHORN, Walter (1966) *When Americans Complain.* Cambridge: Harvard University Press.

GIBBS, James L. Jr. (1969) "Law and Personality: Signposts for a New Direction," in Laura NADER (ed.) *Law in Culture and Society.* Chicago: Aldine.

——————— (1967) "The Kpelle Moot," in Paul BOHANNON (ed.) *Law and Warfare.* Garden City: The Natural History Press.

——————— (1962) "Poro Values and Courtroom Procedures in a Kpelle Chiefdom," 18 *Southwestern Journal of Anthropology* 341.

GILES, F.T. (1949) *The Magistrates' Courts.* Harmondsworth: Penguin Books.

GLUCKMAN, Max (1965) *Politics, Law and Ritual in Tribal Society.* New York: New American Library.

——————— (1955) *The Judicial Process Among the Barotse of Northern Rhodesia.* Manchester: The University Press.

GOUGH, E. Kathleen (1955) "The Social Structure of a Tanjore Village," in McKim MARRIOTT (ed.) *Village India.* Chicago: University of Chicago Press.

GRACE, Roger (1970) "Justice, Chinese Style," 75 *Case and Comment* 50.

GREER, Scott (1962) *The Emerging City.* New York: The Free Press.

——————— (1956) "Urbanism Reconsidered," 21 *American Sociological Review* 22.

GREUEL, Peter J. (1971) "The Leopard-Skin Chief: An Examination of Political Power Among the Nuer," 73 *American Anthropologist* 1115.

GROSSMAN, Joel B. and Austin SARAT (1973) "Courts and Conflict Resolution: Some Observations on the Choice of Dispute Settlement Forum and its Political Impact." Presented at the IX World Congress of the International Political Science Association in Montreal.

GULLIVER, Philip H. (1969) "Introduction and Dispute Settlement Without Courts," in Laura NADER (ed.) *Law in Culture and Society.* Chicago: Aldine.

——————— (1963) *Social Control in an African Society.* Boston: Boston University Press.

HAGER, Philip (1972) "Neighborhood Court Judges Its Own Juvenile Offenders," *Los Angeles Times,* Dec. 25, 1972.

HAHM, Pyong-Choon (1969) "The Decision Process in Korea," in Glendon SCHUBERT and Daniel J. DANIELSKI (eds.) *Comparative Judicial Behavior.* New York: Oxford University Press.

HIRSCHMAN, Albert (1970) *Exit, Voice and Loyalty.* Cambridge: Harvard University Press.

HITCHCOCK, John T. (1960) "Surat Singh, Head Judge," in Joseph B. CASAGRANDE (ed.) *In the Company of Man.* New York: Harper & Brothers.

HOWELL, P.O. (1954) *A Manual of Nuer Law.* London: Oxford University Press.

HUNT, Eva and Robert HUNT (1969) "The Role of Courts in Rural Mexico," in Philip BOCK (ed.) *Peasants in the Modern World.* Albuquerque: University of New Mexico Press.

JONES, Edgar A. Jr. (1964) "Power and Prudence in the Arbitration of Labor Disputes: A Venture in Some Hypotheses," 11 *U.C.L.A. Law Review* 675.

92   LAW AND SOCIETY / FALL 1974

KAUFMAN, Michael T. (1971) "Abbie Hoffman Accused Before a 'Court' of Peers," *New York Times*, Sept. 2, 1971.

KAWASHIMA, Takeyoshi (1963) "Dispute Resolution in Contemporary Japan," in Arthur T. VON MEHREN (ed.) *Law in Japan: The Legal Order in a Changing Society.* Cambridge: Harvard University Press.

KIDDER, Robert L. (1973) "Courts and Conflict in an Indian City: A Study in Legal Impact," 11 *Journal of Commonwealth Political Studies* 121.

KNOWLES, William H. (1958) "Mediation and the Psychology of Small Groups," 9 *Labor Law Journal* 780.

LANSING, John B. and Nancy BARTH (1964) *Residential Location and Urban Mobility: A Multivariate Analysis.* Ann Arbor: Institute for Social Relations, University of Michigan.

LESLIE, Gerald R. (1967) *The Family in Social Context.* New York: Oxford University Press.

LEWIS, Oscar (1965) "Further Observations on the Folk-Urban Continuum and Urbanization with Special Reference to Mexico City," in Philip M. HAUSER and Leo F. SCHNORE (eds.) *The Study of Urbanization.* New York: John Wiley & Sons.

LIEBMAN, Donald A. and Jeffrey A. SCHWARTZ (1973) "Police Programs in Domestic Crisis Intervention: A Review," in John R. SNIBBE and Homa M. SNIBBE (eds.) *The Urban Policeman in Transition.* Springfield, Ill.: Charles C. Thomas.

LITWAK, Eugene (1960a) "Occupational Mobility and Extended Family Cohesion," 25 *American Sociological Review* 9.

_____ (1960b) "Geographic Mobility and Extended Family Cohesion," 25 *American Sociological Review* 385.

LLEWELLYN, Karl N. and E. Adamson HOEBEL (1941) *The Cheyenne Way.* Norman: University of Oklahoma Press.

LOWY, Michael J. (1973) Review, 75 *American Anthropologist* 953.

LUBMAN, Stanley (1967) "Mao and Mediation: Politics and Dispute Resolution in Communist China," 55 *California Law Review* 1284.

MAYER, Adrian C. (1960) *Caste & Kinship in Central India.* Berkeley: University of California Press.

McGONAGLE, John J. Jr. (1972) "Arbitration of Consumer Disputes," 27 *Arbitration Journal* 65.

METZGER, Duane (1960) "Conflict in Chulsanto," 30 *Alpha Kappa Deltan* 35.

MILLER, Walter B. (1955) "Two Concepts of Authority," 57 *American Anthropologist* 271.

MOORE, Sally Falk (1973) "Law and Social Change: The Semi-Autonomous Social Field as an Appropriate Subject of Study," 7 *Law & Society Review* 719.

_____ (1970) "Politics, Procedures and Norms in Changing Chagga Law," 60 *Africa* 321.

NADEL, S.F. (1951) *The Foundations of Social Anthropology.* London: Cohen & West.

NADER, Laura (1972) "Up the Anthropologist—Perspectives Gained from Studying Up," in Dell HYMES (ed.) *Reinventing Anthropology.* New York: Pantheon.

_____ (1969) "Styles of Court Procedure," in Laura NADER (ed.) *Law in Culture and Society.* Chicago: Aldine.

_____ (1965) "The Anthropological Study of Law," 67 *American Anthropologist* (pt. 2) 3.

_____ and Duane METZGER (1963) "Conflict Resolution in Two Mexican Communities," 65 *American Anthropologist* 584.

_____ and Barbara YNGVESSON (1973) "On Studying the Ethnography of Law and Its Consequences," in John J. HONIGMANN (ed.) *Handbook of Social and Cultural Anthropology.* Chicago: Rand McNally.

NELSON, Douglas (1949) "The Small Claims Court," 22 *Wisconsin Bar Bulletin* 237.

NIMKOFF, M.R. and Russell MIDDLETON (1968) "Types of Family and Types of Economy," in Robert F. WINCH and Louis Wolf GOODMAN (eds.) *Selected Studies in Marriage and the Family* (3rd ed.). New York: Holt, Rinehart and Winston.

PARSONS, Talcott (1965) "The Normal American Family," in Seymour M. FARBER, Piero MUSTACCHI and Rober H.L. WILSON (eds.) *Man and Civilization: The Family's Search for Survival.* New York: McGraw-Hill.

—————————— (1951) *Towards a General Theory of Action.* New York: Harper & Row.

POSPISIL, Leopold (1973) "Anthropology of Law: A Rejoinder to Lowy," 75 *American Anthropologist* 1170.

—————————— (1971) *Anthropology of Law: A Comparative Theory.* New York: Harper & Row.

—————————— (1967) "Legal Levels and Multiplicity of Legal Systems in Human Societies," 11 *Journal of Conflict Resolution* 2.

—————————— (1964) *Kapauku Papuans and Their Law.* New Haven: Human Relations Area Files Press.

REISS, Ira L. (1971) *The Family System in America.* New York: Holt, Rinehart and Winston.

REISS, Paul J. (1962) "The Extended Kinship System: Correlates of and Attitudes on Frequency of Interaction," 24 *Marriage and Family Living* 333.

ROBERTS, John M. (1965) "Oaths, Autonomic Ordeals, and Power," 67 *American Anthropologist* (pt. 2) 186.

ROSENBERG, Maurice (1965) "Court Congestion: Status, Causes and Proposed Remedies," in H.W. JONES (ed.) *The Courts, the Public and the Law Explosion.* Englewood Cliffs: Prentice-Hall.

ROSENN, Keith S. (1971) "The Jeito: Brazil's Institutional Bypass of the Formal Legal System and Its Developmental Implications," 19 *American Journal of Comparative Law* 514.

ROSSI, Peter Henry (1955) *Why Families Move.* Glencoe: The Free Press.

ROTHENBERGER, John E. (1970) "Law and Conflict Resolution, Politics and Change in a Sunni Moslem Village in Lebanon." Unpublished Ph.D. dissertation, University of California, Berkeley.

RUDOLPH, Lloyd I. and Susanne Hoeber RUDOLPH (1967) *The Modernity of Tradition.* Chicago: University of Chicago Press.

SCHLEGEL, Stuart A. (1970) *Tiruray Justice.* Berkeley: University of California Press.

SCHWARTZ, Richard D. (1954) "Social Factors in the Development of Legal Control: A Case Study of Two Israeli Settlements," 63 *Yale Law Journal* 471.

SEELEY, John R., R. Alexander SIM and Elizabeth W. LOOSLEY (1956) *Crestwood Heights: A Study of the Culture of Suburban Life.* New York: Basic Books.

SHARP, Harry and Morris AXELROD (1956) "Mutual Aid Among Relatives in an Urban Population," in Ronald FREEDMAN, *et al, Principles of Sociology: A Test with Readings.* New York: Holt, Rinehart and Winston.

SIEGAL, Bernard J. and Alan R. BEALS (1960) "Pervasive Factionalism," 62 *American Anthropologist* 394.

SIMMONS, T.W. (1968) "Changing Residence in the City: a Review of Intraurban Mobility," 58 *Geographical Review* 622.

SMITH, Reginald Heber (1924) "Report of the Committee on Small Claims Courts and Conciliation," 22 *Legal Aid Review* 1.

SRINIVAS, M.N. (1954) "A Caste Dispute Among Washermen of Mysore," 7 *The Eastern Anthropologist* 149.

STANFORD LAW REVIEW (1952) "Small Claims Courts as Collection Agencies," 4 *Stanford Law Review* 237.

STATSKY, William P. (1974) "Community Courts: Decentralizing Juvenile Jurisprudence," 3 *Capital University Law Review* 1.

STIRLING, P. (1957) "Land, Marriage and the Law in Turkish Villages," 9 *International Social Science Bulletin* 21.

94   LAW AND SOCIETY / FALL 1974

STOLZ, Preble (1968) "Insurance for Legal Services: A Preliminary
   Study of Feasibility," 35 *University of Chicago Law Review* 417.
SUSSMAN, Marvin B. (1959) "The Isolated Nuclear Family: Fact or
   Fiction," 6 *Social Problems* 333.
SYKES, Gresham M. (1969) "Cases, Courts, and Congestion," in Laura
   NADER (ed.) *Law in Culture and Society*. Chicago: Aldine.
THE SMALL CLAIMS STUDY GROUP (1972) *Little Injustices: Small
   Claims Courts and the American Consumer*. Washington: The
   Center for Auto Safety.
TOCH, Hans (1973) "Change Through Participation (and Vice Versa),"
   in John R. SNIBBE and Homa M. SNIBBE (eds.) *The Urban Police-
   man in Transition*. Springfield, Ill.: Charles C. Thomas.
TOWNSEND, Peter (1957) *The Family Life of Old People*. London:
   Routledge & Kegan Paul.
TURNER, Ralph H. (1970) *Family Interaction*. New York: John Wiley
   & Sons.
VAN VELSEN, J. (1969) "Procedural Informality, Reconciliation, and
   False Comparisons," in Max GLUCKMAN (ed.) *Ideas and Proce-
   dures in African Customary Law*. London: Oxford University Press.
WALD, Patricia M. and Robert L. WALD (1968) "Law and the Griev-
   ances of the Poor," in James M. CAMPBELL, Joseph R. SAHIB and
   David P. STANG (eds.) *Law and Order Reconsidered*. Washington:
   National Commission on the Causes and Prevention of Violence.
WEBER, Max (1968) "Ideal Types and Theory Construction," in May
   BRODBECK (ed.) *Readings in the Philosophy of the Social Sciences*.
   New York: Macmillan.
——————————— (1967) *Max Weber on Law in Economy and Soci-
   ety* (Max RHEINSTEIN, ed.). New York: Simon and Schuster.
WHITFORD, William L. (1968) "Law and the Consumer Transaction:
   A Case Study of the Automobile Warranty," [1968] *Wisconsin Law
   Review* 1006.
WIMBERLEY, Howard (1973) "Legal Evolution: One Further Step," 79
   American Journal of Sociology 78.
WINCH, Robert F. (1968) "Some Observations on Extended Familism
   in the United States," in Robert F. WINCH and Louis Wolf GOOD-
   MAN (eds.) *Selected Studies in Marriage and the Family* (3rd ed.).
   New York: Holt, Rinehart and Winston.
——————————— and Rae Lesser BLUMBERG (1968) "Societal
   Complexity and Familial Organization," in Robert F. WINCH and
   Louis Wolf GOODMAN (eds.) *Selected Studies in Marriage and the
   Family* (3rd ed.). New York: Holt, Rinehart and Winston.
WIRTH, Louis (1938) "Urbanism as a Way of Life," 44 *American Journal
   of Sociology* 1.
WISER, William H. and Charlotte V. Wiser (1969) *Behind Mud Walls*.
   Berkeley: University of California Press.
WORDSWORTH, William (1933) *The Prelude or Growth of a Poet's
   Mind 1805*. London: Oxford University Press.
YAFFE, James (1972) *So Sue Me! The Story of a Community Court*.
   New York: Saturday Review Press.
YALE LAW JOURNAL (1970) "Legal Ethics and Professionalism," 79
   Yale Law Journal 1179.
YNVESSON, Barbara B. (1970) *Decision-Making and Dispute Settle-
   ment in a Swedish Fishing Village: An Ethnography of Law*. Un-
   published Ph.D. dissertation, University of California, Berkeley.
YOUNG, Michael and Peter WILLMOTT (1957) *Family and Kinship in
   East London*. Glencoe: The Free Press.

[4]

THE EMERGENCE AND TRANSFORMATION OF DISPUTES: NAMING, BLAMING, CLAIMING . . .

WILLIAM L.F. FELSTINER
RICHARD L. ABEL
AUSTIN SARAT

The emergence and transformation of disputes, especially before they enter formal legal institutions, is a neglected topic in the sociology of law. We provide a framework for studying the processes by which unperceived injurious experiences are—or are not—perceived (naming), do or do not become grievances (blaming) and ultimately disputes (claiming), as well as for subsequent transformations. We view each of these stages as subjective, unstable, reactive, complicated, and incomplete. We postulate that transformations between them are caused by, and have consequences for, the parties, their attributions of responsibility, the scope of conflict, the mechanism chosen, the objectives sought, the prevailing ideology, reference groups, representatives and officials, and dispute institutions. We believe the study of transformations is important. Formal litigation and even disputing within unofficial fora account for a tiny fraction of the antecedent events that could mature into disputes. Moreover, what happens at earlier stages determines both the quantity and the contents of the caseload of formal and informal legal institutions. Transformation studies spotlight the issue of conflict levels in American society and permit exploration of the question of whether these levels are too low.

I. INTRODUCTION

The sociology of law has been dominated by studies of officials and formal institutions and their work products. This agenda has shaped the way disputes are understood and portrayed. Institutions reify cases by reducing them to records; they embody disputes in a concrete form that can be studied retrospectively by attending to the words used by lay persons and officials and by examining the economic and legal context in which cases occur (Danzig, 1975). But disputes are not things: they are social constructs.[1] Their shapes reflect

---

[1] Viewing cases as things creates a temptation to count them. But we must be careful in doing so, because litigation rates, like crime rates (see Black, 1970), can be "produced" and manipulated (Seidman and Couzens, 1974). Recognizing this pitfall, researchers in many countries have sought to describe the universe of disputes by examining "legal needs" (see Baraquin,

whatever definition the observer gives to the concept.[2] Moreover, a significant portion of any dispute exists only in the minds of the disputants.

These ideas, though certainly not novel, are important because they draw attention to a neglected topic in the sociology of law—the emergence and transformation of disputes—the way in which experiences become grievances, grievances become disputes, and disputes take various shapes, follow particular dispute processing paths, and lead to new forms of understanding.[3] Studying the emergence and transformation of disputes means studying a social process as it occurs. It means studying the conditions under which injuries are peceived or go unnoticed and how people respond to the experience of injustice and conflict. In addition, though the study of crime and litigation rates seems to be derived from and to support the conviction that both are too high—that there is a need for more police and longer prison terms (Wilson, 1975; Wilson and Boland, 1978; cf. Jacob and Rich, 1980), that the courts are congested with "frivolous" suits (Manning, 1977)— the study of the emergence and transformation of disputes may lead to the judgment that *too little* conflict surfaces in our society, that *too few* wrongs are perceived, pursued, and remedied (cf. Nader and Singer, 1976: 262).

Our purpose in this paper is to provide a framework within which the emergence and transformation of disputes can be described. The history of the sociological study of disputing displays a backward movement, starting with those legal institutions most remote from society—appellate courts—and gradually moving through trial courts, legislatures, administrative agencies, prosecutors, and the police to a focus on disputes and disputing in society and the role of the

---

1975; Cass and Sackville, 1975; Curran, 1977; Royal Commission on Legal Services, 1979; Royal Commission on Legal Services in Scotland, 1980; Colvin *et al.*, 1978; Schuyt *et al.*, 1978); Tieman and Blankenburg, 1979; Valétas, 1976). Yet these studies also reify the social process of disputing since the measure of need invariably reflects the researcher's theory and values, thereby necessarily distorting the social landscape of disputes (see Lewis, 1973; Griffiths, 1977; 1980; Marks, 1976; Mayhew, 1975).

[2] Another way to define disputes is to adopt the definitions of civil or criminal law, in which case we will see the social world through the eyes of the existing political structure. Such a view accepts conventional understandings as adequate and conventional ideas of justice as acceptable. Alternatively, we can resist the temptation to impose ourselves on the people we study and attempt to learn how disputants themselves define their experiences. Each of these approaches has important consequences in the study of disputing.

[3] We have not, of course, invented either the field or the term "transformation." For earlier discussions, see particularly Aubert (1963), Mather and Yngvesson (1981), and Cain (1979).

citizenry in making law.[4] The transformation perspective places disputants at the center of the sociological study of law; it directs our attention to individuals as the creators of opportunities for law and legal activity: people make their own law, but they do not make it just as they please.[5]

II. WHERE DISPUTES COME FROM AND HOW THEY DEVELOP

We come to the study of transformations with the belief that the antecedents of disputing are as problematic and as interesting as the disputes that may ultimately emerge. We begin by setting forth the stages in the development of disputes and the activities connecting one stage to the next. Trouble, problems, personal and social dislocation are everyday occurrences. Yet, social scientists have rarely studied the capacity of people to tolerate substantial distress and injustice (but see Moore, 1979; Janeway, 1980). We do, however, know that such "tolerance" may represent a failure to perceive that one has been injured; such failures may be self-induced or externally manipulated. Assume a population living downwind from a nuclear test site. Some portion of that population has developed cancer as a result of the exposure and some has not. Some of those stricken know that they are sick and some do not. In order for disputes to emerge and remedial action to be taken, an unperceived injurious experience (unPIE, for short) must be transformed into a perceived injurious experience (PIE). The uninformed cancer victims must learn that they are sick. The transformation perspective directs our attention to the differential transformation of unPIEs into PIEs. It urges us to examine, in this case, differences in class, education, work situation, social networks, etc. between those who become aware of their cancer and those who do not, as well as attend to the possible manipulation of information by those responsible for the radiation.

---

[4] Studies of public knowledge and opinion about law are only partially an exception, for they relegate the public to a largely passive role as receptor of and reactor to law (see Sarat, 1977).

[5] Cf. Marx (1976: 72): "Men make their own history, but they do not make it just as they please; they do not make it under circumstances chosen by themselves, but under circumstances directly encountered, given, and transmitted from the past."

Our perspective is influenced by the work of anthropologists who have observed forum choice in non-Western societies (e.g., Nader and Todd, 1978); economists concerned with responses to consumer dissatisfaction (e.g., Hirschman, 1970); and others who have measured or observed the way individuals manage personal problems (Gellhorn, 1966; Levine and Preston, 1970; Abel-Smith *et al.*, 1973; Morris *et al.*, 1973; Friedmann, 1974; Burman *et al.*, 1977; Smith *et al.*, 1979; Cain, 1979; Macaulay, 1979; Nader, 1980b).

634   LAW & SOCIETY / 15:3-4

There are conceptual and methodological difficulties in studying this transformation. The conceptual problem derives from the fact that unPIE is inchoate, PIE in the sky so to speak. It can only be bounded by choosing someone's definition of what is injurious. Frequently this will not be a problem. An injurious experience is any experience that is disvalued by the person to whom it occurs. For the most part, people agree on what is disvalued. But such feelings are never universal. Where people do differ, these differences, in fact, generate some of the most important research questions: why do people who perceive experience similarly *value* it differently, why do they *perceive* similarly valued experience differently, and what is the relation between valuation and perception? From a practical perspective, the lack of consensus about the meaning of experiences does not interfere with any of these tasks, since their purpose is to map covariation among interpretation, perception, and external factors. But if, on the other hand, the research objective is to provide a census of injurious experiences, then the lack of an agreed-upon definition is more serious. In a census, the researcher must either impose a definition upon subjects and run the risk that the definition will fail to capture all injurious experience or permit subjects to define injurious experience as they wish and run the risk that different subjects will define the same experience differently and may include experiences the researcher does not find injurious.

The methodological obstacle is the difficulty of establishing who in a given population has experienced an unPIE. Assume that we want to know why some shipyard workers perceive they have asbestosis and others do not. In order to correlate perception with other variables, it is necessary to distinguish the sick workers who do not know they are sick from those who actually are not sick. But the very process of investigating perception and illness by inquiring about symptoms is likely to influence both. These social scientific equivalents of the uncertainty principle in physics and psychosomatic disease in medicine will create even more acute problems where the subject of inquiry is purely psychological: a personal slight rather than a somatically based illness.

Sometimes it is possible to collect the base data for the study of unPIEs by means of direct observation. For instance, house buyers injured by unfair loan contracts could be identified from inspection of loan documents. On other occasions, hypotheses about the transformation of unPIE to

PIE could be tested directly by inference from aggregate data. Assume that 30 percent of a population exposed to a given level of radiation will develop cancer. We study such a group and find that only ten percent know they are sick. We hypothesize that years of formal schooling are positively associated with cancer *perception*. This hypothesis can be tested by comparing the educational level of the known ten percent with that of the balance of the population. For as long as schooling is not associated with developing cancer, the mean number of school years of the former should be higher than that of the latter. Nevertheless, in many cases it will be difficult to identify and explain transformations from unPIE to PIE. This first transformation—saying to oneself that a particular experience has been injurious—we call *naming*. Though hard to study empirically, naming may be the critical transformation; the level and kind of disputing in a society may turn more on what is initially perceived as an injury than on any later decision (cf. Cahn, 1949; Barton and Mendlovitz, 1960). For instance, asbestosis only became an acknowledged "disease" *and* the basis of a claim for compensation when shipyard workers stopped taking for granted that they would have trouble breathing after ten years of installing insulation and came to view their condition as a problem.

The next step is the transformation of a perceived injurious experience into a grievance. This occurs when a person attributes an injury to the fault of another individual or social entity. By including fault within the definition of grievance, we limit the concept to injuries viewed both as violations of norms and as remediable. The definition takes the grievant's perspective: the injured person must feel wronged and believe that something might be done in response to the injury, however politically or sociologically improbable such a response might be. A grievance must be distinguished from a complaint against no one in particular (about the weather, or perhaps inflation) and from a mere wish unaccompanied by a sense of injury for which another is held responsible (I might like to be more attractive). We call the transformation from perceived injurious experience to grievance *blaming*: our diseased shipyard worker makes this transformation when he holds his employer or the manufacturer of asbestos insulation responsible for his asbestosis.

The third transformation occurs when someone with a grievance voices it to the person or entity believed to be responsible and asks for some remedy. We call this

636   LAW & SOCIETY / 15:3-4

communication *claiming*. A claim is transformed into a dispute when it is rejected in whole or in part. Rejection need not be expressed by words. Delay that the claimant construes as resistance is just as much a rejection as is a compromise offer (partial rejection) or an outright refusal.

The sociology of law should pay more attention to the early stages of disputes and to the factors that determine whether naming, blaming, and claiming will occur. Learning more about the existence, absence, or reversal of these basic transformations will increase our understanding of the disputing process and our ability to evaluate dispute processing institutions. We know that only a small fraction of injurious experiences ever mature into disputes (e.g., Best and Andreasen, 1977: 708-711; Burman *et al.*, 1977: 47). Furthermore, we know that most of the attrition occurs at the early stages: experiences are not perceived as injurious; perceptions do not ripen into grievances; grievances are voiced to intimates but not to the person deemed responsible. A theory of disputing that looked only at institutions mobilized by disputants and the strategies pursued within them would be seriously deficient. It would be like constructing a theory of politics entirely on the basis of voting patterns when we know that most people do not vote in most elections. Recognizing the bias that would result, political scientists have devoted considerable effort to describing and explaining political apathy (see Di Palma, 1970). Sociologists of law need to explore the analogous phenomenon—grievance apathy.

The early stages of naming, blaming, and claiming are significant, not only because of the high attrition they reflect, but also because the range of behavior they encompass is greater than that involved in the later stages of disputes, where institutional patterns restrict the options open to disputants. Examination of this behavior will help us identify the social structure of disputing. Transformations reflect social structural variables, as well as personality traits. People do—or do not—perceive an experience as an injury, blame someone else, claim redress, or get their claims accepted because of their *social position* as well as their individual characteristics. The transformation perspective points as much to the study of social stratification as to the exploration of social psychology.

Finally, attention to naming, blaming, and claiming permits a more critical look at recent efforts to improve "access to justice." The public commitment to formal legal equality, required by the prevailing ideology of liberal legalism, has resulted in substantial efforts to equalize access at the later stages of disputing, where inequality becomes more visible and implicates official institutions; examples include the waiver of court costs, the creation of small claims courts, the movement toward informalism, and the provision of legal services (see R. Abel, 1979c). Access to justice is supposed to reduce the unequal distribution of advantages in society; paradoxically it may amplify these inequalities. The ostensible goal of these reforms is to eliminate bias in the ultimate transformation: disputes into lawsuits. If, however, as we suspect, these very unequal distributions have skewed the earlier stages by which injurious experiences become disputes, then current access to justice efforts will only give additional advantages to those who have already transformed their experiences into disputes. That is, these efforts may accentuate the effects of inequality at the earlier, less visible stages, where it is harder to detect, diagnose, and correct (cf. R. Abel, 1978: 339).

III. THE CHARACTERISTICS OF TRANSFORMATION

PIEs, grievances, and disputes have the following characteristics: they are subjective, unstable, reactive, complicated, and incomplete. They are *subjective* in the sense that transformations need not be accompanied by any observable behavior. A disputant discusses his problem with a lawyer and consequently reappraises the behavior of the opposing party. The disputant now believes that his opponent was not just mistaken but acted in bad faith. The content of the dispute has been transformed in the mind of the disputant, although neither the lawyer nor the opposing party necessarily knows about the shift.

Since transformations may be nothing more than changes in feelings, and feelings may change repeatedly, the process is *unstable*. This characteristic is notable only because it differs so markedly from the conventional understanding of legal controversies. In the conventional view of disputes, the sources of claims and rejections are objective events that happened in the past. It is accepted that it may be difficult to get the facts straight, but there is rarely an awareness that the events themselves may be transformed as they are processed. This view is psychologically naive: it is insensitive to the effect of feelings on the attribution of motive and to the consequences of such attributions for the subject's understanding of behavior (Loftus, 1978).

A focus on transformations also expands, if it does not introduce, the notion of *reactivity*. Since a dispute is a claim and a rejection, disputes are reactive by definition—a characteristic that is readily visible when parties engage in bargaining or litigation. But attention to transformations also reveals reactivity at the earlier stages, as individuals define and redefine their perceptions of experience and the nature of their grievances in response to the communications, behavior, and expectations of a range of people, including opponents, agents, authority figures, companions, and intimates. For instance, in a personal communication, Jane Collier has pointed out that "in hunter-gatherer societies a man cannot overlook his wife's infidelities or *other men* will begin to treat him as if he was unable to defend what he claimed as his. In agrarian societies, such as Spain, a man or woman cannot afford to overlook anything that might be construed as an insult to honor because *others* will then begin treating that person as if they had no honor" [emphasis added] (cf. Starr, 1978: 174-175).

Even in ordinary understanding, disputing is a *complicated* process involving ambiguous behavior, faulty recall, uncertain norms, conflicting objectives, inconsistent values, and complex institutions. It is complicated still further by attention to changes in disputant feelings and objectives over time. Take the stereotypical case of personal injury arising out of an automobile accident. A conventional analysis (e.g., the one often borrowed from economics) assumes that the goals of the defendant driver are to minimize his responsibility and limit the complainant's recovery.[6] A transformation view, on the other hand, suggests that the defendant's objectives may be both less clear and less stable. Depending on his insurance position, his own experience, his empathy for, relationship to, and interaction with the injured person, and the tenor of discussions he may have with others about the accident and its aftermath, the defendant may at various times wish to maximize rather than minimize both his own fault and the complainant's recovery or to take some intermediate position.[7] A transformation approach would seek to identify these

---

[6] Our point is not that economic *theory* would necessarily have any difficulty in coping with these complications or others, but that economic *analysis* as practiced often ignores them and is content with psychological oversimplification. See, e.g., Phillips and Hawkins, 1976.

[7] Automobile guest statutes, which make it difficult for a gratuitous guest injured in an automobile to hold his host liable for damages, were enacted with precisely these factors in mind. See *Brown* v. *Merlo* (106 Cal. Rptr. 388, Sup. Ct., 1973); *Schwalbe* v. *Jones* (128 Cal. Rptr. 321, Sup. Ct., 1976); *Cooper* v. *Bray* (148 Cal. Rptr. 148, Sup. Ct., 1978).

activities and their effects in order to account for such shifts in objective.

To grasp the role of an institution or official in an ongoing conflict, as well as the meaning and outcome of the conflict for the people involved, requires insight into the origins, context, life history, and consequences of the conflict—insight that can only be obtained from the participants. This is the theory of the extended case method in legal anthropology (see Turner, 1957; Van Velsen, 1964; Mitchell, 1956; Epstein, 1967). If to this view we add attention to transformations, we realize that the sequence of behaviors that constitute generating and carrying on a dispute has a tendency to avoid closure. People never fully relegate disputes to the past, never completely let bygones be bygones (R. Abel, 1973: 226-229): there is always a residuum of attitudes, learned techniques, and sensitivities that will, consciously or unconsciously, color later conflict. Furthermore, there is a continuity to disputing that may not be terminated even by formal decision. The end of one dispute may create a new grievance, as surely as a decision labels one party a loser or a liar. Even where such labeling is avoided, it is rare that any process explores and resolves all aspects of all disputant grievances, and new claims may emerge from the recesses of untouched dissatisfactions (see Turk, 1976: 286; Graber and Colton, 1980: 17).

IV. SUBJECTS AND AGENTS OF TRANSFORMATION

One way to organize the study of the transformations of PIEs, grievances, and disputes is to identify what is being transformed (the subjects of transformation) and what does the transforming (the agents of transformation). Unfortunately, it is not possible to present subjects and agents in a simple matrix, since every factor can be construed as both.

Parties

Neither the identity nor the number of parties is fixed. New information about and redefinition of a conflict can lead a party to change his views about appropriate adversaries or desirable allies. Both may also be changed by officials of dispute processing agencies. The new parties, especially if they are groups like the NAACP, ACLU, or Sierra Club, may adopt a lawsuit as part of a campaign to use the courts as a mechanism of social change (see Casper, 1972: ch. 5; Weisbrod *et al.*, 1978; Tushnet, n.d.) or to mobilize political activity (Handler, 1978), although social and political movements may also lose

640   LAW & SOCIETY / 15:3-4

momentum as a collective struggle is translated into an individual lawsuit (e.g., school desegregation; see Wollenberg, 1977). Parties may be dropped as well as added. A grievance that was originally experienced collectively may be individualized in the process of becoming a dispute; tort claims as a response to harm caused by unsafe conditions and disciplinary hearings as a response to labor disputes are examples.

Obviously, the parties to a conflict are central agents, as well as objects, in the transformation process. Their behavior will be a function of personality as it interacts with prior experience and current pressures. Experience includes involvement in other conflicts; contact with reference groups, representatives, and officials; and familiarity with various forms of dispute processing and remedies. For instance, among the newly enrolled members of a prepaid legal services plan, those who have previously consulted a lawyer are more likely to use their membership privileges than are those who have not (Marks *et al.*, 1974: 63-64). Personality variables that may affect transformations include risk preferences, contentiousness, and feelings about personal efficacy, privacy, independence, and attachment to justice (rule-mindedness). Both experience and personality are in turn related to social structural variables: class, ethnicity, gender, age (see Curran, 1977; Griffiths, 1977; Best and Andreasen, 1977: Table 15).

The relationship between the parties (cf. Black, 1973) also has significance for transformations: the sphere of social life that brings them together (work, residence, politics, recreation)—which may affect the cost of exit (see Felstiner, 1974: 79-80, 83-84)—their relative status (see Starr, 1978; R. Abel, 1979a: 245-246), and the history of prior conflict shape the way in which they will conduct their dispute. In addition, strategic interaction between the parties in the course of a conflict may have a major transformational role. An unusual example is the party who seeks proactively to elicit grievances against himself: the retail seller who asks purchasers about complaints (Ross and Littlefield, 1978: 202), the employer who provides an anonymous suggestion box, even the neurotic spouse or lover who invites recriminations. But more common are the new elements disputes take on, the rise and fall in animosity and effort that occurs in response to or in anticipation of the "moves" of the opposition.

Attributions

Attribution theory (see Kelley and Michela, 1980: 458) asserts that the causes a person assigns for an injurious experience will be important determinants of the action he or she takes in response to it; those attributions will also presumably affect perception of the experience as injurious. People who blame themselves for an experience are less likely to see it as injurious, or, having so perceived it, to voice a grievance about it; they are more likely to do both if blame can be placed upon another, particularly when the responsible agent can be seen as intentionally causing or aggravating the problem (see Vidmar and Miller, 1980: 576-577; Coates and Penrod, 1981). But attributions themselves are not fixed. As moral coloration is modified by new information, logic, insight, or experience, attributions are changed, and they alter the participants' understanding of their experience. Adversary response may be an important factor in this transformation, as may the nature of the dispute process. Some processes, such as counseling, may drain the dispute of moral content and diffuse responsibility for problems; others, like direct confrontation or litigation, may intensify the disputant's moral judgment and focus blame. Thus the degree and quality of blame, an important subject of transformations, also produces further transformations.

Scope

The scope of conflict—the extent of relevant discourse about grievances and claims—is affected both by the objectives and behavior of disputants and by the processual characteristics of dispute institutions. A hypothetical case frequently used in mediator training involves a man's wife and his lover. The wife has hit the lover with a rock, and the latter has complained to the police; at arraignment the judge has referred the women to mediation. The discussion there focuses initially on the rock incident and then expands to include the battle for the man's affections. The scope of this dispute is thus complicated by the confrontation between the women during the rock incident, narrowed to that incident alone as the dispute is handled by police and court, and then broadened to re-embrace the original conflict plus the rock incident through interaction between the disputants and the mediator. Some types of dispute processing seek to narrow the disputes with which they deal in order to produce a construction of events that appears manageable. Others are alive to context and

642   LAW & SOCIETY / 15:3-4

circumstance. They encourage a full rendering of events and exploration of the strands of interaction, no matter where they lead. The scope of conflict, in turn, affects the identity of the participants, the tactics used, and the outcomes that become feasible.

Choice of Mechanisms

The grievant's choice of an audience to whom to voice a complaint and the disputant's choice of an institution to which to take a controversy are primarily functions of the person's objectives and will change as objectives change.[8] Mechanisms may also be determined by exogenous factors such as the whims of court clerks (see Felstiner and Williams, 1980: 19; cf. R. Abel, 1969: Table III and accompanying text; 1979d: 188) and lawyers who prefer not to try cases (see Rosenthal, 1974: 110, 115) or who cool out consumers in order to maintain good relations with retailers (Macaulay, 1979: 137).[9] Once a mechanism—court, administrative agency, mediator, arbitrator, or psychotherapist—is set in motion, it determines the rules of relevance, cast of actors, costs, delays, norms, and remedies.

Objectives Sought

A party may change his objectives in two ways: what he seeks or is willing to concede and how much. Stakes go up or down as new information becomes available, a party's needs change, rules are adjusted, and costs are incurred. Delay, frustration, and despair may produce a change in objectives: victims of job discrimination frequently want the job (or promotion) or nothing at the outset but later become willing to settle for money (see E. Abel, 1981; Crowe, 1978). As Aubert (1963: 33) noted, the relationship between objectives and mechanisms is reciprocal: not only do objectives influence the choice of mechanisms, but mechanisms chosen may alter

---

[8] Objectives, on the other hand, will also be influenced by audiences. Lloyd-Bostock notes:

> It is not that the victim does not know his legal rights or how much he *could* receive. In a situation which is unfamiliar, he lacks specific norms of his own and does not feel competent to generate them for himself from more general principles because there is a range of possibilities. What he *feels* is, therefore, often largely the result of what his lawyer, trades union, the police, friends and others have suggested to him since his accident (1980: 24).

[9] To generalize, when clients encounter lawyers in one-shot relationships (e.g., divorce, criminal defense, personal injury), the lawyers' primary allegiance is often to others (insurance claims agents, police, judges, other lawyers), whereas clients who deal regularly with lawyers demand and receive greater loyalty (see R. Abel, 1981; Galanter, 1974: 114-119; 1981).

objectives. Because courts, for instance, often proceed by using a limited number of norms to evaluate an even more circumscribed universe of relevant facts, "the needs of the parties, their wishes for the future, cease to be relevant to the solution" (Aubert, 1963: 33). Even where a legal remedy is anticipatory—alimony, worker's compensation, or tort damages for future loss—the legal system frequently prefers to award a lump sum rather than order periodic payments. Finally, the experience of disputing may stimulate a participant to take steps to avoid similar disputes in the future, or to structure his behavior so as to place him in a stronger position should a dispute occur (e.g., Macaulay, 1966: 167, 204).

Ideology

The individual's sense of entitlement to enjoy certain experiences and be free from others is a function of the prevailing ideology, of which law is simply a component. The consumer's dissatisfaction with a product or service may have been influenced by the campaigns of activists, like Ralph Nader, who assert that consumers have a right to expect high quality.[10] Legal change may sometimes be a highly effective way of transforming ideology to create a sense of entitlement. This is the sense in which, contrary to conventional wisdom, you *can* legislate morality. Although it would be foolish to maintain that after *Brown* v. *Board of Education* every minority child had a sense of entitlement to integrated education, made a claim against segregation, and engaged in a dispute when that claim was rejected, surely this has happened more often *since* than before 1954. Following a recent television program in Chicago in which a woman subjected to a strip search during a routine traffic citation described her successful damage claim against the police department, *hundreds* of women telephoned the station with similar stories. In this instance, a legal victory transformed shame into outrage, encouraging the voicing of grievances, many of which may have become disputes. When the original victim chose a legal mechanism for her complaint, a collective grievance against police practices was individualized and depoliticized. When she broadcast her legal victory on television, the legal

---

10 This belief may explain why consumers from higher socioeconomic strata exhibit a higher level of dissatisfaction with their purchases—it is not the goods and services that are worse but the expectations that are more demanding, partly as a result of the consumer movement which, in its composition, is exclusively middle-class. See Best and Andreasen (1977: 707-709).

dispute was collectivized and repoliticized. Ideology—and law—can also instill a sense of disentitlement. The enactment of worker's compensation as the "solution" to the problem of industrial accidents early in this century may have helped convince workers to rely on employer paternalism to ensure their safety and relinquish claims to control the workplace (Weinstein, 1967).[11]

Reference Groups

Disputes may be transformed through interaction with audiences or sponsors. A tenant's dispute with a landlord may be the cause around which a tenants' association is formed; a worker's grievance against a foreman may become the stimulus to a union organizing drive or a rank-and-file movement within an existing union. This transformation may not only make an individual dispute into a collective one: it also may lead to economic or political struggle displacing legal procedures. This is especially important in the remedy-seeking behavior of disadvantaged groups. The movement from law to politics, and the accompanying expansion of the scope of disputing, are prompted and guided by the reaction of a wide social network to individual instances of injustice. Absent the support of such a network, no such movement is likely to occur (Scheingold, 1974: ch. 12). Whether that support is provided depends on a number of independent variables: the subculture of the audience—which will define the experience as injurious or harmless, encourage or discourage the expression of the grievance, and prefer certain dispute processing strategies; and the social composition of the audience—whether it is made up of peers or superiors. These variables, in turn, are influenced by social structural factors—for instance, whether the network in which the individual is situated is open or closed (Bott, 1955). In an open network, where ego is related (separately) to the members but they are not related to each other, the audience is likely to respond individually, often seeking to resolve the dispute through the exercise of superordinate influence. In a closed network, where everybody is related to everybody, the likelihood of a collective response is much greater.

---

[11] OSHA, which is based on the proposition that private paternalism proved inadequate, may have the opposite effect (see, e.g., Mendeloff, 1979).

Representatives and Officials

Lawyers, psychotherapists, union officials, social workers, government functionaries, and other agents and public officials help people understand their grievances and what they can do about them. In rendering this service, they almost always produce a transformation: the essence of professional jobs is *to define the needs of the consumer* of professional services (Johnson, 1972: 45). Generally, this leads to a definition that calls for the professional to provide such services (Larson, 1977: xvii; R. Abel, 1979b: 86-88; Illich, 1977; 1980).

Of all of the agents of dispute transformation lawyers are probably the most important. This is, in part, the result of the lawyer's central role as gatekeeper to legal institutions and facilitator of a wide range of personal and economic transactions in American society (Parsons, 1962). It is obvious that lawyers play a central role in dispute decisions. Yet relatively few studies of lawyer behavior have been informed, even implicitly, by a transformation perspective (but see Blumberg, 1967; Macaulay, 1979; Cain, 1979; Rosenthal, 1974). We know more about the structure of the bar (see, e.g., Laumann and Heinz, 1977) and about particular ethical problems in the practice of law (see Carlin, 1966; Freedman, 1977) than we do about how lawyers interact with clients and what difference it makes.

Critics of professionals argue that they "create" at least some of the needs they satisfy (see, e.g., Illich, 1977). Lawyers exercise considerable power over their clients. They maintain control over the course of litigation (Rosenthal, 1974: 112-113) and discourage clients from seeking a second opinion or taking their business elsewhere (Steele and Nimmer, 1976: 956-962). There is evidence that lawyers often shape disputes to fit their own interests rather than those of their clients. Sometimes they systematically "cool out" clients with legitimate grievances. In consumer cases lawyers may be reluctant to press claims for fear of offending potential business clients (Macaulay, 1979).[12] In defending the accused criminal, lawyers may prefer negotiating a plea bargain to trying the case (see Blumberg, 1967: 110-115; see generally *Law & Society Review*, 1979). In tort litigation they prefer to settle, and may offer package deals to claims adjusters (see Rosenthal, 1974: 103; Ross, 1970: 82; Schwartz and Mitchell, 1970: 1133). In other

---

[12] For the inhibiting effect of such attitudes on *pro bono* representation, see Ashman (1972: 43); see generally Handler *et al.* (1978: ch. 5, 6).

646   LAW & SOCIETY / 15:3-4

cases they may amplify grievances: some divorce lawyers recommend litigation for which a substantial fee can be charged, rather than engage in difficult, problematic, and unprofitable negotiations about reconciliation (see O'Gorman, 1963: 146).

Lawyers may affect transformations in another way—by rejecting requests for assistance or providing only minimal help and thereby arresting the further development of a dispute, at least through legal channels. Limited data suggest that lawyers respond differently to different categories of clients. This differential lawyer response contributes to variation in dispute behavior between poor and middle class, corporate entities and individuals, normal and deviant, members of ethnic majorities and minorities, and young and old (Maddi and Merrill, 1971: 17-19; Handler *et al.*, 1978: ch. 5; Lochner, 1975: 449-453; Curran, 1977: 149-152).

Of course, lawyers also produce transformations about which we may be more enthusiastic. They furnish information about choices and consequences unknown to clients; offer a forum for testing the reality of the client's perspective; help clients identify, explore, organize, and negotiate their problems; and give emotional and social support to clients who are unsure of themselves or their objectives (see Mnookin and Kornhauser, 1979: 985).

One of the reasons that data about lawyers and dispute transformation are so incomplete and atheoretical is the paucity of observational studies of lawyer-client relationships.

> Research on lawyer-client relationships is long overdue . . . while there have been hundreds of studies of doctor-patient communication, including many which relied mainly on observation, there are hardly any parallel studies of lawyer-client communication. . . . Only about fifteen years ago did social scientists begin to investigate what lawyers do. . . . However, none of these studies emphasized direct observation of lawyers' handling of clients as the main topic and method of study. Rosenthal's more recent, pioneering research (1974) made lawyer-client relations its main focus, but it too employed interviews as the primary source of data (Danet *et al.*, 1980: 906).

Since Danet and her associates wrote these comments, two studies of lawyer-client relations have been published. Cain (1979: 335) reports that "in the sixty-seven of the eighty-two cases which I observed and recorded the client announced his need and set the objective for the solicitor." Her lawyers thus translated client objectives expressed in everyday discourse into legal language and, when successful, delivered the objective the client originally sought. The minority of cases in which the solicitor refused to accept the client's objectives are explained (1979: 344) in terms of the practitioners' lack of professional integration and dependence upon a patron.

Macaulay's (1979) recent study of the way lawyers handle consumer problems with product quality reports quite different results. Macaulay suggests a civil equivalent to what Blumberg (1967) termed the "practice of law as a confidence game" in criminal courts. Consumers bring to lawyers their grievances against retailers based on lay perceptions of negligence, defect, or fraud. Most often the amount of money involved is relatively small. Typically (although not always) the lawyer "cools out" the client, convincing him or her that the grievance is not serious, cannot be remedied, or simply is not worth pursuing. "Those few [consumers] who do seek legal services will get only what the lawyer sees as appropriate—some will get turned away with little more than token gestures, while a very few will recover their full statutory remedies through legal action" (Macaulay, 1979: 130).

Enforcement personnel—police, prosecutors, regulatory agencies—may also produce transformations: seeking disputes in order to advance a public policy or generate a caseload that will justify increased budget demands; discouraging disputes because of personnel shortages; or selectively encouraging those disputes that enhance the prestige of the agency and discouraging those that diminish its significance or call for skills it lacks or are thought to be inappropriate (see Skolnick, 1966: 196; Wilson, 1975).

Dispute Institutions

The transformation effects of dispute institutions have been analyzed at some length (e.g., R. Abel, 1973). Courts, which fall at one extreme along most of the dimensions useful for describing dispute institutions, may transform the content of disputes because the substantive norms they apply differ from rules of custom or ordinary morality, and their unique procedural norms may narrow issues and circumscribe evidence.

> A highly personal and idiosyncratic situation from the point of view of the parties is . . . classified as an instance of a general category. . . . Once the issues are narrowed in this way there is no need to inquire into the general situation. . . . Most of the time . . . [what is preferred] is not to know why anything has happened, but rather *what* occurred, or even more narrowly, what can be *shown* . . . to have occurred (Moore, 1977: 182-183).

Courts may transform disputes by individualizing remedies.[13] Some of the victims of a defective product may want to force the manufacturer to alter the production process. But because courts award only money damages for unintentional torts, even those victims' concept of an acceptable outcome is transformed from a collective good (safety) into individual enrichment, a transformation greatly encouraged by the lawyer's interest in creating a fund out of which his fee can be paid.[14]

Because of the monopoly exercised by lawyers, the esoteric nature of court processes and discourse, and the burdens of pretrial procedure, the *attitude* of disputants may be altered by their minimal role in the courtroom and the way they are treated there (Simon, 1978: 98, 115). In effect, their "property" interest in the dispute is expropriated by lawyers and the state (Christie, 1977). The rediscovery of the victim in the criminal prosecution is one recognition of this. Furthermore, delays caused by court overload or foot-dragging by an adversary may transform what disputants would otherwise consider a useful procedure into pointless frustration.

The nature and potential transformational effects of courts can be seen best if we contrast litigation with another technique for handling conflict—psychotherapy. Like law, therapy individualizes conflicts and remedies. In most other ways, however, it sharply contrasts with courts and lawyers. Disputants are encouraged to describe the conflict and express their feelings about it in whatever terms they find comfortable. Since mental health professionals are trained to use anger to reduce hostility, disputants will not need to deny their feelings. The nonjudgmental posture and reflective responses of the therapist should provide emotional support for disputants, who are urged to examine the pattern of their own responses to the behavior of others. They may find, for instance, that progress toward a solution may be obstructed not by the dilatory tactics or opposition of an adversary but rather by their own reluctance to act. One objective of the process is to increase

---

[13] Even class actions are often merely collections of individual disputes, aggregated for reasons of convenience and efficiency, rather than a form of collective action aimed at achieving a group objective, such as a shift in control over production decisions.

[14] We acknowledge that in making money damages the quintessential remedy, courts are, in a sense, giving people what they "want." But what people "want" is powerfully structured by legal institutions and the media. Although it is difficult to document this process in action, we know that at the turn of the century, before money compensation for injuries was commonplace, workers demanded radical improvements in industrial safety, and only the intransigence of employers compelled them to accept the workers' compensation system instead (cf. Eastman, 1978).

the disputant's understanding of the motives, feelings, and behavior of others. Thus, where the outcome of successful litigation is usually an order directed to an adversary, the outcome of a successful psychotherapeutic intervention may be a change in the client.

In between courts and psychotherapy there are many other dispute institutions—arbitration, mediation, administrative hearings, and investigations—that use ingredients of each process in different combinations but always effect a transformation.[15]

V. THE IMPORTANCE OF STUDYING TRANSFORMATIONS

The study of transformations approaches disputing through individual perceptions, behavior, and decision making. Yet this perspective is useful in studying dispute institutions as well, since "broad patterns of court usage are created by the cumulative choices of individual actors" (Collier, 1973: 251; see also R. Abel, 1979d: 169). Other dispute institutions are also reactive, their caseloads largely determined by the decisions of individuals rather than by institutional planners (Felstiner, 1975: 699). Even proactive institutions are to some extent dependent upon the perceptions, grievances, and ongoing disputes within the population they seek to reach (cf. Black, 1973).

Because transformation studies begin with the individual, they enable researchers to examine perceptions, grievances, and conflicts that are never institutionalized as disputes (cf. Steele, 1977: 672-675). Unarticulated grievances, lumped claims, and bilateral disputes certainly are numerically more significant than are the cases that reach courts and administrative agencies but are rarely studied by researchers (but see Miller and Sarat, 1981; Strauss, 1978).[16] By directing attention to dispute antecedents, the study of transformations should illuminate both the ways in which differential

---

[15] Regardless of whether one is ultimately deterministic, random events necessarily play an important role in transforming *particular* experiences, grievances, and disputes.

A third theme in Koch's review of disputes between neighbors is the importance of chance, of consequences which nobody intended becoming causes of further conflict which nobody sought. A few nuts are stolen, but no scuffle is intended; injuries occur, but no killing is intended; discovered trying to steal a pig in retaliation, the thief is killed . . . (Felstiner, 1976: 1020).

[16] Gulliver's recent book on negotiations (1979), for instance, does not even concern itself with disagreements until they have been transferred to a public domain. All of his references to disputes in the U.S. are labor cases submitted to government mediation.

experience and access to resources affect the number and kinds of problems that mature into disputes and the consequences for individuals and society when responses to injurious experiences are arrested at an early stage (e.g., depoliticization, apathy, anomie).

Evaluation research on the effectiveness of different forms of dispute processing would also be improved if it considered transformations. Conventional evaluation is inclined to explore the attitude of disputants when a process has run its course (see, e.g., Davis *et al.*, 1980b: 50, 54; Cook *et al.*, 1980: 45). Lacking a baseline—the content of the original problem, the nature of the claim as first expressed, or the earlier forms the dispute may have assumed—the evaluator cannot make an independent assessment of the final condition. Nor can one tell how far, at each stage, the process departed from some standard—what the disputant would have liked at that point or perhaps what a professional believes the disputant could have obtained (see, e.g., Rosenthal, 1974; Baldwin and McConville, 1977). This is not to say that the effectiveness of a dispute process is necessarily measured by its ability to uncover and deal with the origin of the dispute. The disputant may no longer view the original problem as important, since a central tenet of transformation theory is that a transformed dispute can actually become *the* dispute. But whether or not such a transformation has taken place, judgments about effectiveness could be improved by the detailed dispute histories that can best be captured by transformation studies.

Much research on disputing in the U.S. measures and explains decisions made by parties by interviewing participants after the dispute is over (see, e.g., Trubek, 1981). This methodology has important limitations, since it requires the respondent to recall the events of a terminated dispute (see Bohannan, 1957: vii). One problem is the distortion in recall when the respondent is questioned about motives and interaction. The errors arise less from the mechanical difficulty in remembering details of past events than from the tendency of subsequent experience to distort those memories. When asked to explain why he acted or failed to act, it is difficult for a respondent to formulate an answer that is uncolored by the consequences of the course he actually chose. Similarly, when asked what he expected an opposing party to do, a respondent's answer is likely to be influenced (to an unknown degree) by the actual behavior of the opponent. Yet such inquiries are necessarily central to an adequate explanation of disputing behavior. Most steps in disputing have alternatives: whether to make a claim, hire a lawyer, accept an offer, appeal, prosecute, or mediate. The best available evidence of the dynamics of these decisions is likely to be the testimony of those who made them, but that evidence is unreliable if markedly retrospective. One aim of transformation research, therefore, is to produce direct and reliable data about motives and interactions by studying them contemporaneously. Only in this way is it possible to catalogue the antecedents of a dispute before the issue is publicly joined, to examine the form in which claims are made and, earlier still, the way in which grievances and injurious experience are first perceived.

Disputing involves the creation and revision of perceptions and attitudes about oneself, one's opponent, agents, dispute content, dispute process, and dispute institutions and personnel. Transformations result from these social psychological processes and are themselves responsible for some of them. Ruhnka and Weller (1979), for example, found that positive attitudes toward, and support for, small claims courts vary inversely with the extent of respondent's experience in such courts, and that this relationship is equally true for "winners" and "losers"; other researchers have found similar inverse relationships with attitudes toward other courts and lawyers (Curran, 1977: 234-239) and the criminal process (Casper, 1978; see generally Sarat, 1977). Transformation research, by focusing on agents and studying attitudes longitudinally, should be able to document this negative shift in opinion and develop hypotheses about *why* it occurs.

We noted earlier that transformation studies render problematic one of the most fundamental political judgments about disputing—that there is too much of it, that Americans are an over-contentious people, far too ready to litigate (e.g., Rosenberg, 1972; Ehrlich, 1976; Kline, 1978). The transformation perspective suggests that there may be too *little* conflict in our society. Many studies are "court-centered." They assess conflict from the point of view of courts which perceive their resources to be limited (cf. Heydebrand, 1979). From this viewpoint, any level of conflict that exceeds the court's capacities is "too much." Things look very different, however, if we start with the *individual* who has suffered an injurious experience. That is what the transformations point of view makes us do. It encourages inquiry into why so few such individuals even get some redress. So the transformation perspective naturally prompts questions that have been largely

652   LAW & SOCIETY / 15:3-4

ignored thus far: why are Americans so slow to perceive injury, so reluctant to make claims, and so fearful of disputing—especially of litigating?[17] One hypothesis tentatively advanced in some early research is that the cult of competence, the individualism celebrated by American culture, inhibits people from acknowledging—to themselves, to others, and particularly to authority—that they have been injured, that they have been bettered by an adversary (e.g., Best and Andreasen, 1977: 709; Menkel-Meadow, 1979: 40).[18]

Transformation studies should also enable us to be more specific about the "culture" of different dispute processing agents and institutions (cf. Friedman, 1969). For instance, the conventional wisdom maintains that divorce lawyers exacerbate conflict, mistrust, and stress. The current interest in custody mediation is more a reflection of skepticism about the usefulness of lawyers (and the adversary process that is their stock in trade) than a failure of confidence in the wisdom of family court judges. Yet *all* lawyers do not mismanage custody cases. Transformation studies that observe lawyer-client interactions over time could tell us which values, experiences, techniques, contexts, or personalities differentiate constructive lawyers from those who tend to complicate an already difficult problem (see Kressel *et al.*, 1979: 255). They could also tell us when clients (and not their lawyers) use litigation for purposes of perpetuating family conflict rather than resolving it (e.g., the "Lesser" case in Goldstein and Katz, 1965: 518-559).

VI. CONCLUSION

The importance of studying the emergence and transformation of disputes should not blind us to its difficulties. Since the study of transformations must focus on the minds of respondents, their attitudes, feelings, objectives, and motives (as these change over time), it must be longitudinal and based

---

[17] See Bohannan (1967), Moriarty (1975), Nader and Singer (1976: 282). For an analysis of the civil litigation rates of African countries, see R. Abel (1979d: 190-195). For historical studies showing declining litigation in the United States, see Grossman and Sarat (1975), Friedman and Percival (1976a); but see Lempert (1978). See generally *Law & Society Review* (1974-75).

[18] In testing this hypothesis, it might be useful to compare Far Eastern societies with even lower levels of litigation, usually explained by the desire to avoid giving offense rather than the fear of receiving it (see, e.g., Kawashima, 1969; Hahm, 1968), with societies displaying much higher levels of disputing, such as those in the Mediterranean and parts of Africa, where culture mandates an immediate, public response to any affront (see, e.g., R. Abel, 1979b; Starr, 1978; Peristiany, 1965). For a fascinating study of attitudes toward injury in a non-Western culture, see Upham (1976).

upon a high level of rapport between researcher and informant. The difficulties in such research are considerable: the most obvious problems arise in devising techniques that minimize reactivity to researcher suggestion while providing researchers with adequate signals about the timeliness of a new wave of interviews.

In order to identify the salient influences on transformations, it is necessary to select for research substantive areas of disputing where high levels of variance can be expected. But different substantive fields are likely to exhibit variation at different stages. For instance, there is probably a low level of PIEs in the relationship between lay persons and professionals but a high level in landlord-tenant interactions; a low level of follow-through on consumer disputes but a high level in claims concerning serious personal injuries. As a result, the development of an empirical understanding of transformations will require many studies with limited objectives rather than a few large-scale projects. Several substantive areas deserve immediate attention, not only because they satisfy these requirements but also because they have been the subject of earlier research that can provide historical data, a baseline for comparison, tentative hypotheses, and methodological guidance. Those fields are personal injury, especially auto accidents (e.g., Conard, 1964; Franklin et al., 1961; Hunting and Neuwirth, 1962; Widiss, 1975; Burman et al., 1977; Royal Commission, 1978; Walker and Maclean, 1980; Lloyd-Bostock, 1980; Genn, 1980); consumer disputes (e.g., Whitford, 1968; Whitford and Kimball, 1974; Steele, 1975; 1977; Best and Andreasen, 1977; Macaulay, 1963; Ross and Littlefield, 1978; Hannigan, 1977; Caplovitz, 1963; 1974; King and McEvoy, 1976; National Institute of Consumer Justice, 1972a; Small Claims Court Study Group, 1972; Warland et al., 1975; Nader, 1980); and family conflict (e.g., MacGregor et al., 1970; Marshall and May, 1932-33; Gellhorn, 1954; Virtue, 1956; Parnas, 1970; Chambers, 1979; Mnookin and Kornhauser, 1979; University of Pennsylvania Law Review, 1953).

Although the emergence and transformation of disputes is personal and individualized, it has an important political dimension. Ultimately what we are concerned with is the capacity of people to respond to trouble, problems, and injustice. We believe that the study of dispute processing has been too removed from the actual difficulties and choices that accompany the recognition that one's life is troubled and that relief from trouble is uncertain, contingent, and costly.

Recognition and action may not be appropriate or desirable in every instance. We do believe, however, that a healthy social order is one that minimizes barriers inhibiting the emergence of grievances and disputes and preventing their translation into claims for redress.

References

ABEL, Emily K. (1981) "Collective Protest and the Meritocracy: Faculty Women and Sex Discrimination Lawsuits," *Feminist Studies* (forthcoming).

ABEL, Richard L. (1981) "Legal Services," in M. Olsen and M. Micklin (eds.), *Frontiers of Applied Sociology*. New York: Holt, Rinehart and Winston (forthcoming).

_____ (1979a) "The Rise of Capitalism and the Transformation of Disputing: From Confrontation Over Honor to Competition for Property," 27 *UCLA Law Review* 223.

_____ (1979b) "The Rise of Professionalism," 6 *British Journal of Law and Society* 82.

_____ (1979c) "Socializing the Legal Profession: Can Redistributing Lawyers' Services Achieve Social Justice?" 1 *Law & Policy Quarterly* 5.

_____ (1979d) "Western Courts in Non-Western Settings: Patterns of Court Use in Colonial and Neo-Colonial Africa," in S. B. Burman and B. E. Harrell-Bond (eds.), *The Imposition of Law*, New York: Academic Press.

_____ (1978) "From the Editor," 12 *Law & Society Review* 33.

_____ (1973) "A Comparative Theory of Dispute Institutions in Society," 8 *Law & Society Review* 217.

_____ (1969), "Customary Laws of Wrongs in Kenya: An Essay in Research Method," 17 *American Journal of Comparative Law* 573.

ABEL-SMITH, Brian, Michael ZANDER, and Rosiland BROOKE (1973) *Legal Problems and the Citizen: A Study in Three London Boroughs*. London: Heinemann.

ASHMAN, Alan (1972) *The New Private Practice: A Study of Piper & Marbury's Neighborhood Law Office*. Chicago: National Legal Aid and Defender Association.

AUBERT, Vilhelm (1963) "Competition and Dissensus: Two Types of Conflict and of Conflict Resolution," 7 *Journal of Conflict Resolution* 26.

BALDWIN, John and Michael MC CONVILLE (1977) *Negotiated Justice*. London: Martin Robertson.

BARAQUIN, Yves (1975) *Les Français et la justice civile: Enquête psychosociologique auprès des justiciables*. Paris: La Documentation Française.

BARTON, Alan and Saul MENDLOVITZ (1960) "The Experience of Injustice as a Research Problem," 13 *Journal of Legal Education* 24.

BEST, Arthur and Alan ANDREASEN (1977) "Consumer Response to Unsatisfactory Purchases: A Survey of Perceiving Defects, Voicing Complaints, and Obtaining Redress," 11 *Law & Society Review* 701.

BLACK, Donald J. (1973) "The Mobilization of Law," 2 *Journal of Legal Studies* 125.

BLUMBERG, Abraham S. (1967) "The Practice of Law as a Confidence Game: Organizational Co-optation of a Profession," 1 *Law & Society Review* 15.

BOHANNAN, Paul (1967) "Introduction," in P. Bohannan (ed.), *Law and Warfare*. Garden City, NY: Natural History Press.

_____ (1957) *Justice and Judgment Among the Tiv*. London: Oxford University Press.

BOTT, Elizabeth (1955) "Urban Families: Conjugal Roles and Social Networks," 8 *Human Relations* 345.

BURMAN, S. B., H. GENN, and J. LYONS (1977) "The Use of Legal Services by Victims of Accidents in the Home—A Pilot Study," 40 *Modern Law Review* 47.

CAHN, Edmund (1949) *The Sense of Injustice: An Anthropocentric View of Law*, New York: New York University Press.

CAIN, Maureen (1979) "The General Practice Lawyer and the Client: Towards a Radical Conception," 7 *International Journal of the Sociology of Law* 331.

CAPLOVITZ, David (1974) *Consumers in Trouble: A Study of Debtors in Default*. New York: Free Press.

———— (1963) *The Poor Pay More: Consumer Practices of Low-Income Families*. New York: Free Press.

CARLIN, Jerome E. (1966) *Lawyers' Ethics: A Survey of the New York City Bar*. New York: Russell Sage.

CASPER, Jonathan D. (1978) "Having Their Day in Court: Defendant Evaluations of the Fairness of Their Treatment," 12 *Law & Society Review* 237.

———— (1972) *Lawyers Before the Warren Court: Civil Liberties and Civil Rights, 1957-66*. Urbana: University of Illinois Press.

CASS, Michael and Ronald SACKVILLE (1975) *Legal Needs of the Poor*. Canberra: Australian Government Publishing Service.

CHAMBERS, David L. (1979) *Making Fathers Pay: The Enforcement of Child Support*. Chicago: University of Chicago Press.

CHRISTIE, Nils (1977) "Conflicts as Property," 17 *British Journal of Criminology* 1.

COATES, Dan and Steven PENROD (1981) "Social Psychology and the Emergence of Disputes," 15 *Law & Society Review* 655.

COLLIER, Jane (1973) *Law and Social Change in Zinacantan*. Stanford: Stanford University Press.

COLVIN, Selma, David STAGER, Larry TAMAN, Janet YALE, and Frederick H. ZEMANS (1978) "The Market for Legal Services: Paraprofessionals and Specialists," Working Paper 10. Toronto: Professional Organizations Committee.

CONARD, Alfred F. (1964) "The Economic Treatment of Automobile Injuries," 63 *Michigan Law Review* 279.

COOK, Royer F., Janice A. ROEHL, and David I. SHEPPARD (1980) *Neighborhood Justice Centers Field Test, Executive Summary and Final Evaluation Report*, Washington, D.C.: U.S. Government Printing Office.

CROWE, Patricia Ward (1978) "Complainant Reactions to the Massachusetts Commission Against Discrimination," 12 *Law & Society Review* 217.

CURRAN, Barbara A. (1977) *The Legal Needs of the Public: The Final Report of a National Survey*. Chicago: American Bar Foundation.

DANET, Brenda, Kenneth B. HOFFMAN, and Nicole C. KERMISH (1980) "Obstacles to the Study of Lawyer-Client Interaction: The Biography of a Failure," 14 *Law & Society Review* 905.

DANZIG, Richard (1975) "*Hadley* v. *Baxendale*: A Study in the Industrialization of the Law," 4 *Journal of Legal Studies* 249.

DAVIS, Robert C., Martha TICHANE, and Deborah GRAYSON (1980) *Mediation and Arbitration as Alternatives to Prosecution in Felony Arrest Cases*, New York: Vera Institute of Justice.

DI PALMA, Giuseppe (1970) *Apathy and Participation*, New York: Free Press.

EASTMAN, Crystal (1978) "From Reform to Socialist Revolution," in B. W. Cook (ed.), *On Women and Revolution*. New York: Oxford University Press.

EHRLICH, Thomas (1976) "Legal Pollution," *New York Times Magazine* 17 (February 8).

EPSTEIN, A. L. (ed.) (1967) *The Craft of Social Anthropology*. New York: Tavistock.

FELSTINER, William L. F. (1976) "Review of K-F Koch, War and Peace in Jalemo: The Management of Conflict in Highland New Guinea," 23 *UCLA Law Review* 1017.

———— (1974) "Influences of Social Organization on Dispute Processing," 9 *Law & Society Review* 63.

FELSTINER, William L. F. and Lynne A. WILLIAMS (1980) *Community Mediation in Dorchester, Massachusetts*. Washington, D.C.: U.S. Government Printing Office.

FRANKLIN, Marc A., Robert H. CHANIN, and Irving MARK (1961) "Accidents, Money and the Law: A Study of the Economics of Personal Injury Litigation," 61 *Columbia Law Review* 1.

FREEDMAN, Monroe (1977) *Lawyers' Ethics in an Adversary System*. Indianapolis: Bobbs-Merrill.

FRIEDMAN, Lawrence M. (1969) "Legal Culture and Social Development," 4 *Law & Society Review* 29.

FRIEDMAN, Lawrence M. and Robert V. PERCIVAL (1976a) "A Tale of Two Courts:

Litigation in Alameda and San Benito Counties," 10 *Law & Society Review* 267.

GALANTER, Marc (1974) "Why the 'Haves' Come Out Ahead: Speculations on the Limits of Legal Change," 9 *Law & Society Review* 95.

GELLHORN, Walter (1966) *When Americans Complain*. Cambridge: Harvard University Press.

—— (1954) *Children and Families in the Courts of New York City*. New York: Columbia University Press.

GENN, Hazel (1980) *The Use of Legal Services by Victims of Accidental Injury*. Oxford: Centre for Socio-Legal Studies.

GOLDSTEIN, Joseph and Jay KATZ (1965) *The Family and the Law*. New York: Free Press.

GRABER, Edith E. and David L. COLTON (1980) "The Limits of Effective Legal Action: The Use of the Labor Injunction in Teacher Strikes." Presented at the annual meeting of the Society for the Study of Social Problems, New York.

GRIFFITHS, John (1980) "A Comment on Research into 'Legal Needs,'" in E. Blankenburg (ed.), *Innovations in the Legal Services*. Konigstein, West Germany: Verlag Anton Hain.

—— (1977) "Review of 'The Distribution of Legal Services in the Netherlands,'" 4 *British Journal of Law and Society* 260.

GROSSMAN, Joel B. and Austin SARAT (1975) "Litigation in the Federal Courts: A Comparative Perspective," 9 *Law & Society Review* 321.

GULLIVER, Philip H. (1979) *Disputes and Negotiations: A Cross-Cultural Perspective*. New York: Academic Press.

HAHM, Pyong-Choon (1967) *The Korean Political Tradition and Law*. Seoul: Hollym.

HANDLER, Joel F. (1978) *Social Movements and the Legal System: A Theory of Law Reform and Social Change*. New York: Academic Press.

HANDLER, Joel F., Ellen Jane HOLLINGSWORTH, and Howard S. ERLANGER (1978) *Lawyers and the Pursuit of Legal Rights*. New York: Academic Press.

HANNIGAN, John A. (1977) "The Newspaper Ombudsman and Consumer Complaints: An Empirical Assessment," 11 *Law & Society Review* 679.

HEYDEBRAND, Wolf V. (1979) "The Technocratic Administration of Justice," 2 *Research in Law and Sociology* 29.

HIRSCHMAN, Albert O. (1970) *Exit, Voice and Loyalty: Responses to Decline in Firms, Organizations and States*. Cambridge: Harvard University Press.

HUNTING, Roger B. and Gloria S. NEUWIRTH (1962) *Who Sues in New York City? A Study of Automobile Accident Claims*. New York: Columbia University Press.

ILLICH, Ivan (1978) *Toward a History of Needs*. New York: Pantheon Books.

—— (1977) *Disabling Professions*. London: Marion Boyars.

JACOB, Herbert and Michael J. RICH (1980) "The Effects of the Police on Crime: A Second Look," 15 *Law & Society Review* 109.

JANEWAY, Elizabeth (1980) *Powers of the Weak*. New York: Alfred A. Knopf.

JOHNSON, Terence C. (1972) *Professions and Power*. London: Macmillan.

KAWASHIMA, Takeyoshi (1969) "Dispute Resolution in Japan," in V. Aubert (ed.), *Sociology of Law*, Harmondsworth: Penguin Books.

KELLEY, Harold H. and John N. MICHAELA (1980) "Attribution Theory and Research," in M. R. Rosenzweig and L. W. Porter (eds.), *Annual Review of Psychology*. Palo Alto: Annual Reviews, Inc.

KING, Donald W. and Kathleen A. MC EVOY (1976) *A National Survey of the Complaint Handling Procedures Used by Consumers*. Rockville, MD: King Research.

KLINE, J. Anthony (1978) "Curbing California's Colossal Legal Appetite," *Los Angeles Times* (February 12), Part VI.

KRESSEL, Kenneth, Martin LOPEZ-MORILLAS, Janet WEINGLASS, and Morton DEUTSCH (1979) "Professional Intervention in Divorce: The Views of Lawyers, Psychotherapists and Clergy," in G. Levinger and O. C. Moles (eds.), *Divorce and Separation*. New York: Basic Books.

LARSON, Magali Sarfatti (1977) *The Rise of Professionalism: A Sociological Analysis*. Berkeley: University of California Press.

LAUMANN, Edward O. and John P. HEINZ (1977) "Specialization and Prestige in the Legal Profession: The Structure of Deference," 1977 *American Bar Foundation Research Journal* 155.

LAW & SOCIETY REVIEW (1979) "Plea Bargaining," 13(2) *Law & Society Review* (Special Issue).

––––– (1975) "Litigation and Dispute Processing: Part II," 9(3) *Law & Society Review* (Special Issue).

––––– (1974) "Litigation and Dispute Processing: Part I," 9(1) *Law & Society Review* (Special Issue).

LEMPERT, Richard O. (1978) "More Tales of Two Courts: Exploring Changes in the 'Dispute Settlement Function' of Trial Courts," 13 *Law & Society Review* 91.

LEVINE, Felice J. and Elizabeth PRESTON (1970) "Community Resource Orientation Among Low Income Groups," 1970 *Wisconsin Law Review* 80.

LEWIS, Philip (1973) "Unmet Legal Needs," in P. Morris, R. White, and P. Lewis (eds.), *Social Needs and Legal Action*. London: Martin Robertson.

LLOYD-BOSTOCK, Sally (1980) *Fault and Liability for Accidents: The Accident Victim's Perspective*. Oxford: Centre for Socio-Legal Studies.

LOCHNER, Philip R., Jr. (1975) "The No Fee and Low Fee Legal Practice of Private Attorneys," 9 *Law & Society Review* 431.

LOFTUS, Elizabeth (1978) "The Development of Meaning," 62 *Modern Language Journal* 80.

MACAULAY, Stewart (1979) "Lawyers and Consumer Protection Laws," 14 *Law & Society Review* 115.

––––– (1966) *Law and the Balance of Power: The Automobile Manufacturers and Their Dealers*. New York: Russell Sage.

––––– (1963) "Non-Contractual Relations in Business: A Preliminary Study," 28 *American Sociological Review* 55.

MAC GREGOR, Oliver Ross, Louis BLOM-COOPER, and Colin GIBSON (1970) *Separated Spouses: A Study of the Matrimonial Jurisdiction of the Magistrates' Courts*. London: Duckworth.

MADDI, Dorothy L. and Frederic R. MERRILL (1971) *The Private Practicing Bar and Legal Services for Low-Income People*. Chicago: American Bar Foundation.

MANNING, Bayless (1977) "Hyperlexis: Our National Disease," 71 *Northwestern University Law Review* 767.

MARKS, F. Raymond (1976) "Some Research Perspectives for Looking at Legal Need and Legal Services Delivery Systems: Old Forms or New?" 11 *Law & Society Review* 191.

MARKS, F. Raymond, Robert Paul HALLUER, and Richard CLIFTON (1974) *The Shreveport Plan: An Experiment in the Delivery of Legal Services*. Chicago: American Bar Foundation.

MARSHALL, Leon and Geoffrey MAY (1932-33) *The Divorce Court. Vol. I: Maryland; Vol. II: Ohio*. Baltimore: John Hopkins University Press.

MARX, Karl (1976) "The Eighteenth Brumaire of Louis Bonaparte," in I. Howe (ed.), *Essential Works of Socialism*. New Haven: Yale University Press.

MATHER, Lynn and Barbara YNGVESSON (1981) "Language, Audience, and the Transformation of Disputes," 15 *Law & Society Review* 775.

MAYHEW, Leon H. (1975) "Institutions of Representation: Civil Justice and the Public," 9 *Law & Society Review* 401.

MENDELOFF, John (1979) *Regulating Safety: An Economic and Political Analysis of Occupational Safety and Health Policy*. Cambridge: MIT Press.

MENKEL-MEADOW, Carrie (1979) *The 59th Street Legal Clinic: Evaluation of an Experiment*. Chicago: American Bar Association.

MILLER, Richard E. and Austin SARAT (1981) "Grievances, Claims, and Disputes: Assessing the Adversary Culture," 15 *Law & Society Review* 525.

MITCHELL, James C. (1956) *The Yao Village*. Manchester: Manchester University.

MNOOKIN, Robert H. and Lewis KORNHAUSER (1979) "Bargaining in the Shadow of the Law: The Case of Divorce," 88 *Yale Law Journal* 950.

MOORE, Barrington (1979) *Injustice*. New York: M. E. Sharp.

MOORE, Sally Falk (1977) "Individual Interests and Organizational Structures: Dispute Settlements as 'Events of Articulation,'" in I. Hamnett (ed.), *Social Anthropology and Law*, New York: Academic Press.

MORIARTY, Thomas (1975) "A Nation of Willing Victims," *Psychology Today* 44 (April).

MORRIS, Pauline, Jenny COOPER, and Anthea BYLES (1973) "Public Attitudes to Problem Definition and Problem Solving: A Pilot Study," 3 *British Journal of Social Work* 301.

NADER, Laura (1980) (ed.) *No Access to Law: Alternatives to the American Judicial System.* New York: Academic Books.

NADER, Laura and Linda SINGER (1976) "Dispute Resolution and the Law in the Future: What Are the Choices?" 51 *California State Bar Journal* 281.

NADER, Laura and Harry F. TODD, Jr. (eds.) (1978) *The Disputing Process: Law in Ten Societies.* New York: Columbia University Press.

NATIONAL INSTITUTE OF CONSUMER JUSTICE (1972) *Redress of Consumer Grievances.* Boston: National Institute of Consumer Justice.

O'GORMAN, Hubert (1963) *Lawyers and Matrimonial Cases: A Study of Informal Pressures in Private Professional Practice.* New York: Columbia University Press.

PARNAS, Raymond I. (1970) "Judicial Response to Intra-Family Violence," 54 *Minnesota Law Review* 585.

PARSONS, Talcott (1962) "A Sociologist Looks at the Legal Profession," in W. Evan (ed.), *Law and Sociology.* New York: Free Press.

PERISTIANY, J. G. (ed.) (1965) *Honour and Shame: The Values of Mediterranean Society.* London: Weidenfeld and Nicholson.

PHILLIPS, Jenny and Keith HAWKINS (1976) "Some Economic Aspects of the Settlement Process: A Study of Personal Injury Claims," 39 *Modern Law Review* 1.

ROSENBERG, Maurice (1972) "Let's Everybody Litigate?" 50 *Texas Law Review* 1349.

ROSENTHAL, Douglas (1974) *Lawyer and Client: Who's in Charge?* New York: Russell Sage.

ROSS, H. Laurence (1979) *Settled Out of Court.* Chicago: Aldine.

ROSS, H. Laurence and Neil O. LITTLEFIELD (1978) "Complaint as a Problem-Solving Mechanism," 12 *Law & Society Review* 199.

ROYAL COMMISSION ON CIVIL LIABILITY AND COMPENSATION FOR PERSONAL INJURY (1978) *Report*, 3 volumes. London: HMSO (Cmnd. 7504-1).

ROYAL COMMISSION ON LEGAL SERVICES IN SCOTLAND (1980) *Report*, 2 volumes. Edinburgh: HMSO (Cmnd. 7846-1).

RUHNKA, John and Steven WELLER, with John A. MARTIN (1978) *Small Claims Courts: A National Examination.* Williamsburg, VA: National Center for State Courts.

SARAT, Austin (1977) "Studying American Legal Culture: An Assessment of Survey Evidence," 11 *Law & Society Review* 427.

SCHEINGOLD, Stuart (1974) *The Politics of Rights.* New Haven: Yale University Press.

SCHUYT, Kees, Kees GROENENDIJK, and Ben SLOOT (1978) "Access to the Legal System and Legal Services Research," *1977 European Yearbook in Law and Sociology* 98.

SCHWARTZ, Murray L. and Daniel J. B. MITCHELL (1970) "An Economic Analysis of the Contingent Fee in Personal-Injury Litigation," 22 *Stanford Law Review* 1125.

SEIDMAN, David and Michael COUZENS (1974) "Getting the Crime Rate Down: Political Pressure and Crime Reporting," 8 *Law & Society Review* 457.

SIMON, William H. (1978) "The Ideology of Advocacy: Procedural Justice and Professional Ethics," 1978 *Wisconsin Law Review* 29.

SKOLNICK, Jerome H. (1966) *Justice Without Trial: Law Enforcement in Democratic Society.* New York: John Wiley.

SMALL CLAIMS COURT STUDY GROUP (1972) *Little Injustices: Small Claims Courts and the American Consumer.* Washington, D.C.: Center for Auto Safety.

SMITH, Alan, John BRYANT, and Deborah BOND (1979) *A Pilot Study of Dispute Treatment in Leamington: A Report.* Coventry: University of Warwick School of Law.

STARR, June (1978) *Dispute and Settlement in Rural Turkey.* Leiden: E. J. Brill.

STEELE, Eric H. (1977) "Two Approaches to Contemporary Dispute Behavior and Consumer Problems," 11 *Law & Society Review* 667.

——— (1975a) "Fraud, Dispute and the Consumer: Responding to Consumer Complaints," 123 *University of Pennsylvania Law Review* 1107.

——— (1975b) "The Dilemma of Consumer Fraud: Prosecute or Mediate," 61 *American Bar Association Journal* 1230.

STEELE, Eric H. and Raymond T. NIMMER (1976) "Lawyers, Clients, and Professional

Regulation," 1976 *American Bar Foundation Research Journal* 917.

STRAUSS, Anselm (1978) *Negotiations: Varieties, Contexts, Processes, and Social Order.* San Francisco: Jossey-Bass.

TIEMANN, Fritz and Erhard BLANKENBURG (1979) "Working Paper on the Evaluation of a Legal Need Survey in West Berlin." Berlin: Wissenschaftszentrum.

TRUBEK, David M. (1981) "The Construction and Deconstruction of a Disputes-Focused Approach: An Afterword." 15 *Law & Society Review* 727.

TURNER, Victor (1957) *Schism and Continuity in an African Society: A Study of Ndembu Village Life.* Manchester: Manchester University Press.

TURK, Austin (1976) "Law as a Weapon in Social Conflict," 23 *Social Problems* 276.

TUSHNET, Mark (n.d.) "Organizational Structure and Legal Strategy: The NAACP's Campaign Against Segregated Education, 1925-1950," unpublished manuscript.

UNIVERSITY OF PENNSYLVANIA LAW REVIEW (1953) "Note: The Administration of Divorce: A Philadelphia Study," 101 *University of Pennsylvania Law Review* 1204.

UPHAM, Frank K. (1976) "Litigation and Moral Consciousness in Japan: An Interpretive Analysis of Four Japanese Pollution Suits," 10 *Law & Society Review* 579.

VALETAS, Marie-France (1976) *Aide Judiciare et Accès á la Justice.* Paris: Centre de Recherches pour l'Etude et l'Observation des Conditions de Vie.

VAN VELSEN, J. (1964) *The Politics of Kinship: A Study in Social Manipulation among the Lakeside Tonga.* Manchester: Manchester University Press.

VIDMAR, Neil and Dale T. MILLER (1980) "Social Psychological Processes Underlying Attitudes Toward Legal Punishment," 14 *Law & Society Review* 565.

VIRTUE, Maxine (1956) *Family Cases in Court.* Durham: Duke University Press.

WALKER, Alan and Mavis MACLEAN (1980) *Financial Compensation for Personal Injury: A Case Study in Law and Social Policy.* Oxford: Centre for Socio-Legal Studies.

WARLAND, Rex H., Robert O. HERRMANN, and Jane WILLITS (1975) "Dissatisfied Consumers: Who Gets Upset and Who Takes Action," 9 *Journal of Consumer Affairs* 148.

WEINSTEIN, James (1967) "Big Business and the Origin of Workman's Compensation," 8 *Labor History* 1560.

WEISBROD, Burton A., Joel F. HANDLER, and Neil K. MONESAR (eds.) (1978) *Public Interest Law: An Economic and Institutional Analysis.* Berkeley: University of California Press.

WHITFORD, William C. (1968) "Law and the Consumer Transaction: A Case Study of the Automobile Warranty," 1968 *Wisconsin Law Review* 1006.

WHITFORD, William C. and Spencer L. KIMBALL (1974) "Why Process Consumer Complaints? A Case Study of the Office of the Commissioner of Insurance in Wisconsin," 1974 *Wisconsin Law Review* 639.

WIDISS, Alan I. (1975) "Accident Victims Under No-Fault Automobile Insurance: A Massachusetts Survey," 61 *Iowa Law Review* 1.

WILSON, James Q. (1975) *Thinking About Crime.* New York: Basic Books.

WILSON, James Q. and Barbara BOLAND (1978) "The Effect of the Police on Crime," 12 *Law & Society Review* 367.

WOLLENBERG, Charles M. (1977) *All Deliberate Speed: Segregation and Exclusion in California Schools, 1855-1975.* Berkeley: University of California Press.

[5]

A TALE OF TWO COURTS: LITIGATION IN ALAMEDA AND SAN BENITO COUNTIES*

LAWRENCE M. FRIEDMAN

Stanford University

ROBERT V. PERCIVAL

Stanford University

American scholarship has lavished most of its attention on appellate courts, paying little attention to courts on the bottom rungs of the ladder. This is true of studies of both past and present courts.[1] But the trial court is the court with the most direct contact with the man in the street, for both civil and criminal matters. Here he meets the law face-to-face. And, although federal courts are certainly important, state trial courts handle by far the larger volume of work.

This paper reports on a study of the *civil* load of two trial courts in California between 1890 and 1970. One court sits in an urban county, the other in a rural county. We tried to measure how the work of these courts changed over time. We expected to find that trial courts have come to do less and less work in settling disputes and that most of their labor is now routine, administrative, cut-and-dried. This hypothesis was confirmed. We also expected to find major differences between the rural and the urban court. But here, it turned out, we were surprised. A common fate overtook both courts; and essentially, our data tell a single story, which holds for city and country alike.

I. THE FUNCTIONS OF TRIAL COURTS

The functions of courts[2] change as their societies change.

---

* Research on this article was supported by National Science Foundation Grant GS 33821. We wish to thank E. Allen John, Jr., Marilyn Epstein, and Marc Warsowe for their great help with the research on which this article is based; and Richard Danzig, Willard Hurst, and Earl Pomeroy for their valuable comments.

1. There have been exceptions—for example, Francis W. Laurent's study of a century of work of the local courts of Chippewa County, Wisconsin. Francis W. Laurent, *The Business of a Trial Court: 100 Years of Cases* (1950); Charles Clark and Harry Shulman, *A Study of Law Administration in Connecticut* (1937).

2. On the functions of trial courts in general, see Lawrence M. Fried-

268   LAW & SOCIETY / WINTER 1975

American society, over the last century, has undergone massive change; hence we expect some alteration in the work of the courts as well. One of the aims of this study is to investigate changes in such functions. We begin with some brief remarks about *dispute settlement*, one of the basic functions of courts.

A. Dispute Settlement

Dispute settlement—the resolution of genuine differences between parties[3] is the function that most clearly fits the traditional picture of court operations. One thinks of wise King Solomon, confronted by two women each of whom claimed to be the mother of a single child; or the judges among the Barotse, described by Max Gluckman;[4] or, closer to home, two quarreling neighbors, each claiming title to a piece of land; or a seller suing a buyer who refuses to pay the price of a carload of lumber; or an action for libel and slander. In all these cases, private parties invoke the aid of courts—that is, a strong third party (the judge), backed by the power of the state—in an attempt to resolve disputes with another private party. Sometimes, both parties have agreed between themselves to lay their cases before the judge; more often, perhaps, one party (the plaintiff) forces the other party (the defendant) into court.

Dispute settlement is a broad term, which covers many different kinds of activity. Among courts that settle disputes, we can distinguish two polar types of procedure or attitude. One type emphasizes social harmony. The aim is to end a quarrel, patch up a rift in the social fabric, set things right again within a family or tribe. This style has been observed most notably by anthropologists studying judicial process in less developed societies. In these societies, judges are wise men, elders, respected chiefs; the public eagerly attends trials. Fees are small; procedure is simple and non-technical; there are no "legal" norms and rules, distinct from other norms and rules in society; there are few if any special rules of evidence, and little attention is paid

man, "Trial Courts and Their Work in the Modern World," *Jahrbuch für Rechtssoziologie und Rechtstheorie* (forthcoming).

   This study focusses on two functions: dispute settlement, and routine administration. There are other functions, for example, social control (primarily criminal cases, hence not treated here) and review of governmental actions, where government is defendant in a civil suit. Government plaintiffs appeared in less than 3% of the cases studied; governmental defendants in only 4%.

3. On the definition of a dispute, see Richard L. Abel, "A Comparative Theory of Dispute Institutions in Society," 8 *Law & Society Review* 217, 226-7 (1973).

4. Max Gluckman, *The Judicial Process Among the Barotse of Northern Rhodesia* (1955).

to formal legal doctrine. Justice will be swift, and, normally, will be in tune with norms widely shared in the community.[5]

This style of decision making is clearly useful and appropriate in simple societies. It helps keep society on an even keel; conflicts do not get out of hand. Disputes get settled, and at the same time, trials and proceedings serve a kind of educational function; they crystallize and publicize community norms. Public opinion encourages people to bring their troubles to court. Because law is not technical but popular, people understand when to invoke it, and they accept the decisions of the courts as legitimate.

The courts in most modern, Western societies are supposed to represent a different style of decision making. These courts are expensive, technical, and slow, compared to the courts discussed above. Legal norms are *not* the same as social norms. The law speaks a different language, and, in formal proceedings the layman must use a lawyer as translator and go-between. In this sense, then, justice is far from open. Nor is it "open" in the physical sense. To be sure, there are seats at trials for the public. A sensational murder trial will draw a crowd; but few people come to an ordinary trial. Judge and jury will deliberate in secret. Rules of evidence screen out "irrelevant" evidence, under rather rigid standards. Western courts often seem primarily interested in determining which party is (legally) right, and which party is (legally) wrong. The search for the "issue" takes priority over the search for the best social solution, the solution that best preserves or restores harmony in human relations.

The reader will note that these two styles of decision making are associated with different types of society. The social harmony style is associated with small, face-to-face, agricultural or hunting societies; the legalistic style with highly technical, urban societies where people deal constantly with strangers. For this reason, the typical dispute which a court must handle will differ in the two types. In a modern, Western case, it is not usual that the parties to the lawsuit stand in some sort of human relationship. Consider the typical automobile accident case. It is a cold-blooded matter, a matter of dollars and cents, brought between strangers. The courts, in fact, have no particular talent for, or interest in developing the expressive, personal aspects of the case, if any. Where cases present such aspects, the court

5. *Id., op. cit.*; Floyd Fallers, *Law Without Precedent* (1969); Laura Nader, "Styles of Court Procedure," in *Law in Culture and Society* (Laura Nader, ed. 1969).

studiously ignores them, at least in the formal proceedings and in the formal decision.[6] Rather, the court will seem to strive to narrow the issues, in a "professional" way; the aim is to handle some precise point of law or of fact.

The assumption, furthermore, is that social change will bring about change in the *style* of a court.[7] As society moves from a rural, face-to-face mode of life, to a technical, urban mode of life, dispute settlement becomes more "legal." There is, in short, a rather vague hypothesis that predicts style of court from certain economic, social, and demographic facts. Dispute settlement in a big city court will be more legal, and less "social" than in a rural court.

B.   Routine Administration

The idea of dispute settlement is strong in the imagery of courts. But courts perform other functions, too. One of these we will call *routine administration*. A matter is *routine* when a court has no disputed question of law or fact to decide. *Routine administration* means the processing or approving of undisputed matters. Courts make and keep records, register formalities, stamp their approval on claims or on changes of status; they handle uncontested divorces; render judgment in cases of petty debt; probate uncontested wills; handle petitions for change of name. In these matters there is almost never any real dispute— at least none that comes before the court. When hubsand or wife files for divorce, there has usually *been* some dispute; but the court does not resolve it. Typically, the parties do not go to court at all, until they have worked matters out and are ready for the rubber stamp.[8]

6. It would, in fact, be improper for a judge, in a lawsuit that Smith brings against Jones, to consider the effect of the suit on their relationship as neighbors, or as brothers-in-law. Some courts—family and juvenile courts—have a mandate to take personal relationships into account. And judges may, in hidden or subconscious ways, re-act to aspects of a case which strictly speaking they ought not legally consider. Still, there is evidence of the "trained incapacity" of judges to handle expressive, social aspects of cases. See, for example, Rüdiger Lautmann's study of the German judiciary, *Justiz —die Stille Gewalt* (1972); Richard Danzig, "Toward the Creation of a Complementary, Decentralized System of Criminal Justice," 26 *Stan. L. Rev.* 1 (1973).

   Of course, both pictures (of the Western court, and the court of the simple society) are exaggerations—or, if you will, ideal types. Trial courts in the United States and other countries can and do dispense a kind of justice more tailored to the specific situation of the parties, through informal means—in pre-trial proceedings, for example.

7. *See* Lawrence M. Friedman, *The Legal System: A Social Science Perspective* 260 (1975).

8. We should not jump to the conclusion, however, that courts and the doctrine they make have no effect on patterns of out-of-court settle-

Friedman & Percival / A TALE OF TWO COURTS 271

To call these matters routine is not to deny their importance. They may—and do—have an important effect, in the mass; but in the particular case, they are small in size and in consequence. And what the court does hardly fits the usual understanding of adjudication.[9]

Routine administration is not a characteristic of the social harmony courts described by anthropologists. It is a modern, Western phenomenon. Societies that are bureaucratic and busy need this kind of formalization far more than hunters and gatherers do. We would expect to find this function becoming more frequent as we approach the present day, and we would expect it to correlate closely with urban and industrial growth. Of our two courts, one is urban, the other is not. The study covers a period of time (1890 to 1970) in which Alameda County urbanized and industrialized more rapidly and profoundly than San Benito. We expect, then, to find great differences in decision-making style, and in the functions performed by the courts. We should see these differences already in 1890, and by 1970 they should be even clearer.

II. QUANTITATIVE INDICATORS OF COURT FUNCTIONS

How can we measure the functions performed by courts? Some inferences arise from the type of cases courts handle, but this is not terribly reliable. A property case, for example, may require the court to resolve a hotly-contested dispute; a contract case may lay bare complex commercial controversy; on the other hand, many "property" or "contract" cases are simply routine. Divorce and tort cases, too, can be bitterly contested, though usually they are not. The procedural history and *outcome* of cases may be more reliable indicators. Of cases *filed*, how many ac-

---

ment. "The law" that a court is likely to apply is an important factor in the bargaining that takes place in settlement of auto accident cases, for example. See Alfred F. Conard *et al.*, *Automobile Accident Costs and Payments* (1964); H. Laurence Ross, *Settled Out of Court: The Social Process of Insurance Claims Adjustment* (1970). Compare Galanter's concept of the "appended" settlement system, that is, a dispute settlement system, which though unofficial is "normatively and institutionally appended to the official system." He gives settlement of auto injuries as an example. Marc Galanter, "Why the 'Haves' Come Out Ahead: Speculations on the Limits of Legal Change," 9 *Law & Society Review* 95, 126 (1974).

9. Of course, sometimes, even in routine matters, a serious issue needing exceptional training and skill to handle may abruptly arise. Most probate proceedings are routine; but once in a while a will is contested or a claim disputed. Arguably the judge must stand by, like a doctor at a hospital, in case of emergency. Many uncontested, routine cases are fossilized forms of what were once areas of more vigorous adjudication: divorce and debt collection, for example.

tually go to trial, how many are settled out of court or voluntarily dropped? What percentage of cases do plaintiffs win? One might expect plaintiffs to win most cases, even contested cases, since people bring lawsuits when they feel a reasonable hope of prevailing. But by the same token, defendants do not resist when resistance is hopeless. When plaintiffs win in an overwhelming percentage of cases, it is a sign that the cases are routine. Similarly, courts produce formal opinions or findings when they resolve real disputes; rarely when the matter is routine.

It is harder to be precise about the two styles of dispute settlement. The nature of the case and the parties provide some clue. Are the parties relatives, or are they strangers? Is it a family case, or a commercial case? But basically, the presence of the "social harmony" style can only be detected by feel, that is, by careful examination of the files.

The raw materials of the study are the civil casefiles of the Superior Courts in two California counties. These files were sampled at twenty-year intervals from 1890 to 1970, that is, in 1890, 1910, 1930, 1950, and 1970. Eighteen-ninety was chosen as the starting point, partly because it was the first census year after the court reform that established the system of Superior Courts. In 1890, California was still a young state, compared to the states of the Eastern seaboard. It was yet to experience its greatest urban growth and industrial development.

III. THE COUNTIES

Alameda and San Benito are the two counties of the study. Although their borders are less than fifty miles apart, at opposite ends of the Santa Clara Valley in west-central California, they are profoundly different in demographic character. Alameda County is densely populated, part of a sprawling megalopolis. It fronts on the eastern shore of San Francisco Bay, directly across from San Francisco and its peninsula. The county has an area of 840 square miles, stretching from the Contra Costa foothills on the northeast to the Santa Clara County border on the south. Oakland, the county seat and largest city, is located along San Francisco Bay in the county's northwest corner. From this point, a string of suburb-cities, some with populations over 100,000, now sprawl along freeway paths to the north and south, engulfing the western portion of the county in the Bay Area megalopolis.

San Benito County is bounded on the north by the Pajaro River and the southern edge of Santa Clara County. The county

Friedman & Percival / A TALE OF TWO COURTS   273

extends seventy miles to the south, averaging twenty-five miles in east-west width. Hollister is the county seat and only town of size. It is set in a lowland area at the southern end of the Santa Clara Valley, in the northern part of the county. Nearly everyone in the county lives and works in this area, between the hamlet of Tres Piños eight miles to the southwest and San Juan Bautista, an equal distance to the west.[10] The rest of the county is mountainous, except for one small lowland area, along the east-central edge of the county. The 5,000-foot high Diablo Mountains dominate the county's landscape in the east and central areas; the Gabilan Range separates the county from Monterey County to the west. Pinnacles National Monument, an area of spectacular rock formations, set aside by President Theodore Roosevelt in 1908, is among the Gabilans.

A. Population

San Benito County has always been rural and sparsely populated. Its growth rate has been, for California, relatively slow. Its population was 6,412 in 1890; in 1970 it was 18,226. Alameda County was already somewhat urban in 1890; two-thirds of its people lived in cities of over 5,000. Alameda grew from 93,864 in 1890 to over a million in 1970 (Table 1). In 1910, over 90% of Alameda's population lived in urban areas. In 1970, Alameda was virtually all urban (99%), by the standards of the United States census.

TABLE 1. POPULATION STATISTICS FOR ALAMEDA AND SAN BENITO COUNTIES

County	1890	1910	1930	1950	1970
ALAMEDA					
Total population	93,864	246,131	474,883	740,315	1,073,184
Percent increase		162.2%	92.9%	55.9%	45.0%
Population density (/sq. mi.)	133.3	336.2	647.9	1,010.0	1,464.1
Percent urban	69.2%	90.5%	92.5%	94.7%	99.0%
Percent rural	30.8%	9.5%	7.5%	5.3%	1.0%
Percent black	0.8%	1.5%	2.1%	9.4%	15.0%
SAN BENITO					
Total population	6,412	8,041	11,311	14,370	18,226
Percent increase	—	25.4%	40.7%	27.0%	26.8%
Population density (/sq. mi.)	6.4	5.8	8.1	10.3	13.1
Percent urban	0.0%	0.0%	33.2%	34.1%	42.0%
Percent rural	100.0%	100.0%	66.8%	65.9%	58.0%
Percent black	1.0%	0.9%	0.4%	0.2%	0.3%

Source: U.S. Census Bureau

10. Ronald L. Chatham, *The Geography of San Benito County, California*, 2 (1962).

San Benito is still basically rural. Hollister, the county seat, grew enough to be classified as an urban area by 1930; a third of the county's population lived there. In 1970, Hollister had a population of some 8,000 and contained 42% of the county's population. No other city in the county was large enough to be called urban, either technically or practically.

Alameda's population is more racially diverse than San Benito's. Oakland has a large black population, mostly added after World War II. More than 15% of Alameda's population is black; few blacks live in San Benito (0.3%). But Spanish was the mother tongue of over 30% of San Benito's population in 1970.[11]

B. The Economy

The economies of the counties are markedly different. San Benito's economy revolves around agriculture. In 1890 the county produced over one million dollars in farm products, compared to $390,000 in manufactured goods. Alameda County, too, was once a rich agricultural area, but its location also suited it for manufacturing and trade, and these in time predominated. In 1890 Alameda County produced over $12-million worth of manufactured goods; its agricultural areas yielded $2.6-million.[12] In 1930, 53% of those employed in San Benito had agricultural jobs; only 4% of Alameda's workers worked in agriculture. By 1970, agriculture had become less labor-intensive, but it remained the dominant occupation in San Benito. Over 20% of those employed in the county worked on farms.[13] Only about half of one per cent still worked in agriculture in Alameda. County-wide income statistics also reflect the difference between an urban industrial economy and a farm economy. The per capita income in Alameda in 1970, $3,718, was 34% higher than in San Benito ($2,782).[14]

---

11. U.S. Department of Commerce, Bureau of the Census, *1970 Census of Population*, Vol. I, *Characteristics of the Population*, Part 6, 1035 (1973).

12. U.S. Department of Interior, Census Office, *Report of the Statistics of Agriculture at the Eleventh Census: 1890*, 200 (1895); U.S. Department of the Interior, Census Office, *Report on Manufacturing Industries in the United States at the Eleventh Census: 1890*, Part 1, 353, 355 (1895).

13. U.S. Department of Commerce, Bureau of the Census, *Fifteenth Census of the United States: 1930*, Vol. III, *Population*, Part 1, 273, 275 (1932); U.S. Department of Commerce, Bureau of the Census, *1970 Census, supra*, note 11 at 1048, 1050.

14. U.S. Department of Commerce, *1970 Census, supra*, note 11, at 1058, 1060.

C. Historical Development

Before 1874, the area in San Benito was part of Monterey County. The Gabilan Mountains cut off the residents from access to the county seat on the coast. They put pressure on the legislature which created the new county in 1874. Its western boundary ran along the Gabilan range, the eastern along the Diablo Mountains, after later additions from Fresno and Merced Counties.

The oldest settlement in the county is San Juan Bautista in the northwest corner of the county, where a mission was founded in 1797. The mission was secularized in the early 1830's. Shortly thereafter, the Mexican government made large land grants to settlers.[15] Fifty people lived in San Juan Bautista at the time of the American takeover.[16]

When adventurers and immigrants began to pour into California, after 1848, a few settled in what is now San Benito County. Patrick Breen, father of the first county judge, arrived with his family in 1848; he ran a hotel. Colonel W. W. Hollister, accompanied by a flock of sheep, left Ohio in 1851, and began a sheep ranch in 1855 in the county. In 1968 fifty farmers formed the San Justo Homestead Association and bought the Colonel's ranch. Hollister, named in honor of the Colonel, became the county seat in 1874.[17]

Cattle ranching dominated the economy until the mid-1860's. In the next decade wheat became the principal crop, then later hay and barley.[18] In 1873 the San Benito branch of the Southern Pacific railroad was extended from Hollister eight miles south to Tres Piños, and this town became the main agricultural shipping point for the surrounding area.

A shortage of cheap power and water, and distance from population centers, handicapped San Benito County; industry never developed. For a brief period the New Idria Quicksilver Mine, in the southeastern part of the county, produced a significant share of the world's quicksilver. Even today there is little industry, except for some agricultural processing plants. San Benito is less than an hour's drive from the southern flank of the Bay

---

15. Chatham, *supra*, note 10, at 137; see also *History of San Benito County* (1881); Lawrence M. Friedman, "San Benito 1890: Legal Snapshot of a County," 27 *Stan. L. Rev.* 687 (1975).
16. National Society of Colonial Dames, *Counties and Courthouses of California* 32-33 (1964).
17. Chatham, *supra*, note 10, at 144, n.34.
18. Chatham, *supra*, note 10, at 149-53.

megalopolis, but, as an observer in 1962 remarked, "In many re-spects, time has bypassed San Benito County."[19]

The history of Alameda also begins with a mission—San Jose de Guadalupe, founded in 1797. The mission, located in the fer-tile south-central portion of the county, was secularized by 1840. In the early part of the 19th century, Alameda's land was divided into a number of immense "ranchos," including the great Rancho de San Antonio, granted to Luis Maria Peralta. Peralta died in 1851, and a year later the town of Oakland was incorporated on land once part of his domain.[20]

Alameda County was created in 1853. First Alvarado, then San Leandro was the county seat.[21] In 1873 the county seat was moved to Oakland, a port and railroad terminus, already undergoing rapid growth. In 1870, there were 24,000 people in Alameda County. By 1880, the county's population reached nearly 63,000; over half lived in Oakland. By 1900 the county's population had doubled again, to 130,197; 66,960 lived in Oakland. This rapid growth has continued until the present, though at a declining rate. Alameda is part of a great metropolitan area, laced with freeways, and stretching all along the bayside half of the county. Oakland is a major metropolis; other cities in the county are also quite sizeable—Berkeley, for example, home of the University of California, and Fremont, site of a General Motors plant, each have more than 100,000 people.

IV. THE STUDY

As we have mentioned, the basic materials for this study were drawn from civil casefiles of the superior courts of the two counties, for the years 1890, 1910, 1930, 1950, and 1970. The case load of San Benito is small, and hence every case was examined in each of these years. In Alameda, with its enormous caseloads, a sample had to be taken. One hundred cases were taken at random from the files in 1890, 1910, and 1930. In 1950 and 1970, sufficient cases were taken to represent 2% of the cases. In all, 1176 cases were included in the study—677 from Alameda and 499 from San Benito.

The table below records the number of cases filed in the two counties, for the years in question, and also gives the case-load per 1,000 population. This last figure is, however, difficult to interpret, because, as we shall see, there are other courts that

19. Chatham, *supra*, note 10, at 4.
20. Mildred B. Hoover, *Historical Spots in California* 23 (1937).
21. Leslie J. Freeman, *Historic San Leandro, California* 34, 40 (1940).

Friedman & Percival / A TALE OF TWO COURTS   277

handle civil litigation, and the concept of a "case" requires some elucidation, too.

TABLE 2. SUPERIOR COURT CASELOAD PER COUNTY

	1890	1910	1930	1950	1970
ALAMEDA					
Cases	716	3,320	5,112	7,049	11,811
Population	93,864	246,131	474,883	740,315	1,073,184
Cases per 1,000 population	7.6	13.5	10.8	9.5	11.0
SAN BENITO					
Cases	31	29	101	150	188
Population	6,412	8,041	11,311	14,370	18,226
Cases per 1,000 population	4.8	3.6	8.9	10.4	10.2

Throughout the period, the Superior Courts were not exclusively trial courts. At all times between 1890 and 1970, inferior trial courts functioned in the counties and the Superior Courts had jurisdiction over appeals from certain of these courts.[22] In all, more than 97% of the cases in the two courts were original.[23] Less than 3% were appeals, and all of these were tried *de novo* in the Superior Court.[24] The records of these inferior courts are very incomplete,[25] and the Superior Court has always had a far broader jurisdiction.[26] Still, these courts—small claims courts, police courts, municipal courts, justice courts—handle, and have handled, a tremendous volume of work. For example, for the fiscal year 1969-70 (California judicial statistics are gath-

22. CAL. CODE CIVIL PROC. § 904.2 (appeals from Municipal Courts), § 904.3 (appeals from Justice Courts), § 117j (appeals from Small Claims Courts). These statutes providing for such appeals are authorized by CAL. CONST. ART. VI § 11. CAL. CODE CIVIL PROC. § 77 provides for an appellate department of Superior Courts.

23. In Alameda County: 94.5% in 1890, 96.3% in 1910, 96.0% in 1930, 99.3% in 1950, 98.7% in 1970. In San Benito County: 93.5% in 1890, 96.7% in 1910, 99.0% in 1930, 100.0% in 1950, and 98.7% in 1970.

24. CAL. CODE CIVIL PROC. § 117j currently requires a trial *de novo* when appeals from Small Claims Courts reach the Superior Court. Until 1968, a trial *de novo* was also required of appeals from Justice Courts by CAL. CODE CIVIL PROC. § 983. Section 904.3 which replaced § 983 no longer embodies this requirement.

25. This is most acute for the earliest periods. Sporadic early records do survive; and newspaper accounts add significant information. See Friedman, *supra*, note 15.

26. CAL. CONST. ART. VI §§ 10-11 established Superior Courts as courts of general jurisdiction, with the lower limit on their jurisdiction determined by statutes establishing inferior courts of limited jurisdiction. For the years 1890 and 1910 in our study, the civil jurisdiction of Superior Courts extended to cases where the amount in controversy was $300 or more. This jurisdictional floor had been increased to $2,000 by 1930 and $3,000 by 1950. The present law, in force in 1970, gives Justice Courts jurisdiction up to $1,000 (CAL. CODE CIVIL PROC. § 112), and Municipal Courts jurisdiction up to $5,000 (CAL. CODE CIVIL PROC. § 89). Superior Courts have jurisdiction over civil cases where the amount in controversy is $5,000 or more.

Law and Society

ered on this basis), the municipal courts of the state disposed of 424,247 civil cases (not counting parking cases). In the Oakland-Piedmont municipal court (the district is the most populous in Alameda County), there were 8,275 small claims filings, 1,724 tort filings, and 8,652 miscellaneous civil filings.[27]

The presence of these inferior courts, and the fact that jurisdictional limits have changed with the years, means that one cannot compare the caseload of Superior Courts over time as strictly and as rigorously as one would like. Their presence makes it difficult to tell how much the actual functions of the courts have changed between 1890 and 1970. The jurisdictional floor of the Superior Court has gone up over the years from $300 to $3,000. Claims for small amounts, which once appeared in Superior Court, would now show up in one of the inferior courts. Of course, the value of the dollar has also changed. But even if we converted the jurisdictional floor into constant dollars, the correspondence between the two sets of figures would still be inexact over time. Indeed, the presence of these courts means that our data can not conclusively demonstrate that there are no courts in which genuine "disputes" among ordinary people may be heard, and rather cheaply and efficiently. But other studies suggest that the inferior courts too are not functioning in any way as "people courts."[28] Rather, the existence of these courts solves one of the major mysteries of the data: the disappearance of cases of debt collection.[29] In California, great numbers of debts are collected through the inferior courts.

Yet there *are* large debts, and the greater mystery is their disappearance from the records. The mystery of the Superior Courts is not so much the vanishing of individual, middle-class litigant, as the vanishing of the business and corporate litigant. The Supreme Courts were and are the basic, fundamental courts for important cases. Any important case must start there; if, for some rare reason, such a case begins in a municipal court, it will go to the Superior Court on appeal. Yet, as we shall see, where

---

27. Administrative Office of the California Courts, Annual Report, *Judicial Statistics for the Fiscal Year 1969-70* 131, 192 (1971).

28. *See* Beatrice A. Moulton, "The Persecution and Intimidation of the Low Income Litigant as Performed by the Small Claims Courts in California," 21 *Stan. L. Rev.* 1667 (1969).

29. In England, the county courts, the basic civil courts, function primarily as collection agencies. The defendants are consumers and occasional small tradesmen; the English county court is where a grocer or the owner of a clothing store goes to collect money his customers owe. See, for the history of these courts, Brian Abel-Smith and Robert Stevens, *Lawyers and the Courts: A Sociological Study of the English Legal System, 1750-1965,* (1967), especially 33-35.

we might expect a great volume of activity, we find instead a void.

One other possible alternative should be mentioned. The United States is a federal system. Is it not conceivable that important cases are funneled into the federal courts? The federal courts handle cases arising under federal laws; they may also hear cases between residents of different states.[30] The business world is increasingly interstate; perhaps important business cases overwhelmingly gravitate into federal courts.

There is no doubt that federal courts are an important part of the judicial system, and that the volume of work they do is increasing. This is largely due to the fact that federal regulation is ubiquitous in the 20th century. It seems extremely doubtful that much ordinary civil litigation has been lost to the federal courts. It is true that patent litigation, labor, anti-trust, and bankruptcy matters, not to mention issues of civil rights and civil liberties, will be brought to federal court. But this still leaves an enormous range of disputes that could or must be centered in state courts. Yet, for 1970, the number of ordinary court cases from Alameda and San Benito counties, filed in federal court, was about 1% of the number of Superior Court cases in the two counties.[31] At present, a case whose sole federal basis is diversity of citizenship cannot enter federal court unless the amount in controversy is $10,000 or more. In California, municipal courts now may hear cases worth up to $5,000; but any ordinary cases of debt or property worth between $5,000 and $10,000

---

30. 28 U.S. Code § 1332 (1971).

31. In 1970, of the 2,887 civil cases filed in Federal District Court for the Northern District of California (the district encompassing both Alameda and San Benito counties), only 359 (12.4%) could be classified as ordinary civil litigation of the kind likely to be found in state trial courts. The rest were divided among cases in which the federal government was a party (679) and private cases involving: prisoner petitions (966), marine personal injury (383), antitrust (90), copyright and patent (76), labor suits (57), the Federal Employers Liability Act (1) and unclassified subjects (276). Administrative Office of the U.S. Courts, *Annual Report of the Director, 1970*, 238-39 (1971).

Although the federal statistics do not indicate the county of origin for these cases, Alameda and San Benito counties accounted for only around one-fifth (21.7%) of the population of the Northern District of California in 1970. 28 U.S.C. § 84 (1971); Bureau of Census, *1970 Census of Population, General Social and Economic Characteristics, California* 380 (1972). Assuming a rough proportionality between population and case filings, Alameda and San Benito counties would account for only 79 ordinary civil cases in federal court in 1970 (21.7% of 359). Even the inclusion of these counties' share of private unclassified cases would only increase this total to 139 (adding 21.7% of 276) and many of these additional cases would not represent ordinary civil litigation. When this figure is compared with the approximately 12,000 civil cases in the superior courts of Alameda and San Benito counties in 1970, it is small indeed (around 1%).

must be brought to Superior Court; there is no other forum. Hence we should expect to find many cases today in Superior Court that occupy this band of space—with too much at stake for municipal court, too little for federal. These expectations are not met. Indeed, at all times, there existed such a band (though the threshold amounts varied). That cases within the band have virtually disappeared by 1970, argues against the hypothesis that federal courts have picked up a function state courts were gradually losing.

A. The Docket

What kind of cases do the two courts hear? How has the docket changed over time? A number of broad trends become apparent upon examining the incidence of types of cases in our study (Tables 3 and 4, Figures 1 and 2).

In both counties the percentage of *family* and *tort* cases filed rose dramatically from 1890 to 1970: the proportion of *property* and *contract* cases fell quite drastically. The family cases are primarily uncontested divorces in which the court basically does nothing except to stamp its approval on arrangements which the parties have already agreed to before coming to court. Contemporary *tort* cases generally stem from automobile accidents. At first glance, there seem to be substantial disputes in some of these cases, but the defendant's insurance company will settle almost all of them before they go to trial (Figure 7). Neither in family nor in tort cases do courts often resolve a true "dispute" between two contending parties. And in the family cases, there is not the slightest trace, in either county, of the social harmony mode.

In both counties, contract and property cases were the most frequent kinds of litigation in 1890. Not by any means were all of these cases contested even then (see Table 5). Property cases fell from around a quarter of all cases in 1890 to less than 4% of each county's cases in 1970. In Alameda County in 1890, 57% of the cases were classified as contract or property. Such cases constituted only 18% of the 1970 docket, a difference significant at the .1% level. The trend appears even more marked in San Benito. Three-fifths of San Benito's 1890 docket were property or contract cases. By 1970, such cases amounted to about one in eight; the difference here too is significant at the .1% level. Three of every five cases were routine family matters. Nearly half of all the "cases" in San Benito in 1970 were routine petitions for dissolution of marriage. Corporation or labor cases rarely occur.

Friedman & Percival / A TALE OF TWO COURTS 281

TABLE 3. TYPE OF CASE—ALAMEDA COUNTY

ALAMEDA COUNTY	1890		1910		1930		1950		1970	
Number of cases (% of total)	100	(14.0%)	100	(3.0%)	100	(2.0%)	141	(2.0%)	236	(2.0%)
TYPE OF CASE— number (%)										
FAMILY	18	(18.0)	23	(23.0)	20	(20.0)	58	(41.1)	122	(51.7)
Divorce or Annulment	16	(16.0)	23	(23.0)	18	(18.0)	57	(40.4)	106	(44.9)
Other Family	2	(2.0)	0	(0.0)	2	(2.0)	1	(0.7)	16	(6.8)
CONTRACTS	33	(33.0)	31	(31.0)	28	(28.0)	21	(14.9)	37	(15.7)
Promissory Notes	17	(17.0)	11	(11.0)	10	(10.0)	8	(5.7)	3	(1.3)
Construction Contracts & Debts	6	(6.0)	5	(5.0)	0	(0.0)	3	(2.1)	2	(0.8)
Contracts Between Merchants	0	(0.0)	3	(3.0)	3	(3.0)	1	(0.7)	2	(0.8)
Wage Claims	0	(0.0)	3	(3.0)	1	(1.0)	4	(2.8)	2	(0.8)
Consumer Sales-Chattel Fin.	0	(0.0)	1	(1.0)	1	(1.0)	0	(0.0)	1	(0.4)
Insurance	0	(0.0)	0	(0.0)	1	(1.0)	0	(0.0)	5	(2.1)
Other Contracts & Debts	10	(10.0)	8	(8.0)	12	(12.0)	5	(3.5)	22	(9.3)
PROPERTY	24	(24.0)	20	(20.0)	11	(11.0)	13	(9.2)	6	(2.3)
Land Transfer & Marketing	20	(20.0)	17	(17.0)	5	(5.0)	12	(8.5)	3	(1.3)
Land Use	1	(1.0)	1	(1.0)	1	(1.0)	0	(0.0)	0	(0.0)
Landlord & Tenant	3	(3.0)	2	(2.0)	3	(3.0)	0	(0.0)	3	(1.3)
Personal Property	0	(0.0)	0	(0.0)	2	(2.0)	1	(0.7)	0	(0.0)
TORTS	6	(6.0)	5	(5.0)	28	(28.0)	32	(22.7)	64	(27.1)
Auto Accidents	0	(0.0)	0	(0.0)	19	(19.0)	23	(16.3)	45	(19.1)
Other Personal Injury	3	(3.0)	4	(4.0)	5	(5.0)	7	(5.0)	15	(6.4)
Other Torts	3	(3.0)	1	(1.0)	4	(4.0)	2	(1.4)	4	(1.7)
GOVERNMENTAL	13	(13.0)	18	(18.0)	8	(8.0)	7	(5.0)	3	(1.3)
Municipal Assessments	7	(7.0)	15	(15.0)	0	(0.0)	0	(0.0)	0	(0.0)
State-Local Govt. Admin.	5	(5.0)	2	(2.0)	3	(3.0)	4	(2.8)	1	(0.4)
Nuisance	0	(0.0)	0	(0.0)	3	(3.0)	0	(0.0)	0	(0.0)
Condemnation	1	(1.0)	1	(1.0)	2	(2.0)	3	(2.1)	2	(0.8)
CORPORATIONS & LABOR	1	(1.0)	2	(2.0)	2	(2.0)	5	(3.5)	3	(1.3)
Business Associations	1	(1.0)	2	(2.0)	1	(1.0)	2	(1.4)	2	(0.8)
Non-Business Associations	0	(0.0)	0	(0.0)	0	(0.0)	0	(0.0)	0	(0.0)
Competition/Trade Reg./Labor	0	(0.0)	0	(0.0)	1	(1.0)	3	(2.1)	1	(0.4)
PERSONAL FINANCE/ INHERITANCE	2	(2.0)	1	(1.0)	2	(2.0)	3	(2.1)	0	(0.0)
Insolvency Petition	2	(2.0)	0	(0.0)	0	(0.0)	0	(0.0)	0	(0.0)
Succession/ Fiduciary	0	(0.0)	1	(1.0)	2	(2.0)	3	(2.1)	0	(0.0)
MISCELLANEOUS	3	(3.0)	0	(0.0)	1	(1.0)	2	(1.4)	1	(0.4)
Enforcement of Judgments	2	(2.0)	0	(0.0)	0	(0.0)	0	(0.0)	1	(0.4)
Miscellaneous	1	(1.0)	0	(0.0)	1	(1.0)	2	(1.4)	0	(0.0)

282 LAW & SOCIETY / WINTER 1976

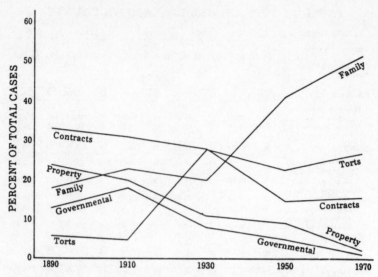

Figure 1. **Type of Case—Alameda County (1890-1970)**

TABLE 4. TYPE OF CASE—SAN BENITO COUNTY

SUPERIOR COURT	1890		1910		1930		1950		1970	
Cases sampled (% of total)	31	(100%)	29	(100%)	101	(100%)	150	(100%)	188	(100%)
TYPE OF CASE— number (%)										
FAMILY	6	(19.3)	11	(37.9)	28	(28.7)	61	(40.6)	116	(61.7)
Divorce or Annulment	5	(16.1)	9	(31.0)	24	(23.8)	53	(35.3)	93	(49.5)
Other Family	1	(3.2)	2	(6.9)	4	(4.0)	8	(5.3)	23	(12.2)
CONTRACTS	10	(32.3)	11	(37.9)	31	(30.8)	41	(27.3)	17	(9.1)
Promissory Notes	4	(12.9)	6	(20.7)	13	(12.9)	6	(4.0)	5	(2.7)
Construction Contracts & Debts	0	(0.0)	0	(0.0)	1	(1.0)	2	(1.3)	0	(0.0)
Contracts Between Merchants	0	(0.0)	0	(0.0)	0	(0.0)	0	(0.0)	0	(0.0)
Wage Claims	2	(6.5)	0	(0.0)	3	(3.0)	3	(2.0)	1	(0.5)
Consumer Sales/ Chattel Fin.	1	(3.2)	0	(0.0)	1	(1.0)	6	(4.0)	0	(0.0)
Insurance	0	(0.0)	0	(0.0)	0	(0.0)	1	(0.7)	0	(0.0)
Other Contracts &, Debts	3	(9.7)	5	(17.2)	13	(12.9)	23	(15.3)	10	(5.3)
PROPERTY	8	(25.8)	5	(17.2)	15	(14.9)	12	(9.0)	6	(3.2)
Land Transfer & Marketing	8	(25.8)	3	(10.3)	14	(13.9)	10	(6.7)	4	(2.1)
Land Use	0	(0.0)	2	(6.9)	0	(0.0)	0	(0.0)	1	(0.5)
Landlord & Tenant	0	(0.0)	0	(0.0)	1	(1.0)	2	(1.3)	1	(0.5)
Personal Property	0	(0.0)	0	(0.0)	0	(0.0)	0	(0.0)	0	(0.0)
TORTS	1	(3.2)	0	(0.0)	20	(19.9)	26	(17.3)	36	(19.2)
Auto Accidents	0	(0.0)	0	(0.0)	16	(15.9)	17	(11.3)	27	(14.4)
Other Personal Injury	0	(0.0)	0	(0.0)	0	(0.0)	6	(4.0)	7	(3.7)
Other Torts	1	(3.2)	0	(0.0)	4	(4.0)	3	(2.0)	2	(1.1)
GOVERNMENTAL	2	(6.5)	1	(3.4)	2	(2.0)	4	(2.7)	2	(1.1)
Municipal Assessments	0	(0.0)	0	(0.0)	0	(0.0)	0	(0.0)	0	(0.0)
State-Local Govt. Admin.	2	(6.5)	0	(0.0)	0	(0.0)	0	(0.0)	1	(0.5)
Nuisance	0	(0.0)	0	(0.0)	0	(0.0)	0	(0.0)	1	(0.5)
Condemnation	0	(0.0)	1	(3.4)	2	(2.0)	4	(2.7)	0	(0.0)

Friedman & Percival / A TALE OF TWO COURTS 283

CORPORATIONS & LABOR	1	(3.2)	1	(3.4)	2	(2.0)	1	(0.7)	6	(3.2)
Business Associations	1	(3.2)	1	(3.4)	2	(2.0)	1	(0.7)	0	(0.0)
Non-Business Associations	0	(0.0)	0	(0.0)	0	(0.0)	0	(0.0)	1	(0.5)
Competition/Trade Reg/Labor	0	(0.0)	0	(0.0)	0	(0.0)	0	(0.0)	5	(2.7)
PERSON FINANCE/ INHERITANCE	1	(3.2)	0	(0.0)	0	(0.0)	2	(1.3)	0	(0.0)
Insolvency Petition	0	(0.0)	0	(0.0)	0	(0.0)	0	(0.0)	0	(0.0)
Succession/Fiduciary	1	(3.2)	0	(0.0)	0	(0.0)	2	(1.3)	0	(0.0)
MISCELLANEOUS	2	(6.5)	0	(0.0)	3	(3.0)	2	(1.3)	2	(1.1)
Enforcement of Judgments	0	(0.0)	0	(0.0)	3	(3.0)	0	(0.0)	1	(0.5)
Miscellaneous	2	(6.5)	0	(0.0)	0	(0.0)	2	(1.3)	1	(0.5)
UNKNOWN	0	(0.0)	0	(0.0)	0	(0.0)	1	(0.7)	3	(1.6)

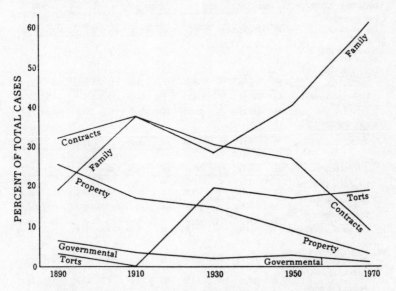

Figure 2. **Type of Case—San Benito County (1890-1970)**

Yet we feel confident that, as the economy develops, the volume of *private* transactions which use legal forms, or which take account of legal rules and processes, rises tremendously. Contracts are made, corporations formed, and property changes hands. The law (statutes, decisions of appellate courts, administrative proceedings) may significantly affect the form and legitimacy of these private transactions; yet in both counties we find a decline in formal resort to courts, to adjudicate disputes arising out of legal transactions. Surprisingly, San Benito (rural, non-industrial) and Alameda (urban, industrial) differ not at all in these regards. In both, the incidence of cases of economic disputes has fallen off, and the incidence of routine cases has risen.

284   LAW & SOCIETY / WINTER 1976

TABLE 5. PERCENT OF CASES TRIED

	1890	1910	1930	1950	1970
ALAMEDA					
All cases	36.0	25.0	48.0	29.1	16.1
Contracts	30.3	22.6	57.1	19.0	27.0
Property	54.2	55.0	63.6	53.8	33.3
SAN BENITO					
All cases	25.8	37.9	19.8	20.0	11.7
Contracts	40.0	18.2	19.4	17.1	17.6
Property	12.5	100.0	33.3	33.3	50.0

TABLE 6.   CASE DISPOSITION—ALAMEDA COUNTY

ALAMEDA COUNTY	1890		1910		1930		1950		1970	
Cases Sampled (% of total)	100	(14.0%)	100	(3.0%)	100	(2.0%)	141	(2.0)%	236	(2.0%)
TYPE OF DISPOSITION— number (%)										
VOLUNTARY DISMISSAL	29	(29.0)	35	(35.0)	23½	(23.5)	49½	(35.1)	77	(32.6)
With. Settlement	11	(11.0)	10	(10.0)	9½	(9.5)	28	(19.9)	30½	(12.9)
Unknown if Settlement	18	(18.0)	25	(25.0)	14	(14.0)	21½	(15.2)	46½	(19.7)
CASE DROPPED— INCOMPLETE FILE	9	(9.0)	11	(11.0)	13	(13.0)	11	(7.8)	34	(14.4)
UNCONTESTED JUDGMENT	29	(29.0)	32	(32.0)	19	(19.0)	48	(34.0)	87½	(37.1)
Ex Parte Petition Granted	4	(4.0)	2	(2.0)	0	(0.0)	2	(1.4)	1	(0.4)
Default Judgments— Divorce	10	(10.0)	17	(17.0)	9	(9.0)	27½	(19.5)	67	(28.4)
Default Judgment— Non-Divorce	11	(11.0)	13	(13.0)	5	(5.0)	10	(7.1)	15	(6.4)
Consent Judgment	4	(4.0)	0	(0.0)	5	(5.0)	8½	(6.0)	4½	(1.9)
CONTESTED JUDGMENT TO PLAINTIFF	27	(27.0)	10	(10.0)	30	(30.0)	32½	(23.0)	28½	(12.1)
Contested Decree (Summ. J.)	0	(0.0)	0	(0.0)	0	(0.0)	5	(3.5)	½	(0.2)
Judgment on Pleadings	0	(0.0)	0	(0.0)	1	(1.0)	0	(0.0)	0	(0.0)
Trial Verdict for Plaintiff	27	(27.0)	10	(10.0)	29	(29.0)	27½	(19.5)	28	(11.9)
JUDGMENT FOR DEFENDANT OR DISMISSAL	5	(5.0)	11	(11.0)	14½	(14.5)	10	(7.1)	5	(2.1)
Invol. Dimissal Before Trial	2	(2.0)	1	(1.0)	1½	(1.5)	0	(0.0)	0	(0.0)
Trial Verdict for Defendant	3	(3.0)	7	(7.0)	12	(12.0)	9	(6.4)	5	(2.1)
Invol. Dismissal at Trial	0	(0.0)	3	(3.0)	1	(1.0)	0	(0.0)	0	(0.0)
Default Judgm't for Defend't	0	(0.0)	0	(0.0)	0	(0.0)	1	(0.7)	0	(0.0)
J in other case decides	0	(0.0)	1	(1.0)	0	(0.0)	0	(0.0)	0	(0.0)
OTHER	1	(1.0)	1	(1.0)	0	(0.0)	0	(0.0)	4	(1.7)
Third Party Wins at Trial	1	(1.0)	1	(1.0)	0	(0.0)	0	(0.0)	0	(0.0)
Case Still Pending	0	(0.0)	0	(0.0)	0	(0.0)	0	(0.0)	2	(0.8)
Transferred to Muni Court	0	(0.0)	0	(0.0)	0	(0.0)	0	(0.0)	2	(0.8)

(Totals ending in ½ represent multiple-party cases that reached different dispositions relative to two different parties defendant.)

Friedman & Percival / A TALE OF TWO COURTS 285

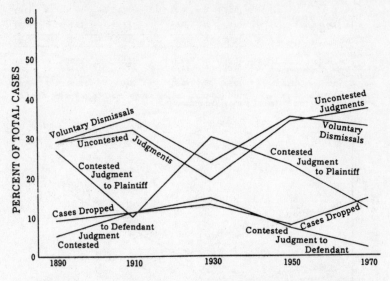

Figure 3. **Case Disposition—Alameda County (1890-1970)**

TABLE 7. CASE DISPOSITION—SAN BENITO COUNTY

SUPERIOR COURT	1890		1910		1930		1950		1970	
Cases sampled (% of total)	31	(100%)	29	(100%)	101	(100%)	150	(100%)	188	(100%)
TYPE OF DISPOSITION— number (%)										
VOLUNTARY DISMISSAL	3	(9.7)	0	(0.0)	16	(15.9)	32	(21.3)	36½	(19.4)
With Settlement	0	(0.0)	0	(0.0)	6	(5.9)	8	(5.3)	5	(2.7)
Unknown if Settlement	3	(9.7)	0	(0.0)	10	(9.9)	24	(16.0)	31½	(16.8)
CASE DROPPED/ INCOMPLETE FILE	8	(25.8)	7	(24.1)	33	(32.8)	35	(23.3)	25	(13.3)
UNCONTESTED JUDGMENT	13	(41.9)	11	(37.9)	31	(30.8)	63	(42.0)	101	(53.7)
Ex Parte Petition Granted	3	(9.7)	3	(10.3)	10	(9.9)	12	(8.0)	11	(5.8)
Default Judgment— Divorce	4	(12.9)	7	(24.1)	9	(8.9)	18	(12.0)	59	(31.4)
Default Judgment— Non-Divorce	6	(19.4)	1	(3.4)	12	(11.9)	18	(12.0)	9½	(5.0)
Consent Judgment	0	(0.0)	0	(0.0)	0	(0.0)	14	(9.3)	21½	(11.5)
CONTESTED JUDGMENT TO PLAINTIFF	5	(16.1)	6	(20.7)	14	(13.9)	12	(8.0)	11	(5.9)
Contested Decree (Summ. J.)	0	(0.0)	0	(0.0)	0	(0.0)	1	(0.7)	4	(2.1)
Judgment on Pleadings	0	(0.0)	0	(0.0)	0	(0.0)	0	(0.0)	0	(0.0)
Trial Verdict for Plaintiff	8	(25.8)	6	(20.7)	14	(13.9)	11	(7.4)	7	(3.7)
JUDGMENT FOR DEF. OR DISMISSAL	2	(6.5)	5	(17.2)	6	(5.9)	7	(4.7)	4½	(2.4)
Invol. Dismissal before Trial	0	(0.0)	1	(3.4)	0	(0.0)	1	(0.7)	1½	(0.9)
Trial Verdict for Defendant	2	(6.5)	4	(13.8)	5	(4.9)	6	(4.0)	1	(0.5)

Continued overleaf

Invol. Dismissal at Trial ____	0	(0.0)	0	(0.0)	0	(0.0)	0	(0.0)	2	(1.1)
Default Judgment for Defendant ____	0	(0.0)	0	(0.0)	1	(1.0)	0	(0.0)	0	(0.0)
OTHER ____	0	(0.0)	0	(0.0)	1	(1.0)	1	(0.7)	10	(5.3)
Removed to U.S. Dist. Court ____	0	(0.0)	0	(0.0)	1	(1.0)	0	(0.0)	0	(0.0)
Change of Venue ____	0	(0.0)	0	(0.0)	0	(0.0)	1	(0.7)	7	(3.7)
Indefinite Continuance ____	0	(0.0)	0	(0.0)	0	(0.0)	0	(0.0)	3	(1.6)

(Totals ending in ½ represent multiple-party cases which reached different dispositions relative to two different parties defendant.)

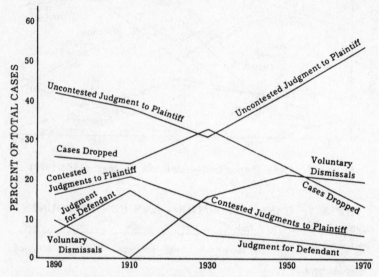

Figure 4. **Case Disposition—San Benito County (1890-1970)**

B. Case Disposition

Another indication of the role courts play is provided by examination of how cases are resolved (Tables 6 and 7, Figures 3 and 4). As uncontested judgments—mostly judgments by default—rise, in both counties the percentage of contested judgments for defendants) falls, dropping from 32.0% to 14.2% in Alameda (significant at the .1% level) and from 22.6% to 8.3% in San Benito (although because of the small number of 1890 cases in the sample, this result is not statistically significant). San Benito has a higher incidence of dissolution petitions; here the proportion of cases disposed of by uncontested judgments rises to over half of all cases. This is evidence of the shift toward administration, away from dispute settlement. The trend is equally striking if we take the percentage of *judgments* which are contested. In Alameda, the proportion of judgments which are uncontested has risen from 47.5% in 1890 to 71.9% in 1970 (significant at the .2% level). In San Benito 86.7% of the judgments are now uncontested, as opposed to 65% in 1890 (significant at the .2% level). Here, too, Alameda seems, surprisingly enough, less routinized and perfunctory than San Benito, where less than one case in ten is contested.

C. Proportion of Plaintiff Victories

We suggested that the percentage of cases which plaintiffs win is an indicator of degree of routinization of judicial process. Where there are genuine disputes, one might still expect plaintiffs to win most of their cases; but not 90 to 95 percent. In Alameda, plaintiffs won 96% of the judgments in 1970; in San Benito, 97%. Similar findings have been reported in other jurisdictions.[32] This too indicates movement towards a routine administrative role. In San Benito, the percentage of plaintiff victories was slimmest in 1910 (77%); in Alameda it was slimmest in 1930 (77%), perhaps indicating a greater dispute-settlement role than in 1890 when the ratio is greatest for Alameda. In Alameda, contested cases were most frequent and voluntary dismissals least frequent in 1930 (44.5% contested judgments, 23.5% voluntary dismissals); in San Benito in 1910 (37.9% contested judgments, 0% voluntary dismissals).

D. Percent of Cases Brought to Trial

One index of dispute settlement is the percentage of cases brought to formal trial. In both counties the incidence of trials has substantially declined between 1890 and 1970 (Table 8, Figure 5). In 1890, more than one out of every three cases filed in Alameda County was brought to trial. Today less than one in six has such a life cycle (a difference significant at the .1% level). The trend is also pronounced in San Benito; trial incidence fell from one in four in 1890, to only one of nine today (significant at the 5% level). Again, this is a strong trend away from dispute settlement; and, again, the incidence of dispute

---

32. Craig Wanner, "The Public Ordering of Private Relations," Part II, 9 *Law & Society Review* 293 (1975). In New Haven and Waterbury Connecticut, in the period roughly between 1919 and 1930, plaintiffs won 83% of their cases. Clark and Shulman, *supra*, note 1, at 41. See also Marc Galanter, "Why the 'Haves' Come Out Ahead; Speculations on the Limits of Legal Change," 9 *Law & Society Review* 95 (1974).

In England, where the county courts have been used as routine debt collection courts, the same disparities appear. For example, in Durham County Court, in a single day, Feb. 13, 1911, there were 111 cases entered on the record books. In only 3 of these was judgment entered for defendant (plaintiffs won 80; seven were marked "paid;" in 12, defendant was not served; in eight the case was struck out or withdrawn). Durham County Court, P.R.O. AK2 no. 10. Plaint and Minute Book B 18ff, 1910-11. Aggregate statistics present a similar picture; for example, in 1870, 912,795 cases were entered in county court; 523,340 went to judgment; plaintiffs won 505,744 of these judgments; there were 8,185 non-suits and only 9,411 judgments for defendant. *Civil Judicial Statistics, 1870*, xi.

288   LAW & SOCIETY / WINTER 1976

settlement—represented here by percent of cases tried—is lower in the rural county.

Figure 5 indicates that the decline in the rate of trials has not been continuous; it rose briefly in San Benito in 1910, sharply in Alameda in 1930. This pattern resembles that of the case disposition statistics. It was in 1930 that automobile accident cases first appeared in the data in substantial numbers. In Alameda, in 1930, these cases were brought to trial more often than they were

TABLE 8. TRIALS & HEARINGS HELD—BY TYPE

ALAMEDA COUNTY	1890		1910		1930		1950		1970	
Cases sampled (% of total)	100	(14.0%)	100	(3.0%)	100	(2.0%)	141	(2.0%)	236	(2.0%)
TRIALS & HEARINGS HELD	36	(36.0)	25	(25.0)	48	(48.0)	41	(29.1)	38	(16.1)
Trials	32	(32.0)	22	(22.0)	48	(48.0)	39	(27.7)	36	(15.3)
Jury Trials	2	(2.0)	0	(0.0)	7	(7.0)	5	(3.5)	2	(0.8)
Non-Jury w/o Opin. or Findings	8	(8.0)	9	(9.0)	8	(8.0)	19	(13.5)	21	(8.9)
Non-Jury with Opin. or Findings	22	(22.0)	13	(13.0)	33	(33.0)	15	(10.6)	11	(4.7)
Hearings	4	(4.0)	3	(3.0)	0	(0.0)	2	(1.4)	2	(0.8)
Without Opinion or Findings	3	(3.0)	2	(2.0)	0	(0.0)	2	(1.4)	2	(0.8)
With Opinion or Findings	2	(2.0)	1	(1.0)	0	(0.0)	0	(0.0)	0	(0.0)
SAN BENITO COUNTY	1890		1910		1930		1950		1970	
Cases sampled (% of total)	31	(100%)	29	(100%)	101	(100%)	150	(100%)	188	(100%)
TRIAL & HEARINGS HELD	8	(25.8)	11	(37.9)	20	(19.8)	30	(20.0)	22	(11.7)
Trials	8	(25.8)	9	(31.0)	20	(19.8)	29	(19.3)	20	(10.7)
Jury Trials	1	(3.2)	0	(0.0)	0	(0.0)	9	(6.0)	6	(3.2)
Non-Jury w/o Opin. or Findings	2	(6.5)	4	(13.8)	14	(13.9)	14	(9.3)	10	(5.3)
Non-Jury with Opin or Findings	5	(16.1)	5	(17.2)	6	(5.9)	6	(4.0)	4	(2.1)
Hearings	0	(0.0)	2	(6.9)	0	(0.0)	1	(0.7)	2	(1.1)
Without Opinion or Findings	0	(0.0)	2	(6.9)	0	(0.0)	1	(0.7)	2	(1.1)
With Opinion or Findings	0	(0.0)	0	(0.0)	0	(0.0)	0	(0.0)	0	(0.0)

Figure 5. **Percent of Cases Brought to Trial or Hearing**
Alameda San Benito Counties 1890-1970

settled out of court; today less than one in ten is brought to trial there (Figure 6). Auto accident cases, however do not account completely for the sharp rise in trials in 1930; this remains, for the present, unexplained.

E. Percent of Trials With Formal Opinions

A rough indicator of the extent of dispute settlement by courts is the proportion of cases tried in which the court writes a formal opinion, or makes formal findings of fact or law. The incidence of such cases is quite similar to the incidence of trials themselves, as shown in Table 8 and Figure 7. With the exception of Alameda in 1930, formal opinions or findings in non-jury trials have declined steadily in both counties. In 1890, in both counties, judges made such opinions or findings in over 70% of non-jury trials. Today they are made in only 34% of such cases in Alameda and 29% in San Benito (the change from 1890 is significant at the .4% level for Alameda, and the .6% level for San Benito). Courts feel less necessity to justify their actions formally, perhaps because of the increased routinization of their work. Again, differences between the two counties are small; if anything, the rural court works in a slightly more perfunctory way.

F. Costs of Litigation—Time and Delay

Delays and costs may be important factors that act to discourage litigation in modern courts. Formal litigation today is

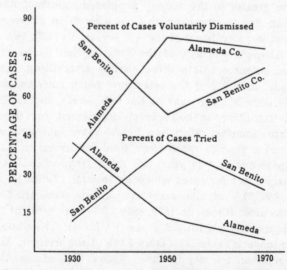

Figure 6. **Auto Accident Cases—Percent Tried and Percent Voluntarily Dismissed**
Alameda & San Benito Counties 1930-1970

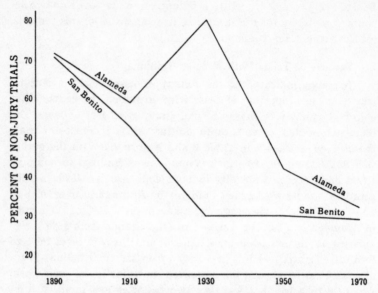

Figure 7. **Percent of Non-Jury Trials with Formal
Opinion or Findings**
Alameda & San Benito Counties 1890-1970

much slower than before (Tables 9 and 10, Figures 8 and 9)—
despite the increase in routinization of procedures and results.
Delays are greater in the densely populated county of Alameda
than in San Benito (three-month final disposition difference between counties; significant at the .1% level). In 1890, 44% of the
cases in Alameda and 52% of the cases in San Benito reached
their final outcome within three months after filing. In 1970,
in Alameda, only 9% of the cases now reach such an outcome
(the difference is significant at the .1% level); in San Benito,
only 26% (significant at the 2% level) are cleared from the docket
within three months. Most San Benito cases take between six
months and a year to reach their final outcomes; in Alameda
delays up to one to two years are more frequent. Delays are
particularly great for cases which go to trial (Table 11, Figure
10). In 1890, 72% of such cases in Alameda were tried within
six months after filing. In 1970, only 13% were brought to trial
within six months (significant at the .1% level). The actual trials
also take longer (Table 12). Only 6.1% of the trials in Alameda
took longer than one day in 1890. Today, 27% of the Alameda
trials—63% of San Benito trials—take longer than one day.

G. Volume of Litigation

Studies in a number of counties suggest an inverse relationship between economic growth and volume of formal litigation.[33] That is, highly developed economic systems do *not* show growth in their litigation rates; on the contrary, rates tend to stabilize or decline in the face of rapid economic growth.

TABLE 9. PERCENT OF CASES REACHING INITIAL DISPOSITION WITHIN SPECIFED TIME PERIODS

ALAMEDA COUNTY	1890	1910	1930	1950	1970
Data available/ total sample	(91/100)	(91/100)	(87/100)	(130/141)	(199/236)
Less than one month	23.1%	7.7%	5.0%	20.8%	3.0%
Less than two months	41.8	15.4	23.0	31.5	13.6
Less than three months	47.3	22.0	33.3	40.8	24.6
Less than six months	64.8	47.3	66.9	53.8	45.7
Less than one year	75.8	68.1	87.4	74.6	69.3
Less than two years	89.0	83.5	96.6	94.6	92.0

SAN BENITO COUNTY	1890	1910	1930	1950	1970
Data available/ total sample	(23/31)	(22/29)	(68/101)	(112/150)	(150/188)
Less than one month	34.8%	31.8%	35.3%	30.4%	12.6%
Less than two months	47.8	45.5	50.0	43.8	31.3
Less than three months	70.0	63.6	54.4	54.5	45.3
Less than six months	82.6	72.7	70.6	72.2	64.7
Less than one year	100.0	77.3	85.3	88.4	89.3
Less than two years	100.0	100.0	94.1	96.4	98.0

TABLE 10. PERCENT OF CASES REACHING FINAL DISPOSITION WITHIN SPECIFIED TIME PERIODS

ALAMEDA COUNTY	1890	1910	1930	1950	1970
Data available/ total sample	(91/100)	(90/100)	(87/100)	(124/141)	(193/236)
Less than one month	18.7%	6.7%	5.7%	8.1%	2.1%
Less than two months	35.2	11.1	10.3	13.7	6.2
Less than three months	44.0	14.4	18.4	18.5	9.3
Less than six months	60.4	34.4	42.5	28.2	18.7
Less than one year	73.6	53.3	65.5	46.0	53.4
Less than two years	85.7	75.6	89.7	79.8	87.0

SAN BENITO COUNTY	1890	1910	1930	1950	1970
Data available/ total sample	(23/31)	(21/29)	(68/101)	(109/150)	(145/188)
Less than one month	30.4%	14.3%	29.4%	18.3%	8.1%
Less than two months	39.1	28.6	39.7	27.5	19.6
Less than three months	52.2	33.3	44.1	36.7	26.4
Less than six months	69.6	47.6	55.9	49.5	39.9
Less than one year	95.7	47.6	69.1	60.6	82.4
Less than two years	95.7	95.2	88.2	84.4	85.3

33. See the important work of José Juan Toharia, *Cambio Social y Vida Jurídica en España, 1900-1970* (1974); a study of the volume of civil litigation at first instance in Sweden and Denmark, between 1930 and 1970, showed similar results. In Sweden, the volume actually decreased; in Denmark, litigation grew in absolute numbers, but not in proportion to the population. Britt-Mari P. Blegvad, P.O. Bolding, Ole Lando, *Arbitration as a Means of Solving Conflicts* 103-105 (1973). The rate of litigation has been static or declining in England, too, since about the turn of the century. Friedman, *supra*, note 2. Findings similar to Toharia's are reported by Carlos José Gutierrez, in a study of Costa Rican litigation, as yet unpublished.

292   LAW & SOCIETY / WINTER 1976

TABLE 11. PERCENT OF CASES REACHING TRIAL WITHIN SPECIFIED TIME PERIODS

ALAMEDA COUNTY	1890	1910	1930	1950	1970
Data available/ trials in sample	(36/36)	(24/25)	(48/48)	(37/40)	(38/38)
Less than one month	25.0%	12.5%	2.1%	24.3%	5.3%
Less than two months	47.2	12.5	14.6	32.4	7.9
Less than three months	50.0	20.8	22.9	40.5	7.9
Less than six months	72.2	41.7	66.7	48.6	13.2
Less than one year	83.3	54.2	83.3	78.4	50.0
Less than two years	100.0	91.7	95.8	94.6	84.2

SAN BENITO COUNTY	1890	1910	1930	1950	1970
Data available/ trials in sample	(5/8)	(11/11)	(20/20)	(27/30)	(20/22)
Less than one month	60.0%	27.3%	28.6%	11.1%	5.0%
Less than two months	80.0	36.4	33.3	18.5	15.0
Less than three months	80.0	54.5	42.9	29.6	25.0
Less than six months	80.0	54.5	66.7	66.7	60.0
Less than one year	100.0	63.6	81.0	81.5	85.0
Less than two years	100.0	100.0	95.2	96.3	100.0

TABLE 12. DURATION OF TRIALS

ALAMEDA COUNTY	1890		1910		1930		1950		1970	
Data available/ trials in sample	(33/36)		(19/25)		(38/48)		(33/40)		(37/38)	
One day or less	31	(93.9)	16	(84.2)	24	(63.2)	22	(66.7)	27	(73.0)
More than one day	2	(6.1)	3	(15.8)	14	(36.8)	11	(33.3)	10	(27.0)

SAN BENITO COUNTY	1890		1910		1930		1950		1970	
Data available/ trials in sample	(1/8)		(6/11)		(3/20)		(21/30)		(11/22)	
One day or less	1	(100.0)	5	(83.3)	3	(100.0)	11	(52.4)	4	(36.4)
More than one day	0	(0.0)	1	(16.7)	0	(0.0)	10	(47.6)	7	(63.6)

Why should this be so? The idea is that formal court processes are slow, expensive, technical. Court process is, from the economic standpoint, inefficient; and society will take no steps to encourage it for ordinary civil disputes. That formal court processes are inefficient and irrelevant to economic life, is quite consistent with our data. But it is not so clear that the two counties confirm the prediction that litigation declines as an economy develops. The rate of cases per 1,000 population in the two counties was shown in Table 2. A number of interesting facts emerge from this table. One is the convergence of the counties. In 1890, urban Alameda was more litigious than rural San Benito; differences today are very small.

Compared to 1890, both counties show an apparent rise in cases per 1,000 population. But the rate in Alameda in 1910 was higher than it is today; and San Benito's ratio declined slightly between 1950 and 1970. And the figures are too crude to be used as indicators of litigation rates. For one thing, they do not take into account either the federal courts or the inferior trial courts. For another thing, they do not take into account the nature of the cases litigated. Before we can speak of "litigation rates" we must define litigation: is an uncontested divorce "litigation?"

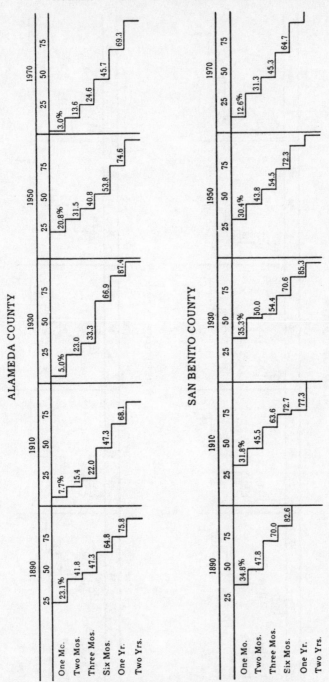

Figure 8. **Time from Filing to Initial Disposition**
Alameda & San Benito Counties 1890-1970

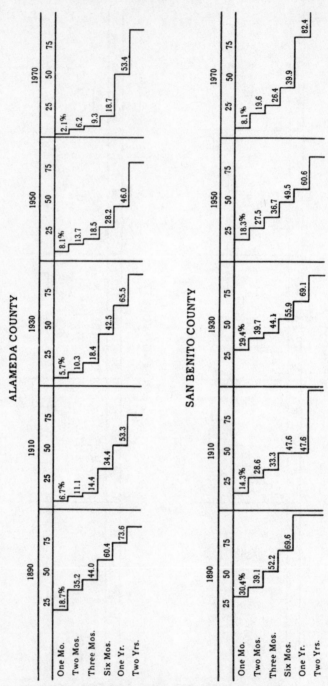

Figure 9. **Time from Filing to Final Disposition**
Alameda & San Benito Counties 1890-1970

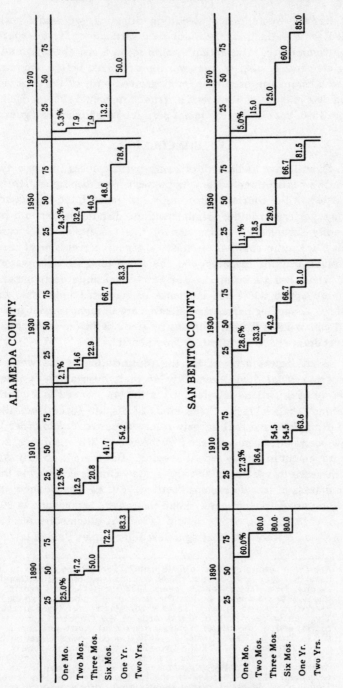

Figure 10. **Time from Filing to Trial**
Alameda & San Benito Counties 1890-1970

To test the hypothesis of declining litigation, we would really need some valid measure of dispute settlement, for all courts, in a community. "Litigation" would mean a proceeding containing elements of dispute, that were not resolved before one party filed a complaint, or perhaps not resolved without the intervention of a judge. Perhaps such a "true" rate would show a decline since 1890; but our figures do not permit us the luxury of a guess.

V. CONCLUSION

Quantitative indicators of court performances in these two counties confirm one general hypothesis: the dispute settlement function in the courts is declining.[34] In general, the trial courts today perform routine administration; dispute settlement has steadily shrunk as a proportion of their caseload. Most cases today are quite routine. In 1890, a higher percentage of cases involved genuine disputes, and the work of the courts was on the whole less stereotyped. The rate of uncontested judgments has multiplied while the incidence of contested judgments has fallen. A smaller percentage of cases are brought to trial today, and courts issue formal opinions or findings in far fewer cases. Court delays have significantly lengthened.

What factors account for the routinization of the work of modern courts? One possibility is that uncertainty—a prime breeder of litigation—has declined in the law; that rules are more "settled" than in 1890. Some kinds of dispute (over land titles for example) have been largely resolved, or reduced to order by new social arrangements, such as the use of title insurance, and improvement in county record-keeping. But there is no easy way to measure this factor in the aggregate. Our assumption is that some areas of law do become "settled;" but as they do, new uncertainties replace old ones. Land titles were less chaotic in 1930 than in 1890; but as this problem faded, the automobile accident more than replaced it, creating a new and complex field of law.

---

34. Are these results specific to California? There is no reason to believe that they are. A spot check was made of records of Camden County, New Jersey, for the years 1892 and 1966. The records of this county show more or less the same progression. In the earlier year contract and property cases predominate; tort cases are rare. This can be seen both in the records of the Camden County trial courts, and in records of New Jersey circuit court judgments, on file in Trenton, New Jersey. By 1970, the pattern of litigation had come to resemble that of the two California counties. Family law cases are handled by separate chancery courts in New Jersey; such cases rose from a miniscule number to a dominant position in the percentage of cases decided on the trial court level in New Jersey. Time did not, however, permit comparison of urban and rural courts in New Jersey. Replication of this study in other parts of the country would be useful.

Friedman & Percival / A TALE OF TWO COURTS 297

For another possible explanation, one may point to factors associated with *urbanization* and the particular brand of economic development that has occurred in the United States. The population in 1970 is mobile and rootless. Overwhelmingly, people live in metropolitan areas. They deal primarily with strangers. The ordered social relations of small towns and traditional courts—a world of face to face relations—has vanished.

In this light, we might expect the modern court in San Benito to resemble its 1890 ancestor, and traditional courts, more closely than we would expect of the Alameda court. Surprisingly, however, the data of 1970 do not show much difference between the counties. On the contrary, San Benito's courts play, if anything, a more routinized role than the courts in urban Alameda. In San Benito, more cases involve routine matters, a larger proportion are uncontested, fewer are brought to trial, and courts more rarely issue formal opinions or findings.

There is a general assumption in the literature that "modernization" brings about a general shift from social-harmony litigation to a more formal style of dispute-settlement. Our data suggests a rather different kind of evolution. To be sure, in 1890 it was already true that precious little of the work of the court conformed to the social harmony style. That had perhaps already virtually vanished in the United States, unless one were to find it in the justice courts, which is doubtful. Did it ever exist? The records of colonial courts suggest that at the very dawn of American history there were institutions that came closer to the anthropologists' model.[35] But by 1890, the Superior Court of Alameda was already an urban court; and as for San Benito, while it was a small community, it was hardly a tightly-knit, traditional community. On the contrary, it was a raw and new community—a community of recent arrivals, transients, strangers.[36] If anything, it is more of a face-to-face community today; and yet the social harmony style is even more absent.

The evolution, then, does not go from social harmony to legalistic style, and find a resting point. Rather, dispute settlement vanishes completely from the courts; it is replaced by routine administration. Whether the legalistic style was an intermediate phase, or whether the development was directly from social

---

35. For pictures of these courts at work, see Joseph H. Smith, *Colonial Justice in Western Massachusetts (1639-1702): The Pynchon Court Record* (1961); Paul M. McCain, *The County in North Carolina before 1750* (1954).
36. See Friedman, *supra*, note 25.

harmony style to routine, our data does not allow us to state with confidence.

Our evidence shows, then, that in the two California courts—one sitting in a bustling urban metropolis, the other not—the dispute settlement function has shriveled to almost nothing; the routine administrative function has become predominant.

This seems on the surface rather curious. Certainly, disputes still arise in society, and they probably must be settled. Yet for some reason, they are not settled in court. Of course, it *is* theoretically possible that fewer disputes go to court than in an earlier period because the *number* of disputes has fallen. We have no way to measure the number of disputes that *might* go to court, if court were costless and freely accessible. Nor do we have any information about the *relative* number of disputes in San Benito County, compared to Alameda, now or in any other period. It is barely possible that, when genuine disputes do occur in San Benito, a larger proportion of them may actually be taken to court than in Alameda. But there is no obvious reason why the number of actual "disputes" should be so low in the two counties; and the most likely assumption is that the court itself—its style, its mode of operation—discourages its use for dispute settlement, rather than that the number of issues or disputes has declined.

Apparently, litigation is not worthwhile, for the potential litigant; it is too costly, in other words; "Costs" may mean dollar costs. Delays and technicalities are also costly, because of the disruption and expense they may inflict, and the uncertainties they may introduce into outcomes. All of these costs in fact did rise during the 19th century, although the data are fragmentary. As costs rise, so does the threshold at which litigation becomes worthwhile.

But this pushes our inquiry back one step; it does not answer the basic question. If courts have become too "costly," why has society permitted this to happen? Why have there not been arrangements to keep the dispute settlement function of courts alive, and healthy and productive? Why has a situation been allowed to develop in which full scale court proceedings on the whole move slowly, cost a great deal, and proceed by rules that are a closed book to the average man—indeed, to the average businessman? Over the last two centuries, the *use* of courts for dispute settlement seems to have declined, while all other *economic* indicators in society have risen. Does this make sense?

Friedman & Percival / A TALE OF TWO COURTS 299

A. Law and Development

Let us, for simplicity, assume economic growth as a goal widely shared in early nineteenth century American society.[37] How could legal process contribute to this end? First of all, it was necessary to dismantle restrictions that restrained the free flow of commerce. Second, new legal arrangements might be instituted or encouraged that would stimulate trade and manufacture. A flourishing economy, a growing economy is an economy of increasing _volume_. The more of society's goods traded on the market, the better; the higher the turnover, the better.

The economy, then, was to be left as free as possible, not for its own sake, but because free trade would foster prosperity. Business, left to its own devices, would develop tools—forms and techniques—that permitted and encouraged rapid trade. Such forms would be highly standard; they would permit rapid, routine, trouble-free use, as much as was humanly possible. A vigorous market is one in which people absorb losses in the short run, and continue to trade. They do not break off commercial relationships in the midst of a competitive situation, nor do they funnel transactions through courts. Any legal agency which exercises discretion and is careful, slow and individuating, cannot help but interrupt the flow of trade. It is not healthy, then, for the economy, unless parties stay out of court except as a last resort.

Hence, costs are permitted to rise. No invisible cartel raises costs, but costs go up, and they are allowed to; there is little countervailing subsidy. Ordinary disputes, between members of the middle class, slowly drain out of the system. Business also tends to avoid the courts.[38] Business can afford to litigate, but does not welcome the disruptiveness of litigation. For business, too, legal norms (especially procedural ones) disappoint legitimate expectations. This formalization is a cost which society has also allowed to rise, as lawyers professionalize, courts conceptualize, and the law becomes more "scientific."

Hence, too, the relative decline in litigation, although, as we have seen, this is not so easy to attest in our two courts. One must remember that the decline in disputed proceedings in court does not mean that "the law" (in a broader sense) is of declin-

---

37. J. Willard Hurst, _Law and the Conditions of Freedom in the 19th Century United States_ (1964); Lawrence M. Friedman, _A History of American Law_ 157-58 (1973); Harry N. Scheiber, _Ohio Canal Era, A Case Study of Government and the Economy, 1820-1861_ (1969).

38. See Stewart Macaulay, "Non-Contractual Relations in Business: A Preliminary Study," 28 _Am. Soc. Rev._ 55 (1963).

ing importance in a developing country; quite the contrary. As the economy expands, so does the use of legal instruments: contracts, checks, deeds, articles of incorporation, wills, mortgages. The number of transactions which take legal form increases more rapidly than the population. But this does *not* mean more "trials" and more use of formal courts to "settle disputes." In modern society, most transactions are private, that is, they take place without the intervention of the state.[39] Thousands of other transactions use the courts, but only in a routine way— to collect debts, legitimize status, and so on.

Routinization, then, accompanies a lowering of the public demand for settlement of disputes in formal courts. Much of the remaining docket hangs on from sheer necessity. One *must* go to court to win legal freedom to remarry, for example. It is a routine but necessary step. For the rest, ordinary people are deterred by the cost, the torpor, the technicality of court proceedings. Businessmen prefer to handle matters themselves, or go to arbitration, which is perhaps less disruptive, and where an arbitrator is more likely than a judge to understand the issues, as businessmen define them. Administrative bodies (zoning boards, workmen's compensation boards) settle many others of society's disputes.

In short, the dispute-settlement trial becomes rarer and rarer. The court system does not expand; the number of judges remains more or less static. The system is rationalized and "improved;" but it remains foreign to the average potential litigant. At the trial level, formal court systems gradually lose their share of dispute settlement cases. Their work becomes, in large part, routine administration.

B. City and Country

The most surprising result of the study, however, is the striking similarity between the two counties. San Benito is small, and the population is thin. In Oakland, one can talk about "crowded" city courts;" but certainly not in Hollister. There is less delay in San Benito, and the court is not rushed or overburdened. Yet little of consequence takes place in court. San Benito is still a small society; yet the main function of its Superior Court is to rubber stamp petitions for dissolution of marriage.

---

39. These private transactions are affected by law; they make use of formalities specifically validated by positive law, or they depend on the advice or consent of a lawyer or notary.

This fact allows us to reject the hypothesis that routinization is to be explained by "industrialization" or "urbanization." There is little industry in San Benito, and no real city. But San Benito is part of an urban, industrial *society*. It is not isolated from modern influence. It is an hour's drive from the Bay Area megalopolis. The mass media lace all communities together; people in Hollister watch the same programs, read much the same news, eat much the same food, as people elsewhere in the country. They are part of a common culture.

It is a culture in which there seems to be factors in the structure of courts—and, more fundamentally, in social attitudes—which have combined to make "going to court" obsolete, as part of the normal life-cycle of dispute settlement. We cannot identify these factors precisely. But their influence on the work of the courts is far more powerful than the gross demographic differences between "cities" and "small towns."

Whatever the causes, the figures for these two courts show a general movement from *dispute settlement* to *routine administration* over the past century. We believe this is a national phenomenon, too. It is a development which may pose problems for society. No doubt courts are still very useful, in a number of ways; but they are almost totally unused by ordinary individuals to resolve *personal* problems. The overwhelming majority of business disputes also avoid the courts. Citizen and businessmen alike either seek out some other agency, or make use of resources within the family, group, or trade association—or, as is frequently the case, handle the matter entirely on their own.[40] The judicial system is often elaborately praised. The praise rings hollow if, as it appears, factors at work militate against the use of the system. We must ask, what are the institutions that have replaced the courts, and how do they operate? And, where no institutions have appeared to fill what may well be a gap, we must ask, what has society gained and lost, as an ancient structure of decision passes into history?

---

40. That is, parties or potential parties may choose to make use of "rival" institutions, such as arbitration. See Britt-Mari P. Blegvad, *et. al.*, *supra*, note 33, or what William Felstiner calls "avoidance." Avoidance is a technique of withdrawal (for example, "consumers switching their trade from one retail merchant to another after a dispute") or it may take the form of "lumping it," where "the salience of the dispute is reduced not so much by limiting the contacts between the disputants, but by ignoring the dispute, by declining to take any or much action in response to the controversy." William L.F. Felstiner, "Influences of Social Organization on Dispute Processing," 9 *Law & Society Review* 63, 76, 81 (1974); see also Richard L. Abel, "A Comparative Theory of Dispute Institutions in Society," 8 *Law & Society Review* 217 (1974).

Part II
Law and the Channelling of Power

[6]

THE PRACTICE OF LAW AS CONFIDENCE GAME

Organizational Cooptation of a Profession

Abraham S. Blumberg

State University of New York at Stony Brook

A RECURRING THEME in the growing dialogue between sociology and law has been the great need for a joint effort of the two disciplines to illuminate urgent social and legal issues. Having uttered fervent public pronouncements in this vein, however, the respective practitioners often go their separate ways. Academic spokesmen for the legal profession are somewhat critical of sociologists of law because of what they perceive as the sociologist's preoccupation with the application of theory and methodology to the examination of legal phenomena, without regard to the solution of legal problems. Further, it is felt that "... contemporary writing in the sociology of law . . . betrays the existence of painfully unsophisticated notions about the day-to-day operations of courts, legislatures and law offices." [1] Regardless of the merit of such criticism,

EDITOR'S NOTE: *In an essay contest sponsored by the Institute on American Freedoms for graduate students in sociology, this article (submitted under the title of: Covert Contingencies in the Right to the Assistance of Counsel) won first prize, in the amount of $1,000, in February 1967.*
AUTHOR'S NOTE: *The article is a revised version of a paper read at the meetings of the American Sociological Association, Miami Beach, Florida, August 30, 1966.*

1. H. W. Jones, *A View From the Bridge,* Law and Society: Supplement to Summer, 1965 Issue of SOCIAL PROBLEMS 42 (1965). See G. Geis, *Sociology, Criminology, and Criminal Law,* 7 SOCIAL PROBLEMS 40–47 (1959) ; N. S. Timasheff, *Growth and Scope of Sociology of Law,* in MODERN SOCIOLOGICAL THEORY IN CONTINUITY AND

LAW AND SOCIETY REVIEW

scant attention—apart from explorations of the legal profession itself—
has been given to the sociological examination of legal institutions, or
their supporting ideological assumptions. Thus, for example, very little
sociological effort is expended to ascertain the validity and viability of
important court decisions, which may rest on wholly erroneous assumptions about the contextual realities of social structure. A particular
decision may rest upon a legally impeccable rationale; at the same time
it may be rendered nugatory or self-defeating by contingencies imposed
by aspects of social reality of which the lawmakers are themselves
unaware.

Within this context, I wish to question the impact of three recent
landmark decisions of the United States Supreme Court; each hailed
as destined to effect profound changes in the future of criminal law
administration and enforcement in America. The first of these, *Gideon
v. Wainwright*, 372 U.S. 335 (1963) required states and localities hence-
forth to furnish counsel in the case of indigent persons charged with
a felony.[2] The Gideon ruling left several major issues unsettled, among
them the vital question: What is the precise point in time at which
a suspect is entitled to counsel?[3] The answer came relatively quickly

CHANGE 424–49 (H. Becker & A. Boskoff, eds. 1957), for further evaluation of the
strained relations between sociology and law.

2. This decision represented the climax of a line of cases which had begun to
chip away at the notion that the Sixth Amendment of the Constitution (right to
assistance of counsel) applied only to the federal government, and could not be held
to run against the states through the Fourteenth Amendment. An exhaustive historical
analysis of the Fourteenth Amendment and the Bill of Rights will be found in C.
Fairman, *Does the Fourteenth Amendment Incorporate the Bill of Rights? The Original
Understanding*, 2 STAN. L. REV. 5–139 (1949). Since the Gideon decision, there is
already evidence that its effect will ultimately extend to indigent persons charged
with misdemeanors—and perhaps ultimately even traffic cases and other minor offenses.
For a popular account of this important development in connection with the right to
assistance of counsel, see A. LEWIS, GIDEON'S TRUMPET (1964). For a scholarly historical analysis of the right to counsel see W. M. BEANEY, THE RIGHT TO COUNSEL IN
AMERICAN COURTS (1955). For a more recent comprehensive review and discussion of
the right to counsel and its development, see Note, *Counsel at Interrogation*, 73 YALE
L.J. 1000–57 (1964).

With the passage of the Criminal Justice Act of 1964, indigent accused persons in
the federal courts will be defended by federally paid legal counsel. For a general discussion of the nature and extent of public and private legal aid in the United States
prior to the Gideon case, see E. A. BROWNELL, LEGAL AID IN THE UNITED STATES (1961);
also R. B. VON MEHREN, et al., EQUAL JUSTICE FOR THE ACCUSED (1959).

3. In the case of federal defendants the issue is clear. In Mallory v. United States,
354 U.S. 449 (1957), the Supreme Court unequivocally indicated that a person under
federal arrest must be taken "without any unnecessary delay" before a U.S. commissioner

THE PRACTICE OF LAW AS CONFIDENCE GAME

in *Escobedo v. Illinois*, 378 U.S. 478 (1964), which has aroused a storm of controversy. Danny Escobedo confessed to the murder of his brother-in-law after the police had refused to permit retained counsel to see him, although his lawyer was present in the station house and asked to confer with his client. In a 5–4 decision, the court asserted that counsel must be permitted when the process of police investigative effort shifts from merely investigatory to that of accusatory: "when its focus is on the accused and its purpose is to elicit a confession—our adversary system begins to operate, and, under the circumstances here, the accused must be permitted to consult with his lawyer."

As a consequence, Escobedo's confession was rendered inadmissible. The decision triggered a national debate among police, district attorneys, judges, lawyers, and other law enforcement officials, which continues unabated, as to the value and propriety of confessions in criminal cases.[4] On June 13, 1966, the Supreme Court in a 5–4 decision underscored the principle enunciated in *Escobedo* in the case of *Miranda v. Arizona*.[5] Police interrogation of any suspect in custody, without his consent, unless a defense attorney is present, is prohibited by the self-incrimination provision of the Fifth Amendment. Regardless of the relative merit of the various shades of opinion about the role of counsel in criminal cases, the issues generated thereby will be in part resolved as additional

---

where he will receive information as to his rights to remain silent and to assistance of counsel which will be furnished, in the event he is indigent, under the Criminal Justice Act of 1964. For a most interesting and richly documented work in connection with the general area of the Bill of Rights, see C. R. SOWLE, POLICE POWER AND INDIVIDUAL FREEDOM (1962).

4. See N.Y. Times, Nov. 20, 1965, p. 1, for Justice Nathan R. Sobel's statement to the effect that based on his study of 1,000 indictments in Brooklyn, N.Y. from February–April, 1965, fewer than 10% involved confessions. Sobel's detailed analysis will be found in six articles which appeared in the New York Law Journal, beginning November 15, 1965, through November 21, 1965, titled *The Exclusionary Rules in the Law of Confessions: A Legal Perspective—A Practical Perspective*. Most law enforcement officials believe that the majority of convictions in criminal cases are based upon confessions obtained by police. For example, the District Attorney of New York County (a jurisdiction which has the largest volume of cases in the United States), Frank S. Hogan, reports that confessions are crucial and indicates "if a suspect is entitled to have a lawyer during preliminary questioning . . . any lawyer worth his fee will tell him to keep his mouth shut", N.Y. Times, Dec. 2, 1965, p. 1. Concise discussions of the issue are to be found in D. Robinson, Jr., *Massiah, Escobedo and Rationales For the Exclusion of Confessions*, 56 J. CRIM. L. C. & P.S. 412-31 (1965) ; D. C. Dowling, *Escobedo and Beyond: The Need for a Fourteenth Amendment Code of Criminal Procedure*, 56 J. CRIM. L. C. & P.S. 143-57 (1965).

5. Miranda v. Arizona, 384 U.S. 436 (1966).

LAW AND SOCIETY REVIEW

cases move toward decision in the Supreme Court in the near future. They are of peripheral interest and not of immediate concern in this paper. However, the *Gideon, Escobedo,* and *Miranda* cases pose interesting general questions. In all three decisions, the Supreme Court reiterates the traditional legal conception of a defense lawyer based on the ideological perception of a criminal case as an *adversary, combative* proceeding, in which counsel for the defense assiduously musters all the admittedly limited resources at his command to *defend* the accused.[6] The fundamental question remains to be answered: Does the Supreme Court's conception of the role of counsel in a criminal case square with social reality?

The task of this paper is to furnish some preliminary evidence toward the illumination of that question. Little empirical understanding of the function of defense counsel exists; only some ideologically oriented generalizations and commitments. This paper is based upon observations made by the writer during many years of legal practice in the criminal courts of a large metropolitan area. No claim is made as to its methodological rigor, although it does reflect a conscious and sustained effort for participant observation.

COURT STRUCTURE DEFINES ROLE OF DEFENSE LAWYER

The overwhelming majority of convictions in criminal cases (usually over 90 per cent) are not the product of a combative, trial-by-jury process at all, but instead merely involve the sentencing of the individual after a negotiated, bargained-for plea of guilty has been entered.[7]

---

6. Even under optimal circumstances a criminal case is a very much one-sided affair, the parties to the "contest" being decidedly unequal in strength and resources. See A. S. Goldstein, *The State and the Accused: Balance of Advantage in Criminal Procedure,* 69 YALE L.J. 1149–99 (1960).

7. F. J. DAVIS et al., SOCIETY AND THE LAW: NEW MEANINGS FOR AN OLD PROFESSION 301 (1962); L. ORFIELD, CRIMINAL PROCEDURE FROM ARREST TO APPEAL 297 (1947).

D. J. Newman, *Pleading Guilty for Considerations: A Study of Bargain Justice,* 46 J. CRIM. L. C. & P.S. 780–90 (1954). Newman's data covered only one year, 1954, in a midwestern community, however, it is in general confirmed by my own data drawn from a far more populous area, and from what is one of the major criminal courts in the country, for a period of fifteen years from 1950 to 1964 inclusive. The English experience tends also to confirm American data, see N. WALKER, CRIME AND PUNISHMENT IN BRITAIN: AN ANALYSIS OF THE PENAL SYSTEM (1965). See also D. J. NEWMAN, CONVICTION: THE DETERMINATION OF GUILT OR INNOCENCE WITHOUT TRIAL (1966),

THE PRACTICE OF LAW AS CONFIDENCE GAME

Although more recently the overzealous role of police and prosecutors in producing pretrial confessions and admissions has achieved a good deal of notoriety, scant attention has been paid to the organizational structure and personnel of the criminal court itself. Indeed, the extremely high conviction rate produced without the features of an adversary trial in our courts would tend to suggest that the "trial" becomes a perfunctory reiteration and validation of the pretrial interrogation and investigation.[8]

The institutional setting of the court defines a role for the defense counsel in a criminal case radically different from the one traditionally depicted.[9] Sociologists and others have focused their attention on the deprivations and social disabilities of such variables as race, ethnicity, and social class as being the source of an accused person's defeat in a criminal court. Largely overlooked is the variable of the court organization itself, which possesses a thrust, purpose, and direction of its own. It is grounded in pragmatic values, bureaucratic priorities, and administrative instruments. These exalt maximum production and the particularistic career designs of organizational incumbents, whose occupational and career commitments tend to generate a set of priorities. These priorities exert a higher claim than the stated ideological goals of "due process of law," and are often inconsistent with them.

Organizational goals and discipline impose a set of demands and conditions of practice on the respective professions in the criminal court, to which they respond by abandoning their ideological and professional commitments to the accused client, in the service of these higher claims of the court organization. All court personnel, including the

---

for a comprehensive legalistic study of the guilty plea sponsored by the American Bar Foundation. The criminal court as a social system, an analysis of "bargaining" and its functions in the criminal court's organizational structure, are examined in my forthcoming book, THE CRIMINAL COURT: A SOCIOLOGICAL PERSPECTIVE, to be published by Quadrangle Books, Chicago.

8. G. FEIFER, JUSTICE IN MOSCOW (1965). The Soviet trial has been termed "an appeal from the pretrial investigation" and Feifer notes that the Soviet "trial" is simply a recapitulation of the data collected by the pretrial investigator. The notions of a trial being a "tabula rasa" and presumptions of innocence are wholly alien to Soviet notions of justice. . . . "the closer the investigation resembles the finished script, the better . . ." *Id.* at 86.

9. For a concise statement of the constitutional and economic aspects of the right to legal assistance, see M. G. PAULSEN, EQUAL JUSTICE FOR THE POOR MAN (1964) ; for a brief traditional description of the legal profession see P. A. Freund, *The Legal Profession*, Daedalus 689–700 (1963).

accused's own lawyer, tend to be coopted to become agent-mediators[10] who help the accused redefine his situation and restructure his perceptions concomitant with a plea of guilty.

Of all the occupational roles in the court the only private individual who is officially recognized as having a special status and concomitant obligations is the lawyer. His legal status is that of "an officer of the court" and he is held to a standard of ethical performance and duty to his client as well as to the court. This obligation is thought to be far higher than that expected of ordinary individuals occupying the various occupational statuses in the court community. However, lawyers, whether privately retained or of the legal-aid, public defender variety, have close and continuing relations with the prosecuting office and the court itself through discreet relations with the judges via their law secretaries or "confidential" assistants. Indeed, lines of communication, influence and contact with those offices, as well as with the Office of the Clerk of the court, Probation Division, and with the press, are essential to present and prospective requirements of criminal law practice. Similarly, the subtle involvement of the press and other mass media in the court's organizational network is not readily discernible to the casual observer. Accused persons come and go in the court system schema, but the structure and its occupational incumbents remain to carry on their respective career, occupational and organizational enterprises. The individual stridencies, tensions, and conflicts a given accused person's case may present to all the participants are overcome, because the formal and informal relations of all the groups in the court setting require it. The probability of continued future relations and interaction must be preserved at all costs.

This is particularly true of the "lawyer regulars" *i.e.*, those defense lawyers, who by virtue of their continuous appearances in behalf of defendants, tend to represent the bulk of a criminal court's non-indigent case workload, and those lawyers who are not "regulars," who appear almost casually in behalf of an occasional client. Some of the "lawyer regulars" are highly visible as one moves about the major urban centers of the nation, their offices line the back streets of the courthouses, at times sharing space with bondsmen. Their political "visibility" in terms of local club house ties, reaching into the judge's chambers and prose-

---

10. I use the concept in the general sense that Erving Goffman employed it in his ASYLUMS: ESSAYS ON THE SOCIAL SITUATION OF MENTAL PATIENTS AND OTHER INMATES (1961).

THE PRACTICE OF LAW AS CONFIDENCE GAME

cutor's office, are also deemed essential to successful practitioners. Previous research has indicated that the "lawyer regulars" make no effort to conceal their dependence upon police, bondsmen, jail personnel. Nor do they conceal the necessity for maintaining intimate relations with all levels of personnel in the court setting as a means of obtaining, maintaining, and building their practice. These informal relations are the *sine qua non* not only of retaining a practice, but also in the negotiation of pleas and sentences.[11]

The client, then, is a secondary figure in the court system as in certain other bureaucratic settings.[12] He becomes a means to other ends of the organization's incumbents. He may present doubts, contingencies, and pressures which challenge existing informal arrangements or disrupt them; but these tend to be resolved in favor of the continuance of the organization and its relations as before. There is a greater community of interest among all the principal organizational structures and their incumbents than exists elsewhere in other settings. The accused's lawyer has far greater professional, economic, intellectual and other ties to the various elements of the court system than he does to his own client. In short, the court is a closed community.

This is more than just the case of the usual "secrets" of bureaucracy which are fanatically defended from an outside view. Even all elements of the press are zealously determined to report on that which will not offend the board of judges, the prosecutor, probation, legal-aid, or other officials, in return for privileges and courtesies granted in the past and to be granted in the future. Rather than any view of the matter in terms of some variation of a "conspiracy" hypothesis, the simple explanation is one of an ongoing system handling delicate tensions, managing the trauma produced by law enforcement and administration, and re-

---

11. A. L. Wood, *Informal Relations in the Practice of Criminal Law*, 62 AM. J. Soc. 48–55 (1956); J. E. CARLIN, LAWYERS ON THEIR OWN 105–09 (1962); R. GOLDFARB, RANSOM—A CRITIQUE OF THE AMERICAN BAIL SYSTEM 114–15 (1965). In connection with relatively recent data as to recruitment to the legal profession, and variables involved in the type of practice engaged in, will be found in J. Ladinsky, *Careers of Lawyers, Law Practice, and Legal Institutions*, 28 AM. Soc. REV. 47–54 (1963). See also S. WARKOV & J. ZELAN, LAWYERS IN THE MAKING (1965).

12. There is a real question to be raised as to whether in certain organizational settings, a complete reversal of the bureaucratic-ideal has not occurred. That is, it would seem, in some instances the organization appears to exist to serve the needs of its various occupational incumbents, rather than its clients. A. ETZIONI, MODERN ORGAN-IZATIONS 94–104 (1964).

quiring almost pathological distrust of "outsiders" bordering on group paranoia.

The hostile attitude toward "outsiders" is in large measure engendered by a defensiveness itself produced by the inherent deficiencies of assembly line justice, so characteristic of our major criminal courts. Intolerably large caseloads of defendants which must be disposed of in an organizational context of limited resources and personnel, potentially subject the participants in the court community to harsh scrutiny from appellate courts, and other public and private sources of condemnation. As a consequence, an almost irreconcilable conflict is posed in terms of intense pressures to process large numbers of cases on the one hand, and the stringent ideological and legal requirements of "due process of law," on the other hand. A rather tenuous resolution of the dilemma has emerged in the shape of a large variety of bureaucratically ordained and controlled "work crimes," short cuts, deviations, and outright rule violations adopted as court practice in order to meet production norms. Fearfully anticipating criticism on ethical as well as legal grounds, all the significant participants in the court's social structure are bound into an organized system of complicity. This consists of a work arrangement in which the patterned, covert, informal breaches, and evasions of "due process" are institutionalized, but are, nevertheless, denied to exist.

These institutionalized evasions will be found to occur to some degree, in all criminal courts. Their nature, scope and complexity are largely determined by the size of the court, and the character of the community in which it is located, *e.g.*, whether it is a large, urban institution, or a relatively small rural county court. In addition, idiosyncratic, local conditions may contribute to a unique flavor in the character and quality of the criminal law's administration in a particular community. However, in most instances a variety of stratagems are employed—some subtle, some crude, in effectively disposing of what are often too large caseloads. A wide variety of coercive devices are employed against an accused-client, couched in a depersonalized, instrumental, bureaucratic version of due process of law, and which are in reality a perfunctory obeisance to the ideology of due process. These include some very explicit pressures which are exerted in some measure by all court personnel, including judges, to plead guilty and avoid trial. In many instances the sanction of a potentially harsh sentence is utilized as the visible alternative to pleading guilty, in the case of

THE PRACTICE OF LAW AS CONFIDENCE GAME

recalcitrants. Probation and psychiatric reports are "tailored" to organizational needs, or are at least responsive to the court organization's requirements for the refurbishment of a defendant's social biography, consonant with his new status. A resourceful judge can, through his subtle domination of the proceedings, impose his will on the final outcome of a trial. Stenographers and clerks, in their function as record keepers, are on occasion pressed into service in support of a judicial need to "rewrite" the record of a courtroom event. Bail practices are usually employed for purposes other than simply assuring a defendant's presence on the date of a hearing in connection with his case. Too often, the discretionary power as to bail is part of the arsenal of weapons available to collapse the resistance of an accused person. The foregoing is a most cursory examination of some of the more prominent "short cuts" available to any court organization. There are numerous other procedural strategies constituting due process deviations, which tend to become the work style artifacts of a court's personnel. Thus, only court "regulars" who are "bound in" are really accepted; others are treated routinely and in almost a coldly correct manner.

The defense attorneys, therefore, whether of the legal-aid, public defender variety, or privately retained, although operating in terms of pressures specific to their respective role and organizational obligations, ultimately are concerned with strategies which tend to lead to a plea. It is the rational, impersonal elements involving economies of time, labor, expense and a superior commitment of the defense counsel to these rationalistic values of maximum production[13] of court organization that prevail, in his relationship with a client. The lawyer "regulars" are frequently former staff members of the prosecutor's office and utilize the prestige, know-how and contacts of their former affiliation as part

---

13. Three relatively recent items reported in the New York Times, tend to underscore this point as it has manifested itself in one of the major criminal courts. In one instance the Bronx County Bar Association condemned "mass assembly-line justice," which "was rushing defendants into pleas of guilty and into convictions, in violation of their legal rights." N.Y. Times, March 10, 1965, p. 51. Another item, appearing somewhat later that year reports a judge criticizing his own court system (the New York Criminal Court), that "pressure to set statistical records in disposing of cases had hurt the administration of justice." N.Y. Times, Nov. 4, 1965, p. 49. A third, and most unusual recent public discussion in the press was a statement by a leading New York appellate judge decrying "instant justice" which is employed to reduce court calendar congestion ". . . converting our courthouses into counting houses . . ., as in most big cities where the volume of business tends to overpower court facilities." N.Y. Times, Feb. 5, 1966, p. 58.

of their stock in trade. Close and continuing relations between the lawyer "regular" and his former colleagues in the prosecutor's office generally overshadow the relationship between the regular and his client. The continuing colleagueship of supposedly adversary counsel rests on real professional and organizational needs of a *quid pro quo,* which goes beyond the limits of an accommodation or *modus vivendi* one might ordinarily expect under the circumstances of an otherwise seemingly adversary relationship. Indeed, the adversary features which are manifest are for the most part muted and exist even in their attenuated form largely for external consumption. The principals, lawyer and assistant district attorney, rely upon one another's cooperation for their continued professional existence, and so the bargaining between them tends usually to be "reasonable" rather than fierce.

FEE COLLECTION AND FIXING

The real key to understanding the role of defense counsel in a criminal case is to be found in the area of the fixing of the fee to be charged and its collection. The problem of fixing and collecting the fee tends to influence to a significant degree the criminal court process itself, and not just the relationship of the lawyer and his client. In essence, a lawyer-client "confidence game" is played. A true confidence game is unlike the case of the emperor's new clothes wherein that monarch's nakedness was a result of inordinate gullibility and credulity. In a genuine confidence game, the perpetrator manipulates the basic dishonesty of his partner, the victim or mark, toward his own (the confidence operator's) ends. Thus, "the victim of a con scheme must have some larceny in his heart." [14]

Legal service lends itself particularly well to confidence games. Usually, a plumber will be able to demonstrate empirically that he has performed a service by clearing up the stuffed drain, repairing the leaky faucet or pipe—and therefore merits his fee. He has rendered, when summoned, a visible, tangible boon for his client in return for the requested fee. A physician, who has not performed some visible surgery or otherwise engaged in some readily discernible procedure in connection with a patient, may be deemed by the patient to have "done nothing" for him. As a consequence, medical practitioners may simply

---

14. R. L. Gasser, *The Confidence Game,* 27 FED. PROB. 47 (1963).

The Practice of Law as Confidence Game

prescribe or administer by injection a placebo to overcome a patient's potential reluctance or dissatisfaction in paying a requested fee, "for nothing."

In the practice of law there is a special problem in this regard, no matter what the level of the practitioner or his place in the hierarchy of prestige. Much legal work is intangible either because it is simply a few words of advice, some preventive action, a telephone call, negotiation of some kind, a form filled out and filed, a hurried conference with another attorney or an official of a government agency, a letter or opinion written, or a countless variety of seemingly innocuous, and even prosaic procedures and actions. These are the basic activities, apart from any possible court appearance, of almost all lawyers, at all levels of practice. Much of the activity is not in the nature of the exercise of the traditional, precise professional skills of the attorney such as library research and oral argument in connection with appellate briefs, court motions, trial work, drafting of opinions, memoranda, contracts, and other complex documents and agreements. Instead, much legal activity, whether it is at the lowest or highest "white shoe" law firm levels, is of the brokerage, agent, sales representative, lobbyist type of activity, in which the lawyer acts for someone else in pursuing the latter's interests and designs. The service is intangible.[15]

The large scale law firm may not speak as openly of their "contacts," their "fixing" abilities, as does the lower level lawyer. They trade instead upon a facade of thick carpeting, walnut panelling, genteel low pressure, and superficialities of traditional legal professionalism. There are occasions when even the large firm is on the defensive in connection with the fees they charge because the services rendered or results obtained do not appear to merit the fee asked.[16] Therefore, there is a recurrent problem in the legal profession in fixing the amount of fee, and in justifying the basis for the requested fee.

Although the fee at times amounts to what the traffic and the conscience of the lawyer will bear, one further observation must be made with regard to the size of the fee and its collection. The defendant in a criminal case and the material gain he may have acquired during the course of his illicit activities are soon parted. Not infrequently the ill gotten fruits of the various modes of larceny are sequestered by a

---

15. C. W. Mills, White Collar 121-29 (1951); J. E. Carlin *supra*, note 11.
16. E. O. Smigel, The Wall Street Lawyer 309 (1964).

defense lawyer in payment of his fee. Inexorably, the amount of the fee is a function of the dollar value of the crime committed, and is frequently set with meticulous precision at a sum which bears an uncanny relationship to that of the net proceeds of the particular offense involved. On occasion, defendants have been known to commit additional offenses while at liberty on bail, in order to secure the requisite funds with which to meet their obligations for payment of legal fees. Defense lawyers condition even the most obtuse clients to recognize that there is a firm interconnection between fee payment and the zealous exercise of professional expertise, secret knowledge, and organizational "connections" in their behalf. Lawyers, therefore, seek to keep their clients in a proper state of tension, and to arouse in them the precise edge of anxiety which is calculated to encourage prompt fee payment. Consequently, the client attitude in the relationship between defense counsel and an accused is in many instances a precarious admixture of hostility, mistrust, dependence, and sycophancy. By keeping his client's anxieties aroused to the proper pitch, and establishing a seemingly causal relationship between a requested fee and the accused's ultimate extrication from his onerous difficulties, the lawyer will have established the necessary preliminary groundwork to assure a minimum of haggling over the fee and its eventual payment.

In varying degrees, as a consequence, all law practice involves a manipulation of the client and a stage management of the lawyer-client relationship so that at least an *appearance* of help and service will be forthcoming. This is accomplished in a variety of ways, often exercised in combination with each other. At the outset, the lawyer-professional employs with suitable variation a measure of sales-puff which may range from an air of unbounding selfconfidence, adequacy, and dominion over events, to that of complete arrogance. This will be supplemented by the affectation of a studied, faultless mode of personal attire. In the larger firms, the furnishings and office trappings will serve as the backdrop to help in impression management and client intimidation. In all firms, solo or large scale, an access to secret knowledge, and to the seats of power and influence is inferred, or presumed to a varying degree as the basic vendible commodity of the practitioners.

The lack of visible end product offers a special complication in the course of the professional life of the criminal court lawyer with respect to his fee and in his relations with his client. The plain fact is that an accused in a criminal case always "loses" even when he has

THE PRACTICE OF LAW AS CONFIDENCE GAME

been exonerated by an acquittal, discharge, or dismissal of his case. The hostility of an accused which follows as a consequence of his arrest, incarceration, possible loss of job, expense and other traumas connected with his case is directed, by means of displacement, toward his lawyer. It is in this sense that it may be said that a criminal lawyer never really "wins" a case. The really satisfied client is rare, since in the very nature of the situation even an accused's vindication leaves him with some degree of dissatisfaction and hostility. It is this state of affairs that makes for a lawyer-client relationship in the criminal court which tends to be a somewhat exaggerated version of the usual lawyer-client confidence game.

At the outset, because there are great risks of nonpayment of the fee, due to the impecuniousness of his clients, and the fact that a man who is sentenced to jail may be a singularly unappreciative client, the criminal lawyer collects his fee *in advance*. Often, because the lawyer and the accused both have questionable designs of their own upon each other, the confidence game can be played. The criminal lawyer must serve three major functions, or stated another way, he must solve three problems. First, he must arrange for his fee; second, he must prepare and then, if necessary, "cool out" his client in case of defeat[17] (a highly likely contingency); third, he must satisfy the court organization that he has performed adequately in the process of negotiating the plea, so as to preclude the possibility of any sort of embarrassing incident which may serve to invite "outside" scrutiny.

In assuring the attainment of one of his primary objectives, his fee, the criminal lawyer will very often enter into negotiations with the accused's kin, including collateral relatives. In many instances, the accused himself is unable to pay any sort of fee or anything more than a token fee. It then becomes important to involve as many of the accused's kin as possible in the situation. This is especially so if the attorney hopes to collect a significant part of a proposed substantial fee. It is not uncommon for several relatives to contribute toward the

---

17. Talcott Parsons indicates that the social role and function of the lawyer can be therapeutic, helping his client psychologically in giving him necessary emotional support at critical times. The lawyer is also said to be acting as an agent of social control in the counseling of his client and in the influencing of his course of conduct. See T. PARSONS, ESSAYS IN SOCIOLOGICAL THEORY 382 et seq. (1954); E. Goffman, *On Cooling the Mark Out: Some Aspects of Adaptation to Failure*, in HUMAN BEHAVIOR AND SOCIAL PROCESSES 482–505 (A. Rose ed., 1962). Goffman's "cooling out" analysis is especially relevant in the lawyer-accused client relationship.

fee. The larger the group, the greater the possibility that the lawyer will collect a sizable fee by getting contributions from each.

A fee for a felony case which ultimately results in a plea, rather than a trial, may ordinarily range anywhere from $500 to $1,500. Should the case go to trial, the fee will be proportionately larger, depending upon the length of the trial. But the larger the fee the lawyer wishes to exact, the more impressive his performance must be, in terms of his stage managed image as a personage of great influence and power in the court organization. Court personnel are keenly aware of the extent to which a lawyer's stock in trade involves the precarious stage management of an image which goes beyond the usual professional flamboyance, and for this reason alone the lawyer is "bound in" to the authority system of the court's organizational discipline. Therefore, to some extent, court personnel will aid the lawyer in the creation and maintenance of that impression. There is a tacit commitment to the lawyer by the court organization, apart from formal etiquette, to aid him in this. Such augmentation of the lawyer's stage managed image as this affords, is the partial basis for the *quid pro quo* which exists between the lawyer and the court organization. It tends to serve as the continuing basis for the higher loyalty of the lawyer to the organization; his relationship with his client, in contrast, is transient, ephemeral and often superficial.

DEFENSE LAWYER AS DOUBLE AGENT

The lawyer has often been accused of stirring up unnecessary litigation, especially in the field of negligence. He is said to acquire a vested interest in a cause of action or claim which was initially his client's. The strong incentive of possible fee motivates the lawyer to promote litigation which would otherwise never have developed. However, the criminal lawyer develops a vested interest of an entirely different nature in his client's case: to limit its scope and duration rather than do battle. Only in this way can a case be "profitable." Thus, he enlists the aid of relatives not only to assure payment of his fee, but he will also rely on these persons to help him in his agent-mediator role of convincing the accused to plead guilty, and ultimately to help in "cooling out" the accused if necessary.

It is at this point that an accused-defendant may experience his first sense of "betrayal." While he had perhaps perceived the police and prosecutor to be adversaries, or possibly even the judge, the accused

THE PRACTICE OF LAW AS CONFIDENCE GAME

is wholly unprepared for his counsel's role performance as an agent-mediator. In the same vein, it is even less likely to occur to an accused that members of his own family or other kin may become agents, albeit at the behest and urging of other agents or mediators, acting on the principle that they are in reality helping an accused negotiate the best possible plea arrangement under the circumstances. Usually, it will be the lawyer who will activate next of kin in this role, his ostensible motive being to arrange for his fee. But soon latent and unstated motives will assert themselves, with entreaties by counsel to the accused's next of kin, to appeal to the accused to "help himself" by pleading. *Gemeinschaft* sentiments are to this extent exploited by a defense lawyer (or even at times by a district attorney) to achieve specific secular ends, that is, of concluding a particular matter with all possible dispatch.

The fee is often collected in stages, each installment usually payable prior to a necessary court appearance required during the course of an accused's career journey. At each stage, in his interviews and communications with the accused, or in addition, with members of his family, if they are helping with the fee payment, the lawyer employs an air of professional confidence and "inside-dopesterism" in order to assuage anxieties on all sides. He makes the necessary bland assurances, and in effect manipulates his client, who is usually willing to do and say the things, true or not, which will help his attorney extricate him. Since the dimensions of what he is essentially selling, organizational influence and expertise, are not technically and precisely measurable, the lawyer can make extravagant claims of influence and secret knowledge with impunity. Thus, lawyers frequently claim to have inside knowledge in connection with information in the hands of the D.A., police, probation officials or to have access to these functionaries. Factually, they often do, and need only to exaggerate the nature of their relationships with them to obtain the desired effective impression upon the client. But, as in the genuine confidence game, the victim who has participated is loathe to do anything which will upset the lesser plea which his lawyer has "conned" him into accepting.[18]

---

18. The question has never been raised as to whether "bargain justice," "copping a plea," or justice by negotiation is a constitutional process. Although it has become the most central aspect of the process of criminal law administration, it has received virtually no close scrutiny by the appellate courts. As a consequence, it is relatively free of legal control and supervision. But, apart from any questions of the legality of bargaining, in terms of the pressures and devices that are employed which tend to violate due process of law, there remain ethical and practical questions. The system

In effect, in his role as double agent, the criminal lawyer performs an extremely vital and delicate mission for the court organization and the accused. Both principals are anxious to terminate the litigation with a minimum of expense and damage to each other. There is no other personage or role incumbent in the total court structure more strategically located, who by training and in terms of his own requirements, is more ideally suited to do so than the lawyer. In recognition of this, judges will cooperate with attorneys in many important ways. For example, they will adjourn the case of an accused in jail awaiting plea or sentence if the attorney requests such action. While explicitly this may be done for some innocuous and seemingly valid reason, the tacit purpose is that pressure is being applied by the attorney for the collection of his fee, which he knows will probably not be forthcoming if the case is concluded. Judges are aware of this tactic on the part of lawyers, who, by requesting an adjournment, keep an accused incarcerated awhile longer as a not too subtle method of dunning a client for payment. However, the judges will go along with this, on the ground that important ends are being served. Often, the only end served is to protect a lawyer's fee.

The judge will help an accused's lawyer in still another way. He will lend the official aura of his office and courtroom so that a lawyer can stage manage an impression of an "all out" performance for the accused in justification of his fee. The judge and other court personnel will serve as a backdrop for a scene charged with dramatic fire, in which the accused's lawyer makes a stirring appeal in his behalf. With a show of restrained passion, the lawyer will intone the virtues of the accused and recite the social deprivations which have reduced him to his present state. The speech varies somewhat, depending on whether the accused has been convicted after trial or has pleaded guilty. In the main, however, the incongruity, superficiality, and ritualistic character of the total performance is underscored by a visibly impassive, almost bored reaction on the part of the judge and other members of the court retinue.

Afterward, there is a hearty exchange of pleasantries between the lawyer and district attorney, wholly out of context in terms of the sup-

---

of bargain-counter justice is like the proverbial iceberg, much of its danger is concealed in secret negotiations and its least alarming feature, the final plea, being the one presented to public view. See A. S. TREBACH, THE RATIONING OF JUSTICE 74–94 (1964); Note, *Guilty Plea Bargaining: Compromises by Prosecutors to Secure Guilty Pleas*, 112 U. PA. L. REV. 865–95 (1964).

THE PRACTICE OF LAW AS CONFIDENCE GAME

posed adversary nature of the preceding events. The fiery passion in defense of his client is gone, and the lawyers for both sides resume their offstage relations, chatting amiably and perhaps including the judge in their restrained banter. No other aspect of their visible conduct so effectively serves to put even a casual observer on notice, that these individuals have claims upon each other. These seemingly innocuous actions are indicative of continuing organizational and informal relations, which, in their intricacy and depth, range far beyond any priorities or claims a particular defendant may have.[19]

Criminal law practice is a unique form of private law practice since it really only appears to be private practice.[20] Actually it is bureaucratic practice, because of the legal practitioner's enmeshment in the authority, discipline, and perspectives of the court organization. Private practice, supposedly, in a professional sense, involves the maintenance of an organized, disciplined body of knowledge and learning; the individual practitioners are imbued with a spirit of autonomy and service, the earning of a livelihood being incidental. In the sense that the lawyer in the criminal court serves as a double agent, serving higher organizational rather than professional ends, he may be deemed to be engaged in bureaucratic rather than private practice. To some extent the lawyer-client "confidence game," in addition to its other functions, serves to conceal this fact.

---

19. For a conventional summary statement of some of the inevitable conflicting loyalties encountered in the practice of law, see E. E. CHEATHAM, CASES AND MATERIALS ON THE LEGAL PROFESSION 70–79 (2d ed. 1955).

20. Some lawyers at either end of the continuum of law practice appear to have grave doubts as to whether it is indeed a profession at all. J. E. Carlin, *op. cit. supra* note 11, at 192; E. O. Smigel *supra*, note 16, at 304–305. Increasingly, it is perceived as a business with widespread evasion of the Canons of Ethics, duplicity and chicanery being practiced in an effort to get and keep business. The poet, Carl Sandburg, epitomized this notion in the following vignette: "Have you a criminal lawyer in this burg?" "We think so but we haven't been able to prove it on him." C. SANDBURG, THE PEOPLE, YES 154 (1936).

Thus, while there is a considerable amount of dishonesty present in law practice involving fee splitting, thefts from clients, influence peddling, fixing, questionable use of favors and gifts to obtain business or influence others, this sort of activity is most often attributed to the "solo," private practice lawyer. See A. L. Wood, *Professional Ethics Among Criminal Lawyers*, SOCIAL PROBLEMS 70–83 (1959). However, to some degree, large scale "downtown" elite firms also engage in these dubious activities. The difference is that the latter firms enjoy a good deal of immunity from these harsh charges because of their institutional and organizational advantages, in terms of near monopoly over more desirable types of practice, as well as exerting great influence in the political, economic and professional realms of power.

THE CLIENT'S PERCEPTION

The "cop-out" ceremony, in which the court process culminates, is not only invaluable for redefining the accused's perspectives of himself, but also in reiterating publicly in a formally structured ritual the accused person's guilt for the benefit of significant "others" who are observing. The accused not only is made to assert publicly his guilt of a specific crime, but also a complete recital of its details. He is further made to indicate that he is entering his plea of guilt freely, willingly, and voluntarily, and that he is not doing so because of any promises or in consideration of any commitments that may have been made to him by anyone. This last is intended as a blanket statement to shield the participants from any possible charges of "coercion" or undue influence that may have been exerted in violation of due process requirements. Its function is to preclude any later review by an appellate court on these grounds, and also to obviate any second thoughts an accused may develop in connection with his plea.

However, for the accused, the conception of self as a guilty person is in large measure a temporary role adaptation. His career socialization as an accused, if it is successful, eventuates in his acceptance and redefinition of himself as a guilty person.[21] However, the transformation is ephemeral, in that he will, in private, quickly reassert his innocence. Of importance is that he accept his defeat, publicly proclaim it, and find some measure of pacification in it.[22] Almost immediately after his

---

21. This does not mean that most of those who plead guilty are innocent of any crime. Indeed, in many instances those who have been able to negotiate a lesser plea, have done so willingly and even eagerly. The system of justice-by-negotiation, without trial, probably tends to better serve the interests and requirements of guilty persons, who are thereby presented with formal alternatives of "half a loaf," in terms of, at worst, possibilities of a lesser plea and a concomitant shorter sentence as compensation for their acquiescence and participation. Having observed the prescriptive etiquette in compliance with the defendant role expectancies in this setting, he is rewarded. An innocent person, on the other hand, is confronted with the same set of role prescriptions, structures and legal alternatives, and in any event, for him this mode of justice is often an ineluctable bind.

22. "Any communicative network between persons whereby the public identity of an actor is transformed into something looked on as lower in the local scheme of social types will be called a 'status degradation ceremony.'" H. Garfinkel, *Conditions of Successful Degradation Ceremonies*, 61 AM. J. Soc. 420–24 (1956). But contrary to the conception of the "cop out" as a "status degradation ceremony," is the fact that it is in reality a charade, during the course of which an accused must project an appropriate and acceptable amount of guilt, penitence and remorse. Having adequately

The Practice of Law as Confidence Game

plea, a defendant will generally be interviewed by a representative of the probation division in connection with a presentence report which is to be prepared. The very first question to be asked of him by the probation officer is: "Are you guilty of the crime to which you pleaded?" This is by way of double affirmation of the defendant's guilt. Should the defendant now begin to make bold assertions of his innocence, despite his plea of guilty, he will be asked to withdraw his plea and stand trial on the original charges. Such a threatened possibility is, in most instances, sufficient to cause an accused to let the plea stand and to request the probation officer to overlook his exclamations of innocence. The table that follows is a breakdown of the categorized responses of a random sample of male defendants in Metropolitan Court[23] during 1962, 1963, and 1964 in connection with their statements during presentence probation interviews following their plea of guilty.

It would be well to observe at the outset, that of the 724 defendants who pleaded guilty before trial, only 43 (5.94 per cent) of the total group had confessed prior to their indictment. Thus, the ultimate judicial process was predicated upon evidence independent of any confession of the accused.[24]

As the data indicate, only a relatively small number (95) out of the total number of defendants actually will even admit their guilt, following the "cop-out" ceremony. However, even though they have

---

feigned the role of the "guilty person," his hearers will engage in the fantasy that he is contrite, and thereby merits a lesser plea. It is one of the essential functions of the criminal lawyer that he coach and direct his accused-client in that role performance. Thus, what is actually involved is not a "degradation" process at all, but is instead, a highly structured system of exchange cloaked in the rituals of legalism and public professions of guilt and repentance.

23. The name is of course fictitious. However, the actual court which served as the universe from which the data were drawn, is one of the largest criminal courts in the United States, dealing with felonies only. Female defendants in the years 1950 through 1964 constituted from 7–10% of the totals for each year.

24. My own data in this connection would appear to support Sobel's conclusion (see note 4 *supra*), and appears to be at variance with the prevalent view, which stresses the importance of confessions in law enforcement and prosecution. All the persons in my sample were originally charged with felonies ranging from homicide to forgery; in most instances the original felony charges were reduced to misdemeanors by way of a negotiated lesser plea. The vast range of crime categories which are available, facilitates the patterned court process of plea reduction to a lesser offense, which is also usually a socially less opprobious crime. For an illustration of this feature of the bargaining process in a court utilizing a public defender office, see D. Sudnow, *Normal Crimes: Sociological Features of the Penal Code in a Public Defender Office,* 12 Social Problems 255–76 (1964).

LAW AND SOCIETY REVIEW

TABLE 1

Defendant Responses as to Guilt or Innocence After Pleading Guilty

N = 724   Years — 1962, 1963, 1964

NATURE OF RESPONSE		N OF DEFENDANTS
INNOCENT (Manipulated)	"The lawyer or judge, police or D.A. 'conned me' "	86
INNOCENT (Pragmatic)	"Wanted to get it over with" "You can't beat the system" "They have you over a barrel when you have a record"	147
INNOCENT (Advice of counsel)	"Followed my lawyer's advice"	92
INNOCENT (Defiant)	"Framed"— Betrayed by "Complainant," "Police," "Squealers," "Lawyer," "Friends," "Wife," "Girlfriend"	33
INNOCENT (Adverse social data)	Blames probation officer or psychiatrist for "Bad Report," in cases where there was pre-pleading investigation	15
GUILTY	"But I should have gotten a better deal" Blames lawyer, D.A., Police, Judge	74
GUILTY	Won't say anything further	21
FATALISTIC (Doesn't press his "Innocence," won't admit "Guilt")	"I did it for convenience" "My lawyer told me it was only thing I could do" "I did it because it was the best way out"	248
NO RESPONSE		8
TOTAL		724

affirmed their guilt, many of these defendants felt that they should have been able to negotiate a more favorable plea. The largest aggregate of defendants (373) were those who reasserted their "innocence" following their public profession of guilt during the "cop-out" ceremony. These defendants employed differential degrees of fervor, solemnity and credibility, ranging from really mild, wavering assertions of innocence which were embroidered with a variety of stock explanations and rationalizations, to those of an adamant, "framed" nature. Thus, the "Innocent" group, for the most part, were largely concerned with under-

THE PRACTICE OF LAW AS CONFIDENCE GAME

scoring for their probation interviewer their essential "goodness" and "worthiness," despite their formal plea of guilty. Assertion of his innocence at the post plea stage, resurrects a more respectable and acceptable self concept for the accused defendant who has pleaded guilty. A recital of the structural exigencies which precipitated his plea of guilt, serves to embellish a newly proffered claim of innocence, which many defendants mistakenly feel will stand them in good stead at the time of sentence, or ultimately with probation or parole authorities.

Relatively few (33) maintained their innocence in terms of having been "framed" by some person or agent-mediator, although a larger number (86) indicated that they had been manipulated or "conned" by an agent-mediator to plead guilty, but as indicated, their assertions of innocence were relatively mild.

A rather substantial group (147) preferred to stress the pragmatic aspects of their plea of guilty. They would only perfunctorily assert their innocence and would in general refer to some adverse aspect of their situation which they believed tended to negatively affect their bargaining leverage, including in some instances a prior criminal record.

One group of defendants (92), while maintaining their innocence, simply employed some variation of a theme of following "the advice of counsel" as a covering response, to explain their guilty plea in the light of their new affirmation of innocence.

The largest single group of defendants (248) were basically fatalistic. They often verbalized weak suggestions of their innocence in rather halting terms, wholly without conviction. By the same token, they would not admit guilt readily and were generally evasive as to guilt or innocence, preferring to stress aspects of their stoic submission in their decision to plead. This sizable group of defendants appeared to perceive the total court process as being caught up in a monstrous organizational apparatus, in which the defendant role expectancies were not clearly defined. Reluctant to offend anyone in authority, fearful that clear cut statements on their part as to their guilt or innocence would be negatively construed, they adopted a stance of passivity, resignation and acceptance. Interestingly, they would in most instances invoke their lawyer as being the one who crystallized the available alternatives for them, and who was therefore the critical element in their decision-making process.

In order to determine which agent-mediator was most influential in altering the accused's perspectives as to his decision to plead or go

LAW AND SOCIETY REVIEW

to trial (regardless of the proposed basis of the plea), the same sample of defendants were asked to indicate the person who first suggested to them that they plead guilty. They were also asked to indicate which of the persons or officials who made such suggestion, was most influential in affecting their final decision to plead.

The following table indicates the breakdown of the responses to the two questions:

TABLE 2

Role of Agent-Mediators in Defendant's Guilty Plea

PERSON OR OFFICIAL	FIRST SUGGESTED PLEA OF GUILTY	INFLUENCED THE ACCUSED MOST IN HIS FINAL DECISION TO PLEAD
JUDGE	4	26
DISTRICT ATTORNEY	67	116
DEFENSE COUNSEL	407	411
PROBATION OFFICER	14	3
PSYCHIATRIST	8	1
WIFE	34	120
FRIENDS AND KIN	21	14
POLICE	14	4
FELLOW INMATES	119	14
OTHERS	28	5
NO RESPONSE	8	10
TOTAL	724	724

It is popularly assumed that the police, through forced confessions, and the district attorney, employing still other pressures, are most instrumental in the inducement of an accused to plead guilty.[25] As Table 2 indicates, it is actually the defendant's own counsel who is

---

25. Failures, shortcomings and oppressive features of our system of criminal justice have been attributed to a variety of sources including "lawless" police, overzealous district attorneys, "hanging" juries, corruption and political connivance, incompetent judges, inadequacy or lack of counsel, and poverty or other social disabilities of the defendant. See A. BARTH, LAW ENFORCEMENT VERSUS THE LAW (1963), for a journalist's account embodying this point of view; J. H. SKOLNICK, JUSTICE WITHOUT TRIAL: LAW ENFORCEMENT IN DEMOCRATIC SOCIETY (1966), for a sociologist's study of the role of the police in criminal law administration. For a somewhat more detailed, albeit legalistic and somewhat technical discussion of American police procedures, see W. R. LaFAVE, ARREST: THE DECISION TO TAKE A SUSPECT INTO CUSTODY (1965).

THE PRACTICE OF LAW AS CONFIDENCE GAME

most effective in this role. Further, this phenomenon tends to reinforce the extremely rational nature of criminal law administration, for an organization could not rely upon the sort of idiosyncratic measures employed by the police to induce confessions and maintain its efficiency, high production and overall rational-legal character. The defense counsel becomes the ideal agent-mediator since, as "officer of the court" and confidant of the accused and his kin, he lives astride both worlds and can serve the ends of the two as well as his own.[26]

While an accused's wife, for example, may be influential in making him more amenable to a plea, her agent-mediator role has, nevertheless, usually been sparked and initiated by defense counsel. Further, although a number of first suggestions of a plea came from an accused's fellow jail inmates, he tended to rely largely on his counsel as an ultimate source of influence in his final decision. The defense counsel, being a crucial figure in the total organizational scheme in constituting a new set of perspectives for the accused, the same sample of defendants were asked to indicate at which stage of their contact with counsel was the suggestion of a plea made. There are three basic kinds of defense counsel available in Metropolitan Court: Legal-aid, privately retained counsel, and counsel assigned by the court (but may eventually be privately retained by the accused).

TABLE 3

Stage at Which Counsel Suggested Accused to Plead

N = 724

CONTACT	COUNSEL TYPE							
	PRIVATELY RETAINED		LEGAL-AID		ASSIGNED		TOTAL	
	N	%	N	%	N	%	N	%
FIRST	66	35	237	49	28	60	331	46
SECOND	83	44	142	29	8	17	233	32
THIRD	29	15	63	13	4	9	96	13
FOURTH OR MORE	12	6	31	7	5	11	48	7
NO RESPONSE	0	0	14	3	2	4	16	2
TOTAL	190	100	487	101*	47	101*	724	100

* Rounded percentage.

26. Aspects of the lawyer's ambivalences with regard to the expectancies of the various groups who have claims upon him, are discussed in H. J. O'Gorman, *The Ambivalence of Lawyers*, paper presented at the Eastern Sociological Association meetings, April 10, 1965.

LAW AND SOCIETY REVIEW

The overwhelming majority of accused persons, regardless of type of counsel, related a specific incident which indicated an urging or suggestion, either during the course of the first or second contact, that they plead guilty to a lesser charge if this could be arranged. Of all the agent-mediators, it is the lawyer who is most effective in manipulating an accused's perspectives, notwithstanding pressures that may have been previously applied by police, district attorney, judge or any of the agent-mediators that may have been activated by them. Legal-aid and assigned counsel would apparently be more likely to suggest a possible plea at the point of initial interview as response to pressures of time. In the case of the assigned counsel, the strong possibility that there is no fee involved, may be an added impetus to such a suggestion at the first contact.

In addition, there is some further evidence in Table 3 of the perfunctory, ministerial character of the system in Metropolitan Court and similar criminal courts. There is little real effort to individualize, and the lawyer's role as agent-mediator may be seen as unique in that he is in effect a double agent. Although, as "officer of the court" he mediates between the court organization and the defendant, his roles with respect to each are rent by conflicts of interest. Too often these must be resolved in favor of the organization which provides him with the means for his professional existence. Consequently, in order to reduce the strains and conflicts imposed in what is ultimately an over-demanding role obligation for him, the lawyer engages in the lawyer-client "confidence game" so as to structure more favorably an otherwise onerous role system.[27]

CONCLUSION

Recent decisions of the Supreme Court, in the area of criminal law administration and defendant's rights, fail to take into account three crucial aspects of social structure which may tend to render the more libertarian rules as nugatory. The decisions overlook (1) the nature of courts as formal organization; (2) the relationship that the lawyer-regular *actually* has with the court organization; and (3) the character of the lawyer-client relationship in the criminal court (the routine rela-

---

27. W. J. Goode, *A Theory of Role Strain*, 25 AM. Soc. REV. 483–96 (1960); J. D. Snoek, *Role Strain in Diversified Role Sets*, 71 AM. J. Soc. 363–72 (1966).

THE PRACTICE OF LAW AS CONFIDENCE GAME

tionships, not those unusual ones that are described in "heroic" terms in novels, movies, and TV).

Courts, like many other modern large-scale organizations possess a monstrous appetite for the cooptation of entire professional groups as well as individuals.[28] Almost all those who come within the ambit of organizational authority, find that their definitions, perceptions and values have been refurbished, largely in terms favorable to the particular organization and its goals. As a result, recent Supreme Court decisions may have a long range effect which is radically different from that intended or anticipated. The more libertarian rules will tend to produce the rather ironic end result of augmenting the *existing* organizational arrangements, enriching court organizations with more personnel and elaborate structure, which in turn will maximize organizational goals of "efficiency" and production. Thus, many defendants will find that courts will possess an even more sophisticated apparatus for processing them toward a guilty plea!

---

28. Some of the resources which have become an integral part of our courts, *e.g.*, psychiatry, social work and probation, were originally intended as part of an ameliorative, therapeutic effort to individualize offenders. However, there is some evidence that a quite different result obtains, than the one originally intended. The ameliorative instruments have been coopted by the court in order to more "efficiently" deal with a court's caseload, often to the legal disadvantage of an accused person. See F. A. ALLEN, THE BORDERLAND OF CRIMINAL JUSTICE (1964); T. S. SZASZ, LAW, LIBERTY AND PSYCHIATRY (1963) and also Szasz's most recent, PSYCHIATRIC JUSTICE (1965); L. Diana, *The Rights of Juvenile Delinquents: An Appraisal of Juvenile Court Procedures,* 47 J. CRIM. L. C. & P.S. 561–69 (1957).

[7]

WHY THE "HAVES" COME OUT AHEAD: SPECULATIONS ON THE LIMITS OF LEGAL CHANGE*

MARC GALANTER

This essay attempts to discern some of the general features of a legal system like the American by drawing on (and rearranging) commonplaces and less than systematic gleanings from the literature. The speculative and tentative nature of the assertions here will be apparent and is acknowledged here wholesale to spare myself and the reader repeated disclaimers.

I would like to try to put forward some conjectures about the way in which the basic architecture of the legal system creates and limits the possibilities of using the system as a means of redistributive (that is, systemically equalizing) change. Our question, specifically, is, under what conditions can litigation[1] be redistributive. taking litigation in the broadest sense of the presentation of claims to be decided by courts (or court-like

---

* This essay grew out of a presentation to Robert Stevens' Seminar on the Legal Profession and Social Change at Yale Law School in the autumn of 1970. while the author was Senior Fellow in the School's Law and Modernization Program. It has gathered bulk and I hope substance in the course of a succession of presentations and revisions. It has accumulated a correspondingly heavy burden of obligation to my colleagues and students. I would like to acknowledge the helpful comments of Richard Abel. James Atleson, Guido Calabresi, Kenneth Davidson. Vernon Dibble. William L.F. Felstiner. Lawrence M. Friedman. Marjorie Girth. Paul Goldstein, Mark Haller. Stephen Halpern. Charles M. Hardin. Adolf Homberger. Geoffrey Hazard. Quintin Johnstone. Patrick L. Kelley, David Kirp. Arthur Leff, Stuart Nagel. Philippe Nonet. Saul Touster, David M. Trubek and Stephen Wasby on earlier drafts, and to confer on them the usual dispensation.

The development of this essay was linked in many places to a contemporaneous project on the Deployment Process in the Implementation of Legal Policy supported by the National Science Foundation. I am grateful to the Foundation for affording me the opportunity to pursue several lines of inquiry touched on here. The Foundation bears no responsibility for the views set forth here.

An earlier version was issued as a working paper of the Law and Modernization Program: yet another version of the first part is contained in the proceedings (edited by Lawrence Friedman and Manfred Rehbinder) of the Conference on the Sociology of the Judicial Process, held at Bielefeld. West Germany in September. 1973.

1. "Litigation" is used here to refer to the pressing of claims oriented to official rules. either by actually invoking official machinery or threatening to do so. Adjudication refers to full-dress individualized and formal application of rules by officials in a particular litigation.

agencies) and the whole penumbra of threats, feints, and so forth, surrounding such presentation.

For purposes of this analysis, let us think of the legal system as comprised of these elements:

A body of authoritative normative learning—for short, RULES

A set of institutional facilities within which the normative learning is applied to specific cases—for short, COURTS

A body of persons with specialized skill in the above—for short, LAWYERS

Persons or groups with claims they might make to the courts in reference to the rules, etc.—for short, PARTIES

Let us also make the following assumptions about the society and the legal system:

It is a society in which actors with different amounts of wealth and power are constantly in competitive or partially cooperative relationships in which they have opposing interests.

This society has a legal system in which a wide range of disputes and conflicts are settled by court-like agencies which purport to apply pre-existing general norms impartially (that is, unaffected by the identity of the parties).

The rules and the procedures of these institutions are complex; wherever possible disputing units employ specialized intermediaries in dealing with them.

The rules applied by the courts are in part worked out in the process of adjudication (courts devise interstitial rules, combine diverse rules, and apply old rules to new situations). There is a living tradition of such rule-work and a system of communication such that the outcomes in some of the adjudicated cases affect the outcome in classes of future adjudicated cases.

Resources on the institutional side are insufficient for timely full-dress adjudication in every case, so that parties are permitted or even encouraged to forego bringing cases and to "settle" cases,—that is, to bargain to a mutually acceptable outcome.

There are several levels of agencies, with "higher" agencies announcing (making, interpreting) rules and other "lower" agencies assigned the responsibility of enforcing (implementing, applying) these rules. (Although there is some overlap of function in both theory and practice, I shall treat them as distinct and refer to them as "peak" and "field level" agencies.)

Not all the rules propounded by "peak" agencies are effective at the "field level," due to imperfections in communication, shortages of resources, skill, understanding, commitment and so forth. (Effectiveness at the field level will be referred to as "penetration."[2])

I. A TYPOLOGY OF PARTIES

Most analyses of the legal system start at the rules end and work down through institutional facilities to see what effect the rules have on the parties. I would like to reverse that procedure and look through the other end of the telescope. Let's think about the different kinds of parties and the effect these differences might have on the way the system works.

Because of differences in their size, differences in the state of the law, and differences in their resources. some of the actors in the society have many occasions to utilize the courts (in the broad sense) to make (or defend) claims; others do so only rarely. We might divide our actors into those claimants who have only occasional recourse to the courts (one-shotters or OS) and repeat players (RP) who are engaged in many similar litigations over time.[3] The spouse in a divorce case, the auto-injury claimant, the criminal accused are OSs; the insurance company, the prosecutor, the finance company are RPs. Obviously this is an oversimplification; there are intermediate cases such as the professional criminal.[4] So we ought to think of OS-RP as a con-

---

2. Cf. Friedman (1969:43) who defines penetration as "the number of actors and spheres of action that a particular rule . . . actually reaches."

3. The discussion here focuses on litigation, but I believe an analagous analysis might be applied to the regulatory and rule-making phases of legal process. OSs and RPs may be found in regulatory and legislative as well as adjudicative settings. The point is nicely epitomized by the observation of one women's movement lobbyist:

> By coming back week after week . . . we tell them not only that we're here, but that we're here to stay. We're not here to scare anybody. . . . The most threatening thing I can say is that we'll be back. *New York Times*, Jan. 29, 1974, p. 34, col. 7-8.

For an interesting example of this distinction in the regulatory arena, see Lobenthal's (1970:20 ff.) description of the regulation of parking near a pier, contrasting the "permanent" shipping company and longshoreman interests with the OS pier visitors, showing how regulation gravitates to the accommodation of the former. This is. of course, akin to the "capture by the regulated" that attends (or afflicts) a variety of administrative agencies. See, e.g., Bernstein (1955); Edelman (1967).

4. Even the taxpayer and the welfare client are not pure OSs. since there is next year's tax bill and next month's welfare check. Our

tinuum rather than as a dichotomous pair. Typically, the RP is a larger unit and the stakes in any given case are smaller (relative to total worth). OSs are usually smaller units and the stakes represented by the tangible outcome of the case may be high relative to total worth, as in the case of injury victim or the criminal accused). Or, the OS may suffer from the opposite problem: his claims may be so small and unmanageable (the shortweighted consumer or the holder of performing rights) that the cost of enforcing them outruns any promise of benefit. See Finklestein (1954: 284-86).

Let us refine our notion of the RP into an "ideal type" if you will—a unit which has had and anticipates repeated litigation, which has low stakes in the outcome of any one case, and which has the resources to pursue its long-run interests.[5] (This does not include every real-world repeat player; that most common repeat player, the alcoholic derelict, enjoys few of the advantages that may accrue to the RP [see below]. His resources are too few to bargain in the short run or take heed of the long run.[6]) An OS, on the other hand, is a unit whose claims are too large (relative to his size) or too small (relative to the cost of remedies) to be managed routinely and rationally.

We would expect an RP to play the litigation game differently from an OS. Let us consider some of his advantages:

(1) RPs, having done it before, have advance intelligence; they are able to structure the next transaction and build a record. It is the RP who writes the form contract, requires the security deposit, and the like.

(2) RPs develop expertise and have ready access to specialists.[7] They enjoy economies of scale and have low start-up costs for any case.[8]

concept of OS conceals the difference between pure OSs—persons such as the accident victim who get in the situation only once—and those who are in a continuing series of transactions (welfare clients or taxpayers) but whose resources permit at most a single crack at litigation.

5. Of course a Repeat Player need not engage in adjudication (or even in litigation). The term includes a party who makes or resists claims which may occupy any sector of the entire range of dispute processing mechanisms discussed in section V below. Perhaps the most successful RPs are those whose antagonists opt for resignation.

6. On the "processing" of these parties and their limited strategic options, see Foote (1956); Spradley (1970: Chap. 6).

7. Ironically, RPs may enjoy access to competent paraprofessional help that is unavailable to OSs. Thus the insurance company can, by employing adjusters, obtain competent and experienced help in routine negotiations without having to resort to expensive professionally qualified personnel. See Ross (1970:25) on the importance of the insurance adjuster in automobile injury settlements.

8. An intriguing example of an RP reaping advantage from a combination of large scale operations and knowledgeability is pro-

(3) RPs have opportunities to develop facilitative informal relations with institutional incumbents.[9]

(4) The RP must establish and maintain credibility as a combatant. His interest in his "bargaining reputation" serves as a resource to establish "commitment" to his bargaining positions. With no bargaining reputation to maintain, the OS has more difficulty in convincingly committing himself in bargaining.[10]

(5) RPs can play the odds.[11] The larger the matter at issue

vided by Skolnick's (1966:174 ff.) account of professional burglars' ability to trade clearances for leniency.

9. See, for example, Jacob's (1969:100) description of creditor colonization of small claims courts:

> ... the neutrality of the judicial process was substantially compromised by the routine relationships which developed between representatives of frequent users of garnishment and the clerk of the court. The clerk scheduled cases so that one or two of the heavy users appeared each day. This enabled the clerk to equalize the work flow of his office. It also consolidated the cases of large creditors and made it unnecessary for them to come to court every day. It appeared that these heavy users and the clerk got to know each other quite well in the course of several months. Although I observed no other evidence of favoritism toward these creditors, it was apparent that the clerk tended to be more receptive toward the version of the conflict told by the creditor than disclosed by the debtor, simply because one was told by a man he knew and the other by a stranger.

The opportunity for regular participants to establish relations of trust and reciprocity with courts is not confined to these lowly precincts. Scigliano (1971:183-84) observes that:

> The Government's success in the Supreme Court seems to owe something . . . to the credit which the Solicitor General's Office has built up with the Court . . . in the first place, by helping the Court manage its great and growing burden of casework. . . . He holds to a trickle what could be a deluge of Government appeals. . . . In the second place by ensuring that the Government's legal work is competently done. So much so that when the Justices or their clerks want to extract the key issues in a complicated case quickly. they turn. according to common report, to the Government's brief.
> [Third.]   The Solicitor General gains further credit . . . by his demonstrations of impartiality and independence from the executive branch.

10. See Ross (1970:156 ff.); Schelling (1963:22 ff., 41). An offsetting advantage enjoyed by some OSs deserves mention. Since he does not anticipate continued dealings with his opponent, an OS can do his damnedest without fear of reprisal next time around or on other issues. (The advantages of those who enjoy the luxury of singlemindedness are evidenced by some notorious examples in the legislative arena, for instance. the success of prohibitionists and of the gun lobby.) Thus there may be a bargaining advantage to the OS who (a) has resources to damage his opponent: (b) is convincingly able to threaten to use them. An OS can burn up his capital. but he has to convince the other side he is really likely to do so. Thus an image of irrationality may be a bargaining advantage. See Ross (1970:170n.); Schelling (1963:17). An OS may be able to sustain such an image in a way that an RP cannot. But cf. Leff (1970a:18) on the role of "spite" in collections and the externalization to specialists of "irrational" vengeance.

11. Ross (1970:214) notes that in dealing with the injury claimant,

looms for OS, the more likely he is to adopt a minimax strategy (minimize the probability of maximum loss). Assuming that the stakes are relatively smaller for RPs, they can adopt strategies calculated to maximize gain over a long series of cases, even where this involves the risk of maximum loss[12] in some cases.[13]

(6) RPs can play for rules as well as immediate gains. First, it pays an RP to expend resources in influencing the making of the relevant rules by such methods as lobbying.[14] (And his accumulated expertise enables him to do this persuasively.)

(7) RPs can also play for rules in litigation itself, whereas an OS is unlikely to. That is, there is a difference in what they regard as a favorable outcome. Because his stakes in the immediate outcome are high and because by definition OS is unconcerned with the outcome of similar litigation in the future, OS will have little interest in that element of the outcome which might influence the disposition of the decision-maker next time around. For the RP, on the other hand, anything that will favorably influence the outcomes of future cases is a worthwhile result. The larger the stake for any player and the lower the probability of repeat play, the less likely that he will be concerned with the rules which govern future cases of the same kind. Consider two parents contesting the custody of their only child, the prizefighter vs. the IRS for tax arrears, the convict facing the death penalty. On the other hand, the player with small stakes in the present case and the prospect of a series of similar cases

---

the insurance adjuster enjoys the advantage of "relative indifference to the uncertainty of litigation . . . the insurance company as a whole in defending large numbers of claims is unaffected by the uncertainty with respect to any one claim. . . . from the claimant's viewpoint [litigation] involves a gamble that may be totally lost. By taking many such gambles in litigating large numbers of cases the insurance company is able to regard the choice between the certainty and the gamble with indifference."

12. That is, not the whole of RPs' worth, but the whole matter at issue in a single claim.

13. Cf. the overpayment of small claims and underpayment of large claims in automobile injury cases. Franklin, Chanin and Mark (1961); Conard, *et al.* (1964). If small claim overpayment can be thought of as the product of the transaction costs of the defendants (and, as Ross [1970:207] shows, organizational pressures to close cases), the large claim underpayment represents the discount for delay and risk on the part of the claimant. (Conard, *et al.* 1964:197-99).

14. Olson's analysis (1965:36ff. 127) suggests that their relatively small number should enhance the capacity of RPs for coordinated action to further common interests. See note 127.

(the IRS. the adoption agency, the prosecutor) may be more interested in the state of the law.

Thus, if we analyze the outcomes of a case into a tangible component and a rule component,[15] we may expect that in case 1, OS will attempt to maximize tangible gain. But if RP is interested in maximizing his tangible gain in a series of cases 1 . . . n, he may be willing to trade off tangible gain in any one case for rule gain (or to minimize rule loss).[16] We assumed that the institutional facilities for litigation were overloaded and settlements were prevalent. We would then expect RPs to "settle" cases where they expected unfavorable rule outcomes.[17] Since they expect to litigate again, RPs can select to adjudicate (or appeal) those cases which they regard as most likely to produce favorable rules.[18] On

---

15. This can be done only where institutions are simultaneously engaged in rule-making and dispute-settling. The rule-making function, however, need not be avowed; all that is required is that the outcome in Case 1 influence the outcome in Case 2 in a way that RP can predict.

16. This is not to imply that rule loss or gain is the main determinant of settlement policy. First, the RP must litigate selectively. He can't fight every case. Second, rules are themselves the subject of dispute relatively rarely. Only a small fraction of litigation involves some disagreement between the parties as to what the rules are or ought to be. Dibble (1973).

   In addition. the very scale that bestows on RPs strategic advantages in settlement policy exposes them to deviations from their goals. Most RPs are organizations and operate through individual incumbents of particular roles (house counsel, claims adjuster, assistant prosecutor) who are subject to pressures which may lead them to deviate from the optimization of institutional goals. Thus Ross (1970:220-21) notes that insurance companies litigate large cases where. although settlement would be "rational" from the overall viewpoint of the company, it would create unacceptable career risk to incumbents. Newman (1966:72) makes a similar observation about prosecutors' offices. He finds that even where the probability of conviction is slim "in cases involving a serious offense which has received a good deal of publicity . . . a prosecutor may prefer to try the case and have the charge reduction or acquittal decision made by the judge or jury."

17. The assumption here is that "settlement" does not have precedent value. Insofar as claimants or their lawyers form a community which shares such information. this factor is diminished—as it is, for example, in automobile injury litigation where, I am told, settlements have a kind of precedent value.

18. Thus the Solicitor General sanctions appeal to the Supreme Court in one-tenth of the appealable defeats of the Government, while its opponents appeal nearly half of their appealable defeats. Scigliano points out that the Government is more selective because:

   In the first place, lower-court defeats usually mean much less to the United States than they do to other parties. In the second place, the government has. as private litigants do not. an independent source of restraint upon the desire to litigate further (1971:169).

   Appellants tend to be winners in the Supreme Court—about two-thirds of cases are decided in their favor. The United States government wins about 70% of the appeals it brings.

   What sets the government apart from other litigants is that

the other hand, OSs should be willing to trade off the
possibility of making "good law" for tangible gain.
Thus, we would expect the body of "precedent" cases—
that is, cases capable of influencing the outcome of future cases—to be relatively skewed toward those favorable to RP.[19]

Of course it is not suggested that the strategic configuration of the parties is the sole or major determinant

it wins a much higher percentage of cases in which it is the
appellee (56% in 1964-66). (1971:178).

Scigliano assigns as reasons for the government's success in the
Supreme Court not only the "government's agreement with the
court on doctrinal position" but the "expertise of the Solicitor General's Office" and "the credit which the Solicitor General has developed with the Court." (1971:182).

More generally, as Rothstein (1974:501) observes:

The large volume litigant is able to achieve the most favorable forum: emphasize different issues in different
courts; take advantage of difference in procedure among
courts at the state and federal level; drop or compromise
unpromising cases without fear of heavy financial loss;
stall some cases and push others; and create rule conflicts
in lower courts to encourage assumption of jurisdiction in
higher courts. Cf. Hazard (1965:68).

19. Macaulay (1966:99-101) in his study of relations between the automobile manufacturers and their dealers recounts that the manufacturers:

. . . had an interest in having the [Good Faith Act] construed to provide standards for their field men's conduct.
Moreover they had resources to devote to the battle. The
amount of money involved might be major to a canceled
dealer, but few, if any cases involved a risk of significant
liability to the manufacturers even if the dealer won. Thus
the manufacturers could afford to fight as long as necessary to get favorable interpretations to set guidelines for
the future. While dealers' attorneys might have to work
on a contingent fee, the manufacturers already had their
own large and competent legal staffs and could afford to
hire trial and appellate specialists. . . . an attorney on a
contingent fee can afford to invest only so much time in a
particular case. Since the manufacturers were interested
in guidelines for the future, they could afford to invest, for
example, $40.000 worth of attorneys' time in a case they
could have settled for $10,000. Moreover, there was the
factor of experience. A dealer's attorney usually started
without any background in arguing a case under the Good
Faith Act. On the other hand, a manufacturer's legal staff
became expert in arguing such a case as it faced a series
of these suits. It could polish its basic brief in case after
case and even influence the company's business practices
—such as record keeping—so that it would be ready for any
suit.

. . . While individual dealers decide whether or not to file
a complaint. the manufacturer. as any fairly wealthy defendant facing a series of related cases, could control the
kinds of cases coming before the courts in which the Good
Faith Act could be construed. It could defend and bring
appeals in those cases where the facts are unfavorable to
the dealer. and it could settle any where the facts favor the
dealer. Since individual dealers were more interested in
money than establishing precedents . . . the manufacturers
in this way were free to control the cases the court would
see.

The net effect . . . was to prompt a sequence of cases
favorable to the manufacturers.

of rule-development. Rule-development is shaped by a relatively autonomous learned tradition, by the impingement of intellectual currents from outside, by the preferences and prudences of the decision-makers. But courts are passive and these factors operate only when the process is triggered by parties. The point here is merely to note the superior opportunities of the RP to trigger promising cases and prevent the triggering of unpromising ones. It is not incompatible with a course of rule-development favoring OSs (or, as indicated below, with OSs failing to get the benefit of those favorable new rules).

In stipiulating that RPs can play for rules, I do not mean to imply that RPs pursue rule-gain as such. If we recall that not all rules penetrate (i.e. ,become effectively applied at the field level) we come to some additional advantages of RPs.

(8) RPs, by virtue of experience and expertise, are more likely to be able to discern which rules are likely to "penetrate" and which are likely to remain merely symbolic commitments. RPs may be able to concentrate their resources on rule-changes that are likely to make a tangible difference. They can trade off symbolic defeats for tangible gains.

(9) Since penetration depends in part on the resources of the parties (knowledge, attentiveness, expert sevices, money), RPs are more likely to be able to invest the matching resources necessary to secure the penetration of rules favorable to them.

It is not suggested that RPs are to be equated with "haves" (in terms of power, wealth and status) or OSs with "have-nots." In the American setting most RPs are larger, richer and more powerful than are most OSs, so these categories overlap, but there are obvious exceptions. RPs may be "have-nots" (alcoholic derelicts) or may act as champions of "have-nots" (as government does from time to time); OSs such as criminal defendants may be wealthy. What this analysis does is to define a position of advantage in the configuration of contending parties and indicate how those with other advantages tend to occupy this position of advantage and to have their other advantages reinforced and augmented thereby.[20] This position of advantage is one of

---

20. Of course. even within the constraints of their strategic position. parties may fare better or worse according to their several capacities to mobilize and utilize legal resources. Nonet (1969: Chap.

the ways in which a legal system formally neutral as between "haves" and "have-nots" may perpetuate and augment the advantages of the former.[21]

Digression on Litigation-mindedness

We have postulated that OSs will be relatively indifferent to the rule-outcomes of particular cases. But one might expect the absolute level of interest in rule-outcomes to vary in different populations: in some there may be widespread and intense concern with securing vindication according to official rules that overshadows interest in the tangible outcomes of disputes: in others rule outcomes may be a matter of relative indifference when compared to tangible outcomes. The level and distribution of such "rule mindedness" may affect the relative strategic position of OSs and RPs. For example, the more rule minded a population, the less we would expect an RP advantage in managing settlement policy.

But such rule mindedness or appetite for official vindication should be distinguished from both (1) readiness to resort to official remedy systems in the first place and (2) high valuation of official rules as symbolic objects. Quite apart from relative concern with rule-outcomes, we might expect populations to differ in their estimates of the propriety and gratification of litigating in the first place.[22] Such atti-

---

IV) refers to this as "legal competence"—that is, the capacity for optimal use of the legal process to pursue one's interests, a capacity which includes information, access, judgment, psychic readiness, and so forth.

An interesting example of the effects of such competence is provided by Rosenthal (1970: Chap. 2) who notes the superior results obtained by "active" personal injury plaintiffs. ("Active" clients are defined as those who express special wants to their attorneys, make follow-up demands for attention, marshall information to aid the lawyer, seek quality medical attention, seek a second legal opinion, and bargain about the fee.) He finds such "active" clients drawn disproportionately from those of higher social status (which presumably provides both the confidence and experience to conduct themselves in this active manner).

The thrust of the argument here is that the distribution of capacity to use the law beneficially cannot be attributed solely or primarily to personal characteristics of parties. The personal qualities that make up competence are themselves systematically related to social structure, both to general systems of stratification and to the degree of specialization of the parties. The emphasis here differs somewhat from that of Nonet, who makes competence central and for whom, for example, organization is one means of enhancing competence. This analysis views personal competence as operating marginally within the framework of the parties' relations to each other and to the litigation process. It is submitted that this reversal permits us to account for systematic differentials of competence and for the differences in the structure of opportunities which face various kinds of parties when personal competence is held constant.

21. The tendency for formal equality to be compatible with domination has been noted by Weber (1954: 188-91) and Ehrlich (1936: 238), who noted "The more the rich and the poor are dealt with according to the same legal propositions, the more the advantage of the rich is increased."

22. Cf. Hahm (1969): Kawashima (1963) for descriptions of cultural settings in which litigation carries high psychic costs. (For the

tudes may affect the strategic situation of the parties. For example, the greater the distaste for litigation in a population, the greater the barriers to OSs pressing or defending claims, and the greater the RP advantages, assuming that

coexistence of anti-litigation attitudes with high rates of litigation, see Kidder [1971].) For a population with a greater propensity to litigate consider the following account (*New York Times*, Oct. 16, 1966) of contemporary Yugoslavia:

> Yugoslavs often complain of a personality characteristic in their neighbors that they call inat, which translates roughly as "spite." . . . One finds countless examples of it chronicled in the press. . . . the case of two neighbors in the village of Pomoravije who had been suing each other for 30 years over insults began when one "gave a dirty look" to the other's pet dog.

> Last year the second district court in Belgrade was presented with 9000 suits over alleged slanders and insults. . . . . Often the cases involve tenants crowded in apartment buildings. In one building in the Street of the October Revolution tenants began 53 suits against each other.

> Other causes of "spite" suits . . . included "a bent fence, a nasty look." Business enterprises are not immune and one court is handling a complaint of the Zastava Company of Knic over a debt of 10 dinars (less than 1 cent).

> In the countryside spite also appears in such petty forms as a brother who sued his sister because she gathered fruit fallen from a tree he regarded as his own. . . .

> Dr. Mirko Barjakterevic, professor of ethnology at Belgrade University . . . remarked that few languages had as many expressions for and about spite as Serbian and that at every turn one hears phrases like, "I'm going to teach him a lesson," and "I don't want to be made a fool of."

Consider, too, Frake's ("Litigation in Lipay: A Study in Subanum Law" quoted in Nader [1965:21]) account of the prominence of litigation among the Lipay of the Philippines:

> A large share, if not the majority, of legal cases deal with offenses so minor that only the fertile imagination of a Subanum legal authority can magnify them into a serious threat to some person or to society in general. . . . A festivity without litigation is almost as unthinkable as one without drink. If no subject for prosecution immediately presents itself, sooner or later, as the brew relaxes the tongues and actions, someone will make a slip.

> In some respects a Lipay trial is more comparable to an American poker game than to out legal proceedings. It is a contest of skill, in this case of verbal skill, accompanied by social merry-making, in which the loser pays a forfeit. He pays for much the same reason we pay a poker debt: so he can play the game again. Even if he does not have the legal authority's ability to deal a verbalized "hand," he can participate as a defendant, plaintiff, kibitzer, singer, and drinker. No one is left out of the range of activities associated with litigation.

> Litigation nevertheless has far greater significance in Lipay than this poker-game analogy implies. For it is more than recreation. Litigation, together with the rights and duties it generates, so pervades Lipay life that one could not consistently refuse to pay fines and remain a functioning member of society. Along with drinking, feasting, and ceremonializing, litigation provides patterned means of interaction linking the independent nuclear families of Lipay into a social unit, even though there are no formal group ties of comparable extent. The importance of litigation as a social activity makes understandable its prevalence among the peaceful and, by our standards, "law-abiding" residents of Lipay.

such sentiments would affect OSs. who are likely to be individuals, more than RPs, who are likely to be organizations.[23]

It cannot be assumed that the observed variations in readiness to resort to official tribunals is directly reflective of a "rights consciousness" or appetite for vindication in terms of authoritative norms.[24] Consider the assertion that the low rate of litigation in Japan flows from an undeveloped "sense of justiciable rights" with the implication that the higher rate in the United States flows from such rights-consciousness.[25] But the high rate of settlements and the low rate of appeals in the United States suggest it should not be regarded as having a population with great interest in securing moral victories through official vindication.[26] Mayhew (1973:14, Table I) reports a survey in which a sample of Detroit area residents were asked how they had wanted to see their "most serious problem" settled. Only a tiny minority (0% of landlord-tenant problems; 2%

---

23. Generally, sentiments against litigation are less likely to affect organizations precisely because the division of labor within organizations means that litigation will be handled impersonally by specialists who do not have to conduct other relations with the opposing party (as customers. etc.). See Jacob (1969:78 ff.) on the separation of collection from merchandizing tasks as one of the determinants of creditor's readiness to avail of litigation remedies. And cf. the suggestion (note 16 above) that in complex organizations resort to litigation may be a way to externalize decisions that no one within the organization wants to assume responsibility for.

24. Cf. Zeisel, Kalven & Buchholz (1959: Chap. 20). On the possibility of explaining differences in patterns of litigation by structural rather than cultural factors. see Kidder's (1971: Chap. IX) comparison of Indian and American litigation.

25. Henderson (1968:488) suggests that in Japan, unlike America,

> . . . popular sentiment for justiciable rights is still largely absent. And, if dispute settlement is the context from which much of the growth. social meaning and political usefulness of justiciable rights derive—and American experience suggests it is—then the traditional tendency of the Japanese to rely on sublegal conciliatory techniques becomes a key obstacle in the path toward the rule-of-law envisioned by the new constitution.

He notes that

> In both traditional and modern Japan, conciliation of one sort or another has been and still is effective in settling the vast majority of disputes arising in the gradually changing social context. (1968:449).

Finding that Californians resorted to litigation about 23 times as often as Japanese. he concludes (1968:453) that traditional conciliation is employed to settle most "disputes that would go to court in a country with a developed sense of justiciable right."

Henderson (1968:454) seems to imply that "in modern society [people] must comport thereselves according to reasonable and enforceable principles rather than haggling, negotiating and jockeying about to adjust personal relationships to fit an ever-shifting power balance among individuals."

Cf. Rabinowitz (1968: Part III) for a "cultural" explanation for the relative unimportance of law in Japanese society. (Non-ego-developed personality. non-rational approach to action, extreme specificity of norms with high degree of contextual differentiation.)

26. For an instructive example of response to a claimant who wants vindication rather than a tidy settlement. see Katz (1969:1492):

> When I reported my client's instructions not to negotiate settlement at the pretrial conference. the judge appointed an impartial psychiatrist to examine Mr. Lin.

of neighborhood problems; 4% of expensive purchase problems; 9% of public organization problems; 31% of discrimination problems) reported that they sought "justice" or vindication of their legal rights: "most answered that they sought resolution of their problems in some more or less expedient way."

Paradoxically, low valuation of rule-outcomes in particular cases may co-exist with high valuation of rules as symbolic objects. Edelman (1967: chap. 2) distinguishes between remote, diffuse, unorganized publics, for whom rules are a source of symbolic gratification and organized, attentive publics directly concerned with the tangible results of their application. Public appetite for symbolic gratification by the promulgation of rules does not imply a corresponding private appetite for official vindication in terms of rules in particular cases. Attentive RPs on the other hand may be more inclined to regard rules instrumentally as assets rather than as sources of symbolic gratification.

We may think of litigation as typically involving various combinations of OSs and RPs. We can then construct a matrix such as Figure 1 and fill in the boxes with some well-known if only approximate American examples. (We ignore for the moment that the terms OS and RP represent ends of a continuum, rather than a dichotomous pair.)

FIGURE 1
A TAXONOMY OF LITIGATION BY STRATEGIC CONFIGURATION OF PARTIES

Initiator, Claimant

	One-Shotter	Repeat Player
One-Shotter	Parent v. Parent (Custody) Spouse v. Spouse (Divorce) Family v. Family Member (Insanity Commitment) Family v. Family (Inheritance) Neighbor v. Neighbor Partner v. Partner OS vs OS I	Prosecutor v. Accused Finance Co. v. Debtor Landlord v. Tenant I.R.S. v. Taxpayer Condemnor v. Property Owner RP vs OS II
Repeat Player	Welfare Client v. Agency Auto Dealer v. Manufacturer Injury Victim v. Insurance Company Tenant v. Landlord Bankrupt Consumer v. Creditors Defamed v. Publisher OS vs RP III	Union v. Company Movie Distributor v. Censorship Board Developer v. Suburban Municipality Purchaser v. Supplier Regulatory Agency v. Firms of Regulated Industry RP vs RP IV

Defendant

108   LAW AND SOCIETY / FALL 1974

On the basis of our incomplete and unsystematic examples, let us conjecture a bit about the content of these boxes:

Box I: OS vs. OS

The most numerous occupants of this box are divorces and insanity hearings. Most (over 90 per cent of divorces, for example) are uncontested.[27] A large portion of these are really pseudo-litigation, that is, a settlement is worked out between the parties and ratified in the guise of adjudication. When we get real litigation in Box I, it is often between parties who have some intimate tie with one another, fighting over some unsharable good, often with overtones of "spite" and "irrationality." Courts are resorted to where an ongoing relationship is ruptured; they have little to do with the routine patterning of activity. The law is invoked *ad hoc* and instrumentally by the parties. There may be a strong interest in vindication, but neither party is likely to have much interest in the long-term state of the law (of, for instance, custody or nuisance). There are few appeals, few test cases, little expenditure of resources on rule-development. Legal doctrine is likely to remain remote from everyday practice and from popular attitudes.[28]

Box II: RP vs. OS

The great bulk of litigation is found in this box—indeed every really numerous kind except personal injury cases, insanity hearings, and divorces. The law is used for routine processing of claims by parties for whom the making of such claims is a regular business activity.[29] Often the cases here take the form

---

27. For descriptions of divorce litigation, see Virtue (1956); O'Gorman (1963); Marshall and May (1932).

28. For an estimate of the discrepancy between the law and popular attitudes in a "Box I" area, see Cohen, Robson and Bates (1958).

29. Available quantitative data on the configuration of parties to litigation will be explored in a sequel to this essay. For the moment let me just say that the speculations here fit handily with the available findings. For example, Wanner (1974), analyzing a sample of 7900 civil cases in three cities, found that business and governmental units are plaintiffs in almost six out of ten cases; and that they win more, settle less and lose less than individual plaintiffs. Individuals, on the other hand, are defendants in two thirds of all cases and they win less and lose more than do government or business units. A similar preponderance of business and governmental plaintiffs and individual defendants is reported in virtually all of the many studies of small claims courts. E.g., Pagter et al. (1964) in their study of a metropolitan California small claims court find that individuals made up just over a third of the plaintiffs and over 85% of defendants. A later survey of four small-town California small claims courts (Moulton 1969:1660) found that only 16% of plaintiffs were individuals—but over 93% of defendants.

of stereotyped mass processing with little of the individuated attention of full-dress adjudication. Even greater numbers of cases are settled "informally" with settlement keyed to possible litigation outcome (discounted by risk, cost, delay).

The state of the law is of interest to the RP, though not to the OS defendants. Insofar as the law is favorable to the RP it is "followed" closely in practice[30] (subject to discount for RP's transaction costs).[31] Transactions are built to fit the rules by creditors, police, draft boards and other RPs.[32] Rules favoring OSs may be less readily applicable, since OSs do not ordinarily plan the underlying transaction, or less meticulously observed in practice, since OSs are unlikely to be as ready or able as RPs to invest in insuring their penetration to the field level.[33]

---

30. The analysis here assumes that, when called upon, judges apply rules routinely and relentlessly to RPs and OSs alike. In the event, litigation often involves some admixture of individuation, kadijustice, fireside equities, sentimentality in favor of the "little guy." (For a comparison of two small claims courts in one of which the admixture is stronger, see Yngvesson (1965)). It also involves some offsetting impurities in favor of frequent users. See Note 9 above and Note 59 below.

31. Cf. Friedman (1967:806) on the zone of "reciprocal immunities" between, for example, landlord and tenant, afforded by the cost of enforcing their rights. The foregoing suggests that these immunities may be reciprocal, but they are not necessarily symmetrical. That is, they may differ in magnitude according to the strategic position of the parties. Cf. Vaughan's (1968:210) description of the "differential dependence" between landlord and low-income tenant. He regards this as reflecting the greater immediacy and constancy of the tenant's need for housing, the landlord's "exercise of privilege in the most elemental routines of the relationship," greater knowledge, and the fact that the landlord, unlike the tenant, does not have all his eggs in one basket (i.e., he is, in our terms, an RP).

> Whereas each tenant is dependent upon one landlord, the landlord typically diffuses his dependency among many tenants. As a result, the owner can rather easily retain an independent position in each relationship.

A similar asymmetry typically attends relations between employer and employee, franchiser and franchisee, insurer and insured, etc.

32. See note 74 below. Cf. Skolnick's (1966:212ff) description of police adjustment to the exclusionary rule.

33. Similarly, even OSs who have procured favorable judgments may experience difficulty at the execution stage. Even where the stakes loom large for OSs, they may be too small to enlist unsubsidized professional help in implementation. A recent survey of consumers who "won" in New York City's Small Claims Court found that almost a third were unable to collect. Marshalls either flatly refused to accept such judgments for collection or "conveyed an impression that, even if they did take a small claims case, they would regard it as an annoyance and would not put much work into it." *New York Times*, Sept. 19, 1971. A subsequent survey (Community Service Society 1974:16) of 195 successful individual plaintiffs in two Manhattan Small Claims Courts revealed that "only 50% of persons who received *judgments* were able to collect these through their own efforts or through use of sheriffs and marshals." (Plaintiffs who received settlements were more successful, collecting in 82% of the cases.) Cf. the finding of Hollingsworth, *et al* (1973: Table 16) that of winning small claims plaintiffs in Hamilton County only 31% of individuals and unrepresented proprietorships collected half or more of the judgment amount; the

Box III: OS vs. RP

All of these are rather infrequent types except for personal injury cases which are distinctive in that free entry to the arena is provided by the contingent fee.[34]   In auto injury claims, litigation is routinized and settlement is closely geared to possible litigation outcome.   Outside the personal injury area, litigation in Box III is not routine.   It usually represents the attempt of some OS to invoke outside help to create leverage on an organization with which he has been having dealings but is now at the point of divorce (for example, the discharged employee or the cancelled franchisee).[35]   The OS claimant generally has little interest in the state of the law; the RP defendant, however, is greatly interested.

Box IV: RP vs. RP

Let us consider the general case first and then several special cases.   We might expect that there would be little litigation in Box IV, because to the extent that two RPs play with each other repeatedly,[36] the expectation of continued mutually beneficial interaction would give rise to informal bilateral controls.[37] This seems borne out by studies of dealings among businessmen[38]

---

corresponding figure for corporations and represented proprietorships was 55%.

34. Perhaps high volume litigation in Box III is particularly susceptible to transformation into relatively unproblematic administrative processing when RPs discover that it is to their advantage and can secure a shift with some gains (or at least no losses) to OSs.   Cf. the shift from tort to workman's compensation in the industrial accident area (Friedman and Ladinsky [1967]) and the contemporary shift to no-fault plans in the automobile injury area.

35. Summers (1960:252) reports that

> more than ¾ of the reported cases in which individuals have sought legal protection of their rights under a collective agreement have arisen out of disciplinary discharge.

The association of litigation with "divorce" is clear in Macaulay (1963, 1969) and other discussions of commercial dealings.   (Bonn 1972b:573 ff.).   Consumer bankruptcy, another of the more numerous species of litigation in Box III, might be thought of as representing the attempt of the OS to effectuate a "divorce."

36. For example, Babcock (1969:53-54) observes that what gives the suburb its greatest leverage on any one issue is the builder's need to have repeated contact with the regulatory powers of the suburb on various issues.

37. The anticipated beneficial relations need not be with the identical party but may be with other parties with whom that party is in communication.   RPs are more likely to participate in a network of communication which cheaply and rapidly disseminates information about the behavior of others in regard to claims and to have an interest and capacity for acquiring and storing that information.   In this way RPs can cheaply and effectively affect the business reputation of adversaries and thus their future relations with relevant others.   Leff (1970a; 26 ff.); Macaulay (1963:64).

38. . . . why is contract doctrine not central to business exchanges?
    Briefly put, private, between-the-parties sanctions usually

and in labor relations. Official agencies are invoked by unions trying to get established and by management trying to prevent them from getting established. more rarely in dealings between bargaining partners.[39] Units with mutually beneficial relations do not adjust their differences in courts. Where they rely on third parties in dispute-resolution, it is likely to take a form (such as arbitration or a domestic tribunal) detached from official sanctions and applying domestic rather than official rules.

However. there are several special cases. First, there are those RPs who seek not furtherance of tangible interests, but vindication of fundamental cultural commitments. An example would be the organizations which sponsor much church-state litigation.[40] Where RPs are contending about value differences (who is right) rather than interest conflicts (who gets what) there is less tendency to settle and less basis for developing a private system of dispute settlement.[41]

Second. government is a special kind of RP. Informal controls depend upon the ultimate sanction of withdrawal and refusal to continue beneficial relations.[42] To the extent that

---

exist. work and do not involve the costs of using contract law either in litigation or as a ploy in negotiations. . . . most importantly. there are relatively few one-shot. but significant, deals. A businessman usually cares about his reputation. He wants to do business again with the man he is dealing with and with others. Friedman and Macaulay (1967:805).

39. Aspin (1966:2) reports that 70 to 75% of all complaints to the NLRB about the unfair labor practices of companies are under the single section [8(a)(3)] which makes it an unfair labor practice for employers to interfere with union organizing. These make up about half of *all* complaints of unfair labor practices.

40. In his description of the organizational participants in church-state litigation. Morgan (1968:chap. 2) points out the difference in approach between value-committed "separationist purists" and their interest-committed "public schoolmen" allies. The latter tend to visualize the game as non-zero-sum and can conceive of advantages in alliances with their parochial-school adversaries. (1968:58n).

41. Cf. Aubert's (1963:27 ff.) distinction between conflict careers based upon conflicts of interest and those arising from conflicts of value.

42. This analysis is illuminated by Hirschman's distinction between two modes of remedial action by customers or members disappointed with the performance of organizations: (1) exit (that is. withdrawal of custom or membership); and (2) voice ("attempts at changing the practices and policies and outputs of the firm from which one buys or the organizations to which one belongs") [1970:30]. Hirschman attempts to discern the conditions under which each will be employed and will be effective in restoring performance. He suggests that the role of voice increases as the opportunities for exit decline. but that the possibility of exit increases the effectiveness of the voice mechanism. (1970:34. 83). Our analysis suggests that it is useful to distinguish those instances of voice which are "internal." that is. confined to expression to the other party, and those which are external. that is. seek the intervention of third parties. This corresponds roughly to the distinction between two-party and three-party dispute settlement. We might then restate the assertion to suggest that internal voice is

112   LAW AND SOCIETY / FALL 1974

withdrawal of future association is not possible in dealing with government, the scope of informal controls is correspondingly limited. The development of informal relations between regulatory agencies and regulated firms is well known. And the regulated may have sanctions other than withdrawal which they can apply; for instance, they may threaten political opposition. But the more inclusive the unit of government, the less effective the withdrawal sanction and the greater the likelihood that a party will attempt to invoke outside allies by litigation even while sustaining the ongoing relationship. This applies also to monopolies. units which share the government's relative immunity to withdrawal sanctions.[43] RPs in monopolistic relationships will occasionally invoke formal controls to show prowess, to give credibility to threats, and to provide satisfactions for other audiences. Thus we would expect litigation by and against government to be more frequent than in other RP vs. RP situations. There is a second reason for expecting more litigation when government is a party. That is, that the notion of "gain" (policy as well as monetary) is often more contingent and problematic for governmental units than for other parties, such as businesses or organized interest groups. In some cases courts may, by profferring authoritative interpretations of public policy, redefine an agency's notion of gain. Hence government parties may be more willing to externalize decisions to the courts. And opponents may have more incentive to litigate against government in the hope of securing a shift in its goals.

A somewhat different kind of special case is present where plaintiff and defendant are both RPs but do not deal with each other repeatedly (two insurance companies, for example.) In the government/monopoly case, the parties were so inextricably bound together that the force of informal controls was limited; here they are not sufficiently bound to each other to give informal controls their bite; there is nothing to withdraw from! The large one-time deal that falls through, the marginal enterprise— these are staple sources of litigation.

Where there is litigation in the RP vs. RP situation, we might expect that there would be heavy expenditure on rule-develop-

---

effective where there is a plausible threat of sanction (including exit and external voice).

43. The potency of the monopolistic character of ties in promoting resort to third parties is suggested by the estimate that in the Soviet Union approximately one million contract disputes were arbitrated annually in the early 1960's. (Loeber, 1965:128, 133). Cf. Scott's (1965:63-64) suggestion that restricted mobility (defined in terms of job change) is associated with the presence of formal appeal systems in business organizations.

ment, many appeals, and rapid and elaborate development of the doctrinal law. Since the parties can invest to secure implementation of favorable rules, we would expect practice to be closely articulated to the resulting rules.

On the basis of these preliminary guesses, we can sketch a general profile of litigation and the factors associated with it. The great bulk of litigation is found in Box II; much less in Box III. Most of the litigation in these Boxes is mass routine processing of disputes between parties who are strangers (not in mutually beneficial continuing relations) or divorced[44]—and between whom there is a disparity in size. One party is a bureaucratically organized "professional" (in the sense of doing it for a living) who enjoys strategic advantages. Informal controls between the parties are tenuous or ineffective; their relationship is likely to be established and defined by official rules; in litigation, these rules are discounted by transaction costs and manipulated selectively to the advantage of the parties. On the other hand, in Boxes I and IV, we have more infrequent but more individualized litigation between parties of the same general magnitude, among whom there are or were continuing multi-stranded relationships with attendant informal controls. Litigation appears when the

---

44. That is, the relationship may never have existed, it may have "failed" in that it is no longer mutually beneficial, or the parties may be "divorced." On the incompatibility of litigation with ongoing relations between parties, consider the case of the lawyer employed by a brokerage house who brought suit against his employer in order to challenge New York State's law requiring fingerprinting of employees in the securities industry.

> They told me, "Don, you've done a serious thing: you've sued your employer." And then they handed me [severance pay] checks. They knew I had to sue them. Without making employer a defendant, it's absolutely impossible to get a determination in court. It was not a matter of my suing them for being bad guys or anything like that and they knew it.
>
> ... the biggest stumbling block is that I'm virtually blacklisted on Wall Street. . . .

His application for unemployment compensation was rejected on the ground that he had quit his employment without good cause, having provoked his dismissal by refusing to be fingerprinted. *New York Times*, March 2, 1970. It appears that, in the American setting at any rate, litigation is not only incompatible with the maintainance of continuing relationships, but with their subsequent restoration. On the rarity of successful reinstatement of employees ordered reinstated by the NLRB, see Aspin (1966). Bonn (1972: 262) finds this pattern even among users of arbitration, which is supposedly less lethal to continuing relations than litigation. He found that in 78 cases of arbitration in textiles, "business relations were resumed in only fourteen." Cf. Golding's (1969:90) observation that jural forms of dispute-settlement are most appropriate where parties are not involved in a continuing relationship. But the association of litigation with strangers is not invariate. See the Yugoslav and Lipay examples in note 22 above. Cf. the Indian pattern described by Kidder (1971) and by Morrison (1974:39) who recounts that his North Indian villagers "commented scornfully that GR [a chronic litigant] would even take a complete stranger to law—proof that his energies were misdirected."

relationship loses its future value; when its "monopolistic" character deprives informal controls of sufficient leverage and the parties invoke outside allies to modify it; and when the parties seek to vindicate conflicting values.

II. LAWYERS

What happens when we introduce lawyers? Parties who have lawyers do better.[45] Lawyers are themselves RPs. Does their presence equalize the parties, dispelling the advantage of the RP client? Or does the existence of lawyers amplify the advantage of the RP client? We might assume that RPs (tending to be larger units) who can buy legal services more steadily, in larger quantities, in bulk (by retainer) and at higher rates, would get services of better quality. They would have better information (especially where restrictions on information about legal services are present).[46] Not only would the RP get more talent to begin with, but he would on the whole get greater continuity, better record-keeping, more anticipatory or preventive work, more experience and specialized skill in pertinent areas, and more control over counsel.

One might expect that just how much the legal services factor would accentuate the RP advantage would be related to the way in which the profession was organized. The more members of the profession were identified with their clients (i.e., the less they were held aloof from clients by their loyalty to courts or an autonomous guild) the more the imbalance would be accentuated.[47] The more close and enduring the lawyer-client relation-

---

45. For example, Ross (1970:193) finds that automobile injury claimants represented by attorneys recover more frequently than unrepresented claimants; that among those who recover, represented claimants recover significantly more than do unrepresented claimants with comparable cases. Claimants represented by firms recovered considerably more than claimants represented by solo practitioners; those represented by negligence specialists recovered more than those represented by firm attorneys. Similarly, Mosier and Soble (1973:35ff) find that represented tenants fare better in eviction cases than do unrepresented ones. The advantages of having a lawyer in criminal cases are well-known. See, for instance, Nagel (1973).

46. As it happens, the information barriers vary in their restrictiveness. The American Bar Association's Code of Professional Responsibility

> permits advertising directed at corporations, banks, insurance companies, and those who work in the upper echelons of such institutions . . . [while proscribing] most forms of dissemination of information which would reach people of "moderate means" and apprise them of their legal rights and how they can find competent and affordable legal assistants to vindicate those rights. (Burnley 1973:77).

On the disparate effect of these restrictions, cf. note 51.

47. The tension between the lawyer's loyalties to the legal system and to his client has been celebrated by Parsons (1954:381 ff.)

ship, the more the primary loyalty of lawyers is to clients rather than to courts or guild, the more telling the advantages of accumulated expertise and guidance in overall strategy.[48]

What about the specialization of the bar? Might we not expect the existence of specialization to offset RP advantages by providing OS with a specialist who in pursuit of his own career goals would be interested in outcomes that would be advantageous to a whole class of OSs? Does the specialist become the functional equivalent of the RP? We may divide specialists into (1) those specialized by field of law (patent, divorce, etc.), (2) those specialized by the kind of party represented (for example, house counsel), and (3) those specialized by both field of law and "side" or party (personal injury plaintiff, criminal defense, labor). Divorce lawyers do not specialize in husbands or wives,[49]

---

and Horsky (1952: chap. 3). But note how this same deflection of loyalty from the client is deplored by Blumberg (1967) and others. The difference in evaluation seems to depend on whether the opposing pull is to the autonomous legal tradition, as Parsons (1954) and Horsky (1952) have it, or to the maintanance of mutually beneficial interaction with a particular local institution whose workings embody some admixture of the "higher law" (see note 82 below) with parochial understandings, institutional maintenance needs, etc.

48. Although this is not the place to elaborate it, let me sketch the model that underlies this assertion. (For a somewhat fuller account, see International Legal Center, 1973: 4ff.). Let us visualize a series of scales along which legal professions might be ranged:

		A	B
1.	Basis of Recruitment	Restricted	_____ Wide
2.	Barriers to Entry	High	_____ Low
3.	Division of Labor		
	a. Coordination	Low	_____ High
	b. Specialization	Low	_____ High
4.	Range of Services and Functions	Narrow	_____ Wide
5.	Enduring Relationships to Client	Low	_____ High
6.	Range of Institutional Settings	Narrow	_____ Wide
7.	Identification with Clients	Low	_____ High
8.	Identification with Authorities	High	_____ Low
9.	Guild Control	Tight	_____ Loose
10.	Ideology	Legalistic	_____ Problem-solving

It is suggested that the characteristics at the A and B ends of the scale tend to go together, so that we can think of the A and B clusters as means of describing types of bodies of legal professionals, for example, the American legal profession (Hurst 1950: Horsky 1952: Pt. V.; Carlin 1962, 1966: Handler 1967: Smigel 1969) would be a B type, compared to British barristers (Abel-Smith and Stevens 1967) and French *avocats* (Le Paulle 1950); Indian lawyers (Galanter 1968-69), an intermediate case. It is suggested that some characteristics of Type B professions tend to accentuate or amplify the strategic advantages of RP parties. Consideration of, for instance, the British bar, should warn us against concluding that Type B professions are necessarily more conservative in function than Type A. See text, at footnote 145.

49. Which is not to deny the possibility that such "side" specializa-

116   LAW AND SOCIETY / FALL 1974

nor real-estate lawyers in buyers or sellers. But labor lawyers and tax lawyers and stockholders-derivative-suit lawyers do specialize not only in the field of law but in representing one side. Such specialists may represent RPs or OSs. Figure 2 provides some well-known examples of different kinds of specialists:

FIGURE 2

A TYPOLOGY OF LEGAL SPECIALISTS

Lawyer

		Specialized by Party	Specialized by Field and Party	Specialized by Field
Client	RP	"House Counsel" or General Counsel for Bank, Insurance Co. etc. Corporation Counsel for Government Unit	Prosecutor Personal Injury Defendant Staff Counsel for NAACP Tax Labor/Management Collections	Patent
	OS	"Poverty Lawyers" Legal Aid	Criminal Defense Personal Injury Plaintiff	Bankruptcy Divorce

Most specializations cater to the needs of particular kinds of RPs. Those specialists who service OSs have some distinctive features:

First, they tend to make up the "lower echelons" of the legal profession. Compared to the lawyers who provide services to RPs, lawyers in these specialties tend to be drawn from lower socio-economic origins, to have attended local, proprietary or part-time law schools, to practice alone rather than in large firms, and to possess low prestige within the profession.[50] (Of course the correlation is far from perfect; some lawyers who represent OSs do not have these characteristics and some representing RPs do. However, on the whole the difference in professional standing is massive).

Second, specialists who service OSs tend to have problems of mobilizing a clientele (because of the low state of information among OSs) and encounter "ethical" barriers imposed by the profession which forbids solicitation, advertising, referral fees,

---

tion might emerge. One can imagine "women's liberation" divorce lawyers—and anti-alimony ones—devoted to rule-development that would favor one set of OSs.

50. On stratification within the American legal profession see Ladinsky (1963); Lortie (1959); Carlin (1966). But cf. Handler (1967).

advances to clients, and so forth.[51]

Third, the episodic and isolated nature of the relationship with particular OS clients tends to elicit a stereotyped and uncreative brand of legal services. Carlin and Howard (1965:385) observe that:

> The quality of service rendered poorer clients is . . . affected by the non-repeating character of the matters they typically bring to lawyers (such as divorce, criminal, personal injury): this combined with the small fees encourages a mass processing of cases. As a result, only a limited amount of time and interest is usually expended on any one case—there is little or no incentive to treat it except as an isolated piece of legal business. Moreover, there is ordinarily no desire to go much beyond the case as the client presents it, and such cases are only accepted when there is a clear-cut cause of action: i.e., when they fit into convenient legal categories and promise a fairly certain return.

Fourth, while they are themselves RPs, these specialists have problems in developing optimizing strategies. What might be good strategy for an insurance company lawyer or prosecutor—trading off some cases for gains on others—is branded as unethical when done by a criminal defense or personal injury plaintiff lawyer.[52] It is not permissible for him to play his series of OSs as if they constituted a single RP.[53]

Conversely, the demands of routine and orderly handling of a whole series of OSs may constrain the lawyer from maximizing advantage for any individual OS. Rosenthal (1970:172) shows that "for all but the largest [personal injury] claims an attorney loses money by thoroughly preparing a case and not settling it early."

For the lawyer who services OSs, with his transient clientele, his permanent "client" is the forum, the opposite party, or the intermediary who supplies clients. Consider, for example, the dependence of the criminal defense lawyer on maintaining coop-

---

51. See Reichstein (1965); Northwestern University Law Review (1953). On the differential impact of the "Canons of Ethics" on large law firms and those lawyers who represent OSs, see Carlin (1966); Schuchman (1968); Christianson (1970:136).

52. ". . . the canons of ethics would prevent an attorney for a [one-shotter] . . . from trying to influence his client to drop a case that would create a bad precedent for other clients with similar cases. On the other hand, the canons of ethics do not prevent an attorney from advising a corporation that some of its cases should not be pursued to prevent setting a bad precedent for its other cases." (Rothstein 1974:502).

53. Ross (1970:82) observes the possibility of conflict between client and

> the negligence specialist. who negotiates on a repeated basis with the same insurance companies. [H]is goal of maximizing the return from any given case may conflict with the goal of maximizing returns from the total series of cases he represents.

For a catalog of other potential conflicts in the relationship between specialists and OS clients, see O'Connell (1971:46-47).

erative relations with the various members of the "criminal court community."[54]   Similarly, Carlin notes that among metropolitan individual practitioners whose clientele consists of OSs, there is a deformation of loyalty toward the intermediary.

> In the case of those lawyers specializing in personal injury, local tax, collections, criminal, and to some extent divorce work, the relationship with the client . . . is generally mediated by a broker or business supplier who may be either another lawyer or a layman. In these fields of practice the lawyer is principally concerned with pleasing the broker or winning his approval, more so than he is with satisfying the individual client. The source of business generally counts for more than the client, especially where the client is unlikely to return or to send in other clients. The client is then expendable: he can be exploited to the full. Under these conditions, when a lawyer receives a client . . . he has not so much gained a client as a piece of business, and his attitude is often that of handling a particular piece of merchandise or of developing a volume of a certain kind of merchandise.[55]

The existence of a specialized bar on the OS side should overcome the gap in expertise, allow some economies of scale, provide for bargaining commitment and personal familiarity. But this is short of overcoming the fundamental strategic advantages of RPs—their capacity to structure the transaction, play the odds, and influence rule-development and enforcement policy.

Specialized lawyers may, by virtue of their identification with parties, become lobbyists, moral entrepreneurs, proponents of reforms on the parties' behalf. But lawyers have a cross-cutting interest in preserving complexity and mystique so that client contact with this area of law is rendered problematic.[56]   Lawyers

---

54. Blumberg (1967: 47) observes
     > [defense] counsel, whether privately retained or of the legal aid variety, have close and continuing relations with the prosecuting office and the court itself. Indeed, lines of communication, influence and contact with those offices, as well as with the other subsidiary divisions of the office of the clerk and the probation division and with the press are essential to the practice of criminal law. Accused persons come and go in the court system, but the structure and its personnel remain to carry on their respective careers, occupational, and organizational enterprises. . . . the accused's lawyer has far greater professional, economic, intellectual, and other ties to the various elements of the court system than to his own client.

     Cf. Skolnick (1967): Battle (1971). On the interdependence of prosecutor and public defender, see Sudnow (1965: 265, 273).
55. Carlin (1962: 161-62). On the "stranger" relationship between accident victim client and lawyer, see Hunting and Neuwirth (1962: 109).
56. Cf. Consumer Council (1970: 19). In connection with the lawyer's attachment to (or at least appreciation of) the problematic character of the law, consider the following legend, carried at the end of a public service column presented by the Illinois State Bar Association and run in a neighborhood newspaper:
     > No person should ever apply or interpret any law without consulting his attorney. Even a slight difference in the facts may change the result under the law. (*Woodlawn Booster*, July 31, 1963).

should not be expected to be proponents of reforms which are optimum from the point of view of the clients taken alone. Rather, we would expect them to seek to optimize the clients' position without diminishing that of lawyers. Therefore, specialized lawyers have an interest in a framework which keeps recovery (or whatever) problematic at the same time that they favor changes which improve their clients' position within this framework. (Consider the lobbying efforts of personal injury plaintiffs and defense lawyers.) Considerations of interest are likely to be fused with ideological commitments: the lawyers' preference for complex and finely-tuned bodies of rules, for adversary proceedings, for individualized case-by-case decision-making.[57] Just as the culture of the client population affects strategic position, so does the professional culture of the lawyers.

III. INSTITUTIONAL FACILITIES

We see then that the strategic advantages of the RP may be augmented by advantages in the distribution of legal services. Both are related to the advantages conferred by the basic features of the institutional facilities for the handling of claims: passivity and overload.

These institutions are passive, first, in the sense that Black refers to as "reactive"—they must be mobilized by the claimant—giving advantage to the claimant with information, ability to surmount cost barriers, and skill to navigate restrictive procedural requirements.[58] They are passive in a further sense that once

---

Where claims become insufficiently problematic they may drop out of the legal sphere entirely (such as social security). In high-volume and repetitive tasks which admit of economies of scale and can be rendered relatively unproblematic, lawyers may be replaced by entrepreneurs—title companies, bank trust departments—serving OSs on a mass basis (or even serving RPs, as do collection agencies). Cf. Johnstone and Hopson (1967:158ff).

57. Stumpf, *et al.* (1971:60) suggest that professional responses to OEO legal services programs require explanation on ideological ("the highly individualized, case-by-case approach . . . as a prime article of faith") as well as pecuniary grounds. On the components of legalism as an ideology, see Shklar (1964:1-19). Of course this professional culture is not uniform but contains various subcultures. Brill's (1973) observations of OEO poverty lawyers suggest that crucial aspects of professional ideology (e.g., the emphasis on courts, rules and adjudication) are equally pronounced among lawyers who seek far-reaching change through the law.

58. Black (1973:141) observes the departures from the passive or "reactive" stance of legal institutions tend to be skewed along class lines:

... governments disproportionately adopt proactive systems of legal mobilization when a social control problem primarily involves the bottom of the social-class system. .... The common forms of legal misconduct in which upper status citizens indulge, such as breach of contract and warranty, civil negligence, and various forms of trust violation and corruption, are usually left to the gentler hand of a reactive mobilization process.

in the door the burden is on each party to proceed with his case.[59]
The presiding official acts as umpire, while the development of
the case. collection of evidence and presentation of proof are left
to the initiative and resources of the parties.[60]   Parties are treated as if they were equally endowed with economic resources, investigative opportunities and legal skills (Cf. Homberger [1971:
641]).   Where, as is usually the case, they are not, the broader
the delegation to the parties, the greater the advantage conferred
on the wealthier,[61] more experienced and better organized

---

59. The passivity of courts may be uneven.   Cf. Mosier and Soble's
(1973:63) description of Detroit landlord-tenant court:

> If a tenant was unrepresented. the judge ordinarily did not
> question the landlord regarding his claims, nor did the
> judge explain defenses to the tenant. The most common
> explanation given a tenant was that the law permitted him
> only ten days to move and thus the judge's hands were
> tied.   In addition, judges often asked tenants for receipts
> for rent paid and corroboration of landlord-breach claims.
> In contrast, the court supplied complaint and notice forms
> to the landlords and clerks at the court helped them to fill
> out the forms if necessary.   In addition. the in-court ob-
> servers noticed during the beginning of the study that the
> court would not dismiss a nonappearing landlord's case un-
> til completion of the docket call, which took approximately
> forty-five minutes (which the tenant sat and waited), but
> extended no similar courtesy to tardy tenants.   However.
> once the surprised observers questioned the court personnel
> about the practice. it was changed; thereafter, tenants had
> thirty minutes after the call within which to appear.
>
> The disparities in help given to landlords and tenants and
> the treatment of late landlords and tenants are an indica-
> tion of the perhaps inevitable bias of the court toward the
> landlord. Most of the judges and court personnel have a
> middle-class background and they have become familiar
> with many landlords and attorneys appearing regularly in
> the court. The court had years of experience as a vehicle
> for rent collection and eviction where no defenses could be
> raised. The judges and clerks repeatedly hear about ten-
> ants who fail to pay rent or did damage to the premises.
> while they probably never have the opportunity to observe
> the actual condition of the housing that the landlords are
> renting.

60. Homberger (1970:31-31). For a description of more "active" courts
see Kaplan, *et al.* (1958:1221 ff); Homberger (1970). Our description is of courts of the relatively passive variety typical of
"common law" systems, but should not be taken as implying
that "civil law" systems are ordinarily or typically different in
practice. Cf. Merryman (1969:124). The far end of a scale of
institutional "activism" might be represented by institutions like
the Soviet Procuracy (Berman 1963:238ff). And, of course, even
among common law courts passivity is relative and variable.
Courts vary in the extent to which they exercise initiative for the
purpose of developing a branch of the law (the "Lord Mansfield
Syndrome"—see Lowry 1973) or actively protecting some class of
vulnerable parties.

61. As Rothstein (1974:506) sums it up, counsel fees and

> [c]ourt costs, witness fees (especially for experts), investi-
> gation costs. court reporters fees. discovery costs, tran-
> script costs. and the cost of any bond needed to secure op-
> ponents' damages, all make litigation an expensive task.
> thereby giving the advantage to those with large financial
> resources.

party.[62]

The advantages conferred by institutional passivity are accentuated by the chronic overload which typically characterizes these institutions.[63] Typically there are far more claims than there are institutional resources for full dress adjudication of each. In several ways overload creates pressures on claimants to settle rather than to adjudicate:

(a) by causing delay (thereby discounting the value of recovery);

(b) by raising costs (of keeping the case alive);

(c) by inducing institutional incumbents to place a high value on clearing dockets, discouraging full-dress adjudication in favor of bargaining, stereotyping and routine processing;[64]

(d) by inducing the forum to adopt restrictive rules to discourage litigation.[65]

Thus, overload increases the cost and risk of adjudicating and shields existing rules from challenge, diminishing opportunities for rule-change.[66] This tends to favor the beneficiaries of existing rules.

---

62. A further set of institutional limitations should be mentioned here: limitations on the scope of matters that courts hear; the kind of relief that they can give; and on their capacity for systematic enforcement are discussed below. (pp. 136 ff).

63. On the limited supply of institutional facilities, consider Saari's (1967) estimate that in the early 1960's total governmental expenditures for civil and criminal justice in the United States ran about four to five billion dollars annually. (Of this, about 60% went for police and prosecution, about 20% for corrections, and 20% for courts.) This amounted to about 2.5% of direct expenditures of American governments. In 1965-66 expenditures for the judiciary represented 1/17 of 1% of the total federal budget; 6/10 of 1% of state budgets; something less than 6% of county and 3% of city budgets.

64. The substitution of bargaining for adjudication need not be regarded as reflecting institutional deficiency. Even in criminal cases it may seem providential:

It is elementary, historically and statistically, that systems of courts—the number of judges, prosecutors and courtrooms—have been based on the premise that approximately 90 percent of all [criminal] defendants will plead guilty, leaving only 10 percent, more or less, to be tried. . . . . The consequences of what might seem on its face a small percentage change in the rate of guilty pleas can be tremendous. . . . in Washington, D.C. . . . the guilty plea rate dropped to 65 percent . . . [T]welve judges out of fifteen in active service were assigned to the criminal calendar and could barely keep up. . . . [T]o have this occur in the National Capital, which ought to be a model for the nation and show place for the world, was little short of disaster (Burger, 1970:931).

65. On institutional coping with overload, see Friedman (1967:798ff).

66. Cf. Foote (1956:645) on the rarity of appeal in vagrancy cases. Powell and Rohan (1968:177-78) observe that the ordinary week-to-week or month-to-month rental agreement

Second, by increasing the difficulty of challenging going practice, overload also benefits those who reap advantage from the neglect (or systematic violation) of rules which favor their adversaries.

Third, overload tends to protect the possessor—the party who has the money or goods—against the claimant.[67] For the most part, this amounts to favoring RPs over OSs, since RPs typically can structure transactions to put themselves in the possessor position.[68]

Finally, the overload situation means that there are more commitments in the formal system than there are resources to honor them—more rights and rules "on the books" than can be vindicated or enforced. There are, then, questions of priorities in the allocation of resources. We would expect judges, police, administrators and other managers of limited institutional facilities to be responsive to the more organized, attentive and influential of their constituents.[69] Again, these tend to be RPs.

Thus, overloaded and passive institutional facilities provide the setting in which the RP advantages in strategic position and legal services can have full play.[70]

is tremendously important sociologically in that occupancy thereunder conditions the home life of a very substantial fraction of the population. On the other hand, the financial smallness of the involved rights results in a great dearth of reported decisions from the courts concerning them. Their legal consequences are chiefly fixed in the 'over the counter' mass handling of 'landlord and tenant' cases of the local courts. So this type of estate, judged sociologically is of great importance, but judged on the basis of its jurisprudential content is almost negligible.

67. In the criminal process, too, the "possessor" (i.e.. of defendant's mobility) enjoys great advantages. On the higher likelihood of conviction and of severe sentencing of those detained before trial, see Rankin (1964) and Wald (1964). Engle (1971) finds that among those convicted pre-trial status explains more of the variation in sentencing severity than any of 23 other factors tested.

68. See Leff (1970a:22) on the tendency of RP creditors to put themselves in the possessor position. shifting the costs of "due process" to the OS debtor. There are, however, instances where OSs may use overload to advantage: for instance, the accused out on bail may benefit from delay. Cf. Engle's (1971) observation of the "weakening effect of time on the prosecutor's position." Rioters or rent-strikers may threaten to demand jury trials, but the effectiveness of this tactic depends on a degree of coordination that effectuates a change of scale.

69. For example, the court studied by Zeisel, *et al.* (1959:7) "had chosen to concentrate all of its delay in the personal injury jury calendar and to keep its other law calendars up to date, granting blanket preferment to all commercial cases . . . and to all non-jury personal injury cases." (Recovery in the latter was about 20% lower than jury awards in comparable cases [1959:119]).

70. This analysis has not made separate mention of corruption, that is. the sale by incumbents of system outcomes divergent from those prescribed by authoritative norms. Insofar as such activities are analytically distinguishable from favorable priorities and "benign neglect" it should be noted that. since such enterprise on any considerable scale is confined to the organized, professional and

Galanter / LEGAL CHANGE 123

IV. RULES[71]

We assume here that rules tend to favor older, culturally dominant interests.[72] This is not meant to imply that the rules are explicitly designed to favor these interests,[73] but rather that those groups which have become dominant have successfully articulated their operations to pre-existing rules.[74] To the extent

---

wealthy, this provides yet another layer of advantage to some classes of "haves."

71. I would like to emphasize that the term "rules" is used here as shorthand for all the authoritative normative learning. It is unnecessary for the purpose at hand to take a position on the question of whether all of that learning consists of rules or whether principles, policies, values, and standards are best understood as fundamentally different. It is enough for our purposes to note that this learning is sufficiently complex that the result in many cases is problematic and unknowable in advance.

72. Even assuming that every instance of formulating rules represented a "fair" compromise among "have" and "have-not" interests, we should expect the stock of rules existing at any given time to be skewed toward those which favor "haves." The argument (cf. Kennedy 1973:384-5) goes like this: At the time of its formulation, each rule represents a current consensus about a just outcome as among competing interests. Over time the consensus changes, so that many rules are out of line with current understandings of fairness. Rule-makers (legislative, administrative and judicial) can attend to only some of all the possible readjustments. Which ones they will attend to depends in large measure on the initiative of those affected in raising the issue and mobilizing support to obtain a declaration of the more favorable current consensus. "Haves" (wealthy, professional, repeat players) enjoy a superior ability to elicit such declarations (cf. p. 100 ff); they are thus likely to enjoy the timely benefits of shifts of social consensus in their favor. OSs, on the other hand, will often find it difficult to secure timely changes in the rules to conform to a new consensus more favorable to them. Thus RPs will be the beneficiaries of the time-lag between crystallized rules and current consensus. Thus, even with the most favorable assumptions about rule-making itself, the mere fact that rules accrue through time, and that it requires expenditure of resources to overcome the lag of rules behind current consensus, provides RPs with a relatively more favorable set of rules than the current consensus would provide.

73. This is sometimes the case; consider, for instance, the rules of landlord-tenant. Ohlhausen (1936) suggests that rules as to the availability of provisional remedies display a pronounced pattern of favoring claims of types likely to be brought by the "well to do" over claims of types brought by the impecunious.

74. Thus the modern credit seller-lender team have built their operation upon the destruction of the purchaser's defenses by the holder in due course doctrine originally developed for the entirely different purpose of insuring the circulation of commercial paper. See Rosenthal (1971:377ff). Shuchman (1971:761-62) points out how in consumer bankruptcies:

Consumer creditors have adjusted their practices so that sufficient proof will be conveniently available for most consumer loans to be excepted from discharge under section 17a (2). They have made wide use of renewals, resetting, and new loans to pay off old loans, with the result that the consumers' entire debt will often be nondischargeable. Section 17a(2) constitutes, in effect, an enabling act—a skeletal outline that the consumer creditor can fill in to create nondischargeable debts—that operated to defeat the consumer's right to the benefits of a discharge in bankruptcy.

Similarly, Shuchman (1969) shows how RP auto dealers and financial institutions have developed patterns for resale of repossessed automobiles that meet statutory resale requirements but which per-

that rules are evenhanded or favor the "have-nots," the limited resources for their implementation will be allocated. I have argued. so as to give greater effect to those rules which protect and promote the tangible interests of organized and influential groups. Furthermore, the requirements of due process, with their barriers or protections against precipitate action, naturally tend to protect the possessor or holder against the claimant.[75] Finally, the rules are sufficiently complex[76] and problematic (or capable of being problematic if sufficient resources are expended to make them so) that differences in the quantity and quality of legal services will affect capacity to derive advantages from the rules.[77]

Thus. we arrive at Figure 3 which summarizes why the "haves" tend to come out ahead. It points to layers of advantages enjoyed by different (but largely overlapping) classes of "haves" —advantages which interlock, reinforcing and shielding one another.

V. ALTERNATIVES TO THE OFFICIAL SYSTEM

We have been discussing resort to the official system to put forward (or defend against) claims. Actually, resort to this system by claimants (or initiators) is one of several alternatives. Our analysis should consider the relationship of the characteristics of the total official litigation system to its use *vis-à-vis* the alternatives. These include at least the following:

(1) Inaction—"lumping it," not making a claim or complaint. This is done all the time by "claimants" who lack information

mit subsequent profitable second sale and in addition produce substantial deficiency claims. More generally, recall the often-noted adaptive powers of regulated industry which manage, in Hamilton's (1957: chap. 2) terms, to convert "regulations into liberties" and "controls into sanctions."

75. For some examples of possessor-defendants exploiting the full panoply of procedural devices to raise the cost to claimants, see Schrag (1969); Macaulay (1966:98). Large (1972) shows how the doctrines of standing, jurisdiction and other procedural hurdles, effectively obstruct application of favorable substantive law in environmental litigation. Facing these rules in serial array, the environmentalists win many skirmishes but few battles.

76. Cf. the observation of Tullock (1971:48-49) that complexity and detail—the "maze" quality of legal rules—in itself confers advantages on "people of above average intelligence, with literary and scholarly interests"—and by extension on those who can develop expertise or employ professional assistance.

77. For an example of the potency of a combination of complexity and expertise in frustrating recovery, see Laufer (1970). Of course. the advantage may derive not from the outcome. but from the complexity. expense and uncertainty of the litigation process itself. Borkin (1950) shows how, in a setting of economic competition among units of disparate size and resources. patent litigation may be used as a tactic of economic struggle. Cf. Hamilton (1957:75-76).

FIGURE 3
WHY THE "HAVES" TEND TO COME OUT AHEAD

Element	Advantages	Enjoyed by
PARTIES	— ability to structure transaction — specialized expertise, economies of scale — long-term strategy — ability to play for rules — bargaining credibility — ability to invest in penetration	— repeat players large, professional*)
LEGAL SERVICES	— skill. specialization. continuity	— organized professional* wealthy
INSTITU-TIONAL FACILITIES	— passivity — cost and delay barriers — favorable priorities	— wealthy, experienced, organized — holders, possessors — beneficiaries of existing rules — organized, attentive
RULES	— favorable rules — due process barriers	— older, culturally dominant — holders, possessors

* in the simple sense of "doing it for a living"

or access[78] or who knowingly decide gain is too low, cost too high (including psychic cost of litigating where such activity is repugnant). Costs are raised by lack of information or skill. and also include risk. Inaction is also familiar on the part of official complainers (police, agencies, prosecutors) who have incomplete information about violations. limited resources, policies about *de minimus*, schedules of priorities, and so forth.[79]

(2) "Exit"—withdrawal from a situation or relationship by moving, resigning, severing relations. finding new partners, etc.

---

78. On the contours of "inaction." see Levine and Preston (1970); Mayhew and Riess (1969); Ennis (1967); Republic Research, Inc. (1970); Hallauer (1972).

79. See Rabin (1972) and Miller (1969) (prosecutors); LaFave (1965) and Black (1971) (police): and generally, Davis (1969). Courts are not the only institutions in the legal system which are chronically overloaded. Typically, agencies with enforcement responsibilities have many more authoritative commitments than resources to carry them out. Thus "selective enforcement" is typical and pervasive: the policies that underlie the selection lie. for the most part. beyond the "higher law." On the interaction between enforcement and rule-development, see Gifford (1971).

This is of course a very common expedient in many kinds of trouble. Like "lumping it," it is an alternative to invocation of any kind of remedy system—although its presence as a sanction may be important to the working of other remedies.[80] The use of "exit" options depends on the availability of alternative opportunities or partners (and information about them), the costs of withdrawal, transfer, relocation, development of new relationships, the pull of loyalty to previous arrangements—and on the availability and cost of other remedies.[81]

(3) Resort to some unofficial control system—we are familiar with many instances in which disputes are handled outside the official litigation system. Here we should distinguish (a) those dispute-settlement systems which are normatively and institutionally appended to the official system (such as settlement of auto-injuries, handling of bad checks) from (b) those settlement systems which are relatively independent in norms and sanctions (such as businessmen settling disputes *inter se*, religious groups, gangs).

What we might call the "appended" settlement systems merge imperceptibly into the official litigation system. We might sort them out by the extent to which the official intervention approaches the adjudicatory mode. We find a continuum from situations where parties settle among themselves with an eye to the official rules and sanctions, through situations where official intervention is invoked, to those in which settlement is supervised and/or imposed by officials, to full-dress adjudication. All along this line the sanction is supplied by the official system (though not always in the manner prescribed in the "higher law")[82] and the norms or rules applied are a version of the official rules. although discounted for transaction costs and distorted by their selective use for the purposes of the parties.

80. On exit or withdrawal as a sanction. see note 42 and text there. For an attempt to explore propensities to choose among resignation, exit, and voice in response to neighborhood problems, see Orbell and Uno (1972). "Exit" would seem to include much of what goes under the rubric of "self-help." Other common forms of self-help, such as taking possession of property, usually represent a salvage operation in the wake of exit by the other party. Yet other forms. such as force, are probably closer to the private dispute settlement systems discussed below.

81. There are. of course, some cases (such as divorce or bankruptcy) in which exit can be accomplished only by securing official certification or permission: that is. it is necessary to resort to an official remedy system in order to effectuate exit.

82. This term is used to refer to the law as a body of authoritative learning (rules. doctrines. principles) as opposed to the parochial embodiments of this higher law, as admixed with local understandings, priorities. and the like.

FIGURE 4

"APPENDED" DISPUTE-SETTLEMENT SYSTEMS

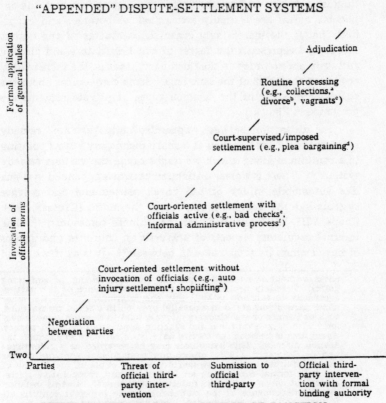

OFFICIAL THIRD-PARTY AS SOURCE OF SANCTION

a. Jacob (1969).
b. O'Gorman (1963); Virtue (1956).
c. Foote (1956); Spradley (1970).
d. Newman (1966: chap. 3); McIntyre and Lippman (1970).
e. Beutel (1957:287 ff.); cf. the operation of the Fraud and Complaint Department at McIntyre (1968:470-71).
f. Woll (1960); cf. the "formal informal settlement system" of the Motor Vehicles Bureau, described by Macaulay (1966:153 ff.).
g. Ross (1970).
h. Cameron (1964:32-36).

From these "appended" systems of discounted and privatized official justice, we should distinguish those informal systems of "private justice" which invoke other norms and other sanctions. Such systems of dispute-settlement are typical among people in continuing interaction such as an organized group, a trade, or a university.[83] In sorting out the various types according to the

83. "Private" dispute settlement may entail mainly bargaining or negotiation between the parties (dyadic) or may involve the invocation of some third party in the decision-making position. It is hypothesized that parties whose roles in a transaction or relationship are complementaries (husband-wife, purchaser-supplier, landlord-tenant) will tend to rely on dyadic processes in which group norms

extent and the mode of intervention of third parties. we can distinguish two dimensions: the first is the degree to which the applicable norms are formally articulated, elaborated. and exposited, that is the increasingly organized character of the norms. The second represents the degree to which initiative and binding authority are accorded to the third party, that is, the increasingly organized character of the sanctions. Some conjectures about the character of some of the common types of private systems are presented in Figure 5.

Our distinction between "appended" and "private" remedy systems should not be taken as a sharp dichotomy but as pointing to a continuum along which we might range the various remedy systems.[84] There is a clear distinction between appended systems like automobile injury or bad check settlements and private systems like the internal regulation of the mafia (Cressey, 1969: Chaps. VIII, IX; Ianni, 1972), or the Chinese community.[85] The internal regulatory aspects of universities, churches and groups of businessmen lie somewhere in between.[86] It is as if we could

enter without specialized apparatus for announcing or enforcing norms. Precisely because of the mutual dependence of the parties, a capacity to sanction is built into the relationship. On the other hand, parties who stand in a parallel position in a set of transactions, such as airlines or stockbrokers *inter se.* tend to develop remedy systems with norm exposition and sanction application by third parties. Again, this is because the parties have little capacity to sanction the deviant directly. This hypothesis may be regarded as a reformulation of Schwartz' (1954) proposition that formal controls appear where informal controls are ineffective and explains his finding of resort to formal controls on an Israeli moshav (cooperative settlement) but not in a kibbutz (collective settlement). In this instance, the interdependence of the kibbutzniks made informal controls effective. while the "independent" moshav members needed formal controls. This echos Durkheim's (1964) notion of different legal controls corresponding to conditions of organic and mechanical solidarity. A corollary to this is suggested by re-analysis of Mentschikoff's (1961) survey of trade association proclivity to engage in arbitration. Her data indicate that the likelihood of arbitration is strongly associated with the fungibility of goods (her categories are raw. soft and hard goods). Presumably dealings in more unique hard goods entail enduring purchaser-supplier relations which equip the parties with sanctions for dyadic dispute-settlement. sanctions which are absent among dealers in fungible goods. Among the latter. sanctions take the form of exclusion from the circle of traders. and it is an organized third party (the trade association) that can best provide this kind of sanction.

84. The distinction is not intended to ignore the overlap and linkage that may exist between "appended" and "private" systems. See, for example. Macaulay's (1966:151 ff.) description of the intricate interweaving of official, appended and private systems in the regulation of manufacturer-dealer relations: Randall's (1968: Chap. 8) account of the relation between official and industry censorship; Aker's (1968:470) observation of the interpenetration of professional associations and state regulatory boards.

85. On internal regulation in Chinese communities in the United States. see Doo (1973); Light (1972. chap. 5, especially 89-94); Grace (1970).

86. Cf. Mentschikoff's (1961) discussion of various species of commercial arbitration. She distinguishes casual arbitrations conducted by the American Arbitration Association which emphasize general legal

Galanter / LEGAL CHANGE 129

visualize a scale stretching from the official remedy system through ones oriented to it through relatively independent systems based on similar values to independent systems based

FIGURE 5

"PRIVATE" REMEDY SYSTEMS

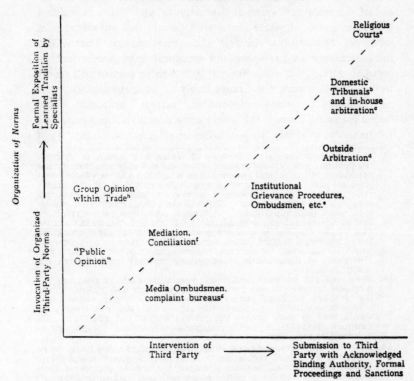

Organization of Norms

Formal Exposition of Learned Tradition by Specialists

Invocation of Organized Third-Party Norms

Religious Courts[a]

Domestic Tribunals[b] and in-house arbitration[c]

Outside Arbitration[d]

Group Opinion within Trade[h]

Institutional Grievance Procedures, Ombudsmen, etc.[e]

Mediation, Conciliation[f]

"Public Opinion"

Media Ombudsmen. complaint bureaus[g]

Intervention of Third Party →

Submission to Third Party with Acknowledged Binding Authority, Formal Proceedings and Sanctions

Organization of Sanctions

a. Columbia J. of Law and Social Problems (1970, 1971); Shriver (1966); Ford (1970:457-79).
b. E.g., The International Air Transport Association (Gollan1970); professional sports leagues and associations (Goldpaper 1971).
c. Mentscnikoff (1961:859).
d. Bonn (1972); Mentschikoff (1961:856-57).
e. Gellnorn. 1966: Anderson (1969:chaps IV, V).
f. E.g., labor-management (Simkin [1971:chap. 3]); MacCallum (1967).
g. E.g., newspaper "action-line" columns. Better Business Bureaus
h. Macaulay (1963:63-64); Leif (1970a:29 ff).

norms and standards and where the "ultimate sanction . . . is the rendering of judgment on the award by a court . . . ." (1961:858) from arbitration within

> self-contained trade groups [where] the norms and standards of the group itself are being brought to bear by the arbitrators (1961:857)

and the ultimate sanction is an intra-group disciplinary proceeding.

on disparate values.[87]

Presumably it is not accidental that some human encounters are regulated frequently and influentially by the official and its appended systems while others seem to generate controls that make resort to the official and its appended systems rare. Which human encounters are we likely to find regulated at the "official" end of our scale and which at the "private" end? It is submitted that location on our scale varies with factors that we might sum up by calling them the "density" of the relationship. That is, the more inclusive in life-space and temporal span a relationship between parties,[88] the less likely it is that those parties will resort to the official system[89] and more likely that the relationship will be regulated by some independent "private" system.[90] This seems plausible because we would expect inclusive and enduring relationships to create the possibility of effective sanctions;[91] and

---

87. The dotted extension of the scale in Table 6 is meant to indicate the possibility of private systems which are not only structurally independent of the official system but in which the shared values comprise an oppositional culture. Presumably this would fit, for example, internal dispute settlement among organized and committed criminals or revolutionaries. Closer to the official might be the sub-cultures of delinquent gangs. Although they have been characterized as deviant sub-cultures, Matza (1964: chap. 2, esp. 59 ff.) argues that in fact the norms of these groups are but variant readings of the official legal culture. Such variant readings may be present elsewhere on the scale; for instance, businessmen may not recognize any divergence of their notion of obligatory business conduct from the law of contract.

88. Since dealings between settlement specialists such as personal injury and defense lawyers may be more recurrent and inclusive than the dealings between parties themselves, one might expect that wherever specialist intermediaries are used, the remedy-system would tend to shift toward the private end of our spectrum. Cf. Skolnick (1967:69) on the "regression to cooperation" in the "criminal court community."

89. Not only is the transient and simplex relationship more likely to be subjected to official regulation, it is apparently more amenable to formal legal control. See, for example, the greater success of anti-discrimination statutes in public accommodation than in housing and in housing than in employment (success here defined merely as a satisfactory outcome for the particular complainant). See Lockard (1968:91,122,138). Mayhew (1968:245 ff; 278 ff.) provides an interesting demonstration of the greater impact of official norms in housing than in employment transactions in spite of the greater evaluative resistance to desegregation in the latter.

90. The capacity of continuing or "on-going" relationships to generate effective informal control has been often noted (Macaulay 1963:63-64; Yngvesson 1973). It is not temporal duration *per se* that provides the possibility of control, but the serial or incremental character of the relationship, which provides multiple choice points at which parties can seek and induce adjustment of the relationship. The mortgagor-mortgagee relationship is an enduring one, but one in which there is heavy reliance on official regulation, precisely because the frame is fixed and the parties cannot withdraw or modify it. Contrast landlord-tenant, husband-wife or purchaser-supplier, in which recurrent inputs of cooperative activity are required, the withholding of which gives the parties leverage to secure adjustment. Schelling (1963:41) suggests a basis for this in game theory: threats intended to deter a given act can be delivered with more credibility if they are capable of being decomposed into a number of consecutive smaller threats.

91. Conversely, the official system will tend to be used where such

FIGURE 6

A SCALE OF REMEDY SYSTEMS FROM
OFFICIAL TO PRIVATE

REMEDY SYSTEMS

	OFFICIAL		APPENDED			PRIVATE	
	Adjudication	Routine Processing	Structurally Interstitial (Officials Participating)	Oriented to Official	Articulated to Official	Independent	Oppositional
EXAMPLES		Collections Divorce	Plea bargaining, bad check recovery	Auto injury settlement	Businessmen	Churches, Chinese community	Gangs	Mafia, Revolutionaries

we would expect participants in such relationships to share a value consensus[92] which provided standards for conduct and legitimized such sanctions in case of deviance.

The prevalance of private systems does not necessarily imply that they embody values or norms which are competing or opposed to those of the official system. Our analysis does not impute the plurality of remedy systems to cultural differences as such. It implies that the official system is utilized when there is a disparity between social structure and cultural norm. It is used, that is, where interaction and vulnerability create encounters and relationships which do not generate shared norms (they may be insufficiently shared or insufficiently specific) and/or do not give rise to group structures which permit sanctioning these norms.[93]

---

sanctions are unavailable. that is, where the claimee has no hope of any stream of benefits from future relations with the claimant (or those whose future relation with claimee will be influenced by his response to the claim). Hence the association of litigation with the aftermath of "divorce" (marital, commercial or organizational) or the absence of any "marriage" to begin with (e.g., auto injury, criminal). That is, government is the remedy agent of last resort and will be used in situations where one party has a loss and the other party has no expectation of any future benefit from the relationship.

92. This does not imply that the values of the participants are completely independent of and distinct from the officially authoritative ones. More common are what we have referred to (note 87 above) as "variant readings" in which elements of authoritative tradition are re-ordered in the light of parochial understandings and priorities. For example, the understanding of criminal procedure by the police (Skolnick [1966:219 ff.]) or of air pollution laws by health departments (Goldstein and Ford [1971:20 ff.]). Thus the variant legal cultures of various legal communities at the field or operating level can exist with little awareness of principled divergence from the higher law.

93. This comports with Bohannan's (1965:34 ff.) notion that law comprises a secondary level of social control in which norms are re-institutionalized in specialized legal institutions. But where Bohannan implies a constant relationship between the primary institutionalization of norms and their reinstitutionalization in specialized legal institutions, the emphasis here is on the difference in the extent to which relational settings can generate self-corrective remedy systems. Thus it suggests that the legal level is brought into play where the original institutionalization of norms is incomplete, either in the norms or the institutionalization.

Bohannan elaborates his analysis by suggesting (1965:37 ff.) that the legal realm can be visualized as comprising various regions of which the "Municipal systems of the sort studied by most jurists deal with a single legal culture within a unicentric power system." (In such a system. differences between institutional practice and legal prescription are matters of phase or lag.) Divergences from unity (cultural, political. or both) define other regions of the legal realm: respectively, colonial law, law in stateless societies and international law.

The analysis here suggests that "municipal systems" themselves may be patchworks in which normative consensus and effective unity of power converge only imperfectly. Thus we might expect a single legal system to include phenomena corresponding to other regions of his schema of the legal realm. The divergence of the "law on the books" and the "law in action" would not then be ascribable

Figure 7 sketches out such relationships of varying density and suggests the location of various official and private remedy systems.

FIGURE 7

RELATIONSHIP BETWEEN DENSITY OF SOCIAL
RELATIONSHIPS AND TYPE OF REMEDY SYSTEM

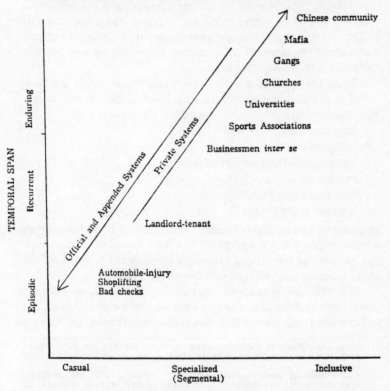

It restates our surmise of a close association between the density of relationships and remoteness from the official system.[94] We

solely to lag or "phase" (1965:37) but rather would give expression to the discontinuity between culture and social structure.

94. The association postulated here seems to have support in connection with a number of distinct aspects of legal process:
Presence of legal controls: Schwartz (1954) may be read as asserting that relational density (and the consequent effectiveness of informal controls) is inversely related to the presence of legal controls (defined in terms of the presence of sanction specialists).
Invocation (mobilization) of official controls: Black (1971:1097) finds that readiness to invoke police and insistence of complainants on arrest is associated with "relational distance" between the parties. Cf. Kawashima's (1963:45) observation that in Japan, where litigation was rare between parties to an enduring relationship regulated

may surmise further that on the whole the official and appended systems flourish in connection with the disputes between parties of disparate size which give rise to the litigation in Boxes II and III of Figure I. Private remedy systems. on the other hand, are more likely to handle disputes between parties of comparable size.[95] The litigation in Boxes I and IV of Figure 1, then, seems to represent in large measure the breakdown (or inhibited development) of private remedy systems. Indeed, the distribution of litigation generally forms a mirror image of the presence of private remedy systems. But the mirror is, for the various reasons discussed here, a distorting one.

From the vantage point of the "higher law" what we have called the official system may be visualized as the "upper" layers of a massive "legal"[96] iceberg, something like this:

Adjudication

Litigation

Appended Settlement Systems

Private Settlement Systems

Exit Remedies/Self Help

Inaction ("lumping it")

The uneven and irregular layers are distinct although they merge imperceptibly into one another.[97] As we proceed to discuss possible reforms of the official system, we will want to consider the kind of impact they will have on the whole iceberg.

We will look at some of the connections and flows between layers mainly from the point of view of the construction of the iceberg itself, but aware that flows and connections are also in-

---

by shared ideals of harmony, resort to officials was common where such ties were absent, as in cases of inter-village and usurer-debtor disputes.
Elaboration of authoritative doctrine: Derrett (1959:54) suggests that the degree of elaboration of authoritative learned doctrine in classical Hindu law is related to the likelihood that the forums applying such doctrine would be invoked, which is in turn dependent on the absence of domestic controls.

95. There are, of course, exceptions, such as the automobile manufacturers' administration of warranty claims described by Whitford (1968) or those same manufacturers' internal dealer relations tribunals described by Macaulay (1966).

96. The iceberg is not properly a legal one. hence the quotation marks. That is, I do not mean to impute any characteristics that might define the "legal" (officials, coercive sanctions, specialists, general rules) to all the instances in the iceberg. It is an iceberg of potential claims or disputes and the extent to which any sector of it is legalized is problematic. Cf. Abel (1974).

97. Contrast the more symmetrical "great pyramid of legal order" envisioned by Hart and Sacks (1958:312). Where the Hart and Sacks pyramid portrays private and official decision-making as successive moments of an integrated normative and institutional order. the present "iceberg" model suggests that the existence of disparate systems of settling disputes is a reflection of cultural and structural discontinuities.

fluenced by atmospheric (cultural) factors such as appetite for vindication, psychic cost of litigation, lawyers' culture and the like.

VI. STRATEGIES FOR REFORM

Our categorization of four layers of advantage (Figure 3) suggests a typology of strategies for "reform" (taken here to mean equalization—conferring relative advantage on those who did not enjoy it before.) We then come to four types of equalizing reform:

(1) rule-change

(2) improvement in institutional facilities

(3) improvement of legal services in quantity and quality

(4) improvement of strategic position of have-not parties

I shall attempt to sketch some of the possible ramifications of change on each of these levels for other parts of the litigation system and then discuss the relationship between changes in the litigation system and the rest of our legal iceberg. Of course such reforms need not be enacted singly, but may occur in various combinations. However, for our purposes we shall only discuss, first, each type taken in isolation and then, all taken together.

A. Rule-change

Obtaining favorable rule changes is an expensive process. The various kinds of "have-nots" (Figure 3) have fewer resources to accomplish changes through legislation or administrative policy-making. The advantages of the organized, professional, wealthy and attentive in these forums are well-known. Litigation, on the other hand, has a flavor of equality. The parties are "equal before the law" and the rules of the game do not permit them to deploy all of their resources in the conflict, but require that they proceed within the limiting forms of the trial. Thus, litigation is a particularly tempting arena to "have-nots," including those seeking rule change.[98] Those who seek change through the courts tend to represent relatively isolated interests, unable to carry the day in more political forums.[99]

98. Hazard (1970:246-47) suggests that the attractions of the courts include that they are open as of right, receptive to arguments based on principle and offer the advocate a forum in which he bears no responsibility for the consequences of having his arguments prevail.

99. Dolbeare (1967:63). Owen (1971:68, 142) reports the parallel finding that in two Georgia counties "opinion leaders and influentials seldom use the court, except for economic retrieval." Cf. Howard's (1969:346) observation that ". . . adjudication is preeminently a method for individuals, small groups and minorities who lack access

Litigation may not, however, be a ready source of rule-change for "have-nots." Complexity, the need for high inputs of legal services and cost barriers (heightened by overloaded institutional facilities) make challenge of rules expensive. OS claimants, with high stakes in the tangible outcome, are unlikely to try to obtain rule changes. By definition, a test case—litigation deliberately designed to procure rule-change—is an unthinkable undertaking for an OS. There are some departures from our ideal type: OSs who place a high value on vindication by official rules or whose peculiar strategic situation makes it in their interest to pursue rule victories.[100] But generally the test-case involves some organization which approximates an RP.[101]

The architecture of courts severely limits the scale and scope of changes they can introduce in the rules. Tradition and ide-

---

to or sufficient strength within the political arena to mobilize a favorable change in legislative coalitions."

100. There are situations in which no settlement is acceptable to the OS. The most common case, perhaps, is that of the prisoner seeking post-conviction remedies. He has "infinite" costless time and nothing further to lose. Other situations may be imagined in which an OS stands only to gain by a test case and has the resources to expend on it. Consider. for example, the physician charged with ten counts of illegal abortion. Pleading guilty to one count if the state dropped the others and agreeing to a suspended sentence would still entail the loss of his license. Every year of delay is worth money, win or lose: the benefits of delay are greater than the costs of continued litigation.

When the price of alternatives becomes unacceptably high, we may find OSs swimming upstream against a clear rule and strategic disadvantage. (Cf. the explosion of selective service cases in the 1960's.) Such a process may be facilitated by, for example, the free entry afforded by the contingent fee. See Friedman and Ladinsky's (1967) description of the erosion of the fellow servant rule under the steady pounding of litigation by injured workman with no place else to turn and free entry.

101. See Vose (1967) on the test-case strategy of the NAACP in the restrictive covenant area. By selecting clients to forward an interest (rather than serving the clients) the NAACP made itself an RP with corresponding strategic advantages over the opposite parties (neighborhood associations). The degree of such organizational support of litigation is a matter of some dispute. Participation by organized interest groups in litigation affecting municipal powers is described in Vose (1966); but Dolbeare (1967:40), in his study of litigation over public policy issues in a suburban county, found a total absence of interest-group sponsorship and participation in cases at the trial court level. Vose (1972:332) concludes a historical review by observing that:

Most constitutional cases before the Supreme Court . . . are sponsored or supported by an identifiable voluntary association . . . [This] has been markedly true for decades.

But Hakman (1966. 1969) found management of Supreme Court litigation by organized groups pursuing coherent long-range strategies to be relatively rare. But see Casper (1970) who contends that civil liberties and civil rights litigation in the Supreme Court is increasingly conducted by lawyers who are "group advocates" (that is. have a long-term commitment to a group with whose aims they identify) or "civil libertarians" (that is. have an impersonal commitment to the vindication of broad principles) rather than advocates. He suggests that the former types of representation lead to the posing of broader issues for decision.

ology limit the kinds of matters that come before them; not patterns of practice but individual instances, not "problems" but cases framed by the parties and strained through requirements of standing, case or controversy, jurisdiction, and so forth. Tradition and ideology also limit the kind of decision they can give. Thus, common law courts for example, give an all-or-none,[102] once-and-for-all[103] decision which must be justified in terms of a limited (though flexible) corpus of rules and techniques.[104] By tradition, courts cannot address problems by devising new regulatory or administrative machinery (and have no taxing and spending powers to support it); courts are limited to solutions compatible with the existing institutional framework.[105] Thus, even the most favorably inclined court may not be able to make those rule-changes most useful to a class of "have-nots."

Rule-change may make use of the courts more attractive to "have-nots." Apart from increasing the possibility of favorable outcomes, it may stimulate organization, rally and encourage litigants. It may directly redistribute symbolic rewards to "have-nots" (or their champions). But tangible rewards do not always follow symbolic ones. Indeed, provision of symbolic rewards to "have-nots" (or crucial groups of their supporters) may decrease capacity and drive to secure redistribution of tangible benefits.[106]

Rule-changes secured from courts or other peak agencies do not penetrate automatically and costlessly to other levels of the

---

102. Although judicial decisions do often embody or ratify compromises agreed upon by the parties, it is precisely at the level of rule promulgation that such splitting the difference is seen as illegitimate. On the ideological pressures limiting the role of compromise in judicial decision see Coons (1964).

103. Cf. Kalven (1958:165). There are, of course, exceptions, such as alimony, to this "once and for all" feature.

104. Hazard (1970:248-50) points out that courts are not well-equipped to address problems by devising systematic legal generalization. They are confined to the facts and theories presented by the parties in specific cases; after deciding the case before them, they lose their power to act; they have little opportunity to elicit commentary until after the event; and generally they can extend but not initiate legal principles. They have limited and rapidly diminishing legitimacy as devisers of new policy. Nor can courts do very much to stimulate and maintain political support for new rules.

105. See generally Friedman (1967:esp. 821); Hazard (1970:248-50). The limits of judicial competence are by no means insurmountable. Courts do administer bankrupt railroads, recalcitrant school districts, offending election boards. But clearly the amount of such affirmative administrative re-ordering that courts can undertake is limited by physical resources as well as by limitations on legitimacy.

106. See Lipsky (1970:176 ff.) for an example of the way in which provision of symbolic rewards to more influential reference publics effectively substituted for the tangible reforms demanded by rent-strikers. More generally, Edelman (1967:chap. 2) argues that it is precisely unorganized and diffuse publics that tend to receive symbolic rewards, while organized professional ones reap tangible rewards.

Law and Society

system, as attested by the growing literature on impact.[107] This may be especially true of rule-change secured by adjudication, for several reasons:

(1) Courts are not equipped to assess systematically the impact or penetration problem. Courts typically have no facilities for surveillance, monitoring, or securing systematic enforcement of their decrees. The task of monitoring is left to the parties.[108]

(2) The built-in limits on applicability due to the piecemeal character of adjudication. Thus a Mobilization for Youth lawyer reflects:

> . . . What is the ultimate value of winning a test case? In many ways a result cannot be clearcut . . . if the present welfare-residency laws are invalidated, it is quite possible that some other kind of welfare-residency law will spring up in their place. It is not very difficult to come up with a policy that is a little different, stated in different words, but which seeks to achieve the same basic objective. The results of test cases are not generally self-executing . . . It is not enough to have a law invalidated or a policy declared void if the agency in question can come up with some variant of that policy, not very different in substance but sufficiently different to remove it from the effects of the court order.[109]

(3) The artificial equalizing of parties in adjudication by insulation from the full play of political pressures—the "equality" of the parties, the exclusion of "irrelevant" material, the "independence" of judges—means that judicial outcomes are more likely to be at variance with the existing constellation of political forces than decisions arrived at in forums lacking such insulation. But resources that cannot be employed in the judicial process can reassert themselves at the implementation stage, especially where institutional overload requires another round of decision making (what resources will be deployed to implement which rules) and/or private expenditures to secure implementation. Even where "have-nots" secure favorable changes at the rule

---

107. For a useful summary of this literature, see Wasby (1970). Some broad generalizations about the conditions conducive to penetration may be found in Grossman (1970: 545 ff.) ; Levine (1970: 599 ff.).

108. Cf. Howard's (1969: 365ff) discussion of the relative ineffectualness of adjudication in voter registration and school integration (as opposed to subsequent legislative/administrative action) as flowing from judicial reliance on party initiative.

109. Rothwax (1969: 143). An analogous conclusion in the consumer protection field is reached by Leff (1970b: 356). ("One cannot think of a more expensive and frustrating course than to seek to regulate goods or 'contract' quality through repeated law-suits against inventive 'wrongdoers.' ") Leff's critique of Murray's (1969) faith in good rules to secure change in the consumer marketplace parallels Handler's (1966) critique of Reich's (1964a, 1964b) prescription of judicial review to secure change in welfare administration. Cf. Black's (1973: 137) observation that institutions which are primarily reactive, requiring mobilization by citizens. tend to deal with specific instances rather than general patterns and, as a consequence. have little preventive capacity.

level, they may not have the resources to secure the penetration of these rules.[110] The impotence of rule-change, whatever its source, is particularly pronounced when there is reliance on unsophisticated OSs to utilize favorable new rules.[111]

Where rule-change promulgated at the peak of the system does have an impact on other levels, we should not assume any isomorphism. The effect on institutional facilities and the strategic position of the parties may be far different than we would predict from the rule change. Thus, Randall's study of movie censorship shows that liberalization of the rules did not make censorship boards more circumspect; instead, many closed down and the old game between censorship boards and distributors was replaced by a new and rougher game between exhibitors and local government-private group coalitions.[112]

B. Increase in Institutional Facilities

Imagine an increase in institutional facilities for processing claims such that there is timely full-dress adjudication of every claim put forward—no queue, no delay, no stereotyping. Decrease in delay would lower costs for claimants, taking away this advantage of possessor-defendants. Those relieved of the necessity of discounting recovery for delay would have more to spend on legal services. To the extent that settlement had been induced by delay (rather than insuring against the risk of unacceptable loss), claimants would be inclined to litigate more and settle less. More litigation without stereotyping would mean more contests, including more contesting of rules and more rule change. As discounts diminished, neither side could use settlement policy to prevent rule-loss. Such reforms would for the most part benefit OS claimants, but they would also improve the position of those RP claimants not already in the possessor position, such as the prosecutor where the accused is free on bail.

---

110. Consider for example the relative absence of litigation about schoolroom religious practices clearly in violation of the Supreme Court's rules, as reported by Dolbeare and Hammond (1971). In this case RPs who were able to secure rule-victories were unable or unwilling to invest resources to secure the implementation of the new rules.

111. See, for example. Mosier and Soble's (1973:61-64) study of the Detroit Landlord-Tenant Court, where even after the enactment of new tenant defenses (landlord breach, retaliation), landlords obtained all they sought in 97% of cases. The new defenses were raised in only 3% of all cases (13% of the 20% that were contested) although, the authors conclude. "many defendants doubtless had valid landlord-breach defenses."

112. Randall (1968:chap. 7). Cf. Macaulay's (1966:156) finding that the most important impact of the new rules was to provide leverage for the operation of informal and private procedures in which dealers enjoyed greater bargaining power in their negotiations with manufacturers.

This assumes no change in the *kind* of institutional facilities. We have merely assumed a greater quantitative availability of courts of the relatively passive variety typical of (at least) "common law" systems in which the case is "tried by the parties before the court . . . ." (Homberger, 1970:31). One may imagine institutions with augmented authority to solicit and supervise litigation, conduct investigations, secure, assemble and present proof; which enjoyed greater flexibility in devising outcomes (such as compromise or mediation); and finally which had available staff for monitoring compliance with their decrees.[113]   Greater institutional "activism" might be expected to reduce advantages of party expertise and of differences in the quality and quantity of legal services. Enhanced capacity for securing compliance might be expected to reduce advantages flowing from differences in ability to invest in enforcement. It is hardly necessary to point out that such reforms could be expected to encounter not only resistance from the beneficiaries of the present passive institutional style, but also massive ideological opposition from legal professionals whose fundamental sense of legal propriety would be violated.[114]

C. Increase in Legal Services

The reform envisaged here is an increase in quantity and quality of legal services to "have-nots" (including greater availability of information about these services).[115] Presumably this would lower costs, remove the expertise advantage, produce more litigation with more favorable outcomes for "have-nots," perhaps with more appeals and more rule challenges, more new rules

---

113. Some administrative agencies approximate this kind of "activist" posture. Cf. Nonet's (1969:79) description of the California Industrial Accident Commission:

> When the IAC in its early days assumed the responsibility of notifying the injured worker of his rights, of filing his application for him, of guiding him in all procedural steps, when its medical bureau checked the accuracy of his medical record and its referees conducted his case at the hearing, the injured employee was able to obtain his benefits at almost no cost and with minimal demands on his intelligence and capacities.

In the American setting, at least such institutional activism seems unstable; over time institutions tend to approximate the more passive court model. See Nonet (1969: chaps. 6-7) and generally Bernstein (1955: chap. 7) on the "judicialization" of administrative agencies.

114. Perhaps the expansive political role of the judiciary and the law in American society is acceptable precisely because the former is so passive and the latter so malleable to private goals. Cf. Selznick's (1969:225ff) discussion of the "privatization" and "voluntarization" of legal regulation in the United States.

115. This would, of course, require the relaxation of barriers on information flow now imposed under the rubric of "professional ethics." See notes 46 and 51 above.

in their favor. (Public defender, legal aid, judicare, and pre-payment plans approximate this in various fashions.) To the extent that OSs would still have to discount for delay and risk, their gains would be limited (and increase in litigation might mean even more delay). Under certain conditions, increased legal services might use institutional overload as leverage on behalf of "have-nots." Our Mobilization for Youth attorney observes:

> . . . if the Welfare Department buys out an individual case, we are precluded from getting a principle of law changed, but if we give them one thousand cases to buy out, that law has been effectively changed whether or not the law as written is changed. The practice is changed; the administration is changed; the attitude to the client is changed. The value of a heavy case load is that it allows you to populate the legal process. It allows you to apply remitting pressure on the agency you are dealing with. It creates a force that has to be dealt with, that has to be considered in terms of the decisions that are going to be made prospectively. It means that you are not somebody who will be gone tomorrow, not an isolated case, but a force in the community that will remain once this particular case has been decided.
>
> As a result . . . we have been able, for the first time to participate along with welfare recipients . . . in a rule-making process itself. . . . (Rothwax, 1969: 140-41).

The increase in quantity of legal services was accompanied here by increased coordination and organization on the "have-not" side, which brings us to our fourth level of reform.

D. Reorganization of Parties

The reform envisaged here is the organization of "have-not" parties (whose position approximates OS) into coherent groups that have the ability to act in a coordinated fashion, play long-run strategies, benefit from high-grade legal services, and so forth.

One can imagine various ways in which OSs might be aggregated into RPs. They include (1) the membership association-bargaining agent (trade unions, tenant unions); (2) the assignee-manager of fragmentary rights (performing rights associations like ASCAP); (3) the interest group-sponsor (NAACP, ACLU, environmental action groups).[116] All of these forms involve upgrading capacities for managing claims by gathering and utilizing information, achieving continuity and persistence, employing expertise, exercising bargaining skill and so forth. These advantages are combined with enhancement of the OS party's strategic

---

116. For some examples of OSs organizing and managing claims collectively see Davis and Schwartz (1967) and various pieces in Burghardt (1972) (tenant unions); McPherson (1972) (Contract Buyers League); Shover (1966) (Farmers Holiday Association—mortgagors); Finklestein (1954) (ASCAP—performing rights); Vose (1967) (NAACP); Macaulay (1966) (automobile dealers).

142   LAW AND SOCIETY / FALL 1974

position either by aggregating claims that are too small relative to the cost of remedies (consumers, breathers of polluted air, owners of performing rights); or by reducing claims to manageable size by collective action to dispel or share unacceptable risks (tenants, migrant workers).[117]   A weaker form of organization would be (4) a clearing-house which established a communication network among OSs.   This would lower the costs of information and give RPs a stake in the effect OSs could have on their reputation.   A minimal instance of this is represented by the "media ombudsman"—the "action line" type of newspaper column.   Finally, there is governmentalization—utilizing the criminal law or the administrative process to make it the responsiblity of a public officer to press claims that would be unmanageable in the hands of private grievants.[118]

---

117. A similar enhancement of prowess in handling claims may sometimes be provided commercially, as by collection agencies.   Nonet (1969:71) observes that insurance coverage may serve as a form of organization:

> When the employer buys insurance [against workman's compensation claims], he not only secures financial coverage for his losses, but he also purchases a claims adjustment service and the legal defense he may need.   Only the largest employers can adequately develop such services on their own. . . .   Others find in their carrier a specialized claims administration they would otherwise be unable to avail themselves of . . . . to the employer, insurance constitutes much more than a way of spreading individual risks over a large group.   One of its major functions is to pool the resources of possibly weak and isolated employers so as to provide them with effective means of self-help and legal defense.

118. On criminalization as a mode of aggregating claims, see Friedman (1973:258).   This is typically a weak form of organization, for several reasons.   First, there is so much law that officials typically have far more to do than they have resources to do it with, so they tend to wait for complaints and to treat them as individual grievances. For example, the Fraud and Complaint Bureau described by McIntyre (1968) or the anti-discrimination commission described by Mayhew (1968).   Cf. Selznick's (1969:225) observations on a general "tendency to turn enforcement agencies into passive recipients of privately initiated complaints. . . .   The focus is more on settling disputes than on affirmative action aimed at realizing public goals." Second, enforcers have a pronounced tendency not to employ litigation against established and respectable institutions.   Consider, for instance, the patterns of air pollution enforcement described by Goldstein and Ford (1971) or the Department of Justice position that the penal provisions of the Refuse Act should be brought to bear only on infrequent or accidental polluters, while chronic ones should be handled by more conciliatory and protracted administrative procedures.   (1 Env. Rptr. Cur. Dev. No. 12 at 288 [1970]).   Compare the reaction of Arizona's Attorney General to the litigation initiated by the overzealous chief of his Consumer Protection Division, who had recently started an investigation of hospital pricing policies.

> I found out much to my shock and chagrin that anybody who is anybody serves on a hospital board of directors and their reaction to our hospital inquiry was one of defense and protection.

> My policy concerning lawsuits . . . is that we don't sue anybody except in the kind of emergency situation that would involve [a business] leaving town or sequestering money or records. . . .   I can't conceive any reason why hospitals in

An organized group is not only better able to secure favorable rule changes, in courts and elsewhere, but is better able to see that good rules are implemented.[119] It can expend resources on surveillance, monitoring, threats, or litigation that would be uneconomic for an OS. Such new units would in effect be RPs.[120] Their encounters with opposing RPs would move into Box IV of Figure I. Neither would enjoy the strategic advantages of RPs over OSs. One possible result, as we have noted in our discussion of the RP v. RP situation, is delegalization, that is, a movement away from the official system to a private system of dispute-settlement; another would be more intense use of the official system.

Many aspects of "public interest law" can be seen as approximations of this reform. (1) The class action is a device to raise the stakes for an RP, reducing his strategic position to that of an OS by making the stakes more than he can afford to play the odds on,[121] while moving the claimants into a position in which they enjoy the RP advantages without having to undergo the outlay for organizing. (2) Similarly, the "community organizing" aspect of public interest law can be seen as an effort to create a unit (tenants, consumers) which can play the RP game. (3) Such a change in strategic position creates the possibility of a test-case strategy for getting rule-change.[122] Thus "public in-

---

this state are going to make me sue them.
(*New York Times*, 1973).

119. On the greater strategic thrust of group-sponsored complaints in the area of discrimination, see Mayhew (1968:168-73).

120. Paradoxically, perhaps, the organization of OSs into a unit which can function as an RP entails the possibility of internal disputes with distinctions between OSs and RPs reappearing. On the re-emergence of these disparities in strategic position within, for example, unions, see Atleson (1967:485 ff.) (finding it doubtful that Title I of the LMRDA affords significant protection to "single individuals"). Cf. Summers (1960): Atleson (1971) on the poor position of individual workers *vis-a-vis* unions in arbitration proceedings.

121. As an outspoken opponent of class actions puts it:
When a firm with assets of, say, a billion dollars is sued in a class action with a class of several million and a potential liability of, say $2 billion. it faces the possibility of destruction. . . . The potential exposure in broad class actions frequently exceeds the net worth of the defendants, and corporate management naturally tends to seek insurance against whatever slight chance of success plaintiffs may have (Simon, 1972:289-90).
He then cites "eminent plaintiff's' counsel" to the effect that:
I have seen nothing so conducive to settlement of complex litigation as the establishment by the court of a class . . . whereas, if there were no class. it would not be disposed of by settlement.

122. The array of devices for securing judicial determination of broad patterns of behavior also includes the "public interest action" in which a plaintiff is permitted to vindicate rights vested in the general public (typically by challenging exercises of government power). (Homberger, 1974). Unlike the class action, plaintiff does

terest law" can be thought of as a combination of community organizing, class action and test-case strategies, along with increase in legal services.[123]

VII. REFORM AND THE REST OF THE ICEBERG

The reforms of the official litigation system that we have imagined would. taken together, provide rules more favorable to the "have nots." Redress according to the offficial rules, undiscounted by delay, strategic disability, disparities of legal services and so forth could be obtained whenever either party found it to his advantage. How might we expect such a utopian upgrading of the official machinery to affect the rest of our legal iceberg?

We would expect more use of the official system. Those who opted for inaction because of information or cost barriers and those who "settled" at discount rates in one of the "appended" systems would in many instances find it to their advantage to use the official system. The appended systems, insofar as they are built on the costs of resort to the official system, would either be abandoned or the outcomes produced would move to approximate closely those produced by adjudication.[124]

On the other hand, our reforms would, by organizing OSs, create many situations in which *both* parties were organized to pursue their long-run interest in the liltigation arena. In effect, many of the situations which occupied Boxes II and III of Figure 1 (RP v. OS, OS v. RP)—the great staple sources of litigation— would now be moved to Box IV (RP v. RP). We observed earlier that RPs who anticipate continued dealings with one another tend to rely on informal bilateral controls. We might expect then that the official system would be abandoned in favor of private systems of dispute-settlement.[125]

---

not purport to represent a class of particular individuals (with all the procedural difficulties of that posture) and unlike the classic test case he is not confined to his own grievance. but is regarded as qualified by virtue of his own injury to represent the interests of the general public.

123. However, there may be tensions among these commitments. Wexler (1970), arguing for the primacy of "organizing" (including training in lay advocacy) in legal practice which aims to help the poor, points to the seductive pull of professional notions of the proper roles and concerns of the lawyer. Cf. Brill's (1973) portrayal of lawyers' professional and personal commitment to "class action'" cases (in which the author apparently includes all "test cases'") as undercutting their avowed commitment to facilitate community organization. On the inherent limits of "organizing" strategies, see note 127.

124. That is. the "reciprocal immunities" (Friedman 1967:806) built on transaction costs of remedies would be narrowed and would be of the same magnitude for each party.

125. This is in Boxes II and III of Figure 1. where both parties are now RPs. But presumably in some of the litigation formerly in Box I.

Thus we would expect our reforms to produce a dual movement: the official and its appended systems would be "legalized"[126] while the proliferation of private systems would "de-
legalize" many relationships. Which relationships would we expect to move which way? As a first approximation, we might
expect that the less "inclusive" relationships currently handled
by litigation or in the appended systems would undergo legalization, while relationships at the more inclusive end of the scale
(Figure 7) would be privatized. Relationships among strangers
(casual, episodic, non-recurrent) would be legalized; more dense
(recurrent, inclusive) relationships between parties would be
candidates for the development of private systems.

Our earlier analysis suggests that the pattern might be more
complex. First, for various reasons a class of OSs may be relatively incapable of being organized. Its size, relative to the size
and distribution of potential benefits, may require disproportionately large inputs of coordination and organization.[127] Its shared
interest may be insufficiently respectable to be publicly acknowledged (for instance, shoplifters, homosexuals until very recently). Or recurrent OS roles may be staffed by shifting population for whom the sides of the transaction are interchangeable.[128]
(For instance, home buyers and sellers, negligent motorists and
accident victims.)[129] Even where OSs are organizable, we recall

one side is capable of organization but the other is not, so new instances of strategic disparity might emerge. We would expect these
to remain in the official system.

126. That is, in which the field level application of the official rules has
   moved closer to the authoritative "higher law" (see note 82.)

127. Olson (1965) argues that capacity for coordinated action to further
   common interests decreases with the size of the group: ". . . relatively small groups will frequently be able voluntarily to organize
   and act in support of their common interests, and some large groups
   normally will not be able to do so." (1965:127). Where smaller
   groups can act in their common interest, larger ones are likely to
   be capable of so acting only when they can obtain some coercive
   power over members or are supplied with some additional selective
   incentives to induce the contribution of the needed inputs of organizational activity. (On the reliance of organizations on these selective incentives, see Salisbury [1969] and Clark and Wilson [1961].)
   Such selective incentives may be present in the form of services provided by a group already organized for some other purpose. Thus
   many interests may gain the benefits of organization only to the extent that those sharing them overlap with those with a more organizable interest (consider, for instance, the prominence of labor unions
   as lobbyists for consumer interests).

128. Cf. Fuller's (1969:23) observation that the notion of duty is most
   understandable and acceptable in a society in which relationships
   are sufficiently fluid and symmetrical so that duties "must in theory
   and practice be reversible."

129. Curiously these relationships have the character which Rawls (1958:
   98) postulates as a condition under which parties will agree to
   be bound by "just" rules; that is, no one knows in advance the
   position he will occupy in the proposed "practice." The analysis
   here assumes that while high turnover and unpredictable inter-
   change of roles may approximate this condition in some cases, one

146   LAW AND SOCIETY / FALL 1974

that not all RP v. RP encounters lead to the development of private remedy systems. There are RPs engaged in value conflict; there are those relationships with a governmental or other monopoly aspect in which informal controls may falter; and finally there are those RPs whose encounters with one another are nonrecurring. In all of these we might expect legalization rather than privatization.

Whichever way the movement in any given instance, our reforms would entail changes in the distribution of power. RPs would no longer be able to wield their strategic advantages to invoke selectively the enforcement of favorable rules while securing large discounts (or complete shielding by cost and overload) where the rules favored their OS opponents.

Delegalization (by the proliferation of private remedy and bargaining systems) would permit many relationships to be regulated by norms and understandings that departed from the official rules. Such parochial remedy systems would be insulated from the impingement of the official rules by the commitment of the parties to their continuing relationship. Thus, delegalization would entail a kind of pluralism and decentralization. On the other hand, the "legalization" of the official and appended systems would amount to the collapse of species of pluralism and decentralization that are endemic in the kind of (unreformed) legal system we have postulated. The current prevalence of appended and private remedy systems reflects the inefficiency, cumbersomeness and costliness of using the official system. This inefficient, cumbersome and costly character is a source and shield of a kind of decentralization and pluralism. It permits a selective application of the "higher law" in a way that gives effect at the operative level to parochial norms and concerns which are not fully recognized in the "higher law" (such as the right to exclude low status neighbors,[130] or police dominance

---

of the pervasive and important characteristics of much human arranging is that the participants have a pretty good idea of which role in the arrangement they will play. Rawls (1971:136ff) suggests that one consequence of this "veil of ignorance" (". . . no one knows his place in society, his class position or social status; nor does he know his fortune in the distribution of natural assets and abilities, his intelligence and strength and the like") is that "the parties have no basis for bargaining in the usual sense" and concludes that without such restriction "we would not be able to work out any definite theory of justice at all." "If knowledge of particulars is allowed, then the outcome is biased by arbitrary contingencies." If we posit knowledge of particulars as endemic, we may surmise that a "definite theory of justice" will play at most a minor role in explaining the legal process.

130. On exclusion of undesirable neighbors, see Babcock (1969); of undesirable sojourners, see the banishment policy described in Foote (1956).

in encounters with citizens[131]). If the insulation afforded by the costs of getting the "higher law" to prevail were eroded, many relationships would suddenly be exposed to the "higher law" rather than its parochial counterparts. We might expect this to generate new pressures for explicit recognition of these "subterranean" values or for explicit decentralization.

These conjectures about the shape that a "reformed' legal system might take suggest that we take another look at our unreformed system, with its pervasive disparity between authoritative norms and everyday operations. A modern legal system of the type we postulated is characterized structurally by institutional unity and culturally by normative universalism. The power to make, apply and change law is reserved to organs of the public, arranged in unified hierarchic relations, commited to uniform application of universalistic norms.

There is, for example, in American law (that is, in the higher reaches of the system where the learned tradition is propounded) an unrelenting stress on the virtues of uniformity and universality and a pervasive distaste for particularism, compromise and discretion.[132] Yet the cultural attachment to universalism is wedded to and perhaps even intensifies diversity and particularism at the operative level.[133]

The unreformed features of the legal system then appear as a device for maintaining the partial dissociation of everyday practice from these authoritative institutional and normative commitments. Structurally, (by cost and institutional overload) and culturally (by ambiguity and normative overload) the unreformed system effects a massive covert delegation from the most authoritative rule-makers to field level officials (and their constituencies) responsive to other norms and priorities than are

---

131. See the anguished discovery (Seymour 1974:9) of this by a former United States Attorney in his encounter with local justice:

> When the police officer had finished his testimony and left the stand. I moved to dismiss the case as a matter of law, pointing out that the facts were exactly the same as in the case cited in the annotation to the statute. I asked the judge to please look at the statute and read the case under it. Instead he looked me straight in the eye and announced, "Motion denied."

132. It seems hardly necessary to adduce examples of this pervasive distaste of particularism. But consider Justice Frankfurter's admonition that "We must not sit like a kadi under a tree dispensing justice according to conditions of individual expediency." *Terminiello v. Chicago*, 337 U.S. 1, 11 (1948). Or Wechsler's (1959) castigation of the Supreme Court for departing from the most fastidiously neutral principles.

133. As Thurman Arnold observed, our law "compels the necessary compromises to be carred on *sub rosa*, while the process is openly condemned. . . . Our process attempts to outlaw the 'unwritten law.' " (1962:162). On the co-existence of stress on uniformity and rulefulness with discretion and irregularity, see Davis (1969).

contained in the "higher law."[134] By their selective application of rules in a context of parochial understandings and priorities, these field level legal communities produce regulatory outcomes which could not be predicted by examination of the authoritative "higher law."[135]

Thus its unreformed character articulates the legal system to the discontinuities of culture and social structure: it provides a way of accommodating cultural heterogeneity and social diversity while propounding universalism and unity; of accommodating vast concentrations of private power while upholding the supremacy of public authority; of accommodating inequality in fact while establishing equality at law; of facilitating action by great collective combines while celebrating individualism. Thus "unreform"—that is, ambiguity and overload of rules, overloaded and inefficient institutional facilities, disparities in the supply of legal services, and disparities in the strategic position of parties—is the foundation of the "dualism"[136] of the legal system. It permits unification and universalism at the symbolic level and diversity and particularism at the operating level.[137]

---

134. Cf. Black's (1973:142-43) observations on "reactive" mobilization systems as a form of delegation which perpetuates diverse moral subcultures as well as reinforces systems of social stratification (141).

135. Some attempts at delineating and comparing such "local legal cultures'" are found in Jacob (1969); Wilson (1968); Goldstein and Ford (1971). It should be emphasized that such variation is not primarily a function of differences at the level of rules. All of these studies show considerable variation among localities and agencies governed by the same body of rules.

136. I employ this term to refer to one distinctive style of accommodating social diversity and normative pluralism by combining universalistic law with variable application, local initiative and tolerated evasion. (Cf. the kindred usage of this term by Rheinstein [1972: chaps. 4, 10] to describe the divorce regime of contemporary western nations characterized by a gap between "the law of the books and the law in action;" and by ten Broek [1964a, 1965] to describe the unacknowledged co-existence of diverse class-specific bodies of law.) This dualistic style might be contrasted to, among others, (a) a "millet" system in which various groups are explicitly delegated broad power to regulate their own internal dealings through their own agencies (cf. Reppetto, 1970); (b) official administration of disparate bodies of "special law" generated by various groups (for example, the application of their respective "personal laws'" to adherents of various religions in South Asian countries. See Galanter [1968].) Although a legal system of the kind we have postulated is closest to dualism, it is not a pure case, but combines all three. For some observations on changes in the relation of government law to other legal orderings, see Weber (1954: 16-20, 140-49).

137. The durability of "dualism" as an adaptation is reinforced by the fact that it is "functional" not only for the larger society, but that each of its "moieties" gives support to the other: the "higher law'" masks and legitimates the "operating level": the accommodation of particularistic interests there shields the "higher law" from demands and pressures which it could not accommodate without sacrificing its universalism and semblance of autonomy. I do not suggest that this explains why some societies generate these "dual" structures.

VIII. IMPLICATIONS FOR REFORM:
THE ROLE OF LAWYERS

We have discussed the way in which the architecture of the legal system tends to confer interlocking advantages on overlapping groups whom we have called the "haves." To what extent might reforms of the legal system dispel these advantages? Reforms will always be less total than the utopian ones envisioned above. Reformers will have limited resources to deploy and they will always be faced with the necessity of choosing which uses of those resources are most productive of equalizing change. What does our analysis suggest sbout strategies and priorities?

Our analysis suggests that change at the level of substantive rules is not likely in itself to be determinative of redistributive outcomes. Rule change is in itself likely to have little effect because the system is so constructed that changes in the rules can be filtered out unless accompanied by changes at other levels. In a setting of overloaded institutional facilities, inadequate costly legal services, and unorganized parties, beneficiaries may lack the resources to secure implementation; or an RP may restructure the transaction to escape the thrust of the new rule. (Leff, 1970b; Rothwax, 1969:143; Cf. Grossman, 1970). Favorable rules are not necessarily (and possibly not typically) in short supply to "have-nots;" certainly less so than any of the other resources needed to play the litigation game.[138] Programs of equalizing reform which focus on rule-change can be readily absorbed without any change in power relations. The system has the capacity to change a great deal at the level of rules without corresponding changes in everyday patterns of practice[139] or distribution of tangible advantages. (See, for example, Lipsky, 1970: chap. 4,5). Indeed rule-change may become a symbolic substitute for redistribution of advantages. (See Edelman, 1967:40).

The low potency of substantive rule-change is especially the case with rule-changes procured from courts. That courts can sometimes be induced to propound rule-changes that legislatures would not make points to the limitations as well as the possibilities of court-produced change. With their relative insulation from retaliation by antagonistic interests, courts may more easily

---

138. Indeed the response that reforms must wait upon rule-change is one of the standard ploys of targets of reform demands. See, for example, Lipsky's (1970:94-96) housing officials' claim that implementation of rent-strikers' demands required new legislation, when they already had the needed power.

139. Compare Dolbeare and Hammond's (1971:151) observation, based on their research into implementation of the school prayer decisions, that "images of change abound while the status quo, in terms of the reality of people's lives, endures."

propound new rules which depart from prevailing power relations. But such rules require even greater inputs of other resources to secure effective implementation. And courts have less
capacity than other rule-makers to create institutional facilities
and re-allocate resources to secure implementation of new rules.
Litigation then is unlikely to shape decisively the distribution
of power in society. It may serve to secure or solidify symbolic
commitments. It is vital tactically in securing temporary advantage or protection, providing leverage for organization and articulation of interests and conferring (or withholding) the mantle
of legitimacy.[140] The more divided the other holders of power,
the greater the redistributive potential of this symbolic/tactical
role. (Dahl, 1958:294).

Our analysis suggests that breaking the interlocked advantages of the "haves" requires attention not only to the level of
rules, but also to institutional facilities, legal services and organization of parties. It suggests that litigating and lobbying have
to be complemented by interest organizing, provisions of services
and invention of new forms of institutional facilities.[141]

The thrust of our analysis is that changes at the level of
parties are most likely to generate changes at other levels. If
rules are the most abundant resource for reformers, parties capable of pursuing long-range strategies are the rarest. The presence of such parties can generate effective demand for high
grade legal services—continuous, expert, and oriented to the long
run—and pressure for institutional reforms and favorable rules.
This suggests that we can roughly surmise the relative strategic
priority of various rule-changes. Rule changes which relate directly to the strategic position of the parties by facilitating organization, increasing the supply of legal services (where these in
turn provide a focus for articulating and organizing common
interests) and increasing the costs of opponents—for instance
authorization of class action suits, award of attorneys fees and
costs, award of provisional remedies—these are the most powerful fulcrum for change.[142] The intensity of the opposition to

---

140. On litigation as an organizational tool, see the examples given by
    Gary Bellow in *Yale Law Journal* (1970:1087-88).
141. Cf. Cahn and Cahn's (1970:1016 ff.) delineation of the "four princi-
    pal areas where the investment of . . . resources would yield critic-
    ally needed changes: the creation (and legitimation) of new jus-
    tice-dispensing institutions, the expansion of the legal manpower
    supply . . . the development of a new body of procedural and sub-
    stantive rights, and the development of forms of group representa-
    tion as a means of enfranchisement," and the rich catalog of exam-
    ples under each heading.
142. The reformer who anticipates "legalization" (see text at note 126
    above) looks to organization as a fulcrum for expanding legal serv-

class action legislation and autonomous reform-oriented legal services[143] such as California Rural Legal Assistance indicates the "haves" own estimation of the relative strategic impact of the several levels.[144]

The contribution of the lawyer to redistributive social change, then, depends upon the organization and culture of the legal profession. We have surmised that court-produced substantive rule-change is unlikely in itself to be a determinative element in producing tangible redistribution of benefits. The leverage provided by litigation depends on its strategic combination with inputs at other levels. The question then is whether the organization of the profession permits lawyers to develop and employ skills at these other levels. The more that lawyers view themselves exclusively as courtroom advocates, the less their willingness to undertake new tasks and form enduring alliances with clients and operate in forums other than courts, the less likely they are to serve as agents of redistributive change. Paradoxically, those legal professions most open to accentuating the advantages of the "haves" (by allowing themselves to be "captured" by recurrent clients) may be most able to become (or have room for, more likely) agents of change, precisely because they provide more license for identification with clients and their "causes" and have a less strict definition of what are properly professional activities.[145]

---

ices, improving institutional facilities and eliciting favorable rules. On the other hand, the reformer who anticipates "de-legalization" and the development of advantageous bargaining relationships/private remedy system may be indifferent or opposed to reforms of the official remedy system that would make it more likely that the official system would impinge on the RP v. RP relationship.

143. It is clear e.g. that what Agnew (1972:930) finds objectionable is the redistributive thrust of the legal services program:

> . . . the legal services program has gone way beyond the idea of a governmentally funded program to make legal remedies available to the indigent. . . . We are dealing, in large part, with a systematic effort to redistribute societal advantages and disadvantages, penalties and rewards, rights and resources.

144. Summed up neatly by the head of OEO programs in California, who, defending Governor Reagan's veto of the California Rural Legal Assistance program, said:

> What we've created in CRLA is an economic leverage equal to that of a large corporation. Clearly that should not be.

Quoted at Stumpf, et al. (1971:65).

145. Cf. Note 48 above. It is submitted that legal professions that approximate "Type B" will not only accentuate the "have" advantages, but will also be most capable of producing redistributive change.

152   LAW AND SOCIETY / FALL 1974

REFERENCES

ABEL, Richard L. (1974) "A Comparative Theory of Dispute Institutions in Society," 8 *Law & Society Review* 217.

ABEL-SMITH, Brian and Robert STEVENS (1967) *Lawyers and the Courts: A Sociological Study of the English Legal System, 1750-1965.* Cambridge: Harvard University Press.

AGNEW, Spiro (1972) "What's Wrong with the Legal Services Program," 58 *A.B.A. Journal* 930.

AKERS, Ronald L. (1968) "The Professional Association and the Legal Regulation of Practice," 2 *Law & Society Review* 463.

ANDERSON, Stanley (1969) *Ombudsman Papers: American Experience and Proposals. With a Comparative Analysis of Ombudsmen Offices by Kent M. Weeks.* Berkeley: Univ. of Cal. Inst. of Govt. Studies.

ARNOLD, Thurman (1962) *The Symbols of Government.* New York: Harcourt Brace and World (First publication, 1935).

ASPIN, Leslie (1966) *A Study of Reinstatement Under the National Labor Relations Act.* Unpublished dissertation, Mass. Inst. of Tech., Dept. of Economics.

ATLESON, James B. (1971) "Disciplinary Discharges, Arbitration and NLRB Deference," 20 *Buffalo Law Review* 355.

——————————— (1967) "A Union Member's Right of Free Speech and Assembly: Institutional Interests and Individual Rights," 51 *Minnesota Law Review* 403.

AUBERT, Vilhelm (1967) "Courts and Conflict Resolution," 11 *Journal of Conflict Resolution* 40.

——————————— (1963) "Competition and Dissensus: Two Types of Conflict and of Conflict Resolution." 7 *Journal of Conflict Resolution* 26.

BABCOCK, Richard S. (1969) *The Zoning Game: Municipal Practices and Policies.* Madison: University of Wisconsin Press.

BATTLE, Jackson B. (1971) "In Search of the Adversary System—The Cooperative Practices of Private Criminal Defense Attorneys," 50 *Texas Law Review* 60.

BERMAN, Harold J. (1963) *Justice in the U.S.S.R.: An Interpretation of Soviet Law.* Revised Ed., Enlarged. New York: Vintage Books.

BERNSTEIN, Marver H. (1955) *Regulating Business by Independent Commission.* Princeton: Princeton University Press.

BEUTEL, Frederick K. (1957) *Some Potentialities of Experimental Jurisprudence as a New Branch of Social Science.* Lincoln: University of Nebraska Press.

BLACK, Donald J. (1973) "The Mobilization of Law," 2 *Journal of Legal Studies* 125.

——————————— (1971) "The Social Organization of Arrest," 23 *Stanford Law Review* 1087.

——————————— (1970) "Production of Crime Rates," 35 *American Sociological Review* 733.

BLANKENBURG, Erhard, Viola BLANKENBURG and Hellmut MORASON (1972) "Der lange Weg in die Berufung," in Rolf BENDER (ed.) *Tatsachen Forschung in der Justiz.* Tubingen: C.B. Mohr, 1972.

BLUMBERG, Abraham S. (1967a) *Criminal Justice.* Chicago: Quadrangle Books.

——————————— (1967b) "The Practice of Law as a Confidence Game," 1 *Law & Society Review* 15.

BOHANNAN, Paul (1965) "The Differing Realms of the Law in The Ethnography of Law," in Laura NADER (ed.) *The Ethnography of Law* (=Part 2 of *American Anthropologist*, Vol. 67, No. 6.).

BONN, Robert L. (1972a) "Arbitration: An Alternative System for Handling Contract Related Disputes," 17 *Administrative Sciences Quarterly* 254.

——————————— (1972b) "The Predictability of Nonlegalistic Adjudication," 6 *Law & Society Review* 563.

BORKIN, Joseph (1950) "The Patent Infringement Suit—Ordeal by Trial," 17 *University of Chicago Law Review* 634.

BRILL, Harry (1973) "The Uses and Abuses of Legal Assistance," No. 31 (Spring) *The Public Interest* 38.

Galanter / LEGAL CHANGE 153

BRUFF, Harold H. (1973) "Arizona's Inferior Courts." 1973 *Law and the Social Order* 1.

BURGER, Warren (1970) "The State of the Judiciary—1970," 56 *A.B.A. Journal* 929.

BURGHARDT, Stephen (ed.) (1972) *Tenants and the Urban Housing Crisis.* Dexter, Mich.: The New Press.

BURNLEY, James H. IV (1973) "Comment. Solicitation by the Second Oldest Profession: Attorneys and Advertising," 8 *Harvard Civil Rights-Civil Liberties Law Review* 77.

CAHN, Edgar S. and Jean Camper CAHN (1970) "Power to the People or the Profession?—The Public Interest in Public Interest Law," 79 *Yale Law Journal* 1005.

CAMERON, Mary Owen (1964) *The Booster and the Snitch: Department Shoplifting.* New York: Free Press of Glencoe.

CARLIN, Jerome E. (1966) *Lawyers' Ethics: A Survey of the New York City Bar.* New York: Russell Sage Foundation.

————— (1962) *Lawyers on Their Own: A Study of Individual Practitioners in Chicago.* New Brunswick: Rutgers University Press.

CARLIN, Jerome E. and Jan HOWARD (1965) "Legal Representation and Class Justice," 12 *U.C.L.A. Law Review* 381.

CASPER, Jonathan D. (1970) "Lawyers Before the Supreme Court: Civil Liberties and Civil Rights, 1957-66," 22 *Stanford Law Review* 487.

CHRISTIANSON, Barlow F. (1970) *Lawyers for People of Moderate Means: Some Problems of Availability of Legal Services.* Chicago: American Bar Foundation.

CLARK, Peter B. and James Q. WILSON (1961) "Incentive Systems: A Theory of Organizations," 6 *Administrative Sciences Quarterly* 129.

COHEN, Julius, Reginald A.H. ROBSON and Alan BATES (1958) *Parental Authority: The Community and the Law.* New Brunswick: Rutgers University Press.

COHN, Bernard S. (1959) "Some Notes on Law and Change in North India," 8 *Economic Development and Cultural Change* 79.

COLUMBIA JOURNAL OF LAW AND SOCIAL PROBLEMS (1971) "Roman Catholic Ecclesiastical Courts and the Law of Marriage," 7 *Columbia Journal of Law and Social Problems* 204.

————— (1970) "Rabbinical Courts: Modern Day Solomons," 6 *Columbia Journal of Law and Social Problems* 49.

COMMUNITY SERVICE SOCIETY, Department of Public Affairs, Special Committee On Consumer Protection (1974) *Large Grievances About Small Causes: New York City's Small Claims Court—Proposals for Improving the Collection of Judgments.* New York: New York City Community Service Society.

CONARD, Alfred F., James N. MORGAN, Robert W. PRATT, JR., Charles F. VOLTZ and ROBERT L. BOMBAUGH (1964) *Automobile Accident Costs and Payments: Studies in the Economics of Injury Reparation.* Ann Arbor: University of Michigran Press.

CONSUMER COUNCIL (1970) *Justice Out of Reach: A Case for Small Claims Courts.* London: Her Majesty's Stationery Office.

COONS, John E. (1964) "Approaches to Court-Imposed Compromise—The Uses of Doubt and Reason," 58 *Northwestern University Law Review* 750.

CRESSEY, Donald R. (1969) *Theft of the Nation: The Structure and Operations of Organized Crime in America.* New York: Harper and Row.

DAHL, Robert A. (1958) "Decision-making in a Democracy: The Supreme Court as a National Policy-maker," 6 *Journal of Public Law* 279.

DAVIS, Gordon J. and Michael W. SCHWARTZ (1967) "Tenant Unions: An Experiment in Private Law Making," 2 *Harvard Civil Rights-Civil Liberties Law Review* 237.

DAVIS, Kenneth Culp (1969) *Discretionary Justice: A Preliminary Inquiry.* Baton Rouge: Louisiana State University Press.

DERRETT, J. Duncan M. (1959) "Sir Henry Maine and Law in India," 1959 (Part I) *Juridical Review* 40.

154   LAW AND SOCIETY / FALL 1974

DIBBLE, Vernon K. (1973) "What Is, and What Ought to Be: A Comparison of Certain Formal Characteristics of the Ideological and Legal Styles of Thought," 79 *American Journal of Sociology* 511.

DOLBEARE. Kenneth M. (1969) "The Federal District Courts and Urban Public Policy: An Exploratory Study (1960-1967)," in J. GROSSMAN and J. TANENHAUS (eds.) *Frontiers of Judicial Research*. New York: John Wiley.

——————————— (1967) *Trial Courts in Urban Politics: State Court Policy Impact and Function in a Local Political System*. New York: John Wiley.

DOLBEARE. Kenneth M. and Phillip E. HAMMOND (1971) *The School Prayer Decisions: From Court Policy to Local Practice.* Chicago: University of Chicago Press.

DOO. Leigh-Wei (1973) "Dispute Settlement in Chinese-American Communities." 21 *American Journal of Comparative Law* 627.

DURKHEIM. Emile (1964) *The Division of Labor in Society.* New York: Free Press.

EDELMAN. Murray (1967) *The Symbolic Uses of Politics.* Urbana: University of Illinois Press.

EHRLICH, Eugen (1936) *Fundamental Principles of the Sociology of Law.* New York: Russell and Russell Publishers.

ENGLE. C. Donald (1971) *Criminal Justice in the City.* Unpublished dissertation. Department of Political Science, Temple University.

ENNIS. Phillip H. (1967) *Criminal Victimization in the United States: A Report of a National Survey.* (President's Commission on Law Enforcement and Administration of Justice, Field Survey II). Washington: Government Printing Office.

FELSTINER. William L.F. (1974) "Influences of Social Organization on Dispute Processing," 9 *Law & Society Review* 63.

FINKLESTEIN, Herman (1954) "The Composer and the Public Interest —Regulation of Performing Rights Societies," 19 *Law and Contemporary Problems* 275.

FOOTE. Caleb (1956) "Vagrancy-type Law and Its Administration," 104 *University of Pennsylvania Law Review* 603.

FORD. Stephen D. (1970) *The American Legal System.* Minneapolis: West Publishing Company.

FRANK, Jerome (1930) *Law and the Modern Mind.* New York: Coward-McCann.

FRANKLIN. Marc, Robert H. CHANIN and Irving MARK (1961) "Accidents, Money and the Law. A Study of the Economics of Personal Injury Litigation," 61 *Columbia Law Review* 1.

FRIEDMAN. Lawrence M. (1973) *A History of American Law.* New York: Simon and Shuster.

——————————— (1969) "Legal Culture and Social Development," 4 *Law & Society Review* 29.

——————————— (1967) "Legal Rules and the Process of Social Change." 19 *Stanford Law Review* 786.

FRIEDMAN. Lawrence M. and Jack LADINSKY (1967) "Social Change and the Law of Industrial Accidents." 67 *Columbia Law Review* 50.

FRIEDMAN. Lawrence M. and Stewart MACAULAY (1967) "Contract Law and Contract Teaching: Past, Present, and Future," 1967 *Wisconsin Law Review* 805.

FULLER, Lon L. (1969) *The Morality of Law.* Revised ed., New Haven: Yale University Press.

GALANTER. Marc (1968-69) "Introduction: The Study of the Indian Legal Profession," 3 *Law & Society Review* 201.

——————————— (1968) "The Displacement of Traditional Law in Modern India." 24 *Journal of Social Issues* 65.

GELLHORN. Walter (1966) *When Americans Complain: Governmental Grievance Procedures.* Cambridge: Harvard University Press.

GIFFORD. Daniel J. (1971) "Communication of Legal Standards. Policy Development and Effective Conduct Regulation." 56 *Cornell Law Review* 409.

GOLDING. Martin P. (1969) "Preliminaries to the Study of Procedural Justice." in G. HUGHES (ed.) *Law, Reason and Justice.* New York: New York University Press.

Galanter / LEGAL CHANGE 155

GOLDSTEIN. Paul and Robert FORD (1971) "The Management of Air Quality: Legal Structures and Official Behavior," 21 *Buffalo Law Review* 1.

GOLDPAPER, Sam (1971) "Judge Rules Caldwell Belongs to ABA Club," *New York Times*, Jan 15, 1971, p. 69.

GOLLAN, David (1970) "Airline Agency Levies Big Fines," *New York Times*, Nov 8, 1970, p. 88.

GRACE, Roger (1970) "Justice, Chinese Style," 75 *Case and Comment* 50.

GROSSMAN, Joel (1970) "The Supreme Court and Social Change: A Preliminary Inquiry," 13 *American Behavioral Scientist* 535.

HAHM, Pyong-Choon (1969) "The Decision Process in Korea," in G. SCHUBERT and D. DANELSKI (eds.) *Comparative Judicial Behavior: Cross-Cultural Studies of Political Decision-Making in the East and West*. New York: Oxford University Press.

HALLAUER, Robert Paul (1972) "Low Income Laborers as Legal Clients: Use Patterns and Attitudes Toward Lawyers," 49 *Denver Law Journal* 169.

HAKMAN, Nathan (1969) "The Supreme Court's Political Environment: The Processing of Noncommercial Litigation," in J. GROSSMAN and J. TANENHAUS (eds.) *Frontiers of Judicial Research*. New York: John Wiley and Sons.

HAMILTON, Walter (1957) *The Politics of Industry*. New York: Alfred A. Knopf.

————— (1966) "Lobbying the Supreme Court—An Appraisal of Political Science Folklore," 35 *Fordham Law Review* 15.

HANDLER, Joel (1967) *The Lawyer and his Community: The Practicing Bar in a Middlesized City*. Madison: University of Wisconsin Press.

————— (1966) "Controlling Official Behavior in Welfare Administration," in Jacobus TENBROEK. *et. al.* (eds.) *The Law of the Poor*. San Francisco: Chandler Publishing Co.

HANDLER, Milton (1971a) "The Shift from Substantive to Procedural Innovations in Antitrust Suits," 26 *Record of N.Y.C. Bar Association* 124.

————— (1971b) "Twenty-Fourth Annual Antitrust Review," 26 *Record of N.Y.C. Bar Association* 753.

HART, Henry M., JR. and Albert M. SACKS (1958) *The Legal Process: Basic Problems in the Making and Application of Law*. Cambridge, Mass.: Harvard Law School. Tentative Edition (Mimeographed).

HAZARD, Geoffrey C., JR. (1970) "Law Reforming in the Anti-Poverty Effort," 37 *University of Chicago Law Review* 242.

————— (1965) "After the Trial Court—the Realities of Appellate Review," in Harry JONES (ed.) *The Courts, the Public and the Law Explosion*. Englewood Cliffs: Prentice Hall.

HENDERSON, Dan Fenno (1968) "Law and Political Modernization in Japan," in Robert E. WARD (ed.) *Political Development in Modern Japan*. Princeton: Princeton University Press.

HIRSCHMAN, Albert O. (1970) *Exit, Voice, and Loyalty: Responses to Decline in Firms, Organizations and States*. Cambridge: Harvard University Press.

HOLLINGSWORTH, Robert J., William B. FELDMAN and David C. CLARK (1973) "The Ohio Small Claims Court: An Empirical Study," 42 *University of Cincinnati Law Review* 469.

HOMBERGER, Adolf (1974) "Private Suits in the Public Interest in the United States of America," 23 *Buffalo Law Review* 343.

————— (1971) "State Class Actions and the Federal Rule," 71 *Columbia Law Review* 609.

————— (1970) "Functions of Orality in Austrian and American Civil Procedure," 20 *Buffalo Law Review* 9.

HORSKY, Charles (1952) *The Washington Lawyer*. Boston: Little, Brown and Co.

HOWARD, J. Woodford, JR. (1969) "Adjudication Considered as a Process of Conflict Resolution: A Variation on Separation of Powers," 18 *Journal of Public Law* 339.

HUNTING,Roger Bryand and Gloria S. NEUWIRTH (1962) *Who Sues in New York City? A Study of Automobile Accident Claims*. New York: Columbia University Press.

HURST, James Willard (1950) *The Growth of American Law: The Law Makers*. Boston: Little, Brown and Co.

IANNI, Francis A.J. (1972) *A Family Business: Kinship and Control in Organized Crime*. New York: Russell Sage Foundation and Basic Books.

156   LAW AND SOCIETY / FALL 1974

INTERNATIONAL LEGAL CENTER (1973) *Newsletter No. 9, July 1973.*
New York: International Legal Center.

JACOB, Herbert (1969) *Debtors in Court: The Consumption of Government Services.* Chicago: Rand McNally.

JOHNSTONE, Quintin and Dan HOPSON, JR. (1967) *Lawyers and Their
Work: An Analysis of the Legal Profession in the United States and
England.* Indianapolis: Bobbs Merrill Co.

KALVEN, Harry, JR. (1958) "The Jury, the Law and the Personal Injury
Damage Award," 19 *Ohio State Law Journal* 158.

KAPLAN, Benjamin, Arthur T. von MEHREN and Rudolf SCHAEFER
(1958) "Phases of German Civil Procedure," 71 *Harvard Law Review*
1193-1268, 1443-72.

KATZ, Marvin (1969) "Mr. Lin's Accident Case: A Working Hypothesis
on the Oriental Meaning of Face in International Relations on the
Grand Scheme," 78 *Yale Law Journal* 1491.

KAWASHIMA, Takeyoshi (1963) "Dispute Resolution in Contemporary
Japan," in A.T. von MEHREN (ed.) *Law in Japan: The Legal Order
in a Changing Society.* Cambridge: Harvard University Press.

KENNEDY, Duncan (1973) "Legal Formality," 2 *Journal of Legal Studies* 351.

KIDDER, Robert L. (1974) "Formal Litigation and Professional Inse-
curity: Legal Entrepreneurship in South India," 9 *Law & Society
Review* 11.

——————————— (1973) "Courts and Conflict in an Indian City: A
Study in Legal Impact," 11 *Journal of Commonwealth Political Studies* 121.

——————————— (1971) *The Dynamics of Litigation: A Study of
Civil Litigation in South Indian Courts.* Unpublished Dissertation,
Northwestern University.

LADINSKY, Jack (1963) "Careers of Lawyers, Law Practice and Legal
Institutions," 28 *American Sociological Review* 47.

LAFAVE, Wayne R. (1965) *Arrest: The Decision to Take a Suspect into
Custody.* Boston: Little, Brown and Co.

LARGE, Donald W. (1972) "Is Anybody Listening? The Problem of Access in Environmental Litigation," 1972 *Wisconsin Law Review* 62.

LAUFER, Joseph (1970) "Embattled Victims of the Uninsured: In Court
with New York's MVAIC, 1959-69," 19 *Buffalo Law Review* 471.

LE VAR, C. Jeddy (1973) "The Small Claims Court: A Case Study of
Process, Politics, Outputs and Factors Associated with Businessmen
Usage." Unpublished Paper.

LEFF, Arthur A. (1970a) "Injury, Ignorance, and Spite—The Dynamics
of Coercive Collection," 80 *Yale Law Journal* 1.

——————————— (1970b) "Unconscionability and the CrowdConsum-
ers and the Common-Law Tradition," 31 *University of Pittsburgh
Law Review* 349.

LEPAULLE, Pierre George (1950) "Law Practice in France," 50 *Columbia Law Review* 945.

LEVINE, Felice J. and Elizabeth PRESTON (1970) "Community Resource Orientation Among Low Income Groups," 1970 *Wisconsin Law
Review* 80.

LEVINE, James P. (1970) "Methodological Concerns in Studying Supreme Court Efficacy," 4 *Law & Society Review* 583.

LIGHT, Ivan H. (1972) *Ethnic Enterprise in America: Business and
Welfare Among Chinese, Japanese and Blacks.* Berkeley: University of California Press.

LIPSKY, Michael (1970) *Protest in City Politics: Rent Strikes, Housing,
and the Power of the Poor.* Chicago: Rand McNally and Co.

LOBENTHAL, Joseph S., JR. (1970) *Power and Put-On: The Law in
America.* New York: Outerbridge and Dienstfrey.

LOCKARD, Duane (1968) *Toward Equal Opportunity: A Study of State
and Local Antidiscrimination Laws.* New York: Macmillan Co.

LOEBER, Dietrich A. (1965) "Plan and Contract Performance in Soviet
Law," in W. LAFAVE (ed.) *Law in the Soviet Society.* Urbana:
University of Illinois Press.

Galanter / LEGAL CHANGE   157

New York Times, "Arizona Losing Consumer Chief," April 22, 1973, p. 39.

LORTIE, Dan C. (1959) "Laymen to Lawmen: Law School, Careers, and Professional Socialization," 29 *Harvard Educational Review* 352.

LOWRY, S. Todd (1973) "Lord Mansfield and the Law Merchant," 7 *Journal of Economic Issues* 605.

LOWY, Michael J. (n.d.) "A Good Name is Worth More than Money: Strategies of Court Use in Urban Ghana." Unpublished paper.

MACAULAY, Stewart (1966) *Law and the Balance of Power: The Automobile Manufacturers and Their Dealers.* New York: Russell Sage Foundation.

————————— (1963) "Non-Contractual Relations in Business: A Preliminary Study," 28 *American Sociological Review* 55.

MacCALLUM, Spencer (1967) "Dispute Settlement in an American Supermarket," in Paul BOHANNAN (ed.) *Law and Warfare.* Garden City, N.Y.: Natural History Press for American Museum of Natural History.

MARSHALL, Leon C. and Geoffrey MAY (1932) *The Divorce Court: Volume One—Maryland.* Baltimore: The Johns Hopkins Press.

MATZA, David (1964) *Delinquency and Drift.* New York: John Wiley.

MAYHEW, Leon H. (1973) "Institutions of Representation." A paper prepared for delivery at the Conference on the Delivery and Distribution of Legal Services, State University of New York at Buffalo, October 12, 1973.

————————— (1971) "Stability and Change in Legal Systems," in Alex INKELES and Bernard BARBER (eds.) *Stability and Social Change.* Boston: Little, Brown and Co.

————————— (1968) *Law and Equal Opportunity: A Study of the Massachusetts Commission Against Discrimination.* Cambridge: Harvard University Press.

MAYHEW, Leon and Albert J. REISS, JR. (1969) "The Social Organization of Legal Contacts," 34 *American Sociological Review* 309.

McINTYRE, Donald M. (1968) "A Study of Judicial Dominance of the Charging Process," 59 *Journal of Criminal Law, Criminology and Police Science* 463.

McINTYRE, Donald M. and David LIPPMAN (1970) "Prosecutors and Early Disposition of Felony Cases," 56 *A.B.A. Journal* 1154.

McPHERSON, James Alan (1972) "In My Father's House There are Many Mansions, and I'm Going to Get Me Some of Them, Too! The Story of the Contract Buyers League," 229(4) *Atlantic Monthly* 51.

MENTSCHIKOFF, Soia (1961) "Commercial Arbitration," 61 *Columbia Law Review* 846.

MERRYMAN, John Henry (1969) *The Civil Law Tradition: An Introduction to the Legal Systems of Western Europe and Latin America.* Stanford, Cal.: Stanford University Press.

MILLER, Frank W. (1969) *Prosecution: the Decision to Charge a Suspect with a Crime.* Boston: Little, Brown and Co.

MORGAN, Richard S. (1968) *The Politics of Religious Conflict: Church and State in America.* New York: Pegasus.

MORRISON, Charles (1974) "Clerks and Clients: Paraprofessional Roles and Cultural Identities in Indian Litigation," 9 *Law & Society Review* 39.

MOSIER, Marilyn Miller and Richard A. SOBLE (1973) "Modern Legislation, Metropolitan Court, Miniscule Results: A Study of Detroit's Landlord-Tenant Court," 7 *University of Michigan Journal of Law Reform* 6.

MOULTON, Beatrice A. (1969) "The Persecution and Intimidation of the Low-Income Litigant as Performed by the Small Claims Court in California," 21 *Stanford Law Review* 1657.

MURPHY, Walter (1959) "Lower Court Checks on Supreme Court Power," 53 *American Political Science Review* 1017.

MURRAY, John E., JR. (1969) "Unconscionability: Unconscionability." 31 *University of Pittsburgh Law Review* 1.

NADER, Laura (1965) "The Anthropological Study of Law," in Laura NADER (ed). *The Ethnography of Law* (= Part 2 of *American Anthropologist,* Volume 67. No. 6).

NAGEL, Stuart S. (1973) "Effects of Alternative Types of Counsel on Criminal Procedure Treatment," 48 *Indiana Law Journal* 404.

158   LAW AND SOCIETY / FALL 1974

NEWMAN, Donald J. (1966) *Conviction: The Determination of Guilt or Innocence Without Trial.* Boston: Little, Brown and Co.

NONET, Philippe (1969) *Administrative Justice: Advocacy and Change in a Government Agency.* New York: Russell Sage Foundation.

NORTHWESTERN UNIVERSITY LAW REVIEW (1953) "Settlement of Personal Injury Cases in the Chicago Area," 47 *Northwestern University Law Review* 895.

O'CONNELL, Jeffrey (1971) *The Injury Industry and the Remedy of No-Fault Insurance.* Chicago: Commerce Clearing House.

O'GORMAN, Hubert (1963) *Lawyers and Matrimonial Cases: A Study of Informal Pressures in Private Professional Practice.* New York: Free Press.

OHLHAUSEN, George C. (1936) "Rich and Poor in Civil Procedure," 11 *Science and Society* 275.

OLSON, Mancur, JR. (1965) *The Logic of Collective Action: Public Goods and the Theory of Groups.* Cambridge: Harvard University Press.

ORBELL, John M. and Toro UNO (1972) "A Theory of Neighborhood Problem Solving: Political Action *vs.* Residential Mobility," 66 *American Political Science Review* 471.

OWEN, Harold J., JR. (1971) *The Role of Trial Courts in the Local Political System: A Comparison of Two Georgia Counties.* Unpublished dissertation, Department of Political Science, University of Georgia.

PAGTER, C.R., R. McCLOSKEY and M. REINIS (1964) "The California Small Claims Court," 52 *California Law Review* 876.

PARSONS, Talcott (1954) "A Sociologist Looks At The Legal Profession," in *Essays in Sociological Theory.* New York: Free Press.

POWELL, Richard R. and Patrick J. ROHAN (1968) *Powell on Real Property.* One Volume Ed. New York: Mathew Bender.

RABIN, Robert L. (1972) "Agency Criminal Referrals in the Federal System: An empirical study of prosecutorial discretion," 24 *Stanford Law Review* 1036.

RABINOWITZ, Richard W. (1968) "Law and the Social Process in Japan," in *Transactions of the Asiatic Society of Japan, Third Series,* Volume X. Tokyo.

RANDALL, Richard S. (1968) *Censorship of the Movies: Social and Political Control of a Mass Medium.* Madison: University of Wisconsin Press.

RANKIN, Anne (1964) "The Effect of Pretrial Detention," 39 *N.Y.U. Law Review* 641.

RAWLS, John (1971) *A Theory of Justice.* Cambridge: Harvard University Press.

———————— (1958) "Justice as Fairness," 68 *The Philosophical Review* 80.

REICH, Charles (1964a) "The New Property," 73 *Yale Law Journal* 733.

———————— (1964b) "Individual Rights and Social Welfare: The Emerging Legal Issues," 74 *Yale Law Journal* 1245.

REICHSTEIN, Kenneth J. (1965) "Ambulance Chasing: A Case Study of Deviation Within the Legal Profession," 3 *Social Problems* 3.

REPPETTO, Thomas (1970) "The Millet System in the Ottoman and American Empires," 5 *Public Policy* 629.

REPUBLIC RESEARCH, INC. (1970) "Claims and Recovery for Product Injury Under the Common Law," in National Commission on Product Safety, Supplemental Studies, Vol. III: *Product Safety Law and Administration: Federal, State, Local and Common Law.* Washington: U.S. Government Printing Office, 237.

ROSENTHAL, Albert J. (1971) "Negotiability—Who Needs It?," 71 *Columbia Law Review* 375.

ROSENTHAL, Douglas E. (1970) *Client Participation in Professional Decision: the Lawyer-Client Relationship in Personal Injury Cases.* Unpublished dissertation. Yale University.

ROSS, H. Laurence (1970) *Settled Out of Court: The Social Process of Insurance Claims Adjustment.* Chicago: Aldine.

ROTHSTEIN, Lawrence E. (1974) "The Myth of Sisyphus: Legal Services Efforts on Behalf of the Poor," 7 *University of Michigan Journal of Law Reform* 493.

ROTHWAX, Harold J. (1969) "The Law as an Instrument of Social Change," in Harold H. WEISSMAN (ed.) *Justice and the Law in the Mobilization for Youth Experience.* New York: New York Association Press.

SAARI, David J. (1967) "Open Doors to Justice—An Overview of Financing Justice in America." 50 *Journal of the American Judicature Society* 296.

SALISBURY, Robert H. (1969) "An Exchange Theory of Interest Groups," 13 *Midwest Journal of Political Science* 1.

SCHELLING, Thomas C. (1963) *The Strategy of Conflict.* New York: Oxford University Press.

SCHRAG, Philip G. (1969) "Bleak House 1968: A Report on Consumer Test Litigation." 44 *N.Y.U. Law Review* 115.

SCHWARTZ, Richard D. (1954) "Social Factors in the Development of Legal Control: A Case Study of Two Israeli Settlements," 63 *Yale Law Journal* 471.

SCIGLIANO, Robert (1971) *The Supreme Court and the Presidency.* New York: Free Press.

SCOTT, William G. (1965) *The Management of Conflict: Appeal Systems in Organizations.* Homewood, Ill.: Irwin/Dorsey.

SELZNICK, Philip with the collaboration of Philippe NONET and Howard M. VOLLMER (1969), *Law, Society and Industrial Justice.* Russell Sage Foundation.

SEYMOUR, Whitney North, JR. (1974) "Frontier Justice: A Run-In With the Law," *The New York Times,* July 21, 1974, § 10, p. 1.

SHKLAR, Judith N. (1964) *Legalism.* Cambridge: Harvard University Press.

SHOVER, John L. (1966) *Cornbelt Rebellion: The Farmers' Holiday Association.* Urbana: University of Illinois Press.

SHRIVER, George H. (ed.) (1966) *America's Religious Heretics: Formal and Informal Trials in American Protestantism.* Nashville: Abdingdon Press.

SHUCHMAN, Philip (1971) "The Fraud Exception in Consumer Bankruptcy," 23 *Stanford Law Review* 735.

——————————— (1969) "Profit on Default: an archival study of automobile repossession and resale," 22 *Stanford Law Review* 20.

——————————— (1968) "Ethics and Legal Ethics: The Propriety of the Canons as a Group Moral Code," 37 *George Washington Law Review* 244.

SIMKIN, William E. (1971) *Mediation and the Dynamics of Collective Bargaining.* Washington: Bureau of National Affairs.

SIMON, William (1972) "Class Actions—Useful Tool or Engine of Destruction," 55 *Federal Rules Decisions* 375.

SKOLNICK, Jerome (1967) "Social Control in the Adversary Process," 11 *Journal of Conflict Resolution* 52.

——————————— (1966) *Justice Without Trial: Law Enforcement in a Democratic Society.* New York: John Wiley.

SMALL CLAIMS STUDY GROUP (1972) "Little Injustices: Small Claims Courts and the American Consumer." A preliminary report to The Center for Auto Safety, Cambridge, Mass.

SMIGEL, Erwin O. (1969) *The Wall Street Lawyer: Professional Organization Man?* Bloomington: Indiana University Press.

SMITH, Regan G. (1970) *The Small Claims Court: a Sociological Interpretation.* Unpublished dissertation, Department of Sociology, University of Illinois.

SPRADLEY, James P. (1970) *You Owe Yourself a Drunk: An Ethnography of Urban Nomads.* Boston: Little, Brown and Co.

STUMPF, Harry P., Henry P. SCHROERLUKE and Forrest D. DILL (1971) "The Legal Profession and Legal Services: Explorations in Local Bar Politics," 6 *Law & Society Review* 47.

SUDNOW, David (1965) "Normal Crimes: Sociological Features of the Penal Code in a Public Defender Office," 12 *Social Problems* 255.

160   LAW AND SOCIETY / FALL 1974

SUMMERS, Clyde (1960) "Individual Rights in Collective Agreements: A Preliminary Analysis," 9 *Buffalo Law Review* 239.

TANNER, Nancy (1970) "Disputing and the Genesis of Legal Principles: Examples from Minangkabau," 26 *Southwestern Journal of Anthropology* 375.

tenBROEK, Jacobus (1964-65) "California's Dual System of Family Law: Its Origin, Development and Present Status," 16 *Stanford Law Review* 257-317, 900-81; 17 *Stanford Law Review* 614-82.

TRUBEK, David M. (1972) "Toward a Social Theory of Law: An Essay on the Study of Law and Development." 82 *Yale Law Journal* 1.

TULLOCK, Gordon (1971) *Logic of the Law*. New York: Basic Books, Inc.

VAUGHAN, Ted R. (1968) "The Landlord-Tenant Relationship in a Low-Income Area," 16 *Social Problems* 208.

VIRTUE, Maxine Boord (1956) *Family Cases in Court: A Group of Four Court Studies Dealing with Judicial Administration.* Durham: Duke University Press.

VOSE, Clement E. (1972) *Constitutional Change: Amendment Politics and Supreme Court Litigation Since 1900.* Lexington, Mass.: D.C. Heath.

————— (1967) *Caucasions Only: The Supreme Court, the NAACP, and the Restrictive Covenant Cases.* Berkeley: University of California Press.

————— (1966) "Interest Groups, Judicial Review, and Local Government," 19 *Western Political Quarterly* 85.

WALD, Patricia (1964) "Foreward: Pretrial Detention and Ultimate Freedom." 39 *N.Y.U. Law Review* 631.

WANNER, Craig (1974a) "The Public Ordering of Private Relations: Part I: Initiating Civil Cases in Urban Trial Courts," 8 *Law & Society Review* 421.

————— (1974b) "The Public Ordering of Private Relations: Part II: Winning Civil Cases in Urban Trial Courts," 9 *Law & Society Review* forthcoming.

————— (1973) "A Harvest of Profits: Exploring the Symbiotic Relationship between Urban Civil Trial Courts and the Business Community," Paper prepared for delivery at the 1973 Annual Meeting of the American Political Science Association.

WASBY, Stephen L. (1970) *The Impact of the United States Supreme Court: Some Perspectives.* Homewood, Ill.: The Dorsey Press.

WEBER, Max (1954), Max RHEINSTEIN (ed.) *Max Weber on Law in Economy and Society.* Cambridge: Harvard University Press.

WECHSLER, Herbert (1959) "Toward Neutral Principles of Constitutional Law," 73 *Harvard Law Review* 1.

WEXLER, Stephen (1970) "Practicing Law for Poor People," 79 *Yale Law Journal* 1049.

WHITFORD, William C. (1968) "Law and the Consumer Transaction: A case study of the automobile warranty," 1968 *Wisconsin Law Review* 1006.

WILSON, James Q. (1968) *Varieties of Police Behavior: The Management of Law and Order in Eight Communities.* Cambridge: Harvard University Press.

WOLL, Peter (1960) "Informal Administrative Adjudication: Summary of Findings," 7 *U.C.L.A. Law Review* 436.

YALE LAW JOURNAL (1970) "The New Public Interest Lawyers," 79 *Yale Law Journal* 1069.

YNGVESSON, Barbara (1973) "Responses to Grievance Behavior: Extended Cases in a Fishing Community," Forthcoming in Michael LOWY (ed). *Choice-Making in the Law.*

————— (1965) "The Berkeley-Albany and Oakland-Piedmont Small Claims Courts: A Comparison of Role of the Judge and Social Function of the Courts." Unpublished paper.

ZEISEL, Hans, Harry KALVEN, JR., and Bernard BUCHHOLZ (1959) *Delay in the Court.* Boston: Little, Brown and Co.

[8]

International Journal of the Sociology of Law 1981, **9**, 245–267

Conservative Conflict and the Reproduction of Capitalism: The Role of Informal Justice*

RICHARD L. ABEL

UCLA Law School, Los Angeles, U.S.A.

Informal alternatives to courts are a major preoccupation of legal reformers and scholars, not just in the United States and Europe but also in the third world, in socialist as well as capitalist nations (see generally Abel, 1982a,b). Informal legal institutions have been the subject of numerous conferences (see, for example, *70 Federal Rules Decisions*, p. 79; *76 Federal Rules Decisions*, p. 277; Fetter, 1978; Sander, 1978) and considerable scholarly research (Blankenberg, Klausa and Rottleuthner, 1979; Cappelletti, 1978 to 1981; Felstiner and Drew, 1976; Nader, 1980) and have generated a literature large enough to inspire several lengthy bibliographies (Sander and Snyder, 1979; Wilkinson, 1980). The National Institute of Justice of the U.S. Department of Justice recently established three Neighborhood Justice Centers (Cook, Roehl and Sheppard, 1980) and these, together with alternative dispute institutions created in more than 110 cities throughout the country (McGillis, 1980), have been the subject of extensive evaluation (see, for example, Felstiner and Williams, 1980; Davis, Tichane and Grayson, 1980). The Royal Commission on Legal Services (1979, chapter 43), the Royal Commission on Legal Services in Scotland (1980, chapters 11, 14), and the Royal Commission on Criminal Procedure (1981) have all expressed interest in simplifying procedure, increasing access, and reducing delay, either by reforming the courts or by creating alternative institutions (see also Economides, 1980).

Notwithstanding all this activity, there is some danger that scholars may create (or at least exaggerate) the importance of the phenomenon of "informalism" by dwelling on it, in much the same way that the media create news. The Dispute Resolution Act of 1980 (P. L. 96–190) was enacted by

* An earlier version of this paper was presented at the Scandinavian–American Exchange on Conflict Management, Stavern, Norway, 31 May to 4 June 1980.

0194-6595/81/030245+23 $02.00/0

246   *R. L. Abel*

Congress but has not been funded, and is not likely to be in the present political climate. The Neighborhood Justice Centers have encountered difficulty in obtaining local support after the termination of their federal grants. Scholarly interest in disputing may say more about the poverty of theory in social studies of law than about the significance of the subject outside academia (Abel, 1980). Yet fads in scholarship and social reform merit analysis, if only to show that they are epiphenomenal. This paper explores the professed reasons for interest in informal alternatives to courts, develops a model of disputing in society that seeks to show the similarities between formal and informal legal institutions as modes of neutralizing conflict, and uses that model to assess the political significance of contemporary concern with informalism.

Informalism as Ideology

The concept of informal justice consists of two, possibly contradictory, ingredients. It clearly refers to alternatives to *courts*, i.e., these are *judicial* institutions, which they declare, modify and apply norms in the process of controlling behavior and handling conflict. What is much less clear is the sense in which these are *alternatives*. This section will therefore examine the claims that advocates of informal justice make for its differences from, and advantages over, formal legal institutions. My purpose is to demystify the ideology of informalism and show its inadequacy as a framework for analysis.

Cost

Informal alternatives are said to be less expensive than courts. But to whom do the savings accrue? To those who use informal alternatives? Would they ever have used the more expensive courts? If not, are they enjoying any savings by being diverted from other responses: two-party negotiation, endurance, or exit? Or are the proponents of informalism more interested in the benefit to those who already use the formal courts regularly and will experience shorter delays as caseload is shifted to informal institutions? And if informal institutions are less expensive perhaps this is because they are *worth* less to their users. Not only are they less well endowed with both coercive power and due process guarantees than formal courts, but participants may also invest less of themselves in the process, so little, in fact, that they get nothing significant in return (*cf.* Christie, 1977). Indeed, this seems a plausible interpretation of the fact that disputants must be compelled to use informal institutions: those alternatives that eschew compulsion tend to have much smaller clienteles (see Cook *et al.*, 1980, p. 106). Contrary to the economistic assumptions of many reformers, disputants may not be bargain hunters.

A completely different measure of expense is cost to the state (or to any other entity, such as a charitable organization) that supports the informal institution. Is the purpose of the institution to reduce the cost to those who use it by shifting some of their expense to the state? If so, we should certainly be concerned to know who is being subsidized to use the institution and who is paying that subsidy (*cf.* Landes and Posner, 1979). Or is the purpose to reduce the cost to the state by transferring litigants to less expensive informal processes? A significant consequence of the diversion of felonies to mediation in New York City, for instance, was the savings in police resources, since officers were not required to testify at arraignment or trial (Davis *et al.*, 1980, p. 67). Yet that is a highly problematic strategy, since reducing court caseloads by creating alternative institutions tends to render courts more attractive to potential litigants, thereby restoring caseloads to their former levels, with the result that the total cost to the state of subsidizing litigation *and* informal alternatives increases significantly (see Haley, 1982). An unacknowledged consequence of the creation of informal alternatives may be to redistribute dispute-settling resources, if those who use courts and those who use informal institutions constitute distinct categories, for instance, business enterprises and individuals. [This is not to deny that business enterprises frequently choose informal alternatives on the their own initiative (see Abel-Smith and Stevens, 1967, pp. 261–262; Macaulay, 1963; Mentschikoff, 1952).]

Access

Informal institutions are said to be more accessible than courts. Cost is obviously an important ingredient in access, but there are others; geography, knowledge, social distance, prior use (see Galanter, 1974; Merry, 1979). Access, like cost can have a number of different, and potentially inconsistent, meanings. It can signify availability. In this sense it is not clear whether we want informal institutions to be highly accessible and to encourage disputing, or highly inaccessible and to discourage it (*cf.* van der Sprenkel, 1962), or to appear accessible while actually being inaccessible. Do we wish to alter patterns of use because we think disputing is intrinsically good or bad or because we have a theory that relates kinds and amounts of disputing to some other social desideratum? Or are we interested in formal access regardless of actual use, in much the same way that most law reform is concerned to change the law on the books without troubling to inquire about consequent changes in the law in action? Proponents certainly want legal institutions to be *equally* available to the entire population, for this is an axiom of liberalism, but they tend to be vague about what such equality means and how it is to be attained within an unequal society. Would equality be satisfied if some disputants had access to courts but others only to informal alternatives?

Process variables and the ideal of formal justice

Informal institutions are said to offer a process that is more desirable for the particular disputes and disputants they handle, or even for all kinds of conflict.

Informal dispute processes are characterized as more humane and caring, speedier, concerned with a broader range of issues and evidence, more comprehensible (because less differentiated linguistically), and open to participation by a wider category of parties (and even non-parties). Yet again these claims are ambiguous. Is the standard of comparison a formal trial, a mediated settlement, or face-to-face negotiations (*cf.* van Velsen, 1969)? Is this the judgment of plaintiffs, defendants, or third parties? Informal processes also co-exist uneasily with the ideology of liberal legalism. In formal courts justice requires conformity with procedural and substantive laws. Why discard these criteria in informal institutions? Are we saying that legal procedures never produce formal justice? Or that they fail to do so only in certain cases? But then how do we recognize such instances? And why do we think that informal institutions can achieve formal justice in an unjust society when formal institutions cannot? Should informal institutions apply official substantive law? Are they better able to do so than formal institutions? If not, what substantive principles should the third party apply: the party's own values? In what cases is it appropriate to abandon substantive law for other normative guidelines? Are the latter preferable because they are imbued with common sense, or are more popular, or less technical? Are informal institutions more democratic in the sense that they are more permeable to diverse normative orders? Or are they better capable of reaching consensus among conflicting norms?

Lay participation

Informal institutions may be valued because they encourage greater lay participation in the process of resolving disputes. But why is it appropriate for the public to be involved in resolving some disputes and not others? And, indeed, why is public participation ever desirable: because it enhances the process, produces outcomes that are more just, or expresses democratic values? Does the public want to participate? The extreme reluctance of Americans to serve on juries (see Alker, Hosticka, and Mitchell, 1976) and the political apathy that leads half the American electorate to abstain from voting even in Presidential races, strongly suggest that most citizens feel neither political interest nor civic obligation. Finally, there is a disconcerting inconsistency between the declining role of the jury in civil cases, where the lay public really do determine outcomes (California voters recently approved overwhelmingly an initiative to halve the number of jurors in civil cases) and advocacy of an informalism in which a new breed of *professionals* (facilitators, mediators, or conciliators) actually exercise control; it is worth noting that arbitration has historically been used to *reduce* the influence of lay juries (Auerbach, 1979).

The value of conflict and litigation

The interest in informalism rests upon attitudes toward conflict and litigation that are ambivalent, perhaps even hypocritical. Advocates of informalism portray all conflict as evil (*cf.* Bohannan, 1969; Haley, 1982; Reifner, 1982) by lumping together forms of illegitimate violence and oppression, street crime, international aggression, and totalitarianism, with *resistance* to political repression, colonialism, racism, sexism, and economic exploitation. They thus identify conflict exclusively with threats to stability, obscuring the fact that many people experience the status quo as oppressive and see themselves as the victims of constant conflict. Yet because conflict is recognized as threatening it must be granted some limited expression, and informal processes are valued as ways of channeling conflict into forms that appear less violent, more just, or simply less revolutionary (Meador, 1978).

The attitude of reformers toward litigation is equally contradictory. Numerous commentators deplore what they describe as the excessive litigiousness of American society (for example, Barton, 1975; Burger, 1977; Ehrlich, 1976; Jones, 1965; Kline, 1978a,b; Manning, 1976; Rosenberg, 1971). They respond with strategies desgned to reduce litigation both by establishing alternatives to draw cases away from the courts and by intimidating potential litigants, compelling indigents to reimburse the state for their legal fees (*Los Angeles Times*, 14 December 1979, Part I, p. 7) or punishing those who litigate and lose (for instance, by imposing liability for costs, or heavier criminal sentences on those who refuse to engage in plea bargaining) (*Law & Society Review*, 1979). Yet the object is not to reduce litigation in general but to rid the courts of *certain kinds* of cases so that judges can handle more cases of other kinds, or handle them better. The attitude toward litigation is somewhat like the invective directed by business against government, except that lawyers (and to a lesser degree litigants) replace bureaucrats as the targets of abuse. The universal experience of the dilatoriness of government, the discourtesy of front-line officials (see Katz *et al.*, 1976; Katz and Danet, 1973), and the inefficiency of large public organizations (see Morris, 1980) can be mobilized, not to reduce government responsibilities but to expand them by creating new procedures and institutions in addition to those that already exist, and to reallocate them selectively.

The concept of informalism as an *alternative* to formal courts is inadequate as either description or prescription. The advantages claimed for informal institutions are vague and often inconsistent. Furthermore, they emphasize qualities internal to those institutions, especially their processual features, a myopic view that is reinforced when informal institutions are evaluated primarily in terms of the satisfaction of individual disputants (for example, Cook *et al.*, 1980, pp. 45–83). But those institutions must have *some* impact on the larger society: even in informal processes disputants win or lose, grievances are expressed or repressed, conflict is transformed, substantive rights are implemented or frustrated. An understanding of informalism must therefore set aside the programmatic assertions of its proponents and instead construct a model of conflict that seeks to identify the social consequences of different forms of legal institutionalization.

Conservative and Liberating Conflict

That the ideology of informalism exaggerates the differences between formal courts and informal alternatives is not surprising: every reform proclaims its novelty. But such distortion hides what seem to me to be far more important similarities between the formal and informal legal institutions of the capitalist state, between adjudication, arbitration, mediation, and conciliation. In order to reveal these common features I will construct two contrasting ideal-typical models of conflict. The first, which I will call conservative conflict, encompasses the processes that typify both formal courts and informal alternatives. It is repetitive, homeostatic, and it preserves the structures of domination that characterize capitalist society. The alternative I will call liberating conflict because it is transformational, disequilibrating, and it challenges those structures of domination (*cf.* Gluckman, 1965, pp. 163–66). Liberating conflict *can* occur within both formal and informal legal institutions, but I will argue below that those institutional structures *tend* to render conflict conservative. And of course conflict that occurs outside legal institutions is not necessarily liberating, the political process can be just as conservative. I want to draw attention to two features of this framework. It is explicitly normative: I am interested in the ways in which institutions shape conflict so as to preserve or challenge structures of domination and exploitation. And it is historically specific: these institutions are part of the state apparatus of advanced capitalism.

Disputant characteristics

People enter into conservative conflict imbued with the attributes that characterize them in the larger society. Among these the most important are that capital and state are organized, whereas workers, citizens, and consumers are disorganized. An extreme instance of this direct translation is the refusal of formal legal institutions to allow new forms of social organization to engage in litigation: constraints on labor unions in the nineteenth century and contemporary restrictions on class actions, intervention, and standing are examples. Individual advantages and disadvantages associated with class, socio-economic status, education, gender, age, and ethnicity retain their significance in conservative conflict. This occurs not through third-party bias, for legal decision makers claim impartiality, thereby mystifying the influence of social inequality, but through differences in the resources each adversary commands. Furthermore, these differences tend to be cumulative and irreversible. Those who are advantaged by their social standing tend to be more successful in their initial encounters and thereby are encouraged to engage in further conservative conflict, and vice versa; this positive or negative reinforcement helps to differentiate what Marc Galanter calls one-shot and repeat-player litigants (1974). Advantage can be displayed visibly (even boastfully) in the conspicuous consumption of extensive and expensive legal services, "papering the opposition to death"; but it can also enter invisibly into the preparations for conflict, including the structure of antecedent transactions, perceptions, the sense of entitlement, and expectations about success (*cf.* Abel, 1979a).

In liberating conflict, existing social structures are transformed, existing patterns of advantage inverted. Organization, for instance, can turn from a source of strength into an Achilles heel: the complex integration of the corporation or state may render it unusually susceptible to pressure on a vital part (e.g., strikes in police or fire departments, or the current political transformation in Poland). Liberating conflict organizes the disorganized, allowing them to see the commonality in their individual grievances and the power that can be gained by aggregating weakness; perceptions are changed, expectations upset. Trades unionism, civil rights, feminism, environmentalism, and consumerism, are obvious examples. But even legal institutions can sometimes be the arena for liberating conflict: revolutionary courts that consciously seek to compensate for prior class advantage illustrate this; so too (if to a far lesser degree) do small claims courts in the United States that forbid legal representation, or doctrines that require judges to disregard unconscionable agreements.

Equality of adversaries

A second, related distinction is that adversaries in conservative conflict can be unequal, even extremely unequal, and usually are, whereas opponents in liberating conflict are roughly equal. In the former the individual confronts some organized entity, either a private corporation or the state (see Galanter, 1975; Wanner, 1974, 1975). This is true whether the individual is making a claim (a dissatisfied consumer seeking a refund or a citizen requesting a welfare benefit) or resisting one (opposing collection of an alleged debt or defending a criminal prosecution). Significant inequalities may also characterize legal conflict between individuals, disputes between estranged spouses being the most frequent example. The reason that conflict between unequals is channeled into legal forms is that the ideology of liberal legalism promises equal justice for all, encouraging relatively weak supplicants to assert their legal rights and simultaneously legitimating the legal victories of corporations and the state as expressions of impersonal law rather than extralegal power. In formal processes, the appearance of equality between patently unequal opponents is enhanced by numerous devices: adversaries are represented by formally equal lawyers; the corporation or state may be replaced by an individual (an official, the prosecutor) who seems more like an equivalent of the individual party; both sides have formally identical opportunities to present evidence and arguments, etc. Prosecutions of particularly heinous crimes or of political dissidents, staged with the full panoply of procedural safeguards and impressive displays of virtuoso rhetoric by lawyers on both sides, are an important means of reaffirming the myth embodied in the iconography of blind justice.

Informal processes use other mechanisms to convey an image of equality: reducing the differentiation of third parties so that they appear equally approachable (rather than equally *un*approachable) by both sides; replacing the awesome state by the individual complainant, who seems a fairer match for the accused; seeking common ground between the two sides by de-emphasizing irreconcilable differences; characterizing proposed outcomes as "compromises", even if only one side is actually giving up anything of significance; excluding some of the more egregious instances of conflict between unequals (preferring, for instance, to handle disputes between individuals); and adopting a therapeutic posture that purports to transcend inequalities. Informalism thus reproduces within intraclass conflict the same structure that formal institutions impose on interclass conflict.

Liberating conflict, by contrast, occurs only between adversaries who are approximately equal (*cf.* Bailey, 1971, p. 19 and n. 17). This statement is certainly counter-intuitive and may even appear absurd. What I mean by it is that, despite the promise of equal treatment held out by legal institutions, (formal or informal) it only makes sense to confront an adversary of roughly equal strength. In situations of patent inequality the weaker party will refrain from asserting a claim and retreat or otherwise avoid battle if made the object of the claim. Even the stronger party may avoid conflict that occurs outside a legal institution capable of mystifying inequalities of power; weakness may thus become a hidden source of strength. International relations, labor relations, and guerilla warfare all illustrate these principles, as do struggles over racism and sexism. A party opposed by a more powerful adversary will seek to enhance its position before openly asserting or resisting a claim; deliberately provoking legal conflict may be one way of doing so. Thus either a symbolic victory (as in many famous constitutional cases) or a symbolic act of oppression (as in political prosecutions) may be a tactic for mobilizing before engaging in liberating conflict.

Normative order

In conservative conflict, the normative order is fully shared by both parties, exhaustive, and internally coherent. In formal legal institutions the judge explicitly imposes this body of norms on the disputants, attributing it to some external authority, a legislature, the constitution, or natural law. Informal institutions disguise authoritative imposition; the third party (mediator, go-between) may suggest that the norms are shared by both parties (emphasizing agreement and downplaying differences); imposition may be relatively invisible because the external authority is diffuse and inchoate (public opinion) or hidden (the threat of resort to formal institutions); or the third party may pretend that the norms are irrelevant, even obstructive. Both formal and informal legal institutions present the normative foundation of the outcome as something that antedates the conflict.

In liberating conflict there is normative dissensus. This does not mean that norms are absent or disregarded; although it is theoretically possible for inconsistent demands to be asserted without any normative justification, this rarely happens (*cf.* Eisenberg, 1976). But it is both conceivable and commonplace for claims to rest on normative bases that are wholly incompatible: an employer's offer of higher wages confronting the demand by employees for greater control over working conditions; a university's insistence upon meritocratic criteria for appointment opposing the demands of women or minorities for some specified level of representation. It is equally distinctive of liberating conflict that the parties themselves create the normative basis that permits a resolution (even if only temporary): create it because normative dissensus implies that no common norms antedated the conflict; and do so themselves because there is no third party on whom to rely.

Role differentiation

Legal conflict is characterized by a very high degree of role differentiation (*cf.* Abel, 1973). In formal institutions the most important role is clearly that of the third party who possesses the power to decide and therefore must take a vow of impartiality and ignorance with respect to both dispute and disputants. But even in informal institutions third parties are expected to be less partisan than the disputants, and this relative impartiality endows them with at least some moral suasion. Third parties are typically assisted by a host of subordinates who occupy their own distinct roles and serve to differentiate the third party still further from the disputants: clerks, bailiffs, and sheriffs in formal institutions, secretaries, intake officers, social workers, and therapists in informal institutions. Even the parties are differentiated: internally structured (corporations, unions, even voluntary associations are bureaucracies since this is the way in which individuals are organized under capitalism) and represented to the outside world by lawyers. Liberating conflict, as an ideal type, displays no role differentiation: there are no intermediaries; parties are unrepresented, internally homogeneous, and non-hierarchical. A group of urban squatters who move into vacant land or buildings might be an example. But since liberating conflict under capitalism pits undifferentiated subordinated groups against differentiated dominant entities (corporate, governmental), the former may tend to adopt a bureaucratic structure, even though this may mean winning a better outcome at the cost of coming to resemble the adversary; union-management conflict may be an example.

Conflict boundaries

Conservative conflict is confined by clearly demarcated, relatively rigid boundaries. These are temporal (conflict has a definite beginning and end), spatial (conflict may only be waged within certain arenas, e.g., the widespread

prohibition on discussing a case that is *sub judice*), institutional (jurisdictional
rules ensure that only one institution will have competence), strategic (violence
is prohibited, rhetoric may be restricted), even linguistic (certain forms must be
used, others cannot be). Rules define the issues that may be raised and the
evidence that may be introduced. Informal legal institutions also bound
conflict, although the novelty or subtlety of the constraints may render them
more difficult to perceive: for instance, parties may be required to abstain from
controversial conduct while the dispute is proceeding (drinking, associating
with friends or lovers), and the restrictions upon language may be even
narrower (accusations may not be tolerated). Because informal legal
institutions rely on formal ones for referrals, and frequently must report the
outcome, they transpose many of the boundaries characteristic of formal
institutions. Procedural rules, like the universe of substantive norms, are
imposed from outside, antedate the encounter, and are agreed, exhaustive, and
internally consistent. Liberating conflict begins untrammeled by procedural
norms; it has no beginning or end and is waged in all arenas, even in several
simultaneously. "All is permitted in love and war". Only the parties themselves
can limit it; but they tend to subordinate process to outcome. Conservative
conflict may be encapsulated as an incident in ongoing liberating conflict; the
reverse cannot occur.

Chronological focus

The distinction just made suggests a reinterpretation of another opposition
frequently encountered in the dispute settlement literature (e.g., Aubert, 1963;
Nader, 1969). Conflict in formal legal institutions is said to be retrospective,
concerned to evaluate past events, interested in causation and in ascertaining
responsibility; informal, therapeutic institutions are prospective, preoccupied
with devising a solution for the future. Though this opposition is reasonably
accurate and useful I suggest that formal and informal legal institutions are
similar in that they bound conflict by focusing on *either* the past *or* the future
whereas liberating conflict is concerned with *both*. Regardless of what they may
profess, formal legal institutions are fundamentally uninterested in the future
(but *cf*. Eisenberg and Yeazell, 1980): they have a limited number of remedies
to choose from and care little what happens to the parties after these remedies
have been formally granted or denied (doctrines of *res judicata* and collateral
estoppel preclude reconsideration). A recurrent justification for legal relief is to
restore the *status quo ante*. Informal legal institutions curtail examination of the
past; they prohibit the attribution of blame or praise because it may prejudice
future relationships, and they tend to view people as lacking free will and urge
accommodation to the inevitable. There are no final judgments for therapy
never ends. Both kinds of legal institution thus render conflict conservative by
ignoring either the past or the future. Liberating conflict, by contrast, engages
in a normative evaluation of the past in order to influence the future (e.g., the

Nuremberg trials, the inquiry demanded by Iran into American complicity with the Shah, or Solzhenitsyn's call for an inquest into the Gulags). Thus scrutiny of the past is shaped by an interest in the future, and an acceptable future is deemed to rest on thorough historical analysis and moral assessment of the past.

Outcome

In conservative conflict the outcome, like the norms that guide and justify it, is externally imposed. The source of authority may be a judge (in formal institutions) or the diffuse sanction of public opinion (in informal institutions). In this sense both popular courts in revolutionary regimes and tribal moots in pre-industrial societies may exhibit conservative conflict. They share with formal courts the paternalistic assumption that someone other than the disputants (the judge, the state, the Party, the community) knows what is best. In liberating conflict the outcome is produced by the parties alone, though these will often be groups rather than individuals. This distinction has an ironic corollary. Conservative conflict is terminated decisively by a final judgment; yet because the parties do not construct this outcome but rather submit to it, a judicial decree is often followed by liberating conflict over whether it will be implemented. Problems of enforcement are endemic in formal legal institutions. Although we know less about conflict within informal institutions, there is every reason to expect similar problems to recur, if the aftermath of divorce (Chambers, 1979; Goode, 1956), the unenforceability of small claims judgments (Yngvesson and Hennessey, 1975, pp. 254–55), and the lack of finality in tribal dispute processing (Abel, 1973, pp. 231–32) are any guide. If and when the parties in liberating conflict finally agree upon an outcome, it will be relatively stable, unless they change their minds or are feigning agreement for tactical purposes.

The outcome of conservative conflict, like the process itself, perpetuates the status quo. By this I mean not only that distributions of wealth and power are preserved (e.g., tort and contract law both protect the income stream of tort victims and contractual parties) but even more that fundamental party characteristics are reproduced. Corporate entities, public and private, have their corporate identity strengthened. Individuals obtain remedies, pre-eminently money damages, that accentuate their individuality, distinguishing them from others by what they do and do not receive and intensifying differences of class and stratum. Liberating conflict transforms parties, disaggregating those that were corporate (for instance, by dividing public policymakers from bureaucratic staff, or capitalists from employees) and organizing previously atomistic individuals (for instance, by producing an outcome that treats them equally and corporately, involving them in new behaviours and conferring joint responsibility rather than making them the passive recipients of an award of money).

Informal Justice as Conservative Conflict

Although I argued in the previous section that both formal and informal legal institutions under capitalism tend to render conflict conservative they are not, for that reason, identical. The questions thus remain: why do we find an emphasis on informal legal institutions today, and what are their social significance?

I have suggested elsewhere (1979b), as have others (e.g., Pound, 1922, p. 54; *cf.* Galanter, 1979a), that formalism and informalism are alternatives in an endless cycle. Some have criticized this view: it is unduly idealist; the end-state of any completed cycle is always different from the beginning; this is at most a description, not an explanation, since the dynamic of the alteration is not stated. I accept these criticisms but still think there is a core of truth in the notion of cycles within capitalism. Those who manage legal institutions (judges, legislators, high executive officials, élite lawyers, legal scholars) are engaged in a continuous effort to legitimate the legal system, at least to themselves, whether or not anyone else is listening or being persuaded; they are constantly building twentieth century Potemkin villages. But the contradictions inherent in the dominant ideology of liberal legalism, between form and substance, the promise of equality and the fact of inequality, constantly erode legitimacy. Yet capitalism cannot escape from this ideology, which justifies both the exercise of state power and its limits. In the endless projects of legitimation within the legalist paradigm, informalism has the attraction of the relatively new, an untested solution whose flaws are not yet apparent. Furthermore, by focusing attention upon experimental peripheral institutions, the program of informalism deflects criticism from those older formal institutions that lie at the core of the legal system.

But this is still a very partial account; it suggests why reformers have turned away from the courts but not why they have turned toward informal institutions (to supplement courts, not to replace them). I think such an explanation must begin with the contemporary backlash to the "rights explosion" of the last few decades. The enemies of the welfare state contend that it has created too many substantive rights, placed too many restrictions upon capital, and constrained both state and capital within too many formal procedures. These forces have recently made substantial political gains, a fact that itself requires explanation, though it is beyond the scope of this paper. Formal legal rights (both substantive and procedural) express classical liberal theory, which consistently has been an important weapon of the oppressed in resisting domination and exploitation. If these rights were invented by the bourgeoisie in the course of overthrowing feudalism, the proletariat and other oppressed groups have also been able to use them in struggling against capitalism (*cf.* Marx, 1963). Informalism, by contrast, expresses positivist theories, developed in the last century and a half, which justify domination, authority, the exercise of control from above, whether in the substantive criminal law, criminal procedure, penology, mental institutions, education, or the workplace (*cf.* Christie, n.d.). Classic liberalism is the ideology of the revolutionary phase of capitalism, whereas positivism is the ideology of capitalism triumphant. The movement from formalism to informalism thus reflects and carries forward a shift in power from the less privileged to the more.

Sometimes the dominant class openly declares this to be its goal: substantive welfare rights, the minimum wage, restraints on commercial fraud and overreaching, the regulation of occupational health and safety, environmental protection, are said to be too "expensive", to reduce "efficiency" or "productivity", to render a country less competitive in the international economy. But because such explicit attacks draw attention to the opposed interests of privileged and oppressed and thus intensify political and economic conflict, the backlash to the rights explosion has generally been couched in the language of process. Process values appear neutral: informalism does not *obviously* favor any group or category. Like proposals to reorganize government or reduce bureaucracy, informalism thus promises reform without conflict, relief from expensive and pointless procedural intricacies without sacrifice by anyone.

Yet if the advocates of informalism seek to portray it as neutral, this mystifies its true significance. Informal processes commonly characterize their outcomes as compromise solutions in which nobody wins or loses. But compromise produces unbiased results only when opponents are equal; compromise between unequals inevitably reproduces inequality. Informal institutions claim to be cheaper and thus more accessible than formal, thereby appealing to the value of equality of opportunity so fundamental to liberalism. Yet enhanced opportunity leads to equal opportunity and equal use only when the potential users are themselves equal. In a class society, a slight reduction of the barriers to access will marginally enlarge the category of privileged users without altering the distinction between use and non-use or the consequences of differential use. Disputants themselves are able to see through the pretensions of informalism: although they may be willing to submit a controversy with an equal to an informal process, they strongly prefer formal institutions when confronting a clearly superior adversary (for example, Buckle and Buckle, 1980; Merry, 1982).

These preliminary examples suggest that the social significance of informalism often may best be revealed by treating its public pronouncements as Orwellian newspeak and inverting them. Let me begin with what is perhaps the central claim: that informalism represents a relaxation of authority, a reduction in domination, an amelioration of coercion. I would argue, on the contrary, that informalism has the potential to subject additional forms of behavior to legal authority, thereby expanding the scope of state control and transforming liberating conflict into conservative (*cf.* Cohen, 1979; Foucault, 1977). First, to the extent that informal institutions handle cases that would otherwise go to court (though the numbers are probably fairly small), they reduce court caseload and thus delay, rendering courts more attractive to disputants, who may choose to litigate conflicts that previously would have been resolved outside of court. Second, to the extent that informal institutions deal with disputes that would not have been litigated they subject those conflicts, too, to the conservative influence of legal forms. This latter influence is not randomly distributed across the population: by their location, staffing, subject matter, jurisdiction, and processual characteristics, informal institutions are targeted at workers, the poor, inner-city residents, women, and ethnic minorities. They handle problems that those who are relatively privileged (in terms of wealth, income, education, ethnicity) solve without state intervention, either by dealing directly with their adversaries (for example, addressing consumer complaints to sellers) (Best and Andreasen, 1977; Hannigan, 1977) or by taking them to private therapists (for example, family conflict) (*cf.* Hollingshead and Redlich, 1958). In other words, if informal institutions render law more accessible to the disadvantaged, they also render the disadvantaged more accessible to the state, and the latter consequence may be the more significant. In assessing the validity of this hypothesis it is essential to bear in mind two contradictory pressures. On the one hand, informal institutions, like so many conspicuous reforms, are of symbolic importance; because they will be systematically underfunded, only a few exemplary institutions will probably be created. The elimination of all appropriations for the Dispute Resolution Act is symptomatic. On the other hand, those relatively few institutions that seek permanent funding will need to develop large caseloads in order to justify their existence according to the prevailing standards of bureaucratic efficiency (Cook *et al.*, 1980).

One reason why informal institutions have the potential to legalize more behavior and new kinds of behavior is that they appear non-coercive. Although there is a continuum of coerciveness, with arbitration at one end and conciliation or facilitated negotiation at the other, all informal processes present themselves as less coercive than courts or administrative agencies. Informal institutions generate this image out of a composite of elements: they blur the distinction between public and private (using private forms to implement state programs); appear to respond passively to the desires of disputants to resolve their conflicts rather than exercising state control affirmatively; involve the parties more actively in the settlement process (without actually surrendering control); frame the outcome as a compromise. But despite appearances, coercion continues to play a significant role. Non-coercive procedures are often backed by implicit coercion: the threat of initiating or reviving a criminal prosecution frequently underlies an "agreed" solution; reluctance to "agree" may be overcome, or nullified, by the residual alternative of compulsory arbitration (Davis *et al.*, 1980; Harrington, 1980). The process may itself be the punishment, judging, stigmatizing, and thereby controlling the participants in the dispute (*cf.* Feeley, 1979). All of this exemplifies a very fundamental tendency in the mode of social control under advanced capitalism: as the state perfects its monopoly of force it no longer needs to exercise power as openly or brutally and can rely, instead, on less coercive forms of control (Poulantzas, 1978, chapter 3). But as coercion becomes less visible and more subtle it is more readily extended to new areas of behavior: persuasion is appropriate in many realms of social interaction where compulsion would be obviously excessive. Furthermore, it evokes less resistance: citizens have greater difficulty in recognizing it and less justification for insisting on formal procedures as a means of protection.

The significance of informal institutions is further mystified by analogizing the state to the family. Half a century ago Jerome Frank (1931) advanced a crude Freudian interpretation of popular faith in law as expressing the need for an omnipotent, omniscient father. Harold Berman (1963) has described the conscious paternalism of Soviet criminal courts. John Griffiths (1970) has argued for a family model of the criminal law, as an alternative to both due process and law and order models. And western scholars often speak admiringly of the identification between ruler and father in eastern societies, which endows the former with the latter's authority. Once this parallel between state and family is accepted, conflict is no longer conflict; there are no truly irreconcilable interests, only misunderstandings. *All* behavior is of interest to the informal institution *qua* family. Informalism explicitly rejects the basic liberal tenet "everything that is not forbidden is allowed" substituting, instead, the principle that everything is either forbidden, or discouraged, or encouraged, or mandated, but never irrelevant or neutral. Because this model denies the possibility of structural opposition between the parental third party and the disputants, because the former is seen as motivated only by solicitude and concern, the latter possess no rights. Where the juvenile court was justified by the failure of parents to control or nurture their children, and the domestic relations court by the dissolution of the family, informal institutions have generalized the role of state as surrogate family. If disputants are children and the third party is a parent it is proper, indeed inevitable, that the former should be totally dependent on the latter. There is no punishment, only tutelage; indeed, rewards are the preferred response.

This formulation, like the characterization of informal institutions as non-coercive, is both false and dangerous. Once again we get closer to the truth if we invert the claim: the state has not come to resemble the family; rather, the family has become ever more transparent to the state (*cf.* Donzelot, 1979; Lasch, 1977). The image of the family that inspires informalism is naive, if not hypocritical. Families are not islands of calm in a sea of dissension; they are driven by sexual, generational, and sibling conflict. It is ironic that the family should be invoked as a model of harmonious interaction at a time when its principal bonds (parent–child and spousal) are both disintegrating under social and economic pressures and the object of ideological attack. But this is hardly surprising: social formations often seek legitimation by identifying with what they are displacing – capitalism with the feudal order (Polanyi, 1957), bourgeois professionalism with aristocratic patron/client relationships (Larson, 1977), the contemporary welfare state with *laissez-faire* capitalism.

State institutions, no matter how informal, cannot replicate behavior within the family and certainly not the idealization of that behavior. A third party does not really care about the disputants, at least not the way one member of a family cares about the others; the intermediary did not live with the parties before the controversy, will not be stuck with them after it is concluded, and has no strong feelings about them. The third party is parental in much the way that airlines, banks, or oil companies are "friendly" (*cf.* Simon, 1978, p. 109). The interests of the third party diverge significantly from those of the disputants: the former takes pride in possessing and exhibiting technical skills in managing people, needs (and wants) to enhance the authority of the dispute institution, and must satisfy bureaucratic pressures to move cases. And because the third party does not control significant rewards (the disputants are not really concerned what the third party thinks about them) negative sanctions must be the primary response.

Just as ostensibly non-coercive institutions insinuate coercion, so institutions that appear to proffer solicitude foster dependence, on the state if they are public bodies, on capitalist enterprises (large manufacturers and retailers, the media) if they are creatures of the latter (Palen, 1979; Ross and Littlefield, 1978). They do this by reproducing and extending the relationship between the helping professional and the needy consumer of services, a paradigmatic form of domination in advanced capitalism (Illich, 1977; Larson, 1977, pp. 241–44). The fact that these institutions are informal extends dependence by creating new categories of professionals (arbitrators, mediators, conciliators) who are less expensive to produce than legally-trained professionals (Marquart and Wheat, 1980, p. 473). The state or corporation can therefore hire more of them and use them to handle conflicts that have less monetary significance than the disputes presently taken to courts or other formal institutions. The fact that these institutions are informal also lulls the client's sense of dependence (and that of us, the observers), just as it masked coercion. But informal institutions do truly foster dependence: there is neither mutuality nor equality between professional and client; the former is competent, knowledgeable, uninvolved (even if these qualities may be less accentuated than they are in lawyers); the latter, incompetent, ignorant, and in the midst of a crisis (psychological, social, economic), is reduced to a passive consumer of the helping service. Informal conflict management is simply the latest service provided by constantly expanding welfare state bureaucracies and capitalist enterprises (the two increasingly indistinguishable) in the movement toward social democracy and corporate paternalism.

Informal institutions not only channel conflict into conservative forms, they also distract attention from conflict that is potentially liberating. Just as nineteenth century French penal institutions diverted attention from illegality by focusing on delinquency (Foucault, 1979, Part 4, Chapter 2) and contemporary American courts ignore political questions in obedience to the "passive virtues" (Bickel, 1962) or in pursuit of an illusory neutrality (Wechsler, 1961), so informal legal institutions, by circumscribing their jurisdiction, help to assign to oblivion whatever conflict is excluded.

First, they define who can claim and what they can claim. Only individuals can be grievants before most informal institutions; hence they discourage organizing (thereby reproducing existing social imbalances, since many respondents are already organized). They also rule out many possible solutions: a tenant may ask a landlord to make repairs but cannot insist on restructuring the landlord-tenant relationship; the purchaser of a defective product may request a replacement but cannot require the manufacturer to redesign the product. Control over property, the capitalist enterprise, and the state apparatus cannot be challenged.

Second, informal institutions define the locus of significant conflict – typically the neighborhood (Beresford and Cooper, 1977; Cratsley, 1978; Danzig, 1973; Fisher, 1975). Here again, as in the self-conscious identification of informalism with family, a symbol that evokes strong nostalgic yearnings (the community) is held out as a model at a time when it has almost totally atrophied as an actual pattern of behavior (in this it recalls conservative appeals to states' rights). Co-residence simply is not the primary locus for social interaction in urban America (*cf.* Sennett, 1977). Hence disputes within the neighborhood tend to be trivial, quarrels over noise, or pets, or fences (Baumgartner, 1980). The neighborhood usually does not witness conflict between worker and capitalist, subordinate and superordinate, citizen and state, human being and polluter. Even racial conflict is largely excluded by residential segregation.

Third, informal institutions define the adversaries against whom claims can be made. Often this limitation is extremely narrow: only individuals can be respondents. This may restrict the institution to managing intra-class conflict between spouses, parents and children, and neighbors. Such a limitation implicitly denies the existence or denigrates the importance of inter-class conflict, it fosters the privatization of life, the cult of the personal. But even a broader definition of respondent tends to include only the petty bourgeoisie (the local landlord or small grocery store) (Cook *et al.*, 1980) and low-level public employees (the garbageman or cop on the beat) not monopoly capitalists or those state officials who set policy. It is because such adversaries are relatively powerless, and thus roughly comparable to the grievants, that informal institutions can relax rules of procedure and present the result as fair compromise. Informal institutions thus not only define legitimate conflict as the dissatisfaction of the consumer, the disharmony between equal individuals (thereby denying the existence of irreconcilable, structural conflicts between classes or between citizen and state), they simultaneously pursue the classic strategy of domination, *divide et imperium,* in much the same way that colonial regimes tolerated or established dispute mechanisms, subjugating indigenous peoples in the name of indirect rule (*cf.* Abel, 1979c; Galanter, 1979b; Santos, 1977).

10

Conclusions

In this paper I have sought to understand the significance of the growth of informal justice within the state apparatus of advanced capitalism. I began by noting that its proponents stress the divergence from formal legal institutions in order both to promote informalism and to present it as a major reform of the capitalist legal system. Yet analysis of their claims reveals them to be vague, contradictory, and empirically dubious. Furthermore, advocates of informalism largely confine their vision to what happens within the legal system and emphasize institutional style. I argued that we must, instead, examine the impact of legal institutions on society. In particular, I urged that we ask whether each institution renders conflict conservative or liberating. The answer, I believe, is that the legal institutions of the capitalist, whether formal or informal, usually render conflict conservative.

We are familiar with the ways in which formal legal institutions have guided many categories of potentially liberating conflict into conservative channels: the arbitration of labor struggles; school desegregation lawsuits in response to racial conflict; administrative hearings for complaints of sex discrimination in employment; individualized grievance mechanisms for prisoners, consumers, tenants, and welfare recipients; state regulatory agencies as a result of environmental activism. Informal institutions perform a similar function but in their own distinctive fashion. By disguising coercion, centralization, and dominance, they extend state control to new behavior. By offering a hearing to certain grievances (thereby cooling out the grievants) they convey the powerful (if implicit) message that other grievances are illegitimate or insignificant. Also unlike civil (though like criminal) courts, they direct their attention largely at the dominated classes.

There is some evidence that informal justice is coming to play a greater role in controlling conflict, although the magnitude of this trend, and its explanation, are unclear. We appear to be reaching the end of a long period, dating back to the end of the nineteenth century, during which formal legal institutions have been the dominant mode of managing conflict: substantive rights have expanded, administrative agencies have proliferated, the compulsory arbitration of labor disputes has become widespread, the criminal justice system has grown enormously, and we have seen the rise of state-funded legal services and foundation-supported public interest law. These formal rights, institutions, and procedures are not about to disappear, but their further growth may be checked and they may experience significant retrenchment. The reasons for this remain obscure. The fiscal crisis of the state may require a reduction of services, but economic forces do not specify that these must be mechanisms of social control. The political weakness of the dominated classes may permit the state to withdraw welfare rights granted earlier, but the source of this weakness is itself uncertain, though it is clearly related to the capitalist economic crisis. Finally, though ideas alone are never a sufficient explanation for institutional change, the dominant ideology of capitalism, liberal legalism, does appear to induce perpetual oscillation between formalism and informalism as modes of legitimation.

How successful are informal legal institutions likely to be in rendering conflict conservative? Here again the answer seems clear, they can only fail. No legal institution, formal or informal, can resolve the contradictions of capitalism or eliminate the exploitation and domination that generate conflict. Formal legal institutions repeatedly engender the liberating conflict they try to contain. Workers threatened with unsafe conditions reject the protection of regulatory agencies and the promise of compensation after they are injured and simply stop production or walk off the job (*Whirlpool Corp.* v. *Marshall,* 100 S.Ct. 883, 1980). Ethnic minorities subjected to constant police violence cannot be pacified with internal review procedures and lawsuits and will finally respond violently, as they recently did in Miami. A community faced with toxic wastes that are producing miscarriages, birth defects, and sick children, like those in the Love Canal, may shortcircuit governmental bureaucracy by taking officials hostage until residents are provided with alternative accommodation (Brown, 1980; *Los Angeles Times,* 20 May 1980, Part I, p. 20).

Informal legal institutions have their own limitations. From the viewpoint of the capitalist state, their drawback is that they cannot effectively manage conflict and remain informal. If they take the latter course they will atrophy, like the conciliation services attached to family courts. If they choose the former they will have to become more openly coercive; but this will generate opposition and compel the liberal state to respond by adopting formal procedures, witness the history of the juvenile court. Members of oppressed groups are likely to find informal procedures uncongenial for other reasons, because they want to resist exploitation and domination, not reach an accommodation with it. They want a public hearing and moral vindication; if informal institutions do not provide this, grievants will find other arenas. Finally, informal (like formal) institutions retain the potential to advance liberation. Indeed, they must express some of the aspirations of the disputants or the latter would shun them altogether. And these institutions sometimes do offer a more humane process, a mechanism for extending welfare rights, greater participation by the parties, exploration of a wider range of issues, and less dependence upon professionals.

Yet both formal and informal legal institutions under capitalism ultimately present the project of liberation with the same dilemma. Most of the time those institutions successfully contain conflict and render it conservative. But even when conflict remains liberating, those who struggle will seek to embody their success in a legal institution, formal or informal: a substantive rule, a new process, an administrative agency. They will do so for several reasons: the hegemony of liberal legalism, the high cost to the participants of continuing the struggle, and the fact that legal institutions do represent important ideals of substantive and procedural justice (if only imperfectly). But the result is the

264   *R. L. Abel*

creation of yet another legal institution that ultimately serves to render further conflict conservative and to strengthen capitalism. For the reasons sketched above, no institution can fully succeed in this task and each will engender resistance. The dialectic of liberation is unending.

Acknowledgements

I am grateful to Nils Christie for inviting me to the Scandinavian–American Exchange on Conflict Management, the German Marshall Fund for supporting the conference, and all the participants for their instruction, stimulation and comments. I have also received valuable criticism from Robert Kidder, Carrie Menkel-Meadow, Udo Reifner, my colleagues in our critical legal studies group in Los Angeles, and Boaventura de Sousa Santos, whose article in this journal (1980, **8,** 379–397) has strongly influenced me.

References

Abel, R. L. (1973) A comparative theory of dispute institutions in society. *Law & Society Review* **8,** 217–347.

Abel, R. L. (1979a) Socializing the legal profession: can redistributing lawyers' services achieve social justice? *Law & Policy Quarterly* **1,** 5–51.

Abel, R. L. (1979b) Delegalization: a critical review of its ideology, manifestations and social consequences. In *Alternative Rechtsformen und Alternativen zum Recht*. (Blankenburg, E., Klausa, E. & Rottleuthner, H., Eds). Westdeutscher Verlag: Opladen, pp. 27–47 (*Jahrbuch für Rechtssoziologie und Rechtstheorie*, band 6).

Abel, R. L. (1979c) Theories of litigation in society: "modern" dispute institutions in "tribal" society and "tribal" dispute institutions in "modern" society as alternative legal forms. In *Alternative Rechtsformen und Alternativen zum Recht*. (Blankenburg, E., Klausa, E. & Rottleuthner, H., Eds). Westdeutscher Verlag: Opladen, pp. 165–91 (*Jahrbuch für Rechtssoziologie und Rechtstheorie*, band 6).

Abel, R. L. (1980) Redirecting social studies of law. *Law & Society Review* **14,** 805–29.

Abel, R. L. (Ed.) (1982a) *The Politics of Informal Justice: The American Experience*. Academic Press: New York (forthcoming).

Abel, R. L. (Ed.) (1982b) *The Politics of Informal Justice: Comparative Studies*. New York: Academic Press (forthcoming).

Abel-Smith, B. & Stevens, R. (1967) *Lawyers and the Courts: A Sociological Study of the English Legal System, 1750–1965*. Heinemann: London.

Alker, Jr. H. R., Hosticka, C. & Mitchell, M. (1976) Jury selection as a biased social process. *Law & Society Review* **11,** 9–42.

Aubert, V. (1963) Competition and dissensus: two types of conflict and of conflict resolution. *Journal of Conflict Resolution* **7,** 26.

Auerbach, J. S. (1979) Informal (in)Justice? The Legalization of Informal Dispute Settlement in Modern America. Part I: Conciliation and Arbitration (unpublished).

Bailey, F. G. (1971) Gifts and poison. In *Gifts and Poison*(Bailey, F. G., Ed.). Blackwell: Oxford, pp. 1–25.

Barton, J. H. (1975) Behind the legal explosion. *Stanford Law Review* **27,** 567–84.

Baumgartner, M. P. (1980) Social Control in a Suburban Town: An Ethnographic Study. PhD. dissertation, Sociology, Yale University.

Beresford, R. & Cooper, J. (1977) A neighborhood court for neighborhood suits. *Judicature* **61**, 185-90.

Berman, H. J. (1963) *Justice in the U.S.S.R: An Interpretation of Soviet Law* (Rev. Ed.). Vintage Books: New York.

Best, A. & Andreasen, A. R. (1977) Consumer response to unsatisfactory purchases: a survey of perceiving defects, voicing complaints, and obtaining redress. *Law & Society Review* **11**, 701-42.

Bickel, A. (1962) *The Least Dangerous Branch: The Supreme Court at the Bar of Politics*. Yale University Press: New Haven.

Blankenburg, E., Klausa, E. & Rottleuthner, H. (Eds) (1979) *Alternative Rechtsformen und Alternativen zum Recht*. Westdeutscher Verlag: Opladen (*Jahrbuch für Rechtssoziologie und Rechtstheorie*, band 6).

Bohannan, P. (1967) Introduction. In *Law and Warfare* (Bohannan, P., Ed.). Natural History Press: Garden City, N.Y.

Brown, M. (1980) *Laying Waste: The Poisoning of America by Toxic Chemicals*. Pantheon: New York.

Buckle, L. G. & Thomas-Buckle, S. R. (1980) Bringing Justice Home: Some Thoughts about the Neighborhood Justice Center Policy. Presented at the joint meeting of the Law and Society Association and the ISA Research Committee on Sociology of Law, Madison, 5 June.

Burger, W. E. (1977) Our vicious legal spiral. *Judges' Journal* **16**, 23-24, 48-49.

Cappelletti, M. (Gen. Ed.) (1978-1981) *Access to Justice*, 5 volumes. Giuffre: Milan and Sijthoff and Noordhoff: Alphen aan de Rijn.

Chambers, D. L. (1979) *Making Fathers Pay: The Enforcement of Child Support*. University of Chicago Press: Chicago.

Christie. N. (1977) Conflicts as property. *British Journal of Criminology* **17**, 1-15.

Christie, N. (n.d.) Limits to Pain (unpublished).

Cohen, S. (1979) The punitive city: notes on the dispersal of social control. *Contemporary Crises* **3**, 339-63.

Cook, R. F., Roehl, J. A. & Sheppard, D. I. (1980) *Neighborhood Justice Centers Field Test: Final Evaluation Report*. U.S. Department of Justice, National Institute of Justice, Office of Program Evaluation: Washington, D.C.

Cratsley, J. C. (1978) Community courts: offering alternative resolution within the judicial system. *Vermont Law Review* **3**, 1-69.

Danzig, R. (1973) Toward the creation of a complementary decentralized system of justice. *Stanford Law Review* **26**, 1.

Davis, R. C., Tichane, M. & Grayson, D. (1980) *Mediation and Arbitration as Alternatives to Prosecution in Felony Arrest Cases: An Evaluation of the Brooklyn Dispute Resolution Center (First Year)*. Vera Institute of Justice: New York.

Donzelot, J. (1979) *The Policing of Families*. Pantheon: New York.

Economides, K. (1980) Small claims and procedural justice. *British Journal of Law and Society* **7**, 111-21.

Ehrlich, T. (1976) Legal pollution. *New York Times Magazine* 17, (8 February).

Eisenberg, M. A. (1976) Private ordering through negotiation: dispute settlement and rule making. *Harvard Law Review* **89**, 376.

Eisenberg, T. & Yeazell, S. C. (1980) The ordinary and extraordinary in institutional litigation. *Harvard Law Review* **93**, 465.

Feeley, M. (1979) *The Process Is the Punishment*. Russell Sage: New York.

Felstiner, W. L. F. & Drew, A. B. (1976) *European Alternatives to Criminal Trials and Their Applicability in the United States*. University of Southern California: Los Angeles, CA.

Felstiner, W. L. F. & Williams, L. A. (1980) *Community Mediation in Dorchester, Massachusetts*. U.S. Department of Justice, National Institute of Justice: Washington, D.C.

Fetter, T. J. (Ed.) (1978) *State Courts: A Blueprint for the Future*. National Center for State Courts: Williamsburg, VA.

Fisher. E. A. (1975) Community courts: an alternative to conventional criminal adjudication. *American University Law Review* **24**, 1253-91.

Foucault, M. (1977) *Discipline and Punish: The Birth of the Prison*. Pantheon: New York.

Frank, J. (1931) *Law and the Modern Mind*. Brentanos: New York.

266 *R. L. Abel*

Fried, C. (1976) The lawyer as friend: the moral foundations of the lawyer client relation. *Yale Law Journal* **85,** 1060.

Galanter, M. (1974) Why the "haves" come out ahead: speculations on the limits of legal change. *Law & Society Review* **9,** 95–160.

Galanter, M. (1979a) Legality and its discontents: a preliminary assessment of current theories of legalization and delegalization. In *Alternative Rechtsformen und Alternativen zum Recht.* (Blankenburg, E., Klausa, E. & Rottleuthner, H., Eds). Westdeutscher Verlag: Opladen, pp. 11–26 (*Jahrbuch für Rechtssoziologie und Rechtstheorie*, band 6).

Galanter, M. (1979b) *Justice in Many Rooms.* University of Wisconsin Law School, Disputes Processing Research Program: Madison (Working Paper 1979–4).

Gluckman, M. (1965) *Politics, Law and Ritual in Tribal Society.* Basil Blackwell: Oxford.

Goode, W. J. (1956) *Women in Divorce.* Free Press: Glencoe, IL.

Griffiths, J. (1970) Ideology in criminal procedure or a third "model" of the criminal process. *Yale Law Journal* **79,** 359.

Haley, J. O. (1981) The politics of informal justice: the Japanese experience 1922–1942. In Abel, 1982b.

Hannigan, J. A. (1977) The newspaper ombudsman and consumer complaints: an empirical assessment. *Law & Society Review* **11,** 679–700.

Harrington, C. (1980) Voluntariness, consent and coercion in adjudicating minor disputes. In *Policy Implementation: Choosing Between Penalties and Incentives.* (Brigham, J. & Brown, D.. Eds) Sage Publications: Beverly Hills, CA.

Hollingshead, A. B. & Redlich, F. (1958) *Social Class and Mental Illness.* Wiley: New York.

Illich, I. *et al.* (1977) *Disabling Professions.* Marion Boyers: London.

Jones, H. W. (Ed.) (1965) *The Courts, the Public, and the Law Explosion.* Prentice-Hall: Englewood Cliffs, N.J.

Katz, D., Gutek, B. A., Kahn, R. L. & Barton, E. (1975) *Bureaucratic Encounters: A Pilot Study in the Evaluation of Government Services.* Survey Research Center: Ann Arbor, MI.

Katz, E. & Danet, B. (Eds) (1973) *Bureaucracy and the Public: a reader in official-client relations.* Basic Books: New York.

Kline, J. A. (1978a) Curbing California's colossal legal appetite. *Los Angeles Times,* Part IV, p. 1 (12 February).

Kline, J. A. (1978b) Law reform and the courts: more power to the people or the profession? *California State Bar Journal* **53,** 14.

Landes, W. M. & Posner, R. A. (1979) Adjudication as a private good. *Journal of Legal Studies* **8,** 235–284.

Larson, M. S. (1977) *The Rise of Professionalism; A Sociological Analysis.* University of California Press: Berkeley.

Lasch, C. (1977) *Haven in a Heartless World: The Family Besieged.* Basic Books: New York.

Law & Society Review (1979) Plea bargaining. *Law & Society Review* **13,** (Special Issue, Winter).

Macaulay, S. (1963) Non-contractual relations in business: a preliminary study. *American Sociological Review* **28,** 55.

McGillis, D. (1980) *Dispute Processing Projects: A Preliminary Directory.* Harvard Law School, Center for Criminal Justice: Cambridge.

Manning, B. (1976) Hyperlexis: our national disease. *Northwestern University Law Review* **71,** 767.

Marquardt, R. G. & Wheat, E. M. (1980) Hidden allocators: administrative law judges and regulatory reform. *Law & Policy Quarterly* **2,** 472–94.

Marx, K. (1963) *The Eighteenth Brumaire of Louis Bonaparte.* International Publishers: New York.

Meador, D. J. (1978) Statement. In *Hearings before the Subcommittee on Courts, Civil Liberties, and the Administration of Justice of the Committee on the Judiciary, House of Representatives, 95th Congress, 2nd Session, on S. 957: Dispute Resolution Act.* U.S.G.P.O.: Washington, DC. pp. 60–2.

Mentschikoff, S. (1952) The significance of arbitration – a preliminary inquiry. *Law and Contemporary Problems* **17,** 699.

Merry, S. E. (1979) Going to court: strategies of dispute management in an American urban neighborhood. *Law & Society Review* **13,** 871–925.

Conservative conflict and informal justice   267

Merry, S. E. (1981) The social organization of mediation in non-industrial societies: implications for informal community justice in America. In Abel, 1982b.

Morris, C. R. (1980) *The Cost of Good Intentions: New York City and the Liberal Experiment, 1960–1975*. Norton: New York.

Nader, L. (1969) Introduction. In *Law in Culture and Society* (Nader, L., Ed.). Aldine: Chicago.

Nader, L. (Ed.) (1980) *No Access to Law: Alternatives to the American Judicial System*. Academic Press: New York.

Palen, F. S. (1979) Media ombudsmen: a critical review. *Law & Society Review* **13**, 799–850.

Polanyi, K. (1957) *The Great Transformation: the Political and Economic Origins of our Time*. Beacon Press: Boston (first published 1944).

Poulantzas, N. (1978) *State, Power Socialism*. New Left Books: London.

Pound, R. (1922) *An Introduction to the Philosophy of Law*. Yale University Press: New Haven.

Rosenberg, M. (1971) Let's everybody litigate? *Texas Law Review* **50**, 1349–68.

Ross, H. L. & Littlefield, N. O. (1978) Complaint as a problem-solving mechanism. *Law & Society Review* **12**, 199–216.

Royal Commission on Criminal Procedure (1981). *Report* H.M.S.O.: London (Cmnd 8092).

Royal Commission on Legal Services (1979) *Final Report*, vol. I. H.M.S.O.: London (Cmnd 7648).

Royal Commission on Legal Services in Scotland (1980) *Report*, vol. I. H.M.S.O.: Edinburgh (Cmnd 7846).

Sander, F. E. A. (1978) *Report on the National Conference on Minor Disputes Resolution*. American Bar Association: Chicago.

Sander, F. E. A. & Snyder, F. E. (1979) *Alternative Methods of Dispute Settlement – A Selected Bibliography*. American Bar Association, Division of Public Service Activities: Washington, D.C.

Santos, B. de S. (1977) The law of the oppressed: the construction and reproduction of legality in Pasargada. *Law & Society Review* **12**, 5–126.

Santos, B. de S. (1980) Law and community: the changing nature of state power in late capitalism. *International Journal of the Sociology of Law* **8**, 379–397.

Sennett, R. (1977) *The Fall of Public Man*. Knopf: New York.

Simon, W. H. (1978) The ideology of advocacy: procedural justice and professional ethics. *Wisconsin Law Review* **1978**, 29–144.

van der Sprenkel, S. (1962) *The Legal Institutions of Manchu China: a sociological analysis*. Athlone Press: London.

van Velsen, J. (1969) Procedural informality, reconciliation and false comparisons. In *Ideas and Procedures in African Customary Law* (Gluckman, M., Ed.). Oxford University Press: New York.

Wechsler, H. (1961) Toward neutral principles of constitutional law. In *Principles, Politics and Fundamental Law*. Harvard University Press: Cambridge.

Wilkinson, P. J. (1980) *The Social Organization of Disputes and Dispute Processing and Methods for the Investigation of Their Social, Legal and Interactive Properties: A Bibliography in Three Parts*. Centre for Socio-Legal Studies: Oxford.

Yngvesson, B. & Hennessey, P. (1975) Small claims, complex disputes: a review of the small claims literature. *Law & Society Review* **9**, 219–74.

Date received: January 1981

[9]

The Corporate Advantage: A Study of the Involvement of Corporate and Individual Victims in a Criminal Justice System*

JOHN HAGAN, *University of Wisconsin–Madison*

ABSTRACT

The legal conceptualization of corporate entities as juristic persons has both obscured and enhanced their influence in the criminal justice process. We point to several consequences of this influence: greater success of corporate than individual actors in getting individual offenders convicted, greater formal equality in the treatment of individuals prosecuted for crimes against corporate than individual victims, and greater satisfaction of corporate than individual victims with their experiences in the criminal justice system. We discuss the apparent paradox that an increase in formal equality may accompany higher rates of conviction for individuals accused of crimes against "juristic persons," and emphasize the important advantages a formal rational system of criminal law can provide these corporate entities. Making the role of corporate entities explicit is one way of adding a structural dimension that is lacking in contemporary criminal justice research.

To the extent that criminologists have talked in recent years about corporate entities and criminal law (e.g., Schrager and Short), they have been most concerned with the illegal and unethical activities of commercial organizations, and with the failure of the criminal law to deal with them (e.g., Ermann and Lundman). The point of this important and growing body of work is to demonstrate that commercial organizations are ineffectively pursued as criminals. Yet there is another, potentially more important, aspect of this situation. That is that corporate entities are nonetheless very active participants in the criminal justice process, pursuing through the police and courts many individuals who commit crimes against them. In other words, corporate entities not only have successfully avoided large-scale criminal prosecutions, they also have proven themselves effective in using

*Presented at the 1980 meetings of the American Sociological Association. I wish to express my gratitude to the Ministry of the Solicitor General of Canada for providing financial support for this study. The views expressed in this paper are my own and are not intended to represent the views of the Solicitor General of Canada.

criminal prosecutions to penalize those who offend them. It is the latter part of this imbalanced situation that we will examine in this paper.

Corporate Entities as Juristic Persons

We will follow Coleman (14) in interchangeably using the terms corporate entity and corporate actor to refer not only to what are commonly called corporations, but also to other collective entities such as churches, associations, unions, and schools, all of whom may enlist the criminal law to prosecute and convict individuals who commit crimes against them. These corporate entities are juristic persons who for legal purposes are treated much like natural persons. Indeed, it may be this apparent legal equivalence drawn between juristic and natural persons that has distracted social scientists from considering the distinctive roles these respective parties play in the criminal justice system. Thus, the formal legal assumption is that juristic and natural persons have equal rights and interests in law as a protection against those who offend against them. However, this assumption is a formal legal abstraction that is inconsistent with social and economic inequalities that differentiate corporate and individual entities. In other words, the juristic person is a legal form (Balbus) that obscures more than it reveals. Coleman states the problem clearly when he notes that ". . . a symmetric allocation of rights between corporations and persons can lead in practice to an asymmetric realization of interests" (76); and when he concludes that ". . . among the variety of interests that men have, those interests that have been successfully collected to create corporate actors are the interests that dominate the society" (49). Our concern in this paper is with how, and with what consequences, corporate advantages in the criminal justice process may have been achieved. The work of Max Weber is relevant to these issues.

The Ideas at Issue

THE DOMINATION OF LAW

Weber regarded the law, criminal and civil, as bearing a close correspondence to the economy, and to the corporate entities that comprise it. The connecting link in this system of thought was the notion of logical formalism, or formal rationality. In fact, much of Weber's work on law addressed a fundamental question that ultimately was left unresolved: Did formal rationality in legal thought contribute to the rise of capitalism, or, alternatively, did capitalism contribute to the rise of logical rationality in legal thought? Regardless of the answer given to this question, Weber made the following point quite clear, "The tempo of modern business communication requires a promptly and predictably functioning legal system," or, said differently, "The universal predominance of the market consociation requires . . . a legal system the functioning of which is *calculable* in accordance with rational rules" (40). Thus corporate entities have a generalized interest in formal rational legal processes, and a mainstay of formal rationality is the domination of law.

By domination, Weber means the probability that commands will be followed. *A key form of domination for our purposes involves the probability that corporate victims will be better able than individual victims to get individual offenders convicted.* Weber notes that such forms of domination are sustained in large part by efforts to raise or cultivate their legitimacy. Thus ". . . the continued existence of every domination . . . always has the strongest need of self-justification through appealing to the principles of legitimation" (336). Weber concludes that "*Rationally* consociated conduct of a dominational structure finds its typical expression in *bureaucracy*, and therefore the purest type of legal domination is that which is carried on by and through a bureaucratic administrative staff." The effectiveness of bureaucracy in the service of this goal is readily explained:

Bureaucracy tends toward *formalistic impersonality*. The ideal official administers his office *sine ira et studio*, without hatred or passion, hence also without 'love' or 'enthusiasm'; under the pressure of a plain sense of duty, 'without regard of person' he treats equally all persons who find themselves in factually equal situations (xliii, emphasis in original).

Thus one key feature of a bureaucratically organized criminal justice system is the presumed capacity to rise above consideration of the extralegal characteristics of the persons it processes. Such a system is expected instead to deal only with legally relevant aspects of offenders' cases. Note that this expectation directly contradicts the instrumental Marxist assumption that discrimination against economic and ethnic minorities is an inevitable product of criminal justice decision-making in a capitalist society (Chambliss and Seidman; Quinney). In contrast to this expectation, we have argued that corporate entities should have an objective interest in the very feature of formal impersonality that a bureaucratically organized criminal justice system is expected to provide: it is this feature that adds the legitimacy, and in turn the predictability and calculability, that are essential to successful commercial enterprise.

If the above reasoning is correct, in historical as well as cross-sectional data, *we should expect the participation of corporate actors as victims in the criminal justice process to be characterized by an increased formal equality in the treatment of offenders.* However, it is essential to underline the word *formal* here, because as Balbus suggests, ". . . the systemic application of an equal scale to systemically unequal individuals necessarily tends to

Law and Society

reinforce systemic inequalities . . ." (652). That is, it is important to emphasize that although individual offenders might be treated more equally when
corporate victims are involved, collectively, they would still fare worse because, as a *group*, they would experience a higher probability of conviction.

    A final implication of the above discussion is that corporate actors
will not only be anxious to make use of the criminal justice system, but also
that they will more easily coordinate their goals with the organizational
priorities of this system. Both organization forms have an interest in the
bureaucratic pursuit of the formal rational application of law. Furthermore,
as bureaucracies themselves, many corporate actors may be better suited
than individuals to work effectively with the criminal justice system. For
example, the element of formal impersonality may better equip corporate
actors to decide which crimes against them are more promising cases for
criminal prosecution. As well, because corporate actors may be more impersonal as well as less involved emotionally in their cases, they may be
less likely to intrude on the criminal justice process once a case is under
way; or, in the course of a case to indicate a change of preference with
regard to the prosecution of it. Thus corporate victims may work more
effectively than individual victims with criminal justice organizations, and
*corporate actors may therefore be more satisfied than individuals with the results
they achieve*. This type of prediction is anticipated by Coleman's observation
that corporate actors (including not only corporations but also government
agencies like those that constitute the criminal justice system) prefer to
work with other corporate actors as compared to individuals. Coleman
captures the irony and significance of this situation when he notes that
"These preferences are often rationally based: the corporate actor ordinarily stands to gain more from a transaction with another corporate actor
than from one with a person. But the rational basis makes the preference
no less real in its consequences for persons."

    Three testable hypotheses are contained in the above discussion:

1. that *corporate actors will be more successful than individuals in obtaining
convictions against offenders*,
2. that *equal treatment of offenders will be more likely to accompany corporate than
individual victim involvement in the criminal justice system*, and
3. that *corporate actors will be more satisfied than individuals with the work of this
system*.

This paper presents a cross-sectional empirical test of these hypotheses.
First, however, it will be useful to provide a brief discussion of the changing historical role of victims in the criminal justice system. The thesis of
this discussion is that the historical emergence of corporate entities has
been associated with significant changes in the role of the crime victim.

THE ROLE OF THE VICTIM VIEWED HISTORICALLY

If the Weberian picture of corporate participation in the criminal justice process we have provided is correct, it should be possible to identify historical changes in the role of crime victims that correspond to changes in the surrounding economy and society (see Tigar and Levy). Such changes can be identified. In their broadest outline: a resort to blood feuds directly involved victims in achieving criminal justice as then conceived in tribal societies; a form of private prosecution and compensation continued to involve victims, but with some notable modifications, in feudal societies; and the emergence of modern capitalism found victims of crime replaced by public prosecutors in pursuit of a more impersonal, formal rational form of justice.

Thus, early societies, based on kinship ties and tribal organization, functioned without centralized systems of criminal justice and they assigned a prominent role to presumed victims in resolving criminal disputes through blood feuds. In these societies, victims and their kin were expected to put things right by avenging what they perceived as crimes against them: "All crime was against the family; it was the family that had to atone, or carry out the blood-feud" (Traill, 5).

Feudalism and Christianity were accompanied by a gradual elimination of blood feuding and an emerging system of compensations. What is significant in this is that as feudalism developed, between 700 and 1066, lords and bishops gradually replaced kinship groups as recipients of the compensatory payments (Hibbert; Jeffrey). This was a very significant beginning of the decoupling (Hagan et al., a) of victims from an emerging criminal justice system. Gradually, the state began to receive a part of the compensation payments. Schafer notes that "Before long the injured person's right to restitution began to shrink, and after the Treaty of Verdun divided the Frankish Empire, the fine that went to the state gradually replaced it entirely" (14). Thus, it was now the state that was replacing the victim as a central actor in the criminal justice process. Finally, although the proceedings of this period (including oaths and ordeals) could be quite formal, at least from a modern viewpoint, they also were quite irrational (see Maine; Thayer).

The transition in England to a more modern form of criminal justice occurred during the reign of Henry II (1154–1189). During this period the feudal system of law disappeared and a system of common law emerged (Jeffrey). Nonetheless, a system of private prosecutions based on the initiative taken by victims of crime remained in effect in England well into the nineteenth century. In fact, the final decline of the victim's role in the criminal justice system did not begin until the Enlightenment, with the work of Cesare Beccaria. Writing in the eighteenth century, Beccaria applied the "principle of utility" in arguing that criminal law should serve the

998 / Social Forces Volume 60:4, June 1982

interests of society rather than the individual victim. What is significant throughout this work is the effort to model a criminal justice system on the same principles of calculation and reason that formed the foundations of modern capitalism (for elaboration of this point, see Halevy). Thus Balbus is able to note direct parallels between the emergence of modern legal forms and the commodity forms that characterize modern capitalism.

With Beccaria and Bentham, then, the formal rationality that Weber associates with modern capitalism found a very fundamental expression. The most important implication of this was that victims should play no direct role in criminal justice decisions about prosecution and punishment. From the utilitarian viewpoint, the crime is against *society*, and the *state* must therefore use calculation and reason in pursuing its prosecution and in deterring its repetition. However, as indicated earlier, in England the right and power to accuse, collect evidence and manage prosecutions for the state resided with individual citizens well into the nineteenth century (McDonald). Indeed this access to the law was regarded as an important right of private citizens, and it was not until the middle of the nineteenth century that the principal inadequacy of this arrangement was acknowledged: namely, that offenders were escaping prosecution because victims could not afford to exercise their legal rights. After several unsuccessful attempts to solve this problem in other ways, the office of the Director of Public Prosecutions was established in England in 1879. The ultimate effect of this change, and those discussed above, was a final loosening of the coupling of the victim to the criminal justice system, and a new autonomy for the state in overseeing victim-offender disputes.

It is clear then that a new kind of criminal justice emerged alongside the rise of the corporate form and the emergence of modern capitalism. It is our argument that this new form of criminal justice is particularly effective in promoting and legitimating use of the criminal law for the protection of corporate property against individuals. Put simply, our argument is that the new autonomy of the state in matters of criminal justice better serves corporate than individual interests. The remainder of this paper is an empirical exploration of this argument.

Prior Research

In spite of the importance we have attached in this discussion to corporate victims of crime, very little empirical attention has been given to them. Several victimization surveys involving corporate actors have been conducted as part of the National Crime Survey Program in the United States (U.S. Department of Justice). However, only two types of commercial crime, robbery and burglary, are considered in this work, and the sampling is restricted almost entirely to commercial establishments. Beyond this, a small collection of articles on crimes against businesses has been brought together in a single volume (Smigel and Ross); there are several studies of shoplifting and its control (e.g., Cameron; Hindelang; Robin); and the United States government has made some attempt to collect information on the costs of several types of commercial victimization (U.S. Department of Commerce). Among these sources, it is the victimization research that is most instructive.

Victimization data collected on burglary and robbery in thirteen American cities (U.S. Department of Justice) are brought together, and weighted to produce population estimates, in Appendices 1.1 and 1.2 of this paper. These data provide preliminary support for our focus on the corporate influence on criminal law. For example, as might be expected given the opportunities and benefits of crimes against corporate actors, both for burglary and robbery, the per capita rates of victimization of commercial establishments are higher than for individuals and households. Across the thirteen cities, on a per capita basis, commercial establishments experience more than three times the burglaries and five times the robberies as households and individuals. Furthermore, in every city, for both burglary and robbery, commercial establishments are more likely than individuals and households to report the victimizations they experience to the police. Across the thirteen cities, approximately three-quarters (76.1 percent) of the commercial burglary victims report their experiences to the police, while about half (51.6 percent) of the household burglary victims report their experiences to the police. Similarly, 82 percent of the commercial robberies and 57 percent of the individual robberies are reported to the police. Undoubtedly, this difference is influenced by the types and amounts of corporate insurance coverage. Nonetheless, it remains significant that on a per capita basis, commercial victims are much more likely than individual victims to require and make use of the system. Of course, individuals and households outnumber commercial organizations, so that when the above findings are weighted back to the population, commercial establishments are reduced in their apparent significance. Even then, however, we find that commercial establishments are very important clients of the criminal justice system. Thus across the thirteen American cities, commercial establishments are responsible for more than a third, and in some cities (e.g., Cincinnati in the case of burglary and Miami in the case of robbery) more than half, of both the burglaries and robberies reported to the police. In sum, the representation of commercial victims in the criminal justice process is large and disproportionate.

Some comments should be added to these findings. First, these data deal with burglary and robbery only, while thefts (by employees and customers) are clearly the most frequent crimes experienced by commercial victims. Second, these data consider only commercial establishments, ignoring other kinds of corporate victims. Finally, these data stop at the point

1000 / Social Forces Volume 60:4, June 1982

where victims indicate that they reported incidents to the police. Thus the picture provided by victimization data is suggestive, but partial. Research reported in the remainder of this paper considers in greater detail the involvement of corporate victims in the criminal justice process, in one Canadian jurisdiction.

The Current Research

The data analyzed in this paper consist of cases involving victims of crime for whom an offender is charged in a collection of suburban communities adjacent to Toronto, Canada. The restriction to cases where an offender is charged is deliberate. We have already shown with victimization data that commercial organizations are more likely than individual victims to report crimes against them to the police. We now want to consider the role of these victims in the criminal justice system. Focusing on cases where charges are laid increases the likelihood that the victims we consider have something more than a passing contact with the system.

Several kinds of data are considered. First, a population of 1,000 cases drawn from police department files from September 1976 to January 1977 is used to establish parameters for the jurisdiction under study. Then a stratified sample of 400 post-disposition interviews with 200 individual and 200 corporate victims is analyzed. The interviews with the individual victims represent the latter half of a panel design involving before and after court contacts which took place between June 1976 and December 1978; the corporate interviews began in September 1977 and continued until September 1978. Individual victims for whom an offender was charged were eliminated from the sampling frame in three circumstances: if the victim was a juvenile, if the crime was against a person's property and resulted in less than five dollars damage, or if the crime was against a person who could not, or would not, recall it. The panel design involving individual victims began with 305 victims and stopped after 200 of these victims could be reached for the follow-up, post-disposition interview.[1]

In establishing the sampling frame for the corporate interviews, two research decisions had to be made. First, which member of the corporate entity should be interviewed? Our decision was to have the interviewer determine who in the organization was most responsible for making decisions to charge, and other decisions, in the relevant case. In practice, this arrangement seemed to work effectively; however, it also raised the second issue to be faced. That issue was: Which cases involving corporate victims should be considered? Many corporate actors—especially the retail department stores—were victimized repeatedly. It would have made little sense to interview representatives of these organizations repeatedly. Instead we formulated as a sampling criterion that each organization was to be interviewed only once about a crime (involving a charged suspect) which was representative of those experienced. This was done in one of two ways. Working with a listing of all cases involving corporate victims for whom an accused was charged, we first sorted the cases by organization. Again as in the case of individual victims, property crimes involving less than five dollars in losses were not considered. If a modal type of case for a corporate victim was present (e.g., shoplifting for many retail stores), a case for interview was selected among these at random. Alternatively, if no modal type of case existed, a case was selected at random from the larger grouping. The resulting sampling frame was made up of cases involving 334 corporate actors.

The variables and their values included in our analysis are listed in Appendix 2.1. Our analysis focuses first on a set of court outcomes: whether the defendant was held for a bail hearing, convicted, and the type of sentence received; and second on victims' reactions to these outcomes: the perceived appropriateness of the disposition and the overall satisfaction with the outcome of the case.

There may be initial discomfort with the idea of considering cases involving corporate and individual victims in a single analysis; a discomfort that probably follows from the observation that some types of cases, for example shoplifting, only involve corporate actors. However, it is not at all clear that this fact makes shoplifting cases *qualitatively* different from other offenses committed against corporate actors and individuals. Certainly the law provides no separate offense category for shoplifting (i.e., the charge is typically theft), and we have noted that it treats both corporate and individual victims as "persons." Furthermore, Sellin and Wolfgang have demonstrated that shoplifting and other types of property crimes can be located, along with a variety of other crimes that cause bodily injury, on a common scale of seriousness. Their point, empirically confirmed, is that in everyday life, and particularly in everyday law enforcement, certain equivalences can and must be formed (348). Beyond this, our argument is that differences between cases involving corporate actors and individuals are a matter of degree, not kind, involving such things as the impersonality versus intimacy involved in the victim–accused relationship. Consideration of such variables is a part of our analysis, an analysis that successfully accounts for an important difference in the outcomes of cases involving corporate and individual victims.

A wide range of independent variables are considered in the analysis, some deriving from our theoretical interests, others from the conventions of this kind of criminal justice research (e.g., Hagan et al., b). For example, in the first part of the analysis, dealing with court outcomes, we consider a number of characteristics of the victim: whether the victim is an individual or a corporate entity, and if the former, the victim's sex and SES; the seriousness of the victimization as measured by the Sellin–Wolfgang scale; whether property was returned to the victim, the willingness of the victim to accept any responsibility for the crime, whether the victim gave testimony, the intimacy of the victim–accused relationship,[2] and whether the victim is a repeat player in the sense of having experienced the same type of crime previously. If the victim is a corporate actor, we consider whether it is involved in retailing, public or private in its base, local to multinational in scale, the number of employees in the representative's division, the number of organization units, the number of employees in the organization, the centralization of the organization and the perceived relationship between the organization and its clients. A number of characteristics of the accused were also taken from police files for this part of the analysis, including the marital status, sex, condition at arrest, and employment status of the accused. Information from the files were also used to determine whether a statement was taken from the accused, the police perception of the demeanor of the accused, and the number of prior convictions, the most serious prior disposition, and the number of charges against the accused. Finally, for this first part of the analysis we included from these files information on whether the victim mobilized the police, filed the complaint, whether a warrant was issued, and the initial decision whether to hold the person for a bail hearing. The last variable was included only for the adjudication and sentencing outcomes, to determine if early processing decisions are coupled to those made later.

There is some overlap in the independent variables included in the first and second parts of the analysis. The type of victim and crime, seriousness of victimization, return of property to the victim, victim responsibility, the relationship between victim and accused, and whether the victim mobilized the police, filed the complaint and gave testimony, are all considered as before. Similarly, four traits of the accused—employment status, prior convictions, most serious prior disposition, and number of other charges—are included in the same way as before. In addition to these variables, we consider a number of others that come from our interviews and that plausibly influence the response to court outcomes.

The remorse of the accused, as perceived by the victim, is included as measured in a Likert-type scale. We also consider characteristics attributed to the accused by the victim, measured in the form of a summed semantic differential scale that includes evaluations of the accused as honest–dishonest, responsible–irresponsible, kind–cruel, gentle–brutal, safe–dangerous, good–bad, predictable–unpredictable, stable–unstable, mature–immature, friendly–unfriendly. Victim ratings of the importance of five goals of sentencing—reformation, general deterrence, individual deterrence, punishment, and incapacitation—are considered. As well, a summed five-item law and order scale (see Hagan, a) is included. A "citizen responsibility" scale was constructed in the same way from responses to two items: (1) there isn't much individual citizens can do to prevent crime, and

(2) preventing crime is the job of the police, not the job of the average citizen. Separate consideration is given to the victim's belief in free will ("To what extent do you believe that human beings act on their own free will?") and conceptions of individual responsibility ("Do you feel that human beings should be responsible for their actions?"), both coded as Likert scales. Consideration is also given to whether the victim attended trial and to the victim's knowledge of the disposition. Victims who did not know the disposition were told it before being asked to respond to the case outcomes. The last of the independent variables we include is the disposition of the case. We are interested not only in the direct effect of this variable on the victim's response to the criminal justice process, but also in the effects of statistically holding this variable constant.

Tabular and regression techniques are used to analyze our data. Two of our five dependent variables are binary and violate technical assumptions of homosedasticity. Under these conditions, ordinary least-squares regression may produce inefficient, though unbiased, parameter estimates. We therefore ran weighted least-squares solutions as well as ordinary least-squares regressions when the binary dependent variables were involved. This procedure produced changes in some coefficients, but no alterations in substantive conclusions. To conserve space and maintain consistency, we present only the results of the ordinary least-squares regressions in this paper. Unless otherwise indicated, in the regression phase of the analysis we consider only those effects that are statistically significant at the .10 level,[3] with betas of .10 and larger. Throughout the analysis we focus on those factors that distinguish the involvement of corporate and individual victims in the criminal justice process.

THE ANALYSIS

The preliminary part of the analysis compared the population and interview data (see Hagan, b, ch. 2) to determine if any systematic sources of error or bias were present in the latter. Although no important discrepancies were discovered, several findings did stand out. First, we found that nearly two-thirds of the victims in the population were corporate entities ($N=643$), while just over a third were individuals ($N=357$). As well, both in the population and in the interviews significantly more corporate (79.5 and 75.0 percent) than individual victims (65.5 and 62.2 percent) saw accused persons in their cases convicted. We analyze this relationship between type of victim and likelihood of conviction further in a moment. Meanwhile, we can note that these preliminary findings are certainly consistent with our first hypothesis about corporate influence in the criminal justice process; that is, that corporate actors are more successful than individuals in obtaining convictions against offenders.

Before pursuing our multivariate analysis, several additional bivari-

1004 / Social Forces Volume 60:4, June 1982

ate relationships are presented in Table 1. The first two findings in this table reveal that corporate victims are more likely than individual victims to believe they could have prevented the incident and less likely to believe that crime prevention is the job of police. The implication is that corporate victims are well aware of the fact that they present more opportunities for crime than individuals, and that they could, and perhaps should, assume a greater responsibility for the crimes committed against them. As we have indicated, however, the paradox of this situation is that corporate victims are more likely to see accused persons convicted.

Table 1 also establishes several other things: individual victims are significantly more likely to know the accused, attend court, and know the case outcome. These indicators suggest that corporate victims are more detached from the accused, and decoupled from the criminal justice system, than are individual victims. We note these findings here because, as we suggest later, they may make for a more formal rational influence of corporate victims on the criminal justice process.

Finally, there is evidence in Table 1, consistent with our third hypothesis above, that corporate victims respond more positively to the criminal justice experience than do individual victims. Corporate victims are less likely than individual victims to be dissatisfied with the sentences the courts generally impose, and more likely to be satisfied with the competence of the police, the overall outcome of the case, and with the specific sentence imposed in the immediate case. All but the last of these differences is statistically significant. In other words, and perhaps with good reason, corporate victims express a greater satisfaction with the criminal justice system than do individual victims. Since some of this satisfaction may derive from the greater success of corporate victims in obtaining convictions, we go on next to a multivariate analysis of this success.

In Table 2 we use a step-wise multiple regression procedure to assess the impact of several variables on the greater success of corporate victims in obtaining convictions. These variables were selected in terms of our expectations about corporate participation in the criminal justice process. Thus the first of the variables is the victim–accused relationship, measured in terms of the intimacy, or conversely, the impersonality, of this relationship. Our expectation is that an impersonal relationship is more likely to allow a sustained prosecution, while intimacy between the victim and accused more often does not. Second, we consider the presence of a statement from the accused. Offenders who make incriminating statements are more easily convicted, and corporate entities may be able to use their resources more selectively in picking cases for prosecution where such statements can be generated. As well, we include the demeanor of the accused. One aspect of good demeanor, as perceived by the police, is an acknowledgment of guilt; again, corporate victims may be better able to generate cases with accused persons who have been reduced to this de-

Table 1. TYPE OF VICTIM BY RESPONSE TO VICTIMIZATION AND COURT EXPERIENCE

	Perceived Ability to Prevent Incident	Prevention of crime Job of Police	Knowledge of Offender	Attended Court	Knowledge of Case Outcome	Sentences Generally Too Easy	Satisfaction with Police Competence	Satisfied with Sentence	Satisfied with Overall Outcome
Individual	10.5% (21)	18.0% (36)	40.0% (80)	57.0% (114)	50.5% (101)	64.0% (128)	79.5% (159)	43.5% (87)	53.0% (106)
Organization	26.5 (53)	9.0 (18)	18.0 (36)	21.0 (42)	26.0 (52)	53.0 (106)	88.5 (177)	46.0 (92)	66.0 (132)
	$x^2=11.02$	$x^2=8.21$	$x^2=23.51$	$x^2=55.20$	$x^2=29.02$	$x^2=5.25$	$x^2=5.25$	$x^2=3.27$	$x^2=16.35$
	$p=.001$	$p=.004$	$p=.001$	$p=.001$	$p=.001$	$p=.072$	$p=.014$	$p=.351$	$p=.006$

1006 / Social Forces Volume 60:4, June 1982

Table 2. DECOMPOSITION OF THE EFFECT OF TYPE OF VICTIM ON ADJUDICATION (N=400)

		(1)		(2)		(3)		(4)		(5)	
		B	F	B	F	B	F	B	F	B	F
1.	Type of victim	.16	10.18	.14	7.17	.12	5.63	.09	2.99	.09	3.12
2.	Statement taken			.22	21.15	.18	11.94	.18	11.91	.17	11.63
3.	Accused demeanor					-.14	6.83	-.14	6.93	-.13	6.68
4.	Victim-accused relationship							-.12	5.39	-.12	5.62
5.	Repeat player									-.07	2.21
	Mediated effect			.02		.02		.03		.00	

meanor. Finally, we consider whether the victim is a repeat player, in the sense of having been a victim previously of a similar crime (Galanter). Corporate entities are more likely to be repeat players ($r=.53$), and this experience may be expected to improve their prospects for successful prosecutions. The above variables were introduced into regression equations in Table 2 in the order that they increased the explained variance in convictions.

Examination of Table 2 reveals that three of the above four variables are indeed involved in the success of corporations in obtaining convictions. Thus the statistical significance of the type of victim was reduced below the .05 level after the introduction of three of these variables.[4] The largest of the mediated effects (.03) in Table 2 is produced by the introduction of the victim–accused relationship. In other words, the impersonality of corporate actors is a key factor in their higher rate of convictions. Only slightly less important is the apparent ability of corporate victims to select and/or generate accused persons who give statements to the police and who demonstrate cooperative demeanor (both mediated effects = .02). The only variable that does not operate as expected is whether the victim is a repeat player. Apparently this experience does not *directly* account for the success of organizations. Indeed, the correlation between this experience and convictions is only .07. On the other hand, we have found evidence that corporate entities seem more generally to choose cases for prosecution with an eye toward what the courts are most likely to convict. Said differently, corporate entities choose their cases impersonally and strategically, a pattern that would seem to promote the formal rational enforcement of criminal law.

There was no evidence in our data that corporate victims were any more likely than individual victims to see accused persons held for a bail hearing or severely sentenced. However, a comparison in Tables 3 and 5 of factors producing these outcomes in cases of individual and corporate

Table 3. CORRELATION AND REGRESSION COEFFICIENTS FOR INDIVIDUAL VICTIMS

Independent Variables	Bail (N=188)				Adjudication (N=188)				Sentence (N=130)			
	r	b	B	F	r	b	B	F	r	b	B	F
Seriousness of victimization	.17	.02	.15	4.20**					.31	.08	.29	11.07**
Return of property					.23	.18	.15	3.70**	-.13	-.03	-.15	3.02*
Victim-accused relationship												
Accused condition at arrest	.20	.14	.17	5.11**								
Accused employment status	-.08	-.11	-.14	3.85**	-.30	-.22	-.23	9.47**	-.16	-.26	-.16	3.87*
Statement taken	.16	.18	.22	8.59**								
Accused demeanor	.17	.17	.19	7.05**								
Accused most serious disposition	.36	.11	.35	14.38**					.38	.18	.30	6.21
Number of charges against accused					-.12	-.06	-.23	7.98**				
Complaint	-.15	-.10	-.13	3.28*								
Warrant		--			-.18	-.27	-.19	6.52**				
Victim's sex	.07	-.12	-.15	3.67*					-.06	-.40	-.26	8.49**
	R^2 = .29				R^2 = .25				R^2 = .38			
	Intercept = .15				Intercept = .64				Intercept = 3.41			

*Significant at the .10 level.
**Significant at the .05 level.

1008 / Social Forces Volume 60:4, June 1982

Table 4. RESULTS OF DUMMY VARIABLE REGRESSIONS INVOLVING SEX OF VICTIM AND INVOLVEMENT WITH THE ACCUSED

Dummy Variables	Bail				Adjudication				Sentence			
	r	b	B	F	r	b	B	F	r	b	B	F
Female victim-involved with accused	-.06	.08	.09	1.24	-.14	-.02	-.02	.04	-.12	.12	.06	.49
Female victim-not involved with accused	-.02	.12	.13	2.91*	.02	.03	.02	.08	.18	.42	.22	6.15**

*Significant at the .10 level.

**Significant at the .05 level.

Table 5. CORRELATION AND REGRESSION COEFFICIENTS FOR ORGANIZATION VICTIMS

Independent Variables	Bail (N=200)				Adjudication (N=200)				Sentence (N=157)			
	r	b	B	F	r	b	B	F	r	b	B	F
Seriousness of victimization									.32	.08	.19	7.29**
Victim responsibility					-.16	-.12	-.12	3.17*				
Victim testimony									-.06	-.33	-.13	3.41*
Accused marital status					.13	.07	.12	2.78*	-.23	-.23	-.17	4.96*
Accused condition at arrest					.06	.16	.13	3.43*				
Accused employment status	-.16	-.14	-.16	4.93**								
Statement taken					.26	.26	.32	16.85**	.26	.47	.28	11.66**
Accused demeanor					-.21	-.12	-.14	3.59*				
Accused prior convictions	.42	.03	.29	7.44**								
Accused most serious disposition	.39	.06	.18	2.77*					.39	.53	.27	12.39**
Number of charges against accused					-.04	-.04	-.13	2.87*				
Mobilization					.15	.14	.17	6.34***				
Bail decision					.15	.15	.15	3.94***				
Number of employees					.10	.01	.14	3.32*				
	$R^2 = .27$				$R^2 = .28$				$R^2 = .47$			
	Intercept = .09				Intercept = 1.11				Intercept = 2.87			

*Significant at the .10 level.
**Significant at the .05 level.

1010 / Social Forces Volume 60:4, June 1982

victims reveals some striking differences that are consistent with our earlier discussion. For example, in cases with individual victims (see Table 3), the independent variable that most consistently predicts bail, adjudication, and sentencing decisions is the employment status of the accused. In these cases, unemployed accused are more likely to be held for bail ($B = -.14$), convicted ($B = -.23$), and sentenced severely ($B = -.16$). It may be possible to legally justify detention of an unemployed accused for a bail hearing in terms of formal standards for the making of these decisions (see Morden; Nagel). However, similar justifications do not exist at conviction and sentencing, and measured against normative expectations about equality before the law, these effects therefore may be extra-legal. In contrast, in Table 5, where cases involving corporate victims are considered, the employment status of the accused does *not* play a significant role at conviction and sentencing. These findings support our second hypothesis that formally equal treatment of offenders increases with corporate involvement in the criminal justice system.

Of related interest is the finding that persons accused of crimes against women are more likely than are persons accused of crimes against men to be held for a bail hearing ($B = -.15$) and to be sentenced severely ($B = -.26$). Interpretation of these effects is complicated by the fact that they only become apparent when other variables are held constant ($r = .07$ and $-.06$). Our concern in offering an interpretation of these effects was with the complicating role that the victim's relationship with the accused might play. To explore this we created two dummy variables representing female victims who *were* and *were not* intimately involved with the accused.[5] The "omitted category" for these dummy variables was *male* victims *un*involved with the accused. The results of substituting these dummy variables for their component parts in the regression equations of Table 3 are presented in Table 4. These results reveal two things: (1) offender involvement with female victims lessens the probability of conviction ($r = -.14$), and when conviction occurs, tends to result in more lenient sentencing ($r = -.12$); (2) other variables held constant, offenders accused of crimes against female victims with whom they are uninvolved are more likely to be held for bail hearings ($B = .13$) and receive severe sentences ($B = .22$). In other words, female victims who are uninvolved with the offender receive greater protective treatment from the courts than do female victims who are involved with the accused. These results suggest another type of inequality before the law that accompanies disputes between individuals.

Rather different findings emerge in Table 5, where cases involving corporate victims are considered. For example, in addition to the finding pertaining to the employment status of the accused noted above, the two most important determinants of being held for a bail hearing are the number of prior convictions and the most serious prior disposition against the accused. Beyond this, the most consistent influence on adjudication and sentencing is whether the accused was held for a bail hearing ($B = .15$ and .27). Overall, then, there is a tendency in cases involving corporate victims to give greater attention to legal variables (or in other words to formal rational considerations), and to prior organization decisions. The former finding supports, again, our second hypothesis; the latter reliance on bail decisions at the later stages of adjudication and sentencing suggests a pattern in which decision-making is routinized and reaffirmed as the defendant moves through the criminal justice process. One possible further indication of this routinization is that the largest explained variance in Tables 3 and 4 occurs at the sentencing stage in cases involving corporate victims ($R^2 = .47$). It may be here that the court is most certain of what it is doing. Finally, it is significant to note that at the conviction stage, larger corporate entities are apparently more successful than smaller corporate entities in obtaining convictions (i.e., the Beta for Number of Employees is .14). Insofar as size is a reflection of power and resources, this finding is consistent with our focus on the corporate advantage in the criminal justice process. More generally, the findings from this part of the analysis also support the link we have drawn between formal rationality and the involvement of corporate victims in the criminal justice process.

The final part of our analysis deals with the specific reactions of individual and corporate victims to the sentences imposed in their cases, and with their overall satisfaction with the outcomes in these cases. As earlier, there are clear differences in the responses of individual and corporate victims (see Table 6). Among these, the most significant again involves the employment status of the accused. If the accused is unemployed, individual victims are more likely to think the sentence was too lenient ($B = -.16$) and to be dissatisfied ($B = -.15$) with the overall outcome of the case. The reader will recall the earlier finding that in cases with individual victims, unemployed accused were more likely to be held for a bail hearing, convicted and sentenced severely. In this analysis we have held disposition constant. *Thus, individual victims apparently want more severe sanctioning for unemployed accused than they already receive.* No similar pattern exists when corporate victims are considered. Again, then, the implication is that corporate victims encourage, or at least facilitate, formal equality in the treatment of accused. However, we again emphasize that this gain is offset by the greater collective likelihood of conviction in these cases.

There is further evidence that individual victims who support a "law and order" orientation think sentences in their cases are too lenient and are dissatisfied with their case outcomes ($B = -.18$ and $-.21$). As well, those individual victims who attribute negative characteristics to the accused also find the sentences in their cases too lenient ($B = .25$).

The reactions of corporate victims to their case outcomes are more narrow or circumscribed in character. While individual victims do not vary in their reactions to court outcomes according to their concerns about de-

1012 / Social Forces Volume 60:4, June 1982

Table 6. CORRELATION AND REGRESSION COEFFICIENTS FOR PERCEIVED SENTENCE SEVERITY AND SATISFACTION WITH OUTCOME IN CASES WITH INDIVIDUAL AND ORGANIZATIONAL VICTIMS

	Perceived Sentence Severity, Individual Victims (n=188)				Satisfaction with Case Outcome, Individual Victims (n=188)				Perceived Sentence Severity, Organizational Victims (n=200)				Satisfaction with Case Outcome, Organizational Victims (n=200)			
	r	b	B	F	r	b	B	F	r	b	B	F	r	b	B	F
Seriousness of victimization	.17	.03	.16	3.68*	.17	.14	.24	9.19***					.17	-.79	-.20	6.65***
Victim responsibility	-.11	-.15	-.13	2.67*												
Characteristics attributed to accused	.27	.01	.25	10.50***												
Complainant					-.14	-.72	-.22	8.06***								
General deterrence-victim ranking													-.15	-.19	-.14	2.73*
Individual deterrence-victim ranking									-.19	-.09	-.16	3.09*				
Law and Order attitudes	-.17	-.03	-.18	5.68**	-.18	-.12	-.21	6.92***								
Individual responsibility					.02	.05	.15	3.70*								
Victim testimony					-.07	-.50	-.15	3.01*								
Accused employment status	-.12	-.16	-.16	3.89**	-.08	-.48	-.15	3.62*								
Disposition					-.15	-.26	-.25	9.25***	.19	-.07	-.19	5.50**	-.26	-.25	-.26	11.31***
Trial attendance					-.00	.61	.19	3.68*					.02			

Relationship between
organization and Clients

.16   .24   .16   4.23**

$R^2 = .25$ $R^2 = .25$ $R^2 = .19$ $R^2 = .23$

Intercept = 2.06   Intercept = 3.04   Intercept = 5.15   Intercept = 3.08

*Significant at the .10 level.
**Significant at the .05 level.
***Significant at the .01 level.

1014 / Social Forces Volume 60:4, June 1982

terrence, or for that matter in relation to any other goal of sentencing, corporate victims do. Among corporate victims, a concern with individual deterrence is associated with a perception that the sentence is too lenient ($B = -.16$), and a concern with general deterrence is associated with a dissatisfaction with the overall case outcome ($B = -.14$). The other consistent response of corporate victims is to the actual severity of the disposition in the case. As one might expect, the more lenient the disposition, the more likely the corporate victim is to regard the sentence as too lenient ($B = -.19$) and to be dissatisfied with the overall outcome of the case ($B = -.26$). These findings seem quite consistent with Coleman's observation that insofar as corporate actors come to replace individuals in influencing the allocation of organizational resources, "these decisions . . . are more and more removed from the multiplicity of dampening and modifying interests of which a real person is composed—more and more the resultant of a balance of narrow intense interests of which corporate actors are composed" (49). The corporate attention here seems narrowly focused on the deterrence of future crimes against them.

Discussion and Conclusions

To date, criminal justice research has not given much attention to the structural contexts in which criminal justice decisions are made (see Hagan and Bumiller). One source of this *a*structural attitude is undoubtedly the importance Anglo-American law attaches to individuals. Notions of individual rights permeate our system of criminal law and are reflected in the modern ideal of individualized justice. However, one purpose of this paper is to argue that there is a myth of individualism that is stretched beyond plausibility, for example, by the legal conceptualization of corporate entities as juristic persons who are accorded the same formal status as natural persons. Criminal justice research has accepted uncritically the myth of individualism insofar as it has neglected to explore the consequences of the involvement of these juristic persons as victims in criminal justice decision-making. Making the role of corporate entities explicit in this system is one way of adding a structural dimension to work in this domain.

We hypothesized that the involvement of these new juristic persons in the criminal justice system has resulted in a corporate influence in the criminal justice process that is characterized by (a) the greater success of corporate than individual actors in getting individual offenders convicted, (b) a greater likelihood of formal equality in the treatment of individuals prosecuted for crimes against corporate than individual victims, and (c) a greater satisfaction of corporate than individual victims with their experiences in the criminal justice system. We noted that an increase in formal equality in the treatment of individuals prosecuted for crimes against corporate actors (Hypothesis 2) is offset by the possibility that as a group, these individuals may still be more likely to be convicted for crimes against corporate entities (Hypothesis 1). This combination of possibilities may also serve to increase the legitimacy as well as the efficiency with which criminal justice agencies serve corporate actors, and therefore anticipate the greater satisfaction corporate actors are hypothesized to take from the criminal justice experience (Hypothesis 3). To put all this in Weberian terms, we are suggesting that there is an "elective affinity" between corporate actors and agencies of criminal justice.

There is much in our data that supports the perspective just outlined. Our historical review of victim involvement in criminal justice decision-making revealed that it was not until the Enlightenment and the rise of modern capitalism that the role of the state-supported public prosecutor fully emerged, and consequently reduced the involvement of private victims in criminal justice operations. We noted that this new autonomy of the state might better serve the interests of corporate than individual victims. Thus our review of contemporary victimization data from thirteen American cities revealed that as compared to individuals, commercial organizations experience and report crimes to the police in large and disproportionate numbers. While we have no data to indicate precisely when the increased involvement of corporate actors began, it is reasonable to assume that it has paralleled the tremendous growth of commercial retailing in this century. The purpose of the current study has been to examine how the involvement of corporate victims may influence contemporary criminal justice operations. We have explored this issue within a Canadian jurisdiction.

Overall, our data provide support for the perspective outlined above. For example, corporate actors actually outnumber individuals as victims in the jurisdiction studied.[6] As well, corporate actors are more likely than individuals to obtain convictions, and, the larger the organization, the greater is the likelihood of conviction. The greater success of corporate actors as compared to individuals in obtaining convictions is explained by their more impersonal relationships with the accused, and by their selection of accused who give statements to the police and who convey a demeanor that acknowledges their guilt. The picture that emerges is of corporate entities that use their resources in an impersonal, formal, rational, efficient fashion. One of these resources, the use of private security personnel, deserves further study. It is likely that size of organization acts as a proxy in our data for quantity and quality of private security arrangements. Access to private security may well be a crucial part of what we have called the corporate advantage.

We also considered separately factors that lead to bail, conviction and sentencing decisions in cases involving corporate, as contrasted with individual, victims. Measured against legal standards of equality before the law, we found that the involvement of individual victims is associated

1016 / Social Forces Volume 60:4, June 1982

with the operation of extra-legal factors in the decision-making process. For example, in cases with individual victims, unemployed accused are more likely to be held for a bail hearing, convicted, and sentenced severely. Furthermore, even when the severity of dispositions in these cases is held constant, individual victims of unemployed accused still express a greater desire for severe sanctions and a dissatisfaction with overall case outcome. The implication is that individual victims are a part (although not as large a part as they might wish) of the differential imposition of the sanctions noted above. A different pattern emerges when corporate victims are involved. More influential here are factors that derive from contact of the accused with criminal justice organizations (e.g., bail decisions, prior convictions and dispositions, and statements given to the police) and corporate concerns about individual and general deterrence. Measured against legal expectations, corporate victims again seem to be part of a more formal rational application of law.

We have argued that the form and content of criminal justice found in modern capitalist societies supports and legitimates the use of criminal law for the protection of corporate property against individuals. That is, we have argued that the modern criminal justice system better serves corporate than individual interests. One consequence of this situation is that criminal justice agencies originally thought to have emerged for the purposes of protecting individuals against individuals today are devoting a substantial share of their resources to the protection of large affluent corporate actors. It is important to note that this may not be the unique fate of modern institutions of criminal justice. For example, the post office has long complained of a related set of pressures generated by the growth of commercial enterprise; and it is interesting to note that in the same way commercial retailers have encouraged the development of private security services to do what the criminal courts will not, similar commercial interests have generated a private mail industry to do what the post office will not. Thus the patterns we have observed probably have parallels and consequences beyond those explored in this paper. This is another way of saying that the corporate domination of our everyday lives is probably a more pervasive phenomenon than the subject matter of this paper may unintentionally have implied.

Appendix 1:1. VICTIMIZATION DATA ON BURGLARY IN THIRTEEN AMERICAN CITIES

	Boston	Buffalo	Cincinnati	Houston	Miami	Milwaukee	Minneapolis	New Orleans	Oakland	Pittsburgh	San Diego	San Francisco	Washington	13 cities
Burglary incidents per 1,000 population	149	97	143	164	85	152	177	112	174	93	138	115	75	128.7
Percent reported to police	56%	50%	55%	46%	58%	54%	52%	47%	57%	50%	50%	51%	57%	51.6%
Incidents reported to police weighted to population	17,360 (56.7%)	7,200 (60.4%)	12,375 (48.9%)	32,016 (70.4%)	6,090 (50.4%)	19,926 (76.9%)	14,768 (74.3%)	10,199 (62.8%)	13,224 (56.2%)	8,100 (66.5%)	17,650 (74.4%)	16,932 (64.6%)	11,229 (62.3%)	187,069 (64.2%)
Burglary incidents per 1,000 establishments	576	319	566	518	292	321	436	448	637	293	358	253	330	411.3
Percent reported to police	78%	75%	84%	71%	79%	82%	71%	68%	77%	73%	80%	72%	79%	76.1%
Incidents reported to police weighted to population	13,260 (43.3%)	4,725 (39.6%)	12,936 (51.1%)	13,490 (29.6%)	6,004 (49.6%)	5,986 (23.1%)	5,112 (25.7%)	6,052 (37.2%)	10,318 (43.8%)	4,088 (33.5%)	6,080 (25.6%)	9,288 (35.4%)	6,794 (37.7%)	104,133 (35.8%)
Per capita ratio of commercial to household burglaries	3.9	3.3	4.0	3.2	3.4	2.1	2.5	4.0	3.7	3.2	2.6	2.2	4.4	3.2
Total number of incidents reported to police weighted to population	30,620	11,925	25,311	45,506	12,094	25,912	19,880	16,251	23,542	12,188	23,730	26,220	18,023	291,202

1018 / Social Forces Volume 60:4, June 1982

Appendix 1:2. VICTIMIZATION DATA ON ROBBERY IN THIRTEEN AMERICAN CITIES

	Boston	Buffalo	Cincinnati	Houston	Miami	Milwaukee	Minneapolis	New Orleans	Oakland	Pittsburgh	San Diego	San Francisco	Washington	13 Cities
Robbery Incidents per 1,000 population	31	16	15	17	10	18	21	18	22	15	11	29	17	18.5
Percent reported to police	53%	51%	51%	47%	65%	51%	49%	53%	53%	56%	46%	44%	63%	57%
Incidents reported to police weighted to population	5,989 (64.9%)	2,295 (73.0%)	2,091 (54.6%)	6,157 (60.8%)	1,430 (43.4%)	4,182 (80.0%)	2,793 (67.9%)	3,392 (54.6%)	2,650 (52.4%)	2,744 (65.3%)	2,438 (74.0%)	6,160 (66.1%)	4,914 (70.4%)	47,235 (63.8%)
Robbery Incidents per 1,000 establishments	132	56	72	140	104	49	91	173	137	77	49	80	88	96.0
Percent reported to police	83%	77%	87%	78%	69%	95%	88%	83%	83%	97%	85%	77%	90%	82%
Incidents reported to police weighted to population	3,237 (35.1%)	847 (27.0%)	1,740 (45.4%)	3,978 (39.2%)	1,863 (56.6%)	1,045 (20.0%)	1,320 (32.1%)	2,822 (45.4%)	2,407 (47.6%)	1,455 (34.7%)	855 (26.0%)	3,157 (33.9%)	2,070 (29.6%)	26,796 (36.2%)
Per capita ratio of commercial to personal robberies	4.3	3.5	4.8	8.2	10.4	2.7	4.3	9.6	6.2	5.1	4.5	2.8	5.2	5.2
Total number of incidents reported to police weighted to population	9,226	9,142	3,831	10,135	3,293	5,227	4,113	6,214	5,057	4,199	3,293	9,317	6,984	74,031

The Corporate Advantage / 1019

Appendix 2:1. VARIABLES, VALUES AND DESCRIPTIVE STATISTICS FOR ANALYSES

	Values	$\bar{x}$	s
Independent Variables:			
Individual & Organizations			
Type of victim	Individual=0	.50	.50
	Organization=0		
Type of crime	Person=0		
	Property=1		
Seriousness of victimization	Sellin-Wolfgang scale	3.36	2.47
Return of property to victim	Property not returned=0	.37	.48
	Property returned=1		
Victim responsibility	Denies responsibility=0	1.26	.44
	Accepts responsibility=1		
Victim testimony	Victim did not testify=0	.23	.43
	Victim testified		
Victim-accused relationship	Intimacy scale	6.45	4.25
Repeat player	No=0		
	Yes=1		
Accused marital status	Divorced, separated, common law=0	1.05	.65
	Single=1		
	Married, widowed=2		
Accused sex	Female=0	.88	.33
	Male=1		
Accused condition at arrest	Sober=0	.23	.42
	Intoxicated=1		
Accused employment status	Unemployed=0	.44	.50
	Employed=1		
Accused demeanor	Good=0	.67	.47
	Bad or indifferent=1		
Accused prior convictions	Actual number	2.98	4.80
Accused most serious prior disposition	None=0	1.18	1.26
	Fine=1		
	Probation=2		
	Prison=3		
Number of charges	Actual number	.56	1.61
Statement taken	No statement=0	.39	.49
	Statement taken=1		
Warrant	No warrant=0	.14	.35
	Warrant executed=1		
Mobilization	Other than by victim=0	.56	.50
	By victim=1		
Complaint	Other than victim=0	.27	.44
	Victim=1		
Perceived remorse of accused	Likert scale (high to low)	2.90	.75
Characteristics attributed to accused	Summated semantic differential (positive to negative)	42.53	7.93
Reformation-victim ranking	Likert scale (high to low)	1.56	.91
General deterrence-victim ranking	Likert scale (high to low)	1.92	1.03
Individual deterrence-victim ranking	Likert scale (high to low)	1.64	.92
Punishment-victim ranking	Likert scale (high to low)	2.58	1.24
Incapacitation-victim ranking	Likert scale (high to low)	2.46	1.17
Law and order attitudes	Summated Likert scale (high to low)	11.70	2.96
Citizen responsibility	Summated Likert scale (high to low)	7.78	1.58
Belief in free will	Likert scale (high to low)	7.28	2.63
Individual responsibility	Likert scale (high to low)	5.58	3.83
Knowledge of disposition	No=0	.39	.49
	Yes=1		

Continued overleaf

1020 / Social Forces Volume 60:4, June 1982

Appendix 2:1. Continued

Disposition	Withdrawn, dismissed or acquitted=0 Absolute discharge=1 Peace bond or fine=2 Probation=3 Prison=4	2.39	1.46
Trial	Victim did not attend=0 Victim attended=1	.39	.49

Independent Variables
  Organizations Only

Type of organization	Retail=0 Other=1	.42	.49
Organizational base	Private=1 Public=0	1.38	.49
Scale of organization	Local=1 Regional=2 Provincial=3 Interprovincial=4 National=5 Multinational=6	3.20	2.04
Number of employees in division	Actual number	99.76	342.85
Number of organizational units	Actual number	44.18	126.41
Number of employees in organization	Actual number	352,359.91	449,393.03
Centralization of organization	Likert scale (decentralized to centralized)	3.52	1.09
Relationship between organization and clients	Likert scale (decentralized to centralized)	3.90	.87

Dependent Variables
  Individuals & Organizations

Bail hearing	Not held for hearing=0 Held for hearing=1	.21	.40
Adjudication	Not guilty=0 Guilty=1	.72	.45
Sentence	Absolute discharge=1 Peace bone or fine=2 Probation=3 Prison=4	2.96	.83
Perceived severity of disposition	Too severe=1 About right=2 Not severe enough=3	2.45	.52
Satisfaction with outcome	Very satisfied=1 Satisfied=2 Neutral=3 Dissatisfied=4 Very Dissatisfied=5	2.69	1.52

Notes

1. An examination of the population and sample data revealed no systematic evidence of error or bias in the latter (Hagan, b, ch. 2). The panel design forms the basis for an analysis reported in Hagan (b, ch. 3–4). Only the follow-up interviews are used here.

2. Our measure of the intimacy of the victim–accused relationship is based on ordinally ranked responses to five interview questions: How well did you know the offender? How frequently did you talk to the offender? Did you know the offender's name? Would you say that you generally liked the offender before this incident? Did you feel that the offender generally liked you before this incident? Responses to these items were combined into an additive measure of intimacy.

The Corporate Advantage / 1021

3. Our decision to use the .10 level is based on the exploratory character of the research.
4. Introduction of additional variables reduced the statistical significance of this relationship below the .10 level used elsewhere in this paper, however, the mediating influences of subsequent variables were not sufficiently large to justify substantive discussion.
5. Our measure of the intimacy of the victim's involvement with the accused is the scale discussed in note 2, dichotomized at the mean.
6. How this suburban Canadian jurisdiction compares to other jurisdictions is, of course, an issue that calls for further research.

References

Balbus, Issac. 1977. "Commodity Form and Legal Form: An Essay on the 'Relative Autonomy' of the Law." *Law & Society Review* 11:571–88.

Beccaria, Cesare. 1963. *On Crimes and Punishments*. Translated by Henry Paolucci. Indianapolis: Bobbs-Merrill.

Bentham, Jeremy. 1970. *An Introduction to the Principles of Morals and Legislation*. Edited by J. H. Burns and H. L. A. Hart. University of London: Athlone Press.

Cameron, Mary O. 1965. *The Booster and the Snitch*. New York: Free Press.

Chambliss, William, and Robert Seidman. 1971. *Law, Order and Power*. Reading, Ma.: Addison-Wesley.

Coleman, James. 1974. *Power and the Structure of Society*. New York: Norton.

Ermann, M. David, and Richard J. Lundman. 1980. *Corporate Deviance: Toward a Sociology of Deviance, Social Problems and Crime*. New York: Holt, Rinehart & Winston.

Galanter, Marc. 1974. "Why the Have's Come Out Ahead." *Law & Society Review* 9:95–160.

Gower, L. C. B. 1969. *The Principles of Modern Company Law*. London: Stevens.

Hagan, John. a:1975. "Law, Order and Sentencing: A Study of Attitude in Action." *Sociometry* 38:374–84.

———. b:1980. A Study of Victim Involvement in the Criminal Justice System. Final Report to Solicitor General Canada.

Hagan, John, and Kristen Bumiller. 1982. "Making Sense of Sentencing: A Review and Critique of Sentencing Research." In Alfred Blumstein (ed.), *Research on Sentencing*. Washington: National Academy of Sciences.

Hagan, John, J. Hewitt, and D. Alwin. a:1979. "Ceremonial Justice: Crime and Punishment in a Loosely Coupled System." *Social Forces* 58(2):506–27.

Hagan, John, Ilene Nagel, and Celesta Albonetti. b:1980. "The Differential Sentencing of White Collar Offenders in Ten Federal District Courts." *American Sociological Review* 45:802–20.

Halevy, Eli. 1960. *The Growth of Philosophic Radicalism*. Translated by Mary Morris. Boston: Beacon Press.

Hibbert, Christopher. 1963. *The Roots of Evil: A Social History of Crime and Punishment*. Boston: Little, Brown.

Hindelang, Michael. 1974. "Decisions of Shoplifting Victims to Invoke the Criminal Justice Process." *Social Problems* 21:580–93.

Jeffrey, Clarence R. 1957. "The Development of Crime in Early English Society." *Journal of Criminal Law, Criminology and Police Science* 47(6):647–66.

McDonald, William F. 1976. "Towards a Bicentennial Revolution in Criminal Justice: The Return of the Victim." *American Criminal Law Review* 13(4):649–73.

Maine, (Sir) Henry James Sumner. 1960. *Ancient Law*. London: Dent.

Morden, Peter. 1980. *A Multivariate Analysis of Bail Decisions Involving the Police*. Unpublished masters thesis, University of Toronto.

1022 / Social Forces Volume 60:4, June 1982

Nagel, Ilene. 1980. "The Behavior of Formal Law: A Study of Bail Decisions." Indiana University. Unpublished manuscript.

Quinney, Richard. 1970. *The Social Reality of Crime*. Boston: Little, Brown.

Robin, Gerald D. 1967. "The Corporate and Judicial Disposition of Employee Thieves." *Wisconsin Law Review* (Summer):685–702.

Schafer, Stephen. 1977. *Victimology: The Victim and His Criminal*. Reston, Virginia: Reston.

Schrager, Laura Shill, and James F. Short, Jr. 1978. "Toward a Sociology of Organizational Crime." *Social Problems* 25(4):407–19.

Sellin, Thorston, and Marvin E. Wolfgang. 1964. *The Measurement of Delinquency*. New York: Wiley.

Smigel, Erwin O., and H. Laurence Ross, (eds.). 1970. *Crimes Against Bureaucracy*. New York: Van Nostrand Reinhold.

Thayer, James Bradley. 1898. *A Preliminary Treatise on Evidence at the Common Law*. Boston: Little, Brown.

Tigar, Michael, and Madeleine Levy. 1977. *Law and the Rise of Capitalism*. New York: Monthly Review Press.

Traill, H. D. 1899. *Social England*. Vol. 1. New York: Putnam.

U.S. Department of Commerce. 1974. *The Costs of Crimes Against Business*. Washington: GPO.

U.S. Department of Justice. 1975. *Criminal Victimization in Thirteen American Cities*. Washington: GPO.

Weber, Max. 1969. *Max Weber on Law in Economy and Society*. Translation by Max Rheinstein. Cambridge: Harvard University Press.

[10]

AMERICAN SOCIOLOGICAL REVIEW

October 1967   Volume 32, No. 5

THE POLICE ON SKID-ROW: A STUDY OF PEACE KEEPING *

Egon Bittner

Langley Porter Neuropsychiatric Institute

Following the distinction proposed by Banton, police work consists of two relatively different activities: "law enforcement" and "keeping the peace." The latter is not determined by a clear legal mandate and does not stand under any system of external control. Instead, it developed as a craft in response to a variety of demand conditions. One such condition is created by the concentration of certain types of persons on skid-row. Patrolmen have a particular conception of the social order of skid-row life that determines the procedures of control they employ. The most conspicuous features of the peace keeping methods used are an aggressively personalized approach to residents, an attenuated regard for questions of culpability, and the use of coercion, mainly in the interest of managing situations rather than persons.

THE prototype of modern police organization, the Metropolitan Police of London, was created to replace an antiquated and corrupt system of law enforcement. The early planners were motivated by the mixture of hardheaded business rationality and humane sentiment that characterized liberal British thought of the first half of the nineteenth century.[1] Partly to meet the objections of a parliamentary committee, which was opposed to the establishment of the police in England, and partly because it was in line with their own thinking, the planners sought to produce an instrument that could not readily be used in the play of internal power politics but which would, instead, advance and protect conditions favorable to industry and commerce and to urban civil life in general. These intentions were not very specific and had to be reconciled with the existing structures of governing, administering justice, and keeping the peace. Consequently, the locus and mandate of the police in the modern polity were ill-defined at the outset. On the one hand, the new institution was to be a part of the executive branch of government, organized, funded, and staffed in accordance with standards that were typical for the entire system of the executive. On the other hand, the duties that were given to the police organization brought it under direct control of the judiciary in its day-to-day operation.

The dual patronage of the police by the executive and the judiciary is characteristic for all democratically governed countries. Moreover, it is generally the case, or at least it is deemed desirable, that judges *rather than* executive officials have control over police use and procedure.[2] This preference is based

* This research was supported in part by Grant 64-1-35 from the California Department of Mental Hygiene. I gratefully acknowledge the help I received from Fred Davis, Sheldon Messinger, Leonard Schatzman, and Anselm Strauss in the preparation of this paper.

[1] The bill for a Metropolitan Police was actually enacted under the sponsorship of Robert Peel, the Home Secretary in the Tory Government of the Duke of Wellington. There is, however, no doubt that it was one of the several reform tendencies that Peel assimilated into Tory politics in his long career. Cf. J. L. Lyman, "The Metropolitan Police Act of 1829," *Journal of Criminal Law, Criminology and Police Science,* 55 (1964), 141–154.

[2] Jerome Hall, "Police and Law in a Democratic Society," *Indiana Law Journal,* 28 (1953), 133–177. Though other authors are less emphatic on this point, judicial control is generally taken for granted. The point has been made, however, that in modern times judicial control over the police has been asserted mainly because of the default of any other general controlling authority, cf. E. L. Barrett, Jr.

on two considerations. First, in the tenets of the democratic creed, the possibility of direct control of the police by a government in power is repugnant.[3] Even when the specter of the police state in its more ominous forms is not a concern, close ties between those who govern and those who police are viewed as a sign of political corruption.[4] Hence, mayors, governors, and cabinet officers—although the nominal superiors of the police—tend to maintain, or to pretend, a hands-off policy. Second, it is commonly understood that the main function of the police is the control of crime. Since the concept of crime belongs wholly to the law, and its treatment is exhaustively based on considerations of legality, police procedure automatically stands under the same system of review that controls the administration of justice in general.

By nature, judicial control encompasses only those aspects of police activity that are directly related to full-dress legal prosecution of offenders. The judiciary has neither the authority nor the means to direct, supervise, and review those activities of the police that do not result in prosecution. Yet such other activities are unavoidable, frequent, and largely within the realm of public expectations. It might be assumed that in this domain of practice the police are under executive control. This is not the case, however, except in a marginal sense.[5] Not only are police departments generally free to determine what need be done and how, but

aside from informal pressures they are given scant direction in these matters. Thus, there appear to exist two relatively independent domains of police activity. In one, their methods are constrained by the prospect of the future disposition of a case in the courts; in the other, they operate under some other consideration and largely with no structured and continuous outside constraint. Following the terminology suggested by Michael Banton, they may be said to function in the first instance as "law officers" and in the second instance as "peace officers."[6] It must be emphasized that the designation "peace officer" is a residual term, with only some vaguely presumptive content. The role, as Banton speaks of it, is supposed to encompass all occupational routines not directly related to making arrests, without, however, specifying what determines the limits of competence and availability of the police in such actions.

Efforts to characterize a large domain of activities of an important public agency have so far yielded only negative definitions. We know that they do not involve arrests; we also know that they do not stand under judicial control, and that they are not, in any important sense, determined by specific executive or legislative mandates. In police textbooks and manuals, these activities receive only casual attention, and the role of the "peace officer" is typically stated in terms suggesting that his work is governed mainly by the individual officer's personal wisdom, integrity, and altruism.[7] Police departments generally keep no records of procedures that do not involve making arrests. Policemen, when asked, insist that they merely use common sense when acting as "peace officers," though they tend to emphasize the elements of experience and practice in discharging the role adequately. All this ambiguity is the more remarkable for the fact that peace keeping tasks, i.e., procedures not involving the formal legal remedy of arrest, were explicitly built into the program of the modern police from the outset.[8]

"Police Practice and the Law," *California Law Review*, 50 (1962), 11–55.

[3] A. C. German, F. D. Day and R. R. J. Gallati, *Introduction to Law Enforcement*, Springfield, Ill.: C. C Thomas, 1966; "One concept, in particular, should be kept in mind. A dictatorship can never exist unless the police system of the country is under the absolute control of the dictator. There is no other way to uphold a dictatorship except by terror, and the instrument of this total terror is the secret police, whatever its name. In every country where freedom has been lost, law enforcement has been a dominant instrument in destroying it" (p. 80).

[4] The point is frequently made; cf. Raymond B. Fosdick, *American Police Systems*, New York: Century Company, 1920; Bruce Smith, *Police Systems in the United States*, 2nd rev. ed., New York: Harper, 1960.

[5] The executive margin of control is set mainly in terms of budgetary determinations and the mapping of some formal aspects of the organization of departments.

[6] Michael Banton, *The Policeman in the Community*, New York: Basic Books, 1964, pp. 6–7 and 127 ff.

[7] R. Bruce Holmgren, *Primary Police Functions*, New York: William C. Copp, 1962.

[8] Cf. Lyman, *op. cit.*, p. 153; F. C. Mather, *Public Order in the Age of the Chartists*, Manchester: Manchester University Press, 1959, chap-

POLICE ON SKID-ROW

The early executives of the London police saw with great clarity that their organization had a dual function. While it was to be an arm of the administration of justice, in respect of which it developed certain techniques for bringing offenders to trial, it was also expected to function apart from, and at times in lieu of, the employment of full-dress legal procedure. Despite its early origin, despite a great deal of public knowledge about it, despite the fact that it is routinely done by policemen, no one can say with any clarity what it means to do a good job of keeping the peace. To be sure, there is vague consensus that when policemen direct, aid, inform, pacify, warn, discipline, roust, and do whatever else they do without making arrests, they do this with some reference to the circumstances of the occasion and, thus, somehow contribute to the maintenance of the peace and order. Peace keeping appears to be a solution to an unknown problem arrived at by unknown means.

The following is an attempt to clarify conceptually the mandate and the practice of keeping the peace. The effort will be directed not to the formulation of a comprehensive solution of the problem but to a detailed consideration of some aspects of it. Only in order to place the particular into the overall domain to which it belongs will the structural determinants of keeping the peace in general be discussed. By structural determinants are meant the typical situations that policemen perceive as *demand conditions* for action without arrest. This will be followed by a description of peace keeping in skid-row districts, with the object of identifying those aspects of it that constitute a *practical skill*.

Since the major object of this paper is to elucidate peace keeping practice as a skilled performance, it is necessary to make clear how the use of the term is intended.

Practical skill will be used to refer to those methods of doing certain things, and to the information that underlies the use of the methods, that *practitioners themselves* view as proper and efficient. Skill is, therefore, a stable orientation to work tasks that is relatively independent of the personal feel-

ings and judgments of those who employ it. Whether the exercise of this skilled performance is desirable or not, and whether it is based on correct information or not, are specifically outside the scope of interest of this presentation. The following is deliberately confined to a description of what police patrolmen consider to be the reality of their work circumstances, what they do, and what they feel they must do to do a good job. That the practice is thought to be determined by normative standards of skill minimizes but does not eliminate the factors of personal interest or inclination. Moreover, the distribution of skill varies among practitioners in the very standards they set for themselves. For example, we will show that patrolmen view a measure of rough informality as good practice vis-a-vis skid-row inhabitants. By this standard, patrolmen who are "not rough enough," or who are "too rough," or whose roughness is determined by personal feelings rather than by situational exigencies, are judged to be poor craftsmen.

The description and analysis are based on twelve months of field work with the police departments of two large cities west of the Mississippi. Eleven weeks of this time were spent in skid-row and skid-row-like districts. The observations were augmented by approximately one hundred interviews with police officers of all ranks. The formulations that will be proposed were discussed in these interviews. They were recognized by the respondents as elements of standard practice. The respondents' recognition was often accompanied by remarks indicating that they had never thought about things in this way and that they were not aware how standardized police work was.

STRUCTURAL DEMAND CONDITIONS OF PEACE KEEPING

There exist at least five types of relatively distinct circumstances that produce police activities that do not involve invoking the law and that are only in a trivial sense determined by those considerations of legality that determine law enforcement. This does not mean that these activities are illegal but merely that there is no legal directive that informs the acting policeman whether what he does must be done or how it is to be done. In these circumstances, policemen act

ter IV. See also Robert H. Bremer, "Police, Penal and Parole Policies in Cleveland and Toledo," *American Journal of Economics and Sociology*, 14 (1955), 387-398, for similar recognition in the United States at about the turn of this century.

as all-purpose and terminal remedial agents, and the confronted problem is solved in the field. If these practices stand under any kind of review at all, and typically they do not, it is only through internal police department control.

1. Although the executive branch of government generally refrains from exercising a controlling influence over the direction of police interest, it manages to extract certain performances from it. Two important examples of this are the supervision of certain licensed services and premises and the regulation of traffic.[9] With respect to the first, the police tend to concentrate on what might be called the moral aspects of establishments rather than on questions relating to the technical adequacy of the service. This orientation is based on the assumption that certain types of businesses lend themselves to exploitation for undesirable and illegal purposes. Since this tendency cannot be fully controlled, it is only natural that the police will be inclined to favor licensees who are at least cooperative. This, however, transforms the task from the mere scrutiny of credentials and the passing of judgments, to the creation and maintenance of a network of connections that conveys influence, pressure, and information. The duty to inspect is the background of this network, but the resulting contacts acquire additional value for solving crimes and maintaining public order. Bartenders, shopkeepers, and hotel clerks become, for patrolmen, a resource that must be continuously serviced by visits and exchanges of favors. While it is apparent that this condition lends itself to corrupt exploitation by individual officers, even the most flawlessly honest policeman must participate in this network of exchanges if he is to function adequately. Thus, engaging in such exchanges becomes an occupational task that demands attention and time.

Regulation of traffic is considerably less complex. More than anything else, traffic control symbolizes the autonomous authority of policemen. Their commands generally are met with unquestioned compliance. Even when they issue citations, which seemingly refer the case to the courts, it is common practice for the accused to view the allegation as a finding against him and to pay the fine. Police officials emphasize that it is more important to be circumspect than legalistic in traffic control. Officers are often reminded that a large segment of the public has no other contacts with the police, and that the field lends itself to public relations work by the line personnel.[10]

2. Policemen often do not arrest persons who have committed minor offences in circumstances in which the arrest is technically possible. This practice has recently received considerable attention in legal and sociological literature. The studies were motivated by the realization that "police decisions not to invoke the criminal process determine the outer limits of law enforcement."[11] From these researches, it was learned that the police tend to impose more stringent criteria of law enforcement on certain segments of the community than on others.[12] It was also learned that, from the perspective of the administration of justice, the decisions not to make arrests often are based on compelling reasons.[13] It is less well appreciated that policemen often not only refrain from invoking the law formally but also employ alternative sanctions. For example, it is standard practice that violators are warned not to repeat the offense. This often leads to patrolmen's "keeping an eye" on certain persons. Less frequent, though not unusual, is the practice of direct disciplining of offenders, especially when they are juveniles, which occasionally involves inducing them to repair the damage occasioned by their misconduct.[14]

The power to arrest and the freedom not to arrest can be used in cases that do not involve patent offenses. An officer can say to a person whose behavior he wishes to control, "I'll let you go this time!" without

---

[9] Smith, *op. cit.*, pp. 15 ff.

[10] Orlando W. Wilson, "Police Authority in a Free Society," *Journal of Criminal Law, Criminology and Police Science,* 54 (1964), 175–177.

[11] Joseph Goldstein, "Police Discretion Not to Invoke the Criminal Process," *Yale Law Journal,* 69 (1960), 543.

[12] Jerome Skolnick, *Justice Without Trial,* New York: Wiley, 1966.

[13] Wayne LaFave, "The Police and Nonenforcement of the Law," *Wisconsin Law Review* (1962), 104–137 and 179–239.

[14] Nathan Goldman, *The Differential Selection of Juvenile Offenders for Court Appearance,* National Research and Information Center, National Council on Crime and Delinquency, 1963, pp. 114 ff.

indicating to him that he could not have been arrested in any case. Nor is this always deliberate misrepresentation, for in many cases the law is sufficiently ambiguous to allow alternative interpretations. In short, not to make an arrest is rarely, if ever, merely a decision not to act; it is most often a decision to act alternatively. In the case of minor offenses, to make an arrest often is merely one of several possible proper actions.

3. There exists a public demand for police intervention in matters that contain no criminal and often no legal aspects.[15] For example, it is commonly assumed that officers will be available to arbitrate quarrels, to pacify the unruly, and to help in keeping order. They are supposed also to aid people in trouble, and there is scarcely a human predicament imaginable for which police aid has not been solicited and obtained at one time or another. Most authors writing about the police consider such activities only marginally related to the police mandate. This view fails to reckon with the fact that the availability of these performances is taken for granted and the police assign a substantial amount of their resources to such work. Although this work cannot be subsumed under the concept of legal action, it does involve the exercise of a form of authority that most people associate with the police. In fact, no matter how trivial the occasion, the device of "calling the cops" transforms any problem. It implies that a situation is, or is getting, out of hand. Police responses to public demands are always oriented to this implication, and the risk of proliferation of troubles makes every call a potentially serious matter.[16]

4. Certain mass phenomena of either a regular or a spontaneous nature require direct monitoring. Most important is the controlling of crowds in incipient stages of disorder. The specter of mob violence frequently calls for measures that involve coercion, including the use of physical force. Legal theory allows, of course, that public officials are empowered to use coercion in situations of imminent danger.[17] Unfortunately, the doctrine is not sufficiently specific to be of much help as a rule of practice. It is based on the assumption of the adventitiousness of danger, and thus does not lend itself readily to elaborations that could direct the routines of early detection and prevention of untoward developments. It is interesting that the objective of preventing riots by informal means posed one of the central organizational problems for the police in England during the era of the Chartists.[18]

5. The police have certain special duties with respect to persons who are viewed as less than fully accountable for their actions. Examples of those eligible for special consideration are those who are under age [19] and those who are mentally ill.[20] Although it is virtually never acknowledged explicitly, those receiving special treatment include people who do not lead "normal" lives and who occupy a pariah status in society. This group includes residents of ethnic ghettos, certain types of bohemians and vagabonds, and persons of known criminal background. The special treatment of children and of sick persons is permissively sanctioned by the law, but the special treatment of others is, in principle, opposed by the leading theme of legality and the tenets of the democratic faith.[21] The important point is not that such persons are arrested more often than others, which is quite true, but that they are per-

---

[15] Elaine Cumming, Ian Cumming and Laura Edell, "Policeman as Philosopher, Guide and Friend," *Social Problems*, 12 (1965), 276–286.

[16] There is little doubt that many requests for service are turned down by the police, especially when they are made over the telephone or by mail, cf. LaFave, *op. cit.*, p. 212, n. 124. The uniformed patrolman, however, finds it virtually impossible to leave the scene without becoming involved in some way or another.

[17] Hans Kelsen, *General Theory of Law and State*, New York: Russell & Russell, 1961, pp. 278–279; H. L. A. Hart, *The Concept of Law*, Oxford: Clarendon Press, 1961, pp. 20–21.

[18] Mather, *op. cit.*; see also, Jenifer Hart, "Reform of the Borough Police, 1835–1856," *English History Review*, 70 (1955), 411–427.

[19] Francis A. Allen, *The Borderland of Criminal Justice*, Chicago: University of Chicago Press, 1964.

[20] Egon Bittner, "Police Discretion in Emergency Apprehension of Mentally Ill Persons," *Social Problems*, 14 (1967), 278–292.

[21] It bears mentioning, however, that differential treatment is not unique with the police, but is also in many ways representative for the administration of justice in general; cf. J. E. Carlin, Jan Howard and S. L. Messinger, "Civil Justice and the Poor," *Law and Society*, 1 (1966), 9–89; Jacobus tenBroek (ed.) *The Law of the Poor*, San Francisco: Chandler Publishing Co., 1966.

ceived by the police as producing a special problem that necessitates continuous attention and the use of special procedures.

The five types of demand conditions do not exclude the possibility of invoking the criminal process. Indeed, arrests do occur quite frequently in all these circumstances. But the concerns generated in these areas cause activities that usually do not terminate in an arrest. When arrests are made, there exist, at least in the ideal, certain criteria by reference to which the arrest can be judged as having been made more or less properly, and there are some persons who, in the natural course of events, actually judge the performance.[22] But for actions not resulting in arrest there are no such criteria and no such judges. How, then, can one speak of such actions as necessary and proper? Since there does not exist any official answer to this query, and since policemen act in the role of "peace officers" pretty much without external direction or constraint, the question comes down to asking how the policeman himself knows whether he has any business with a person he does not arrest, and if so, what that business might be. Furthermore, if there exists a domain of concerns and activities that is largely independent of the law enforcement mandate, it is reasonable to assume that it will exercise some degree of influence on how and to what ends the law is invoked in cases of arrests.

Skid-row presents one excellent opportunity to study these problems. The area contains a heavy concentration of persons who do not live "normal" lives in terms of prevailing standards of middle-class morality. Since the police respond to this situation by intensive patrolling, the structure of peace keeping should be readily observable. Needless to say, the findings and conclusions will not be necessarily generalizable to other types of demand conditions.

THE PROBLEM OF KEEPING THE PEACE
IN SKID-ROW

Skid-row has always occupied a special place among the various forms of urban life.

While other areas are perceived as being different in many ways, skid-row is seen as completely different. Though it is located in the heart of civilization, it is viewed as containing aspects of the primordial jungle, calling for missionary activities and offering opportunities for exotic adventure. While each inhabitant individually can be seen as tragically linked to the vicissitudes of "normal" life, allowing others to say "here but for the Grace of God go I," those who live there are believed to have repudiated the entire role-casting scheme of the majority and to live apart from normalcy. Accordingly, the traditional attitude of civic-mindedness toward skid-row has been dominated by the desire to contain it and to salvage souls from its clutches.[23] The specific task of containment has been left to the police. That this task pressed upon the police some rather special duties has never come under explicit consideration, either from the government that expects control or from the police departments that implement it. Instead, the prevailing method of carrying out the task is to assign patrolmen to the area on a fairly permanent basis and to allow them to work out their own ways of running things. External influence is confined largely to the supply of support and facilities, on the one hand, and to occasional expressions of criticism about the overall conditions, on the other. Within the limits of available resources and general expectations, patrolmen are supposed to know what to do and are free to do it.[24]

[22] This is, however, true only in the ideal. It is well known that a substantial number of persons who are arrested are subsequently released without ever being charged and tried, cf. Barret, *op. cit.*

[23] The literature on skid-row is voluminous. The classic in the field is Nels Anderson, *The Hobo*, Chicago: University of Chicago Press, 1923. Samuel E. Wallace, *Skid-Row as a Way of Life*, Totowa, New Jersey: The Bedminster Press, 1965, is a more recent descriptive account and contains a useful bibliography. Donald A. Bogue, *Skid-Row in American Cities*, Chicago: Community and Family Center, University of Chicago, 1963, contains an exhaustive quantitative survey of Chicago skid-row.

[24] One of the two cities described in this paper also employed the procedure of the "round-up" of drunks. In this, the police van toured the skid-row area twice daily, during the mid-afternoon and early evening hours, and the officers who manned it picked up drunks they sighted. A similar procedure is used in New York's Bowery and the officers who do it are called "condition men." Cf. *Bowery Project*, Bureau of Applied Social Research, Columbia University, Summary Report of a Study Undertaken under Contract Approved by the Board of Estimates, 1963, mimeo., p. 11.

Patrolmen who are more or less permanently assigned to skid-row districts tend to develop a conception of the nature of their "domain" that is surprisingly uniform. Individual officers differ in many aspects of practice, emphasize different concerns, and maintain different contacts, but they are in fundamental agreement about the structure of skid-row life. This relatively uniform conception includes an implicit formulation of the problem of keeping the peace in skid-row.

In the view of experienced patrolmen, life on skid-row is fundamentally different from life in other parts of society. To be sure, they say, around its geographic limits the area tends to blend into the surrounding environment, and its population always encompasses some persons who are only transitionally associated with it. Basically, however, skid-row is perceived as the natural habitat of people who lack the capacities and commitments to live "normal" lives on a sustained basis. The presence of these people defines the nature of social reality in the area. In general, and especially in casual encounters, the presumption of incompetence and of the disinclination to be "normal" is the leading theme for the interpretation of all actions and relations. Not only do people approach one another in this manner, but presumably they also expect to be approached in this way, and they conduct themselves accordingly.

In practice, the restriction of interactional possibilities that is based on the patrolman's stereotyped conception of skid-row residents is always subject to revision and modification toward particular individuals. Thus, it is entirely possible, and not unusual, for patrolmen to view certain skid-row inhabitants in terms that involve non-skid-row aspects of normality. Instances of such approaches and relationships invariably involve personal acquaintance and the knowledge of a good deal of individually qualifying information. Such instances are seen, despite their relative frequency, as exceptions to the rule. The awareness of the possibility of breakdown, frustration, and betrayal is ever-present, basic wariness is never wholly dissipated, and undaunted trust can never be fully reconciled with presence on skid-row.

What patrolmen view as normal on skid-row—and what they also think is taken for granted as "life as usual" by the inhabitants—is not easily summarized. It seems to focus on the idea that the dominant consideration governing all enterprise and association is directed to the occasion of the moment. Nothing is thought of as having a background that might have led up to the present in terms of some compelling moral or practical necessity. There are some exceptions to this rule, of course: the police themselves, and those who run certain establishments, are perceived as engaged in important and necessary activities. But in order to carry them out they, too, must be geared to the overall atmosphere of fortuitousness. In this atmosphere, the range of control that persons have over one another is exceedingly narrow. Good faith, even where it is valued, is seen merely as a personal matter. Its violations are the victim's own hard luck, rather than demonstrable violations of property. There is only a private sense of irony at having been victimized. The overall air is not so much one of active distrust as it is one of irrelevance of trust; as patrolmen often emphasize, the situation does not necessarily cause all relations to be predatory, but the possibility of exploitation is not checked by the expectation that it will not happen.

Just as the past is seen by the policeman as having only the most attenuated relevance to the present, so the future implications of present situations are said to be generally devoid of prospective coherence. No venture, especially no joint venture, can be said to have a strongly predictable future in line with its initial objectives. It is a matter of adventitious circumstance whether or not matters go as anticipated. That which is not within the grasp of momentary control is outside of practical social reality.

Though patrolmen see the temporal framework of the occasion of the moment mainly as a lack of trustworthiness, they also recognize that it involves more than merely the personal motives of individuals. In addition to the fact that everybody *feels* that things matter only at the moment, irresponsibility takes an *objectified* form on skid-row. The places the residents occupy, the social relations they entertain, and the activities that engage them are not meaningfully connected over time. Thus, for example, address, occupation, marital status, etc., matter much

less on skid-row than in any other part of
society. The fact that present whereabouts,
activities, and affiliations imply neither continuity nor direction means that life on skid-
row lacks a socially structured background
of accountability. Of course, everybody's
life contains some sequential incongruities,
but in the life of a skid-row inhabitant every
moment is an accident. That a man has no
"address" in the future that could be in some
way inferred from where he is and what he
does makes him a person of *radically reduced
visibility*. If he disappears from sight and one
wishes to locate him, it is virtually impossible
to systematize the search. All one can know
with relative certainty is that he will be
somewhere on some skid-row and the only
thing one can do is to trace the factual con-
tiguities of his whereabouts.

It is commonly known that the police are
expert in finding people and that they have
developed an exquisite technology involving
special facilities and procedures of sleuthing.
It is less well appreciated that all this technology builds upon those socially structured
features of everyday life that render persons
findable in the first place.

Under ordinary conditions, the query as
to where a person is can be addressed, from
the outset, to a restricted realm of possibilities that can be further narrowed by looking
into certain places and asking certain persons. The map of whereabouts that normally
competent persons use whenever they wish
to locate someone is constituted by the basic
facts of membership in society. Insofar as
membership consists of status incumbencies,
each of which has an adumbrated future that
substantially reduces unpredictability, it is
itself a guarantee of the order within which
it is quite difficult to get lost. Membership is
thus visible not only now but also as its own
projection into the future. It is in terms of
this prospective availability that the skid-row
inhabitant is a person of reduced visibility.
His membership is viewed as extraordinary
because its extension into the future is *not*
reduced to a restricted realm of possibilities.
Neither his subjective dispositions, nor his
circumstances, indicate that he is oriented to
any particular long-range interests. But, as
he may claim every contingent opportunity,
his claims are always seen as based on slight

merit or right, at least to the extent that
interfering with them does not constitute a
substantial denial of his freedom.

This, then, constitutes the problem of
keeping the peace on skid-row. Considerations of momentary expediency are seen as
having unqualified priority as maxims of
conduct; consequently, the controlling influences of the pursuit of sustained interests
are presumed to be absent.

THE PRACTICES OF KEEPING THE PEACE IN SKID-ROW

From the perspective of society as a whole,
skid-row inhabitants appear troublesome in
a variety of ways. The uncommitted life
attributed to them is perceived as inherently
offensive; its very existence arouses indignation and contempt. More important, however, is the feeling that persons who have
repudiated the entire role-status casting system of society, persons whose lives forever
collapse into a succession of random moments, are seen as constituting a practical
risk. As they have nothing to foresake, nothing is thought safe from them.[25]

The skid-row patrolman's concept of his
mandate includes an awareness of this presumed risk. He is constantly attuned to the
possibility of violence, and he is convinced
that things to which the inhabitants have
free access are as good as lost. But his concern is directed toward the continuous condition of peril *in the area* rather than *for
society in general*. While he is obviously
conscious of the presence of many persons
who have committed crimes outside of skid-
row and will arrest them when they come
to his attention, this is a peripheral part of
his routine activities. In general, the skid-row
patrolman and his superiors take for granted
that his main business is to keep the peace

---

[25] An illuminating parallel to the perception of
skid-row can be found in the more traditional concept of vagabondage. Cf. Alexandre Vexliard, *Introduction a la Sociologie du Vagabondage*, Paris:
Libraire Marcel Riviere, 1956, and "La Disparition
du Vagabondage comme Fleau Social Universel,"
Revue de L'Instut de Sociologie (1963), 53–79.
The classic account of English conditions up to the
19th century is C. J. Ribton-Turner, *A History of
Vagrants and Vagrancy and Beggars and Begging*,
London: Chapman and Hall, 1887.

and enforce the laws *on skid-row*, and that he is involved only incidentally in protecting society at large. Thus, his task is formulated basically as the protection of putative predators from one another. The maintenance of peace and safety is difficult because everyday life on skid-row is viewed as an open field for reciprocal exploitation. As the lives of the inhabitants lack the prospective coherence associated with status incumbency, the realization of self-interest does not produce order. Hence, mechanisms that control risk must work primarily from without.

External containment, to be effective, must be oriented to the realities of existence. Thus, the skid-row patrolman employs an approach that he views as appropriate to the *ad hoc* nature of skid-row life. The following are the three most prominent elements of this approach. First, the seasoned patrolman seeks to acquire a richly particularized knowledge of people and places in the area. Second, he gives the consideration of strict culpability a subordinate status among grounds for remedial sanction. Third, his use and choice of coercive interventions is determined mainly by exigencies of situations and with little regard for possible long range effects on individual persons.

The Particularization of Knowledge. The patrolman's orientation to people on skid-row is structured basically by the presupposition that if he does not know a man personally there is very little that he can assume about him. This rule determines his interaction with people who live on skid-row. Since the area also contains other types of persons, however, its applicability is not universal. To some such persons it does not apply at all, and it has a somewhat mitigated significance with certain others. For example, some persons encountered on skid-row can be recognized immediately as outsiders. Among them are workers who are employed in commercial and industrial enterprises that abut the area, persons who come for the purpose of adventurous "slumming," and some patrons of second-hand stores and pawn shops. Even with very little experience, it is relatively easy to identify these people by appearance, demeanor, and the time and place of their presence. The patrolman maintains an impersonal attitude toward them,

and they are, under ordinary circumstances, not the objects of his attention.[26]

Clearly set off from these outsiders are the residents and the entire corps of personnel that services skid-row. It would be fair to say that one of the main routine activities of patrolmen is the establishment and maintenance of familiar relationships with individual members of these groups. Officers emphasize their interest in this, and they maintain that their grasp of and control over skid-row is precisely commensurate with the extent to which they "know the people." By this they do not mean having a quasi-theoretical understanding of human nature but rather the common practice of individualized and reciprocal recognition. As this group encompasses both those who render services on skid-row and those who are serviced, individualized interest is not always based on the desire to overcome uncertainty. Instead, relations with service personnel become absorbed into the network of particularized attention. Ties between patrolmen, on the one hand, and businessmen, managers, and workers, on the other hand, are often defined in terms of shared or similar interests. It bears mentioning that many persons live *and* work on skid-row. Thus, the distinction between those who service and those who are serviced is not a clearcut dichotomy but a spectrum of affiliations.

As a general rule, the skid-row patrolman possesses an immensely detailed factual knowledge of his beat. He knows, and knows a great deal about, a large number of residents. He is likely to know every person who manages or works in the local bars, hotels, shops, stores, and missions. Moreover, he probably knows every public and private place inside and out. Finally, he ordinarily remembers countless events of the past which he can recount by citing names, dates and places with remarkable precision. Though there are always some threads missing in the fabric of information, it is continuously woven and mended even as it is being used. New facts, however, are added to the texture,

---

[26] Several patrolmen complained about the influx of "tourists" into skid-row. Since such "tourists" are perceived as seeking illicit adventure, they receive little sympathy from patrolmen when they complain about being victimized.

not in terms of structured categories but in terms of adjoining known realities. In other words, the content and organization of the patrolman's knowledge is primarily ideographic and only vestigially, if at all, nomothetic.

Individual patrolmen vary in the extent to which they make themselves available or actively pursue personal acquaintances. But even the most aloof are continuously greeted and engaged in conversations that indicate a background of individualistic associations. While this scarcely has the appearance of work, because of its casual character, patrolmen do not view it as an optional activity. In the course of making their rounds, patrolmen seem to have access to every place, and their entry causes no surprise or consternation. Instead, the entry tends to lead to informal exchanges of small talk. At times the rounds include entering hotels and gaining access to rooms or dormitories, often for no other purpose than asking the occupants how things are going. In all this, patrolmen address innumerable persons by name and are in turn addressed by name. The conversational style that characterizes these exchanges is casual to an extent that by nonskid-row standards might suggest intimacy. Not only does the officer himself avoid all terms of deference and respect but he does not seem to expect or demand them. For example, a patrolman said to a man radiating an alcoholic glow on the street, "You've got enough of a heat on now; I'll give you ten minutes to get your ass off the street!" Without stopping, the man answered, "Oh, why don't you go and piss in your own pot!" The officer's only response was, "All right, in ten minutes you're either in bed or on your way to the can."

This kind of expressive freedom is an intricately limited privilege. Persons of acquaintance are entitled to it and appear to exercise it mainly in routinized encounters. But strangers, too, can use it with impunity. The safe way of gaining the privilege is to respond to the patrolman in ways that do not challenge his right to ask questions and issue commands. Once the concession is made that the officer is entitled to inquire into a man's background, business, and intentions, and that he is entitled to obedience, there opens a field of colloquial license. A patrolman

seems to grant expressive freedom in recognition of a person's acceptance of his access to areas of life ordinarily defined as private and subject to coercive control only under special circumstances. While patrolmen accept and seemingly even cultivate the rough *quid pro quo* of informality, and while they do not expect sincerity, candor, or obedience in their dealings with the inhabitants, they do not allow the rejection of their approach.

The explicit refusal to answer questions of a personal nature and the demand to know why the questions are asked significantly enhances a person's chances of being arrested on some minor charge. While most patrolmen tend to be personally indignant about this kind of response and use the arrest to compose their own hurt feelings, this is merely a case of affect being in line with the method. There are other officers who proceed in the same manner without taking offense, or even with feelings of regret. Such patrolmen often maintain that their colleagues' affective involvement is a corruption of an essentially valid technique. The technique is oriented to the goal of maintaining operational control. The patrolman's conception of this goal places him hierarchically above whomever he approaches, and makes him the sole judge of the propriety of the occasion. As he alone is oriented to this goal, and as he seeks to attain it by means of individualized access to persons, those who frustrate him are seen as motivated at best by the desire to "give him a hard time" and at worst by some darkly devious purpose.

Officers are quite aware that the directness of their approach and the demands they make are difficult to reconcile with the doctrines of civil liberties, but they maintain that they are in accord with the general freedom of access that persons living on skid-row normally grant one another. That is, they believe that the imposition of personalized and far-reaching control is in tune with standard expectancies. In terms of these expectancies, people are not so much denied the right to privacy as they are seen as not having any privacy. Thus, officers seek to install themselves in the center of people's lives and let the consciousness of their presence play the part of conscience.

When talking about the practical necessity of an aggressively personal approach, officers do not refer merely to the need for maintaining control over lives that are open in the direction of the untoward. They also see it as the basis for the supply of certain valued services to inhabitants of skid-row. The coerced or conceded access to persons often imposes on the patrolman tasks that are, in the main, in line with these persons' expressed or implied interest. In asserting this connection, patrolmen note that they frequently help people to obtain meals, lodging, employment, that they direct them to welfare and health services, and that they aid them in various other ways. Though patrolmen tend to describe such services mainly as the product of their own altruism, they also say that their colleagues who avoid them are simply doing a poor job of patrolling. The acceptance of the need to help people is based on the realization that the hungry, the sick, and the troubled are a potential source of problems. Moreover, that patrolmen will help people is part of the background expectancies of life on skid-row. Hotel clerks normally call policemen when someone gets so sick as to need attention; merchants expect to be taxed, in a manner of speaking, to meet the pressing needs of certain persons; and the inhabitants do not hesitate to accept, solicit, and demand every kind of aid. The domain of the patrolman's service activity is virtually limitless, and it is no exaggeration to say that the solution of every conceivable problem has at one time or another been attempted by a police officer. In one observed instance, a patrolman unceremoniously entered the room of a man he had never seen before. The man, who gave no indication that he regarded the officer's entry and questions as anything but part of life as usual, related a story of having had his dentures stolen by his wife. In the course of the subsequent rounds, the patrolman sought to locate the woman and the dentures. This did not become the evening's project but was attended to while doing other things. In the densely matted activities of the patrolman, the questioning became one more strand, not so much to be pursued to its solution as a theme that organized the memory of one more man known individually. In all this, the officer followed the precept formulated by a somewhat more articulate patrolman: "If I want to be in control of my work and keep the street relatively peaceful, I have to know the people. To know them I must gain their trust, which means that I have to be involved in their lives. But I can't be soft like a social worker because unlike him I cannot call the cops when things go wrong. I am the cops!" [27]

The Restricted Relevance of Culpability. It is well known that policemen exercise discretionary freedom in invoking the law. It is also conceded that, in some measure, the practice is unavoidable. This being so, the outstanding problem is whether or not the decisions are in line with the intent of the law. On skid-row, patrolmen often make decisions based on reasons that the law probably does not recognize as valid. The problem can best be introduced by citing an example.

A man in a relatively mild state of intoxication (by skid-row standards) approached a patrolman to tell him that he had a room in a hotel, to which the officer responded by urging him to go to bed instead of getting drunk. As the man walked off, the officer related the following thoughts: Here is a completely lost soul. Though he probably is no more than thirty-five years old, he looks to be in his fifties. He never works and he hardly ever has a place to stay. He has been on the street for several years and is known as "Dakota." During the past few days, "Dakota" has been seen in the company of "Big Jim." The latter is an invalid living on some sort of pension with which he pays for a room in the hotel to which "Dakota" referred and for four weekly meal tickets in one of the restaurants on the street. Whatever is left he spends on wine and beer. Occasionally, "Big Jim" goes on drinking sprees in the company of someone like "Dakota." Leaving aside the consideration that there is probably a homosexual background to the association, and that it is not right that "Big Jim" should have to support the drinking habit of someone else, there is the more important risk that if "Dakota" moves in with "Big Jim" he will

---

[27] The same officer commented further, "If a man looks for something, I might help him. But I don't stay with him till he finds what he is looking for. If I did, I would never get to do anything else. In the last analysis, I really never solve any problems. The best I can hope for is to keep things from getting worse."

Law and Society

very likely walk off with whatever the latter keeps in his room. "Big Jim" would never dream of reporting the theft; he would just beat the hell out of "Dakota" after he sobered up. When asked what could be done to prevent the theft and the subsequent recriminations, the patrolman proposed that in this particular case he would throw "Big Jim" into jail if he found him tonight and then tell the hotel clerk to throw "Dakota" out of the room. When asked why he did not arrest "Dakota," who was, after all, drunk enough to warrant an arrest, the officer explained that this would not solve anything. While "Dakota" was in jail "Big Jim" would continue drinking and would either strike up another liaison or embrace his old buddy after he had been released. The only thing to do was to get "Big Jim" to sober up, and the only sure way of doing this was to arrest him.

As it turned out, "Big Jim" was not located that evening. But had he been located and arrested on a drunk charge, the fact that he was intoxicated would not have been the real reason for proceeding against him, but merely the pretext. The point of the example is not that it illustrates the tendency of skid-row patrolmen to arrest persons who would not be arrested under conditions of full respect for their legal rights. To be sure, this too happens. In the majority of minor arrest cases, however, the criteria the law specifies are met. But it is the rare exception that the law is invoked merely because the specifications of the law are met. That is, compliance with the law is merely the outward appearance of an intervention that is actually based on altogether different considerations. Thus, it could be said that patrolmen do not really enforce the law, even when they do invoke it, but merely use it as a resource to solve certain pressing practical problems in keeping the peace. This observation goes beyond the conclusion that many of the lesser norms of the criminal law are treated as defeasible in police work. It is patently not the case that skid-row patrolmen apply the legal norms while recognizing many exceptions to their applicability. Instead, the observation leads to the conclusion that in keeping the peace on skid-row, patrolmen encounter certain matters they attend to by means of coercive action, e.g., arrests. In doing this,

they invoke legal norms that are available, and with some regard for substantive appropriateness. Hence, the problem patrolmen confront is not which drunks, beggars, or disturbers of the peace should be arrested and which can be let go as exceptions to the rule. Rather, the problem is whether, when someone "needs" to be arrested, he should be charged with drunkenness, begging, or disturbing the peace. Speculating further, one is almost compelled to infer that virtually any set of norms could be used in this manner, provided that they sanction relatively common forms of behavior.

The reduced relevance of culpability in peace keeping practice on skid-row is not readily visible. As mentioned, most arrested persons were actually found in the act, or in the state, alleged in the arrest record. It becomes partly visible when one views the treatment of persons who are not arrested even though all the legal grounds for an arrest are present. Whenever such persons are encountered and can be induced to leave, or taken to some shelter, or remanded to someone's care, then patrolmen feel, or at least maintain, that an arrest would serve no useful purpose. That is, whenever there exist means for controlling the troublesome aspects of some person's presence in some way alternative to an arrest, such means are preferentially employed, provided, of course, that the case at hand involves only a minor offense.[28]

The attenuation of the relevance of culpability is most visible when the presence of legal grounds for an arrest could be questioned, i.e., in cases that sometimes are euphemistically called "preventive arrests." In one observed instance, a man who attempted to trade a pocket knife came to the attention of a patrolman. The initial encounter was attended by a good deal of levity

---

[28] When evidence is present to indicate that a serious crime has been committed, considerations of culpability acquire a position of priority. Two such arrests were observed, both involving checkpassers. The first offender was caught *in flagrante delicto*. In the second instance, the suspect attracted the attention of the patrolman because of his sickly appearance. In the ensuing conversation the man made some remarks that led the officer to place a call with the Warrant Division of his department. According to the information that was obtained by checking records, the man was a wanted checkpasser and was immediately arrested.

and the man willingly responded to the officer's inquiries about his identity and business. The man laughingly acknowledged that he needed some money to get drunk. In the course of the exchange it came to light that he had just arrived in town, traveling in his automobile. When confronted with the demand to lead the officer to the car, the man's expression became serious and he pointedly stated that he would not comply because this was none of the officer's business. After a bit more prodding, which the patrolman initially kept in the light mood, the man was arrested on a charge involving begging. In subsequent conversation the patrolman acknowledged that the charge was only speciously appropriate and mainly a pretext. Having committed himself to demanding information he could not accept defeat. When this incident was discussed with another patrolman, the second officer found fault not with the fact that the arrest was made on a pretext but with the first officer's own contribution to the creation of conditions that made it unavoidable. "You see," he continued, "there is always the risk that the man is testing you and you must let him know what is what. The best among us can usually keep the upper hand in such situations without making arrests. But when it comes down to the wire, then you can't let them get away with it."

Finally, it must be mentioned that the reduction of the significance of culpability is built into the normal order of skid-row life, as patrolmen see it. Officers almost unfailingly say, pointing to some particular person, "I know that he knows that I know that some of the things he 'owns' are stolen, and that nothing can be done about it." In saying this, they often claim to have knowledge of such a degree of certainty as would normally be sufficient for virtually any kind of action except legal proceedings. Against this background, patrolmen adopt the view that the law is not merely imperfect and difficult to implement, but that on skid-row, at least, the association between delict and sanction is distinctly occasional. Thus, to implement the law naively, i.e., to arrest someone *merely* because he committed some minor offense, is perceived as containing elements of injustice.

Moreover, patrolmen often deal with situations in which questions of culpability are profoundly ambiguous. For example, an officer was called to help in settling a violent dispute in a hotel room. The object of the quarrel was a supposedly stolen pair of trousers. As the story unfolded in the conflicting versions of the participants, it was not possible to decide who was the complainant and who was alleged to be the thief, nor did it come to light who occupied the room in which the fracas took place, or whether the trousers were taken from the room or to the room. Though the officer did ask some questions, it seemed, and was confirmed in later conversation, that he was there not to solve the puzzle of the missing trousers but to keep the situation from getting out of hand. In the end, the exhausted participants dispersed, and this was the conclusion of the case. The patrolman maintained that no one could unravel mysteries of this sort because "these people take things from each' other so often that no one could tell what 'belongs' to whom." In fact, he suggested, the terms owning, stealing, and swindling, in their strict sense, do not really belong on skid-row, and all efforts to distribute guilt and innocence according to some rational formula of justice are doomed to failure.

It could be said that the term "curb-stone justice" that is sometimes applied to the procedures of patrolmen in skid-rows contains a double irony. Not only is the procedure not legally authorized, which is the intended irony in the expression, but it does not even pretend to distribute deserts. The best among the patrolmen, according to their own standards, use the law to keep skid-row inhabitants from sinking deeper into the misery they already experience. The worst, in terms of these same standards, exploit the practice for personal aggrandizement or gain. Leaving motives aside, however, it is easy to see that if culpability is not the salient consideration leading to an arrest in cases where it is patently obvious, then the practical patrolman may not view it as being wholly out of line to make arrests lacking in formal legal justification. Conversely, he will come to view minor offense arrests made solely because legal standards are met as poor craftsmanship.

The Background of Ad Hoc *Decision Making.* When skid-row patrolmen are pressed to explain their reasons for minor offense arrests, they most often mention that it is done for the protection of the arrested person. This, they maintain, is the case in virtually all drunk arrests, in the majority of arrests involving begging and other nuisance offenses, and in many cases involving acts of violence. When they are asked to explain further such arrests as the one cited earlier involving the man attempting to sell the pocket knife, who was certainly not arrested for his own protection, they cite the consideration that belligerent persons constitute a much greater menace on skid-row than any place else in the city. The reasons for this are twofold. First, many of the inhabitants are old, feeble, and not too smart, all of which makes them relatively defenseless. Second, many of the inhabitants are involved in illegal activities and are known as persons of bad character, which does not make them credible victims or witnesses. Potential predators realize that the resources society has mobilized to minimize the risk of criminal victimization do not protect the predator himself. Thus, reciprocal exploitation constitutes a preferred risk. The high vulnerability of everybody on skid-row is public knowledge and causes every seemingly aggressive act to be seen as a potentially grave risk.

When, in response to all this, patrolmen are confronted with the observation that many minor offense arrests they make do not seem to involve a careful evaluation of facts before acting, they give the following explanations: First, the two reasons of protection and prevention represent a global background, and in individual cases it may sometimes not be possible to produce adequate justification on these grounds. Nor is it thought to be a problem of great moment to estimate precisely whether someone is more likely to come to grief or to cause grief when the objective is to prevent the proliferation of troubles. Second, patrolmen maintain that some of the seemingly spur-of-the-moment decisions are actually made against a background of knowledge of facts that are not readily apparent in the situations. Since experience not only contains this information but also causes it to come to mind, patrolmen claim to have developed a special sensitivity for qualities of appearances that allow an

intuitive grasp of probable tendencies. In this context, little things are said to have high informational value and lead to conclusions without the intervention of explicitly reasoned chains of inferences. Third, patrolmen readily admit that they do not adhere to high standards of adequacy of justification. They do not seek to defend the adequacy of their method against some abstract criteria of merit. Instead, when questioned, they assess their methods against the background of a whole system of *ad hoc* decision making, a system that encompasses the courts, correction facilities, the welfare establishment, and medical services. In fact, policemen generally maintain that their own procedures not only measure up to the workings of this system but exceed them in the attitude of carefulness.

In addition to these recognized reasons, there are two additional background factors that play a significant part in decisions to employ coercion. One has to do with the relevance of situational factors, and the other with the evaluation of coercion as relatively insignificant in the lives of the inhabitants.

There is no doubt that the nature of the circumstances often has decisive influence on what will be done. For example, the same patrolman who arrested the man trying to sell his pocket knife was observed dealing with a young couple. Though the officer was clearly angered by what he perceived as insolence and threatened the man with arrest, he merely ordered him and his companion to leave the street. He saw them walking away in a deliberately slow manner and when he noticed them a while later, still standing only a short distance away from the place of encounter, he did not respond to their presence. The difference between the two cases was that in the first there was a crowd of amused bystanders, while the latter case was not witnessed by anyone. In another instance, the patrolman was directed to a hotel and found a father and son fighting about money. The father occupied a room in the hotel and the son occasionally shared his quarters. There were two other men present, and they made it clear that their sympathies were with the older man. The son was whisked off to jail without much study of the relative merits of the conflicting claims. In yet another case, a middle-aged woman was forcefully evacuated from a bar even after the bartender explained that her loud behavior was merely a response to goading by some foul-mouth youth.

In all such circumstances, coercive control is exercised as a means of coming to grips with situational exigencies. Force is used against particular persons but is incidental to the task. An ideal of "economy of intervention" dictates in these and similar cases that the person whose presence is most likely to perpetuate the troublesome development be removed. Moreover, the decision as to who is to be removed is arrived at very quickly. Officers feel considerable pressure to act unhesitatingly, and many give accounts of situations that got out of hand because of desires to handle cases with careful consideration. However, even when there is no apparent risk of rapid proliferation of trouble, the tactic of removing one or two persons is used to control an undesirable situation. Thus, when a patrolman ran into a group of four men sharing a bottle of wine in an alley, he emptied the remaining contents of the bottle into the gutter, arrested one man—who was no more and no less drunk than the others—and let the others disperse in various directions.

The exigential nature of control is also evident in the handling of isolated drunks. Men are arrested because of where they happen to be encountered. In this, it matters not only whether a man is found in a conspicuous place or not, but also how far away he is from his domicile. The further away he is, the less likely it is that he will make it to his room, and the more likely the arrest. Sometimes drunk arrests are made mainly because the police van is available. In one case a patrolman summoned the van to pick up an arrested man. As the van was pulling away from the curb the officer stopped the driver because he sighted another drunk stumbling across the street. The second man protested saying that he "wasn't even half drunk yet." The patrolman's response was "OK, I'll owe you half a drunk." In sum, the basic routine of keeping the peace on skid-row involves a process of matching the resources of control with situational exigencies. The overall objective is to reduce the total amount of risk in the area. In this,

practicality plays a considerably more important role than legal norms. Precisely because patrolmen see legal reasons for coercive action much more widely distributed on skid-row than could ever be matched by interventions, they intervene not in the interest of law enforcement but in the interest of producing relative tranquility and order on the street.

Taking the perspective of the victim of coercive measures, one could ask why he, in particular, has to bear the cost of keeping the aggregate of troubles down while others, who are equally or perhaps even more implicated, go scot-free. Patrolmen maintain that the *ad hoc* selection of persons for attention must be viewed in the light of the following consideration: Arresting a person on skid-row on some minor charge may save him and others a lot of trouble, but it does not work any real hardships on the arrested person. It is difficult to overestimate the skid-row patrolman's feeling of certainty that his coercive and disciplinary actions toward the inhabitants have but the most passing significance in their lives. Sending a man to jail on some charge that will hold him for a couple of days is seen as a matter of such slight importance to the affected person that it could hardly give rise to scruples. Thus, every indication that a coercive measure should be taken is accompanied by the realization "I might as well, for all it matters to him." Certain realities of life on skid-row furnish the context for this belief in the attenuated relevance of coercion in the lives of the inhabitants. Foremost among them is that the use of police authority is seen as totally unremarkable by everybody on skid-row. Persons who live or work there are continuously exposed to it and take its existence for granted. Shopkeepers, hotel clerks, and bartenders call patrolmen to rid themselves of unwanted and troublesome patrons. Residents expect patrolmen to arbitrate their quarrels authoritatively. Men who receive orders, whether they obey them or not, treat them as part of life as usual. Moreover, patrolmen find that disciplinary and coercive actions apparently do not affect their friendly relations with the persons against whom these actions are taken. Those who greet and chat with them are the very same men who have been disciplined, arrested, and ordered around in the past, and who expect to be thus treated again in the future. From all this, officers gather that though the people on skid-row seek to evade police authority, they do not really object to it. Indeed, it happens quite frequently that officers encounter men who welcome being arrested and even actively ask for it. Finally, officers point out that sending someone to jail from skid-row does not upset his relatives or his family life, does not cause him to miss work or lose a job, does not lead to his being reproached by friends and associates, does not lead to failure to meet commitments or protect investments, and does not conflict with any but the most passing intentions of the arrested person. Seasoned patrolmen are not oblivious to the irony of the fact that measures intended as mechanisms for distributing deserts can be used freely because these measures are relatively impotent in their effects.

SUMMARY AND CONCLUSIONS

It was the purpose of this paper to render an account of a domain of police practice that does not seem subject to any system of external control. Following the terminology suggested by Michael Banton, this practice was called keeping the peace. The procedures employed in keeping the peace are not determined by legal mandates but are, instead, responses to certain demand conditions. From among several demand conditions, we concentrated on the one produced by the concentration of certain types of persons in districts known as skid-row. Patrolmen maintain that the lives of the inhabitants of the area are lacking in prospective coherence. The consequent reduction in the temporal horizon of predictability constitutes the main problem of keeping the peace on skid-row. Peace keeping procedure on skid-row consists of three elements. Patrolmen seek to acquire a rich body of concrete knowledge about people by cultivating personal acquaintance with as many residents as possible. They tend to proceed against persons mainly on the basis of perceived risk, rather than on the basis of culpability. And they are more interested in reducing the aggregate total of troubles in the area than in evaluating individual cases according to merit.

There may seem to be a discrepancy between the skid-row patrolman's objective of preventing disorder and his efforts to maintain personal acquaintance with as many persons as possible. But these efforts are principally a tactical device. By knowing someone individually the patrolman reduces ambiguity, extends trust and favors, but does not grant immunity. The informality of interaction on skid-row always contains some indications of the hierarchical superiority of the patrolman and the reality of his potential power lurks in the background of every encounter.

Though our interest was focused initially on those police procedures that did not involve invoking the law, we found that the two cannot be separated. The reason for the connection is not given in the circumstance that the roles of the "law officer" and of the "peace officer" are enacted by the same person and thus are contiguous. According to our observations, patrolmen do not act alternatively as one or the other, with certain actions being determined by the intended objective of keeping the peace and others being determined by the duty to enforce the law. Instead, we have found that *peace keeping occasionally acquires the external aspects of law enforcement*. This makes it specious to inquire whether or not police discretion in invoking the law conforms with the intention of some specific legal formula. The real reason behind an arrest is virtually always the actual state of particular social situations, or of the skid-row area in general.

We have concentrated on those procedures and considerations that skid-row patrolmen regard as necessary, proper, and efficient relative to the circumstances in which they are employed. In this way, we attempted to disclose the conception of the mandate to which the police feel summoned. It was entirely outside the scope of the presentation to review the merits of this conception and of the methods used to meet it. Only insofar as patrolmen themselves recognized instances and patterns of malpractice did we take note of them. Most of the criticism voiced by officers had to do with the use of undue harshness and with the indiscriminate use of arrest powers when these were based on personal feelings rather than the requirements of the situation. According to prevailing opinion, patrolmen guilty of such abuses make life unnecessarily difficult for themselves and for their co-workers. Despite disapproval of harshness, officers tend to be defensive about it. For example, one sergeant who was outspokenly critical of brutality, said that though in general brutal men create more problems than they solve, "they do a good job in some situations for which the better men have no stomach." Moreover, supevisory personnel exhibit a strong reluctance to direct their subordinates in the particulars of their work performance. According to our observations, control is exercised mainly through consultation with superiors, and directives take the form of requests rather than orders. In the background of all this is the belief that patrol work on skid-row requires a great deal of discretionary freedom. In the words of the same sergeant quoted above, "a good man has things worked out in his own ways on his beat and he doesn't need anybody to tell him what to do."

The virtual absence of disciplinary control and the demand for discretionary freedom are related to the idea that patrol work involves "playing by ear." For if it is true that peace keeping cannot be systematically generalized, then, of course, it cannot be organizationally constrained. What the seasoned patrolman means, however, in saying that he "plays by ear" is that he is making his decisions while being attuned to the realities of complex situations about which

he has immensely detailed knowledge. This studied aspect of peace keeping generally is not made explicit, nor is the tyro or the outsider made aware of it. Quite to the contrary, the ability to discharge the duties associated with keeping the peace is viewed as a reflection of an innate talent of "getting along with people." Thus, the same demands are made of barely initiated officers as are made of experienced practitioners. Correspondingly, beginners tend to think that they can do as well as their more knowledgeable peers. As this leads to inevitable frustrations, they find themselves in a situation that is conducive to the development of a particular sense of "touchiness." Personal dispositions of individual officers are, of course, of great relevance. But the license of discretionary freedom and the expectation of success under conditions of autonomy, without any indication that the work of the successful craftsman is based on an acquired preparedness for the task, is ready-made for failure and malpractice. Moreover, it leads to slipshod practices of patrol that also infect the standards of the careful craftsman.

The uniformed patrol, and especially the foot patrol, has a low preferential value in the division of labor of police work. This is, in part, at least, due to the belief that "anyone could do it." In fact, this belief is thoroughly mistaken. At present, however, the recognition that the practice requires preparation, and the process of obtaining the preparation itself, is left entirely to the practitioner.

[11]

The Social Organization of Arrest*

Donald J. Black†

This Article offers a set of descriptive materials on the social conditions under which policemen make arrests in routine encounters. At this level, it is a modest increment in the expanding literature on the law's empirical face. Scholarship on law-in-action has concentrated upon criminal law in general and the world of the police in particular.[1] Just what, beyond the hoarding of facts, these empirical studies will yield, however, is still unclear. Perhaps a degree of planned change in the criminal justice system will follow, be it in legal doctrine or in legal administration. In any event, evaluation certainly appears to be the purpose, and reform the expected outcome, of much empirical research. This Article pursues a different sort of yield from its empirical study: a sociological theory of law.[2] The analysis is self-consciously inattentive to policy reform or evaluation of the police; it is intentionally bloodless in tone. It examines arrest in order to infer patterns relevant to an understanding of all instances of legal control.

The empirical analysis queries how a number of circumstances affect the probability of arrest. The factors considered are: the suspect's race, the legal seriousness of the alleged crime, the evidence available in the field setting, the complainant's preference for police action, the social relationship between the complainant and suspect, the suspect's degree of deference toward the police, and the manner in which the police come to handle an incident, whether in response to a citizen's request or through their own initiative. The inquiry seeks to discover general principles according to

---

* The Article's findings derive from a larger research project under the direction of Professor Albert J. Reiss, Jr., Department of Sociology and Institute of Social Science, Yale University. The project was coordinated at the Center for Research on Social Organization, Department of Sociology, University of Michigan. It was supported by Grant Award 006, Office of Law Enforcement Assistance, U.S. Department of Justice, under the Law Enforcement Assistance Act of 1965, and by grants from the National Science Foundation and the Russell Sage Foundation.

† A.B., 1963, Indiana University; M.A., 1965; Ph.D., 1968, University of Michigan. Assistant Professor of Sociology, Yale University; Lecturer in Law, Yale Law School.

1. *See generally* E. SCHUR, LAW AND SOCIETY (1968); Skolnick, *The Sociology of Law in America: Overview and Trends*, in LAW AND SOCIETY 4 (1965) (supplement to 13 SOCIAL PROBLEMS (1965)); Bordua & Reiss, *Law Enforcement*, in THE USES OF SOCIOLOGY 275 (1967); Manning, *Observing the Police*, in OBSERVING DEVIANCE (J. Douglas ed., forthcoming). The empirical literature is so abundant and is expanding so rapidly that these published bibliographic discussions are invariably inadequate.

2. It should be noted that the Article's approach to legal life differs quite radically from the approach of Philip Selznick, one of the most influential American sociologists of law. Selznick's sociology of law attempts to follow the path of natural law; my approach follows the general direction of legal positivism. In Lon Fuller's language, Selznick is willing to tolerate a confusion of the *is* and *ought*, while I am not. L. FULLER, THE LAW IN QUEST OF ITSELF 5 (1940). *See* P. SELZNICK, LAW, SOCIETY, AND INDUSTRIAL JUSTICE (1969); Selznick, *The Sociology of Law*, 9 INTERNATIONAL ENCYCLOPEDIA OF THE SOCIAL SCIENCES 50 (D. L. Sills ed., 1968); Selznick, *Sociology and Natural Law*, 6 NATURAL L.F. 84 (1961).

which policemen routinely use or withhold their power to arrest, and thus to reveal a part of the social organization[3] of arrest.

The Article begins with a skeletal discussion of the field method. Next follows a brief ethnography of routine police work designed to place arrest within its mundane context. The findings on arrest are then presented, first for encounters involving both a citizen complainant and a suspect, and second for police encounters with lone suspects. The Article finally speculates about the implications of the empirical findings at the level of a general theory of legal control, the focus shifting from a sociology of the police to a sociology of law.

I. Field Method

The data were collected during the summer of 1966 by systematic observation of police-citizen transactions in Boston, Chicago, and Washington, D.C.[4] Thirty-six observers—persons with law, social science, and police administration backgrounds—recorded observations of encounters between uniformed patrolmen and citizens. The observers' training and supervision was, for all practical purposes, identical in the three cities. Observers accompanied patrolmen on all work shifts on all days of the week for seven weeks in each city. Proportionately more of our manhours were devoted to times when police activity is comparatively high, namely evening shifts, and particularly weekend evenings. Hence, to a degree the sample overrepresents the kinds of social disruptions that arise more on evenings and weekends than at other times. The police precincts chosen as observation sites in each city were selected to maximize scrutiny of lower socio-economic, high crime rate, racially homogeneous residential areas. Two precincts were used in both Boston and Chicago, and four precincts were used in Washington, D.C. The Washington, D.C., precincts, however, were more racially integrated than were those in Boston and Chicago.

Observers recorded the data in "incident booklets," forms structurally similar to interview schedules. One booklet was used for each incident. A field situation involving police action was classified as an "incident" if it was brought to the officer's attention by the police radio system, or by a citizen on the street or in the police station, or if the officer himself noticed

3. As used in this Article, the broad concept "social organization" refers to the supraindividual principles and mechanisms according to which social events come into being, are maintained and arranged, change, and go out of existence. Put another way, social organization refers to the descriptive grammar of social events.

4. At this writing, the data are over four years old. However, there has been little reform in routine patrol work since 1966. This is in part because the police work in question—everyday police contact with citizens—is not as amenable to planned change as other forms of police work, such as crowd or riot control, traffic regulation, or vice enforcement. Moreover, the data have value even if they no longer describe contemporary conduct, since they remain useful for developing a theory of law as a behavior system. A general theory of law has no time limits. Indeed, how fine it would be if we possessed more empirical data from legal life past.

a situation and decided that it required police attention. Also included as incidents were a handful of situations which the police noticed themselves but which they chose to ignore.

The observers did not fill out incident booklets in the presence of policemen. In fact, the line officers were told that the research was not concerned with police behavior but only with citizen behavior toward the police and the kinds of problems citizens make for the police.

The observers recorded a total of 5,713 incidents, but the base for the present analysis is only a little more than 5 percent of the total. This attrition results primarily from the general absence of opportunities for arrest in patrol work, where most of the incidents involve non-criminal situations or criminal situations for which there is no suspect. Traffic encounters also were excluded, even though technically any traffic violation presents an opportunity for arrest. Other cases were eliminated because they involved factors that could invisibly distort or otherwise confuse the analysis. The encounters excluded were those initiated by citizens who walked into a police station to ask for help (6 percent of total) or who flagged down the police on the street (5 percent). These kinds of encounters involve peculiar situational features warranting separate treatment, though even that would be difficult, given their statistically negligible number. For similar reasons encounters involving participants of mixed race and mixed social-class status[5] were also eliminated. Finally, the sample of encounters excludes suspects under 18 years of age—legal juveniles in most states—and suspects of white-collar status.[6] Thus, it investigates arrest patterns in police encounters with predominantly blue-collar adult suspects.

II. Routine Police Work

In some respects, selecting arrest as a subject of study implicitly misrepresents routine police work. Too commonly, the routine is equated with the exercise of the arrest power, not only by members of the general public but by lawyers and even many policemen as well. In fact, the daily round of the patrol officer infrequently involves arrest[7] or even encounters with a

---

5. This means that encounters involving a complainant and suspect of different races were excluded. Similarly, the sample would not include the arrest of a black man with a white wife. However, it does not mean the exclusion of encounters where the policeman and suspect were not of the same race.

6. Because field observers occasionally had difficulty in judging the age or social class of a citizen, they were told to use a "don't know" category whenever they felt the danger of misclassification. Two broad categories of social class, blue-collar and white-collar, were employed. Since the precincts sampled were predominantly lower class, the observers labeled the vast majority of the citizen participants blue-collar. In fact, not enough white-collar cases were available for separate analysis. The small number of adults of ambiguous social class were combined with the blue-collar cases into a sample of "predominantly blue-collar" suspects. The observers probably were reasonably accurate in classifying suspects because the police frequently interviewed suspects about their age and occupation.

7. In this Article, "arrest" refers only to transportation of a suspect to a police station. It does not include the application of constraint in field settings, and it does not require formal booking of a

criminal suspect. The most cursory observation of the policeman on the job overturns the imagery of a man who makes his living parcelling citizens into jail.

Modern police departments are geared to respond to citizen calls for service; the great majority of incidents the police handle arise when a citizen telephones the police and the dispatcher sends a patrol car to deal with the situation. The officer becomes implicated in a wide range of human troubles, most not of his own choosing, and many of which have little or nothing to do with criminal law enforcement. He transports people to the hospital, writes reports of auto accidents, and arbitrates and mediates between disputants—neighbors, husbands and wives, landlords and tenants, and businessmen and customers. He takes missing-person reports, directs traffic, controls crowds at fires, writes dogbite reports, and identifies abandoned autos. He removes safety hazards from the streets, and occasionally scoops up a dead animal. Policemen disdain this kind of work, but they do it every day. Such incidents rarely result in arrest; they nevertheless comprise nearly half of the incidents uniformed patrolmen encounter in situations initiated by phone calls from citizens.[8] Policemen also spend much of their time with "juvenile trouble," a police category typically pertaining to distinctively youthful disturbances of adult peace—noisy groups of teenagers on a street corner, ball-playing in the street, trespassing or playing in deserted buildings or construction sites, and rock-throwing. These situations, too, rarely result in arrest. Some officers view handling juvenile trouble as work they do in the service of neighborhood grouches. The same may be said of ticketing parking violations in answer to citizen complaints. All these chores necessitate much unexciting paperwork.

Somewhat less than half of the encounters arising from a citizen telephone call have to do with a crime—a felony or a misdemeanor other than juvenile trouble. Yet even criminal incidents are so constituted situationally as to preclude arrest in the majority of cases, because no suspect is present when the police arrive at the scene. In 77 percent of the felony situations and in 51 percent of the misdemeanor situations the only major citizen participant is a complainant.[9] In a handful of other cases the only citizen present is an informant or bystander. When no suspect is available in the field setting, the typical official outcome is a crime report, the basic document from which official crime statistics are constructed and the operational prerequisite of further investigation by the detective division.

---

suspect with a crime. *See* W. LaFave, Arrest: The Decision to Take a Suspect into Custody 4 (1965).

8. D. Black, Police Encounters and Social Organization: An Observation Study, 51–57, Dec. 15, 1968 (unpublished dissertation in Department of Sociology, University of Michigan). *See also* Cumming, Cumming, & Edell, *Policeman as Philosopher, Guide and Friend*, 12 Social Problems 276 (1965).

9. D. Black, *supra* note 8, at 94.

The minority of citizen-initiated crime encounters where a suspect is present when the police arrive is the appropriate base for a study of arrest. In the great majority of these suspect encounters a citizen complainant also takes part in the situational interaction, so any study of routine arrest must consider the complainant's role as well as those of the police officer and the suspect.[10]

Through their own discretionary authority, policemen occasionally initiate encounters that may be called *proactive* police work, as opposed to the *reactive*, citizen-initiated work that consumes the greater part of the average patrol officer's day.[11] On an evening shift (traditionally 4 p.m. to midnight) a typical work-load for a patrol car is 6 radio-dispatched encounters and one proactive encounter. The ratio of proactive encounters varies enormously by shift, day of week, patrol beat or territory, and number of cars on duty. An extremely busy weekend night could involve 20 dispatches to a single car. Under these rushed conditions the officers might not initiate any encounters on their own. At another time in another area a patrol car might receive no dispatches, but the officers might initiate as many as 8 or 10 encounters on the street. During the observation study only 13 percent of incidents came to police attention without the assistance of citizens.[12] Still, most officers as well as citizens probably think of proactive policing as the form that epitomizes the police function.

The police-initiated encounter is a bald confrontation between state and citizen. Hardly ever does a citizen complainant take part in a proactive field encounter and then only if a policeman were to discover an incident of personal victimization or if a complainant were to step forth subsequent to the officer's initial encounter with a suspect. Moreover, the array of incidents policemen handle—their operational jurisdiction—is quite different when they have the discretion to select situations for attention compared to what it is when that discretion is lodged in citizens. In reactive police work they are servants of the public, with one consequence being that the social troubles they oversee often have little if anything to do with the criminal law. Arrest is usually a situational impossibility. In proactive policing the officer is more a public guardian and the operational jurisdiction is a police choice; the only limits are in law and in departmental policy. In proactive police work, arrest is totally a matter of the officer's own making. Yet the reality of proactive police work has an ironic quality

---

10. In fact, of all the felony cases the police handle in response to a citizen request by telephone, including cases where only a complainant, informant, or bystander is present in the situation, a mere 3% involve a police transaction with a lone suspect. D. Black, *supra* note 8, at 94.

11. The concepts "reactive" and "proactive" derive from the origins of individual action, the former referring to actions originating in the environment, the latter to those originating within the actor. *See* Murray, *Toward a Classification of Interactions*, in TOWARD A GENERAL THEORY OF ACTION 434 (1967).

12. This proportion is based upon the total sample of 5,713 incidents.

about it. The organization of crime in time and space deprives policemen on free patrol of legally serious arrests. Most felonies occur in off-street settings and must be detected by citizens. Even those that occur in a visible public place usually escape the policemen's ken. When the police have an opportunity to initiate an encounter, the occasion is more likely than not a traffic violation. Traffic violations comprise the majority of proactive encounters, and most of the remainder concern minor "disturbances of the peace."[13] In short, where the police role is most starkly aggressive in form, the substance is drably trivial, and legally trivial incidents provide practically all of the grist for arrest in proactive police operations.

Perhaps a study of arrest flatters the legal significance of the everyday police encounter. Still, even though arrest situations are uncommon in routine policing, invocation of the criminal process accounts for more formal-legal cases, more court trials and sanctions, more public controversies and conflicts than any other mechanism in the legal system. As a major occasion of legal control, then, arrest cries out for empirical study.[14]

III. COMPLAINANT AND SUSPECT

The police encounter involving both a suspect and a complainant is a microcosm of a total legal control system. In it are personified the state, the alleged threat to social order, and the citizenry. The complainant is to a police encounter what an interest group is to a legislature or a plaintiff to a civil lawsuit. His presence makes a dramatic difference in police encounters, particularly if he assumes the role of situational lobbyist. This Section will show, *inter alia*, that the fate of suspects rests nearly as much with complainants as it does with police officers themselves.

Of the 176 encounters involving both a complainant and a suspect a

---

13. Much proactive patrol work involves a drunken or disorderly person. Typically, however, arrest occurs in these cases only when the citizen is uncooperative; ordinarily the policeman begins his encounter by giving an order such as "Move on," "Take off," or "Take it easy." Arrest is an outcome of interaction rather than a simple and direct response of an officer to what he observes as an official witness.

14. Earlier observational studies have neglected patterns of arrest in the everyday work of uniformed patrolmen. Emphasis has instead been placed upon detective work, vice enforcement, policing of juveniles, and other comparatively marginal aspects of police control. *See* J. SKOLNICK, JUSTICE WITHOUT TRIAL (1966) (patterns of arrest in vice enforcement); Bittner, *The Police on Skid-Row: A Study of Peace-Keeping*, 32 AM. SOC. REV. 699 (1967); Black & Reiss, *Police Control of Juveniles*, 35 AM. SOC. REV. 63 (1970); Piliavin & Briar, *Police Encounters with Juveniles*, 70 AM. J. SOC. 206 (1964). Several observational studies emphasizing other dimensions of police work also are directly relevant. *See* L. TIFFANY, D. McINTYRE, & D. ROTENBERG, DETECTION OF CRIME (1967); Reiss, & Black, *Interrogation and the Criminal Process*, 374 ANNALS OF THE AM. ACADEMY OF POL. & SOC. SCI. 47 (1967); Project, *Interrogations in New Haven: The Impact of Miranda*, 76 YALE L.J. 1519 (1967). There also have been a number of studies based upon official arrest statistics. *See* N. GOLDMAN, THE DIFFERENTIAL SELECTION OF JUVENILE OFFENDERS FOR COURT APPEARANCE (1963); J. WILSON, VARIETIES OF POLICE BEHAVIOR (1968); Green, *Race, Social Status, and Criminal Arrest*, 35 AM. SOC. REV. 476 (1970); Terry, *The Screening of Juvenile Offenders*, 58 J. CRIM. L.C. & P.S. 173 (1967). For a more speculative discussion *see* Goldstein, *Police Discretion Not to Invoke the Criminal Process: Low-Visibility Decisions in the Administration of Justice*, 69 YALE L.J. 543 (1960). *See generally* W. LAFAVE, *supra* note 7.

little over one-third were alleged to be felonies; the remainder were misdemeanors of one or another variety. Not surprisingly, the police make arrests more often in felony than in misdemeanor situations, but the difference is not as wide as might be expected. An arrest occurs in 58 percent of the felony encounters and in 44 percent of the misdemeanor encounters. The police, then, release roughly half of the persons they suspect of crimes. This strikingly low arrest rate requires explanation.[15]

A. *Evidence*

Factors other than the kind of evidence available to an officer in the field setting affect the probability of arrests, for even exceptionally clear situational evidence of criminal liability does not guarantee that arrest will follow a police encounter.

One of two major forms of evidence ordinarily is present when the police confront a suspect in the presence of a complainant: Either the police arrive at the setting in time to witness the offense, or a citizen—usually the complainant himself—gives testimony against the suspect. Only rarely is some other kind of evidence available, such as a physical clue on the premises or on the suspect's person. On the other hand, in only three of the complainant-suspect encounters was situational evidence entirely absent. In these few cases the police acted upon what they knew from the original complaint as it was relayed to them by radio dispatch and upon what they heard about the crime from the complainant, but they had no other information apparent in the field situation linking the suspect to the alleged crime.

In a great majority of felony situations the best evidence accessible to the police is citizen testimony, whereas in misdemeanor situations the police generally witness the offense themselves. These evidentiary circumstances are roughly equivalent as far as the law of arrest is concerned, since the requirements for a misdemeanor arrest without a formal warrant are more stringent than are those for a felony arrest. In most jurisdictions the police must observe the offense or acquire a signed complaint before they may arrest a misdemeanor suspect in the field. In felony situations, however, they need only have "probable cause" or "reasonable grounds" to believe the suspect is guilty. Thus, though the evidence usually is stronger in misdemeanor than in felony situations, the law in effect compensates the police by giving them more power in the felony situations where they

---

15. At this point a word should be said about the explanatory strategy to be followed in the analysis of data. The Article's approach is radically behavioral or, more specifically, supramotivational, in that it seeks out supraindividual conditions with which the probability of arrest varies. Implicit in this strategy is a conception of arrest as a social event rather than as an individual event. The mental processes of the police and the citizens whose outward behavior our observers recorded are not important to this analysis. At this point the sole object is to delineate aspects of the social context of arrest as a variety of legal intervention.

1094   *STANFORD LAW REVIEW*   [Vol. 23: Page 1087

TABLE 1

ARREST RATES IN CITIZEN-INITIATED ENCOUNTERS
ACCORDING TO TYPE OF CRIME AND MAJOR SITUATIONAL EVIDENCE

Crime	Evidence	Total Number of Incidents	Arrest Rate in Percent
Felony	Police Witness[a]	6	(4)[b]
	Citizen Testimony	45	56
	Other Evidence	1	(0)
	No Evidence	0	(0)
Misdemeanor	Police Witness[a]	52	65
	Citizen Testimony	39	31
	Other Evidence	0	(0)
	No Evidence	3	(0)
All Crimes[c]	Police Witness[a]	58	66
	Citizen Testimony	84	44
	Other Evidence	1	(0)
	No Evidence	3	(0)

[a] This category includes all cases in which the police witness evidence was supplemented by other types of evidence.
[b] Arrest rate figures in parentheses in this and later tables are used whenever the total number of incidents is statistically too small to justify making a generalized assertion of arrest rate.
[c] This excludes 30 cases for which the observer did not ascertain the character of the evidence. Thus the total is 146 cases.

would otherwise be at a disadvantage. Correspondingly the law of arrest undermines the advantage felons in the aggregate would otherwise enjoy.

Table 1 indicates that the police do not use all the legal power they possess. They arrest only slightly over one-half of the felony suspects against whom testimonial evidence is present in the field encounter, although "probable cause" can be assumed to have been satisfied in nearly every such incident. Furthermore, during the observation study the police released 2 of the 6 felony suspects they observed in allegedly felonious activity. These two cases are noteworthy even though based upon a sample several times smaller than the other samples. In misdemeanor situations the arrest rate is about two-thirds when the police observe the offense, while it drops to about one-third when the only evidence comes from a citizen's testimony. An evidentiary legal perspective alone, therefore, cannot account for differentials in police arrest practices. On the other hand, evidence is not irrelevant to arrest differentials. In none of the 3 cases where no evidence was available did the police make an arrest, and where the legal standing of the police was at best precarious—misdemeanor situations with citizen testimonial evidence—the arrest rate was relatively low.

B. *The Complainant's Preference*

While complainants frequently are present when policemen fail to invoke the law against suspects who are highly vulnerable to arrest, the complainants do not necessarily resent police leniency. In 24 percent of the misdemeanor situations and in 21 percent of the felony situations the complainant expresses to the police a preference for clemency toward the suspect.[16] The complainant manifests a preference for an arrest in 34 percent of the misdemeanors and in 48 percent of the felonies. In the remainder of encounters the complainant's preference is unclear; frequently the complainant's outward behavior is passive, especially in misdemeanor situations.

The findings in Table 2 indicate that police arrest practices, in both felony and misdemeanor situations, sharply reflect the complainant's preferences, whether they be compassionate or vindictive. In felony situations where a citizen's testimony links a suspect to the crime, arrest results in about three-fourths of the cases in which the complainant specifies a preference for that outcome. When the complainant prefers no arrest, the police go against his wishes in only about one-tenth of the cases. Passive or unexpressive complainants see the police arrest suspects in a little under two-thirds of the situations where the police have a complainant's testimonial evidence. Thus, when the complainant leaves the decision to arrest wholly in police hands, the police are by no means reluctant to arrest the felony suspect. They become strikingly reluctant only when a complainant exerts pressure on the suspect's behalf.

The findings for misdemeanor situations likewise show police compliance with the complainant's preference and also demonstrate the relevance of situational evidence to the suspect's fate. Encounters where the complainant outwardly prefers arrest and where the police observe the offense itself have an extremely high probability of arrest, 95 percent, a proportion somewhat higher than that for felony situations involving testimonial evidence alone. When the major situational evidence is citizen testimony against a misdemeanor suspect, the proportion drops to 70 percent. On the other hand, even when the police observe the offense, the arrest rate drops to less than one-fifth in those encounters where the complainant outwardly prefers leniency for his adversary. Plainly, therefore, the complainant's preference is a more powerful situational factor than evidence, though the two operate jointly. As might be expected, evidence is particularly consequential

---

16. In such cases a complainant's preference is clear from his response to the question posed by the police. When police did not solicit the complainant's opinion, the observer classified the complainant's preference according to the audible or visible clues available to him. Some complainants made explicit demands upon the police; others appeared more confused and made no attempt to influence the outcome.

TABLE 2

ARREST RATES IN CITIZEN-INITIATED ENCOUNTERS ACCORDING TO TYPE OF CRIME, MAJOR SITUATIONAL EVIDENCE AND COMPLAINANT'S PREFERENCE

Felony

Evidence	Complainant's Preference	Total Number of Incidents	Arrest Rate in Percent
Police Witness	Arrest	2	(1)
	Unclear	4	(3)
	No Arrest	0	(0)
Citizen Testimony	Arrest	23	74
	Unclear	11	64
	No Arrest	11	9
All Felonies[a]	Arrest	25	72
	Unclear	15	67
	No Arrest	11	9

Misdemeanor

Evidence	Complainant's Preference	Total Number of Incidents	Arrest Rate in Percent
Police Witness	Arrest	21	95
	Unclear	23	52
	No Arrest	11	18
Citizen Testimony	Arrest	10	70
	Unclear	15	27
	No Arrest	11	9
All Misdemeanors[b]	Arrest	31	87
	Unclear	38	42
	No Arrest	22	14

[a] Excludes one case of "other evidence" and seven cases in which the observer did not ascertain the evidence.
[b] Excludes three cases of "no evidence" and 23 cases where the type of evidence was not ascertained.

when the complainant expresses no clear preference for police action, and in those cases the suspect is almost twice as likely to be arrested when the police observe the offense as when the major evidence is the complainant's or another citizen's testimony. As noted above, however, the complainant does make his preference clear in the majority of encounters, and that preference appears to be strongly associated with the arrest rate.

C. Relational Distance

When police enter into an encounter involving both a complainant and a suspect they find themselves not only in a narrow legal conflict but also in a conflict between citizen adversaries within a social relationship— one between family members, acquaintances, neighbors, friends, business associates, or total strangers. The data in Table 3 suggest that police arrest practices vary with the relational nature of complainant-suspect conflicts. The probability of arrest is highest when the citizen adversaries have the most distant social relation to one another, i.e., when they are strangers. The felony cases especially reveal that arrest becomes more probable as the relational distance increases. Forty-five percent of suspects are arrested in a family member relationship, 77 percent in a friends, neighbors, acquaintances relationship, and 7 out of 8 or 88 percent in a stranger relationship.[17] In the misdemeanor cases the pattern is not so consistent. Although the likelihood of arrest is still highest in conflicts between strangers, the lowest likelihood is in situations involving friends, neighbors, or acquaintances. When the complainant's preference is unclear, or when he prefers no arrest, no difference of any significance is discernible across the categories of relational distance; the type of social conflict embodied in the police encounter visibly affects arrest probability only when the complainant presses the police to make an arrest.

D. Race, Respect, and the Complainant

Table 4 demonstrates that police arrest blacks at a higher rate than whites. But no evidence supports the view that the police discriminate against blacks. Rather, the race differential seems to be a function of the relatively higher rate at which black suspects display disrespect toward the police. When the arrest rate for respectful black suspects is compared to that for respectful whites, no difference is apparent. Before examining this last finding in detail, however, the importance of citizen respect in itself should be established.

Considering felony and misdemeanor situations together, the arrest

17. Little confidence can be placed in findings based on less than 10 cases. Nevertheless, the Article occasionally mentions such findings when they are strikingly consistent with patterns seen in the larger samples. In no instances, however, do broader generalizations rest upon these inadequate statistical bases.

TABLE 3

ARREST RATES IN CITIZEN-INITIATED ENCOUNTERS ACCORDING TO TYPE OF CRIME, RELATIONAL TIE BETWEEN COMPLAINANT AND SUSPECT, AND COMPLAINANT'S PREFERENCE

	Felony			Misdemeanor		
Relational Tie	Complainant's Preference	Total Number of Incidents	Arrest Rate in Percent	Complainant's Preference	Total Number of Incidents	Arrest Rate in Percent
Family Members	Prefers Arrest	20	55	Prefers Arrest	15	80
	Preference Unclear	8	(6)	Preference Unclear	13	38
	Prefers No Arrest	10	0	Prefers No Arrest	8	(0)
Friends, Neighbors, Acquaintances	Prefers Arrest	5	(4)	Prefers Arrest	11	64
	Preference Unclear	8	(6)	Preference Unclear	15	40
	Prefers No Arrest	0	(0)	Prefers No Arrest	20	5
Strangers	Prefers Arrest	3	(3)	Prefers Arrest	15	87
	Preference Unclear	2	(2)	Preference Unclear	15	47
	Prefers No Arrest	3	(2)	Prefers No Arrest	5	(0)
All Family Members		38	45		36	47
All Friends, Neighbors, Acquaintances		13	77		46	30
All Strangers		8	(7)		35	57

TABLE 4

ARREST RATES IN CITIZEN-INITIATED ENCOUNTERS
ACCORDING TO TYPE OF CRIME AND RACE OF SUSPECT

Crime	Race	Total Number of Incidents	Arrest Rate in Percent
Felony	Black	48	60
	White	11	45
Misdemeanor	Black	75	47
	White	42	38
All Crimes	Black	123	52
	White	53	39

rate for very deferential suspects is 40 percent of 10 cases. For civil suspects it is effectively the same at 42 percent of 71 cases, but it is 70 percent of 37 cases for antagonistic or disrespectful suspects.[18] Unquestionably, the suspect who refuses to defer to police authority takes a gamble with his freedom. This pattern persists in felony and misdemeanor situations when they are examined separately, but the small samples that result from dividing the data by type of crime prevent any more refined comparison than between civil and disrespectful levels of deference. The police make an arrest in 40 percent of the 25 felony encounters in which the suspect is civil, as compared to 69 percent of the 16 felony encounters in which he is disrespectful. In misdemeanor situations the corresponding proportions are 43 percent of 46 cases and 71 percent of 21 cases. In the aggregate of cases, the police are more likely to arrest a misdemeanor suspect who is disrespectful toward them than a felony suspect who is civil. In this sense the police enforce their authority more severely than they enforce the law.

The complainant's preference can erode the impact of the suspect's degree of respect somewhat, but when complainant's preference is held constant, the pattern remains, as Table 5 shows. When the complainant expresses a preference for arrest of his adversary, the police comply more readily if the suspect is disrespectful rather than civil toward them. Table 5 also reveals that, when the complainant desires an arrest and the suspect is civil, the probability of arrest for black and white suspects is almost exactly equal, but black suspects are disrespectful toward the police more often than are whites, a pattern that operates to increase disproportionately the overall black arrest rate.

---

18. The observers classified a suspect's degree of deference on the basis of whatever clues they could cull from his behavior. The observers undoubtedly made classificatory errors from time to time since some suspects, particularly some disrespectful suspects, could be extremely subtle in their communicative demeanor. Some, for example, were exceedingly deferential as a way of ridiculing the police. In the great majority of cases, however, the classifications accurately described the outward behavior to which the police were relating. Of course, the suspects' *feelings* were not necessarily reflected in their behavior.

TABLE 5

ARREST RATES IN CITIZEN-INITIATED ENCOUNTERS ACCORDING TO COMPLAINANT'S PREFERENCE, SUSPECT'S RACE, AND DEGREE OF DEFERENCE

Complainant Prefers Arrest

Race	Suspect's Deference	Total Number of Incidents	Arrest Rate in Percent
Black	Very Deferential	2	(2)
	Civil	19	68
	Antagonistic	12	83
White	Very Deferential	1	(1)
	Civil	15	67
	Antagonistic	4	(2)
Both Races[a]	Very Deferential	3	(3)
	Civil	34	68
	Antagonistic	16	75

Complainant's Preference Is Unclear

Race	Suspect's Deference	Total Number of Incidents	Arrest Rate in Percent
Black	Very Deferential	2	(0)
	Civil	18	33
	Antagonistic	15	93
White	Very Deferential	1	(1)
	Civil	7	(2)
	Antagonistic	3	(1)
Both Races[b]	Very Deferential	3	(1)
	Civil	25	32
	Antagonistic	18	83

Complainant Prefers No Arrest

Race	Suspect's Deference	Total Number of Incidents	Arrest Rate in Percent
Black	Very Deferential	3	(0)
	Civil	13	23
	Antagonistic	4	(1)
White	Very Deferential	1	(0)
	Civil	6	(1)
	Antagonistic	1	(0)
Both Races[c]	Very Deferential	4	(0)
	Civil	19	21
	Antagonistic	5	(1)

[a] Excludes 16 cases for which the suspect's degree of deference was not ascertained.
[b] Excludes 15 cases for which the suspect's degree of deference was not ascertained.
[c] Excludes 18 cases for which the suspect's degree of deference was not ascertained.

When the complainant's preference is unclear the degree of deference of the suspect is especially consequential. The police arrest civil suspects in 32 percent of these cases, while they arrest disrespectful suspects in 83 percent of the cases. This difference is far wider than where the complainant expresses a preference for arrest (68 percent and 75 percent). Especially when the complainant is passive, the suspect carries his fate in his own hands. Under these circumstances blacks more than whites tend, to their own disadvantage, to be disrespectful toward the police.

The small sample of cases rules out a complete analysis of the encounters in which the complainant favors clemency for his adversary. The cases are only adequate for establishing that a civil suspect is less likely to be arrested under these conditions than when the complainant prefers arrest or expresses no preference. Although statistically negligible, it is noteworthy that 4 of the 5 disrespectful suspects were released by the police under these conditions. The evidence suggests that complainants have voices sufficiently persuasive in routine police encounters to save disrespectful suspects from arrest.

IV. Encounters Without Complainants

Police transactions with lone suspects comprise a minority of the encounters with adults, but they nevertheless carry a special significance to a description of police work. There is no complainant available to deflect the outcome, so the encounter is all between the polity and the accused. This kind of situation often arises when citizens call the police but refuse to identify themselves or when they identify themselves but fail to materialize when the police arrive. In these cases the police handle incidents, usually in public places, as the servants of unknown masters. Only rarely do the police themselves detect and act upon crime situations with no prompting from a concerned citizen. This Section treats separately the citizen-initiated and the police-initiated encounters. With no complainant participating, the analysis contains fewer variables. Absent are the complainant's preference and the relational distance between complainant and suspect. Because the police rarely encounter felony suspects without the help of a complaining witness, the legal seriousness of the lone suspect's offense is likewise invariable: Nearly all police-initiated encounters involve misdemeanors. Finally, the situational evidence in the vast majority of lone-suspect encounters is a police officer's claim that he witnessed an offense. The size of the sample is too small to allow separate analysis of encounters resting upon other kinds of evidence or those apparently based only upon diffuse police suspicion. The analysis, therefore, is confined to the effect on arrest rates of suspect's race, the suspect's degree of respect for the police, and the type of police mobilization—*i.e.*, whether a citizen or the police initiated the encounter.

A. *Race, Respect, and the Lone Suspect*

In 67 situations the police witnessed a misdemeanor after being called to the scene by a citizen's telephone request. They arrested a suspect in 49 percent of these cases. In another 45 situations the police witnessed a misdemeanor and entered into an encounter with a suspect wholly upon their own initiative. In these police-initiated encounters the arrest rate was somewhat higher—62 percent. Hence, the police seem a bit more severe when they act completely upon their own authority than when they respond to citizens' calls. Conversely, when a citizen calls the police but avoids the field situation, the officers match the citizen's seeming indifference with their own.

Table 6 shows the arrest rates for blacks and whites in citizen- and police-initiated encounters where no complainant participated. Under both types of mobilization the police arrested blacks at a higher rate, though in police-initiated encounters the difference is statistically negligible, given the sample size. However, just as in encounters involving complainants, the race difference disappeared in lone-suspect encounters when the suspect's level of respect for the police was held constant, as Table 7 shows.

In citizen-initiated encounters black suspects disproportionately show disrespect for the police, and the police reply with a high arrest rate—83 percent. They arrest only 36 percent of the civil black suspects, a rate comparable to that for civil white suspects, 29 percent (a difference of just one case of the 14 in the sample). Considering both races together in citizen-initiated encounters, disrespectful conduct toward the police clearly is highly determinative for a suspect whose illegal behavior is witnessed by

TABLE 6

ARREST RATES IN POLICE ENCOUNTERS WITH SUSPECTS IN
POLICE-WITNESSED MISDEMEANOR SITUATIONS WITHOUT COMPLAINANT PARTICIPATION
ACCORDING TO TYPE OF MOBILIZATION AND SUSPECT'S RACE

Type of Mobilization	Race	Total Number of Incidents	Arrest Rate in Percent
Citizen-Initiated	Black	43	58
	White	24	33
Police-Initiated	Black	28	64
	White	17	59
All Citizen-Initiated Encounters		67	49
All Police-Initiated Encounters		45	62

TABLE 7

Arrest Rates in Police Encounters with Suspects in Police-Witnessed Misdemeanor Situations Without Complainant Participation According to Type of Mobilization, Suspect's Race, and Degree of Deference

	Citizen-Initiated Encounters				Police-Initiated Encounters		
Race	Suspect's Deference	Total Number of Incidents	Arrest Rate in Percent	Race	Suspect's Deference	Total Number of Incidents	Arrest Rate in Percent
Black	Very Deferential	5	(0)	Black	Very Deferential	2	(1)
	Civil	14	36		Civil	13	69
	Antagonistic	18	83		Antagonistic	10	70
White	Very Deferential	3	(1)	White	Very Deferential	1	(0)
	Civil	14	29		Civil	10	70
	Antagonistic	5	(3)		Antagonistic	6	(3)
Both Races[a]	Very Deferential	8	(1)	Both Races[b]	Very Deferential	3	(1)
	Civil	28	32		Civil	23	70
	Antagonistic	23	78		Antagonistic	16	62

[a] Excludes 8 cases for which the suspect's degree of deference was not ascertained.
[b] Excludes 3 cases for which the suspect's degree of deference was not ascertained.

1104   STANFORD LAW REVIEW   [Vol. 23: Page 1087]

the police. A display of respect for the officers, on the other hand, can overcome the suspect's evidentiary jeopardy.

Arrest practices differ to a degree in encounters the police initiate. While again arrest rates for civil blacks and civil whites are the same, no significant difference emerges between the vulnerability of civil suspects and that of suspects disrespectful toward the police. In other words, neither the race nor suspect's degree of respect has predictive effect on arrest rates in police-initiated encounters with misdemeanor suspects. The absence of variance in arrest rates for disrespectful and civil suspects is the major difference between police-initiated and citizen-initiated encounters. Moreover, it is the major anomaly in the findings presented in this Article, one that might disappear if the sample of police-initiated encounters were larger.

V. Generalizations

This section restates the major findings of this study in the form of empirical generalizations which should provide a manageable profile of police behavior in routine situations where arrest is a possibility. When appropriate, inferences are drawn from these materials to more abstract propositions at the level of a general theory of legal control. Arrest patterns may reveal broad principles according to which legal policy is defined, legal resources mobilized, and dispositions made.[19]

A. *Mobilization*

Most arrest situations arise through citizen rather than police initiative. In this sense, the criminal law is invoked in a manner not unlike that of private-law systems that are mobilized through a reactive process, depending upon the enterprise of citizen claimants in pursuit of their own interests. In criminal law as in other areas of public law, although the state has formal, proactive authority to bring legal actions, the average criminal matter is the product of a citizen complaint.

One implication of this pattern is that most criminal cases pass through a moral filter in the citizen population before the state assumes its enforcement role. A major portion of the responsibility for criminal-law enforcement is kept out of police hands. Much like courts in the realm of private law, the police operate as moral servants of the citizenry. A further implication of this pattern of reactive policing is that the deterrence function of the criminal process, to an important degree, depends upon citizen willing-

---

19. These three functional foci of legal control—prescription, mobilization, and disposition—correspond roughly to the legislative, executive, and judicial dimensions of government, though they are useful in the analysis of subsystems of legal control as well as total systems. For instance, the police can be regarded as the major mobilization subsystem of the criminal justice system. Yet the police subsystem itself can be approached as a total system involving prescription, mobilization, and disposition subsystems. *Cf.* H. Lasswell, The Decision Process 2 (1956).

ness to mobilize the criminal law, just as the deterrence function of private law depends so much upon citizen plaintiffs.[20] Sanctions cannot deter illegal behavior if the law lies dormant because of an inefficient mobilization process.[21] In this sense all legal systems rely to a great extent upon private citizens.

B. *Complainants*

Arrest practices sharply reflect the preferences of citizen complainants, particularly when the desire is for leniency and also, though less frequently, when the complainant demands arrest. The police are an instrument of the complainant, then, in two ways: Generally they handle what the complainant wants them to handle and they handle the matter in the way the complainant prescribes.

Often students of the police comment that a community has the kind of police it wants, as if the community outlines the police function by some sort of *de facto* legislative process.[22] That view is vague, if not mistaken. Instead, the police serve an atomized mass of complainants far more than they serve an organized community. The greater part of the police workload is case-by-case, isolated contacts between individual policemen and individual complainants. In this sense the police serve a phantom master who dwells throughout the population, who is everywhere but nowhere at once. Because of this fact, the police are at once an easy yet elusive target for criticism. Their field work evades planned change, but as shifts occur in the desires of the atomized citizenry who call and direct the police, changes ripple into policemen's routine behavior.

The pattern of police compliance with complainants gives police work a radically democratic character. The result is not, however, uniform standards of justice, since the moral standards of complainants doubtlessly vary to some extent across the population. Indeed, by complying with complainants the police in effect perpetuate the moral diversity they encounter in the citizen mass.[23] In this respect again, a public-law system bears similarity

20. Contemporary literature on deterrence is devoted primarily to the role of sanctions in criminal law. *See, e.g.,* Andenaes, *The General Preventive Effects of Punishment,* 114 U. Pa. L. Rev. 949 (1966). *But see* R. Von Jhering, The Struggle for Law (1879).

21. Roscoe Pound concludes that the contingent nature of legal mobilization is one of the major obstacles to the effectiveness of law as a social engineering device. *See* Pound, *The Limits of Effective Legal Action,* 27 Int'l J. Ethics 150 (1917). *See also* H. Jones, The Efficacy of Law 21–26 (1969); Bohannan, *The Differing Realms of the Law,* in The Ethnography of Law 33 (1965) (supplement to 67 Am. Anthropologist 33 (1965)).

22. *See, e.g.,* P. Slater, The Pursuit of Loneliness: American Culture at the Breaking Point 49 (1970).

23. This generalization does not apply to proactive police operations such as vice control or street harassment, which seldom involve a citizen complainant. By definition, street harassment is the selective and abrasive attention directed at people who are, at best, marginally liable to arrest—for example, a police command to "move on" to a group of unconventional youths. Proactive policing may involve an attack on particular moral subcultures. *Compare* J. Clebert, The Gypsies 87–119 (1963), *with* Brown, *The Condemnation and Persecution of Hippies,* Trans-Action, Sept. 1969 at 33, *and* W. Hagan, Indian Police and Judges (1966).

to systems of private law.[24] Both types seem organized, visibly and invisibly, so as to give priority to the demands of their dispersed citizens. Whoever may prescribe the law and however the law is applied, many sovereigns call the law to action.[25] Public-law systems are peculiar in that their formal organization allows them to initiate and pursue cases without complainants as sponsors. Still, the reality of public-law systems such as the police belies their formal appearance. The citizenry continually undermines uniformity in public- as well as private-law enforcement. Perhaps democratic organization invariably jeopardizes uniformity in the application of legal controls.[26]

C. Leniency

The police are lenient in their routine arrest practices; they use their arrest power less often than the law would allow. Legal leniency, however, is hardly peculiar to the police. Especially in the private-law sector[27] and also in other areas of public law,[28] the official process for redress of grievances is invoked less often than illegality is detected. Citizens and public officials display reluctance to wield legal power in immediate response to illegality, and a sociology of law must treat as problematic the fact that legal cases arise at all.

D. Evidence

Evidence is an important factor in arrest. The stronger the evidence in the field situation, the more likely is an arrest. When the police themselves witness a criminal offense they are more likely to arrest the suspect than when they only hear about the offense from a third party. Rarely do the

---

24. *See* Pashukanis, *The General Theory of Law and Marxism* in SOVIET LEGAL PHILOSOPHY III, (H. Babb transl. 1951).

25. This is true historically as well; legal systems usually have made the citizen complainant the *sine qua non* of legal mobilization, except under circumstances posing a direct threat to political order. A well-known example was the Roman legal process, where even extreme forms of personal violence required the initiative of a complainant before government sanctions were imposed. *See generally* A. LINTOTT, VIOLENCE IN REPUBLICAN ROME (1968). A theory of legal control should treat as problematic the capacity and willingness of governments to initiate cases and sanction violators in the absence of an aggrieved citizen demanding justice. *See generally* S. RANULF, MORAL INDIGNATION AND MIDDLE CLASS PSYCHOLOGY: A SOCIOLOGICAL STUDY (1938).

26. The norm of universalism reflected in systems of public law in advanced societies is a norm of impersonalism: The police are expected to enforce the law impersonally. But by giving complainants a strong role in the determination of outcomes, the police personalize the criminal law. This pattern allows fellow family members and friends to mobilize the police to handle their disputes with little danger that the police will impose standards foreign to their relationships. At the level of disputes between strangers, however, the same pattern of police compliance with complainants can, given moral diversity, result in a form of discriminatory enforcement. A law enforcement process that takes no account of the degree of intimacy between complainant and suspect may also upset the peculiar balance of close social relationships. *See* Kawashima, *Dispute Resolution in Contemporary Japan*, in LAW IN JAPAN: THE LEGAL ORDER IN A CHANGING SOCIETY 41 (A. von Mehren ed. 1964).

27. *See, e.g.*, Macaulay, *Non-Contractual Relations in Business: A Preliminary Study*, 28 AM. Soc. REV. 55 (1963).

28. *See, e.g.*, M. Mileski, Policing Slum Landlords: An Observation Study of Administrative Control, June 14, 1971 (unpublished dissertation in Department of Sociology, Yale University).

police confront persons as suspects without some evidence; even more rarely are arrests unsupported by evidence. The importance of situational evidence hardly constitutes a major advance in knowledge. Evidence has a role in every legal process. It is the definition of evidence, not whether evidence is required, that differs across legal systems. It should be emphasized that even when the evidence against a suspect is very strong, the police frequently take action short of arrest. Evidence alone, then, is a necessary but not a sufficient basis for predicting invocation of the law.

E. Seriousness

The probability of arrest is higher in legally serious crime situations than in those of a relatively minor nature. This finding certainly is not unexpected, but it has theoretical significance. The police levy arrest as a sanction to correspond with the defined seriousness of the criminal event in much the same fashion as legislators and judges allocate punishments. The formal legal conception of arrest contrasts sharply with this practice by holding that arrest follows upon detection of any criminal act without distinguishing among levels of legal seriousness. Assuming the offender population is aware that arrest represents legislation and adjudication by police officers, arrest practices should contribute to deterrence of serious crime, for the perpetrator whose act is detected risks a greater likelihood of arrest as well as more severe punishment. The higher risk of arrest, once the suspect confronts the police, may help to offset the low probability of detection for some of the more serious crimes.[29]

F. Intimacy

The greater the relational distance between a complainant and a suspect, the greater is the likelihood of arrest. When a complainant demands the arrest of a suspect the police are most apt to comply if the adversaries are strangers. Arrest is less likely if they are friends, neighbors, or acquaintances, and it is least likely if they are family members. Policemen also write official crime reports according to the same differential.[30] Relational distance likewise appears to be a major factor in the probability of litigation in contract disputes[31] and other private-law contexts.[32] One may generalize that in all

---

29. *See* Black, *Production of Crime Rates*, 35 Am. Soc. Rev. 733, 735 (1970) (remarks on detection differentials in police work).

30. Black, *supra* note 29, at 740. Jerome Hall hypothesizes that relational distance influences the probability of criminal prosecution. J. Hall, Theft, Law and Society 318 (2d ed. 1952).

31. Macaulay, *supra* note 27, at 56.

32. For example, in Japan disputes that arise across rather than within communities are more likely to result in litigation. *See* Kawashima, *supra* note 26, at 45. In American chinatowns disputes that arise between Chinese and non-Chinese are far more likely to result in litigation than disputes between Chinese. *See* Grace, *Justice, Chinese Style*, Case & Com., Jan–Feb., 1970, at 50. The same is true of disputes between gypsies and non-gypsies as compared to disputes between gypsies. *See* J. Clebert, *supra* note 23, at 90. Likewise, in the United States in the first half of the 19th century, crimes committed between Indians generally were left to the tribes. *See* F. Prucha, American Indian

legal affairs relational distance between the adversaries affects the probability of formal litigation. If the generalization is true, it teaches that legal control may have comparatively little to do with the maintenance of order between and among intimates.

Yet the findings on relational distance in police arrest practices may merely reflect the fact that legal control operates only when sublegal control is unavailable.[33] The greater the relational distance, the less is the likelihood that sublegal mechanisms of control will operate. This proposition even seems a useful principle for understanding the increasing salience of legal control in social evolution.[34] Over time the drift of history delivers proportionately more and more strangers who need the law to hold them together and apart. Law seems to bespeak an absence of community, and law grows ever more prominent as the dissolution of community proceeds.[35]

G. *Disrespect*

The probability of arrest increases when a suspect is disrespectful toward the police. The same pattern appears in youth officer behavior,[36] patrol officer encounters with juveniles,[37] and in the use of illegal violence by the police.[38] Even disrespectful complainants receive a penalty of sorts from the police, as their complaints are less likely to receive official recognition.[39] In form, disrespect in a police encounter is much the same as "contempt" in a courtroom hearing. It is a rebellion against the processing system. Unlike the judge, however, the policeman has no special legal weapons in his arsenal for dealing with citizens who refuse to defer to his authority at a verbal or otherwise symbolic level. Perhaps as the legal system further differentiates, a crime of "contempt of police" will emerge. From a radically behavioral standpoint, indeed, this crime has already emerged; the question is when it will be formalized in the written law.

POLICY IN THE FORMATIVE YEARS: THE INDIAN TRADE AND INTERCOURSE ACTS 188–212 (1962). In medieval England the same sort of pattern obtained in the legal condition of the Jews. Ordinary English rules applied to legal dealings between Jews and the King and between Jews and Christians, but disputes between Jew and Jew were heard in Jewish tribunals and decided under Jewish law. *See* 1 F. POLLOCK & F. MAITLAND, THE HISTORY OF ENGLISH LAW 468–75 (2d ed. 1898).

33. *See* L. PEATTIE, THE VIEW FROM THE BARRIO 54–62 (1968) (for a stark illustration of this pattern). *See generally* R. POUND, SOCIAL CONTROL THROUGH LAW 18–25 (1942); S. VAN DER SPRENKEL, LEGAL INSTITUTIONS IN MANCHU CHINA: A SOCIOLOGICAL ANALYSIS (1962); Cohen, *Chinese Mediation on the Eve of Modernization*, 54 CALIF. L. REV. 1201 (1966); Nader, *An Analysis of Zapotec Law Cases*, 3 ETHNOLOGY 404 (1964); Nader & Metzger, *Conflict Resolution in Two Mexican Communities*, 65 AM. ANTHROPOLOGIST 584 (1963); Schwartz, *Social Factors in the Development of Legal Control: A Case Study of Two Israeli Settlements*, 63 YALE L.J. 471 (1954); notes 26, 30–31 *supra*.

34. It is at this level that Pound posits his thesis concerning the priority of sublegal control. R. POUND, *supra* note 33, at 33. *See also* Fuller, *Two Principles of Human Association*, 11 NOMOS 3 (1969); Selznick, *Legal Institutions and Social Controls*, 17 VAND. L. REV. 79 (1963).

35. *See* F. TONNIES, COMMUNITY AND SOCIETY 202 (C. Loomis transl. 1957).

36. Piliavin & Briar, *supra* note 14, at 210.

37. Black & Reiss, *Police Control of Juveniles, supra* note 14, at 74–75.

38. P. CHEVIGNY, POLICE POWER: POLICE ABUSES IN NEW YORK CITY 51–83 (1969); Reiss, *Police Brutality—Answers to Key Questions*, TRANS-ACTION, July–Aug., 1968, at 18; Westley, *Violence and the Police*, 59 AM. J. SOC. 34 (1954).

39. Black, *supra* note 29, at 742–44.

All legal control systems, not only the police and the judiciary, defend their own authority with energy and dispatch. To question or assault the legitimacy of a legal control process is to invite legal invocation, a sanction, or a more serious sanction, whatever is at issue in a given confrontation. Law seems to lash out at every revolt against its own integrity. Accordingly, it might be useful to consider disrespect toward a policeman to be a minor form of civil disorder, or revolution the highest form of disrespect.

H. *Discrimination*

No evidence exists to show that the police discriminate on the basis of race. The police arrest blacks at a comparatively high rate, but the difference between the races appears to result primarily from the greater rate at which blacks show disrespect for the police. The behavioral difference thus lies with the citizen participants, not the police.[40] This finding conflicts with some ideological conceptions of police work, but it is supported by the findings of several studies based upon direct observation of the police.[41] These findings should be taken as a caveat that in general improper or illegal behavior toward blacks does not in itself constitute evidence of discrimination toward blacks. A finding of discrimination or of nondiscrimination requires a comparative analysis of behavior toward each race with other variables such as level of respect held constant. No study of citizen opinions or perceptions[42] or of official statistics[43] can hold these variables constant.

In closing this Section it is important to note that the findings on racial discrimination by the police should not remotely suggest that law is oblivious to social rank. On the contrary, broader patterns in the form and substance of legal control seem at any one time to reflect and to perpetuate existing systems of social stratification. That the degradation of arrest is

---

40. Of course, "discrimination" can be defined to include any *de facto* unequal treatment, regardless of its causes. *See* L. MAYHEW, LAW AND EQUAL OPPORTUNITY 59–60 (1968). The evidence in the Article simply indicates that blacks are treated differently not because they are blacks, but because they manifest other behavioral patterns, such as disrespect for the police, more frequently than whites. The question of why blacks disproportionately show disrespect for the police cannot be addressed with the observational data. We could speculate, for example, that in anticipation of harsh treatment blacks often behave disrespectfully toward the police, thereby setting in motion a pattern that confirms their expectations.

Despite the Article's finding of nondiscrimination the police officers observed did reveal considerable prejudice in their attitudes toward blacks. *See generally* Black & Reiss, *Patterns of Behavior in Police and Citizen Transactions,* in 2 PRESIDENT'S COMMISSION ON LAW ENFORCEMENT AND ADMINISTRATION OF JUSTICE, STUDIES IN CRIME AND LAW ENFORCEMENT IN MAJOR METROPOLITAN AREAS 132–39. *See also* Deutscher, *Words and Deeds: Social Science and Social Policy,* 13 SOCIAL PROBLEMS 235 (1966).

41. *See generally* W. LAFAVE, *supra* note 7; J. SKOLNICK, *supra* note 14, at 83–88; L. TIFFANY, D. McINTYRE, & D. ROTENBERG, *supra* note 14; Piliavin & Briar, *supra* note 14 (despite innuendos to the contrary); Project, *supra* note 14, at 1645, n.9. These studies do not report evidence of discrimination or fail altogether to mention race as an analytically important variable.

42. *E.g.,* Werthman & Piliavin, *Gang Members and the Police,* in THE POLICE: SIX SOCIOLOGICAL ESSAYS 56 (D. Bordua ed. 1967).

43. *See* N. GOLDMAN, *supra* note 14, at 45; J. WILSON, *supra* note 14, at 113; Green, *supra* note 14, at 481.

Law and Society

reserved primarily for the kinds of illegality committed by lower status citizens exemplifies this broader tendency of the law in action.

VI. CONCLUDING REMARKS

A major commitment of this Article is to dislodge the discussion from its grounding in empirical findings and to raise the degree of abstraction to the level of general theory. Statements at this level ignore the boundaries and distinctions that ordinarily contain and constrain generalization about law as a social phenomenon. The various subsystems of law—criminal law, torts, contracts, constitutional law, family law, property law, criminal procedure, administrative law—are assumed to contain common elements. As if this aim were too faint-hearted, a general theory of legal control also seeks to discover patterns present in several functional dimensions of law: prescription, mobilization, and disposition; or, respectively, the articulation of legal policy, the engagement of legal cases by legal organizations, and the situational resolution of legal disputes. This sort of sociology of law shares with jurisprudence the inclusiveness of its subject matter. Each discipline acts upon a longing for a universal understanding of law. For each, the past shares the relevance of the present, and other legal systems illustrate our own. Unlike jurisprudence, however, sociology of law abjures problems of a normative character; unlike sociology of law, jurisprudence bypasses the ordeal of concrete description.

A closing note should state what the Article has not done. Arrest might be examined from a number of other perspectives that have their own vocabulary suited to their own special kind of discourse. For example, arrest may usefully be conceived as one stage in an elaborate processing network, an assembly line of inputs and outputs. This technocratic metaphor has been popular in recent studies of the criminal justice system. Another perspective might see every arrest as a political event. When and how the arrest power is used says much about the nature of a political system and the quality of life within it. Then, too, arrest is part of a job. It is a role performance of a bureaucratic functionary. Police work may be contemplated as it arises from its rich occupational subculture with standards and values that policemen share and enforce among their peers. And every arrest is enveloped by the police bureaucracy. Not surprisingly, therefore, the arrest practices of individual officers are under some degree of surveillance from their superiors as well as their peers. Finally, a study of arrest can inform and benefit from the sociology of face-to-face interaction. The police encounter is a small group with its own morphology, its own dynamics. What happens in an encounter may have less to do with crime and law than with the demands of situational order, with social etiquette or the pressures of group size or spatial configuration. An arrest may be the only means available to a policeman bent on restoring order to a field situation, yet other times it is the surest way to undermine order by making a situation disintegrate.

Some encouragement may be taken from the development of social science to the point where a subject such as arrest can occasion so many diverse perspectives. Diversity of this degree, nevertheless, casts a film of arbitrariness over whatever theoretical framework is chosen. Although the many perspectives available to a study of arrest surely mirror the empirical nature of arrest itself, its theoretical identity is precarious and unstable. Here it is sanction and justice; there input, coercion, expectation, job, criterion, or gesture. Any single theoretical view of arrest is inevitably incomplete.

Part III
Law and the Production
of Social Understandings

[12]

Some Social Functions of Legislation

by Vilhelm Aubert*)

There are not many studies available which deal empirically and in detail with the influence of a particular piece of legislation upon the audience to which it adresses itself. Rather than attempting to summarize the results of these few studies, I shall present more fully the results of one such case study, which deals with the Norwegian Law on Housemaids. Its representativity may be doubted. The topic chosen belongs to the periphery of labor-legislation, and concerns an area of life which presents some unique aspects. Nevertheless, the study may well serve to illustrate the mechanisms involved in the legal influence process.

The report will deal with three problems. First it will present material on the extent to which the manifest functions of the Law have been fulfilled. Secondly, and almost inseparably from this, it will be demonstrated how the successful achievement of the goals of the legislators depends upon the operation of factors outside the Law itself. Finally, it will be shown how the Law, apparently unsuccessful in achieving many of its manifest functions, may have been influenced by latent functions. The term function is used rather loosely, and can mostly be replaced by terms like cause, effect and motive. The functionalist terminology has been retained primarily because the distinction between manifest and latent seems to be obviously useful in this particular kind of analysis, where goals are so clearly and authoritatively stated in the Parliamentary records of the legislative debate.

The manifest functions of the Housemaid Law.

The Law on Housemaids was issued in 1948, but with the proviso that it was to be revised in a few years. With some revisions it is still in force. The Law has a long and tortuous pre-history, which suggest that the field of domestic service is one beset with conflicts from the legislator's point of view. Until the middle of the last century the relationship between the employer and domestic help was regulated by a general Law of Servants. This law was written from the point of view of the employer, stipulating a duty to seek service for the members of the rural landless classes. It established a paternalistic and diffuse relationship between the Master and the Servant, entitling the employer to make any demand upon the servant from which he was not specifically exempt by law. No complementary protection of the servant's interests was guaranteed by the law, but followed to some extent from ingrained customs.

The Law of Servants was gradually abolished as a consequence of a general liberalistic trend in the thinking of the legal authorities. Full freedom of contract reigned in this area from the end of the 19th century until 1948. In the meantime several proposals for new legislation were presented, but did not reach Parliament in the form of a bill. Some of these proposals aimed at protection of the employer's interests, by attempting to provide an ample, qualified and obedient supply of domestic servants. Other proposals were in line with the general trend in labor legislation, attempting to set up obligatory minimum standards to protect the interests of the housemaids. A committee was set up in 1936 to prepare a law. It had a survey conducted on the working conditions of housemaids in Norway, the results of which can to some extent be compared with those from the study we conducted in 1950.

The purpose of the Law of 1948 is simple and onesided. It gives rules to protect the interests of the housemaid. Workinghours are limited to 10 hours a day, including time for meals. Over-time is clearly defined, and a minimum payment for over-time service is stipulated. Over-time beyond a certain number of hours per week is prohibited. The housemaid can demand a written contract and payment every other week. She can demand one free afternoon a week and every other Sunday. Notice terminating employment must be given 2 weeks in advance. Wage-levels remain unregulated, and vacation-regulation follows from another general Law on Vacations. There are some other clauses in the Law which need not concern us here. The law limits the freedom to agree contractually to set the law aside.

The first aim of the empirical study of the impact of the Law on Housemaids, was simply to establish the extent to which behavior conformed to the rules laid down in the Law. A probability sample of 218 housewives and 221 housemaids in Oslo, drawn mostly in pairs, were interviewed on their behavior, information, attitudes and motives in so far as they had a bearing upon the content of the Law on Housemaids. The results with respect to behavior are easily summarized: not more than one tenth of the sampled relationships showed complete conformity to the demands of the Law. Many deviations are of minor importance, however. But the main rule embodied in the law, the 10-hour working day, was set aside in approximately half of the 233 households. In a considerable number of cases the violation was of great magnitude. Most other rules of the Law were likewise frequently violated, although considerable variations occur between the clauses.

The immediate impression of the data is that the law is far from established practice, with the exception of a few rules where behavior is remarkably in conformity. Before we proceed to investigate the causes of conformity and deviance, the influence process itself, some attention must be paid to the clustering of deviance. It would make a difference, although not in strictly legal terms, if the deviations were well distributed, in the sense that violations in one area were compensated by strict obedience or overfulfillment of demands in other areas. Likewise, we must raise the question of whether violations of the established rules might not be compensated by higher wages. If this were the case, the housemaid might see her own interests taken best care of through an agreement which was not in full conformity with the law.

The tendency is for deviations to cluster in a group of households. Occurrence of one type of violation, generally increases the likelihood of other offenses as well. The more frequent the violations, and the greater the magnitude of these, the lower the pay, although households exist in which strenuous and illegal working conditions are compensated by high wages. The high frequencies of households in the high index marginal cells, must be interpreted as a tentative expression of the clustering of violations. Thus, it would be hard to claim that the offenses against the law in general were of such an insignificant magnitude that the lack of strict conformity is without interest. In a large number of cases it is obvious that the working-conditions belong to precisely that category which the legislators aimed to get rid of, and which many of them thought had disappeared long ago.

Sumner claimed in his pioneer study of social norms, that legislation had little or no independent influence upon behavior. But he did not deny that laws were abided by. If they were, it was because they corresponded to, possibly originated in, and were at least supported by the already existing mores. Sumner ascribed little reformatory influence to laws, however. "Vain attempts have been made to control the new order by legislation. The only result is the proof that legislation cannot make mores".[1]) At first glance this seems to be a very adequate summary of the above data, irrespective of the general validity of Sumner's theory. Extensive deviance from the rules of a law is, however, no proof that the law has been without influence. Neither is conformity to rules certain evidence that it has been effective.

In order to measure the effective influence of a law it is necessary to study the variables which intervene between the promulgation of the law and the behavior. One of the most important of these variables is the level of information among the recipients of the legal communication. Thus, various measures of the level of information among housewives and housemaids were collected in the survey.

Some of these refer to the amount of acquaintance with the law itself, while others refer to perceptions of norms, irrespective of their source.

The first, preliminary and open, question which gave an occasion for referring to the Housemaid Law, without explicitly mentioning it, elicited little response. It seemed that there must have been few respondents for whom the new Law played an important and salient part in their daily lives. A question which explicitly directed the attention of the respondents to possible recent changes in the working-conditions of housemaids, and asked for the causes of such change, gave the result that only 3 housewives and 3 housemaids mentioned the law. But as soon as the Housemaid Law was mentioned by the interviewer, 80 % of the housemaids and 81 % of the housewives claimed to have at least heard about the law. Although less than one fifth of the respondents were completely unfamiliar with the Law, 36 % of the housemaids and 26 % of the housewives were unable to mention a single clause in the law. Most of the others mentioned only one area regulated by the law. The 10-hour working day seems to have been the most publicized and most widely known part of the new law.

Table 1 shows how perceptions of norms are distributed among the areas regulated by the Housemaid Law, and with respect to two areas unregulated by the law. In these measures of level of information, no attention has been paid to the sources of information, that is to say, whether it is derived from the law itself, from customs or from personal attitudes and experiences.

There are wide variations in the degree to which the norms underwritten by the law have penetrated individual perceptions. If we disregard the two non-existent rules (on wages and education), the norms fall into two relatively distinct classes. A fair amount of information exist with respect to the norms regulating termination of hire, days off and vacations. But the norms on the length of working-hours, and especially on overtime and periods of wage payment, seem to be

Tabel 1. *The percentage of housemaids and housewives who possess some knowledge about the different clauses of the law.*

Clause	Housemaids	Housewives
Termination of hire	83	76
Days off	76	73
Vacation	76	70
Education (non-existent)	57	71
Wages (non-existent)	48	60
Length of working hours	34	33
Periods of wage payment	23	21
Pay for overtime work	16	25
Extension of overtime work	7	8

"law in books" rather than "law in action". The gap between the two sets of rules must be interpreted in the light of Sumner's hypothesis. The rules which are fairly well-known, happen to be those where the law (on Housemaids or on Vacations) corresponds to existing customs. The other, less known rules, are those where the Law on Housemaids has a more indubitable reformatory function, and lacks sanction in available customs.

Nothing is yet proved with respect to the relative effectiveness of law and custom as far as behavior goes. Unfortunately, we have no information on actual practice with respect to the termination of hire. But as far as days off and vacations go, it seems that the great majority abide by the crucial aspects of the clauses, while the frequent deviations concern details. Tentatively, it may be claimed that customs resigned strongly in the particular area of life under scrutiny here. But it is to be noted, of course, that the survey was conducted only 2 years after the law had been issued. On one point, we find an established practice, contrary to the law, but obviously corresponding to an older custom, namely with respect to the periodic payment of wages.

How can we further test the hypothesis that perceptions of norms derive more from customs than from laws? Obviously by correlating perception of norms to acquaintance with the law. Figure 2 shows that correct perception of norms is closely dependent upon the respondent's degree of contact with the law. Those who have read the law are more frequently aware of the norms in question than those who have only heard about the law, while those who have not even heard about it, are even less aware of the valid norms.

These relationships between contact with the law and perception of norms, are not equally strong with respect to all rules. A great many persons, even those who have not heard of the Housemaid Law, perceive quite correctly the norms regulating termination of hire, days off and vacations. These are precisely the norms which have a strong foundation in available customs, and which for that reason enjoy widespread awareness and support. When we come to the norms on hours of work, overtime and periodic payment of wages, the amount of contact with the law makes a very great difference to the perception of norms. Some contract with the text of the law seems almost to be a prerequisite of correct perception of norms, which would follow from the assumption that these clauses lack support in old customs and attempt to reform the state of affairs.

Table 2 goes contrary to Sumner's hypothesis, however, in another respect. Although the respondents were relatively unaware of the norms of the new law in so far as it has a reformative function, the few who did known the norms were people who had some contact with the law. The evidence is not decisive, however, that the law is the source of their correct perception of the norms. The relationship may to some extent depend upon a common dependence on a third

Table 2. *The percentage of housemaids and housewives who possess some knowledge about the content of the rules, distributed, accoring to whether they have read the law, heard about the law, or not even heard about it.*

Clause	Housewives			Housemaids		
	Read law	Heard about law	Not heard about law	Read law	Heard about law	Not heard about law
Termination of hire	82	86	76	83	82	57
Days off	87	79	61	91	74	54
Vacation	80	85	70	88	74	46
Length of working hours ..	67	35	5	56	31	14
Periods of wage payment ..	36	25	12	46	17	8
Pay for overtime work	26	17	5	39	23	11
Extension of overtime work	28	3	0	26	4	0

and independently operating factor. It may be that those who have read the Law, and have at least heard about it, belong to groups which for reasons unconnected with the law, practice norms similar to those stipulated by the Housemaid Law.

Of the several factors which might be suspected of influencing practice, norms and acquaintance with the law, age appears to be the most important. With respect to actual behaviour the difference between the age groups is a significant among housemaids, but insignificant among housewives. The tendency is consistently in favour of the younger housemaids, with the exception of the very youngest who may not yet have realized their scarcity value, and who are used to the diffuse unprofessional working conditions in a rural household. The housewives become more prone to violate the law as they move up on the age scale; but the change is very moderate, especially in the light of the distribution of norm perception among the age groups.

A strong and consistent relationship exists between the age of the housewife and her level of legal information. Young housewives have more and better information on legal norms than do the older ones, and the fall in information level with age is gradual. Among the housemaids too, a pattern is discernible, which links level of legal information to age. The very young, below 20, are relatively ignorant compared to those between 20 and 30 who again know more than the older ones. The differences are, however, much smaller and less significant than in the case of the housewives.

A difference between housewives and housemaids with respect to level of information on the law and norms has been discernible in all our data. The housewives are usually better informed than the housemaids. It is not surprising that women of the urban middle or upper middle classes should have easier access to legal material than housemaids with little formal education and most often with little training in handling problems of this kind. Only 2 % of them were organized in the Housemaid's Union, which is generally known to enjoy very limited support. Thus, the housemaids have been without that source of support and information which workers can count on in most other areas of labor legislation.

So far the evidence is rather ambiguous with respect to the answer to the crucial question: has the law influenced behavior to any appreciable degree? We have seen that customs may have been a more important factor in determining behavior and perceived norms than the law itself. But we have also seen that contact with the law relates significantly to perceived norms. But then, again, both these factors are closely related to age, as is also behavior, although less clearly so. The influence of age is tied up with changes between the generations in their general demands and perspectives on proper working conditions, derived from larger economic and social trends. How, then, do actual working conditions correlate with the level of information among housewives and housemaids respectively?

There exists a close significant relationship among housewives between information and index of violations, in the expected direction. Among the housemaids there is rather more than less information in the high-violation households than in the low-violation ones, but the relationship is inconsistent and lacks statistical significance. Analysis of relationships between specific violations and corresponding information is inconclusive. It does not yield statistically significant variations in information between violators and (more or less) non-violators. To what extent the relationship found among housemaids is evidence of a direct influence from the law upon behavior, and to what extent it merely mirrors general differences between the generations, is hard to determine. It seems clear that information on the part of the housemaids has little or no bearing upon the actual working conditions. In general they enjoy the most favorable working conditions and are also best informed, if they belong to the 20–30 age-group, but this must depend upon a third and independent factor. At that age the housemaid is in her prime as domestic help, she has some experience and some notion of her scarcity value. More often than not she will be employed by a relatively young housewife, familiar with the law or at least accustomed to modern views on labour-relationships. Given this constellation of housewife and housemaid, one may find the optimum arrangements from the point of view of the law.

Although it is impossible to reach definitive conclusions on the crucial question of how much influence the law as such has exerted, one is left with a general impression that it must have been modest. The enormous development from 1938 to 1950 can certainly not be ascribed to the law. Rather, the drastic changes in actual working conditions, due to the altered situation on the labour market, general increase in welfare, and changes in philosophy, were among the preconditions of the relatively painless acceptance of the Housemaid Law among all political groups in Parliament.

It has to be concluded that the law was, at least for some years, ineffective in the sense that actual working conditions were very far from the norms laid down, and also in the sense that even conformity to the legal norms was rarely due to influence from the law. Why was it not effective, and why did the Parliament tend to overestimate the effects of the law as well as the current status when the law was issued?

There are some specific circumstances in the case of this piece of legislation which might be expected to create difficulties, without therefore necessarily throwing doubt upon the influence of other laws. The recipients, the audience to which this law directs itself, belong to groups which traditionally have had little connection with laws and with public authorities. They are women who are not organized, and thus lack this intermediary with government. The law concerns an area traditionally assumed to be protected against public inspection and control, the home. The place of work is isolated and very different from factories and offices, and the nature of the work-relationship is for profound reasons intrinsically difficult to regulate. It is an area on the border-line between "work" and "private life", where it is sometimes hard to distinguish between the worker and the (slightly inferior) member of the family.[2] Paternalistic, or maternalistic, relations are traditionally very strong, and continuously supported by the usually pronounced age differential between employer and employee (the average age of housewives was 51, of housemaids 36). Many housemaids are very young, inexperienced and unfamiliar with urban living conditions. They look upon their job as temporary. The turn-over is very high, continuously sapping the occupation of its most experienced members, those who might otherwise also have fought for improvements.

We shall leave these impediments aside, however, and concentrate on two other factors which may have counteracted an effective, or effectively enforced, Law on Housemaids. These two factors are of more general relevance, and they seem linked to latent functions which this law shares with other legislation. The first factor has to do with the language employed in the law, and the second has to do with the relationship between substantive and procedural clauses in the law.

The language of the Law.

Most of the respondents had no intimate acquaintance with the new piece of legislation, and even among those who had, compliance with the requirements of the law was far from complete. Both phenomena might in part be due to the

105

technical aspects of the law as a means of communication, to its terminology. Even a cursory reading of the text of the law leaves an impression that some of the clauses must be heavy going for people with limited experience in handling legal or other written texts of this kind. This may deter them from reading as well as lead to misunderstanding and incomprehension when the laws are being read.

In order to test the degree of comprehensibility of the language employed in the Housemaid Law, an experiment in legal interpretation was conducted in the course of the interview with the housewives and housemaids. The essential meaning of the clause chosen for presentation to the respondents, was that the housemaid may not be kept doing over-time more than 10 times in the course of a month. It was a clause with considerable practical significance, and one where the interests of the two parties frequently contrast sharply. The clause represents an average level of complexity among the clauses of the Law on Housemaids. Two questions of interpretation were put, the first whether the clause meant that the house-maid had a duty to work overtime 10 times a month, if the housewife demanded this, the second whether the housewife was permitted to keep her at work more than 10 times, if the housemaid freely consented to do so.

A fairly large number of respondents gave contradictory or don't know answers, while the meaningful answers were rather evenly distributed among correct and false alternatives, although with a preponderance of correct answers. The con-clusion is inescapable, however, that the law is far from being a reliable source of guidance for this particular type of audience. Pure guess-work or the tossing of a coin would not have yielded results drastically different from those found in the experiment.

The interpretation chosen by the respondent is very closely related to her attitude to how the question of overtime ought to be solved. These attitudes were gathered from separate questions, put before the experimental test was admini-stered. Those who were in favor of a certain way of regulating overtime, usually interpreted the law so that it gave support to their view. This is especially striking with respect to the prohibitory character of the 10 times limit. But it is to be noted that the attitudes of housewives and housemaids differ very little on this point. This corresponds to a general tendency, among housewives as well as among housemaids, to believe that the freedom of contract reigns in their mutual relationships. It may very well be that both parties believe a complete freedom of contract to be in their own interest, although the law builds upon the assump-tion that complete freedom of contract unduly favors the employer.

Although it may be claimed that some of the relationships regulated by the Law on Housemaids are intrinsically complex and difficult to disentangle, there can be little doubt that the legislators did not achieve a maximum of clarity and simplicity in the text under scrutiny. Why not? Is the incomprehensibility of the Housemaid Law simply to be written off as a more or less unsystematic result of a legislative mistake, lack of care, ability and foresight? I do not believe so. The Housemaid Law has, above all, become hard to grasp for an audience of housewives and housemaids, because it is written in a language shaped by an entirely different function. It is written in the same kind of terminology as most laws, a terminalogy which has been sharpened and made precise as a means of communication within the legal profession. It has developed as a means to the goal of resolving legal conflicts through the participation of legally trained personnel.

We are dealing here with a separate function of the law, its part in the processes of influence and communication with reference to the total population of lay people. This was also what the legislators mentioned most often, when the Law on Housemaids was under preparation. Yet it was written in the traditional language which lawyers employ when they want to communicate precise messages to other layers. It was not taken into consideration that this might be an area where lawyers are unlikely to become much involved and where the courts would rarely, if ever, be asked to give an opinion. At the time of the study no legal suit originating in the Law on Housemaids had been brought to the attention of the courts or of other legal authorities. Thus, the problem of the function of this law is almost wholly concentrated around its influence upon a lay audience, and around its ability to communicate its message to housewives and housemaids without any legally trained intermediaries. In this respect it had, to a large extent, failed without achieving the subsidiary aim of easing conflict resolution before the courts or among legal representatives of contending parties.

There are several reasons why conflict resolution by means of a court procedure is absent in this area. No official machinery, comparable to the Labor Inspectorate in industrial relations exists to chek the working conditions in households and instigate criminal procedure if violations are found. The initiative is left to the housemaid. For the same reasons that housemaids are unlikely to organize and become acquainted with a new law, they are also very little prone to litigation. It is especially to be noted that their best means of sanction, if they are at all aware of being exploited, is to leave their job at short notice and seek new employment, which will not be hard to find. Thus, a legal solution must have appeared to the thoughtful housemaid to be a costly, cumbersome, unpleasant and ineffective way of achieving good working conditions, when realistically compared to available alternatives.

Although conflict-resolution in legal form should foreseeably have presented itself as a remote possibility to the legislators, the Housemaid Law set out to influence working conditions in the home through the application of a terminology developed in areas where conflict-resolution is frequent and legal intervention

107

the order of the day. We shall give one example of the kind of text which appeared reasonable to the legislators, because it corresponded well with traditional patterns, and appeared no more complex than many other statutory clauses.

"Overtime work is to be compensated by time off or by payment in full, in both cases with an addendum of 25 %. In calculating full payment, the value of food and shelter, to which the housemaid is entitled, must be added to the full payment. The value is to be set in conformity with the rates of the internal revenue office pluss 50 %. In this context it is to be assumed that the working hours in a full job amounts to 200 hours per month".[3]

This method of calculation was not applied in a single household about which we possess information. No doubt it is too complicated to be apprehended and too unwieldy in use. The corresponding clause in the bill was even more complicated, stipulating that the percentage increment should increase during the evening. The Parliamentary Committee on Social Affairs found that a system based upon graduated percentage rates for the various time intervals would be cumbersome to practice and added: "It is of great importance that the minimum requirements of the law should be simple and easy to practice".[4]

Presumably the committee found that the formulation of clause 11, which it suggested, fulfills the requirement of simplicity. Such a conception can only be explained on the basis of the persistence of traditional patterns of legislation. Clause 11 fits nicely into established legislative terminology and juridical style, and it is not more complicated than many other, highly effective, legal rules. Its uselesness in practice is due to the fact that it has to serve as guidance for a class of people who are entirely different from those reached by most laws. This is in practice a law for lay people, not for lawyers. Because they are shaped by the traditional function of facilitating precise communication within the legal profession, many clauses of the housemaid law are unable to fulfil the more pressing function of communicating to housewives and housemaids. A social mechanism which has achieved its form when fulfilling one function, remains unaltered when faced with an entirely different function, and fails correspondingly.

Legislation and group conflicts.

The inaccessibility of the terminology is an impediment to the effective functioning of the Law. So is the weak development of an enforcement machinery and the vagueness of the sanctions which can be invoked against violations. In two respects the procedural rules differ from what is commonly the case in the area of labor legislation. The penal clause has a conditional form, and no inspectorate is set up charged with independent initiative in supervising obedience to the law. The penal clause (18) states that there is "a penalty of fines for those who repeatedly in spite of protests keep their housemaid at work contrary to the rules of this law". It is, furthermore, up to the plaintiff to forward charges of violation.

The penal clause in the Housemaid Law is probably unique in making *repeated* violation, *in spite of protest* from the victim, a condition for sanctions. Areas of life may exist where such a penal clause would still have some force. But in this area it is quite clear that a housemaid who is dissatisfied with her working conditions, and aware of this deviance from the law, will leave her job and seek more satisfactory employment. She will not vainly protest and then instigate cumbersome legal procedures, which would in the end make a continued work relationship intolerable anyway. It is hard to believe that the legislators can have been completely unaware of this state of affairs.

Without a public agency charged with supervision, such a penal clause must become ineffective. In many areas of the law it is, of course, common to leave it to private initiative to instigate legal suits, but not within labour law and other areas of social legislation. Here it is usually left to a public agency to supervise the obedience to the law and to take action against violation. There are several reasons why the legislators do not leave enforcement in these areas to private initiative alone. It may, in part, be due to the fact that these laws frequently aim at the introduction of new habits and modes of thinking, thus making deviance more likely than in areas where the law corresponds to customs and traditional moral conventions. Another reason why public agencies have been set up to supervise the legal enforcement, is that the people protected by the law are often assumed to lack personal independence, and the intellectual or financial qualifications to defend their own rights effectively. These reasons are fully present in the case of the housemaids. The legislators were completely aware of this. Why did they, nevertheless, formulate such a hybrid system of enforcement and sanction?

The answer must be sought in the analysis of a function of legislation which is unrelated to the process of communicating norms and achieving conformity with these in a certain category of the population. This function relates to the need for compromise in the legislative assembly, turning legislative form into a means for resolving or ameliorating group-conflicts. In many cases this corresponds closely to a function which Thurman Arnold formulated thus: "It is part of the function of Law to give recognition to ideals representing the exact opposite of established conduct. Most of its complications arise from the necessity of pretending to do one thing, while actually doing another."5) What is pretended in the penal clause of the Housemaid Law is that effective enforcement of the law is envisaged. And what the legislature is actually doing, is to see to it that the privacy of the home and the interests of housewives are not ignored.

The ambivalence and the conflicting views of the legislators, as they can be gleaned from the penal clause, appear more clearly in the legislative debate. A curious dualism runs throughout the debates. It was claimed on the one hand, that the law is essentially a codification of customs and established practice, rendering effective enforcement inessential. On the other hand, there was a tendency to claim that the Housemaid Law is an important new piece of labor legislation with a clearly reformatory purpose, attempting to change a not wholly acceptable status quo.

One and the same speaker in Parliament might use both kinds of argument on occasion. But there was also a tendency for the Conservatives to lean towards the claim that the Housemaid Law is nothing but a codification of established practice, while the Left would more frequently claim a reformatory function for the Law. Both types of argument may convince a different clientèle. The crucial point here is the remarkable ease with which such apparently contradictory claims were suffused in one and the same legislative action, which in the end received unanimuous support from all political groups. It is also remarkable how references to facts or probable facts could go contrary to available evidence. It suggests that the legislator on occasion moves within a social reality very narrowly circumscribed by his political duties to party ideology and electorate, not to scientific truth.

In some cases it was, no doubt, realistic to claim that the law would in fact do no more than give legal sanction to what was being practised on the basis of custom and convenience. In other cases, however, the reference to practice seems to represent an attempt to draw upon the prestige attached to the status quo, as a means of engineering change. The Departmental Housemaid Committee declared that the main rule establishing a 10 hour working day had already become established practice. They based this assumption upon the statistic from 1938. The conclusion was arrived at by subtracting more than two hours from the gross work hours, based upon some very inaccurate statements in the questionnaires about pause in the work. There can be little doubt that these inferences were wrong, and obviously so. They were arrived at because the housemaid committee wanted to establish a 10 hour working day. It seems unlikely, considering the general 8 hour rule in labor law, that longer hours would have been politically feasible at the time, although it represented a break with the past. The most respectable and the least controversial argument in favor of the rules was, however, the claim that it did on the whole correspond to established practice, and would only affect the exceptional cases which were in real need of reform.

10 years passed between the time when the committee report was completed and the final legislative debate. In the bill as well as in Parliament many voiced the opinion that the scarcity of housemaids in the meantime had led to considerable change in housemaids' working conditions. By and large the legislators seem to have assumed that they were already in conformity with the proposed law. Ac-

cording to the bill the law would not give much protection to those housemaids "who do not themselves have the ability to demand and have enforced reasonable working conditions". For the rest it will "prevent that the conditions with respect to work hours etc. becoming less favorable than is stipulated in the law, in case the opportunities for work once more decline and the competition for housemaids is transformed into a competition for jobs".

Many statements in the Parliamentary Record accord with this. The spokesman for the Law, R. Seweriin (Labor) said: "In many respects the law which is to be issued, merely corroborates established practice." The Minister of Social Affairs, Aasland (Labor) said that ". . . what the Odelsting (Lower House) does today is primarily to codify already established valid law". This opinion was voiced even more strongly by a conservative representative, Thorén: "Today the housemaids may demand the wages they like, and the conditions which are established in the law, the 8 hour day etc. is only what they already have". Liv Tomter (labour) who had served on the Housemaid Committee espoused the hypothese that the proposals of the committee had already born fruit: "We noticed already then (in 1940) that our proposal had a great effect to the advantage of the majority of housemaids in Norway. Thus, the decision to be made here today involves scarcely more than to get practice formalized so that no one shall evade the law".

In the bill of prolongation of the law it is assumed that the working conditions of housemaids are to a large extent better than the minimum standards set by the law. After a mention of the scarcity of housemaids, it is claimed that: "Under these conditions it will, as a rule, not be difficult for the individual housemaid to obtain an arrangement which is more advantageous to her than that established by the housemaid law". In the Parliamentary debate Bondevik (Christian Democrat) claimed that the country was in the midst of a serious crisis because it was so difficult to get domestic help. The Housemaid Law "had made the working conditions and payment much better for the housemaid than previously", he said, and added that "the housemaid may today make almost any demands she may wish to". Under these circumstances only the very wealthy could get domestic servants: "Room with radio and various other luxuries are offered, and wages are so high that an ordinary family cannot afford to hire the needed help. If the family is big, with small children, practically no housemaid will even consider such a job". The speaker saw this development as "a threat to society itself".

The factual premises of all these statements accord poorly with the information gathered in the survey. But it may have been a convenient argument for all concerned. Those who were especially eager to have the law accepted, may have considered a reference to established practice as the most efficient means of influence. For those representatives in Parliament whose identification lies primarily with the housewife, other motives may have led in the same direction. They wanted to express concern for their own interest group, give recognition to its problems, and acclaim it for its responsibilty and non-exploitative behavior. Feeling unable to oppose the law, they felt, possibly, a need to disavow any willingness to revolutionize or change the status quo. They saw a way of reconciling their social consciousness with conservative caution.

At the same time as the legislators referred to established practice as a useful norm, many of them put great emphasis upon the considerable social consequences that would accrue from the law. First of all, a great many claims were made with respect to the achievements of individual clauses in the law. In addition to these, the Parliamentary records also comprise many general statements concerning the consequences of the law. Some emphasize the importance of more certainty and predictability in the work relationships, that the parties know what to expect of each other. Others pointed to an expected increase in the social esteem accorded to housemaids, while still others believed that the law would tend to increase the supply of labor for domestic service.

Most of these statements seem too optimistic in view of our findings. It is not easy to say whether the predictions were more optimistic than may have appeared reasonable at the time, without access to information on the future. But the logical contradiction between this kind of argument and the one to the effect that the law codifies established practice, is undeniable. This contradiction supports the notion that legislative action takes place in an atmosphere of political conflict, and the arguments may have served as a means of ameliorating such conflicts.

Through the place accorded to the status quo arguments as well as the reform arguments, both the housewives and the housemaids got their share of recognition. Symbolically at least Parliament accepted the views of both parties or of their political protagonists, and achieved a "solution" around which everybody might rally. The formulations in the debates served the function of restoring peace and harmony in a situation where opposing interests might tear politicians and others apart.

This function is most apparent in the penal clause of the law, which obviously aims at satisfying both parties. In the Parliamentary records one can find many remarks on the enforcement problem. They are characterized by a considerable amount of ambivalence and inconsistency. In the proposal of the committee, as well as in the bill concern is expressed that the rules to protect the life and health of the domestic help, will not be as effectively enforced as those in the Labor legislation, due to a lack of control in the home. This reserved view is aslo expressed with respect to the clause on work hours: "One must, however, be aware that a strictly legal regulation of the housemaid's work hours in private homes, will be weak in practice, because these rules lack support in a system of public inspection". The committee proposal states: "It will weaken the law a great deal, if no official agency is established to supervise its enforcement. The law is first of all a law of protection for the housemaid. She is the one interested in its effective enforcement. If she were to seek legal aid whenever she has complaints to make, it would certainly imply a significant weakening of the law."

At a later stage in the preparation of the law these arguments were encountered by the argument that any outside interference would aggravate the relationship between the parties. Thus it was found inadvisable to establish a separate agency charged with conflict-resolution, mediation and advise under this particular law. The compromise solution incorporated in the law leaves it to the general Labor Inspectorate to give advise and disseminate information suited to improve the conditions of housemaids. This clause has remained largely ineffective, although statistics show that quite a few housewises sought information about the working conditions of housemaids during the year 1949, although mostly about vacations, which is not regulated in the Housemaid Law, but in the general Law on Vacations.

The bill states that the lack of public inspection and the necessity of relying exclusively on the reports of the parties "render the penal clause less effective than the similar clause in the Law of Labor Protection." Nevertheless it continues with an argument in favor of including penalties: "It is clear, however, that the rules of the Law will have a weak influence upon practice unless they are supported by penalties. The Department has therefore found it necessary to propose a clause of penalties". The legislators seem to have thought that it would be difficult to enforce the Housemaid Law through penalties, at the same time as they found it even less likely to achieve the goals of the law without sanctions.

The peculiar and unique compromise formulation of the penalty clause can only be understood as a resultant of two contradictory forces. On the one hand, the legislators wanted to demonstrate their serious intent in issuing this law. Traditionally this is done by the threat of sanction, by putting "teeth into the law". This must have appeared especially pertinent to those amongst them who made some claims for the reformatory function of the law, and who took it upon themselves to represent the housemaid's point of view. The other side got its share, however, by the obvious inefficiency of the penalty clause, and the utter improbability that it would ever be applied. Thus, the privacy of the home and the interests of the housewife, would in practice be protected, although in principle, on paper, exposed to a slight threat. The substantive law goes wholly in favor of the housemaids, while the procedural norms protect the housewives. The idea of Law Enforcement is upheld, while made ineffective in practice.

The follow-up study of the Housemaid Law.

It might be claimed that the results of the 1950 study would have been very different, if the interval had been longer between the promulgation of the law and the survey. It may very well be that it takes some time before a law of this kind is abided by effectively. To this it may be retorted that a law has more chance of becoming known at the time it is issued, since there will be more debate and publicity then than later. The only way to find out is, of course, to conduct surveys at various times, just after the law has been issued as well as some years later.

An occasion arose to test these contrasting hypotheses with respect to the effects of the Housemaid Law. In 1954 a new legislative committee was appointed with the mandate to reconsider the Housmaid Law, and if necessary recommend amendments to the law. One of the collaborators in the first survey (Eckhoff) was appointed chairman of the committee, and started to prepare a new survey modelled by and large upon the first one. In 1956 the study was conducted not only in Oslo, but also in the three other major cities in Norway, Bergen, Trondheim, and Stavanger. The housewives and housemaids in 528 households were interviewed, 356 of these in Oslo. The 356 households in 1956 are comparable with the 233 in 1950.

During the last 30 years great changes have taken place in the size of the housemaid population, in the country as a whole as well as in the capital. In 1930 there were 120.000 women employed as domestic help in Norway. In 1946 there were 81.000 housemaids, in 1950 there were 50.000. In the 1950's the gradual decline continued, so that in 1962 there were only 19.000 women employed as domestic help. In Oslo in 1938 there were 11.000 housemaids, in 1950 there were 5–6.000 and in 1962 the number was 2.000.

It is indeed a phenomenon which must arouse sociological curiosity that a social group which appears to be so definitely on its way out, should receive so much legislative attention in its final stage, after having had to fend for its interests without legislative support at the time when it constituted a very important part of the working population. It may possibly be explained by a belief that legislation can restore the group to life, by securing for it a new status. It may also be an example of how legislation sometimes serves as an escape into fantasy, magically recreating a situation where the supply of domestic help is plentiful. In a certain sense the absence of housemaids must be more sharply and widely felt today than ever before. There are many more people capable of paying for aids to the comfort of their homes (although few are able to provide for a full-time housemaid); and there are many more gainfully employed women in the middle classes, whose very style of life is related to the assistance of domestic help.

This intensive legislative attention to a small and dwindling group of the population reminds one of a study of the serious legislative concern of the colonial administration with an apparently non-existent group of "leopard-men" in West Africa. If a certain category of roles is needed in a social system, it may be created in fantasy, and for widely divergent reasons. Even the law may participate in this. Law may on occasion move in the sphere of symbolism and magic rather than in the everyday sphere of practical solutions to practical problems.

The continuous and continuing decline of the housemaid as an occupational category also appear in the changing age distribution. The present distribution of age seems to be a result of two tendencies. On the one hand there is a sharp decline in the supply of young recruits. And it must be assumed that most house-maids have entered the occupation at an early age. The drop we find from age group 20–30 to 30–40 is, however, nothing new. There has always been a strong tendency for young housemaids to get married or to find other employment some time in their 20's. The relative and strong increase in size from 30–40 to 40 plus is, however, a recent phenomenon, and it is probably a temporary situation. Most likely it is caused by the normal tendency to drop out somewhere around the age of 30, combined with the emergence in the 40 plus group of the remnants from the period before the war, when the supply of young housemaids was much greater than in succeeding generations. The survey of 1956 revealed that 77 % of the housemaids over 50 had spent 20 years or more in their occupation, that is to say they had been employed before 1936. Of those 40–50, 65 % had been employed before 1936.

The great decline in the number of housemaids after 1950 shows that the Law on Housemaids was unsuccessful in so far as the legislators intended it as a means of improving the status of housemaids so as to make the occupation more attractive. It is, of course, possible that the situation would have deteriorated even more rapidly without the law. But it seems that the law has had little effect upon the supply of domestic help at all.

A comparison of the actual working conditions in the 1950 households with those in the 1956 households should yield information on the effectiveness of the law in terms of its most immediate purpose of creating conformity with the established legal norms. By and large the changes have been very modest between 1950 and 1956. In about half of the households investigated in 1956 the house-maid worked longer than the prescribed 10 hours. Less than 40 % of those who had a claim upon remuneration for overtime work, received such remuneration. Even if they did, the amount paid was too low. No more than 10–15 % of the households exhibited complete conformity to the norms of the law on this point. Relatively few, however, violated the clause which prohibited more than 10 times overtime service in a month. The clause on regular days off was violated by 20–25 %.

It seems safe to conclude from these data that the law has not, through its continued operation during 6 more years, managed to change the distribution of working conditions within the housemaid population very much. As we soon shall see, however, this is not identical with saying that the law has had no effect, or no added effect due to its lenght of operation. It might, on the other hand, be claimed that the slight changes towards closer conformity with the law are due, not to the law, but to the market situation. The dwindling number of housemaids means, of course, that those who remain are increasingly in demand, and should also increasingly be able to set their own conditions. Against this it might possibly be maintained that those who remain in the occupation are increasingly unqualified to look after their own interests in a rational and efficient way.

There is some evidence in favor of the last hypothesis. In 1950 there was an observable relationship between working conditions and age, in favor of the younger housemaids and housewives. This relationship is even more clearcut in 1956, among housemaids as well as among housewives.

The age of the housemaid explains a larger part of the observed variations than does the age of the housewife. These findings are important when interpreted in the light of the changing age distribution. The static situation may be the resultant of two forces, rather than the absence of any force at all. If we assume that the law has had some influence, this will have been counteracted in the distribution of work conditions for the occupation as a whole, by the relative increase of old housemaids. Those housemaids who seem, for one reason or another, to be the least amenable to change and influence from the law, have taken on increased weight in the sample as a whole. But it seems likely that the conditions of work have improved somewhat *within each age group.*

Unfortunately, it is not easy to determine the extent to which this depends upon the law and to what extent it depends upon the market situation. It may also be that unfavorable skewness of the most recent sample from the point of view of legal conformity, is but an example of a more general negative selection. The housemaid occupation may accumulate women who are in one sense or another "disqualified" from marrying or from seeking other employment, by age, low intelligence, passivity, origin in very underprivileged groups or in remote and economically backward districts. Such a selection process might outweigh the influence of the law, even if this influence were far from negligible, viewed in islolation.

To penetrate into the possible causal connections between the law and behavior, we must once more consider the spread of information about the law and the knowledge of its norms. The tendency to mention the law in response to the open, preliminary questions, was not different from what was found in 1950. The same is by and large true of the response to the questions about whether the housewife or housemaid had heard about the law, read about it, read the text itself, or actually had the text of the law in her possession. More than 4/5 claimed to have heard about the law, one half to have read it, one fourth to have read the text, while a little more than one tenth possessed the text itself. The last three questions revealed that more housewives than housemaids were acquainted with the law. Also the ability to mention the most important clauses of the law seemed to be approximately the same as it was in 1950, although there were some improvements.

The distribution of legal knowledge between the various age groups was uneven in 1950 and 1956. In both surveys the younger housewives tend to be better acquainted with the law than the older ones. The changes occurring between 1950 and 1956 were small among those below 50, but quite considerable among the older ones, especially in the group above 70. To these groups, whose members have had housemaids for long periods of time, it seems that the passing of time after promulgation of the law has increased the likelihood of knowledge. Among the housemaids we do not find the same clear differentiation between the age groups. Between 1950 and 1956 small changes have occurred. The only statistically significant difference is found in the 30–50 age group with respect to the percentage who had heard about the law.

There is a remarkable correspondence between these results and those obtained in 1950, with respect to the rank order of clauses as well as with respect to the percentage familiar with the content of each clause. The clauses fall once more into two distinct classes, those with support in older customs and those which apparently still lack such support. The amount of correspondence suggests that very little has happened in terms of dissemination of legal information during the past 6 years.

There exists a relationship between actual contact with the law and correctness in perception of legal norms. It is quite clear that perception of norms is closely related to the degree of contact with the law. And it seems probable that the correct perception of norms, especially of the lesser known norms, is caused by contact with the law. Variations seem to be greater between the various degrees of contact with the law among housewives than among housemaids. This corresponds well with many other findings in the 1956 survey as well as in that of 1950.

In 1950 it was found that not only the amount of contact with the law, but also the perception of individual norms, was related to age. This was the case in 1956 as well. For all age groups taken together there are practically no changes, neither for housewives nor for housemaids. If we consider the age groups above 50 among the housewives, and particularly those above 70, there seems, however, to have been some improvement in knowledge. These old housewives are still lagging behind the younger ones, but not to the same extent as in 1950. It does suggest that the law has been able to reach some housewives, given an extended time of operation. But among the housemaids no comparable development can be discerned.

We have found that some dissemination of knowledge has taken place during the years between 1950 and 1956, and that this new information has reached especially that category of employers which in 1950 offered their domestic help the poorest conditions of work. This makes one very curious to see how a new test of the relationship between knowledge and behavior would turn out. This crucial test yielded a rather inconclusive answer in the 1950 study, suggesting that many fairly knowledgable housewives still deviated from the law, while many of those who conformed well were relatively ignorant of the law and its norms. Among the housemaids, knowledge seemed unrelated to the conditions of work obtained.

In 1956 there is a highly significant relationship between knowledge and behavior among the housewives. There is a gradual deterioration of working conditions as one goes from those with much knowledge to those with somewhat less and finally to those with very little knowledge. Among the housemaids the relationship is less clear, although in favor of those with knowledge. Their chances of avoiding the worst working conditions seem unrelated to knowledge, while the chance of obtaining the best conditions does depend upon the amount of their knowledge, and especially upon not falling in the most ignorant group.

A comparison of the conditions of work in 1950 and 1956 gave the immediate impression that nothing much had happened, that the law could not have had much influence in the past 6 years. A consideration of the unfavourable age shifting leads, however, to a suspension of judgment, since the impact of the law might have been counteracted by a negative selection of housewives and housemaids. We seem now very close to the conclusion that something has indeed happened during the 6 years under scrutiny, making the law more efficient in 1956 than it was in 1950. We have found that the old, and now rather numerous, housewives know more of the law than they did in 1950. And it has been demonstrated that knowledge of the law is significantly related to actual behavior, while this was dubious in 1950.

Before any conclusion is drawn and any further explanation of change is attempted, a possible source of error should be investigated. The correlation might not express a causal relationship between knowledge and behavior. Both might be a function of a third, independent variable. If such a variable is operating, the most likely supposition would be that it was somehow associated with age, since behavior as well as knowledge is related to age. If the housewives age is kept constant and the variation in behavior between the more and less knowledgeable is studied separately for each age group, the differences between the various levels of knowledge with respect to behavior are actually diminished. But the difference does not disappear. And among the housemaids the difference is as clear within each age group as for the sample as a whole.

It seems reasonable to conclude that factors which operate independently of the law may account for some of the relationship found between knowledge and behavior on the housewives' side. But it does not account for all of it. In the group of old housewives we still find a significant relationship between knowledge and actual working conditions, the magnitude of the difference being scarcely less than for the sample as a whole. Among the housemaids we have reason to believe that knowledge of the legal norms does influence the conditions of work obtained, although the influence is modest. There are still fewer housemaids above 40 with good knowledge who achieve good working conditions, than below 40 with little knowledge. And the behavior of housewives below 60 with little knowledge, is still more often in conformity with the law than that of knowledgeable house-wives above 60.

Since it seems reasonable to assume that the law operates more effectively in 1956 than it did 6 years previously, it is necessary to look for an explanation of the change in effectiveness. The nature of the change does not imply that the working conditions have changed much, nor does it imply a vast increase in know-ledge. It is primarily the relationship between knowledge and behavior that has changed. This leads one to assume that whatever it is that has changed, it must be related to motivation to abide by the rules, and the factor must be related to the passsing of time.

One plausible guess seems to be that the law gradually has stimulated a type of communication which is more effective than the reception of mass communi-cated messages. Many studies emphasize the motivation force of *personal influence* as against mass communication. It seems probable that the norms of the House-maid Law are to an increasing degree transmitted by word of mouth among friends, acquaintance and neighbours. The sheer passing of time increases the number of occasions for such personal transmission of information. Thus, what originally was a distant message without much psychological force may gradually have been translated into meaningful personal communication within certain milieus of housewives and housemaids. This may very well be a general process in the ̇semination of legal information and in the strengthening of the motive to by laws. True, it does depend upon the attitude of the opinionleaders, those ̇d at the gate of the informal communication net-works and decide

119

whether a norm emanating from formal authority should be permitted inside and transmitted with explicit or tacit approval. This would not necessarily be the case with all the clauses of the Housemaid Law. But some of its central standards of behavior would probably be acceptable to those who form opinion. Only 8 % of the housewives said they thought the law was no good. This gives support to our hypothesis that the passing of time permits the activation of personal influence, which has a higher degree of effectiveness than the media of mass communication.

NOTES AND REFERENCES:

*) University of Oslo and Institute for Social Research.

The study which forms the basis of this article has been carried out in cooperation with Torstein Eckhoff, Knut Sveri and Per Norseng. Cf. the joint publication, *En lov i søkelyset* (A Law in the Searchlight). Oslo 1952. The follow-up study was conducted by Eckhoff and Sveri and is published in *Instilling til lov om arbeidsvilkår for hushjelp m.fl.* 1960.

1) WILLIAM GRAHAM SUMNER, *Folkways,* Boston 1906, p. 77.

2) Cf. VILHELM AUBERT, *The Housemaid: An Occupational Role in Crisis.* In S. M. Lipset and N. J. Smelser (Ed.), Sociology, The Progress of a Decade. Englewood Cliffs 1961, pp. 414–420.

3) *Midlertidig lov av 3. desember 1948 om arbeidsvilkår for hushjelp.* § 11, 2.

4) *Innst.* O.XIX, 1948.

5) THURMAN W. ARNOLD, *The Symbols of Government.* New Haven 1935, p. 34.

[13]

BRIT. J. CRIMINOL. Vol. 16 No. 1 JANUARY 1976

THE STAGING OF MAGISTRATES' JUSTICE

Pat Carlen (*Uxbridge*)*

METAPHORIC critiques of judicial proceedings have been done by mainly American writers: Garfinkel (1956), Emerson (1967) and Blumberg (1967), for instance, have all used dramaturgical or game imagery in analyses of courtroom interaction. In England, on the other hand the concern has been different, and largely reformative. Analyses of sentencing patterns (Hood, 1962; King, 1972), surveys of the availability of legal aid (Patterson, 1971) and assessment of bailing procedures (Bottomley, 1970; Dell, 1970)—all have contributed to the current concern with improving, mainly by increasing the availability of legal aid, the quality of justice in general and the quality of magistrates' justice in particular.

Difficult though it would be to deny the immense contributions of the aforementioned studies, both the American theorists and the English investigators have tended either to ignore or to take for granted other, equally consequential, dimensions of socio-legal control: the coercive structures of dread, awe and uncertainty depicted by Camus and Kafka; the coercive structures of resentment, frustration and absurdity depicted by Lewis Carroll and N. F. Simpson. That the masterly descriptions of a Kafka or a Camus are unlikely to be bettered by sociologists is obvious. The idea, however, that such surrealism and psychic coercion properly belong to the world of the French novel, rather than to the local magistrates' court in the High Street, is erroneous. In this paper, based on two years' observation of the Metropolitan magistrates' courts, I shall argue that the staging of magistrates' justice in itself infuses the proceedings with a surrealism which atrophies defendants' ability to participate in them.

The Magistrates' Court as a Theatre of the Absurd

Traditionally and situationally, judicial proceedings are dramatic. Aristotle noted the importance of forensic oratory as a special device of legal rhetoric; playwrights as diverse as Shakespeare and Shaw appreciated the dramatic value of a trial scene; lawyers have always been cognisant of rhetorical presentations.

In 1950, nine years before Goffman's *The Presentation of Self in Everyday Life*, a lawyer, Jerome Frank, discussed the conventional ascription of character which occurs in law courts and which is dependent upon the tacit dimensions of interpersonal knowledge. Such analyses are nowadays the familiar stuff of the dramaturgical perspectives in sociology. Yet people do not only ascribe character to each other. Furniture, stage-props, scenic devices, tacit scheduling programmes, etiquettes of ritual address and reference—in short, all the paraphernalia of social occasions—are, both immediately and documentarily, indexed with consequential social meanings (Mannheim, 1952; Schutz,

*Department of Sociology, Brunel University.

THE STAGING OF MAGISTRATES' JUSTICE

1970). These meanings can be set up as being either mundane (*i.e.* constitutive of and reflecting everyday realities) or puzzling (*i.e.* constitutive of and reflecting alternative realities) or, less often, as being both mundane and puzzling (*i.e.* surrealistic). In hierarchically organised social institutions, however, certain people can monopolise and manipulate the scenic and scheduling arrangements of the most important public settings so that a coercive control, often spurious to the professed aims of the institution, can be maintained.

Within the courtrooms of the magistrates' courts tacit control of their spatial and temporal properties is the monopoly of the police and the judicial personnel. In practice both the staging and the prosecution of the criminal business becomes the responsibility of the police. This renders absurd the judicial rhetoric of an adversary justice, where, so the story goes, both prosecution and defence stand as equals before the law. Indeed, within the courtrooms of the magistrates' courts the ideal of adversary justice is subjugated to an organisational efficiency in whose service body-movement and body-presentation are carefully circumscribed and regulated, bewilderment and embarrassment are openly fostered and aggravated, and uncertainty is callously observed and manipulated. Human creativity is there, certainly, but it is celebrated as much in the covert deployment of tacit control techniques as it is in the innovative judicial action. Whereas, therefore, Goffman's dramaturgical analyses have focused on the everyday realities of the *cinéma vérité*, these notes on the staging of magistrates' justice will focus on the surrealist dimensions of the theatre of the absurd.

Staging the Absurd

Though structurally opposed, the theatre of the absurd and the court of law have several phenomenological features in common. Their central divergence inheres in their opposed structural functions. Thus, whereas dramatists of the absurd intentionally and overtly utilise the plausible and the mundane to construct the overtly senseless and absurd, the mandarins of justice intentionally and covertly utilise the plausible and mundane to construct the covertly senseless and absurd.

In magistrates' courts, as in the theatre of the absurd, mundane and conventional ways of organising and communicating the operative meanings of social occasions are simultaneously exploited and denied. Yet their outcomes are situationally authenticated and the intermeshed structures of surrealism and psychic coercion are difficult to locate. This is because police and judicial personnel systematically present their coercive devices as being nothing more than the traditional, conventional and commonsensical ways of organising and synchronising judicial proceedings.

Space

The spacing and placing of people on public occasions is strategic to their ability to participate effectively in them. Even upon informal social occasions temporary spacing arrangements will at least decide which conversations can

PAT CARLEN

be heard by whom. On the most formal social occasions spacing arrangements, being more rigid, will, in addition to determining the mode and range of verbal interaction, emphasise the relative status of the people present. On ritual occasions, the rules of spacing and placing will, additionally, define the specific territorial rights and duties of those designated as occupiers of particular social space.

A magistrates' court is a very formal and ritualistic social setting; in it social space is pre-formed and distributed by the fixtures and fittings which comprise its definitive physical dimensions. The conditional essence of formality is the maintenance of existing social forms; the *raison d'être* of the criminal law is an assumption of the vulnerability of existing social forms. It is not surprising, therefore, to find that, in the courts, not even the usually implicit rules of spacing and placing are left to chance interpretation. Instead, judicial violation of the mundane expectations which usually enable fully adult people to cope with unfamiliar situations, judicial tolerance of flawed communication systems, and a judicial perversion of the accepted modes of conversational practice, realise a structure of tacit coercion which makes nonsense of recent claims that judicial proceedings are loaded in favour of the defendant (CLRC, 1972; Mark, 1973).

In the courtroom spatial dominance is achieved by structural elevation and the magistrate sits raised up from the rest of the court. The defendant is also raised up to public view but the dock is set lower than the magisterial seat, whilst the rails surrounding it are symbolic of the defendant's captive state. Of all the main protagonists the defendant is the one who is placed farthest away from the magistrate. Between the defendant and the magistrate sit clerk, solicitors, probation officers, social workers, press reporters, police, and any others deemed to be assisting the court in the discharge of its duties. Spatial arrangements, however, which might signify to the onlooker a guarantee of an orderly display of justice, are too often experienced by participants as being generative of a kind of theatrical autism with all the actors talking past each other.

Difficulties of hearing are endemic to magistrates' courts. At one court where microphones are used they distort voices so badly that most people in the courtroom laughingly wince when they are turned on, and visibly sympathise with the lady magistrate who always has them turned off because " they make us sound like Donald Duck ". At other courts they have microphones but do not use them. Magistrates and clerks can go to elaborate lengths to explain the meaning of legal phraseology to defendants who either do not hear them and say " Pardon, sir? " or who nod in the " dazed " or " blank " way noted by so many policemen and probation officers. Acoustics, however, cannot bear total responsibility for the chronic breakdown of communication in magistrates' courts. The placing and spacing of people within the courtroom is a further cause of the series of " pardons " and " blank stares " which characterise and punctuate judicial proceedings.

It has already been stressed that, in the courtroom, defendants and magistrates are set well apart from each other. Distances between bench and dock vary from court to court but in all courts such distances are certainly greater

THE STAGING OF MAGISTRATES' JUSTICE

than those usually, and voluntarily, chosen for the disclosure of intimate details of sexual habits, personal relationships and financial affairs. Certain communications, as Edward Hall has stressed, are conventionally presented as intimate communications, and both their timing and situating are delicately arranged. Indeed, " there are certain things which are difficult to talk about unless one is within the proper conversational zone " (Hall, 1959).

In magistrates' courts, where the vast majority of defendants do not have a solicitor as a " mouthpiece ", defendants are set up in a guarded dock and then, at a distance artificially stretched beyond the familiar boundaries of face-to-face communication, are asked to describe or comment on intimate details of their lives; details which do not in themselves constitute infractions of any law but which are open to public investigation once a person has been accused of breaking the law.

Further, during such sequences of interrogation, defendants' embarrassed stuttering is often aggravated by judicial violation of another taken-for-granted conversational practice. For in conventional social practice the chain-rule of question-answer sequence (Sacks, 1967; Schegloff, 1972) is also accompanied by the assumption that it is the interrogator who demands an answer. In magistrates' courts, however, defendants often find that they are continually rebuked, either for not addressing their answers to the magistrate, or for directing their answers to their interrogators in such a way that the magistrate cannot hear them. As a result, defendants are often in the position of having to synchronise their answers and stances in a way quite divorced from the conventions of everyday life outside the courtroom.

For defendants who often do not immediately distinguish between magistrate and clerk, for defendants who do not comprehend the separate symbolic functions of dock and witness-box, for defendants who may have already spent up to three hours waiting around the squalid environs of the courtroom —the surrealistic dimensions of meaning, emanating from judicial exploitation of courtroom placing and spacing, can have a paralysing effect. A senior probation officer summed up the present situation in the Metropolitan magistrates' courts very well when she commented: " Many of them don't even go into the witness-box because they can't face walking round there. They're too nervous."

Time

Though it is unlikely that absolute control of the situation can be obtained in a cramped courtroom which may have 30 to 40 people in its main area, and over that number in its public gallery, officials, as I have already argued, appear to be well aware of how to facilitate control through exploitation of the courtroom's physical dimensions. Courtroom ceremony is maintained partly to facilitate physical control of defendants and any others who may step out of place, and partly to refurbish the historically sacred meanings attached to law. Yet, because of the volume of criminal business dealt with by magistrates' courts, control of the proceedings is often precarious. Continuous inroads on the putative sanctity of the courtroom are made by the daily wear and tear of judicial proceedings which may involve the consecutive

PAT CARLEN

appearances of 20 or 30 defendants at one court session. A series of brief but complex scenes have to be welded into a fast-moving but judicially satisfying documentary. Lines of spatial demarcation provide the base-lines for the overall performance; once the action starts the movement of documents and persons from the various regions of the court has to be synchronised by the mainly backstage activities of the police.

In the management of social occasions, time, like place, always belongs to somebody or some group. During formal social occasions certain persons are appointed to oversee the timing of events, to ensure both the continuity and punctuation of performances. During judicial proceedings in magistrates' courts the timing of events is monopolised by the police. They are the ones who set up the proceedings; it is their responsibility to see that all defendants arrive at court; it is their job to draw up the charge sheets; it is their job to ensure that all relevant documents are in the hands of the clerk of court. And policemen are very jealous of their competence in programming the criminal business. Like other occupational groups doing a complex job publicly and under constant criticism they have developed plausible accounts to " demonstrate the rationality " (Moore, 1974) of the court's timetable. For instance, when I talked with him, a court inspector appealed to common-sense when he insisted that it was " only sensible " to hear contested cases last: " Think of it from your own point of view: if you'd pleaded guilty you wouldn't want to hang around all afternoon for something that was going to take two minutes." Yet, for the majority of defendants, the court experience is characterised by long periods of waiting unpunctuated by any official explanations about the cause of the delays. Worse, because cases can be arbitrarily switched from courtroom to courtroom, a defendant can have his case heard in one courtroom while his friends (among them, potential witnesses) sit unsuspectingly in the public gallery of an adjacent courtroom. During the long hours of waiting, many defendants become more and more nervous, harbouring fears (usually unfounded) that they will be sent to prison and, in the majority of courts, unable to get either refreshments or the privacy in which to talk to their solicitors or probation officers.

So, defendants, told to arrive at court at 10 a.m., may wait one, two or even three hours before their cases are " called on," but the police do the court lists according to a rationality which is rooted in two strands of situational logic. First, they calculate the time a case will take from their experience of the past performing times of the presiding magistrate and clerk. Secondly, they treat as an organisational norm their assumption that quicker business should take precedence over longer business. What the policemen successfully present as commonsense, however, also has a symbolic pay-off. If, early on in the proceedings, it is established that the court dispenses a swift and sure justice, untarnished by the ambiguity which characterises the later contested cases, then the contested case can, structurally, be presented as the deviant case, the one which needs special justification and management. Successful assertion by the police of their claim to present these cases in their " own time " displays a basic feature of their control over the courtroom situation.

THE STAGING OF MAGISTRATES' JUSTICE

Presentations

Agencies which routinely handle large numbers of people usually develop strategies for promoting their disciplined movement between and within regions. Conventionally, organisational traffic is facilitated by sign-posting, information desks, printed rubrics and organisational maps. In magistrates' courts, however, such information is almost non-existent. Arrows indicate courtroom, gaoler's office and various other offices, but inquiring or first-time defendants are predominantly dependent upon the oral and tactile directions of the police.

Defendants are escorted into the courtroom by the policeman calling the cases. Once the defendant is in the dock the escort acts as a kind of personal choreographer to him. He tells him when to stand up and when to sit down (often in contradiction of the magistrates' directions!), when to speak and when to be quiet, when to leave the dock at the end of the hearing. During the hearing the policeman can tell the defendant to take his hands out of his pockets, chewing-gum out of his mouth, his hat off his head and the smile off his face. Thus, even at the outset, a series of physical checks, aligned with a battery of commands and counter-commands, inhibits the defendant's presentational style. Once he is in the distraught state of mind where he just " wants to get it over ", judicial fears that the defendant might slow down the proceedings by being " awkward " are diminished.

In contrast to their unceremonious and coercive presentation of defendants, magistrates, policemen, solicitors and other court personnel all project visual images of themselves, and verbally embellished images of each other which are designed to personify the absolute propriety of their situated (judicial) actions.

Most court-workers are concerned with maintaining credibility with the magistrate, but magistrates themselves argue that their own authority is invested in the *place* rather than in their trans-situational status as magistrates. They, nonetheless, see the degrees of respect shown for the court as reflections of, and on, the image of the bench, and many of the organisational and cere-monial strategies of stage-management centre around the presentation of the magistrate. His entrance to the courtroom is both staged and heralded. The opening of the court is signalled by the usher calling " All stand " and " Silence in court ". Once everybody in the courtroom is standing in silence, the magistrate enters, his appearance being staged *via* the door of which he has the exclusive use, and which appears to seal off those innermost areas of the court to which the public never has access. Throughout the court hearing the usher ensures that the magistrate is granted deference, interposing himself between those who, without further intermediary, would try to hand docu-ments or letters directly into the magistrate's hands. Each magisterial entrance and exit is marked by the same ceremony.

Inter-professionally and collusively a concerted portrayal of authority and wisdom is maintained by the ceremonial courtesies of complimentary addresses and reference. Frozen in the rhetoric of their own self-justificatory vocabulary the magistrate becomes " Your Worship " and " Your Honour "; the clerk of the court becomes the " learned clerk "; policemen become

53

PAT CARLEN

" public servants "; probation officers and social workers become " these experts who can help you ". What in vulgar parlance might be called the " scratch my back " syndrome becomes in court the rhetorical embroidery on the judicial backcloth. By contrast, the defendant too often becomes just " this man ", unentitled, " Smith ".

Discussion

People who work in a place usually have more control over its particular rules of placing, spacing and ritual etiquettes than do those who pass through it; magistrates' courts are not unusual in these respects. Most defendants do not find it odd or disturbing that the court has its own routine. What they do find frustrating is that, at the very times when they are both subject to and object of its rules, a fog of mystification permeates the court (Grigg, 1965). To speak plainly, the major existential attribute of court proceedings is that they *do* proceed, regardless of the structural inability of many of those present to *hear* what is going on, and despite the structural inability of many of those present to *participate* in what is going on (Dell, 1970).

Given the coercion immanent in the very staging of magistrates' justice, what is one to make of the current arguments that increased legal aid will substantially protect defendants' interests? What is one to make of the suggestion that the advice of a duty solicitor should be available to every defendant?

A most interesting feature of " reformist " socio-legal analyses is that all proposed changes in judicial organisation centre on the defendant. *He* will be assisted, guided, spoken for, represented more often; *he* will be helped to present a more plausible case. If, however, such reforms are truly meant to elevate the defendant from marionette to co-star status, it is arguable, from the analyses presented here, that they must either be accompanied or be preceded by radical changes in the staging of magistrates' justice.

REFERENCES

BOTTOMLEY, A. K. (1970). *Prison Before Trial*. London: Bell.
BLUMBERG, ABRAHAM (1967). " The Practice of Law as a Confidence Game." *Law And Society Review*, Vol. I.
CAMUS, ALBERT (1969). *The Outsider*. Harmondsworth, Middlesex: Penguin.
CARROLL, LEWIS (1971). *Alice in Wonderland*. London: Oxford University Press.
CRIMINAL LAW REVISION COMMITTEE (1972). *Eleventh Report*. London: H.M.S.O.
DELL, S. (1970). *Silent in Court*. London: Bell.
EMERSON, R. M. (1967). *Judging Delinquents*. Chicago: Aldine.
FRANK, JEROME (1950). *Courts on Trial*. Princeton: Princeton University Press.
GARFINKEL, H. (1956). " Conditions of Successful Degradation Ceremonies." *American Journal of Sociology LXI*.
GOFFMAN, E. (1959). *The Presentation of Self in Everyday Life*. Garden City, N.Y.: Doubleday.
HALL, E. T. (1959). *The Silent Language*. Garden City, N.Y.: Doubleday.
HOOD, ROGER (1962). *Sentencing in Magistrates' Courts*. London: Stevens and Sons.

THE STAGING OF MAGISTRATES' JUSTICE

KAFKA, FRANZ (1972). *The Trial*. Harmondsworth, Middlesex: Penguin.

KING, M. (1972). *Bail or Custody*. London: The Cobden Trust.

MANNHEIM, K. (1952). *Essays in the Sociology of Knowledge*. London: Routledge and Kegan Paul.

MARK, ROBERT (1973). *Richard Dimbleby Lecture*. London: B.B.C. Publications.

MOORE, MICHAEL (1974). " Demonstrating the Rationality of an Occupation." *Sociology*, **8**, 1, January.

PATTERSON, A. (1971). *Legal Aid as a Social Service*. London: Cobden Trust.

SACKS, H. (1967). *Transcribed Lectures*. Mimeo.

SCHEGLOFF, E. A. (1972). Notes on a Conversational Practice Formulating Place, in D. Sudnow, *Studies in Social Interaction*. New York: Free Press.

SCHUTZ, A. (1970). *Reflection on the Problems of Relevance*. New Haven: Yale University Press.

SIMPSON, N. (1960). *One Way Pendulum*. London: Faber.

[14]

BRITISH JOURNAL OF LAW & SOCIETY
VOLUME 8, NUMBER 2, WINTER 1981

MAGISTRATES' COURTS AND THE IDEOLOGY OF JUSTICE

DOREEN MCBARNET†[1]

Magistrates' courts have frequently attracted comment for their role as a conveyor belt for the guilty pleas which constitute 95% of their caseload. Far less attention has been paid to their contested trials, even though, as a recent research study for the Royal Commission on Criminal Procedure notes, by far the majority of contested trials are heard before magistrates.[2]

This article draws on observational research into contested trials in magistrates' courts,[3] to consider two very different levels of sociological problem. First there is the plight of the unrepresented defendant, the focal point of most sociological and social policy studies of the courts. This article tries to offer a fresh approach by locating the problem not just in the social class of the defendant or the informal games played by courtroom personnel, but in the structure of magistrates' justice.

Second, there are the ideological problems posed by the departure of the magistrates' courts from central tenets of the rhetoric of justice. This article seeks to locate this departure not just in the practice of magistrates but in the institutional basis of magistrates' justice. It tries to demonstrate the problems posed for the ideology of justice and the legitimations by which they are resolved.

The research on which the article draws was done in Scotland. Legal institutions in Scotland and England do vary and any problems of generalisability are discussed where they arise.[4]

The Unrepresented Defendant

The conviction rate in magistrates' courts is extremely high. According to 1978 statistics, it is 95% for non-indictable offences in English magistrates' courts, 93% for indictable crimes. In Scottish summary courts the rate is 95%.[5] These figures of course include, indeed are mainly made up of, guilty pleas. But the decision to plead guilty is itself partly a product of people's expectation that they have little chance of being found not guilty if they opt for trial by magistrates. Guilty pleas cannot in short be isolated from the expectations of magistrates' justice in general. In any case, a recent Home Office Study shows 75% of contested trials resulted in conviction, ranging, according to the offence, from 60% to 100%.[6]

This high conviction rate, and the associated problems for the defendant

† Centre for Socio-Legal Studies, Oxford.

in winning his case, are usually put down to the fact that the defendant is normally working class and normally unrepresented. Hence Dell's description of unrepresented defendants never getting their case across in court, because they remain *silent in court*, silent through working class inarticulateness or fear.[7]

Carlen would put the defendant's problems down to the games played by courtroom personnel, whereby the accused is the only outsider, the only one who does not know what is going on, what the cues passing between magistrates and policemen or social workers mean.[8] But it is not just a matter of the defendant's class or indeed of informal rules and games that poses him problems in court. In fact the sociological focus on these as the issues has distracted attention from the role of legal policy and formal legal structure. Both of these have to be examined to understand first, why defendants in the magistrates' courts *are* usually unrepresented; second, why being represented professionally is, in the current legal structure, so important.

In Scotland there has been a duty solicitor scheme available at all courts since 1975. But duty stretches only to those in custody and stops at the point of plea — legal advice is available of right only to answer a charge, not to contest it. In England the defendant in the magistrates' court only exceptionally has a lawyer: Bottoms' and McClean's Sheffield study found only 19% represented throughout compared to 99% in the higher courts.[9] The reason for this is simple enough: legal aid, though virtually a right in the higher courts, is not available in any but exceptional cases in the lower courts. Nor do the recommendations of the Royal Commission on legal services augur well for any significant change.[10] Discretion is retained in the award of legal aid in cases triable only by magistrates, and although there is a change of emphasis from the need to find grounds to *award* aid to the need to find grounds to *deny* it, the same basic criteria set down by the Widgery Committee in 1966 still stand.

The reasoning in the Widgery Report was clear enough. It denied that a professional lawyer was normally necessary in the lower courts, implying that points of law, tracing and interviewing witnesses or engaging in expert cross examination were not normally involved. Yet the same report insisted that a professional lawyer *was* necessary for the higher courts:

> 'A layman, however competent, can rarely be relied on to possess the skill and knowledge necessary to put forward the defence effectively tried *on indictment* without the guidance of a lawyer.'[11]

Were the structure and rules of procedure in the two levels of courts essentially different, this distinction might be valid. Differences there are, as we shall see, but not in the proof of a case. The trial, and with it the method of proof and the criteria of proof remain exactly the same. There is the same adversarial structure, the same structure of proof by examination, cross-examination, the same requirement of direct witnesses to provide that proof, the same rules of evidence *and the same requirement that the procedures be rigidly adhered to.* In terms of their structure and procedure these are *not* laymen's courts but highly legalised proceedings.

Carlen underestimates this when she talks of the informal rules of interaction as more significant than the formal procedures and refers to the rules of time, place and order being invoked only to suppress challenges to the court.[12] Procedural pedantics are not just emergency measures: they are what make a trial a trial, and the result is that the accused in the magistrates' courts is not just prevented from challenging the court but is *routinely prevented from participating effectively in his own trial.* In short, from my own observation, the accused is often not so much *silent* in court — inarticulate, afraid or outside the game — but *silenced* in court for not obeying the rules of legal procedure.

Silenced in Court

The trial is organised into a quite definite order of events and at each stage different rules pertain:

(1) the defendant makes his plea
(2) the prosecutor calls his witnesses — usually policemen — and examines them
(3) the defendant can crossexamine each witness, immediately after the prosecutor has examined him — at this stage the rule is that he can only ask questions of the witnesses not make statements on his own behalf
(4) the defendant can, though he need not, move from the dock to the witness box to give his evidence
(5) he is crossexamined in turn
(6) if he has any witnesses he can examine them (again ask questions only) to elicit support for his story
(7) each witness is in turn crossexamined by the prosecutor
(8) each party may sum up.

The defendant's first admissible opportunity to make a statement is at stage 4. But repeatedly he takes up the first invitation to speak, at stage 3, to deliver a statement to the magistrate, only to be rebuffed on procedural grounds. He is likewise interrupted or silenced with each witness until, when it comes to his turn to enter the witness box (and often he starts his statement again in the dock only to be rebuffed or moved), he often rejects the chance or is quite taken aback to have a say. When he does speak he may well find his story interrupted and what seem to be crucial points excluded by the rules of evidence.

Some examples from observed cases demonstrate this quite clearly. Hence Case 29:

Magistrate: How do you know what they (the police) said to Pauline (co-accused)?
Accused: She told us
Magistrate: That's hearsay

183

Or Case 1:

> Accused: Sir I'd left before closing time to go to another pub.
> Magistrate: That's an alibi defence. You didn't intimate that.

(In his summing up later the magistrate declared the defence inadmissible because no warning had been given). In Case 27 the accused's defence depended on his having good reason to use a police phone:

> Magistrate: Would you like to ask the officer any questions Mr. McC?
> Accused: Do you know why I was on the phone?
> Prosecutor: He can't answer that.

Without an understanding of legal procedure, the layman-defendant can find it extremely difficult to actually present his case in court at all.

Of course proving a case usually involves not just stating one's own version of events but undermining one's opponent's. And the conventional means of doing this is via cross-examination. The Widgery Report sees professional cross-examination as rarely needed in summary cases.[13] Yet cross-examination is one of the essential weapons of the adversarial trial. With no cross-examination there is in a sense no trial and with no professional lawyer there tends to be no cross-examination, as observation in court demonstrates.

The defendant's desperate eagerness to get his version of what happened before the court as quickly as possible has two consequences. Making a statement at stage three, when he should be cross-examining not only gets him into a procedural tangle which threatens his chance of making a statement at all, it also gets in the way of his ever cross-examining. The opportunity is not taken up at the procedurally correct time, and is therefore lost for good, as in Case 1:

> Magistrate: Would you like to ask any questions?
> Accused: All I said was "what's happening?"
> Magistrate to policeman:
>   Are you in any doubt that this man was committing the offence?
> Policeman: No
> Accused: I never opened my mouth except to ask what was happening.
> Magistrate: You can't deliver a peroration at this point. Have you (moving on to Accused 2) any questions?

Or case 35:

> Magistrate: At this time you may ask the officer questions from the evidence he's given. Have you any questions?
> Accused: We were just standing talking.
> Magistrate: (To policeman) She says they were just standing talking. Is this so?
> Policeman: No.

184

Magistrate: That's the answer to your question. You may not like it but that's it. Move on to the next question.

Accused: There's nothing else.

Case 29:

Accused: We were playing football and he came up and asked our name and about a TV.

Assessor to policeman:
Did you say this?

Policeman: No

Magistrate: There's your answer. Any other questions?

Case 5:

Magistrate: Any questions?

Accused: I was only violent because I was being punched.

Magistrate: Was he being assaulted?

Policeman: No. We put him on the floor when he entered to await assistance.

Magistrate: That's your answer. Any more questions?

Case 25:

Accused to magistrate:
Well all I can say is

Magistrate: It's him you ask the questions

Accused: No questions then.

And so on. There are dozens of examples from the data — these are not peculiar but *typical* cases, as indeed the Lord Chancellor's office recognises in a series of lectures to magistrates:

> cross-examination and re-examination are difficult matters for unrepresented parties, and the help of the court is often necessary, just as it is necessary in most cases for the court to conduct the examination-in chief.[14]

Magistrates are, in short, expected to help the accused with procedure and indeed to help him cross-examine. And this expectation is often used to justify the lack of legal representation in the lower courts. The defendant's interests are said to be "safe in the hands of the presiding judge"[15] and the assumption is made that the "court will usually be able to turn his statements into questions on his behalf".[16] The problem is that this is *not* cross-examination.

For a start it is too late: once the statement is put the surprise is lost. What is more, once the translated direct question is put, it creates an impasse, a categorical denial, with nothing to pursue further. A competent professional advocate would never take this route. Professional cross-examination proceeds by quite different means, by indirect approaches, by a series of questions on apparently peripheral matters, with a crucial issue casually dropped in en route, by a series of questions leading the witness to an accusation which the witness cannot logically deny without discrediting his previous answers.

For the magistrate to turn a statement into a question does not therefore help the unrepresented accused conduct his cross-examination as a professional might, it simply ensures that his amateur non-cross-examination both terminates and fails. The magistrate's "help" is therefore no substitute for defence advocacy. Nor indeed could it be.

The magistrate can, as all judges can, ask questions, but his *role* remains that of independent judge, he has no involvement in the preparation of cases and he may not take sides. And of course he does not know the defendant's version beforehand, so the questions he asks are necessarily coloured by the only version he has heard, the prosecution's. With the best will in the world he is not in the *structural position* to do the job of defence advocate.

Neither, ironically, is the defendant. Indeed the unrepresented defendant is truly in a dilemma. Without exercising the skills of the advocate or knowledge of the law he cannot participate in his trial, and there is no defence, but if he does demonstrate such skills he is caught in the double bind that he is not supposed to.

Underlying the defendant's inadequate self-defence is not only lack of knowledge and skill but the fact that the expected role of the defendant almost *requires* that he behaves like that, that he rushes in his moral indignation to tell his version rather than coolly making a case. The result is that the accused who does cross-examine rather than make statements invites interruption and criticism, even though he is often pursuing only, if perhaps a little more agitatedly, the same lines that the professional would.

It is, for example, a normal technique of advocates to cross-examine on matters which appear to be peripheral as a way of catching the witness on a crucial matter unawares, or indeed to make something significant of a matter which may not seem so to the witness. Either way the crucial elements are surprise and a continuity of flow in the questioning and a judge would be unlikely to intervene. Unrepresented defendants are not so readily accorded this privilege:

Magistrate: What's that got to do with it? Next question. (Case 1)

Repetition, near repetition, or persistence with a particular line, normal enough advocacy styles invite termination:

Assessor: I think you've covered that. I think we've got the picture. (Case 21)

It is not therefore just as simple as lawyers being able to do things that laymen cannot. Even among defendants competent in the art of self defence, it is harder for the unrepresented defendant to *get away with* the same methods as a lawyer. Indeed to be too au fait with law, procedure and advocacy can mean inviting not just ridicule or interruption but suspicion:

> Magistrate: It seems strange a young girl like you should know all this jargon if you've not been in trouble before. (Case 29)

One defendant who set about cross-examining the first police witness against him with some gusto, was invited drily to cross-examine the second with the quip:

> And remember, we don't want a breach of the peace here. (Case 6)

When one of the accused in Case 1 caught out the police witness on a detail of location, exactly the kind of detail advocates rub their hands over, he was interrupted by the magistrate (who after all had to decide his fate) with the comment:

> I wish you wouldn't be so aggressive — you're slightly offensive.

Another, in Case 29, was admonished for his approach:

> Magistrate: You're still a cocky young whippersnapper. When's your bubble going to be burst? You're a very confident self-opinionated young man.

Dell may point to nerves as a problem for defendants but it would appear from such comments that confidence fares them little better. Defendants *may not* play the role of the confident punch-pulling advocate not only because it clashes with the incompetence and deference routinely demanded of the lower class people who dominate the courts, but because it clashes with the role expected of the *defendant*. The defendant may be diffident, nervous, excited, contrite; he may not be confident, aggressive, cool, calculating, tricky — unless of course he is that rarety, an unrepresented middle class defendant in the lower courts. The inherent characteristics of the competent defendant and the competent advocate make it structurally difficult to get away with playing both roles at once. The accused is thus put in an absurd double bind — damned if he is knowledgeable in the rules, competent in advocacy, damned if he is not.

The problems of the defendant in either getting his case across or undermining his opponent's cannot, then, simply be put down to working class inadequacy or the games played by courtroom personnel. The structure of the trial, in terms of both procedures and roles, itself inhibits the making of a case and leads to the accused being silenced in court.

Underlying all this is a structural paradox. The trial is predicated upon professional knowledge, expertise and adversarial advocacy — but legal policy denies access to it.

The answer, in policy terms, seems simple — provide lawyers. But there are some fundamental reasons why that would not be likely to work. The chances are that even with a lawyer, the defendant in the magistrates' courts would still have the odds weighted against him. The structural paradox is not only a cause but a symptom of a deeper structural and ideological distinction between higher and lower court justice. The magistrates' courts deal in a kind of justice which is in its source, nature and ideology, quite different from the higher courts. They deal in summary justice.

The Structure of Summary Justice

Summary justice is what most people going through the courts — some 98% in both Scotland and England — *experience* as justice, but it clashes violently with the traditional *images* of justice. Other commentators have noted the chaos, casualness and rapidity of the proceedings in magistrates' courts. Few students in my experience emerge from their first visit to the public benches anything but shocked. Certainly the image of justice carried into the court is quickly shattered, and not just by the conveyor belt of guilty pleas. The trials too run counter to all the expectations of a solemn, skilful adversarial joust. Magistrates' justice seems to be another world from the legal system we have learned about in books and films and television.

The statistics, as we have seen, tell the same story. Credibility in the ideology that the scales of justice are tipped to acquitting ten guilty men rather than convicting one innocent man is stretched to breaking point by the work of the summary courts. And not just by its work but by its structure. Examining the legal foundations of summary justice indicates that if the rights of the defendant do not obstruct the conviction process in magistrates' courts too much it is not just because they are not known about or not enforced but because in large measure they do not exist.

Though common law and trial by jury claim a heritage going back to Magna Carta, summary justice is a statutory creation which only came into widespread use in the nineteenth century. It is characterised precisely by its *lack* of many of the attributes of the ideology of law, legality, and a fair trial. The Oxford Dictionary defines summary justice as "proceedings in a court of law carried out rapidly by the omission of certain formalities required by the common law". The lack of representation is but one of many omissions. The judicial definition in Scots law is a procedure:

> without induciae and without indictment and further without any notice to the party of the names of the witnesses that are to be called against him and without the accused being represented by legal adviser unless he chooses to provide himself with one.[17]

The judge might have added, without a record of the proceedings and of course without a jury. Summary justice is thus characterised legally not by positive attributes but by negative ones: it negates many of the procedures held to be necessary in the traditional ideology of due process.

In all sorts of ways the formality of the higher court is abandoned. The indictments by which prosecutions are launched in the superior courts require absolute precision — even the size of the paper and margins were specified in the 1918 rules — but the "information" which initiates the lower court prosecution has no set form, it need not even be written, though it usually is, and not all the elements of the offence need to be stated. Nor as English law puts it can any objection be raised to an "information" on the grounds of defect of substance or form or because the evidence given at the trial varies from it, while the Scottish text, notes generally and succinctly: "No proceeding will be invalidated through a defect which is merely technical".[18]

Hence the administration of the lower courts is often presented favourably — as less formal and legalistic than that of the higher courts, and as more accessible, as a result, to the lay-defendant. But that is hardly borne out by research. In fact, the defendant's *task*, as this article has already tried to show, is still governed by formal procedures, but the defendant's *rights* are greatly reduced.

If the lower courts seem to present a different world from the image we carry in our heads of the higher courts then, it is hardly surprising; in law that is exactly what they are. The law has created two tiers of justice, one which is geared in its ideology and generality at least to the structures of legality,[19] and one which, quite simply and explicitly is not.

This differential structure is of course legitimised. Indeed the same two legitimations occur over and over again. First, both the offences and the penalties involved in magistrates' justice are too trivial for the strictures of due process; second, the issues and processes are such that the niceties of law and lawyers are irrelevant.

The remainder of this paper sets out to analyse these legitimations, to demonstrate their ideological nature, their impact on those who work in the courts, and their ideological accomplishments.

The ideology of triviality

To read law books for information on the magistrates' courts is to come away with the clear impression that what goes on in them is overwhelmingly trivial. They deal with "minor offences", "everyday offences", "the most ordinary cases", "humdrum" events.[20] Legal academics even go so far — rare event — as indulging in jocularity. Coull and Merry's text gives the Scottish police courts, very much the lowest tier of justice, seven lines, largely taken up with the fact that they are empowered,

> inter alia to impose a fine of 50p for 'allowing a chimney to catch or be on fire' or a penalty of £2 for throwing 'any snowball, to the danger or annoyance' of any person.[21]

This dominant image of the triviality of the work of the lower courts is shared by the press. The press benches in magistrates' courts are rarely occupied. The column of offenders and penalties that every local paper carries is the result of a phone call for results. The proceedings themselves are of no interest, except perhaps to provide this week's funny stories for the Diary column. And why not? Much of what happens in the court is funny or pathetic or absurd, and so very trivial, too trivial to attract any serious attention from the press.

Nor indeed from the public: so rare is it for a member of the public to attend summary courts that the public benches are often used as a waiting room for the morning's batch of defendants, from which they can observe their predecessors' fate and shuffle along to each newly vacated space till their turn comes for the dock. To go to these courts as a member of the public is to become an object of curiosity; to sit there taking notes is to invite paroxysms of paranoia.

In the course of the research I have been asked by one police officer on duty if I was "from one of those radical papers" by another if I was "just here to practice your shorthand, dear?" I've been called before the bench to explain myself, had a policeman sent by the magistrate to ask me what I was doing there, been advised not to take notes by a policeman on duty and told by another that taking notes was illegal. The 'public' in the lower court is an unusual phenomenon, and the purveyors of magistrates' justice are somewhat sensitive to anyone seeing their particular brand of justice being done.

More than that, some were just genuinely concerned that I should be wasting my time at the lower courts when I could be watching "juicy cases" and "real judges" elsewhere. *Their* assumption was that the work of *their* court was too trivial to be of interest. So the image of triviality that pervades the lowest ranks of criminal justice has the consequence of removing yet another requisite of due process: that the administration of justice should be public.

One of the objections of the eighteenth century judges to summary justice[22] was that it was "in a private chamber" behind closed doors. The doors were opened in 1848 but the dominant image of triviality helps ensure that the public benches remain empty. It is, after all, difficult to work up a moral panic over, to cite observed cases, taking lead worth 20p from a rubbish tip, "touching cars", or my favourite, "jumping on and off a pavement in a disorderly manner". And however hard the penalties are to those on the receiving end, they can hardly match the salacious fascination of the life and death decisions in Hay's eighteenth century courts.[23]

More specifically it is the relative triviality of the *penalties* that provides the crucial legitimations in law for the lack of due process in summary justice. Due process of law is required in the ideology of democratic justice before a person's liberty may be interfered with. The reasoning which legitimises reducing due process in the lowest courts is based on this premise, but with a refinement. "Liberty" ceases to be an absolute and becomes subject to a measuring rod. The limited penalties available to magistrates means they can interfere less with one's liberty than the higher courts, so defendants in these courts need less due process. The less one's liberty is at risk the less one needs protection. This is perhaps most explicitly stated in the criteria for awarding legal aid. One important condition is where the defendant is "in real jeopardy of losing his liberty or livelihood or suffering imprisonment".[24]

More generally this is in many ways a strange argument. 'Trivial' offences after all still involve state intervention in the citizen's liberty. Indeed if the same due process is not to be awarded to all defendants, it might seem a bit illogical to minimise the legal rights for those who have allegedly infringed least on law and order and maximise them for those who have infringed most. Perhaps it is just that the more unusual the crime and the larger the penalty the more public interest is likely to be aroused and the more justice will be willy-nilly on display. The more criminality in the offence, the more legality in the proceedings might be an odd equation. The more *publicity*, the more legality, is in ideological terms, perfectly understandable. Publicity is not, however, an issue that need trouble lower court justice, closetted from the public eye by its own triviality — or, more accurately, by its own ideology of triviality. Triviality is not just a description but an interpretation, an assessment, and the work of the lower courts could be viewed quite differently.

For a start, offences and penalties may seem trivial from the outside but far from trivial from the perspective of the accused. The James Report rejected the perspective of the defendant as a way of categorising which offences and penalties were serious and which were not, on grounds which stressed its significance but its bureaucratic inconvenience:

> It would be impracticable ... since that importance varies according to his character and position in society.[25]

The same reasoning was, however, used in the Widgery Report to do the opposite, that is, to use the defendant's perspective, *as it varied according to his social status*, to justify discriminating in favour of the middle class in the award of legal aid:

> the seriousness of the consequences likely to result from loss of employment will also differ widely in different circumstances. A young labourer who loses his job in conditions of full employment will obviously not suffer to anything like the same extent as a middle aged black-coated worker who in the loss of his job, sacrifices career prospects, pension rights and may have the greatest difficulty in finding other comparable employment.[26]

One is tempted to conclude from such careful exceptions that the ideology of triviality may ultimately derive less from the triviality of the offences or the penalties but from the triviality in authoritative eyes of *the people*, the lower class, the unemployed, homeless, feeble, who provide the fodder for the lower courts — an implication indeed which is supported by the fact that the only time the lower courts become news is when, for example, Mark Phillips is charged with speeding.

Nor is it just a question of perspective but a question of focus. There is an inherent paradox in the very idea of prosecuting trivial offences. They are too trivial to interest the public but not too trivial for the state to prosecute in the name of the public; too trivial to merit due process of law but not too trivial for the intervention of the law. The ideology of triviality focusses on the offences and penalties, not on the question of prosecution itself. It is these trivial offences after all which are, first, most open to the direct intervention of the state in the sense that the police are often the *only complainants*. A recent Home Office study notes that for offences against public order 86.8% of prosecution cases comprise direct police evidence, and 13.2%

circumstantial evidence. Civilians evidence accounts for precisely 0.0%.[27] Second, they are most open to the imposition of a criminal label on "marginal" behaviour like loitering, and third, most open — because the definitions of offences are so open — to post hoc law-making.[28] In short, it is exactly in the area of minor offences that the operation of the law, in terms of democratic justice, becomes most suspect. If the behaviour involved in the offence is not intrinsically interesting, perhaps the law's processing of that behaviour into an offence is. But contemporary official discourse is more concerned with the quantity of crime than the quality of justice and the lower courts remain something to be laughed at or yawned over for the pettiness of their crimes, not watched with care for the marginality of their legality.

Legal Relevance

The second justification for reducing the strictures of due process — a view that is indeed given some endorsement by socio-legal writers like Mungham and Thomas[29] is that the offences dealt with in the lower courts do not involve much law or require much legal expertise or advocacy. They can therefore be safely left to be dealt with by laymen — by lay magistrates and by the defendants themselves, with lawyers seen as normally unnecessary in the lower courts. According to the Widgery Report, legal aid is rarely necessary for summary offences since:

> The large majority of cases are straightforward and the facts are uncomplicated and clear-cut.[30]

But this view of the lower court is inaccurate in two ways. First empirical study, as already demonstrated, shows that the lower courts are permeated by legalistic and professional consciousness. Second, it is logically confused — it confuses cause and effect — verges indeed on tautology. It might just as readily be argued that minor offences are characterised by simple facts and straightforward cases because there are so rarely lawyers involved.

The 'case' is a construct from an event, not a reproduction of it.[31] The construction of a case as straightforward or as involving points of law is very much the product of the advocate's trade. Case law, after all, develops exactly because advocates present cases which draw subtle distinctions and shades of meaning, in short, complicate the simple, in arguing for the treatment of the case in hand as different from previous precedents. What is more, case law and the development of complicated and difficult legal issues in specific types of offence and case, is predicated largely on the right to appeal on points of law, and both the nature of the appeal procedure in the lower courts and the lack of lawyers to formulate an appeal on a point of law, means that there is little opportunity to develop difficult and complex case law on minor offences.

It is not in the nature of drunkenness, breach of the peace or petty theft to be less susceptible than fraud, burglary or murder to complex legal argument; it is rather in the nature of the procedure by which they are tried. Indeed the James Report implicitly recognises this when it notes that:

> trial on indictment takes longer than summary trial even for a case of similar gravity and complexity.[32]

The "straightforward cases" of the lower courts are themselves legal constructions.

The same is true of the "simple facts". The facts of a case — a case of any sort — are not *all* the elements of the event, but the information allowed in by the rules, presented by the witnesses, and surviving the credibility test of cross-examination. The facts of summary cases may not be simple because of the nature of the offences but because of the lack of professional expertise in manipulation of the rules, persuasive presentation of one's own case and destructive cross-examination of the other side's. It is not that complex facts need lawyers but that lawyers can make 'facts' complex. That is exactly their trade.

Or the facts may be 'simple' not because of the nature of the offence but because of the *definition* of the offence. The openness of the legal definition of what constitutes an offence, and consequent scope for wide police discretion, along with the fact that these offences are normally the result not of citizens' reports but of police-accused encounters, with only the accused's word against the policeman's constituting the case, means that it is extremely difficult to establish a defence. In short, the facts are simple only because they are legally so difficult for the defendant to contest.

Indeed it might be suggested that the openness of the laws defining summary offences argues not for less legal expertise but for more. If the police can legally define almost anything as an offence, then the facts cannot be in dispute and the only way to establish a defence is on a point of law. Consider case 20, the "jumping on and off a pavement in a disorderly manner" case.

One reaction to being charged for that, even if one *was* doing it, might be total disbelief and a defence on the basis of it being absurd to be taken to court for such behaviour at all. But that of course is not a legal defence, just a cut and dried admission of guilt. The accused in this case, the only one of the group charged who pleaded not guilty, defended himself by saying he was not doing anything disorderly, that indeed he had just crossed the road to talk to the others and that he didn't run away because he "didn't expect to be lifted". That was his mistake. The prosecutor even noted in his summing up that

> he may think he wasn't misbehaving as much as the others *but he stayed with them.*

And that was all that was necessary *in law*. The prosecutor had to prove no more than that the defendant was part of a disorderly crowd which he could have left, not that he was actually disorderly himself.

There was therefore no legal defence in denying his behaviour was offensive, not only because that was difficult to maintain against two policemen but because in law it was irrelevant. A relevant defence would have been to take on the meaning of the law, for example, contending that to be "part of a disorderly crowd" requires not just one's presence but active participation. But that would be a point of law: it would require a more sophisticated knowledge of law and legal reasoning than this layman had, and of course, as we've already seen, might require presentation by a lawyer to be given a hearing at all.

The irony is then that because of the openness of the law in minor offences, kept open because there is so little case law to specify meaning, the best route to a defence is to challenge on a point of law. This of course could *establish* that missing case law, but it can't be readily done because no need for lawyers is perceived and the means to raise a point of law are denied. The image of the lower courts as not needing lawyers, which justifies not providing lawyers, is itself a *product* of their absence. The defendant is thus caught up in the vicious circle that lies behind the image of "simple facts" and "straightforward cases".

But, and this is why situational analysis needs to be set in its deeper structural context, providing lawyers would not necessarily make any difference: the ideologies of non-law and triviality pervade the origins and structure of the lower courts and so pervade the attitudes of those who work in them. Remember the police official who helpfully suggested I go to the higher courts for "juicy cases" and "real judges". And lawyers themselves often operate with a different style in the lower courts.

Indeed they are different lawyers. The non-law ideology has its structural expression in the idea that only barristers can act in the higher courts but only solicitors can usually be provided on legal aid in the lower courts. This is not to suggest invidious comparisons between the skills of solicitors and barristers, but merely to indicate that whatever the personal attitudes or competence of the solicitors who do appear in the lower courts the standard of advocacy *required* is pre-set as second class.

Likewise there is a structural expectation that lower courts do not need cases that are well prepared or indeed prepared beforehand at all by either side. With no committal proceedings the defence has no advance warning of the prosecution case it will have to face anyway, while Arguile's book on criminal procedure notes that if a matter arises in the defence evidence that takes the prosecutor by surprise he may call evidence in rebuttal of it *afterwards*:

> This is permitted because summary trials usually owe very little to advance preparation of the case, and the prosecution is therefore more likely to be surprised by unexpected defences.[33]

Lack of skilled preparation or presentation is certainly borne out by observation in courts.[34] and indeed by the criticism of the level of advocacy in the magistrates' courts made to the Royal Commission on Legal Services by the Association of Magisterial Officers. The concern here however is less with assessing the level of performance and attitude of lawyers per se than with teasing out what that demonstrates about the professional lawyer's ideology of the lower courts. On that score, the reply by the Law Society is as telling as the criticism, describing, as it does, the offenders, offences and work of the court in general as "relative trivia" and "the dross of the criminal courts".[35] What these comments suggest is that the profession too is imbued with the dominant images of the lower courts as neither serious enough nor legally relevant enough to need lawyers. To simply prescribe lawyers on tap for the lower courts as a solution to the defendant's dilemma is thus to ignore the much more fundamental structural and ideological realities which lie behind the courtroom situation.

The Accomplishments

These images of the court are not just ideological accomplishments; they also accomplish ideological functions themselves. Carlen points to the marginality of the offences, the lack of ceremony, lack of lawyers in the lower courts, as a problem for the magistrate in presenting the court's work as justice.[36] But the situational problem is in fact resolved structurally. The very same factors are transformed into images of the court as trivial and non-legal: and the effect of those images is that the court never actually has to account for its work anyway. The magistrate may have an existential problem in portraying his work as justice but he rarely has a social problem. For the magistrates' court is a theatre without an audience.

Legal policy has established two tiers of justice. One, the higher courts, is for public consumption, the arena where the ideology of justice is put on display.[37] The other, the lower courts, deliberately structured in defiance of the ideology of justice, is concerned less with subtle ideological messages than with direct control. The latter is closeted from the public eye by the ideology of triviality, so the higher courts alone feed into the public image of what the law does and how it operates. But the higher courts deal with only 2% of the cases that pass through the courts. Almost all criminal law is acted out in the lower courts *without* traditional due process. But of course what happens in the lower courts is not only trivial it is not really law. So the position is turned on its head. The 98% becomes the exception to the rule of "real law" and the working of the law comes to be typified *not* by its routine nature, but by its *atypical*, indeed *exceptional* high court form. Between them the ideologies of triviality and legal irrelevance accomplish the remarkable feats of defining 98% of court cases not only as exceptions to the rule of due process, but also as of no public interest whatsoever. The traditional ideology of justice can thus survive the contradiction that the summary courts blatantly ignore it every day — and that they were set up precisely for that purpose.

NOTES AND REFERENCES

[1] Though much abridged and modified, this article draws on Chapter 7 of D. McBarnet: *Conviction: Law, the State and the Construction of Justice* (1981). It was presented to the Sociology Society, University College Cardiff, on February 3rd, 1981.

[2] J. Vennard, *Contested Trials in Magistrates' Courts*. Royal Commission on Criminal Procedure Research Study No. 6 (1980).

[3] This particular piece of research was part of a larger study of courts in general. See McBarnet, *op.cit*. For the purposes of this article only cases in magistrates' courts are considered. Observed cases are numbered and cited by number.

[4] The Scottish court structure is more complex than the English. Scottish Magistrates' courts are presided over by a single magistrate, lay or stipendiary, laymen sitting with a legally qualified "assessor". More especially, magistrates' courts constitute only one section of Scottish summary justice, much being conducted not by a magistrate but by a sheriff sitting without a jury. Magistrates, however, especially in major cities like the one where this work was done, still deal with a very large number of cases.

[5] Criminal Statistics, England and Wales, 1978 (1979, HMSO Cmnd. 7670) Criminal Statistics, Scotland, 1978 (1979, HMSO Cmnd. 7676).

[6] Vennard *op.cit*.

[7] S. Dell, *Silence in Court*, Occasional Papers in Social Administration, 42 (1971).

[8] P. Carlen, *Magistrates' Justice* (1976).

[9] A. E. Bottoms and J. D. McClean, *Defendants in the Criminal Process* (1976).

[10] Report of the Royal Commission on Legal Services (1979; Cmnd. 7648) 58.

[11] Report of the Departmental Committee on Legal Aid in Criminal Court Proceedings (1966; Cmnd. 2934) 46.

[12] *op.cit*. p. 104.

[13] *op.cit*. p. 47.

[14] Lord Chancellor's office: Lectures for Magistrates (1953) 38.

[15] Widgery Report, *op.cit*. p. 2.

[16] Lord Chancellor's office, *op.cit*. p. 38.

[17] *Lamb* v *Threshie* (1892) 3 White 261.

[18] R. Arguile, *Criminal Procedure* (1969). 55; R. Renton and Brown: *Criminal Procedure according to the law of Scotland* (1972) 278.

[19] Note the reference to "*ideology and generality at least*". There are all sorts of ways in which the higher courts too routinely contravene the rhetoric. See McBarnet *op.cit*.

[20] The issue of triviality is one point where it might be thought that the generalisability of the Scottish data is in question. The magistrates' courts in Scotland are a lower rung than those in England in that much of the work that would be done by magistrates in England is done by sheriffs in Scotland and the assumption is often made that the Scottish magistrates are only allocated the most trivial offences to deal with. There could therefore be an *overstatement* in Scottish magistrates' courts of the triviality of the offences involved compared to England. However, two points should be borne in mind. First the data used here were collected in stipendiary as well as lay magistrates' courts and though lay magistrates may well tend to be allocated very trivial cases, there is less evidence that the stipendiaries are. Secondly, the *descriptions* of magistrates' work just quoted are from English as well as Scottish sources. The first is taken from Arguile *op.cit*. the second from the Lords' Debate on the Magistrates' Courts Bill (1953 Hansard), the third is Scottish (Walker). In short, the *image* of triviality, which is the concern of this article, is the same in both jurisdictions.

[21] J. W. Coull and E. W. Merry, *Principles and Practice of Scots Law* (1971). 25–26.

[22] See McBarnet *op.cit*. ch. 7, Section: 'State struggles and the two tiers of justice'.

[23] D. Hay, 'Property, authority and the law' in *Albion's Fatal Tree* (1975, eds. D. Hay *et. al.*).

[24] Widgery *op.cit.* p. 190.

[25] (1975; Cmnd. 6323) 20.

[26] *op.cit.*p. 46.

[27] Vennard *op.cit.*

[28] See McBarnet *op.cit.* ch. 3.

[29] 'Advocacy and the solicitor-advocate in magistrates' courts in England and Wales' *International Journal of the Sociology of Law* (May 1979).

[30] *op.cit.* p. 17.

[31] For a more detailed analysis see McBarnet *op.cit.* ch. 2.

[32] *op.cit.* p. 13.

[33] *op.cit.* p. 164.

[34] From my own observation, and see P. Darbyshire, *The Role of the Justices' Clerk and the Court Clerk.* Ph.D. Thesis (1978 Birmingham).

[35] Quoted in *The Times* 23 August 1977.

[36] *op.cit.* p. 38.

[37] In appearance at least, see note 19.

[15]

LAY EXPECTATIONS OF THE CIVIL JUSTICE SYSTEM

WILLIAM M. O'BARR
JOHN M. CONLEY

In this paper we present results from a study of small claims litigants' expectations about the civil justice system. Interviews with plaintiffs at the time they file their cases reveal that many people come to court with profound misunderstandings about the authority of civil courts as well as the procedural and evidentiary burdens that the civil justice system imposes. These findings, based on the empirical investigation of litigants' beliefs about and understandings of civil justice, complement experimental studies of procedural justice conducted over the past two decades. We find that litigants are at least as concerned with issues of process as they are with the substantive questions that make up their cases. Yet litigants' preconceptions of procedure are frequently at variance with what the law requires and what will happen in the legal process. Such differences suggest that litigants' expectations and understandings deserve attention in the study of their attitudes toward the legal process.

I. BACKGROUND AND PURPOSE

In their landmark study of procedural justice, Thibaut and Walker (1975) argued that the process used in resolving a dispute strongly influences the disputants' level of satisfaction with the resolution. In a series of laboratory experiments, they showed that disputants' judgments about procedural fairness have an effect on the satisfaction that transcends the outcome of disputes or the likelihood that particular procedures will be advantageous to individual disputants. Their work ultimately led many researchers concerned with fairness and consumer satisfaction to reevaluate the traditional focus on the fairness of outcomes ("distributive fairness") and to concentrate instead on the significance of procedure.

The research reported here is a joint project. The authors alternate priority of authorship in their publications. The research was supported by Grants SES 85-21528 and SES 85-21574 from the Law and Social Science Program of the National Science Foundation. We acknowledge with appreciation the assistance of the officials of the small claims courts and the clerk's office in Denver, Colorado; the persons (identified in this paper by pseudonyms) whose cases we studied; and our research assistants, Mark Bielawski and Rebecca Schaller. Allan Lind provided much assistance with the literature on procedural justice and offered helpful suggestions on earlier drafts of this paper.

LAW & SOCIETY REVIEW, Volume 22, Number 1 (1988)

138   LAY EXPECTATIONS OF CIVIL JUSTICE

Thibaut and Walker's theory of procedural justice has spawned a large and growing literature.[1] A number of researchers have confirmed the basic procedural justice hypothesis with studies of such diverse subjects as criminal defendants (Casper and Tyler, 1986; Landis and Goodstein, 1986), parties to alternative dispute resolution proceedings (Adler *et al.*, 1983), citizens dealing with the police (Tyler and Folger, 1980), citizens evaluating the government benefits they receive against the taxes they pay (Tyler and Caine, 1981; Tyler, Rasinski, and Spodick, 1985), and workers evaluating their employers' decision-making procedures (e.g., Alexander and Ruderman, in press). Much current procedural justice research focuses on why procedural fairness is so important. Thibaut and Walker originally hypothesized that litigants prefer adversary procedures to inquisitorial ones because the former allow the litigants to maintain control over the process of presenting evidence. They later argued (Thibaut and Walker, 1978) that such process control is important to litigants because they see it as promoting equitable, if not necessarily favorable, outcomes. Subsequent researchers have suggested that litigants value process control because they view it as either a means of controlling outcome (Brett and Goldberg, 1983) or a guarantee of the opportunity for self-expression (Tyler, Rasinski, and McGraw, 1985). More recent work has concerned itself with the psychological processes that occasion preference for one procedure over another.

Both the work of Thibaut and Walker and the diverse research it has inspired share the goal of theoretical development through laboratory experimentation designed to explicate structural and/or psychological determinants of litigants' preferences. We have been greatly influenced by this body of work, but our disciplinary background leads us to ask somewhat different questions about procedural justice and the contexts in which it works. As anthropologists we ask about the ethnographic reality of process concerns for everyday litigants who encounter the civil justice system in practical as opposed to laboratory situations. We would have perhaps never formulated such questions without the stimulus of the insights that have come from laboratory research on procedural justice. In turn, we hope that an ethnographic understanding of lay expectations and concerns will make its way into the experimental research effort.

In addition to its relation to the study of procedural justice, the investigation of litigant perceptions of justice is significant in its own right, because it offers an opportunity to understand the theories of law that litigants themselves hold. Felsteiner and Sarat (1986) have demonstrated that the examination of the dialogue between lawyers and their clients in divorce cases can reveal

---

[1] For a comprehensive review of this literature, see Lind and Tyler, in press.

the theories that lawyers use to transform their clients' problems into legally sufficient claims that articulate with the law. Our investigation of the talk of small claims litigants reveals an equally interesting set of insights into the legal process, since the theories of both legal professionals and lay persons interact in the functioning of the legal system.

We interviewed small claims plaintiffs before and after the trial of their cases. Despite the diversity of the plaintiffs' backgrounds and claims, three themes run consistently through their comments. First, litigants are deeply concerned with legal process. By contrast, they seem to have little concern with substance. They tend to view the facts at issue as straightforward and assume that they will be readily understood by the court.

Second, litigants fail to appreciate the purely adversarial nature of civil litigation. In reality, civil litigants (with the aid of a lawyer in more formal courts) must conceive their own case, assemble their own evidence, find and prepare their own witnesses, and present their own case in court, with a passive judicial system providing little assistance. The criminal justice system, by contrast, has an important inquisitorial component: A victim or complaining witness goes to the police, who investigate; if a defendant is charged, the prosecution is in the hands of the authorities, with the victim often acting as a passive observer. As the texts we analyze indicate, many of the litigants in our study come to civil court with a model of procedure more appropriate to the criminal justice system. Moreover, at this point in the process most litigants have little or no awareness that they will encounter—and thus be required to overcome—another substantially different perspective or version of their case.

The third pervasive theme is the misapprehension of the remedial authority of the civil courts. The civil system can compensate but rarely punishes, whereas the criminal system punishes but rarely compensates. Thus, the civil system has no practical authority over an impecunious defendant. Our data indicate, however, that this basic distinction is lost on many litigants, some of whom base their very decision to go to small claims court on an overestimation of the remedial power of civil courts.

II. METHODS

The data on which this analysis is based were collected as a part of a comparative study of small claims courts in Colorado, North Carolina, and Pennsylvania. The overall objective of the larger study is to understand lay versus legal concepts of basic issues such as evidence, procedure, proof, causality, blame, and responsibility.

The study began with interviews of plaintiffs conducted imme-

140   LAY EXPECTATIONS OF CIVIL JUSTICE

diately after they filed their complaints at the courthouse.[2] Our purpose was to gain some understanding of the perceptions, attitudes, and assumptions that litigants bring to the system. For the present analysis, we draw on data from forty-five cases processed in Denver during the summer of 1986. Two law students (one male, one female), who had been trained in open-ended interview techniques conducted the interviews. With as little prompting as possible and a lot of active listening, they spoke with plaintiffs for periods ranging from five minutes to one-half hour. The question at the heart of each interview was: "What is your case about?" The interviewers had a loose agenda of topics covering evidence, procedure, and case facts that they raised in the interview if they were not first brought up by the litigants. The litigants talked about the details of their cases, often providing successive and elaborated versions of "what happened" as the interviews developed. In addition, they talked about their general views of the legal system, of what they had to prove in court, and of what they would use as evidence.

Of the forty-five cases we studied, twenty-eight went forward to trial or other final disposition,[3] usually within a month of our first interview. About a month after most of the cases had gone to court, we attempted to locate all forty-five plaintiffs for follow-up interviews; we were able to interview nineteen. We questioned them about their overall reaction to the small claims system and, more specifically, about the extent to which their experiences had met their expectations, and their satisfaction with both the process and the result.

The analysis of these data consisted of transcribing the interviews and listening repeatedly to the tapes. The authors, along with the research assistants who conducted the interviews, noted issues of relevance to the project and discussed them in workshops.[4] In our effort to comb the data for what we could learn about the issues of interest to us, we also learned about other matters that we had not specifically intended to research. The two

---

[2] Comparable pretrial interviews of defendants have not proved feasible. Despite our theoretical interest in defendants at the pretrial stage, we have had limited success in interviewing them. We suspect that this is due in large part to their dismay and general unhappiness with their status as defendants.

[3] By "other final disposition" we mean entry of a default judgment if either of the parties failed to appear or settlement of the case. In most of the remaining 17 cases, the plaintiff failed to obtain service of process on the defendant, resulting in withdrawal of the complaint or dismissal without prejudice.

[4] We owe a debt to the conversation analysis approach to the study of verbal behavior for what it has taught us about the significance and utility of the fine-grained analysis of speech (Atkinson and Heritage, 1984; Atkinson and Drew, 1979). Our work has been greatly influenced by its methods. However, our goals are different in that we are concerned with the analysis of legal institutions and their functions rather than with the explanation of linguistic interaction per se.

such issues we discuss in this paper—the blurring of the civil/criminal distinction and the views of litigants on inquisitorial versus adversarial procedures—emerged as topics of interest *because the litigants themselves* made us aware of their concerns about these matters through their talk.

The data and analyses reported in this paper are qualitative in nature. An important first step in understanding lay versus legal conceptions of the law is listening to how litigants talk and comparing this to the institutional requirements for how they *should* talk. To the extent that quantification of such complex data would ever be feasible, it is not appropriate even to consider quantification until we have a better understanding of the issues that concern litigants and what they say about them.[5]

We will focus on five cases that illustrate particularly well the range of views expressed by our forty-five subjects on the distinction between civil and criminal law and the nature of the adversary system.[6] The case method has served legal anthropologists at least since Malinowski (1926) used it in his analyses of Trobriand law, and has been widely used by such influential figures as Llewellyn and Hoebel (1941) and Gluckman (1955) as well as more recent legal anthropologists. As in the studies cited, we use the case method to understand how a system works by looking at the details of many specific cases. This approach is particularly useful because it allows us to focus on each case from the perspective of its participants.

III. DATA AND ANALYSIS

We will examine the five illustrative cases to determine what they show about lay perceptions of law and legal procedure. For each case, we present a summary of the facts and include relevant excerpts from the interviews.

Case 1: "$100 Worth of Drunk." The plaintiff, Edward Atkin, is a businessman in his twenties. He owns a large motorcycle that, on the night in question, was parked at the curb

---

[5] We cite as instructive models for this type of qualitative analysis the research of Felsteiner and Sarat (1986) and our own previous work on small claims narratives (O'Barr and Conley, 1985).

[6] In the pretrial interviews, 33 of the 45 plaintiffs made comments relevant to the civil/criminal distinction; 9 of the 33 demonstrated what we judged to be a fundamental misunderstanding of the distinction. Forty-one of the 45 plaintiffs discussed trial procedures, and 10 of them seriously misperceived the adversarial nature of civil justice. Although admittedly sketchy, these figures are noteworthy in two respects. First, we were impressed by the extent to which lay litigants had thought about procedural issues. Second, we were struck by the number of litigants who seriously misunderstood (at least in our subjective judgment) two concepts that are fundamental to our legal system. While we would not presume to draw any statistical conclusions from the latter observation, we note it as a matter of concern and a possible subject for future research.

outside his house. The defendant is an otherwise unidentified woman. Atkin was awakened late at night by his neighbor, who told him that a woman had just "dumped" the motorcycle. According to the neighbor's account, which was based largely on reconstruction and inference, a battered and obviously drunk woman appeared at his door looking for help in finding her own motorcycle. She apparently had just fallen off her bike, which skidded off down the street while she tumbled away in the opposite direction. The neighbor looked up and down the street, and the only motorcycle he saw was Atkin's, which he pointed out to the woman. The neighbor then either saw or heard Atkin's bike fall, and went to his house to tell him. When Atkin went out into the street, the woman was gone, but her bike was lying in the street. Apparently assuming that she would return in the morning, he went back to bed.

The next morning, Atkin waited for the woman for some time, and then called the police to report the accident. His understanding was that the police then "picked her up." In any event, some time thereafter she came to his house to discuss the accident. The details are unclear, but it appears that Atkin took the bike to a repair shop. An initial assessment revealed that the forks were bent, in addition to minor damages to the blinkers and gas tank. The repair estimate for the forks alone was $100, and the woman paid Atkin that amount. According to Atkin, she gave him a receipt for that amount (perhaps she tendered a receipt that he signed and returned). However, while repairing the forks, the shop discovered more extensive structural damage, which would cost several hundred dollars to repair. At this point, the woman—with whom Atkin apparently was in regular communication—balked. Her "attitude," according to Atkin, was that she "couldn't have been more than $100 worth of drunk." When she refused to accept responsibility for the additional damage, Atkin sued, seeking the cost of the repairs to the frame as well as the cost of fixing the blinkers and gas tank, which he had been prepared to forget at the time of the $100 agreement. On the trial date, he went to court with his wife and three witnesses—his neighbor, a mechanic, and a friend who could testify about the bike's condition. The woman did not appear. In a five-minute proceeding, he and the friend testified, and the judge gave him a default judgment. Later, the woman applied to the court for relief from the default judgment. Atkin had to appear at another hearing, at which the judge confirmed the original judgment. When interviewed after the trial, Atkin was in the process of collecting the judgment by garnishing the woman's paycheck.

Edward Atkin is a middle-class businessman. Additionally, he has had experience with small claims court. On one prior occasion, he filed a complaint, the sheriff served the papers, and the defendant accepted responsibility and settled. Atkin's conduct during the present dispute and his interview comments suggest that his background and this previous small claims experience have led him to a reasonably accurate understanding of the civil justice system.

Consider first his conduct. After hearing the story of the drunken woman from his neighbor, his immediate objective was to "talk to her and see if she wanted to settle everything out of court."[7] Toward this end, he left a note on her abandoned bike and waited on his front porch the next morning to see if she would appear. His first thought was compensation, a civil remedy; appropriately, he did not call the police, but waited to see if a settlement was possible.

When the woman did not appear, he finally called the police. He believes (the source of his belief is unclear) that "the police went to her house, picked her up, and cited her for reckless driving." In any event, about a month later she finally appeared, and the parties began negotiating. The negotiations broke down over the extent of the damage for which the woman would assume responsibility, and Atkin filed a small claims action. Significantly, throughout the negotiation, he never spoke to the police—indeed, when the interviewer raised the topic, he responded that he might call them the next day, since he had not spoken with them for months. The most obvious interpretation of this course of conduct is that his objective was compensation rather than punishment, and that he understands that one can achieve compensation through either direct negotiation or the civil justice system. Accordingly, he used the police for the limited purpose of flushing out the wrongdoer, and then dealt with her himself. When he was unable to achieve his objective, he went not to the police but to the civil courts.

Atkin's conduct also reflects a general understanding of the burden placed on him by the adversarial system. On the trial date, he appeared in court with three witnesses and "all these receipts and all my stuff." After he obtained a default judgment, he took the initiative and garnished the woman's paycheck.

Atkin's stated understanding of the nature of civil justice is consistent with his conduct. In Text 1A, drawn from the pretrial interview, after dismissing (perhaps erroneously) the idea of pursuing the woman's insurance company, he describes clearly the alternatives of instigating a criminal prosecution and seeking a civil remedy:

---

[7] Directly quoted passages drawn from this and other interviews are indicated.

144   LAY EXPECTATIONS OF CIVIL JUSTICE

Text 1A[8]

Q₂:	Does she have insurance that would cover it?
Q:	What about um . . . ?
Atkin:	What kind of insurance?
Q₂:	Well, don't for bikes you have to have something like — insurance?
Atkin:	Well, she didn't really hit it with her bike though.
Q₂:	Oh, I see.
Atkin:	See, she got off it.
Q₂:	That's right, yeah, that makes sense.
Atkin:	She got off. It's, it's, it's, uh . . .
Q:	I'd try and make a claim. [*In a joking manner:*] I'd, I'd roll the other bike under it, you know. I'd . . .
All:	[*laughter*]
Atkin:	No, but all I could do, you know, is cite her for, uh, destruction of personal property . . .
Q:	Yeah.
Q₂:	Yeah.
Atkin:	. . . and, what I'm doing now.
Q₂:	Yeah.

On the basis of this evidence, one might well conclude that Atkin has a thorough and accurate understanding of the role of the civil justice system. One might further conclude that his understanding is quite predictable, given his business background and prior legal experience. There is additional evidence, however, that suggests that the proper interpretation is somewhat more complicated. Near the end of the pretrial interview, he talks about his plans for trying the case:

Text 1B

Q:	. . . Do you have it mapped out, have you practiced in front of the mirror, you know, how

---

8 Except where otherwise noted, the texts are drawn from pre-trial interviews. To make the texts accessible to as wide an audience as possible, we have not used special transcribing conventions such as those used by linguists and conversation analysts. We believe, following Ochs (1979), that the act of transcribing is a statement about the theoretical significance of the data. Because we are focusing on the sociolegal issues involved and not on the interaction patterns per se, we believe we are justified in electing to use a straightforward set of conventions that do not bring in issues that we do not intend to discuss. Moreover, as anyone who has worked with transcripts knows, there is never a totally complete transcript. There are always other issues to be noticed, such as prosody, rate, pauses, overlapping, accent, and even nonverbal features when videotapes as opposed to audiotapes are available. In the texts, Q and Q₂ refer respectively to the male and female interviewers.

	you're gonna handle the court case, or, you know, pictures and drawings or [*laughter*]?
Atkin:	Well, no.
Q:	Today we saw one [*a case*] with a diagram and a model truck . . .
Atkin:	[*laughter*] Did you?
Q:	. . . demonstrating how an accident could not have possibly happened.
Atkin:	[*laughter*] No, well, I don't. I don't, you know. I'm not totally unprepared, but I haven't rehearsed either. You know I've got uh, I'm gonna have my neighbor come in.
Q₂:	Uh huh.
Atkin:	And he can tell his story. Uh, I'm gonna have the mechanic come in; he can tell his story. You know, can this actually happen by a bike being tipped over. He can tell them that it can happen.
Q₂:	Right.
Atkin:	Which obvious—, obviously it can happen.
Q₂:	Did he know your bike before? I mean . . .
Atkin:	No, I've got a friend, that's the best I can do as far as that goes, I've got a friend coming in that, uh, knows the bike was in min—, mint condition.
Q₂:	Right.
Atkin:	So I don't know what more I can do, much else I can do, you know.
Q:	Yeah.
Q₂:	If you get that, that's, you know, that's a lot.
Atkin:	And then I'll just ask, answer the referee's questions or judge's questions or whatever.
Q:	Yeah.
Atkin:	I dunno. What can I rehearse?

These remarks suggest that in spite of his background and experience, Atkin has brought to this case some mistaken assumptions about the burden the civil justice system will place on him to produce evidence and prove facts. With the trial a week away, he has not prepared his own testimony, relying instead on an anticipated interrogation by the judge to elicit the facts—a rare occurrence in the small claims courts we have observed. Moreover, he seems not to consider seriously the possibility that the defendant will present a vigorous case of her own, saying, "I don't see how I can go wrong unless she does skip town." (There is in fact a number of plausible defenses she might have presented, including denying that her actions caused the damage to the bike and contending that their $100 arrangement was a final settlement.) Additionally, the interviewers met the neighbor shortly after talking to Atkin and learned that he had not yet contacted this critical witness to insure his appearance and confirm the content of his testimony. Thus, even this relatively sophisticated litigant seems to view the civil court as more active and inquisitorial than it is in reality and to underestimate his own role in prosecuting his case. We cannot assess the effect of this misunderstanding since Atkin won his case by default.

Case 2: "The Thirteen-Hour Day." The plaintiff, Harvey Johnson, is a middle-aged man. The defendant owns a lawn care business. Johnson agreed to work for the defendant cutting lawns. The defendant agreed to pay him $35 per day, which Johnson assumed referred to an eight-hour work day. The first day, the defendant picked him up early in the morning, drove him from house to house, and brought him home at the end of a thirteen-hour day. He paid Johnson $35. The next day, they started early in the morning and worked nine hours. At that point, Johnson said he refused to work until eight at night again, and the man responded, "We're gonna be here as late as we were yesterday." Johnson quit on the spot and demanded to be paid for his hours, but the defendant refused. Johnson took the bus home from the house where they were working.

Johnson then went to the State Labor Board. According to Johnson, they advised him that he was entitled to be paid an hourly wage for all the time he had worked, with time-and-a-half for any hours in excess of eight in a given day. They also told him that they could not collect his money for him, so he should go to small claims court. In filing his suit, he has made detailed calculations of the amount owed him. He began by dividing eight into $35 to get an hourly rate of $4.38. He is claiming two eight-hour days at this rate, plus six hours overtime (five the first day, one the second) at time-and-a-half, for a total of $111.62 (the arithmetic appears to be off by about a dollar). The court records show that Johnson was unable to get service, and dropped the case. We were unable to locate him for a post-trial interview.

The evidence from Case 2 is quite different from what we observed in Case 1. The plaintiff, Johnson, seems to have a profound misunderstanding of the adversarial nature of civil justice and to have experienced dissatisfaction from the very first time the system frustrated his expectations. As the interview progresses, he reveals that his expectations may be derived from his previous dealings with the law. The different legal experiences of Johnson and Edward Atkin, the plaintiff in Case 1, may explain the different attitudes and expectations that they bring to small claims court.

As Johnson states in Text 2A, he has brought the case because of a failure on the part of "the state," which "couldn't catch up with" the defendant and told Johnson to try small claims court. In so doing, the State Labor Board was effectively admitting that its inquisitorial undertaking had failed and suggesting that Johnson try his luck with the adversarial system.

Text 2A

Johnson:	I went by and asked him for my money a few days later. He said that he didn't owe me anything. So, I've been watching uh, Judge Wapner.
Q:	[*laughter*]
Johnson:	He said, "If you have a case . . ."
Q:	"The People's Court?"
Johnson:	Yeah, "People's Court." And uh, so I decided to bring him to court. Well, I took him to the state but the state can't catch up with him. He keeps his equipment in one place and he lives in another place.
Q:	Uh huh.
Johnson:	And it's hard to catch up, the state couldn't catch up with him 'cause they told me to bring it to sm—, small claims court. But the problem that I think I'm going to have is serving the papers, serving him.

Although he had learned something about small claims court from watching "The People's Court" on television, Johnson was unpleasantly surprised by the litigant-driven, adversarial process he confronted. In particular, his responsibility for serving the summons on the elusive defendant runs contrary to his view of how "the law" should function:

Text 2B

Johnson:	And, well, I probably know several guys that I could get to go around and just catch him, and give him the papers, but, uh, it's all left up to me.
Q:	Right.

Law and Society

148   LAY EXPECTATIONS OF CIVIL JUSTICE

Johnson: And um, I thought the law was supposed to be,
                    you know, if you have a case against someone,
                    hey, I think the law, the deputy sheriff should be
                    able anytime up until midnight, anytime, to serve
                    papers.[9]

The reason for Johnson's dissatisfaction with the passive system is itself interesting. As he acknowledges in Text 2B, he knows
"several guys" who might be able to find the defendant. Nonetheless, he states in Text 2C that he is reluctant to see the defendant
until the court date, for he wants their ultimate confrontation to
be mediated by the state:

Text 2C

Johnson: . . . I'll just have to get someone early in the
                    morning or late at night and just wait on
                    him . . .
Q: Yeah.
Johnson: . . . to serve the papers. That's the problem,
                    that's the thing I don't like. See, I don't want, I
                    don't want—he know what I'm doing to him.
                    See, I don't want to have the, I, I don't want to
                    be seeing him until court.

In Text 2D, Johnson discloses the source of his reluctance to confront the defendant—his bad feelings toward him—and makes the
point that this is the only grievance he has thus far with the small
claims process:

Text 2D

Johnson: And I, I don't, I don't, that's, the only thing that
                    I don't like about the courts to start with, is
                    serving him the papers.
Q: Have you ever uh . . .
Johnson: See, I don't, I don't feel good towards him at all.

In some respects, Johnson's expectations reflect a model of
the small claims process that would be more appropriate for the
criminal system. He believes that "the law" should seek out and
serve the defendant while the plaintiff remains anonymously in
the background until the trial. Later in the interview, he suggests
the source of these expectations:

---

[9] In Denver, the county sheriffs will serve summonses, but they work
only during regular business hours. Litigants wanting to sue persons not
available during these hours must find a disinterested party to make service
on their behalf.

Text 2E

Q:	Have you ever uh, you know, gone to a court before like that?
Johnson:	No, not to claims, not to small claims, not suing anybody.
Q:	Uh huh.
Johnson:	When I've ever been to court, I've always been behind the gun in the courtroom, DUIs, disturbing, and things like that, I've always been behind the gun.

Thus, even though Johnson has been influenced to some extent by "The People's Court," his only previous personal experience with the legal system has been as a criminal defendant. He has probably seen the active, inquisitorial arm of "the law" at work. He expects the same when he is the complaining party, and is dissatisfied with the civil justice system when it fails to perform up to his expectations. Since Johnson was ultimately forced to drop his case because of a feature of the system he has specifically complained about (lack of assistance in serving process), it is regrettable that we were unable to question him again about his reactions. Had his case gone to trial, it also would have been interesting to see whether he experienced similar dissatisfaction with such other manifestations of the adversarial system as the burden to produce evidence and to present an affirmative case.[10]

Case 3: "Harassment at the Grocery Store." Plaintiff Lorna Terry, a young woman, sued the owner of a grocery store where she had worked for several days. The owner fired her (this is Terry's version—she said that the owner claims that she quit) and then refused to give her a paycheck. She went to the Colorado Labor Board, where she obtained a "demand notice" calling on the owner to pay her immediately or face a penalty of ten extra days' pay. She served a copy of the notice on the owner, but he still refused to pay her. On the advice of the Labor Board, she filed suit for the overdue pay plus the penalty. Late in the pretrial interview, Terry volunteered that "there's more to this story than what I'm tellin' you, it's a lot more." She then mentioned unspecified "harassments" as well as problems with bill collectors in the store. She believed that the store was on the

---

[10] At one point in the interview, Johnson hinted that he had considered some of these matters. He raised the issue of having to prove that he had done the work and suggested that he might contact some of the homeowners to "see if I can get just one of them to verify that I did [work]." It is unclear, however, what he meant by "verify." Would he arrange for them to come to court, or get written statements, or simply tell them to stand by for a phone call from the judge? The last possibility is not far-fetched, as we have seen a number of litigants suggest in court that the judge should call someone for additional evidence.

150   LAY EXPECTATIONS OF CIVIL JUSTICE

verge of bankruptcy, even though the owner had money in other companies. She was confident that she would get paid, however, since her claim was "registered in the court already." Terry appeared for the trial with her father and her friend Charles, but the defendant did not show up. After a brief informal discussion with the judge, she was awarded a default judgment for $43.85, which she understands to represent ten percent of the amount she claimed. In a posttrial interview, she expressed complete satisfaction with the outcome and the small claims process.

Lorna Terry, the plaintiff, has no apparent prior experience with the law. Nonetheless, she has some accurate ideas about the legal system. For example, she is aware of the principle that a judgment gives its holder priority over many other creditors if the defendant goes bankrupt:

Text 3A

Terry: If he goes bankrupt, I'm still gettin' mine. 'Cause I have mine's registered in court, already. Either way he goes, I'm gettin' mine's. Now I, I feel for the people that's still workin' for him and then try to file after he bankrupts. They don't get nothin'.

Like many other litigants, however, she attributes to the civil court far more power than it actually has. In Text 3B, she considers the question of what will happen if the defendant fails to appear for trial:

Text 3B

Q: I'll be interested to see what that guy's gonna say if he shows up.
Terry: Oh, he, he, no he's gonna show up. Like [*the clerk*] told me, he's got to show up . . .
Q: Uh huh.
Terry: . . . if he's served, he's got to show up.
Q: Uh huh.
Q₂: And if he doesn't, like . . .
[*inaudible*]
Terry: . . . if he doesn't, better, okay, I will win like this [*indicating paper*] says.
Charles: We'll have a warrant out for his arrest if he doesn't show up.
Q₂: Well, you can just get the money, I guess, you know.

Terry:	Okay, it says, "If you do not appear justi—," um, excuse me. "If you do not appear judgment will be made against you for the amount of the plaintiff's claim plus costs of this suit."

In Terry's view, "he's got to show up"; if he does not, she claims two consequences will ensue. First, perhaps informed by the summons that she later quotes, she concludes that "I will win. . . ." Second, according to her companion, the defendant will find "a warrant out for his arrest." The first point is accurate in the limited sense that the court will issue a default judgment—a piece of paper—against an absent defendant. The second point is patently inaccurate, of course, which suggests that Terry did not mean "win" in the limited technical sense but had something more final and meaningful in mind. It is tempting to speculate that her slip in reading from the summons form ("If you do not appear justi—") is more than inadvertent and in fact reflects her view of the court's authority.

The evidence in Text 3C (from the pretrial interview) is consistent with this interpretation. Here Terry expresses her belief that if the defendant fails to appear for trial, "the government" will compensate her, and the defendant will be left to deal with the government—surely something he will want to avoid:

Text 3C

Terry:	Yeah, and then he don't want the government to pay me 'cause he has to pay the government and if he pay the government, he's through. When he don't pay the government, he's through.

Once again, her view seems to be that the civil justice system is an omnipotent, self-directed authority that will recognize the justice of her cause and do whatever is necessary to protect her position.

In an objective sense, the court failed to meet Terry's expectations when it awarded her only $43.85. However, she made it clear in the posttrial interview that she sees considerable value in the outcome. From a purely economic perspective, she recognizes that her victory was insignificant: "If I got to chase him down just for $43, I don't want to." Nonetheless, maintaining her original belief in the power of the system and the documents it generates, she views the judgment as money in the bank: "Now if I needed that $43, I'll take it to him." Moreover, perhaps motivated by the same belief, she concludes that she has achieved something even more important: "Yeah, it came out great . . . . At least he know he can't run over nobody else." Throughout the interview, she reiterated that her experience had been a positive one—thanks to the judge's sense of humor, the trial was "really funny"—and that she was satisfied with the system and would use it again. Thus, the

152   LAY EXPECTATIONS OF CIVIL JUSTICE

very misconceptions about the system that set her up for possible
disappointment ultimately shielded her from it by leading her to
overestimate the practical and legal significance of what she had
accomplished. Terry's reactions also demonstrate the fallacy of assessing the adequacy of the judicial system solely in rational, economic terms.

> *Case 4: "The Former Friends."* The plaintiffs, Mr. and Mrs.
> Winner, are a couple in their twenties. They sued "some old
> friends" who failed to repay a loan. The story is unclear, but it
> appears that the defendants have a recent history of moving
> around the country, living with friends and borrowing money.
> They were living in Arkansas until the Winners suggested that
> they would help them find jobs if they moved to Denver. The
> defendants came and lived with the Winners until, as they put it,
> "We kicked them out. . . . We starved them to death." Then Mr.
> Winner inherited some money, and he and his wife lent or gave
> the defendants $390. After a couple of months passed without
> repayment, the Winners prepared some type of loan document
> that the defendants signed, although they admitted while sign-
> ing that they could not repay the money. The document appar-
> ently required the defendants to make a $50 payment by June
> 17. On June 24, having heard nothing from the defendants, the
> Winners sued. They sought the $390, plus $110 for their ex-
> penses in bringing the suit. According to Mr. Winner, the pur-
> pose of claiming the additional damages was to "make it hurt."
> The defendants did not appear for trial, and the Winners re-
> ceived a default judgment for $400. Although they located the
> defendants, they were unable to collect their money. The Win-
> ners thought the trial itself was fair and were pleased that they
> had damaged the defendants' credit rating, but concluded that
> the whole small claims process was "a waste of our time." In
> particular, they felt that "there should be some way that the city
> or the court or somebody should be able to get our money for
> us."

The Winners claim to have considerable knowledge of the
small claims process, derived largely from watching "The People's
Court."[11]

Text 4A

Q_2:   . . . How'd you know to do, do small claims?
How'd you think of it?

---

[11] We have been struck by the litigants' repeated references to "The People's Court." While we initially joked about the "Wapner factor," we now suspect that the television program is a significant factor in many litigants' decisions to go to small claims courts and an important influence on the way they
prepare their cases.

Mrs. Winner:	I don't know. We just told them, you know, if they didn't pay us, we'd take them to court.
Q₂:	Uh huh.
Mrs. Winner:	We watch Judge Wapner on TV.
Q₂:	Oh yeah. People, a lot of people find out about, you know, small claims, you know, through that.
Mr. Winner:	Yeah.
Q₂:	'Cause if not, you really wouldn't know where, what to do, I guess.
Mrs. Winner:	That's right, that's right. And we wouldn't know to, um, you know, charge them for lost wages and stuff. . . .

The plaintiffs are also aware of the significance the law attaches to written contracts, particularly those sworn to before a notary. Thus, when their exfriends failed to repay the loan, the Winners made them sign a sworn document and advised them of the potential legal consequences of continued failure to repay:

Text 4B

Mr. Winner:	They're some old friends of ours. And it took them a couple of months to finally make payment arrangements with us so I wrote up a contract and they signed it in front of a notary and everything, to pay me $50 a month and, uh, by the 17th of this month and they haven't done so.
Q₂:	Uh huh.
Mr. Winner:	And I told them I'd take them to court, no hesitations. And they've done this . . .
Q₂:	Sure.
Mr. Winner:	. . . they've done this to people before.

As is evident from Text 4C, however, the Winners are aware that the defendants simply do not have the money they owe (recall that the defendants so admitted when they signed the loan document):

Text 4C

Mrs. Winner:	She didn't think we would do it, I don't think.
Q₂:	Oh yeah? So, um, do you think she, they have it?
Mrs. Winner:	No.
Mr. Winner:	They don't have it.
Q₂:	Yeah, so . . .
Mrs. Winner:	They're gonna have to go to court, ah ha ha.

The obvious question is why these plaintiffs, sophisticated in

154   LAY EXPECTATIONS OF CIVIL JUSTICE

some respects about law and procedure, are wasting time and
money on the pursuit of debtors who will be unable to pay a judgment ("judgment-proof" defendants, in lawyers' jargon). Text 4C
provides one clue. Mrs. Winner says, in a mocking tone, "They're
gonna have to go to court, ah ha ha," suggesting that she and her
husband may intend to punish the defendants with the inconvenience and humiliation of a court appearance. Later in the pretrial
interview, however, the Winners provide evidence for a different
interpretation:

Text 4D

Mr. Winner:	You know, I figured I can go up for $390 but I'm losing time from work. I gotta pay these fees and . . .
Q₂:	Sure.
Mrs. Winner:	. . . gas to get down here and everything else.
Q₂:	Yeah, yeah.
Mr. Winner:	I'm gonna make it hurt.
Q₂:	Mmhm.
Mrs. Winner:	[laughter]
Mr. Winner:	Feels good.
Q₂:	Yeah. Well, I understand. Probably can use some money.
Mr. Winner:	Yeah, we sure could.

In Text 4D Mr. Winner says, in reference to his inflated damage calculations, "I'm gonna make it hurt." The clear implication
is that the increased damages will inflict more pain on the defendants, although they lack the resources to pay even the $390 loan.
Mrs. Winner then concludes the interview by responding to the
statement that they "probably can use some money" with "yeah,
we sure could," suggesting some measure of economic motivation
in bringing the case.

To the extent that the Winners' motivation is indeed economic, it rests on an erroneous assumption about the power of a
civil court. In fact, the court merely furnishes a piece of paper
called a judgment, and then provides a mechanism for the successful plaintiff to collect it against the assets of a defendant who will
not pay voluntarily. If the defendant refuses to pay and has no
unencumbered property that can be sold off, the plaintiff is out of
luck. The Winners seem to assume, however, that the court will
somehow force the defendants to produce money they do not have
or perhaps will punish them for their penury. They thus attribute
to the court some of the power of the American criminal system or
of some hypothetical inquisition.

The Winners' erroneous expectations contribute to their ultimate dissatisfaction with the process. In a posttrial interview, Mrs.
Winner described the trial itself as being "real fair" and "real easy

with them not being there," and she did not complain about the amount of the judgment. However, she became increasingly vitriolic when discussing her belief that "the court should be able to go after them." She progressed from stating that "we're pretty unhappy with the overall system" to "it just stinks," observing that her husband "was pretty pissed off about the whole thing." It is significant that for these litigants, dissatisfaction has arisen not because they "lost" in a normative sense nor because the system failed to perform up to its capabilities, but because it lacked capabilities that they had erroneously attributed to it.

Case 5: "The Man on the Street." The plaintiff, James Parker, is a middle-aged man. He is suing a landlord who locked him out of his apartment and seized his personal possessions, all because Parker owed $35. At the time of the interview, he had been living on the street for two weeks. He went to the police immediately after the eviction, but they told him they could not get involved because it was a civil matter. He is seeking recovery of his possessions as well as damages for being forced to live on the street. The police told him that the landlord has a reputation for doing this, and Parker has decided that he will pursue the suit even if the landlord returns his possessions and lets him back in, because "somebody's got to take a stand against him." Parker's name does not appear in the court records, indicating that he never completed the process of filing his complaint. We were unable to locate him for a follow-up interview.

This case is particularly interesting. The plaintiff, James Parker, is a street person in fact and appearance. On this basis alone, one might predict that he would be particularly susceptible to the misconceptions about civil justice that the other four plaintiffs share to a greater or lesser extent. In reality, however, his understanding of the nature and respective roles of the civil and criminal systems is remarkably accurate.

In Text 5A, which is taken from the beginning of the interview, Parker expresses confidence in his legal acumen:

Text 5A

Q: So how did you, you know, how did you hear to uh, come on down here?

Parker: Uh, well, I have some basic knowledge of law. I know I have rights.

Q₂: Sure, sure.

Parker: You can't lock people outside their apartments . . .

Q₂: Right.

Parker: . . . because they owe you $35.

156   LAY EXPECTATIONS OF CIVIL JUSTICE

Immediately thereafter he makes two specific points that seem to justify this self-confidence. First, he acknowledges that the court will decide whether he really owes the $35 in allegedly overdue rent, and that the decision could go against him, notwithstanding the rectitude of his position. Second, he suggests that if the landlord broke the law by locking him out, he may be entitled to damages, which will be somehow related to the two weeks he has been on the street:

Text 5B

Parker:	I'm willing to pay that [$35], but I refuse to pay it until such time 'til we bring it into court. And if he's due that $35, the judge will tell me to pay him that $35.
Q:	Yeah.
Parker:	But, due to the fact he's in violation of the law and I've been living on the streets for two weeks, common sense tells me that he owes me, eh heh, quite a bit as a matter of fact.

Parker thus recognizes two important legal principles: that the outcomes of legal disputes do not always comport with one's sense of natural justice, and that civil courts must usually reduce human problems to matters of dollars and cents.

Later in the interview, he displays an appreciation for the division of responsibility between the civil and criminal systems:

Text 5C

Q₂:	. . . Have you ever seen him, like dealt with him?
Parker:	No, I, after he locked me out the police informed me that there is nothing they could do about it because of some, well, it's a civil matter . . .
Q:	Sure.
Parker:	. . . and they are not gonna get involved with that, but they'll, they're aware of the situation.
Q₂:	Okay.
Q:	Yeah.
Parker:	And, uh, apparently he has a reputation for doing this.
[eight lines of detail omitted]	
Q:	They didn't know about the small claims court?
Parker:	No, um, you can't expect law enforcement officers to know the law.
All:	[*laughter*]

When the landlord locked him out, Parker went to the police, although he understood when they told him there was nothing they could do "because it's a civil matter."[12] Then, despite getting no advice from the laughably ignorant police officers, he determined that the civil small claims court was the place to seek relief.

Some contrary evidence is found in Text 5D. After hearing that his court date is likely to be several weeks away, Parker expresses his belief that the landlord will be forced to return his property sometime sooner.

Text 5D

Q:	. . . I don't, you know, I think, you know, my impression of what we were seeing yesterday [is] that I think it [Parker's court date] would be a matter, you know, of four, five weeks.
Parker:	Yeah.
Q:	I mean, it's like, you know, it's not like huge . . .
Q₂:	It's pretty fast considering, but, you know . . .
Q:	. . . but it's not like days, so, uh . . .
Parker:	Yeah.
Q:	So, uh . . .
Parker:	Well, before the court action, that may be true, but, uh, I still think that, uh, he's required to return my personal property before four or five weeks.

Parker's last statement contrasts with his earlier recognition that it will be up to the judge at trial to decide whether he owes the $35 and is entitled to damages for the landlord's violation of the law. Here he implies that some legal authority, presumably acting on its own initiative, will come forward and compel the landlord to return his property even before the judge has acted. The uncertain basis of his faith is suggested by the lack of a responsible agent in the phrase, "I still think . . . he's required. . . ."

It is also instructive to note these areas in which Parker is unwilling to trust his own legal expertise. In Text 5E, taken from the beginning of the interview, he raises two specific questions concerning the timing of the service and the scheduling of the hearing. Near the end of the interview, he says, with reference to the complaint form, "I'm gonna try to find a lawyer to help me fill these out properly."

Text 5E

Parker:	I was telling the lady outside [the assistant clerk] that I have a lot of questions, because I'm going into this [legal action] blindly.

---

[12] An interesting question is why it is relevant to him that the police are "aware of the situation," if they are powerless to help him. Perhaps he retains some faith in the power of the police to intervene even in a civil matter.

158   LAY EXPECTATIONS OF CIVIL JUSTICE

Q:	Sure.
Parker:	Of course, there's a $9 filing fee.
Q:	Yeah.
Parker:	Okay, and I need to . . .
Q:	They've got that in the big letters.
Parker:	Yeah. They make sure you understand that. I need to find out once this summons is filed, how long will it be before it's served to the landlord, which is one question I got.
Q:	Uh huh.
Parker:	Another question is after you serve the summons, how long before the court date will be established for him to appear in court?

All of Parker's expressed concerns relate to court procedure. He does not ask the interviewers any questions about the substance of the case or the landlord's possible defenses, nor does he suggest that he will need a lawyer's help on such issues. Thus, his remark about "going into this blindly" seems to refer only to procedural details; he appears to trust his "basic knowledge of law" on those larger issues that will determine the outcome of the case. The interesting question is why his legal sophistication does not extend to an appreciation of the difficulties he may encounter in proving his case. The answer may lie in his failure to comprehend the ramifications of an adversary system; in particular, even though Parker understands that lawyers are sometimes necessary, he does not think he will need one to win his case because it has not occurred to him that the landlord will present his own, very different interpretations of the facts and the law. In Parker's view, facts are facts and law is law; he does not appreciate that in an adversary system, facts and law are what the parties make of them.

James Parker is in some respects the most complex of the five plaintiffs we have analyzed. Although a street person, he understands the distinction between civil and criminal law and the functions of civil courts. Despite this understanding, however, he has a vague faith in the power of the court to go beyond its procedural limitations and do what justice requires. Additionally, while concerned about the perils of procedural error, he seems oblivious to the complexities of proving a case, perhaps because he misperceives the adversarial process. Once again, the recurrent themes are the overestimation of the power and initiative of the civil court and the underestimation of the individual litigant's burden in the adversary system.

IV. CONCLUSION

As these five cases illustrate, our ethnographic study of small claims litigants reveals that lay people come to court with expectations about the civil justice system that vary substantially. Three issues are particularly prominent in our interview data. First, many litigants do not seem to comprehend the burden that the adversary system imposes on them. Their comments indicate that they are unprepared to deal with such specific issues as their obligation to locate the defendant, to find and prepare the witnesses, and to make an affirmative presentation. Second, several litigants expressed a serious misunderstanding of the remedial power of the civil courts, believing that the government would pay them if the defendant failed to appear or would somehow "punish" a defendant who could not pay a judgment. Third, these misunderstandings may contribute to litigant dissatisfaction with the small claims process. Sometimes, as in the case of the Winners, the system's failure to live up to an unrealistic expectation may be a direct source of dissatisfaction. However, the Terry case suggests that similar misunderstandings may prevent some litigants from realizing that the system has failed them.

The unifying theme in the interview data is an overestimation of the power and initiative of the civil court. Litigants often see the court as an inquisitorial authority that will recognize the justice of their position and find and punish the wrongdoer, rather than as a largely passive tribunal that renders judgment on the basis of the facts brought before it. Many litigants thus come to the civil court with a model of justice that better fits the criminal system. Understandably, the one plaintiff who had experience with the criminal system had such a model; however, each of the litigants we considered—and numerous other litigants that they represent—shared similar misunderstandings to some extent, irrespective of legal experience or business background.

We do not claim, of course, to have made a statistical showing of a pervasive misconception of the role of civil justice. We do believe, however, that the recurrence of this theme in the unstructured comments of litigants from diverse backgrounds is striking and significant in two important respects.

First, our findings suggest some new issues that complement the general understandings of process that have emerged from nearly two decades of social psychological investigations of procedural justice. Specifically, we find that process is at least as important in the minds of litigants as the substantive issues in their cases. We also find that lay conceptions of process are at variance, often considerable variance, with the realities of the legal process as it is practiced in many small claims courts. We would hope that researchers who focus on procedure would consider the potential

160   LAY EXPECTATIONS OF CIVIL JUSTICE

relevance to their theoretical agenda of the assumptions and folk beliefs that lay people bring to the legal process.

Second, the observation of a discontinuity between lay culture and a powerful institution such as the law is significant in its own right. Traditionally, legal scholarship has examined legal issues from the perspective of those who make and practice law. More recently, social scientists, including procedural justice researchers, have begun to focus on the reactions and attitudes of consumers of justice. Even this research, however, poses questions that the law has defined as important. Accordingly, it assumes, at least implicitly, that lay and legally trained people think about disputes in similar ways. In our present research, we have been repeatedly reminded of the importance of examining legal issues from the perspective of the consumer. In addition to the findings reported here, we have learned, for example, that lay people have ideas about causation, proof, and the structure of adequate accounts that differ markedly from those of the law (O'Barr and Conley, 1985; Conley and O'Barr, forthcoming). This accumulating evidence of fundamental differences in reasoning and communication between lay and legal cultures should be of interest to those who study the cultural background of law as well as those who seek to reform the legal process.

Our findings also make a larger point about the role of ethnography in social science research about legal problems.[13] In the design of experimental studies, some issues can be identified a priori. However, as we learned in our initial studies of law and language (Conley *et al.*, 1978; O'Barr, 1982), other issues, less obvious but equally important, emerge only after lengthy observation of the system being studied. Thus, just as ethnographers should enlist the aid of quantitative specialists before making claims about the frequency or distribution of the behavior they observe, those who do quantitative analysis should acknowledge the role of open-ended ethnographic observation in identifying issues worthy of study.

REFERENCES

ADLER, J.W., D.R. HENSLER, and C.E. NELSON (1983) *Simple Justice*. Santa Monca, CA: Rand.
ALEXANDER, S., and M. RUDERMAN (in press) "The Role of Procedural and Distributive Justice in Organizational Behavior," *Social Justice Review*.
ATKINSON, J. Maxwell, and Paul DREW (1979) *Order in Court: The Organisation of Verbal Interaction in Judicial Settings*. London: Macmillan.
ATKINSON, J. Maxwell, and John HERITAGE (1984) *Structures of Social Action*. New York: Cambridge University Press.

---

[13] The usefulness of combining ethnographic and experimental techniques in legal research is discussed in O'Barr and Lind (1981).

BRETT, J.M., and S.B. GOLDBERG (1983) "Grievance Mediation in the Coal Industry: A Field Experiment," 37 *Industrial and Labor Relations Review* 49.

CASPER, J.D., and T.R. TYLER (1986) "Procedural Justice and Felony Defendants." Presented at the Law and Society Association meetings, Chicago (June).

CONLEY, John M., and William M. O'BARR (forthcoming) "Rules Versus Relationships in Small Claims Narratives," in A. Grimshaw (ed.), *Conflict Talk*. New York: Cambridge University Press.

CONLEY, John M., William M. O'BARR, and E.A. LIND (1978) "The Power of Language: Presentational Style in the Courtroom," 1978 *Duke Law Journal* 1375.

FELSTEINER, W., and A. SARAT (1986) "Law and Strategy in the Divorce Lawyer's Office," 20 *Law & Society Review* 93.

GLUCKMAN, Max (1955) *The Judicial Process Among the Barotse of Northern Rhodesia*. Manchester: Manchester University Press.

LANDIS, J.M., and L.I. GOODSTEIN (1986) "Defendants' Perceptions of the Fairness of Their Criminal Justice Processing: A Model of Outcome Fairness." Presented at the Law and Society Association meetings, Chicago (June).

LIND, E.A., and T.R. TYLER. In press.

LLEWELLYN, K.N., and E.A. HOEBEL (1941) *The Cheyenne Way*. Norman: University of Oklahoma Press.

MALINOWSKI, Bronislaw (1926) *Crime and Custom in Savage Society*. London: Kegan Paul.

O'BARR, William M. (1982) *Linguistic Evidence: Language, Power and Strategy in the Courtroom*. New York: Academic Press.

O'BARR, William M., and John M. CONLEY (1985) "Litigant Satisfaction Versus Legal Adequacy in Small Claims Court Narratives," 19 *Law & Society Review* 661.

O'BARR, William M., and E.A. LIND (1981) "Ethnography and Experimentation—Partners in Legal Research," in B.D. Sales (ed.), *The Trial Process*. New York: Plenum.

OCHS, Elinor (1979) "Transcription as Theory," in E. Ochs and B.B. Scheiflein (eds.), *Developmental Pragmatics*. New York: Academic Press.

THIBAUT, J., and L. WALKER (1978) "A Theory of Procedure," 66 *California Law Review* 541.

—— (1975) *Procedural Justice*. Hillsdale, NJ: Erlbaum.

TYLER, T.R., and A. CAINE (1981) "The Influence of Outcomes and Procedures on Satisfaction with Formal Leaders," 41 *Journal of Personality and Social Psychology* 642.

TYLER, T.R., and R. FOLGER (1980) "Distributional and Procedural Aspects of Satisfaction with Citizen-Police Encounters," 1 *Basic and Applied Psychology* 281.

TYLER, T.R., K. RASINSKI, and K. McGRAW (1985) "The Influence of Perceived Injustice on the Endorsement of Political Leaders," 15 *Journal of Applied Social Psychology* 700.

TYLER, T.R., K. RASINSKI, and N. SPODICK (1985) "The Influence of Voice on Satisfaction with Leaders: Exploring the Meaning of Process Control," 48 *Journal of Personality and Social Psychology* 72.

[16]

WHAT IS PROCEDURAL JUSTICE?: CRITERIA USED BY CITIZENS TO ASSESS THE FAIRNESS OF LEGAL PROCEDURES

TOM R. TYLER

This paper examines procedural justice in the context of citizen experiences with the police and courts. It is based on interviews of 652 citizens with recent personal experiences involving those authorities. I will consider two issues: first, whether the justice of the procedures involved influences citizen satisfaction with outcomes and evaluations of legal authorities; and second, how citizens define "fair process" in such settings. The results replicate those of past studies, which found that procedural justice has a major influence on both satisfaction and evaluation. They further suggest that such procedural justice judgments are complex and multifaceted. Seven issues make independent contributions to citizen judgments about whether the legal authorities acted fairly: (1) the degree to which those authorities were motivated to be fair; (2) judgments of their honesty; (3) the degree to which the authorities followed ethical principles of conduct; (4) the extent to which opportunities for representation were provided; (5) the quality of the decisions made; (6) the opportunities for error correction; and (7) whether the authorities behaved in a biased fashion. I found that the meaning of procedural justice varied according to the nature of the situation, not the characteristics of the people involved.

I. INTRODUCTION

In 1975 Thibaut and Walker hypothesized that litigants' satisfaction with dispute resolution decisions would be independently influenced by their judgments about the fairness of the dispute resolution process. This hypothesis was strongly supported by their data and by subsequent research (see Casper, Tyler, and Fisher, in press; Landis and Goodstein, 1986; Lind, 1982; Lind and Tyler, 1988; Tyler, 1987c; Tyler and Lind, 1986; and Walker and Lind, 1984). In addition, procedural justice concerns have been found to influence evaluations of the legal authorities and institu-

---

The data utilized in this paper were collected using funds provided by the National Science Foundation program in Law and Social Science, Grant SES-8310199. Support for analyzing that data and writing this article was provided by the National Science Foundation, the American Bar Foundation, and the Northwestern University Center for Urban Affairs and Policy Research. I would like to thank Jonathan Casper, E. Allan Lind, Jo Perry, and Christopher Winship for comments on a draft of this paper.

104   CRITERIA USED TO ASSESS PROCEDURAL JUSTICE

tions responsible for settling disputes (Tyler, 1984b, 1987b; Tyler and Caine, 1981; Tyler, Casper, and Fisher, 1987; Tyler and Folger, 1980). It is clear from this research that citizen assessments of the justice of the procedures used by legal authorities to make decisions influence reactions to those decisions.

It is less clear *what* it is about a legal procedure that leads those involved to consider it to be fair.[1] The purpose of this study is to move beyond establishing the existence of procedural justice effects to examining this issue. Consideration of the meaning of procedural justice will involve a test of the importance of the criteria of procedural justice derived from the theories of Thibaut and Walker (1975) and Leventhal (1980).

I will explore the meaning of procedural justice within the arena first utilized by Thibaut and Walker: citizen contact with legal authorities. My focus has, however, been broadened to include both the study of contacts with the police and nondispute-related contacts with the courts. While the resolution of disputes in trial settings, which was examined by Thibaut and Walker, is an important symbol of our legal system that matters a great deal to those citizens involved in such disputes, most citizen contact with legal authorities does not involve disputes or occur in courtrooms. I will explore the natural range of such contact.

I also extend the original focus of Thibaut and Walker beyond judgments of the fairness of experiences to examine citizen judgments about the fairness of authorities. As a result, I can explore whether the same criteria of procedural fairness influence assessments of the fairness of personal treatment and of authorities.

I will examine three questions: (1) the importance of different criteria of fairness in the assessment of the justice of a personally experienced procedure; (2) the relationship of these criteria to each other; and (3) the universality of the importance ratings given to the criteria. Here I will consider the effect of the nature of the event and those involved on the criteria used by citizens to judge whether they received fair treatment.

A. *Potential Procedural Justice Criteria*

Two bodies of theory and research have independently addressed the issue of criteria that might be used by citizens to judge the fairness of a legal procedure: the work of Thibaut and Walker (1975) and the work of Leventhal (1980). Thibaut and Walker differentiated between two aspects of the control that parties might have over the procedure used to resolve a dispute: process control (control over the opportunity to present evidence), and decision control (control over the final decision). Leventhal identified six

---

[1] Another issue that has emerged in recent research is when procedural justice is more or less important (for a review of this work, see Tyler, 1987b, 1987c).

criteria: consistency, the ability to suppress bias, decision quality or accuracy, correctability, representation, and ethicality. Consistency refers to similarity of treatment and outcomes across people or time or both. The ability to suppress bias involves the ability of a procedure to prevent favoritism or other external biases. Decision quality or accuracy means the ability of a procedure to effect solutions of objectively high quality. Correctability means the existence of opportunities to correct unfair or inaccurate decisions. Representation refers to the degree to which parties affected by a decision are allowed to be involved in the decision-making process. Finally, ethicality refers to the degree to which the decision-making process accords with general standards of fairness and morality.

What is striking about these two bodies of theory is the extent to which the criteria they identify as potential bases for evaluating the justice of a procedure do not overlap. The only common criterion is representation (Leventhal's category for process and/or decision control). Even here it is unclear whether in Leventhal's typology representativeness refers to process control, decision control, or both. Leventhal (1980: 43) is ambiguous on this point, suggesting that representation means that "the concerns of those affected should be represented in all phases of the allocation process." The other issues raised by Leventhal are not discussed by Thibaut and Walker.

B.   *The Importance of Procedural Justice Criteria*

Since there are varying criteria for evaluating the fairness of a procedure, it is important to know the weight that those affected by decisions place on each criterion. Research developing from both of the theoretical frameworks outlined above has addressed this issue, with the most extensive exploration provided by Thibaut, Walker, and their students. It has suggested that both types of control are important in procedural evaluations (Thibaut and Walker, 1975). More recent research has supported this, finding either that process control is more important than decision control (Tyler, Rasinski, and Spodick, 1985; Tyler, 1987a) or that only process control matters (Lind *et al.*, 1983).

A second area of research explores the importance of Leventhal's six criteria of procedural justice. The four studies that examined their importance to those affected by decisions found that consistency is the major assessment criterion (Barrett-Howard and Tyler, 1986; Fry and Leventhal, 1979; Fry and Chaney, 1981; Greenberg, 1986). Barrett-Howard and Tyler further divided consistency judgments between those involving consistency across time and those involving consistency across people and found that the latter was the primary means of evaluation.

While the criteria utilized by Leventhal and by Thibaut and

106   CRITERIA USED TO ASSESS PROCEDURAL JUSTICE

Walker have generally been examined separately, one exception to
this approach is a recent study by Sheppard and Lewicki (1987). In
that work managers and management students considered recent
personally experienced incidents of fair and unfair treatment in
dealing with a supervisor and generated the principle that led
them to judge their treatment to be fair or unfair. Three of the
principles outlined above emerged as especially important: consistency, representation, and accuracy.

Overall, there is considerable convergence of the results of
studies exploring criteria of procedural justice. Such studies typically find an emphasis on consistency (Barrett-Howard and Tyler,
1986; Fry and Leventhal, 1979; Fry and Chaney, 1981; Greenberg,
1986; Sheppard and Lewicki, 1987). In addition, Barrett-Howard
and Tyler (1986), Cornelius et al., (1986), and Sheppard and Lewicki (1987) identify accuracy as important, and Barrett-Howard
and Tyler (1986) discover that the related issue of bias suppression
is a factor. Finally, work in the Thibaut and Walker tradition
finds that representation is significant (Houlden et al., 1978; Lind
et al., 1983; Tyler, 1987a; Tyler, Rasinski, and Spodick, 1985), a result consistent with the conclusions of Sheppard and Lewicki.

In this paper, I combine the criteria proposed by Thibaut and
Walker (1975) and Leventhal (1980) to examine the importance of
each to the citizens I interviewed. Only one prior study has conducted such an examination (Sheppard and Lewicki, 1987), and
that effort was limited by the use of a methodology that did not
allow the rated importance of the criteria outlined to be directly
assessed.

C. The Relationship Among Procedural Justice Criteria

The existence of varying criteria of procedural fairness also
raises the question of how those criteria are related. The importance of their relationship lies in the choice of decision-making
procedures. In the distributive justice literature the decisions of
leaders have been regarded as value trade-offs between objectives
that cannot be simultaneously realized. For example, because
many have argued that productivity and social harmony cannot be
achieved at the same time, policy makers have had to move back
and forth between the use of differing rules of distributive justice,
each of which maximizes the attainment of one objective at the expense of the other (see, for example, Okun, 1975). The concern
here is with the extent to which such trade-offs also occur with
procedures.

An example of value trade-offs in the criteria of procedural
fairness can be found in the literature on the psychology of judicial
sentencing, which argues that magistrates can make high-quality
decisions that particularize punishment to the situation of each individual defendant only if they have wide latitude to sentence in-

consistently, that is, to give very different sentences for the same crime (Galegher and Carroll, 1983). This argument suggests that consistency in sentencing is in conflict with decision quality, operationalized in this case by sentences that will effectively rehabilitate criminals.

The major effort to explore the relationship among procedural justice criteria was made by Thibaut and Walker (1975). They focused on one subissue of this general question: the relationship between process and decision control. Their studies and those of others have consistently found a positive relationship between assessments of these two criteria in natural settings. Unfortunately, studies developing out of the Leventhal (1980) framework have not examined the relationship among procedural justice criteria.

The relationship question leads into another issue: the possibility of underlying dimensions of procedural justice. Although Thibaut, Walker, and Leventhal have elaborated a set of potentially important criteria for assessing the fairness of procedures, and Sheppard and Lewicki (1987) have shown that an even broader set of concerns can be generated, these varying criteria may actually reflect several basic dimensions of procedural evaluation. Prior research suggests four potential underlying dimensions: consistency, decision quality, bias suppression, and representation. Consistency is based upon a comparison of the procedure to other procedures experienced either in the past or by others, while the latter three criteria refer to the quality of the process itself.

D. The Universality of Procedural Justice Criteria

It is also important to examine the universality of the meaning of procedural justice, that is, the degree to which the fairness of procedures is always judged by the same criteria. Two extreme positions might be imagined. One would emphasize the stability of criteria, with all citizens judging fairness by the same standards, irrespective of the nature of the dispute resolution or allocation problem. The other would hypothesize that the characteristics of the contact and the citizens involved would influence the criteria used to evaluate the fairness of the procedures chosen to deal with that problem.

Research has suggested that the meaning of justice will vary depending upon the nature of the dispute or allocation involved. Barrett-Howard and Tyler (1986) varied situations along four basic dimensions of interpersonal relations (Deutsch, 1982; Wish *et al.*, 1976; Wish and Kaplan, 1977) and found that in formal settings respondents place more emphasis on bias suppression, decision quality, consistency, and representation. In cooperative situations they focus more on consistency, decision quality, and ethicality. Sheppard and Lewicki (1987) found that the fairness criteria most important to parties affected by a supervisor's decision differed ac-

cording to the nature of the organizational roles of the parties
(also see Lissak and Sheppard 1983; Sheppard *et al.*, 1986).

The present study will test the degree of variation in the
meaning of procedural fairness by examining the effect of differences in the nature of citizen experiences with the police and
courts on the way citizens evaluate whether they have received
fair treatment. In addition, the effect of variation in the type of
people involved in the interaction will be explored.

E. Situational Variations

This study will test the hypothesis that the meaning of procedural justice varies depending upon the circumstances of a citizen
encounter with legal authority. Ideally such a test should be based
on a typology of situations or people or both that leads to theoretically derived predictions about variations induced by circumstances. Unfortunately, no such typology has yet been developed
for the study of either moral issues (Kurtines, 1968) or third-party
conflict resolution. As a result, I derived the dimensions utilized
and predictions about their effects from the literature on procedural justice and conflict resolution more generally.

1. Extensions of Thibaut and Walker. Two dimensions considered are variations of the original Thibaut and Walker (1975) research. The first variation considered was the authority encountered: police or courts. Thibaut and Walker examined formal
courtroom settings. However, I extend the study to less formal
contacts with the police. I examine the degree to which Thibaut
and Walker's findings are specific to courtroom settings and do not
generalize across the larger range of experiences with legal authorities. While formal courtroom trials are important to those involved, they account for only about 20 percent of the surveyed citizen contacts with legal authority.

I hypothesize that informal encounters with the police will be
evaluated more on police efforts to be fair and less on adherence to
formal issues of rights (i.e., on ethicality). I make this prediction
because I anticipate that the more formalized courtroom situation
will draw attention to issues of rights and that ethical standards
will be clearer in that setting.

Thibaut and Walker's focus on disputes was also extended.
Their study of trials led to a focus on disputes between contending
parties. In many cases, however, citizens have contact with legal
authorities for other reasons. For example, they may call the police for help. I hypothesize that disputes, because they involve
contending factions, will lead citizens to place greater weight on
whether they have an opportunity to state their case, on bias (i.e.,
favoring one party over others), and on consistency. In nondispute

settings I expect that respondents will judge procedural justice more heavily in terms of the quality of problem resolution.

2. **Characteristics of the Experience.** Several characteristics of the experience itself may also influence citizen views about the meaning of fair treatment. I hypothesize that citizens will be more concerned with the quality of decisions when the contact with the police or courts is voluntary and more concerned with attention to their rights when it is not.

The favorability of the outcome of a situation may also affect judgments of fairness. Those who have received poor outcomes will focus more on issues of bias, consistency, or dishonesty. Such judgments allow them to determine whether alternative dispute resolution procedures would have produced better outcomes (Folger, 1986a, 1986b). Those who received favorable outcomes, however, will, I hypothesize, tend to emphasize abstract issues such as ethicality. In other words, those who win can afford the luxury of thinking about issues such as their rights.

Citizens may also differ from each other in the degree to which they view it as important to receive favorable outcomes and/or favorable treatment in their dealings with the police or courts. Such variations in importance might influence how they define the meaning of procedural justice. Those to whom outcomes matter more might focus more heavily on outcome-related aspects of procedure such as consistency rather than on issues of ethicality.

3. **Characteristics of the Person.** I predict two types of personal characteristics will influence citizen views about the meaning of fairness. First, citizens may differ in their background characteristics and these differences may influence their views about the meaning of procedural fairness. Six potentially important factors are sex, age, race, education, income, and liberalism. I explored the influence of each. Only one specific prediction could be made based on the literature: The more highly educated and liberal will pay more attention to issues of ethicality in determinations of fairness (McClosky and Brill, 1983; Sullivan *et al.*, 1982).

Respondent's prior views or expectations about the police/courts might also affect their views about important criteria on fair procedure. Such differences are examined through the use of citizen assessments of the equality of the treatment citizens receive from the police/courts. Citizens were asked: 1) whether the police/courts generally treat citizens equally and 2) whether they treat people of the citizen's age, sex, race, or nationality worse than others. These two general assessments were hypothesized to lead to variations in the extent to which issues of bias influenced the meaning of procedural justice. If citizens expected unequal

110   CRITERIA USED TO ASSESS PROCEDURAL JUSTICE

treatment, or knew that it occurred, it was anticipated that they
would assess the fairness of their own experience in terms of the
bias or lack of bias they experienced.

II.   QUESTIONS TO BE ADDRESSED

Before examining the meaning of procedural justice, I considered whether, as prior studies found, procedural justice figured
prominently in citizen reactions to legal authorities. Given that
procedural justice has a key role in mediating reactions to experiences with the police and courts, further analysis will explore
how citizens define fairness.

To answer this question I first explored the impact of procedural justice on several dependent variables. The first is whether
respondents indicated satisfaction with the outcomes and treatment they received from legal authorities. Also important are
their affective reactions to the particular authorities they encountered. Finally, citizen generalizations from particular experiences
to broader views about the authorities are considered, as is their
support for those authorities (see Tyler, 1984b; Tyler and Caine,
1981; Tyler, Rasinski, and McGraw, 1985).

III.   METHOD

A.   *Subjects*

The participants in the study were 1,575 citizens of Chicago interviewed over the telephone during the spring of 1984. I chose respondents from a random sample, with 63 percent of those contacted yielding completed interviews. Of those interviewed, 733
(47 percent) indicated that they had had personal experience with
the Chicago police and/or courts in the previous year; they formed
the sample used. I interviewed those respondents about that experience or, in the case of multiple experiences, their most important
experience.

Of the 733 respondents, 81 had had experiences that were too
superficial for detailed analysis. These situations involved cases in
which the respondent had called the police but not dealt with
them personally. For example, some had reported suspicious behavior in their neighborhood but did not know what activities
were generated by their call; others were told over the phone that
the police could not handle their problem. These respondents
were not included in the study. Hence, the sample size was actually 652. Of this group 47 percent had called the police for help, 31
percent had been stopped by the police, and 23 percent had been to
court.

B. *Questionnaire: The Meaning of Procedural Justice*

1. Control/Representation. The first two potential criteria of procedural justice examined were those proposed by Thibaut and Walker (1975): process control and decision control. They also constitute Leventhal's (1980) dimension of representation.

The extent to which respondents had process control was measured by asking them "how much opportunity" they had had to present their problem or case to the authorities before decisions were made. Most felt that they had either "a great deal" (42 percent) or "some" (20 percent) such opportunity. Only a small group felt that they had "a little" (11 percent) or "not much" (28 percent) chance to state their case.

I measured respondents' perceived decision control by asking them how much influence they had had over the decisions made by the authorities. The majority felt that they had "little" (10 percent) or "not much" decision control (49 percent), with smaller groups indicating "a great deal" (19 percent) or "some" (22 percent) control.

As in prior correlational studies, process and decision control were highly interrelated ($r = .56$; $p < .001$). Because distinguishing between these two issues was not important in this study for such an effort (see Tyler, 1987a), I combined them into a single measure of representation.

2. Consistency. Leventhal's (1980) first criterion of procedural justice is consistency. I examined four types of consistency. First, respondents compared their recent experience to previous ones (consistency across time). Second, they compared their experience to their prior expectations, however derived. Third, they compared their experience to what they thought generally happened to others. Finally, they compared their experience to recent experiences of their friends, family, or neighbors. In each case they separately compared both their outcome and treatment to the standard.

Consistency across time was assessed by asking respondents to compare their outcomes and treatment to their outcomes and treatment in the past. In the case of treatment 54 percent said that their treatment was the same as in the past, 21 percent that it was better, and 11 percent that it was worse (15 percent had had no past experience). Fifty-five percent felt that their outcomes were similar in the past, 18 percent that it was better, and 10 percent that it was worse; again, 15 percent had had no past experience.

I also assessed consistency across people "in similar situations." Sixty-eight percent felt that their treatment was similar to that received by others, 22 percent that it was better, and 10 percent that it was worse. Sixty-four percent felt that their outcome

112   CRITERIA USED TO ASSESS PROCEDURAL JUSTICE

was similar to that of others, 28 percent that it was better, and 9 percent that it was worse.

Looking at consistency with prior expectations, 46 percent indicated that they were treated as they had expected, while 32 percent were treated better and 22 percent were treated worse. Forty-three percent received the outcome they had expected, while 32 percent received a better one and 25 percent a worse one.

Finally, I assessed consistency in relationship to the recent experiences of family, neighbors, and friends. Of the 33 percent who knew of experiences that members of one of these three groups had had in the past year, 58 percent indicated that their treatment was similar to that of the others, 38 percent that it was better, and 4 percent that it was worse. Fifty-four percent indicated that they had received a similar outcome, 32 percent that their outcome was better, and 14 percent that their outcome was worse.

For my analysis I created two indices of consistency: the average of respondent judgments concerning their outcome and the average of respondent judgments concerning their treatment.[2]

3. **Impartiality.** I operationalized impartiality or neutrality in three ways: as a lack of bias, as honesty, and as having made an effort to be fair. I established lack of bias in the authorities' behavior by asking respondents whether their treatment or outcome was influenced by their "race, sex, age, nationality, or some other characteristic of them as a person." In addition, in those cases (18 percent) in which there was a dispute between parties, I asked respondents whether the authorities had favored one party over another. Eleven percent indicated at least one of these types of bias.

I assessed impartiality as honesty by combining responses to two questions: (1) whether the authorities "did anything" that was "improper or dishonest" (21 percent said they had), and (2) whether officials had lied to them (16 percent said yes).

I also assessed the impartiality of the authorities more subjectively by asking respondents to indicate how hard the police or judge had tried to show fairness. Respondents differed widely on this dimension. Thirty-seven percent said that the authorities had tried very hard to be fair, 12 percent that they had tried quite hard, 26 percent that they had tried somewhat hard, and 26 percent that they had not tried hard at all.

4. **Decision Accuracy.** I established the accuracy or quality of decision making by combining responses to two questions. First, respondents reported whether the authorities involved had "gotten

---

2 An alternative approach to creating consistency scales is to create separate scales for consistency with expectancies, across time, across people in general, and across friends and family. Although I also utilized this approach in analyzing the data, I did not report the results because they are weaker than those obtained from the other method.

the information they needed to make good decisions about how to handle" the problem. Eighty percent said that they had. Second, respondents indicated whether the authorities had tried to "bring the problem into the open so that it could be solved." Sixty-three percent said that they had.

5. Correctability. I assessed correctability by asking respondents whether they knew of any "agency or organization" to which they could have "complained" about unfair treatment. Thirty-three percent indicated that they knew of such an agency.

6. Ethicality. Finally, I established ethicality by combining responses to two questions: whether the authorities had been polite to the respondents (83 percent said yes) and whether they had shown concern for their rights (76 percent said yes).

C. Questionnaire: Dependent Variables

The key dependent variable for the analysis of the meaning of procedural justice was the respondents' judgment about the fairness of the process that characterized their experience with the police and/or courts. I asked respondents "how fair" the procedures used by the authorities were and "how fairly" they were treated, with both answers rated on a four-point scale (very fair, somewhat fair, somewhat unfair, and very unfair). Most respondents indicated that the procedures were fair (54 percent, very fair; 24 percent, somewhat fair) and that they were fairly treated (49 percent, very fairly; 32 percent, somewhat fairly).

I also asked respondents to assess the fairness of the authorities with whom they had dealt. They first indicated their assessment of the fairness of "the way the Chicago police [or courts] treat people and handle problems" (66 percent of those who had dealt with the police indicated that they were very or somewhat fair, compared with 53 percent of those who had dealt with the courts). They also gave their opinion of "how often the police [or courts] treat citizens fairly and handle their problems in a fair way" (53 percent said usually or often for the police, compared with 46 percent for the courts) and "how fairly" they thought they would be treated if they dealt with the police and/or courts in the future (90 percent said very or somewhat fairly for the police; 86 percent said the same for the courts). These questions related not to specific legal actors (i.e., a particular police officer) but to the general legal authorities they represent.

D. Does Procedural Justice Matter?

1. Independent Variables. To test the hypothesis that procedural justice is important in reactions to experiences with the police and the courts, I explored the influence of procedural justice

114   CRITERIA USED TO ASSESS PROCEDURAL JUSTICE

upon satisfaction and evaluations, controlling for the influence of distributive fairness and three nonfairness factors: the absolute favorability of the outcomes, the outcome favorability relative to several standards of reference, and the treatment favorability relative to several standards of reference.

I assessed procedural justice in the manner previously outlined. This analysis utilizes the scale assessing the procedural justice of the experience, not the overall procedural fairness of the authorities. I examined distributive justice using judgments of the fairness of the outcome received (57 percent reported it was very fair; 23 percent, somewhat fair) and of whether the authorities gave the case or problem the attention it deserved (58 percent said yes; 14 percent said it received more than it deserved; 28 percent said it received less than it deserved).

The first nonfairness factor considered was outcome favorability, which I measured in two ways. First, the respondents indicated the absolute quality of the outcome. This judgment was then weighted by the self-reported seriousness of the problem to produce an overall favorability rating. The nature of this assessment differed for each of the three types of experience examined. In the case of calls to the police, respondents reported whether the police had solved the problem and, if not, how hard they had tried to do so. For respondents who had been stopped, I asked whether the police had cited them for a violation of the law and/or arrested them and took them to the police station. Respondents involved in court cases reported whether they had won or lost their case.

Respondents also rated outcome favorability in relative terms, that is, in relationship to what they had expected prior to the contact, to what they had received in the past, to what others generally received, and to what their family, friends, or neighbors had received in the past. The nature of these assessments was outlined in our prior discussion of consistency measurement.[3]

---

[3] The use of consistency scales at two points in this analysis highlights an important conceptual problem in procedural justice research. Past studies of the importance of procedural justice in reactions to experiences with legal authorities have been concerned with assessing that influence independent of outcomes. To do so researchers have treated judgments of outcome and treatment quality relative to various standards of comparison as nonfairness-based assessments. This is quite consistent with relative deprivation research, which examines outcome quality relative to various standards of reference (i.e., "Deprivation in comparison to what standard?"). A second question that has been addressed is the meaning of procedural fairness. In that literature consistency of outcome and treatment is viewed (by Leventhal (1980), for example) as one basis for assessing procedural fairness. The difference between the treatment of consistency in these two areas of study suggests that the consistency of the outcome with outcomes received in the past or by others is a judgment that is not necessarily ethically based. When people are judging whether they feel fairly treated, they may also consider consistency of outcome and treatment in making that assessment. So consistency is one criterion that could be used in judging procedural fairness and outcome fairness. It is also a nonfairness-based expectancy judgment.

While past treatments of reactions to contact with the legal system have tended to view nonfairness issues as involving violated expectations for outcomes, which is in keeping with both psychological theories of expectancy (Helson, 1964) and relative deprivation models (Crosby, 1976), it is also possible that respondents would be troubled by violations of how they expected to be treated. As with expectancy theory, such violations need not involve issues of fairness. To assess the impact of nonfairness-based expectancy violation in treatment, I asked respondents to rate their treatment relative to their past expectations and experiences and the experiences of others generally and of their friends, family, or neighbors.

2. **Dependent Variables.** The two dependent variables analyzed were satisfaction and evaluation. Satisfaction questions assessed the citizens' personal satisfaction with their outcome (46 percent, very satisfied; 23 percent, somewhat satisfied; 11 percent, somewhat dissatisfied; 20 percent, very dissatisfied) and treatment (53 percent, very satisfied; 23 percent, somewhat satisfied; 12 percent, somewhat dissatisfied; 12 percent, very dissatisfied). I examined three types of evaluation. First, respondents indicated whether they were angry (22 percent said yes), frustrated (32 percent said yes), or pleased with the authorities (55 percent said yes). I established generalizations to overall evaluations of the type of authorities through respondent ratings of the quality of the service those authorities provided and the extent to which they offered appropriate levels of service and fair treatment. These evaluations corresponded to what political scientists have termed "specific system support." The evaluation scale had fourteen items for the police and ten for the courts. It ranged from 1 to 5, with 3 indicating neutral feelings. Overall respondents had slightly positive feelings about the authorities they had dealt with (mean = 3.41).

Support for legal authorities assessed citizen feelings toward the authorities in a more generalized and affectively tinged way (see Easton, 1965). Support of this type corresponds to what political scientists refer to as "diffuse system support," involving long-term affective attachment to the authorities involved (see Tyler, 1987b). The support scale involved five items and ranged from 1 to 4. Overall, respondents were neutral about the authorities (mean = 2.53).

E. *Dimensions of the Setting*

The work of Thibaut and Walker (1975) focused upon trials. This means that the typical contact citizens had with legal authorities was not of the type studied by Thibaut and Walker. I expanded the focus to include the police and nondisputes.

I established the voluntary nature of the contact by asking the

116   CRITERIA USED TO ASSESS PROCEDURAL JUSTICE

respondents if they had a choice about whether to initiate the contact with the police or courts (62 percent said yes). Outcome favorability ratings ranged from 1 to 8, with high scores indicating favorable outcomes. The scale mean was 5.36. Overall 56 percent of the respondents received outcomes that they reported to be favorable.

The importance of the outcome to the respondents was established by asking them how much they cared about what outcome they received. Sixty-one percent indicated that it was very important. Similarly, 66 percent said that it was very important to them to be well treated.

I assessed prior expectations by asking respondents whether the police or courts generally treat citizens equally or favor some over others. In addition, I asked citizens whether people like themselves (i.e., those of their age, sex, race, nationality, and income) received the same treatment as the average citizen. Seventy-nine percent felt that the authorities they had dealt with generally treated people unequally; 28 percent said that the authorities generally treated people like themselves worse than the average citizen.[4]

I also measured six other respondent characteristics: sex, age, race, education, liberalism, and income. Interviewers indicated the respondents' sex after the interview (55 percent were women). Respondents reported their own age (51 percent were 34 or younger), and identified their race by answering the standard survey question: "What is your racial-ethnic background?" Of those studied, 52 percent were white. Education level was established by asking respondents to indicate the "highest grade or year of school" they had completed. Of those interviewed, 31 percent were college graduates; 28 percent had some college; 24 percent were high school graduates; and 16 percent had not finished high school. I assessed liberalism using a self-report methodology in which respondents classified themselves as conservative (39 per-

---

[4] One difficulty with using respondents' answers to the question of equal treatment as a temporally *prior* expectation is that such an analysis is based on the assumption that prior views truly exist prior to experiences rather than being influenced by them. Since this study is a survey that assesses both sets of views at one point in time, it is possible that whether a person is treated equally by authorities determines their view about whether the police and courts generally treat people equally, rather than their experience being influenced by that prior view. While no definitive test of this possibility can be conducted using cross-sectional data, some evidence of its implausibility can be gathered. If the equality of one's own recent treatment relative to that of others influences one's views about whether the police generally treat citizens equally, we would expect some correlation between these two judgments. However, no such correlation was found in this study. Whether people received treatment that they viewed as equal to that of others was uncorrelated with whether they thought that the police generally provided equal treatment to citizens ($r = .05$; not significant). In other words, citizens' views about the equality of treatment do not develop out of what happens during their recent personal experiences with the police and courts.

cent), moderate (18 percent), or liberal (44 percent). Finally, I measured six categories of self-reported income. Of those interviewed, 38 percent had an annual income of under $15,000; 71 percent, under $30,000; and 90 percent under $50,000.

IV.   RESULTS

A.   The Replication of Procedural Justice Effects

Past studies have consistently found that judgments of the fairness of the procedures that occur when citizens deal with legal authorities influence citizen satisfaction and evaluation of those authorities (see Lind, 1982; Tyler, 1984b; and Tyler, Rasinski, and Griffin, 1986). Prior to exploring the questions that form the heart of this paper, I will test the influence of procedural justice on the satisfaction and evaluation of the respondents in this study, a test which I expect will reveal that procedural justice is again the key issue to citizens.

The first question is the relationship between nonfairness-based judgments and experiences and judgments about distributive and procedural justice. Table 1 shows that although outcome favorability is related to judgments of distributive and procedural fairness (mean $r = .34$), the two are clearly distinct. In other words, as past studies have found, those receiving favorable outcomes think that those outcomes and the procedures used to arrive at them are fairer. On the other hand, favorability and fairness are not identical, and citizens are clearly making distinct fairness judgments. As has also been the case in other studies, distributive fairness and procedural fairness were highly related (mean $r = .61$).

The second question is whether fairness judgments influence satisfaction and evaluation. To address this question I used regression analysis, with satisfaction and evaluation as the dependent variables and both nonfairness- and fairness-based judgments about the citizens' experience as the independent variables. This analysis is shown in Table 2. Table 2 shows combined indexes of outcome and procedural favorability, since a more complex analysis using each judgment as a separate independent variable yields similar results.

The overall importance of fairness can be examined by comparing the increment in the square of the multiple correlation coefficient that occurs when one cluster of variables is entered following another (a "usefulness analysis"). That analysis shows that fairness judgments are the key influence on all five dependent variables. In each case fairness judgments explain a substantial percentage of variance that is unexplained by nonfairness factors (average $R^2 = 24$ percent), while nonfairness factors explain only approximately 1 percent of the variance unexplained by judgments of fairness or nonfairness.

118   CRITERIA USED TO ASSESS PROCEDURAL JUSTICE

Table 1. The Relationship Among Indexes of Outcome and Procedural Favorability and Distributive and Procedural Justice

Index	Outcome Favorability					Procedural Favorability				Fairness		
	Favor-ability	Past Experiences	Expecta-tions	Experiences of Others	Experiences of Friends, Family, or Neighbors	Past Experiences	Expecta-tions	Experiences of Others	Experiences of Friends, Family, or Neighbors	DJ1[a]	DJ2[b]	PJ1[c]
Nonfairness												
Outcomes												
Favorability relative to:												
Past experiences	.22[d]											
Expectations	.42[d]	.43[d]										
Experiences of others	.33[d]	.42[d]	.49[d]									
Experiences of family, friends, or neighbors	.07	.25[d]	.20[e]	.26[d]								
Procedures												
Relative to:												
Past experiences	.14[f]	.47[d]	.26[d]	.23[d]	.14[f]							
Expectations	.32[d]	.34[d]	.47[d]	.31[d]	.08	.21[d]						
Experiences of others	.31[d]	.38[d]	.42[d]	.62[d]	.34[d]	.24[d]	.34[d]					
Experiences of family, friends, or neighbors	-.01	.25[d]	.15[f]	.31[d]	.47[d]	.12[f]	.20[e]	.46[d]				

Fairness												
Distributive												
Fairness	.48d	.44d	.57d	.39d	.22e	.21d	.38d	.37d	.18e			
Deservedness	.50d	.37d	.55d	.37d	.18e	.23d	.32d	.38d	.13f	.61d		
Procedural												
Procedures	.43d	.39d	.51d	.31d	.18e	.21d	.44d	.37d	.13f	.73d	.48d	
Treatment	.41d	.45d	.52d	.39d	.24e	.19d	.46d	.42d	.18e	.73d	.51d	.81d

[a] First distributive justice item—fairness
[b] Second distributive justice item—deservedness
[c] First procedural justice item—procedure
[d] $p < .001$
[e] $p < .01$
[f] $p < .05$

120   CRITERIA USED TO ASSESS PROCEDURAL JUSTICE

Table 2. The Influence of Judgments About Personal Experience on Satisfaction and Evaluation

Independent Variable	Satisfaction						Views of Authorities			
	Outcome		Treatment		Affect		Evaluation		Support	
	R^{2a}	β^b	R^2	β	R^2	β	R^2	β	R^2	β
Nonfairness										
Outcome factors[c]		.08		.06		.04		−.01		−.13
Procedural factors[d]		.00		.09[g]		.07		−.14[f]		−.13[g]
Total (R^2)	.33[e]		.36[e]		.30[e]		.12[e]		.02	
Fairness										
Distributive		.44[e]		.22[e]		.28[e]		.27[e]		.15[g]
Procedural		.33[e]		.54[e]		.45[e]		.43[e]		.42[e]
Total (R^2)	.60[e]		.64[e]		.55[e]		.34[e]		.16[e]	
Total (R^2)	.60[e]		.65[e]		.55[e]		.36[e]		.18[e]	
Usefulness Analysis										
Nonfairness beyond fairness	.00		.01		.00		.02		.02	
Fairness beyond nonfairness	.27		.29		.25		.24		.16	

[a] R^2 = adjusted square of the multiple correlation coefficient
[b] β = standardized regression coefficient
[c] Absolute favorability: outcomes relative to the past, expectations, and experiences of others and friends, family, or neighbors
[d] Treatment relative to the past, expectations, and experiences of others and friends, family, or neighbors
[e] $p < .001$
[f] $p < .01$
[g] $p < .05$

If fairness is examined to see whether distributive or procedural fairness causes the effects observed, both types of fairness are found to matter. As would be expected, distributive fairness has the greater impact when the dependent variable is outcome satisfaction ($\beta = .44$, versus $\beta = .33$ for procedural fairness), while procedural fairness matters more when the dependent variable is satisfaction with treatment ($\beta = .54$, versus $\beta = .22$ for distributive fairness). In the case of evaluations, procedural justice (mean $\beta = .43$) is uniformly more important than distributive justice (mean $\beta = .23$).

B.   *The Meaning of Procedural Justice*

1. The Importance of Differing Procedural Justice Criteria. Based upon prior research I expected several factors to have an important influence on judgments about the fairness of the procedures citizens encounter in their dealings with legal authorities: consistency, accuracy, impartiality, and representation.

I tested the importance of these potential criteria of procedural fairness by looking at the relationship between citizens' judgments that their experiences were characterized by those criteria and their judgments that they were fairly treated. I conducted two types of analysis, the results of which are shown in Table 3. In the first I established the zero order correlation between each potential criterion and judgments of procedural justice. In the second I computed the beta weight for an equation in which all criteria were entered simultaneously. This latter number indicates the independent contribution of each factor.

The results of the regression analysis suggest that the criteria of procedural justice assessed explain most of the variance in citizen judgments about whether fair procedures were used (69 percent). Seven aspects of procedural justice make an independent contribution to assessments of process fairness: the effort of the authorities to be fair; their honesty; whether their behavior is consistent with ethical standards; whether opportunities for representation are given; the quality of the decisions made; whether opportunities to appeal decisions exist; and whether the behavior of the authorities shows bias.

These data provide partial support for the predictions made in the introduction. Impartiality proved to be important, but more in the form of subjective bias, the effort to be fair ($\beta = .30; p < .001$), and honesty ($\beta = .23; p < .001$) than in direct ratings of the degree of bias in the behavior of the authorities ($\beta = .07; p < .01$). Quality was also important ($\beta = .17; p < .001$), as was representation ($\beta = .17; p < .001$).

The results differed from the predictions in two ways. First, the consistency of outcomes and treatment with past experiences, expectations, or the treatment of others, was not important ($\beta =$

122   CRITERIA USED TO ASSESS PROCEDURAL JUSTICE

Table 3. Attributes of a Procedure That Lead Citizens to View It as Fair

Attribute	Fair Procedures				Fair Authorities			
	r^a	Rank	β^b	Rank	r^a	Rank	β^b	Rank
Representation	.62d	3	.17d	4	.35d	3	.12d	3
Consistency	.32d	7	.04		.16d		.03	
Impartiality								
Bias	.43d	5	.07e	7	.26d	5	.05	
Dishonesty	.59d	4	.23d	2	.34d	4	.11f	4
Effort to be fair	.71d	1	.30d	1	.45d	1	.27d	1
Quality of decisions	.37d	6	.17d	5	.15d	6	.02	
Correctability	.04		.14d	6	−.03		.00	
Ethicality	.69d	2	.21d	3	.41d	2	.15d	2
R^{2c}			.69d				.26d	

a r = Pearson correlation
b β = standardized regression coefficient in an equation including all criteria
c R^2 = adjusted square of the multiple correlation coefficient
d $p < .001$
e $p < .01$
f $p < .05$

.04; not significant), although it was expected to be. Second, ethicality (i.e., whether the police and courts followed general principles of fair conduct) mattered ($\beta = .21$; $p < .001$), but prior research had not suggested that it would. The results, in other words, partially supported *and* contradicted the hypotheses.

The results also suggest that the criteria used to assess the fairness of an experience are similar to those used to assess the fairness of the authorities involved. In both cases the effort to be fair, ethicality, honesty, and representation were important. Since the correlation between these two assessments of procedural justice is .51, this is not surprising.

2. **The Relationship Among Procedural Justice Criteria.** A second question of importance is the relationship among the varying criteria of procedural justice outlined. Table 4 shows this relationship, and suggests that the criteria of procedural justice generally have a positive, overlapping quality (mean $r = .30$). In other words, citizens judge the fairness of process by using a variety of positively interrelated criteria.

Given that the varying criteria are clearly not identical, we can also ask about the presence of underlying dimensions. To identify such dimensions, I factor analyzed the criteria. The results, presented in Table 5, indicate that there were two underlying factors. The first (Factor One) includes assessments about the nature of the experience itself; opportunities for representation, impartiality, and the quality of the decisions made. The second (Factor Two) includes assessments that compare the experience to external standards. Consistency compares the experience to past experiences or the experience of others. Ethicality compares the experience to external standards.

3. **The Universality of Procedural Justice Criteria.** The third issue I consider is the extent to which different criteria are used to assess the justice of a procedure by different people or by people in different circumstances. To test for such variations I conducted a series of regression analyses in which the eight criteria of procedural justice were used to predict procedural justice, as in previously outlined analyses. In addition, I entered interaction terms for the interaction of each criterion with the situational/personal difference variable under consideration.

To explore the meaning of the regression results, I divided respondents into two groups using the situational/personal difference variables under consideration. I then performed a regression for each group, with the eight procedural criteria used to predict judgments in that group.

I distinguished two aspects of the experience: the characteristics of the situation and of the person. The six situational characteristics were the authority involved, whether the situation was a

124 CRITERIA USED TO ASSESS PROCEDURAL JUSTICE

Table 4. The Relationship Among the Attributes of a Fair Procedure[a]

| | Attributes | | | | | | | | | | | |
| | Representation | | Consistency | | Impartiality | | | Quality | | | Ethicality | |
Attribute	Process Control	Decision Control	Outcomes	Process	Bias	Dishonesty	Effort	Decisions	Efforts	Correctability	Polite	Concern for Rights
Representation												
Process control												
Decision control	.56[b]											
Consistency												
Outcomes	.03	.03										
Process	.09	.14	.40[b]									
Impartiality												
Bias	.31[b]	.25[b]	.09	.13[b]								
Dishonesty	.33[b]	.25[b]	.07	.17[b]	.36[b]							
Effort	.58[b]	.48[b]	.02	.12	.36[b]	.43[b]						
Quality												
Decisions	.57[b]	.33[b]	.02	.17[b]	.33[b]	.39[b]	.46[b]					
Efforts	.57[b]	.43[b]	.02	.17[b]	.32[b]	.41[b]	.62[b]	.59[b]				
Correctability	.10	.08	.06	.02	.04	.04	.09	.09	.08			
Ethicality												
Polite	.47[b]	.29[b]	.28[b]	.59[b]	.37[b]	.49[b]	.47[b]	.38[b]	.41[b]	.03		
Concern for rights	.48[b]	.35[b]	.22[b]	.56[b]	.38[b]	.53[b]	.58[b]	.51[b]	.57[b]	.05	.59[b]	

[a] Entries are Pearson correlations.
[b] $p < .001$

Table 5. Factor Analysis of the Attributes of a Fair
          Procedure*

Attribute	Factor One	Factor Two
Representation		
Process control	.78	
Decision control	.58	
Consistency		
Outcomes		.42
Process		.75
Impartiality		
Bias	.42	
Dishonesty	.49	
Effort	.75	
Quality		
Decisions	.66	
Efforts	.76	
Correctabililty		
Ethicality		
Polite		.78
Concern for rights	.43	.73

* Entries are from a factor analysis using Varimax rotation.
  Only loadings over 0.4 are listed.

dispute, whether the situation involved choice, whether the outcome was positive or negative, outcome importance, and the importance of fair treatment. Eight personal characteristics were also examined: two types of prior views, education, race, liberalism, sex, age, and income.

Each characteristic divided the respondents into two groups. The six situational characteristics and eight criteria of procedural justice led to forty-eight comparisons. Of those, sixteen were statistically significant (33 percent, a proportion higher than would be expected by chance). This suggests that the nature of the situation influences the meaning of procedural justice. In different situations citizens judge the fairness of procedures using different criteria. Table 6 shows how such judgments differ. I also considered eight personal characteristics, leading to sixty-four comparisons. Of these only five (8 percent) were significant, a level not different from the number of significant findings that would be expected by chance. There is no evidence, therefore, that different types of people think about the meaning of fairness differently.

The first situational characteristic I examined was the extension of Thibaut and Walker (1975) into noncourtroom experiences and nondisputes. I found that citizens dealing with the courts

ERRATA

The following table was incorrectly printed on page 126 of volume 22, number 1.

Table 6. Attributes of a Fair Procedure Under Varying Circumstances[a]

Attribute	Authority			Dispute Present			Choice			Outcome			Outcome Importance			Process Importance		
	Courts	Police	Difference[b]	Yes	No	Difference	Yes	No	Difference	Positive	Negative	Difference	High	Low	Difference	High	Low	Difference
Representation	.15[e]	.18[g]	•	.38[g]	.17[g]	•	.13[g]	.20[f]	•	.15[f]	.18[g]	•	.18[g]	.17[f]	•	.15[g]	.19[g]	•
Consistency	.04	.05		.12[d]	.03		.02	.08[d]		−.04	.09[f]	•	−.04	−.04		−.04	−.07	
Impartiality																		
Bias	.13[d]	.02		.06	.00		.14[f]	.04		.00	.09[f]		.04	.13[e]		.05	.08	
Dishonesty	.21[f]	.26[g]		.15[e]	.23[g]		.22[g]	.23[g]		.31[g]	.21[g]		.26[g]	.15[f]		.23[g]	.25[g]	
Effort	.26[f]	.31[g]	•	.07	.36[g]	•	.35[g]	.24[g]		.20[f]	.32[g]	•	.29[g]	.32[g]		.29[g]	.28[g]	•
Quality	.26[f]	.14[e]		.16	.08[d]		.29[g]	.03	•	.12[d]	.18[f]		.19[g]	.10		.18[g]	.12[e]	•
Correctability	.25[f]	.10[e]	•	.08	.09[e]		.23[g]	.05	•	.09	.16[f]		.13[f]	.14[e]		.17[g]	.03	
Ethicality	.29[f]	.20[g]		.21[f]	.23[g]		.13[f]	.27[g]		.39[g]	.15[f]	•	.19[g]	.27[g]		.25[g]	.18[f]	
R^2	.67	.71		.75	.67		.67	.66		.74	.66		.71	.66		.72	.63	

a Entries are beta weights when all criteria are entered at the same time.

b The significance of the difference in weights is assessed by using a regression equation that includes main effects and interactions terms for all eight criteria.

c R^2 = adjusted square of the multiple correlation coefficient

d $p < .10$

e $p < .05$

f $p < .01$

g $p < .001$

• Interaction terms that are significant at the $p < .10$ level or greater

were more concerned with issues of decision quality, bias, and correctability than were those dealing with the police. There was no evidence for the hypothesized greater attention to ethicality in courtrooms. Why would this be true? One possible explanation lies in the generally low esteem in which the Chicago courts are held by the public. Citizens approaching the courts may not think of them as places that emphasize rights. The police, in contrast, are viewed more positively by citizens. As a result, ethicality mattered equally in both settings. As hypothesized, those dealing with the police focused more on the effort to be fair (a nonsignificant difference).

I found that procedures used for resolving disputes were more likely to be judged in terms of opportunities for input and consistency of treatment (a nonsignificant difference), as hypothesized, but found no bias effect. Nondisputes were more likely to be judged in terms of the efforts made by the police officer or judge to be fair. Earlier I suggested that the general lack of consistency effects found in this study might stem from the fact that most of the respondents' experiences were not disputes between contending parties. This finding supports that suggestion because consistency matters more when disputes are involved. It is also noteworthy that judgments of procedural justice were better explained in the case of disputes ($R^2 = 75$ percent) than nondisputes ($R^2 = 67$ percent).

The two dimensions of the experience itself also showed an effect on the meaning of procedural justice. In the case of choice, citizens who voluntarily contacted the police or courts focused more heavily on the quality of the authorities' decision making, as hypothesized, while those without choice were concerned with the extent to which they had input into the decisions made and whether the police behaved ethically (nonsignificant differences).

Citizens who received a favorable outcome were more concerned with ethicality, as predicted, and also with honesty (a nonsignificant difference). Those who received negative outcomes evaluated procedural justice more heavily in terms of the effort of the authorities to be fair and the consistency of their actions with other situations. Predicted increased concerns with bias and dishonesty among this group were not found. Rather than focus on these issues, respondents reacted to their inference of whether the authorities had made an effort to be fair; in other words, they looked beneath the surface at motives.

Outcome importance was found to have only one influence on the meaning of procedural justice. When outcomes were more important, issues of honesty became more important. Treatment importance produced two effects. Those who regarded being well treated as more important paid more attention to ethicality and to the quality of the decisions made.

V. DISCUSSION

A. *The Importance of Procedural Justice*

The findings reported strongly support the suggestion of prior research that a key determinant of citizen reactions to encounters with legal authorities is the respondents' assessment of the fairness of the procedures used in that contact. There is also a lesser influence of distributive justice. Once such fairness factors are taken into account, there is little independent effect of the favorability of the outcomes or procedures involved.[5]

The results of this examination support the original Thibaut and Walker (1975) hypothesis that the way legal decisions are made affects litigant reactions to those decisions. This support is consistent with other post–Thibaut and Walker findings in the legal arena (Lind, 1982; Walker and Lind, 1984), in the political world (Tyler, 1986a; Tyler, Rasinski, and Griffin, 1986), and in work settings (Folger and Greenberg, 1985; Greenberg and Folger, 1983; Greenberg and Tyler, 1987). Similarly, the finding of effects on the evaluation of authorities is consistent with other recent discoveries of such effects in the legal (Tyler, 1984b; Tyler and Folger, 1980), political (Tyler and Caine, 1981; Tyler, Rasinski, and McGraw, 1985), and organizational (Bies, 1985) arenas. In other words, this result is quite in line with widespread suggestions that those affected by the decisions of third parties in both formal and informal settings react to the procedural justice of the decision-making process at least as much, and often more, than they react to the decision itself (Lind and Tyler, 1988).

B. *The Meaning of Procedural Justice*

These findings indicate that the judgment of procedural justice is complex and multifaceted. Citizens are not using any simple, unidimensional approach to such assessments. Instead, they pay attention to seven distinct aspects of process: the authorities' motivation, honesty, and ethicality; the opportunities for representation; the quality of the decisions; the opportunities for error correction; and the authorities' bias. It is noteworthy that the major criteria used to assess process fairness are those aspects of procedure least linked to outcomes—ethicality, honesty, and the effort to be fair—rather than consistency with other outcomes. This reinforces the earlier suggestion that procedural issues are distinct from concern with outcomes.

Following the lead of Thibaut and Walker, most researchers have focused on issues of process and decision control (i.e., repre-

---

[5] In considering the conclusions of this study, it is important to remember that the data are correlational. As a result, the causal order assumptions cannot be rigorously tested. It should be recognized, therefore, that the conclusions are, of necessity, more tentative than if an experimental design had been used.

sentation) when exploring the meaning of procedural justice. These results suggest that representation, while important, is only one of a number of concerns that define fair processes.

1. **The Effort to Be Fair.** Judgments about "how hard" the authorities tried to be fair emerged as the key overall factor in assessing procedural justice. From an attributional perspective this represents a motive attribution and requires the respondent to think about whether the official involved was motivated to be just. As such it requires more effort than simpler behavioral judgments and might be expected to be avoided. Instead, however, citizens focus on this assessment, even though trait inferences are especially difficult to make and are less reliable when observers can only rely on information from a single interaction (Heider, 1958).

Others have also noted the desire of citizens to infer the motives of authorities. Lane (1986) writes that citizens focus heavily on inferences about the "benevolence" of political leaders, while Bies (Bies and Shapiro, 1987) suggests that workers are very concerned with the "sincerity" of managers. These issues reflect respondents' desire to understand the dispositional tendencies of those making decisions. If they infer a positive disposition, they can trust that, in the long run, the leader will strive to serve their self-interest. It is for this reason that trust is such a key component of legitimacy (Barber, 1983; Tyler, 1986c).

2. **Ethicality.** While concern with ethicality has not figured prominently in past psychological discussions of procedural justice, it has emerged here as an important criterion of procedural fairness. Social scientists, including Leventhal (1980), have suggested that ethical appropriateness might be a key aspect of fair treatment. Lane (1986), for example, has noted its importance in political settings. He argues that one of the most significant aspects of procedural justice to citizens is that the procedures used support their sense of self-respect. Being treated politely and seeing one's rights respected should strongly reinforce self-respect. The general importance of self-respect to overall psychological well-being has also been suggested (Campbell, 1980; Rosenberg, 1979). Its importance in the specific context of encounters with legal authority was suggested by Tyler and Folger (1980), who examined citizen-police contacts and found that a key issue to citizens in such contacts was "recognition of citizen rights" (p. 292). Similar evidence of a concern with interpersonal aspects of encounters with authorities has also been found in research on work organizations (Bies and Shapiro, 1987).

In this paper the concept of ethicality is operationalized in two potentially distinct ways: as politeness and as concern for one's rights. These two items were combined into one index because I found them to be highly correlated ($r = .59$). If they are sepa-

130   CRITERIA USED TO ASSESS PROCEDURAL JUSTICE

rated, concern for one's rights is more strongly related to judgments of procedural justice ($r = .67$) than is politeness ($r = .58$).

3. **Consistency.** Perhaps the most striking deviation from the predictions is the failure to find strong consistency effects in citizen judgments of fairness. In this study citizens are not basing their judgments on a comparison of their outcomes or treatment with other experiences, either their own or of others'. Since consistency has been found to be a major issue in past studies, its insignificance here is puzzling. There are several possible explanations. One is that citizens lack the information necessary to make consistency judgments. Citizens might have contact with the police and courts for a wide variety of reasons, each with its appropriate type of treatment by those authorities. As a result, citizens may be aware of several instances of police or judge behavior but may not know how they relate to their own experience. Since similarity judgments are the key to comparisons (Festinger, 1954), this makes it difficult for citizens to assess relative outcomes and treatment. How, for example, can the result of a call to the police to stop a neighborhood disturbance be compared to not receiving a ticket when stopped for speeding? Citizens may thus lack the knowledge necessary for judging whether their outcomes or treatment were better or worse than those of others.

The idea that citizens can accept differences in treatment or outcomes if those differences are justified by differences in the problems being dealt with has been suggested by Bies and Shapiro (1987). It is also supported by the finding of Cornelius et al. (1986) that inconsistency of treatment does not lead to perceived unfairness if it is justified by differences in the nature of the task.

It may be that the lack of awareness of others' experiences is characteristic of only some populations. Special groups may have greater knowledge about others and rely more on others' experiences when evaluating their own. One such example is criminals. Casper's (1972, 1978) interviews with defendants in prison suggest that criminals have a great deal of knowledge about the typical behavior of the police and courts and use consistency with their expectations as an important basis for evaluating their treatment and sentences.

The difficulties that citizens have acquiring the appropriate information for social comparisons are similar to the more general difficulty they have drawing useful information from indirect sources such as the mass media. In the case of crime information, for example, these difficulties can be traced in part to the failure of the media to present citizens with the situational information they need to compare the factors involved in the crime victimizations they read about or see on television to their own situation and behavior to estimate their crime risks. (Tyler, 1984a; Tyler and Cook, 1984; Tyler and Lavrakas, 1985). In other words, a person can know of instances involving others but lack the contextual information required to apply those data.

If citizens lack the information needed to rely on consistency, that is, on cross-situational comparisons, their alternative is to rely on judgments that can be made with the information that they do have. One type is information about the behavior of the official, which leads to inferences about their efforts to be fair. Others are information about their honesty as well as whether the official followed general ethical standards of conduct.

The need to rely on judgments based on a single experience suggests one reason that ethicality had a strong influence on judgments of procedural justice. Consistency with ethical principles is a type of judgment that allows citizens to assess the quality of police or court conduct within the context of one experience. Irrespective of the problem or issue at dispute, they can feel that the officials involved should follow general ethical guidelines. As a result, such judgments override the difficulties involved in social or temporal comparisons.

C. The Relationship Among Procedural Justice Criteria

These findings confirm the idea of positively interrelated clusters of procedural criteria. Their existence suggests that the choice of procedures for resolving disputes or solving problems does not require making the trade-offs discussed in the literature on distributive justice. Procedures that are viewed as leading to higher quality decisions, for example, are also more ethical and allow more citizen input. In other words, from the citizens' perspective, procedures exist that will promote all aspects of procedural justice simultaneously. This does not mean that the attainment of all criteria can be maximized at one time—it cannot. However, the harsh trade-offs described in the distributive justice literature do not appear in this study of procedural justice.

Factor analysis also suggests two underlying factors that can account for the seven independent criteria identified. The first is made up of experience-based judgments. The second consists of judgments that involve the comparison of the experience to other experiences or external ethical standards.

D. The Universality of Procedural Justice Criteria

The results of the regression analysis suggest that the meaning of procedural justice changes in response to the nature of citizens' experiences with legal authorities. While the pattern of the findings is complex, it points to the conclusion that individuals do not have a single schema of a fair process that they apply on all occasions. Instead, they are concerned with different issues under different circumstances. As a result, it is likely that there are no universally fair procedures for allocation and dispute resolution.

132   CRITERIA USED TO ASSESS PROCEDURAL JUSTICE

Instead, different procedures are appropriate under different circumstances.

As noted, Thibaut and Walker (1975) focused on issues of representation (process and decision control) when examining the meaning of procedural justice. The results of this study suggest that they may have overgeneralized from the dispute context of their own work to a general theory of fair process. In the context of disputes, representation is the most important issue (see Table 6). If the context is broadened, however, other issues emerge.

It is also interesting to note that the characteristics of the person do not influence the criteria used to assess whether a procedure is fair. In other words, different types of people within American culture define the meaning of procedural justice in a similar way. This suggests that definitions of the meaning of justice within particular settings may be part of the cultural beliefs shared by members of our society. This suggestion is also supported by recent ethnographic studies of the courts (Merry, 1985, 1986) and by studies of consensus in judging wrongdoing (Sanders and Hamilton, 1987). The lack of personal differences has very important consequences for interactions among citizens and between citizens and authorities. Since all parties to a problem share a common conception of the meaning of procedural justice, all will focus on similar issues in attempting to find a process for dealing with the question at issue. If this were not the case, police officers and judges would be required to make an initial effort to understand the definition of procedural justice held by each party who appeared before them. Developing agreements on these issues before attempting to choose procedures for resolving every problem legal officials must deal with would be both complex and time-consuming.

These results suggest that legal authorities are aided in their efforts to resolve public problems by shared cultural values about the meaning of procedural justice within the context of particular situations. These common values facilitate the efforts of officials by suggesting the public concerns they ought to focus on to gain citizen acceptance of their efforts. They also facilitate the acceptance of decisions in disputes, since both parties are likely to share a conception of what the authorities should be doing.

These results also suggest that efforts to develop a typology that will clarify when procedural justice will have different meanings should concentrate on developing a situational typology. People think about procedural justice in a similar way even if they differ from each other on background characteristics.

REFERENCES

BARBER, B. (1983) *The Logic and Limits of Trust*. New Brunswick, NJ: Rutgers University Press.

BARRETT-HOWARD, E., and Tom R. TYLER (1986) "Procedural Justice as a Criterion in Allocation Decisions," 50 *Journal of Personality and Social Psychology* 296.

BIES, R. J. (1985) "The Influence of a Leader's Concerns for Task, Teamwork, and Fairness on Subordinates' Satisfaction and Organizational Evaluations." Unpublished, Department of Organizational Behavior, Northwestern University.

BIES, R. J., and D. L. SHAPIRO (1987) "Processual Fairness Judgments: The Influence of Causal Accounts," 1 *Social Justice Review* 199.

CAMPBELL, A. (1980) *The Sense of Well-Being in America*. New York: Mc-Graw-Hill.

CASPER, J. (1978) "Having Their Day in Court: Defendant Evaluations of the Fairness of Their Treatment," 12 *Law & Society Review* 237.

——— (1972) *American Criminal Justice: The Defendant's Perspective*. Englewood Cliffs, NJ: Prentice-Hall.

CASPER, J., Tom R. TYLER, and Bonnie FISHER (in press) "Procedural Justice among Felony Defendants." *Law & Society Review*.

COHEN, J., and P. COHEN (1975) *Applied Multiple Regression/Correlation Analysis for the Behavioral Sciences*. Hillsdale, NJ: Erlbaum.

CORNELIUS, G. W., R. KANFER, and E.A. LIND (1986) "Evaluation Fairness and Work Motivation." Unpublished. University of Illinois.

CROSBY, F. (1976) "A Model of Egoistical Relative Deprivation," 83 *Psychological Review* 85.

DEUTSCH, M., (1982) "Interdependence and Psychological Orientation," in V. J. Derlaga and J. Grzelak (eds.), *Cooperation and Helping Behavior*. New York: Academic Press.

EASTON, D. (1965). *A Systems Analysis of Political Life*. Chicago: University of Chicago Press.

FESTINGER, L. (1954) "A Theory of Social Comparison Processes," 7 *Human Relations* 117.

FOLGER, R. (1986a) "A Referent Cognitions Theory of Relative Deprivation," in J. M. Olson, C. P. Hermann, and M. P. Zanna (eds.), *Social Comparison and Relative Deprivation: The Ontario Symposium*, Vol. 4. Hillsdale, NJ: Erlbaum.

FOLGER, R. (1968b) "Rethinking Equity Theory: A Referent Cognitions Model," in H. W. Bierhoff, R. L. Cohen, and J. Greenberg (eds.), *Justice in Social Relations*. New York: Plenum.

FOLGER, R., and J. GREENBERG (1985) "Procedural Justice: An Interpretive Analysis of Personnel Systems," in K. Rowland and G. Ferris (eds.), *Research in Personnel and Human Resources Management*, Vol. 3. Greenwich, CT: JAI Press.

FRY, W. R., and G. CHANEY (1981) "Perceptions of Procedural Fairness as a Function of Distributive Preferences." Presented at the Annual Meeting of the Midwestern Psychological Association, Detroit (May).

FRY, W. R., and G. S. LEVENTHAL (1979) "Cross Situational Procedural Preferences: A Comparison of Allocation Preferences and Equity Across Different Social Settings." Presented at the Annual Meeting of the Southeastern Psychological Association, Washington, DC (March).

GALEGHER, J., and J. S. CARROLL (1983) "Voluntary Sentencing Guidelines: Prescription for Justice or Patent Medicine?," 7 *Law and Human Behavior* 361.

GREENBERG, J. (1986) "Reactions to Procedural Justice in Payment Distributions: Do the Means Justify the Ends?," 72 *Journal of Applied Psychology* 55.

——— (1986) "Determinants of Perceived Fairness of Performance Evaluations," 71 *Journal of Applied Psychology* 340.

GREENBERG, J., and R. FOLGER (1983) "Procedural Justice, Participation,

134   CRITERIA USED TO ASSESS PROCEDURAL JUSTICE

and the Fair Process Effect in Groups and Organizations," in P. B. Paulus (ed.), *Basic Group Processes*. New York: Springer-Verlag.

GREENBERG, J., and Tom R. TYLER (1987) "Procedural Justice in Organizational Settings," 1 *Social Justice Review* 127.

HEIDER, F. (1958) *The Psychology of Interpersonal Relations*. New York: Wiley.

HELSON, H. (1964) *Adaptation-Level Theory*. New York: Harper and Row.

HOULDEN, P., S. LATOUR, L. WALKER, and J. THIBAUT (1978) "Preference for Modes of Dispute Resolution as a Function of Process and Decision Control," 14 *Journal of Experimental Social Psychology* 13.

KURTINES, W. M. (1986) "Moral Behavior as Rule Governed Behavior: Person and Situation Effects on Moral Decision Making," 50 *Journal of Personality and Social Psychology* 784.

LANDIS, J. M. and L. I. GOODSTEIN (1986) "When Is Justice Fair? An Integrated Approach to the Outcome Versus Procedural Debate." *American Bar Foundation Research Journal* 675.

LANE, R. E. (1986) "Procedural Justice: How One Is Treated vs. What One Gets." Unpublished, Department of Political Science, Yale University.

LEVENTHAL, G. S. (1980) "What Should Be Done with Equity Theory?," in K. J. Gergen, M.S. Greenberg, and R. H. Weiss (eds.), *Social Exchange: Advances in Theory and Research*. New York: Plenum.

LIND, E. A. (1982) "The Psychology of Courtroom Procedure," in N. L. Kerr and R. M. Bray (eds.), *The Psychology of the Courtroom*. New York: Academic.

LIND, E. A., R. I. LISSAK, and A. E. CONLON (1983) "Decision Control and Process Control Effects on Procedural Fairness Judgments," 13 *Journal of Applied Social Psychology* 338.

LIND, E. A., and Tom R. TYLER (1988) *The Social Psychology of Procedural Justice*. New York: Plenum.

LISSAK, R. I., and B. SHEPPARD (1983) "Beyond Fairness: The Criterion Problem in Research on Dispute Intervention," 13 *Journal of Applied Social Psychology* 45.

McCLOSKY, H., and A. BRILL (1983) *Dimensions of Tolerance: What Americans Believe About Civil Liberties*. New York: Russell Sage Foundation.

MERRY, S. E. (1985) "Concepts of Law and Justice among Working-Class Americans: Ideology as Culture." 9 *Legal Studies Forum* 59.

———— (1986) "Everyday Understandings of the Law in Working-Class America." 13 *American Ethnologist* 253.

OKUN, A. M. (1975) *Equality and Efficiency: The Big Tradeoff*. Washington, DC: Brookings Institute.

ROSENBERG, M. (1979) *Conceiving the Self*. New York: Basic.

SANDERS, J., and L. HAMILTON (1987) "Is There a "Common Law" of Responsibility?" 11 *Law and Human Behavior* 277.

SHEPPARD, B. H., and R. J. LEWICKI (1987) "Toward General Principles of Managerial Fairness," *Social Justice Review*.

SHEPPARD, B. H., D. SAUNDERS and J. MINTON (1986) "Determinants of Procedural Choice in Informal Dispute Resolution." Presented at the Annual Meeting of the Law and Society Association, Chicago (June).

SULLIVAN, J. L., J. PIERESON and G. MARCUS (1982) *Political Tolerance and American Democracy*. Chicago: University of Chicago Press.

THIBAUT, J., and L. WALKER (1975) *Procedural Justice: A Psychological Analysis*. Hillsdale, NJ: Erlbaum.

TYLER, Tom R. (1987a) "Conditions Leading to Value-Expressive Effects in Judgments of Procedural Justice: A Test of Four Models," 52 *Journal of Personality and Social Psychology* 333.

———— (1987b) "Procedural Justice, Legitimacy, and Compliance." Unpublished, Department of Psychology, Northwestern University.

———— (1987c) "Procedural Justice Research." 1 *Social Justice Review* 41.

———— (1986a) "Justice and Leadership Endorsement," in R. R. Lau and D. O. Sears (eds.), *Political Cognition*. Hillsdale, NJ: Erlbaum.

———— (1986b) "Justice, Legitimacy and Compliance." Presented at the Meeting of the Law and Society Association, Chicago (May).

———— (1986c) "When Does Procedural Justice Matter in Organizational Settings?," in R. J. Lewicki, B. H. Sheppard, and M. Bazerman (eds.), *Research on Negotiating in Organizations.* Greenwich, CT: JAI Press.

—— (1984a) "Assessing the Risk of Crime Victimization: The Integration of Personal Victimization Experience and Socially Transmitted Information," 40 *Journal of Social Issues* 27.

—— (1984b) "The Role of Perceived Injustice in Defendants' Evaluations of Their Courtroom Experience," 18 *Law & Society Review* 51.

TYLER, Tom R., and A. CAINE (1981) "The Influence of Outcome and Procedures on Satisfaction with Formal Leaders," 41 *Journal of Personality and Social Psychology* 642.

TYLER, Tom R., and F. L. COOK (1984) "The Mass Media and Judgments of Risk: Distinguishing Impact on Personal and Societal Level Judgments," 47 *Journal of Personality and Social Psychology* 693.

TYLER, Tom R., and R. FOLGER (1980) "Distributional and Procedural Aspects of Satisfaction with Citizen-Police Encounters," 1 *Basic and Applied Social Psychology* 281.

TYLER, Tom R., and P. LAVRAKAS (1985) "Cognitions Leading to Personal and Political Behaviors: The Case of Crime," in S. Kraus and R. M. Perloff (eds.), *The Mass Media and Political Thought.* Beverly Hills: Sage.

TYLER, Tom R., and E. A. LIND (1986) "Procedural Processes and Legal Institutions." Presented at the International Conference on Social Justice in Human Relations, Leiden (July).

TYLER, Tom R., K. RASINSKI and E. GRIFFIN (1986) "Alternative Images of the Citizen: Implications for Public Policy," 41 *American Psychologist* 970.

TYLER, Tom R., K. RASINSKI and K. McGRAW (1985) "The Influence of Perceived Injustice on the Endorsement of Political Leaders," 15 *Journal of Applied Social Psychology* 700.

TYLER, Tom R., K. RASINSKI and N. SPODICK (1985) "The Influence of Voice on Satisfaction with Leaders: Exploring the Meaning of Process Control," 48 *Journal of Personality and Social Psychology* 72.

WALKER, L., and E. A. LIND (1984) "Psychological Studies of Procedural Models," in G. M. Stephenson and J. H. Davis (eds.), *Progress in Applied Social Psychology,* Vol. 2. New York: Wiley.

WISH, M., M. DEUTSCH, and S. J. KAPLAN (1976) "Perceived Dimensions of Interpersonal Relations," 33 *Journal of Personality and Social Psychology* 409.

WISH, M., and S. J. KAPLAN (1977) "Toward an Implicit Theory of Interpersonal Communication," 40 *Sociometry* 234.

[17]

". . . The Law Is All Over": Power, Resistance and the Legal Consciousness of the Welfare Poor

Austin Sarat*

I. INTRODUCTION

"For me the law is all over. I am caught, you know; there is always some rule that I'm supposed to follow, some rule I don't even know about that they say. It's just different and you can't really understand." These words were spoken by Spencer, a thirty-five-year-old man on public assistance (general relief), whom I first encountered in the waiting room of a legal services office. I introduced myself and told him that I was interested in talking to him about law and finding out why he was using legal services; I asked if he would be willing to talk with me and allow me to be present when he met with his lawyer. While he seemed, at first, both puzzled and amused that I had, as he put it, "nothing more important to do," he agreed to both of my requests.

As my research unfolded, what Spencer said in our first conversation, ". . . the law is all over," served as a reference point for understanding the meaning and significance of law in the lives of the welfare poor. His words helped me interpret how people on welfare think about law and use legal ideas as well as how they respond to problems with the welfare bureaucracy. In this paper I present that interpretation and describe what I call the legal consciousness of the welfare poor.[1] I suggest that the legal

---

* Support for this research was provided by an Amherst College Faculty Research Grant. I am grateful for the able assistance of Chris Sayler and Jarl Ahlvist. Amrita Basu, Nathaniel Berman, Kristin Bumiller, Lawrence Douglas, Tom Dumm, Patricia Ewick, Joel Handler, Christine Harrington, Sally Merry, Deborah Rhode, Stephanie Sandler, Stuart Scheingold, Carroll Seron, Susan Silbey, Stanton Wheeler and participants in the Law and Society Seminar at Northwestern University, the Amherst Seminar on Legal Ideology and Legal Process and the Legal Theory Workshop at Yale Law School provided helpful comments on earlier versions of this paper.

1. Trubek, *Where the Action Is: Critical Legal Studies and Empiricism*, 36 Stan. L. Rev. 575, 592 (1984) defines legal consciousness as ". . . all the ideas about the nature, function and operation of law held by anyone in society at a given time." I use the term consciousness, but I could have as easily substituted ideology. Indeed for my purposes legal consciousness and legal ideology could be used interchangeably.

Consciousness and ideology are used instead of attitudes because speaking about attitudes toward or about law suggests a radical individuation, a picture of persons influenced by a variety of factors, thinking, choosing, deciding autonomously how and what to think. The language of attitudes links popular views of law with feelings and, in so doing, "diminishes the authority of the attitude holder." *See* Brigham, The Public's Property: Distinguishing Law From Attitude, (1989) (unpublished

consciousness of the welfare poor is a consciousness of power and domination, in which the keynote is enclosure and dependency, and a consciousness of resistance, in which welfare recipients assert themselves and demand recognition of their personal identities and their human needs.

The legal consciousness of the welfare poor is, I will argue, substantially different from other groups in society for whom law is a less immediate and visible presence. Law is, for people on welfare, repeatedly encountered in the most ordinary transactions and events of their lives. Legal rules and practices are implicated in determining whether and how welfare recipients will be able to meet some of their most pressing needs. Law is immediate and powerful because being on welfare means having a significant part of one's life organized by a regime of legal rules invoked by officials to claim jurisdiction over choices and decisions which those not on welfare would regard as personal and private.[2] Thus, Spencer's sense

---

manuscript).

Consciousness and ideology suggest greater structure and constraint. These terms embed the study of ideas in social structure and social relations. They draw attention to the way similarly situated persons come to see the world in similar ways. They suggest that subjectivity is not free floating and autonomous but is, instead, constituted, in a historically contingent manner, by the very objects of consciousness. *See* Harrington and Merry, *Ideological Production: The Making of Community Mediation*, 22 Law & Soc'y Rev. 709, 711 n. 1 (1988).

2. When an individual takes public assistance he or she becomes a legal subject in a rather dramatic and visible way. As Hunt argues, "It is by transforming a human subject into a legal subject that law influences the way in which participants experience and perceive their relations with others." Hunt, *The Ideology of Law*, 19 Law & Soc'y Rev. 11, 15 (1985).

In the United States the transformation of the human subject into a legal subject which is accomplished when someone takes public assistance traditionally has been tainted and stigmatized. *See* W. Ryan, Blaming the Victim (1971). For the welfare poor, the choice is to internalize and accept, or to resist and reject, what Tocqueville once called, the ". . . notarized manifestation of misery, of weakness, of misconduct. . . ." which comes with the acceptance of public assistance. This quotation is taken from G. Himmelfarb, The Idea of Poverty: England in the Early Industrial Age 150 (1983).

Legal rules both establish the conditions for relief and historically have given meaning to being "on welfare" through a system of intrusions, invasions and indignities reserved specifically for welfare recipients. For example under the 'absent' or 'substitute parent' rule, which was invalidated in King v. Smith, 392 U.S. 309 (1968), states would deny AFDC payments if the mother 'cohabits' with any able-bodied man. *See* W. Trattner, Social Welfare and Social Control (1983); J. Handler, The Coercive Social Worker (1973) and M. Katz, In The Shadow of the Poorhouse (1986).

In the last twenty five years, however, efforts have been made to alter that system through the legal recognition of welfare rights and procedural limitations on the power of the welfare bureaucracy. *See* Shapiro v. Thompson, 394 U.S. 618 (1969) and Goldberg v. Kelly, 397 U.S. 254 (1970). Yet such rights and procedural limitations further inscribed the welfare poor in law even as they made the identity constituted by and the meaning of being "on welfare" more complex. Simon, *Rights and Redistribution in the Welfare System*, 38 Stan. L. Rev. 1431 (1986).

During the last decade welfare eligibility standards have been made more stringent, and a continuous process of reporting and review was put into place. Law's hard, bureaucratic face has supplemented, if not altogether replaced, its rights-protecting concerns. "Even before the days of QC [federally mandated quality control] welfare administration required procedures for application, for determining categorical and income eligibility, for establishing benefit levels and for making changes as circumstances require. In current practice this has come to involve visits to welfare offices, forms to fill out, forms to mail in, interviews with workers, investigations and waiting." *See* Bane & Dowling, Trends in the Administration of Welfare Programs 7 (1987) (unpublished manuscript). For recipients this has meant more problems in getting and keeping welfare benefits. It has increased the difficulty and fear associated with the welfare experience and further complicated efforts to make sense of law. *Id.* at 9.

that ". . . the law is all over" is an introduction to the pervasiveness and obtrusiveness of legal rules and practices in the lives of people on welfare.

For Spencer and other welfare recipients law is not a distant abstraction; it is a web-like enclosure in which they are "caught." It is a space which is not their own and which allows them only a "tactical" presence.[3] It is both a metaphorical trap and a material force. Like the man from the country in Franz Kafka's parable "Before the Law," law is, for Spencer and others on welfare, an irresistible and inescapable presence. For them, however, it is an already entered space, an enclosure seen from the inside, an enclosure whose imperative power, whose "supposed to'(s)," is clothed in the categories and abstractions of rules.[4]

The rules Spencer confronts are a series of "they say(s)." The rules speak, but what Spencer hears is the embodied voice of law's bureaucratic guardians. For him, as for Kafka's character, the power of legal rules and practices is derived, at least in part, from the incomplete, yet authoritative, representation of law's categories and abstractions by officials authorized to say what the law is.[5] Legal rules and practices are all around, immediately and visibly present; yet the law itself remains a shadowy presence.

The law that the welfare poor confront is neither a law of reason and justification nor of sacred texts and shared normative commitments. Spencer and others like him are not invited to participate in the interpretation of those texts,[6] and they are included in neither the official explication of welfare law nor in the construction of meaningful accounts of the legal practices they regularly encounter. They are "caught" inside law's rules,

---

3. Here I use the concept of tactics as it is used by de Certeau. For him a "tactic is a calculated action determined by the absence of a proper locus. No delineation of an exteriority, then, provides it with the condition necessary for autonomy. The space of a tactic is the space of the other." *See* The Practice of Everyday Life 36-37 (1987).

4. White notes that a welfare recipient for whom she provided legal representation had the "persistent feeling about being on welfare was, in her words, that she was 'boxed in.' None of the formal rules of welfare set up boundaries to protect her. . . . Yet those rules confined her." *See* Unearthing the Barriers to Women's Speech: Notes Toward a Feminist Vision of Procedural Justice 90 (1989) (unpublished paper).

5. Derrida, *Devant La Loi*, in Kafka and the Contemporary Critical Performance 136 (Avital Ronnell trans. 1987), asks what holds Kafka's man from the country before the law; "is it not its possibility and impossibility, its readability and unreadability, its necessity and prohibition, and those possibilities, as of the relation, repetition and history?"

Other research has noted that welfare is, for welfare recipients, ". . . a mysterious process, one which they do not understand and one which . . . is not visible to them." *See* Briar, *Welfare From Below: Welfare Recipients Views of the Public Welfare System*, 20 Cal. L. Rev. 370, 377 (1966). Indeed two welfare administrators suggest that recently welfare programs have "become more and more mysterious to workers and clients. (We are not sure we understand the AFDC program completely ourselves. . . .)" *See* Bane and Dowling, *supra* note 2, at 11-12. More generally, as Derrida claims, ". . . we know neither who nor what the law is." *See Devant La Loi*, at 144.

6. Cover suggests that ". . . [A]s long as legal interpretation is constituted as violent behavior as well as meaning . . . there will always be a tragic limit to the common meaning achieved. . . . [F]or those who impose the violence . . . justification is important, real and carefully cultivated. Conversely, for the victim, the justification recedes in reality and significance. . . ." *See Violence and the Word*, 95 Yale L.J. 1601, 1629 (1986).

but are, at the same time, excluded from its interpretive community.[7] In all of their dealings with welfare they act on "a terrain imposed . . . and organized by the law of a foreign power."[8] Their law is a law of power and of compulsion, and their experience of being inside, but yet excluded, is one indication of the way that power is exercised over the welfare poor.

While the welfare poor are surrounded and entrapped by legal rules as well as by officials and institutions which claim authority to say what the law is and what the rules mean, they are not, like the man from the country, transfixed or paralyzed. In this paper I argue that the welfare poor subscribe to neither an allegedly hegemonic "myth of rights"[9] nor to a picture of law as autonomous, apolitical, objective, neutral and disinterested.[10] They are not the passive recipients of an ideology encoded in doctrine which is allegedly taken seriously among legal elites.[11] Power and domination are thus only part of the story of the legal consciousness of the welfare poor. Because welfare recipients are trapped or "caught," because they are involved in an ongoing series of transactions with officials visibly engaged in the interpretation and use of rules, the welfare poor have access to inside knowledge not generally available to those whose contacts with law are more episodic or for whom law is less visible. This inside knowledge means, as we will see, that they have few illusions about what law is or what it can do. They are, as a result, able, when the need arises, to respond strategically, to maneuver and to resist the "they say(s)" and "supposed to(s)" of the welfare bureaucracy.

Resistance exists side-by-side with power and domination. Thus, when people like Spencer seek legal assistance or go to legal services they fight the welfare bureaucracy and its "legal order" even as they submit themselves to another of law's domains. They use legal ideas to interpret and make sense of their relationship to the welfare bureaucracy even as they refine those ideas by making claims the meaning and moral content of which are often at variance with dominant understandings.[12] They resist

---

7. For an analysis of the nature and terms of the exclusion of welfare recipients and other members of the public from law's interpretive community see Brigham, *supra* note 1. Such exclusion might give rise to what Wolin calls a "democratic critique of the welfare state." Such a critique asks, "what are the political implications of humanitarianism, of classifying citizens as needy and of making them needful objects of state power. . . ." rather than allowing them to use "power to constitute a collaborative world." The Presence of the Past: Essays on the State and the Constitution 154 (1989).

8. de Certeau, *supra* note 3, at 37.

9. For an examination of the nature of the "myth of rights" see S. Scheingold, The Politics of Rights (1974).

10. For a description of this picture of law see Singer, *"The Player and the Cards": Critical Legal Studies and Nihilism*, 94 Yale L.J. 1 (1984) and Gordon, *New Developments in Legal Theory*, in The Politics of Law 286 (D. Kairys ed. 1982).

11. To assume that they are persuaded by those ideologies, or that they give meaning to law on the terms that law itself provides, would be to see them as ". . . passive, helpless and deluded recipients of the ideas produced by an active and creative ruling class." Merry, *Concepts of Law and Justice Among Working-Class Americans*, 9 Legal Stud. F. 59, 68 (1985).

12. *See* Yngvesson, *Making Law at the Doorway: The Clerk, The Court and The Construction of Community in a New England Town*, 22 Law & Soc'y Rev. 409, 410 (1988).

those understandings by "vigilantly making use of the cracks that particular conjunctions open in . . . proprietary powers. . . ."[13] Yet their use of legal services and legal ideas further inscribes them in the world of state law and helps to reproduce official understandings of law and justice. It is, however, always an incomplete inscription.

Spencer and others like him stand in a contradictory, paradoxical and ambivalent relationship to legal authority, mobilizing one set of legal officials against another, moving from one arena of rules to another,[14] seeking recognition and help while being very dubious about the treatment they receive and seeking to establish spaces for, or moments of, resistance.[15] While they seek *legal* redress for wrongs done in the name of law, they contest what are sometimes said to be key symbols of law and legal authority, in particular the association of law with neutrality, disinterestedness, rule determinacy and rights.[16]

The dynamic of power and resistance that I observed is, of course, played out on the "foreign" terrain of the lawyer's office, and the welfare poor seem very conscious of the fact that neither here nor in their dealings with the welfare bureaucracy are they able to find a "*place* that can be delineated as . . . [their] own and serve as a base from which relations of *exteriority* . . . can be managed."[17] The recognition that ". . . the law is all over" expresses, in spatial terms, the experience of power and domination; resistance involves efforts to avoid further "spatialization" or establish unreachable spaces of personal identity and integrity.

Power and domination are, however, represented in the legal consciousness of the welfare poor in temporal as well as spatial terms;[18] thus, the people I studied often spoke of an interminable waiting that they said marks the welfare experience. In that waiting they are frozen in time as if time itself were frozen; power defines whose time is valued and whose

---

13. de Certeau, *supra* note 3, at 37.

14. As Yngvesson argues, "The power of legal ideologies and law itself derives not only from its constitutive effects, but from . . . contradictions, paradoxes, and impurities as well. . . . Whereas some might see such contradictions, paradoxes, and impurities as weakening the power of law . . . these apparent weaknesses make law available for innumerable uses and provide an extraordinarily wide arc for its compass." *See* Yngvesson, *Inventing Law in Local Settings: Rethinking Popular Culture,*" 98 Yale L.J. 1689, 1693 (1989); *see also* Amherst Seminar, *From the Special Issue Editors, Special Issue: Law and Ideology,* 22 Law & Soc'y Rev. 629, 634 (1988).

15. The concept of resistance is discussed by M. Foucault, Power/Knowledge (trans. C. Gordon et. al. 1980); *see also* Fitzpatrick, Law, Politics and Resistance (1986) (unpublished manuscript). Here I use it to signify behavior or actions seen to be at odds with the expectations of those exercising power in a particular situation.

16. *See* Singer, *supra* note 10; Gordon, *supra* note 10.

17. de Certeau, *supra* note 3, at 36.

18. Greenhouse argues that law has "a mythic dimension, in its self-totalization, its quality of being in time (in that it is a human product) but also out of time (where did it or does it begin or end?) and in its promise of systematic yet permutable meaning. This myth is essentially a temporal one. Specifically the law's implicit claim is to invoke the total system of its own distinctions simultaneously in a way that both individualizes subjects/citizens and orients them toward particular forms of action." *Just in Time: Temporality and Cultural Legitimation in Law,* 98 Yale L.J. 1631, 1640 (1989).

time is valueless. For the welfare poor resistance involves a use of time against space, an insistence on the *immediacy* of their material needs, an attempt to substitute human for bureaucratic time. Thus metaphors of space and time become important signs of the way the welfare poor understand power and resistance as well as a currency for tactical maneuvers within a "world bewitched by the . . . powers of the Other."[19]

To this point I have talked about the welfare poor as if they were a homogeneous group whose legal consciousness and relationship to power and resistance were uniform. There is, however, considerably more fragmentation and division among people on welfare than might be suggested by my repeated references to *the* welfare poor.[20] As Spencer put it, "all welfare recipients aren't the same." He reminded me that the welfare poor are not a natural social group. They neither share a distinctive background nor common ties of sentiment; they vary greatly in their life situations, their ability to survive without public assistance and their disposition to do so.

Spencer insisted that many welfare recipients have lives not unlike my own only without the material comfort which a regular job would provide, that many have stable ties to their community and its major social institutions. They are often regular church-goers, who maintain close relationships with their extended families. They invest heavily in the effort to attain symbols of respectability even as they confront conditions of material deprivation. Others lack such stable social ties and aspirations. They are cut off from their families or do not know the identities of parents and relatives; some are involved in serious drug use and have criminal records.

Spencer helped me see that there are, if you will, at least two ways of life concealed by the singular label—the welfare poor—and that serious antagonisms sometimes occur between people whose lives on welfare are very different. One group defines itself, in part, by differentiating itself from what Spencer referred to as the "welfare crowd." In contrast, as I later came to appreciate, many members of that so-called "crowd" take pleasure in mocking efforts by people like Spencer to maintain "respectability" in the midst of misery. These differences suggest that legal consciousness among people on welfare may be as internally divided and plural as it is different from the legal consciousness of other social groups.

The following analysis describes the way themes of power and resistance weave their way through the legal consciousness of both the respect-

---

19. de Certeau, *supra* note 3, at 36. In the pages that follow references to time and an awareness of time will play an important role as the welfare poor speak about their experiences with the welfare bureaucracy and the legal services office. *See infra* text accompanying notes 30, 42, 51 & 56. For a discussion of the meaning of time in shaping a community's relation to law see Engel, *Law, Time and Community*, 21 Law & Soc'y Rev. 605 (1987); *see also* Greenhouse, *supra* note 18 at 1632-1633.

20. *See* Popkin, Welfare: A View From the Bottom, 48-53 (1988) (unpublished Ph.D. dissertation). *See also* J. Macleod, Ain't No Makin' It: Leveled Aspirations in a Low-Income Neighborhood (1986).

able poor and the welfare crowd. In the next section I describe the research upon which this analysis is based, and I note that the people I studied seemed to experience their relationship with me as a social science investigator in a way which is not unlike the way they experience their relationship with welfare workers and lawyers. The third section describes the way those people talk about and understand law and the relationship between legal services lawyers and the welfare bureaucracy. Section Four analyzes the reasons why the welfare poor bring their problems to lawyers, while the subsequent section examines the discursive construction of those problems and the way law's meaning is created and deployed in the efforts of welfare recipients to obtain legal assistance. The conclusion highlights the dynamic of power and resistance which characterizes the legal consciousness of the welfare poor and suggests that mass legal consciousness is more fragmented and plural than is suggested in some recent accounts.

II. THE RESEARCH

This article is based upon ethnographic observation of legal services offices in two cities with substantial welfare populations. Both are middle-sized New England cities. In each I secured permission to conduct my research from the managing attorney of the legal services office. As a condition of access I assured lawyers and clients that the location and identity of those offices would not be disclosed.

In each city I studied nineteen welfare recipients. Initial contact with those recipients was made in the legal services offices. There I was able to begin to understand how the meaning of law is constructed by watching and listening as welfare recipients attempted to cope with problems involving, among other things, eligibility for welfare and/or the denial, reduction or termination of welfare benefits.[21] For purposes of this paper I have limited my attention to problems involving welfare.

All of the clients were interviewed at least once and some as many as six times. In addition, I was able to interview lawyers in twenty two of these cases. In one office I was able to observe lawyer/client conferences, and I did so in fourteen of the cases I studied in that office. I observed a total of twenty one meetings between lawyers and clients. As part of this research I also spent some time with several of the clients outside of the legal services offices—generally in their homes, and I was able to see how

---

21. Cases were selected to represent the range of issues and problems for which persons on public assistance sought legal assistance. In the thirty-eight cases studied there were twenty-two female clients and sixteen males; fifteen black clients, fourteen whites and nine Hispanics.

Of the thirty eight people in this study twenty eight had been on some form of public assistance for more than one year. Twelve reported that they had, at one time or another, been involved in a fair hearing. Twenty three had never before used a lawyer.

they spoke about their cases and their problems with family members and friends.

Interviews and participant observation are, of course, standard tools of social science, even of an interpretive, critical social science.[22] These techniques are, in one respect, intended to insure the accuracy and reliability of observations; at the same time they, as well as other social science methods, work to establish the authority of social scientists and their descriptions. This was an authority which Spencer, and others I studied, disrupted in both direct and indirect ways.

The first disruption occurred when Spencer ended his brief introduction to the complex legal world of the welfare poor with the admonition—"you can't really understand." Having agreed to play my game, to allow himself to be probed and watched and to submit to my questions and observations, he warned me that his would be an incomplete submission. At first that warning seemed to be no more than a routine conversational marker, but in subsequent conversations Spencer insistently chided me about my inability, the inability of anyone who has not "been on and off welfare forever" to comprehend the life or consciousness of the welfare poor.

The phrase "you can't really understand" was an idiom which recurred as I observed meetings between recipients and their lawyers and listened to what they would say to me about their lives or their problems. In those conversations, people on public assistance hinted that they were withholding something, that something of decisive importance was at best only partially present. They enacted a similar drama of power and resistance whether they were talking to lawyers, caseworkers or the social scientist seeking to understand them.

When the welfare poor insist that their experiences with caseworkers and welfare bureaucracies, lawyers and legal services offices, as well as their encounters with legal rules and their feeling of being "caught" inside the law, separate them from those who have never been on welfare, they claim a privileged knowledge based on a lived experience. They claim that their lived experience establishes a boundary which even the curious social science observer may be unable to cross. Spencer's talk about the difficulty of knowing law's rules was thus not just talk about his own problem; he was, in addition, describing a problem for those who try to understand his world and his way of seeing the law.

At a subsequent point in our conversations, conversations that took place over a two month period, Spencer claimed that being on welfare is "so different" that I could never come to terms with the way recipients thought about anything, and he almost dared me to acknowledge openly

---

22. *See* Trubek & Esser, *Critical Empiricism in American Legal Studies*, 14 Law & Soc. Inquiry 3 (1989); Harrington & Yngvesson, *Interpretive Sociolegal Research*, 15 Law & Soc. Inquiry, (forthcoming 1990).

this possibility.[23] He said, "You gotta think you know a lot, that you are pretty smart. You all pretend you do, but I know how much you know or don't know. Only you'll never tell that I think you can't ever understand us. You couldn't without blowing it bad."

Through this dare and the insistence that I could not understand, Spencer resisted my effort to describe his views about law, and he inverted or disrupted, at least temporarily, the conventional hierarchy in a world which respects social scientists somewhat more than welfare recipients. At the same time, such provocations served, as I think Spencer intended, to insure my continued attention; the more he resisted, the more I persisted. However, this insistence on difference and impenetrability also set my effort to understand and describe the legal consciousness of the welfare poor somewhat in opposition to his effort to control his own story. For him, I fear, no attempt to empathize or to participate in his culture can completely authorize my descriptions or fully differentiate the person who purports to describe his world from the person who would regulate it.[24]

Thus it is not surprising that Spencer remained playfully skeptical about me and my research, engaged enough to talk several times and to let me observe his conversations with his lawyer, yet dubious about what I would do with what he said or what I heard. He was, in the end, most doubtful about what my research would mean to him or other welfare recipients, about what its payoff would be. There was, however, a strange parallel between my effort to understand why he would use legal services and his effort to figure out why I would want to produce such an understanding. As I came to see, this engagement linked with skepticism, this doubt about what good it would all do, was an instruction about how the welfare poor understand their relationship with their lawyers, about why they use legal services to deal with problems with the welfare bureaucracy, and about the complex ways they both submit to and resist power.

III. LAWYERS, CASEWORKERS AND THE AUTONOMY OF THE LEGAL ORDER

"You know it's all pretty much the same. I'm just a welfare recipient whether I'm here (the legal services office) or talking to someone over in the welfare office. It's all welfare, you know, and it seems alike to me. I wish it was different but I've got to live with it this way. They're all the same. Welfare, legal services, it's all the Man." This was Spencer's somewhat indirect answer to my inquiry about whether he expected to be

---

23. The form of the introduction to this paper is, in part, what Van Maanen refers to as a "confessional tale." *See* Van Maanen, Tales of the Field: On Writing Ethnography (1986).

24. The people I studied seemed to be aware of the political dimensions of my activity, of the way we were implicated in relations of power. As Harrington and Yngvesson put it, "The politics of interpretative social research demand attention to power because interpretive work is embedded in social relations." Harrington & Yngvesson, *supra* note 22, at 32.

treated any differently by his legal services lawyer than by welfare workers. In this response he described the legal services office as virtually indistinguishable from the welfare apparatus. Just as Spencer portrayed himself as "caught" in the web of legal rules, he saw the legal services office
caught within the welfare bureaucracy.

Being situated inside that bureaucracy, legal services seems somehow
swallowed up, assimilated, presented as if it was not only inseparable
from but was identical with welfare. In this identity, Spencer's own identity is frozen. Unable to escape the welfare bureaucracy by going to legal
services, he is unable to transcend or leave behind the self constituted by
being on welfare. Whether talking to a caseworker or a lawyer he is
caught yet again, only this time he is, and can be, no more than "just a
welfare recipient."

Other recipients displayed a similar understanding about the relationship of legal services and welfare if not a similar sense of the consequences
of that relationship. Several responded to my query about their expectations concerning legal services by explaining that, as Gary, a young man
on general relief, put it, legal services lawyers and welfare bureaucrats
both "work for the same people. You see it says US Government on their
checks so they can't really pull in opposite directions."[25] Another man
explained that as far as he could tell, "they are both part of government."
For him, lawyers and caseworkers were both there to keep "things from
getting out of hand."[26] Still another man said

> You get what you pay for and . . . [it's] not any different here. . . .
> He's not really my lawyer. You know they have to do this to get
> paid, just like my caseworker, but I can't tell him do this or do that
> or . . . I'm not paying. [Laughs]. That's what it's all about. Being
> on welfare is just like being a child. Have to ask for everything, get
> permission before you can shit. No difference. Doesn't matter
> whether they call it welfare or legal services. It's the same shit.

Ellis, who went to legal services seeking help in dealing with a denial of
general relief, talked about the relationship between law and welfare in
similar terms.

> Welfare didn't just come from nowhere. Somebody had to make it
> up. That's why they got lawyers, you see, to make up rules and stuff

---

25. White, *supra* note 4, at 104.
26. When asked what "things" he was talking about he said,
   Look, it's an old story. We [welfare recipients] are the problem for them. Without us, neither
   of them would have jobs, but they seem to think that we're just problems, problems, problems.
   Nobody likes to be on welfare and nobody likes having to help people on welfare.
As a result, he, like other welfare recipients, worried about disloyalty, about the possibility that lawyer's law might ultimately be turned against him, that his legal services lawyer might ultimately side
with the welfare bureaucracy.

for them. . . . So without welfare those lawyers would have nothing, they'd have no jobs. But the way it works now with legal services, legal services is kind of like an Internal Revenue . . . no that's
the wrong word. What is the word for the police force having their
own inner group, you know, to make sure that cops aren't up to
anything, like don't go too crazy with their guns. Law is like that.
They put these legal services guys there to keep an eye on the welfare people because welfare would fall apart without them. Be a real
big mess. See what I'm saying. They work together . . . not fighting, as if they're opposed. I can even tell from, you know, the way
they are friendly.

For Ellis, welfare is a domain both legally constituted and constitutive
of the legal domain. Legal services lawyers are thus an important part of
an ongoing state activity. In such an activity lawyer's law operates
through regulation and internal surveillance rather than prohibition and
punishment, and legal services lawyers are part of the apparatus that disciplines both the welfare population and others (social workers) who are
in the business of carrying out disciplinary activities.

Here Ellis seems to add some refinement to Spencer's view that it's "all
welfare." Lawyers are inside welfare just as the welfare poor are inside
the law; however, while the latter are denied an identity as anything other
than a "welfare recipient," legal services lawyers are not just another in a
faceless string of welfare bureaucrats. They are inside, in Ellis's view, in a
special and important way.

Such a view helps explain why welfare recipients see the law of the
legal services office as both weak and powerful in relation to the welfare
bureaucracy. It is weak because, in Ellis's words, it "can't rock the boat
without drowning itself;" as he saw it, the interests of legal services lawyers and caseworkers are so closely linked that there are real limits on
what the former are willing or able to do in challenging and criticizing
decisions of the latter. Yet, at the same time, the indispensability of legal
services for the poor to welfare's bureaucratic operation gives lawyer's law
considerable potential leverage.[27]

While legal services lawyers sometimes claim that they are powerless to
help their welfare clients and that there is nothing they can do, at other
times they go to great lengths to help their clients. Sometimes help is
withheld while at other times it is provided. Lawyers can help if they
want to or deny help by proclaiming their own impotence. As a result
they seem to have uncontrollable, if not irresistible, power.

---

27. The view that law is inscribed within the social activities that it is assumed to regulate was
most often articulated when welfare recipients talked about their own problems with welfare. There
were, however, several people who spoke in similar terms about the relationship of prosecutors and
the police and housing court and landlords.

> I'm nobody for her [the lawyer]. . . . She don't work for me and I
> just want her to do like a favor, you know, to make some calls for
> me, but she don't have to and no way I could make her. . . . I'm
> still waiting for her to tell me about what she's going to do. She
> could say like I can't help and that's that. Maybe she's going to
> figure out that I'm nobody and why make waves just for me.

Here, the all too frequent proclamation by legal services lawyers that
there is "nothing I can do" is understood to be an act of power rather
than a confession of authentic weakness, a refusal to help borne of desire
not necessity.

Decisions about whether to help, according to welfare recipients, are
made on the basis of an assessment of their character, whether they are a
"nobody," rather than the merits of their claims or the extent of their
needs. Thus people like Spencer, for whom maintaining an image of "respectability" was an important general concern, frequently criticized welfare and welfare recipients to their lawyers and to me. As one young woman put it, "being on welfare stinks and welfare makes you stink." A
middle aged man receiving food stamps said, as if talking about a class to
which he did not belong, "They [people on public assistance] better clean
up, you see, get straight."[28]

Such criticism puts distance between the individual welfare recipient
seeking legal assistance and the class of recipients as a whole. It gives
voice to the shame and stigma associated with receiving welfare and, in so
doing, ratifies and reinforces the images that produce such shame and
stigma.[29] Going to legal services the welfare poor feel no more in control
of their own destiny than they felt in dealing with the welfare bureaucracy,[30] and their response, their effort to find some way of proving themselves worthy of the help that lawyers can either give or withhold, is a
form of self-injury.

If they could enlist their lawyer's help, the welfare poor imagine that
one phone call, one letter, even one word from their lawyer could make
everything right. Yet, they worry that nothing *will* be done because they
are "nobody" or, as Ellis suggested, the friendship between lawyers and
welfare workers displaces opposition or that nothing *can* be done because,

---

28. Briar, *supra* note 5, at 377, notes that welfare recipients tend to refer to other welfare recipients as "they" not "we." He argues that this self-conscious "estrangement . . . reflects the desire of
. . . recipients to disassociate themselves from the image they have of other recipients . . . [and to
express] opinions about other welfare recipients which usually have been associated primarily with
conservative, anti-welfare groups."

29. As Wolin argues, in the modern welfare state, "Welfare recipients signify a distinct category,
the virtueless citizen. The virtueless citizen has no a priori claim not to be shaped in accordance with
the rational requirements of state policy." Wolin, *supra* note 7, at 162.

30. For these welfare clients, law was just another infantilizing experience. Bane and Dowling
speculate that such infantilization may frustrate the welfare system's alleged goal of encouraging recipients to "become self-supporting." Bane & Dowling, *supra* note 2, at 20. *See also* White, *supra*
note 4.

as Nancy, a long-time recipient of AFDC, said, "the welfare holds all the cards." Even if lawyers take up the grievances that are brought to them, some recipients fear that they will, in the end, reach an impasse in dealing with the welfare bureaucracy. Thus images of power and powerlessness, awesome force and impotence exist side by side.

This is the case with Al, a fifty-eight-year-old recipient of general assistance who lost his benefits when he took a temporary job washing dishes in a local diner. Al went to legal services to find out if there was any way to keep that job and still retain his benefits. But as he told me,

> Listen, there's not much they [legal services lawyers] can do, because why should any caseworker listen. They don't get paid to listen to nobody says.

> QUESTION: Then why did you come to legal services?

> What could I do, just lose everything? They can just tell them what to give me. . . . That is what lawyers do and why they are so good. They'll just tell them and there won't be no trouble.[31]

The linkage of power and powerlessness is also heard in the words of Damian:

> They [lawyers] can do anything they want, just say the word and I'll be back on emergency assistance tomorrow. It's great. . . . Final is what they say, but it's no use because those welfare folks don't care about nobody, not me, not him [the lawyer]. I've seen people scream and cry, but they don't budge, so what can he [the lawyer] do. He ain't going to shoot them, you know, I mean, take a gun and go make them do it.

Al and Damien see their lawyers as both impotent in the face of an unmovable welfare bureaucracy and able, with but a single word, to end their troubles.[32] It is almost as if they exaggerated the imagined power of lawyers to convey to me their own sense of the incredible impenetrability of the welfare system. Yet by conjuring up that image they may also be trying, if inconsistently, to gather the courage to enter a battle they seem unlikely to win. Theirs is an interesting combination of veneration and cynicism. What they venerate, what is "good" or "great," is a law whose power they hope to enlist, while the law about which they express grave

---

31. There is here an odd and interesting juxtaposition of speaking and listening. In one voice Al suggests that lawyers simply "tell" caseworkers what to do; Al speaks about the efficacy of the telling that lawyers do. In another voice he commands me to listen while he tells me that caseworkers don't "listen to nobody."

32. This simultaneous under- and over-estimation of law is a repeated theme among the welfare recipients I studied just as it was among the victims of discrimination studied by K. Bumiller, The Civil Rights Society (1988).

doubts is an apparently frustrated legality swimming upstream against bureaucratic resistance and inertia.

A common perception of virtually everyone I interviewed was that the relationship of legal services and the welfare bureaucracy typifies a legal system whose various elements are tightly interconnected rather than autonomous and separate and where political influence is pervasive. Few of the recipients think that the decisions made by lawyers, welfare bureaucrats or other legal officials are neutral, disinterested, impartial or rule governed.[33] Law is talked about as a thoroughly politicized patronage system which attends to who you are and whom you know; it is a system of contacts and credibility[34] which, at its best, makes "arrangements" to deal with problems.[35] In the welfare context, a good lawyer is able, as Spencer said, to "work something out;" a bad lawyer "can't get it done," "can't do no deal." In this "world of deals,"[36] "everything depends," as he told me, "on who you know in the system. You know, it really does seem to me, I really think it's who you know. How much you want to dish out to get back."

Whether talking specifically about welfare or about other aspects of law, many recipients see no difference between law and politics. "It's all political" was a recurring theme in conversations about the behavior of legal services lawyers, welfare officials, prosecutors and judges. Casey, a thirty-eight-year-old woman, put it this way,

> All lawyers, even the lawyers here have to play politics. You can't get it, but they have to cozy up to my caseworker, you know, convince her that I'm not so bad. Same when my son went to court. It's a political game, that's all it is cause you have a judge and you get whatever you get, understand? The right lawyer, you see the right judge, you get the best sentence of all. Happens everyday. It's a whole political game. . . . I've seen trials that wait 'til certain

---

33. Elaine, a mother of seven receiving AFDC, is one of the few who think this way. As she put it, "Here [the legal services office] it don't matter who you are or what you done. Everybody's alike." While the welfare bureaucracy seems to her to make judgments about people on the basis of who they are and what they do, law as it appears in the legal services office seems evenhanded. In addition, as she saw it, "The law is the law. It should go by the books." While welfare officials ignore rules, the law that she desires would be a coherent, determinate rule system, a system in which rules produce results. Unlike Spencer who experiences rules as a confining trap, or those who see rules being used as weapons against them, Elaine seeks a formalist's paradise.

34. A similar view seems to be held by some segments of the practicing bar. *See* Sarat & Felstiner, *Lawyers and Legal Consciousness: Law Talk in the Divorce Lawyer's Office*, 98 Yale L.J. 1663 (1989). Similar cynicism is noted in Bumiller's research, *supra* note 32. Tyler demonstrates the importance of such understandings of law for theories of procedural justice. *See* T. Tyler, Why People Obey the Law (1990); Tyler, *What Is Procedural Justice?* 22 Law & Soc'y Rev. 103 (1988).

35. This view is especially prevalent among those who had previous experience with lawyers. As one man put it, "Lawyers are pretty much the same. Here [the legal services office] they'll plea bargain just like my lawyer did when I was charged with burglary. Doesn't matter much whether you are innocent, it's the deal that counts."

36. Galanter, *Worlds of Deals*, 34 J. Legal Educ. 268 (1984).

judges are on the bench. Sure, lawyers are lawyers, judges are judges, that's all it is. They always just owe each other favors.

For Casey, the majesty of law is demystified; its power is located in human relations and transactions, in the pettiness of favor-doing and favor-getting. Moreover, it is not like one could get beyond the cozying up and playing politics by appealing over the head of the bureaucratic apparatus to a judicial system attentive to principles not personalities, to precedent not politics. For Casey and others with whom I spoke not only is there no escape from law, there is no escape for law. Lawyers and judges are themselves trapped within "the whole political game."

This favor-doing and favor-getting is just a polite and metaphorical description of corruption. Law is corrupted by politics, and politics itself is nothing but corruption. For Casey the corruption of politics is not simply a matter of bad people doing bad things; it is the essence of the political game. For her, acting politically, organizing and seeking to achieve significant political change is not a normatively viable alternative to law, a way of correcting its problems or seizing control of its instrumentalities. As Frankie, an elderly man with whom I had only one conversation, told me,

> Law is too much political for me. For lack of a better word I'd call it all politics. It's always that way, always going to be that way. . . . Politics as I see it, it's all greed and power. . . . Those simple words greed and power corrupt you by money and by pure 'I'm God and you're nothing' attitude.

However, for Frankie and several of the others in my study, the greatest corruption of the welfare bureaucracy, legal services offices or the law in general is that they are not immune to discrimination. Many welfare recipients believe that race and ethnicity are noticed by legal officials and lawyers (including legal services lawyers) and that money counts, that the "rich" are treated differently than the poor. Frankie put this point quite vividly:

> If you want to know the truth, I think that social workers, lawyers, judges hate Puerto Ricans. There's a lot of us now and that makes all them nervous because welfare's fine for white folks, but giving it to PRs is for them like giving it to animals. What I seen when I was arrested was different cause I'm from Puerto Rico. I was treated different. Same thing here [the legal services office]. I have to get here early and wait longer and I get the young guy who don't know shit. Who can't see it? You just can't.[37]

---

37. Like Spencer, Frankie claims the authority of experience. The only people who cannot see the discrimination to which he is subject is someone like me who is neither Puerto Rican nor a welfare

Others made the same point in different ways:

> If a poor person, okay, murders somebody, they're going to throw
> the book at them. But if some rich guy does something like that,
> they're going to get off. They might not get any time or they might
> get easier time than somebody like me that doesn't have anything.
> You can't really know what I'm saying. You know, it's basically
> money. They sure go harder on somebody's poor than somebody who
> has money. Like when you got nothing, what can you offer? I'm not
> calling it a bribe, but there's some fancy word for it, a person who
> doesn't have anything can't offer anything. They got nothing to de-
> fend themselves with so they've got to come, like me, to legal
> services.

* * *

> Law is for people with money so if I had some cash to pay a lawyer
> it'd be better. If you don't have the money, forget it, you're not going
> to get service. That's how it is, you know, you might not get the help
> you need. But rich people they don't have to worry none about that.
> They walk into the room and everybody stands up.

* * *

> The fact is if you're poor or a minority you don't get as good treat-
> ment from lawyers or anybody. These legal services people they hold
> their noses and just do what they have to do.

Merry notes that working class Americans see law as both inequitable
and, at the same time, somewhat less inequitable than the rest of society.[38]
In her view, law "benefits" from comparisons with other social institutions and practices. Working class court users accept the inequity they
experience because they do not expect anything better. Among welfare
recipients there is a similar tendency to think about law's discrimination
in light of discrimination experienced elsewhere. At worst law is, as
Frankie noted, "just like the rest, no better, no worse;" at best law's attentiveness to race, ethnicity, or wealth "doesn't get in the way."

Thus most of the welfare recipients I studied are more resigned than
angry about law's inequities, inequities which in their view are built into
the very fabric of law's rules and practices. Yet being resigned to the inequity of law does not mean being resigned in the face of particular deci-

---

recipient.
   38.   Merry, *supra* note 11, at 65.

sions, of decisions that hurt not because they impose disabilities in a biased or discriminatory way but because of the pain they inflict or the interests they threaten. The welfare poor worry about having enough to get by on more than about whether they are getting as much as anyone else. As a result, they are able to seek legal assistance and use law, both of which are tainted with and corrupted by political favoritism and discriminatory treatment, without particularly liking the law that they are using. They accept without condoning the unfairness of the system in which they find themselves, and seek ways of working within and around that unfairness.

In all of this—in their understanding of the relationship between legal services and welfare, their notions of the political character of the legal domain, their sense of pervasive inequity and unfairness, their complex understandings of law's blurred boundaries and of the way that blurring of boundaries constructs particular identities and precludes the construction of others—the welfare poor exemplify what Duncan Kennedy meant when he conceded, "We don't need Critical legal theory to be effective practitioners of the de-reification of institutions."[39] The welfare poor are not paralyzed by their understandings or their insight into the highly politicized nature of the legal system. The law as the welfare poor experience and understand it is grounded in the realities of a society in which race, wealth, and power matter, and law is neither more nor less useful because it does not transcend or transform the world as they know it.

IV. THE SEARCH FOR LEGAL ASSISTANCE

When I asked Spencer why, if he could see no real difference between legal services and the welfare office and if he thought that he would "just be a welfare recipient" in the eyes of his lawyer, he had come to talk to a lawyer, he smiled and shook his head as if amazed by the question and confirmed in his sense that I could never understand. However, after a brief pause the smile disappeared and he said, "I'm here cause I can't figure out what's going on . . . you know, how come they stopped my check. . . . I won't let them make me starve and cause all that stuff about, you know, some rule."

Spencer arrived at the legal services office uncertain but defiant. He had tried to find out what was going on by talking with people at the welfare office, but his efforts evaporated in a bureaucratic maze in which no one seemed to know what had happened or to be able to explain to him why his check had stopped. Without the money provided by general relief he could not imagine how he was going to live. Thus he came to legal services to fight what he saw being done to him by "them," and he inter-

---

39. Kennedy & Gabel, *Roll Over Beethoven*, 36 Stan. L. Rev. 1, 31 (1984).

preted the transaction which led to the termination of his welfare benefits as a personal attack. Interpreting his problem this way he denied the bureaucratic legitimacy which accompanies claims that decisions are impersonal and resisted efforts to clothe power in the rhetoric of rules. This tendency to see problems with welfare as personal attacks is quite consistent with views of law as driven by assessments of character or by who, not what, you know. "I won't let them . . ."; here personal power must be deployed against personal power. Given the prospect of starvation, real or imagined, there was no other choice.

Like Spencer, others who seek the help of a legal services lawyer do not see themselves as having a real choice.[40] Chris, an older woman who playfully refused to tell me her age, explained that she had come to legal services when her AFDC benefits were reduced to compensate for a previous overpayment. She said that because of the reduction she was behind in her rent and afraid of being evicted.

> What else could I do when they [welfare workers] won't listen to me. All they do is make me wait so it's getting to be that I'm not going to have a place to live cause my landlord ain't going to let me be there as charity or free. Couldn't think of anything else. These are the only people to go to.

Or as a woman I call Barbara said,

> I tried to get them [the welfare department] to let me know, but no way. You wouldn't think it mattered about getting less money and maybe it doesn't matter to them, but it does if you want to feed your kids. I don't like coming here [to legal services] no more than I like going there [to the welfare office]. No fun sitting, waiting, telling things to another stranger, but I'm at my end.[41]

For Chris and Barbara the search for legal assistance is part of a recurring drama in which they wait to speak only to be unheard, then find another place to wait and engage in yet another ritualistic telling. Waiting is, for them, the experience of being "spatialized," of having someone else's place triumph over their time.[42] Waiting is the physical embodiment of their own weakness. Their experience with the welfare system is, more-

---

40. This is not to suggest that everyone who experiences problems with welfare seeks legal assistance. That surely is not the case. However, those who do seek help describe themselves as lacking any reasonable alternative. In another part of my research I am studying the legal ideology of welfare recipients who do not use legal services when they encounter problems with the welfare system.

41. "No fun . . . telling things to another stranger;" no more fun talking to me than to the lawyer or the caseworker. I wondered then and I wonder now why she talked to me when I could do nothing to help her "feed her kids." The best I could imagine was that I was a stranger who, if nothing else, seemed interested and willing to listen.

42. de Certeau suggests that the powerful "privilege spatial relationships . . . [and] reduce temporal relations to spatial ones. . . ." de Certeau, *supra* note 3, at 38.

over, often one of speaking into a void, of speech without response. What they have to say seems to be ignored or is, at best, impatiently tolerated by caseworkers and other officials.[43] As a result, they went to legal services without great confidence that their voices would register in that setting or that their speech would matter and doubtful about the efficacy of yet another telling to yet another official "stranger."[44] They went because they have exhausted other possibilities and were at the "end." They went even though they were uncertain that legal services lawyers could, or would even if they could, provide help, and even though they were afraid that their trip to the legal services office would ratify the inescapability or legitimize the unresponsiveness of the welfare bureaucracy.

As Marion, who sought legal assistance when welfare told her that there was nothing they could do to help her with a serious debt problem, explained,

> I didn't want to come here, but they [the collection agency] said that I had to come cause unless my check started coming again and I made some payments they were going to take me to court. I got letters and they call me and call me. All this makes me sick, but I didn't know what to do. I was afraid of lawyers, still afraid, and I say maybe he'll agree with the welfare. He'll tell them that it's okay not to send me the check. He'll call the collection agency and tell them I'm no good for it. He could end up against me cause I don't count.

Because the welfare poor understand that they cannot fully escape law's enclosure and that they are all, like Spencer, "caught" in what Dumm calls "the space of law,"[45] and because they are quite conscious of their continuing dependence on welfare, many are also concerned about what will happen if they prevail in their present claims.[46] In such a situation they expect to be labelled "troublemakers" or "bad actors" by welfare officials who, in the future, might use some minor violation of an unknown rule as an excuse to get revenge. At some point those who move within the law from bureaucratic denial to adversarial response will return to the scene of that denial; there they again will be unprotected, and

---

43. In this limited sense, the welfare poor are by no means incited or encouraged to speak. *Contra* 1 M. Foucault, The History of Sexuality (trans. R. Hurley 1980).

44. Many of the people I studied used legal services even though they did not have faith that their voices would matter and even though they did not believe that the legal services lawyer would be able to intervene successfully and straighten out the mess. Briar, *supra* note 5, at 380.

While most of those people were experienced in law's routine bureaucratic encounters and, as a result, familiar with the ambience of law, many had never been to a lawyer before. Inexperienced clients had no idea what a lawyer could do for them or whether a lawyer would do anything.

45. *See* Dumm, *Fear of Law*, 10 Stud. in L. Pol. & Soc'y (forthcoming 1990). *See also* de Certeau, *supra* note 3.

46. *See* White, *supra* note 4, at 76. This concern was widespread among both the "respectable" poor and the "welfare crowd."

will be even more vulnerable, less able to count on the assistance of lawyer's law.[47]

The movement from the welfare office to the legal services office is then for many of the people with whom I spoke an experience of fear, fear that lawyers will not help or that help will provoke vindictiveness or that they will end up further entrapped by rules should their lawyer discover that they have violated some rule about which neither they nor their caseworker know. As a young woman named Marlene said to me before she saw a lawyer about a reduction in her AFDC benefits,

> I don't know, the way the system is now, I think anybody can do practically anything now and be able to get away with it if they look hard enough in the law books. You can't understand this, but you never really know when you've broken some rule. It would be a real bitch if I found out here [the legal service office] that I've violated something on the books.

Or as Eddie, a twenty-one-year-old, told me before he talked to a lawyer about his inability to obtain general relief,

> It's always been, you know, one thing or another, you know, I mean it's got to be one set of rules and regulations. Lawyers are bad with that stuff so be careful. There is always some rule or if that one doesn't give you enough shit then they find another one. They've got rules for every possible thing, but I don't think them rules tell them what to do, I think they tell the rules what to do.[48]

Here again the welfare poor do not distinguish lawyers from caseworkers. They seek legal assistance uncertain about whether the lawyers with whom they speak will take it upon themselves to enforce welfare's complex body of rules and regulations.[49] As welfare recipients seek legal assistance, as they move from the welfare office to the legal services office, they experience a "moment of vertigo that accompanies the movement from a place of protection (or at least of familiarity) to a place of exposure, (and they experience) the vertigo of uncertainty, not knowing

---

47. Some recipients believe a "law of diminishing returns" governs the use of lawyers to deal with the welfare bureaucracy. They believe that the first time a lawyer intervenes caseworkers are more likely to be responsive than they are in subsequent interventions.

48. This last comment is clearly not consistent with law's allegedly hegemonic, formalist mythology. Instead it seems characteristic of the impulses of a legal realism which sees rules as instruments used by officials to accomplish their own purposes, *see* Cohen, *Transcendental Nonsense and the Functional Approach*, 34 Colum. L. Rev. 809 (1935); *see also* Llewellyn, *Some Realism About Realism*, 44 Harv. L. Rev. 1222 (1931), or of an imperial law whose empire is manipulated by powerful mandarins. The way in which lawyers and administrators use the network of rules to maximize their discretion is discussed in Silbey & Bitner, *The Availability of Law*. 4 Law & Pol'y Q. 399 (1982).

49. *See* Blumberg, *The Practice of Law as a Confidence Game*, 1 Law & Soc'y Rev. 15 (1967).

and admitting that one does not know, what threats to well-being lay in wait."[50]

This feeling and this way of thinking about the power and meaning of lawyer's law was, however, by no means uniform. Other recipients, especially those with longstanding, stable ties to the community (the "respectable" poor) saw their legal services lawyer as a tool in an ongoing struggle or, perhaps more accurately as a way of sending a message and asserting a self. Getting a lawyer is as important for the message it sends as for the results it produces. The message sent is a demand for respect, respect regularly denied in encounters with the welfare bureaucracy, a demand which cannot be fully captured by any claim to material benefits.[51] Getting a lawyer makes it possible for some welfare recipients to live honorably with their continuing dependency. While the search for legal assistance may be a futile act insofar as it is understood in purely instrumental terms, it is a gesture that gives these welfare recipients a name, an identity, a way of being heard; it ends the frustrating experience of speaking into a void and of going unnoticed that Chris and Barbara described. It forces recognition through an act of defiance.

Another woman, Bernice, exemplified this view when she said,

> Look, nobody pays attention. I could have spent the rest of my life sitting there waiting for them to pay attention and it wouldn't happen, no way. They got so much going down that I'm just one more person trying to get emergency relief. They don't pay no mind, but when they call, I mean when the lawyer calls, then I'm somebody, something. . . . I'm doing what I'm not supposed to, you see, being good means taking what they say you should get and not asking no questions. Well, I ask questions. I came here [to legal services] to get them to pay attention because they don't want to pay attention. Who knows? Maybe they'll get mad. Probably won't do no good, but why should I just put up with their stuff?

Unlike Kafka's man from the country, Bernice was not content to spend her life waiting to be admitted, to be allowed in. Here the search for legal assistance breaks the spell simply by ending the inertia induced by being on welfare. The search for legal assistance is, on this account, a way of individualizing and humanizing the welfare bureaucracy.

Bernice's explanation of why she went to legal services again portrays lawyers as wielding enormous power, as though a simple act could break through bureaucratic indifference and give someone an identity. Bernice's

---

50. Dumm, *supra* note 45, at 36.

51. Here one can see some limit to the use of the language of need in framing and interpreting problems with the welfare bureaucracy. *See infra* text accompanying note 58. Or perhaps what one sees is a contradiction between that language, with its immediacy and its attention to the material dimensions of welfare problems, and this more expressive, symbolic understanding of the meaning of legal assistance.

search for legal assistance was, however, not so much a search for an identity or an effort to become a "somebody" as it was an expression of her already constituted identity as someone who self-consciously defies the normative expectations of the welfare bureaucracy. Where "questions" are not supposed to be asked, she asks questions.[52]

For her, being on welfare should not require becoming part of the faceless welfare clientele, and should not mean that one is treated, as she put it in another conversation, like "dirt." She was deeply troubled by dissonance between other aspects of her life, especially her role as a lay preacher in her church, and the way she was treated in the welfare office. Getting a lawyer was a way of responding to that treatment and was, at the same time, a strategy of self-assertion, a way of not being "just one more person trying to get emergency relief." For her, getting a lawyer was a way of getting attention and respect and making welfare officials, who seem otherwise unreachable, "mad."[53] It gave her a voice, broke a silence, insured that her complaint would not be ignored even if, in the end, it "won't do no good." For this woman, getting a lawyer was a step across an imagined boundary and a way of showing herself as someone to be reckoned with.[54]

Yet, in the end, the thing that stood out most in Bernice's account of her experience with legal services was her lawyer's failure to remember Bernice's name and her need to look at the file to remember what the case was about in the second of their two brief meetings. As Bernice put it, "She [referring to her lawyer] would probably make a really good caseworker." It is, of course, ironic that the experience with legal services in some ways replicated the experience of impersonality and facelessness that she was trying to overcome by getting a lawyer.

As Bernice described her experience with legal services, it was, in the end, another "insult" to her dignity, another affront in her continuing search for respect. Since she had had previous dealings with legal services lawyers in a dispute with a landlord she was not surprised by this experience, nor did it diminish her sense that merely by seeking legal help she would be noticed in the welfare bureaucracy. Putting up with the indignities of the legal services office allowed her to juxtapose one bureaucracy against another and, in so doing, to get just a little space in which a self could claim recognition.

In contrast to Bernice's use of legal services as an act of defiance necessary to maintain self respect, for Karla, who had been on AFDC for seven

---

52. Merry notes how working class court users employ similar tactics. Getting Justice and Getting Even: Legal Consciousness Among Working Class Americans (forthcoming 1990).

53. Sennett warns that resistance itself may strengthen authority through what he calls the "bonds of rejection." See chapter 1 of Authority (1980).

54. Leff, *Ignorance, Injury and Spite*, 80 Yale L.J. 1 (1970), notes that many people use the law for just such purposes.

months when she received notice that her benefits were being reduced, seeing a lawyer was simply the "approved" thing to do.[55] In fact she went to legal services on the advice of her caseworker: "She told me I could get a fair hearing. I could have them review it, but that maybe it would do me some good to talk to a lawyer about whether that would be a good move. So here I am." Taking this advice was, in her view, exactly what the "good" welfare recipient does. As Karla put it, "I guess it is better to come here than just to bitch and complain about not knowing what is going on."

Echoing this theme, Bob, a forty-year-old man said,

> Come sit in the waiting room [of the welfare office], and you hear all kinds of shit. Certain people get real angry and mad. Then before you know it they're doing some number on their worker, taking it out, being just dumb fuckers. Not me. That's not my way. It's better to come here [to legal services] rather than just getting all frustrated. No hassle for me and this way I don't hassle nobody.

For Karla and Bob, the movement from the caseworker to the lawyer is a journey from one part of the welfare bureaucracy to another, just "another office down the hall" as Bob put it, just another bureaucrat to talk to, just another set of forms to fill out. Resort to the legal services office is a logical next step within the welfare bureaucracy, a step which "respectable" people willingly take rather than being disruptive and making trouble.[56]

V. The Legal Construction of Social Problems: Needs Versus Rules

When welfare recipients take that step what kind of a vocabulary do they use to make sense of, and talk about, the problems they bring to legal services offices? How are legal ideas and concepts used? Do recipients think about welfare as property or as a legally guaranteed entitlement?[57]

---

55. *But see* White, *supra* note 4 (noting that welfare recipients are sometimes explicitly discouraged by their caseworkers from seeking legal services).

56. For still others, the lawyer's office can be both a place of defiance and a place of safety. Why come here? Why? Cause there was nothing else. I'm just moving along in line like I'm supposed to. Anybody's ever been on welfare tell you that, you know, there's always more, someone to talk to. . . . These guys supposed to keep the other guys in line so they don't get away with nothing. They help me, but you know, I don't think they should let me just lose my electric and make me do a repayment so big that I can't get by. See coming here to these guys means I don't buy it and I'm telling them.

This view alleviates fear at the same time it gives the act of going to law its meaning. Because law is for some recipients inscribed in an ambivalent relation to welfare, they can both do what they are "supposed to" and refuse to acquiesce. This image of law makes the journey to the legal services office seem ordinary, expected, appropriate for someone on welfare and, at the same time, it provides a way of standing up to those upon whom one is ultimately dependent.

57. The legal status of welfare has been, during the last two decades, a subject of intense scrutiny. Since Reich's now classic description of the "new property," a variety of substantive and procedural

What kinds of arguments do they deploy in trying to make persuasive appeals to their lawyers?

Maria, a thirty-three-year-old mother of seven, lives with her children in a three bedroom apartment. She describes herself as a regular church-goer and is, by her own account, a "responsible" person and "strict" parent whose children have never "been in trouble." For her, being on welfare is a "shame," but something she "had to do," and she insists that when her children grow up they will never have to take public assistance. They will do something better with their lives than she has done with hers. Maria, like Spencer and others aspiring to "respectability," is openly contemptuous of "the welfare crowd," people who think that they have a "God-given right to live off other people" and who have no other goals or ambitions than to keep getting public assistance. Such people are, in her view, "troublemakers and welfare cheats."

Yet Maria herself is frequently in trouble with her landlord and with the utility company. While she is careful with her money, she cannot figure out a way to "pay everything at once." It is difficult for her to stretch her welfare payment to cover all her expenses, and, as a result, she is often late with her rent or unable to pay her utility bills. Several times she has asked for an increase in her welfare payments, but each time she has been turned down. As she put it, "I never complain. I just tell them how hard it is and hope they give me more help."

However, the first and only time she came to legal services Maria was not seeking an increase in benefits. Early in the winter of 1988, again finding herself short of funds and unable to pay her utility bills, Maria sought help from a private heating assistance program run by the New England Farm Workers Union. Things proceeded smoothly until she was asked to get a letter from her caseworker certifying her continuing eligibility for public assistance and noting the amount of her welfare benefits. She sought legal help when her caseworker refused to write such a letter.

While she had had what she described to her lawyer as the "usual" difficulties with the welfare system, things had never before ". . . come apart, you know, not gotten straight quick." This time she had "lost [her] innocence." She told him that

> I wanted to get some help from New England Farm Workers, you know, to pay heat, for my gas. So the lady there wanted some proof about how much I get from the state. See I get help for my kids . . .

---

rights have been extended to welfare recipients. *See* Reich, *The New Property*, 73 Yale L.J. 733 (1964); Michelman, *Welfare Rights in a Constitutional Democracy*, 1979 Wash. U.L.Q. 659 (1979). The impact of that extension is discussed by Simon, *supra* note 2; Simon, *Legality, Bureaucracy and Class in the Welfare System*, 92 Yale L.J. 1198 (1983); Rosenblatt, *Legal Entitlements and Welfare Benefits*, in The Politics of Law (D. Kairys ed. 1982); Krislov, *The OEO Lawyers Fail to Constitutionalize a Right to Welfare*, 58 Minn. L. Rev. 211 (1973); Epstein, *The Uncertain Quest for Welfare Rights*, 1985 B.Y.U. L. Rev. 201 (1985).

and this lady wanted to know why welfare wasn't giving me the difference, you know to pay my heat. So I called to ask my caseworker if she'd give me some paper to explain, and she refused to give me information about my own self. She said that people from New England Farm Workers, some rule said they were supposed to ask her, not me. But she never sent the information. I think she'd made some mistake, you know, covering up, when I'd run out of protective payments last year. . . . I wanted to kill her. What's she doing? She's trying to kill me and my kids. I'm trying to keep it all together, and it's just what I need. That they know. . . . How can anyone live with small kids without heat? You don't do that to no-body, treat them like a dog, don't do nothing but let them freeze.

Here Maria initially described her problem as a simple request for "information about my own self," talked, at least in the beginning, as if the information being withheld were her property, and openly expressed resentment at being denied something she felt belonged to her. However, the more Maria talked about her problem, the more her initial sense of entitlement was overwhelmed by the immediacy of her "need," and the emphasis on the invasion of her ownership interest gave way to a concern for getting help to pay her utility bill.

Indeed, almost immediately after insisting that the information being withheld was "mine," Maria told her lawyer, "Look, I don't really care about that [whether the caseworker provides the information]. What I gotta have is something to pay my gas. I don't got nothing now so I don't care how, just tell the Farm Workers it's okay." For her, rights talk was less important than obtaining a particular result. She shifted the ground of her appeal to law, moved away from the problem of the caseworker and sought direct action by the lawyer who, in her mind, became a substitute social worker. The lawyer could provide the authority and authoritative help she needed to satisfy the Farm Workers. It made no difference to her who gave them the information they needed just so long as someone would tell them "it's okay."

Maria saw her problem as a bureaucratic foul-up, and, like Spencer, a personal attack clothed in the distant, impersonal, abstract language of rules;[58] she sought legal help as a tool of self-defense and a displacement of her own violent revenge fantasy. While she lived in a world of pressing material need and saw herself, in contrast to welfare cheaters, as asking for "just what I need," her caseworker seemed at best to care about rules and compliance with rules and at worst to be engaged in bureaucratic cover-up. In Maria's view, neither welfare officials nor lawyers should be interested primarily in figuring out whether some rule has or has not been violated; she is impatient with law's technicalities because those technicali-

---

58. Popkin, *supra* note 20, at 104, reports that, unlike Maria, most of the welfare recipients in her sample believe that their caseworkers treat them fairly.

368   Yale Journal of Law & the Humanities   [Vol. 2: 343

ties are all too often used to frustrate her efforts to get help in dealing with pressing problems. Maria knew and understood how her alleged failure to comply with "some rule" was being used, how her caseworker was able to manipulate rule-based arguments to protect bureaucratic, or perhaps even narrowly personal, interests, and to do violence to herself and her children.

As Maria later said to her lawyer, "What's all this stuff about a rule? What rule? Why do they always care about what rule you haven't followed?" What Maria wanted was for her lawyer to break through and ignore her caseworker's invocation of rules and to do exactly what the caseworker refused to do, namely act in response to her immediate life situation. She wanted him to end the violence which was hidden in the abstract talk of rules. Hers was a consciousness of equity working out its continuing battle with a conception of law as rule and rule following; hers was an argument about need seeking to break through bureaucratic rigidity.

By emphasizing human need over rules, Maria identified a recurring tension in the welfare system, a tension between the supposedly humane, moral sensibilities of enlightened professionals and the constraining narrowness of a formally rational organization. Though she was, at least in her own eyes, no troublemaker, she refused to give in and go along when the welfare bureaucracy, supposedly established to help poor people,[59] prevented her from doing what she believed was necessary to protect and provide for her children.[60] She searched for ways, within the existing welfare system, to resist what seemed an unjustifiable decision, and found a language for expressing her resistance within the complex and contradictory character of welfare itself.[61]

Unlike many other welfare recipients, Maria spoke about welfare in very idealistic terms, as a system of "doing for those who can't do for themselves," a system "to make people's lives for the better." In using those terms, she tried to find a way of bridging the gap between her own understanding of law and that of her caseworker; she asserted the superiority of the humane and moral over the bureaucratic and rule-bound. Her idealism was, in this sense, strategic rather than naive; it allowed her to mobilize the rhetoric of welfare itself to deal with that system's apparent failure.

---

59. Lipsky suggests that "The importance of social programs that formally address but fail to meet need is that they give . . . the appearance of systemic responsiveness while implicitly signalling people who remain dependent that they are unlucky or somehow at fault for failing to take advantage of these programs." *See* Lipsky, *Bureaucratic Disentitlement in Social Welfare Programs*, 20 Soc. Serv. Rev. 3, 10 (1984).

60. I. Susser, Norman Street, chapter 5 (1982). *See also* S. Sheehan. A Welfare Mother (1976).

61. As de Certeau argues, "Through procedures that Freud makes explicit with reference to wit, a tactic boldly juxtaposes diverse elements in order suddenly to produce a flash shedding a different light on the language of a place." *See* de Certeau, *supra* note 3, at 37.

In the end, Maria received the assistance she wanted from the Farm Workers, but her understanding of law and of the welfare bureaucracy did not prevail. Her lawyer refused to deal directly with the Farm Workers and explained to her that it would be inappropriate for him to do so. He cited an office policy which prevented him from doing an end-run around the caseworker and insisted, over Maria's objection, on contacting the caseworker and working the problem out with her.[62] What mattered yet again was not the immediacy of Maria's need, but an abstract commitment to a particular way of doing things. Trying to escape what for her was a bureaucratic 'Catch-22' Maria found herself caught up in another maze of bureaucratic policy and routine. While this time she got what she wanted, she was as baffled as ever. She never found out what the rule was that required direct contact between the Farm Workers and her caseworker; nor was she ever informed about what transpired between her lawyer and caseworker. Her lawyer just told her that "things had been taken care of."[63]

The same sense of urgency which Maria brought to the legal services office, and the same language of need which she and Spencer deployed in dealing with their lawyers and with me, was also apparent as other welfare recipients articulated their grievances against the welfare bureaucracy.[64] Because welfare programs are set up to insure minimum levels of subsistence, recipients think that great sensitivity should be shown before benefits are reduced or terminated. Their claims are thus often framed as appeals beyond rules to a minimum standard of decency.[65]

This is illustrated by Ellen, a twenty-eight-year-old mother of four, who came to the legal services office because, as she told her lawyer:

---

62. Unlike other welfare recipients, *see supra* text accompanying note 33, Maria did not think that a good lawyer was one who would make a good deal.

63. As I listened to Maria. I wondered whether I was guilty of the same tendency to abstract, and the same failure to comprehend or take seriously her immediate, material needs which she found so troubling in her dealings with both her caseworker and her lawyer. This worry reappears as I try to put in writing what I learned in the course of studying thirty-eight welfare recipients and as I try to fit their understandings into a framework of debates about legal consciousness. These are, of course, general concerns, concerns that go beyond mv particular research. *See* J. Van Maanen, *supra* note 23; R. Rosaldo, Culture and Truth: The Remaking of Social Analysis (1989); G. Marcus & J. Clifford, Writing Culture: The Poetics and Politics of Ethnography (1986).

In these acts I am rendering abstract and distant what is for the people I studied very real and very close at hand. Such abstraction. as Maria's claim vividly demonstrates, is, in many ways, their enemy. It is what they encounter in their dealings with caseworkers and lawyers; it is part of a conceptual apparatus which leaves people hungry and calls that justice or which responds to a call for help with a discussion of rules.

This is an example of what Bourdieu calls "symbolic violence." As he defines it, symbolic violence is "that form of domination which, transcending the opposition usually drawn between sense relations and power relations. communication and domination, is only exerted *through* the communication in which it is disguised." P. Bourdieu, Outline of a Theory of Practice 237 (1977).

64. *See* Briar, *supra* note 5. at 374.

65. These appeals are at variance with the belief that law is all politics and that it is only "who you know" that counts. These appeals beyond rules coexist with a deep cynicism about the welfare bureaucracy and the legal system.

370   Yale Journal of Law & the Humanities   [Vol. 2: 343

I was receiving food stamps and still we wasn't eating right. So, I got
a temporary job, nothing, not much, just a little more food. And
then, I guess there are so many weeks you're supposed to let them
know you're working. I was getting food stamps and I heard there
was going to be a layoff and they stop my stamps and then the job
goes. Why do that? Why? Don't they think we should eat? I'm not
living high. I'm trying to get enough to eat. That's what this is
about.[66]

> Lawyer: Yeah, there are so many weeks, but before they take
> anything they. . . . Did they tell you before your stamps were
> stopped?
> I . . . I, who knows? Maybe, I can't remember. But who cares. I
> know I'm not getting them anymore.
> Lawyer: It is very important. . . .
> No, not for me. I can't remember.

Ellen seemed surprised by her lawyer's question and tried to redi-
rect their conversation, to get it back to what she cared about and
away from what seemed to her to be an insignificant detail. In this
brief exchange Ellen suggested that she both could not remember
whether she was told before her food stamps were terminated and
that she did not think that she should have to think about or recall it.
Her response was as much a refusal to shift the agenda as it was a
failure of memory.[67]

Two different conceptions of the meaning of Ellen's problem sur-
faced in this exchange. For her, the problem was about getting
enough to eat; for her lawyer, the important question seemed to be
one of notice. His focus on that question parallels the concern of the
welfare people about Ellen's own failure to give them notice when
she was working. Here Ellen could have gone along with her lawyer's conception and agreed to use the issue of notice the way it had
been used against her. Instead she held her ground and, in so doing,
kept alive the question of need, of hunger, of a minimum standard of
decency.

Ellen tried to get her lawyer to understand the situation in those
terms and to get him to communicate that understanding to the welfare people. Yet Ellen did not talk about her loss of food stamps as a
matter of losing something which she had been promised or to which
she was entitled as a matter of law. She said that the welfare people
could not comprehend (they "just can't understand") and deal with
her problem because they had never been hungry. All they are concerned with is making sure that they do not make overpayments, and

---

66. Federal rules require that documentation of earned income be provided on a monthly basis.
Recipients must inform their caseworkers how many hours they work and how much money they
earn and provide proof in the form of check stubs or letters from employers.

67. Welfare recipients frequently do not remember what are for their lawyers important details of
their cases, nor are they able to provide the kind of paper record that their lawyers sometimes think is
essential. As one somewhat sarcastically put it in responding to his lawyer's request for documents, "I
ain't got enough room to keep a filing system and I ain't got a secretary."

they are too eager, in Ellen's words, to "flush" recipients for failing to comply with "some nit-picky" technical requirements.[68] Those requirements, she said, seemed to be more important to them than dealing with her hunger.

Here again we see how an appeal to human decency and a humane professionalism is used as a resource to oppose what appears to be a bureaucratic pathology and an excessively narrow preoccupation with rules. Ellen sought some way of dealing with her lawyer and the welfare bureaucracy without resorting to a formalistic incantation of rights and rules. She resisted her lawyer's repeated efforts to talk about her problem as an issue of failed procedures or violations of rules and to talk about the problem of not having enough to eat in impersonal, abstract terms. In so doing she avoided playing out her sense of grievance in terms with which the welfare bureaucracy would be most familiar and with which they would be most comfortable. As she said, "They know about all that rules and procedures. . . . Let them go hungry for a while and they won't be no talk about that shit."

Like Maria, Ellen deployed a language of persuasion that depended on ideas of right which are necessarily part of the life experience of persons at the margins of subsistence. She insisted that the normative commitments of the welfare community be heard and that the appropriateness of those normative commitments be recognized even as she used the instrumentalities of law to transmit that insistence. In the end, Ellen's food stamps were restored, but as she told me, "I don't know how or why, but I don't think it was because my lawyer ever really knew what I was going through. It was like some kind of game for him: You know some rule they didn't follow and he had caught them. It was no game to me."

Yet for Ellen more was at stake than the articulation of the normative commitments of the welfare community. In using the language of need she appealed to something she assumed was held in common by herself, her caseworker and her lawyer, namely, a shared humanity and a shared aversion to human suffering.[69] It is

---

68. The phrase "being flushed" was used to describe the experience of having one's benefits reduced or terminated. Bane and Dowling talk about the " 'churning' of clients" to refer to a process of "quick termination from and reinstatement to the assistance rolls—until clients complete procedural requirements." *See supra* note 2, at 5.

69. This language, some might argue, suggests that the welfare poor do not use legal ideas in constructing or framing their relations with the welfare bureaucracy. For example, Merry, *supra* note 11, at 65, seems to use law and rights interchangeably and, in so doing, to limit her understanding of the nature of law. Thus in discussing the pervasive use of the language of rights among working class persons experiencing interpersonal problems she says, "*The* legal definition is not the only one possible. . . . The language of rights recurs frequently . . . suggesting that . . . legal concepts are commonly used to interpret the behavior of neighbors, children, and family members" (emphasis added). *See also* Merry, *The Discourse of Mediation and the Power of Naming*," 2 Yale J.L. & Humanities 1, 6 (1990).

The vocabulary of law, however, provides ample room for formulating claims in various ways. *See* Silbey & Sarat, *Dispute Processing in Law and Legal Scholarship*, 66 Den. U. L. Rev. 437 (1989) and Fraser, *Talking About Needs: Interpretative Contests as Political Conflicts in Welfare-State Societies*, 99 Ethics 291 (1989). Because the content of legal rights is built on the basis of various kinds of calculations and considerations, many different conceptions of social relations are encoded in

because she assumed that that was the lowest common denominator among them that she was both so puzzled by the actions of the welfare bureaucracy ("Why? Don't they think we should eat?") and surprised by her lawyer's focus on the notice question.

Ellen, Maria and others like them (generally those who Spencer would call the "respectable" poor) understand law as being about more than rules and compliance. However, they do not think of welfare as a form of property the use and enjoyment of which should be recognized as presumptively theirs,[70] and see denials, reductions or terminations of benefits as invasions, in either the literal or metaphorical sense, of a domain within which they believe themselves to be sovereign.[71] Few spoke about denials, reductions or terminations of benefits as if they had some *a priori* claim to those benefits. However, neither were their grievances phrased in such a manner as to suggest that problems were conceived of as the loss of a mere privilege or gratuity.[72] Recipients interpret loss of food stamps, denials of emergency assistance, reductions in AFDC and similar events in a way that ignores the right/privilege distinction and act as if rational appeals could be made, as if the immediacy of their life situation would have a moral force that would compel attention and response. Keeping this belief alive was an important part of their aspiration to

---

doctrine and many different ways of constructing law are found in communities, welfare bureaucracies and legal services offices.

The legal constitution of social relations is thus multi-layered and complex. In a wide variety of areas, from negligence and nuisance to contracts and antitrust, claims are formulated in terms of the most efficient use of resources, and rights are derived from explicit economic calculations. The adequacy and limits of such calculations are discussed by B. Ackerman, Reconstructing American Law (1984). *See also* Calabresi & Melamed, *Property Rights, Liability Rules and Inalienability*, 85 Harv. L. Rev. 1089 (1972).

The law of welfare, on the other hand, relies on the language of needs, needs tests and needs assessments. Simon argues that a jurisprudence of need was developed by "New Deal social workers and . . . natural rights lawyers." They ". . . found a source of entitlement in the notion of minimum need . . . and sought to develop minimum need as a sufficiently determinate standard to appraise and reform the system." Simon, *supra* note 2, at 1459. So while welfare recipients like Maria and Ellen seldom use the language of rights in an explicit manner, their talk about needs is a way of articulating demands that is, or ought to be, recognizable. However, because this jurisprudence of need has developed its own bureaucratic self-understanding, welfare recipients are often unable to articulate their sense of need in ways that are recognizable to those in charge of the welfare system.

As Fraser puts it, in the welfare system ". . . people's needs are subject to a sort of rewriting operation. Experienced situations and life-problems are translated into administrable needs. And since the latter are not necessarily isomorphic to the former, the possibility of a gap between them arises." *See* Fraser, *Women, Welfare and the Politics of Need Interpretation*," 2 Hypatia 103, 114 (1987). For the welfare bureaucracy, need is a matter of rules and tables which measure it and arrange human situations in a static relationship to those impersonal measures. This way of thinking about need flattens its time dimension and obscures its embeddedness in ongoing human relationships. For welfare recipients, in contrast, need is thought about in terms of obligations to children and the changeable exigencies of life which leave Spencer afraid of starvation, Ellen worried about how she is going to eat and Maria uncertain of how she will keep her children warm during the winter.

70. *See* Reich, *supra* note 57; Michelman, *In Pursuit of Constitutional Welfare Rights*, 121 U. Pa. L. Rev. 962 (1973).

71. Maria's initial insistence that she was entitled to information about herself was an important exception.

72. The welfare recipients I studied would disagree with the argument made by Judge Holtzoff, in Smith v. Board of Comm'rs, 259 F. Supp. 423, 424 (D.D.C. 1966), that "[p]ayments of relief funds are grants and gratuities."

respectability. As Ellen said, "Good people know the difference between right and wrong. They don't have to be told what to do by no rule."

Occasionally one of the welfare recipients who Spencer would have labelled a member of the "welfare crowd" did press their lawyer to redress what they saw as a violation of the welfare system's own rules. Such an appeal was for them, however, a sign of despair if not resignation and hopelessness. The invocation of rules was generally a last-ditch effort to exercise leverage where recipients thought there were no shared values which might be deployed against bureaucratic indifference and insensitivity. It was just one more way in which some recipients tried to "work the angles" or "beat the system at its own game," and it represented an ironic mirroring of the mechanical, formalistic attitude toward rules they encounter in the welfare bureaucracy.

As Louise, middle-aged mother of four, told me, "If you deal with them [caseworkers] long enough, you know, like the rest of the world, they don't give a shit about you. The only thing that you've got on them is when they trip up, when they don't do like the rules say and then you can maybe make a deal."[73] Waiting for the moment "when" caseworkers "trip up" is yet another indication of the conjunction of the tactical and the temporal in the legal consciousness of the welfare poor. Here Louise stands ready to "accept the chance offerings of the moment . . . [to create] surprises" for those whose power defines the usual deployment of advantage and disadvantage.[74]

She went to legal services when she was told that court-ordered support for the child of her third husband would be figured into the calculation of her total family income and that this might result in a reduction of AFDC benefits which had just resumed. As she told her lawyer, such a reduction should be "against the law and . . . illegal for them not to be giving me more. They aren't giving me my rights." She urged her "to find out how the decision was made and whether any rules were broken."[75] In so doing Louise, like other members of the "welfare crowd," talked about the welfare bureaucracy as if it only could be held accountable to its own system of specific and unbending rules.[76]

---

73. Louise had had extensive experience with lawyers, judges and other legal officials before she showed up in the legal services office. Her oldest child, a twelve year old boy, was frequently in trouble with the police and juvenile authorities. In addition, Louise had been in and out of drug programs during the last several years as well as on some form of public assistance throughout most of her life.

74. *See* de Certeau, *supra* note 3, at 37.

75. Louise persisted even after her lawyer said that it was not against the law to include child support in the calculation of total family income. However, she shifted ground slightly and suggested that there should be "something to make sure this doesn't happen." In the end, she was told that there was nothing that could be done.

76. Louise displays a residual formalism which identifies the protection of rights with compliance to law, a formalism traces of which survive in all post-realist reconstructions of law, *see* Tushnet, *Post-Realist Legal Scholarship*, 1980 Wis. L. Rev. 1383 (1980); Sarat, *The "New Formalism" in Disputing and Dispute Processing*, 21 Law & Soc'y Rev. 695 (1988)).

Law and Society

However, Louise was not hopeful that the appeal to rules would produce a beneficial result. As she told me (echoing sentiments described earlier in this paper), "it's all politics. Like even if they broke the rules, who says my lawyer is going to do anything about it." In her view, the rules of law are stacked against welfare recipients, and talk of rights is, in the end, just talk. For her, rule based arguments, though they are not particularly potent, are the last and perhaps only weapons available.

VI. Conclusion

The welfare poor understand that law and legal services are deeply implicated in the welfare system and are highly politicized. As a result, they are both uncertain and afraid when they seek legal assistance. Nevertheless, some use law and lawyers to get the welfare bureaucracy to live up to its own *raison d'etre*. Uncertainty and fear do not defeat hope, and the discourse of need is used to appeal to a humane professionalism or a shared humanity. For others, all that is left by the time they go to legal services is the possibility of defeating the welfare bureaucracy on the basis of a "technicality." Their invocation of rules is an act of desperation as well as a parody of welfare's own bureaucratic pathology. Yet both the discourse of need and rules occur on law's terrain and depend on a vocabulary made available by law itself.[77] Both reaffirm law's dominance even as they are used to challenge the decisions of particular legal officials—or to provide the grounds for a redress of grievances.

The understandings and actions of the welfare poor do not fit easily with images of a population deeply attached to ideas of law's autonomy, neutrality and disinterestedness[78] or a so called "myth of rights."[79] By

---

77. *See* P. Nonet & P. Selznick, Law and Society in Transition: Toward Responsive Law (1978).
78. *See, e.g.*, Singer, *supra* note 10 at 12. *See also* Gordon, *supra* note 10, at 286.

In another work Gordon argues for a less constrained view of the nature of legal consciousness. He suggests that ". . . law figures as a factor in the power relationships of individuals and social classes but [it is] also . . . omnipresent in the very marrow of society. . . . [L]awmaking and law-interpreting institutions have been among the primary sources of the pictures of order and disorder, virtue and vice, reasonableness and craziness, Realism and visionary naivete and some of the most commonplace aspects of social reality that ordinary people carry around with them and use in ordering their lives. To put this another way, the power exerted by a legal regime consists less in the force that it can bring to bear against violators of its rules than in its capacity to persuade people that the world described in its images and categories is the only attainable world in which a sane person would want to live." *See* Gordon, *Critical Legal Histories*, 36 Stan. L. Rev. 57, 109 (1984). Note how Gordon makes the empirical claim that law is "omnipresent" in the consciousness of "ordinary people."

Such an empirical claim is, however, left unexamined by many of those whose treatment of legal consciousness has been limited to judicial opinions. Some argue that such opinions work primarily at the ideological level. They state, "A principal vehicle for the transmission of . . . ideological imagery has been and continues to be 'the law'." Gabel & Feinman, *Contract Law as Ideology*, in The Politics of Law 173 (D. Kairys ed. 1982) Later in this same essay Gabel and Feinman argue that "'The law' does not enforce anything, however, because the law is nothing but ideas and the images they signify. Its purpose is to justify practical norms. . . . The key social function of the [judicial] opinion . . . is . . . to be found in the . . . rhetorical structure of the opinion itself, in the legitimation of the practical norm that occurs through the application of it in the form of a 'legal rule'." (at 181). For an important criticism of this view of law see Cover, *supra* note 6.

adding this paper to the growing body of scholarship on legal ideology and legal consciousness,[80] I intend to highlight divergent strands among the welfare poor and differences between the legal consciousness of the welfare poor and other groups in society. In so doing, I want to suggest that legal consciousness is, like law itself, polyvocal, contingent and variable.[81]

Trubek, *supra* note 1, at 611 identifies two places, both in footnotes, where scholars interested in the doctrinal construction of legal consciousness, *see* Klare, *Labor Law as Ideology*, 4 Indus. Rel. L. J. 450 (1981); Kennedy, *The Structure of Blackstone's Commentaries*, 28 Buffalo L. Rev. 205 (1979), seem to acknowledge the need to study the recipients as well as the producers of law and the possibility that the cultural codes embodied in legal doctrine may not be translated into mass legal consciousness.

My effort to understand legal consciousness and ideology complements the concerns of Critical Legal Studies which Trubek contends rests on ". . . notions about relations among the ideas we hold about law and society, the structures of social life we are engaged in and the actions we take. . . ." *supra* note 1, at 575; *see also* Freeman, *Legitimating Racial Discrimination Through Anti-Discrimination Law*, 62 Minn. L. Rev. 1049 (1978); Klare, *Judicial Deradicalization of the Wagner Act and the Origins of Modern Legal Consciousness*, 62 Minn. L. Rev. 265 (1978); Klare, *Labor Law As Ideology*, 4 Indus. Rel. L. J. 450 (1981). Moreover, Hutchinson, *Introduction*, in Critical Legal Studies 227 (1989) contends that,

> A crucial plank in the Critical platform is the need to appreciate the operation of law as ideology or as a particular mode of consciousness. CLS writers go beyond the marxist notion of ideology as 'false consciousness'. . . . Instead CLS insists that ideology is . . . a lived relation in the world . . . ; law does not so much falsely describe the world, as inscribes it with its own image. Law and legal consciousness are constitutive features of social life and change.

My efforts are, however, critical of those within that movement who embrace a top-down view of the relation of law and society. My own work attempts to illustrate the co-existence of various elements of formalist, realist and post-realist legal thought in contemporary legal consciousness by getting beyond the mandarin materials of elite legal culture and studying other "sites" in which law and legality are produced. For a useful discussion of the relationship of this kind of work to CLS see Trubek & Esser, *supra* note 22, at 31-34. My interest in this kind of research, the effort to describe law as it is seen from the bottom-up, is partially a response to an argument made by Cover, *supra* note 6, at 1629.

79. Scheingold argues that a "myth of rights . . . exercises a compelling influence . . . and provides shared ideals for the great majority. . . . Even otherwise alienated minorities are receptive to values associated with legal ordering. . . . [W]hile we may respond to the myth of rights as groups . . . most of us do respond." *See* Scheingold, *supra* note 9, at 78-79.

There is some evidence to support this view. For example, many of those who have studied public attitudes toward the Supreme Court note a widespread diffusion of such beliefs. *See* Casey, *The Supreme Court and Myth*, 8 Law & Soc'y Rev. 385, 393 (1974); Kressel, *Public Perceptions of the Supreme Court*, 10 Midwest J. Pol. Sci. 167 (1966); Dolbeare, *The Public Views the Supreme Court*, in Law, Politics and the Federal Courts (H. Jacob ed. 1967).

80. *See* Hunt, *supra* note 2; Hay, *Property, Authority and the Criminal Law*, in Albion's Fatal Tree (D. Hay et. al. ed 1975); E. P. Thompson, Whigs and Hunters (1975); Macaulay, *Images of Law in Everyday Life*, 21 Law & Soc'y Rev. 185 (1987); Amherst Seminar, *supra* note 14.

81. These qualities of mass legal consciousness are highlighted in recent sociolegal research that describes the distinctiveness of insider views of law and the variability of legal consciousness within particular social groups. Among legal professionals, for example, there is evidence that lawyers actively debunk the idea of law's neutrality and disinterestedness and of the salience of rights in day-to-day interactions with clients. *See* Sarat & Felstiner, *supra* note 34. Lawyers tell their clients that the legal system is not governed by rules and that judges and other officials allow their own preferences and interests to shape legal decisions. They tell them that rights mean only what judges say they mean.

Other research (see, for example, M. Feeley, The Process Is the Punishment (1979) and Yngvesson, *supra* note 12) suggests that when citizens use judicial institutions they are often introduced to a legal discourse in which formal rights play but one part. *See also* Kennedy, *Toward an Historical Understanding of Legal Consciousness*, 3 Res. Law & Soc. 3 (1980); Kennedy & Gabel, *supra* note 39; Dalton, *An Essay in the Deconstruction of Contract Doctrine*, 94 Yale L. J. 997 (1985). In that context, law speaks the language of individuation and is concerned with preserving relationships and

Such polyvocality, contingency and variability do not, however, dislodge the power of law or the dominance of legal rules and practices. That is surely the case with respect to the situation of poor people who find themselves embedded in the hierarchical relations which characterize the welfare system. Responses to that system are, in de Certeau's sense, tactical,[82] and may, as we have seen, juxtapose differing elements of its official ideology (need as against rule formalism) or deploy particular elements to hold officials to account. In those responses some aspects of the official ideology are incorporated into new ideological configurations by persons seeking to

---

responding to human needs. (In another paper I have tried to track the way in which developments in legal practice and legal scholarship help to produce these various vocabularies of law. See Silbey & Sarat, supra note 69.

Outside such legal institutions, law's meaning seems to vary within, as well as among, different social groups. See Engel, The Oven Bird's Song, 18 Law & Soc'y Rev. 551 (1984); Greenhouse, Courting Difference, 22 Law & Soc'y Rev. 687 (1988); Bumiller, supra note 32; Merry, supra note 11. Engel, for example, shows how residents of "Sander County" think about particular problems (those involving contracts and repayment of debts) in terms of rights even as they resist or ignore rights in dealing with other kinds of issues (personal injuries). While these people see the assertion of rights in contract cases as supportive of a valued moral order in which broken promises create entitlements to legal redress, they think that asserting rights in personal injury cases is simply a cover for greed, self-interest and economic calculation. In addition to this problem-oriented segmentation in legal consciousness, a segmentation that allows residents of Sander County to both use and reject the language of rights, their relations with "outsiders" are thought about in different terms than relations with "neighbors" and long-time residents. Law is regarded as appropriate in dealing with the former and inappropriate in dealing with the latter.

Bumiller shows how the intended beneficiaries of particular legal protections—victims of discrimination—believe in the significance of law and yet refuse to take advantage of its protections. Those people ". . . view law as both protective and destructive. . . . [They fear] that if they seek a legal resolution [to their problem] they will not gain power but [will] lose control over a hostile situation. They resolve the ambiguity by rejecting the relevance of law to their lives," supra note 32, at 4. Their experiences, their grievances, are not understood in terms of rights, and law does not help interpret those experiences or make them meaningful. However, at the same time that law seems irrelevant to their experiences with discrimination, the people with whom Bumiller talked believe that ". . . the law in 'absolute' terms would rectify the injustices done to them." Id., at 104. While rejecting legal protection in one context, they embrace it as an abstract possibility. They see themselves as having rights the content and particular utility of which are not specified.

Perhaps the most extensive empirical investigation of the complexities of contemporary legal consciousness has been carried out by Merry. See Merry, supra note 11; Merry, Everyday Understandings of the Law in Working-Class America, 13 Am. Ethnologist 253 (1986); supra note 52. Merry shows that among working class Americans a wide variety of personal and interpersonal problems, for example, problems involving barking dogs or loud noise, are understood in the language of law and are conceptualized as invasions of property. Supra note 11, at 65. For these people, property rights provide a set of symbols through which experience is interpreted and which highlight particular courses of action while making others seem inappropriate.

But, as Merry says, while members of the working class display a strong attachment to Scheingold's "myth of rights," "their ideology is complex . . . [It incorporates] competing interpretations of the nature of legal regulation and . . . [shifts] with experience with the legal system." Merry, supra note 11, at 60. The more experience those people have with law, the closer they come to the insider view in which rights seem less relevant and less absolute. Like Bumiller's victims of discrimination, Merry's working class court users remain attached to law, at least at a symbolic level. They do so, as Merry suggests, ". . . not because they are deluded or convinced that the possession of legal rights makes them the economic or political equals of the rich, but because the law, from time to time, delivers for them," and because the law is less unequal and less stratified than the society in which they live. Merry, supra note 11, at 68.

82. "Lacking its own place, lacking a view of the whole, limited by blindness . . . resulting from combat at close quarters, limited by the possibilities of the moment, a tactic is determined by the absence of power just as a strategy is organized by the postulation of power." de Certeau, supra note 3, at 38.

resist dominant power while other elements are rejected out-of-hand. Thus the official ideology is "both a resource and a constraint."[83]

Continuing dependency of the kind that the welfare poor experience can and does coexist with conflict and challenge. For them, "the law is all over," but its complex structure provides opportunities for opposition even as it produces fear and uncertainty. As Yngvesson argues,

'[T]he spirit of the law', while embodying the concerns of a powerful and dominant professional elite, is not simply invented at the top but is transformed, challenged and reinvented in local practices that produce a plural legal culture in contemporary America. Recognition of plurality [or difference] does not eclipse the reality of pervasive cultural understandings and values. . . . Hegemony assumes plurality: '[It] does not just passively exist as a form of dominance. It has continually to be renewed, recreated, defended, and modified. It is also continually resisted, limited, altered, challenged by pressures not at all its own.' . . . The interpretation of key symbols . . . is contested, while the dominance of a particular structure of differences in society is left unquestioned. Only by viewing legal culture in this dynamic way can we explain popular consciousness as a force contributing to the production of legal order rather than as simply an anomaly or a pocket of consciousness 'outside' of law, irrelevant to its maintenance and transformation.[84]

My research indicates that the welfare poor frequently contest what are often thought of as the key legitimating symbols of law, in particular the association of law with neutrality, disinterestedness, rule determinacy and rights. They are not "taken in" by those symbols, and, like others with continuous, regular contact with law, they have a realistic, if not cynical, view. They have complex and sophisticated views of the bureaucratic and social relations that obtain between welfare workers and legal services lawyers.

Yet neither their realism nor their sophistication guarantees the production of counter-hegemonic views of law. Continuous, regular contact does not mean that the welfare poor are included, or can establish themselves, as full participants in the construction of legal meanings or in the practices through which power is exercised and domination maintained. Because the welfare poor are in positions of continuing dependency,[85] they must engage in an uphill struggle to make their voices heard and their understandings of right and justice part of the legal order.

They use lawyers in that struggle even though they have little hope of success in battling the welfare bureaucracy and even though neither law

---

83. Merry, *Everyday Understandings, supra* note 81, at 255.
84. Yngvesson, *supra* note 14, at 1693.
85. The meaning of such dependence is discussed by Handler, *Dependent People, the State, and the Modern/Postmodern Search for the Dialogic Community,* 35 UCLA L. Rev. 999 (1988).

nor legal services lives up to its self-proclaimed ideals. They do so because both provide strategic resources in an ongoing, if modest, struggle with the welfare bureaucracy.[86] Law, as well the complex relationship of legal services and welfare, is a social fact the broad parameters of which are not questioned; yet it is a social fact which provides room for maneuver and space for resistance.

It is, however, a social fact about which moral judgments are made. The welfare poor call their caseworkers, and sometimes their lawyers, to account for being inhumane or unfair or for violating the system's own rules. They describe law as corrupt, as institutionalizing privilege and treating the poor differently from others and as working through a system of arrangements and deals. Nevertheless, they are not disillusioned by law's failure to be disinterested, neutral or rule governed because they do not expect law to be that way.[87] They can be critical, and cynical about the possibility of change, without being paralyzed; neither their criticism nor their cynicism prevents them from using one set of rules and practices, lawyer's law, to respond to the rules and practices as well as the recalcitrance and inertia of the welfare bureaucracy.

Law, as they see it, is no better, and no worse, than the social world in which it is embedded. Thus the welfare poor construct a consciousness of law on the basis of their daily deprivation, their experience of unequal, often demeaning treatment, and their search for tools with which to cope with an often unresponsive welfare bureaucracy. Law is, for the welfare poor, embodied in a particular set of lived conditions; theirs is a law of practices, not promises, of material transactions, not abstract ideals.

In all this the welfare poor recognize that their experience is different from that of others in this society, whether they be social scientists seeking to understand the welfare poor or the incompletely identified class of "the rich." Differences arise, in one respect, because the poor operate in a space whose meaning they do not define, but whose dominance can be resisted through a "clever *utilization of time*, of the opportunities it presents and also of the play that it introduces into the foundations of power."[88] Differences arise, in another respect, because the identity of the welfare poor is, in substantial part, legally constructed, and because the legal constitution of their subjectivity is visible in a way the legal constitu-

---

86. For a similar argument in a different context see Merry, Law as Fair, Law as Help: The Texture of Legitimacy in American Society (unpublished manuscript) (1987). As Merry argues, less powerful groups in America "do not generally think that legal ordering has produced a fair and just society. More often, the law serves as a resource in struggles over control. . . . Legitimacy has many facets: it is not only a matter of beliefs and values but also social practices and strategies. Perhaps the power and resilience of the legitimacy of legal authority in American society, despite its failure to live up to its claims of equity and fairness, is the result of its utility. . . ." *Id.*, at 31. *See also* Hyde, *The Concept of Legitimation in the Sociology of Law*, 1983 Wis. L. Rev. 379 (1983).

87. If they are disillusioned at all it is by the failure of the welfare system to take human need seriously.

88. de Certeau, *supra* note 3, at 39.

tion of the subjectivity of others is not.[89] This is what Spencer and others were trying to communicate when they insisted that I would not understand them. The law that is "everywhere" in their lives is given meaning in the particular social relations which comprise the welfare experience. Perhaps Spencer's challenges and his playful skepticism about my research were his way of trying to insure that the "law" of our relationship would be different, and perhaps better, than the law which governed his dealings with caseworkers and lawyers.

---

89.   To talk about the legal constitution of identity is to talk about the way human subjectivity is "created by and through a range of different discourses" and to acknowledge that to some extent the law helps define what it means to be a person. "The creation of legal subjects involves the recognition of 'the law' as the active 'subject' that calls . . . [us] into being." *See* Hunt, *supra* note 2, at 15. Yet the creation of legal subjects is never fully a product of state law. It occurs through complex interactions between state actors and individuals, through the articulation of a vision of the self in legal doctrine and in the appropriation of those visions in social relations. *See, e.g.,* Hunt, *supra* note 2.

Thus many welfare recipients struggle to resist the official definition of their subjectivity. They struggle to maintain their dignity against the impersonality of the bureaucratic settings in which they are engaged. They struggle to escape legal rules which demean them or to create an idea of law through which they can express their normative views. Yet the struggle to escape law or to find a meaningful place within it is, for them, sometimes overwhelmingly difficult since their engagements with the welfare bureaucracy are ongoing and the power differentials within that bureaucracy are so enormous. *See* R. Elman, The Poorhouse State: The American Way of Life on Public Assistance (1966).

Part IV
Law and the Structuring
of Communities

[18]

NON-CONTRACTUAL RELATIONS IN BUSINESS:
A PRELIMINARY STUDY *

STEWART MACAULAY

Law School, University of Wisconsin

Preliminary findings indicate that businessmen often fail to plan exchange relationships completely, and seldom use legal sanctions to adjust these relationships or to settle disputes. Planning and legal sanctions are often unnecessary and may have undesirable consequences. Transactions are planned and legal sanctions are used when the gains are thought to outweigh the costs. The power to decide whether the gains from using contract outweigh the costs will be held by individuals having different occupational roles. The occupational role influences the decision that is made.

WHAT good is contract law? who uses it? when and how? Complete answers would require an investigation of almost every type of transaction between individuals and oganizations. In this report, research has been confined to exchanges between businesses, and primarily to manufacturers.[1] Futhermore, this report will be limited to a presentation of the findings concerning when contract is and is not used and to a tentative explanation of these findings.[2]

This research is only the first phase in a scientific study.[3] The primary research technique involved interviewing 68 businessmen and lawyers representing 43 companies and six law firms. The interviews ranged from a 30-minute brush-off where not all questions could be asked of a busy and uninterested sales manager to a six-hour discussion with the general counsel of a large corporation. Detailed notes of the interviews were taken and a complete report of each interview was dictated, usually no later than the evening after the interview. All but two of the companies had plants in Wisconsin; 17 were manufacturers of machinery but

---

* Revision of a paper read at the annual meeting of the Americal Sociological Association, August, 1962. An earlier version of the paper was read at the annual meeting of the Midwest Sociological Society, April, 1962. The research has been supported by a Law and Policy Research Grant to the University of Wisconsin Law School from the Ford Foundation. I am grateful for the help generously given by a number of sociologists including Robert K. Merton, Harry V. Ball, Jerome Carlin and William Evan.

[1] The reasons for this limitation are that (a) these transactions are important from an economic standpoint, (b) they are frequently said in theoretical discussions to represent a high degree of rational planning, and (c) manufacturing personnel are sufficiently public-relations-minded to cooperate with a law professor who wants to ask a seemingly endless number of questions. Future research will deal with the building construction industry and other areas.

[2] For the present purposes, the what-difference-does-it-make issue is important primarily as it makes a case for an empirical study by a law teacher of the use and nonuse of contract by businessmen. First, law teachers have a professional concern with what the law ought to be. This involves evaluation of the consequences of the existing situation and of the possible alternatives. Thus, it is most relevant to examine business practices concerning contract if one is interested in what commercial law ought to be. Second, law teachers are supposed to teach law students something relevant to becoming lawyers. These business practices

are facts that are relevant to the skills which law students will need when, as lawyers, they are called upon to create exchange relationships and to solve problems arising out of these relationships.

[3] The following things have been done. The literature in law, business, economics, psychology, and sociology has been surveyed. The formal systems related to exchange transactions have been examined. Standard form contracts and the standard terms and conditions that are found on such business documents as catalogues, quotation forms, purchase orders, and acknowledgment-of-order forms from 850 firms that are based in or do business in Wisconsin have been collected. The citations of all reported court cases during a period of 15 years involving the largest 500 manufacturing corporations in the United States have been obtained and are being analyzed to determine why the use of contract legal sanctions was thought necessary and whether or not any patterns of "problem situations" can be delineated. In addition, the informal systems related to exchange transactions have been examined. Letters of inquiry concerning practices in certain situations have been answered by approximately 125 businessmen. Interviews, as described in the text, have been conducted. Moreover, six of my students have interviewed 21 other businessmen, bankers and lawyers. Their findings are consistent with those reported in the text.

none made such items as food products, scientific instruments, textiles or petroleum products. Thus the likelihood of error because of sampling bias may be considerable.[4] However, to a great extent, existing knowledge has been inadequate to permit more rigorous procedures—as yet one cannot formulate many precise questions to be asked a systematically selected sample of "right people." Much time has been spent fishing for relevant questions or answers, or both.

Reciprocity, exchange or contract has long been of interest to sociologists, economists and lawyers. Yet each discipline has an incomplete view of this kind of conduct. This study represents the effort of a law teacher to draw on sociological ideas and empirical investigation. It stresses, among other things, the functions and dysfunctions of using contract to solve exchange problems and the influence of occupational roles on how one assesses whether the benefits of using contract outweigh the costs.

To discuss when contract is and is not used, the term "contract" must be specified. This term will be used here to refer to devices for conducting exchanges. Contract is not treated as synonymous with an exchange itself, which may or may not be characterized as contractual. Nor is contract used to refer to a writing recording an agreement. Contract, as I use the term here, involves two distinct elements: (a) Rational planning of the transaction with careful provision for as many future contingencies as can be foreseen, and (b) the existence or use of actual or potential legal sanctions to induce performance of the exchange or to compensate for non-performance.

These devices for conducting exchanges may be used or may exist in greater or lesser degree, so that transactions can be described relatively as involving a more contractual or a less contractual manner (a) of creating an exchange relationship or (b) of solving problems arising during the course of such a relationship. For example, General Motors might agree to buy all of the Buick Divi-

sion's requirements of aluminum for ten years from Reynolds Aluminum. Here the two large corporations probably would plan their relationship carefully. The plan probably would include a complex pricing formula designed to meet market fluctuations, an agreement on what would happen if either party suffered a strike or a fire, a definition of Reynolds' responsibility for quality control and for losses caused by defective quality, and many other provisions. As the term contract is used here, this is a more contractual method of creating an exchange relationship than is a home-owner's casual agreement with a real estate broker giving the broker the exclusive right to sell the owner's house which fails to include provisions for the consequences of many easily foreseeable (and perhaps even highly probable) contingencies. In both instances, legally enforceable contracts may or may not have been created, but it must be recognized that the existence of a legal sanction has no necessary relationship to the degree of rational planning by the parties, beyond certain minimal legal requirements of certainty of obligation. General Motors and Reynolds might never sue or even refer to the written record of their agreement to answer questions which come up during their ten-year relationship, while the real estate broker might sue, or at least threaten to sue, the owner of the house. The broker's method of *dispute settlement* then would be more contractual than that of General Motors and Reynolds, thus reversing the relationship that existed in regard to the "contractualness" of the *creation* of the exchange relationships.

TENTATIVE FINDINGS

It is difficult to generalize about the use and nonuse of contract by manufacturing industry. However, a number of observations can be made with reasonable accuracy at this time. The use and nonuse of contract in creating exchange relations and in dispute settling will be taken up in turn.

The creation of exchange relationships. In creating exchange relationships, businessmen may plan to a greater or lesser degree in relation to several types of issues. Before reporting the findings as to practices in cre-

---

[4] However, the cases have not been selected because they *did* use contract. There is as much interest in, and effort to obtain, cases of nonuse as of use of contract. Thus, one variety of bias has been minimized.

NON-CONTRACTUAL RELATIONS IN BUSINESS 57

ating such relationships, it is necessary to describe what one can plan about in a bargain and the degrees of planning which are possible.

People negotiating a contract can make plans concerning several types of issues: (1) They can plan what each is to do or refrain from doing; e.g., S might agree to deliver ten 1963 Studebaker four-door sedan automobiles to B on a certain date in exchange for a specified amount of money. (2) They can plan what effect certain contingencies are to have on their duties; e.g., what is to happen to S and B's obligations if S cannot deliver the cars because of a strike at the Studebaker factory? (3) They can plan what is to happen if either of them fails to perform; e.g., what is to happen if S delivers nine of the cars two weeks late? (4) They can plan their agreement so that it is a legally enforceable contract—that is, so that a legal sanction would be available to provide compensation for injury suffered by B as a result of S's failure to deliver the cars on time.

As to each of these issues, there may be a different degree of planning by the parties. (1) They may carefully and explicitly plan; e.g., S may agree to deliver ten 1963 Studebaker four-door sedans which have six cylinder engines, automatic transmissions and other specified items of optional equipment and which will perform to a specified standard for a certain time. (2) They may have a mutual but tacit understanding about an issue; e.g., although the subject was never mentioned in their negotiations, both S and B may assume that B may cancel his order for the cars before they are delivered if B's taxi-cab business is so curtailed that B can no longer use ten additional cabs. (3) They may have two inconsistent unexpressed assumptions about an issue; e.g., S may assume that if any of the cabs fails to perform to the specified standard for a certain time, all S must do is repair or replace it. B may assume S must also compensate B for the profits B would have made if the cab had been in operation. (4) They may never have thought of the issue; e.g., neither S nor B planned their agreement so that it would be a legally enforceable contract. Of course, the first and fourth degrees of planning listed are the extreme cases and

the second and third are intermediate points. Clearly other intermediate points are possible; e.g., S and B neglect to specify whether the cabs should have automatic or conventional transmissions. Their planning is not as careful and explicit as that in the example previously given.

The following diagram represents the dimensions of creating an exchange relationship just discussed with "X's" representing the example of S and B's contract for ten taxi-cabs.

	Definition of Performances	Effect of Contingencies	Effect of Defective Performances	Legal Sanctions
Explicit and careful	X			
Tacit agreement		X		
Unilateral assumptions			X	
Unawareness of the issue				X

Most larger companies, and many smaller ones, attempt to plan carefully and completely. Important transactions not in the ordinary course of business are handled by a detailed contract. For example, recently the Empire State Building was sold for $65 million. More than 100 attorneys, representing 34 parties, produced a 400 page contract. Another example is found in the agreement of a major rubber company in the United States to give technical assistance to a Japanese firm. Several million dollars were involved and the contract consisted of 88 provisions on 17 pages. The 12 house counsel—lawyers who work for one corporation rather than many clients—interviewed said that all but the smallest businesses carefully planned most transactions of any significance. Corporations have procedures so that particular types of exchanges will be reviewed by their legal and financial departments.

More routine transactions commonly are handled by what can be called standardized planning. A firm will have a set of terms and conditions for purchases, sales, or both printed on the business documents used in

Law and Society

these exchanges. Thus the things to be sold and the price may be planned particularly for each transaction, but standard provisions will further elaborate the performances and cover the other subjects of planning. Typically, these terms and conditions are lengthy and printed in small type on the back of the forms. For example, 24 paragraphs in eight point type are printed on the back of the purchase order form used by the Allis Chalmers Manufacturing Company. The provisions: (1) describe, in part, the performance required, e.g., "DO NOT WELD CASTINGS WITHOUT OUR CONSENT"; (2) plan for the effect of contingencies, e.g., ". . . in the event the Seller suffers delay in performance due to an act of God, war, act of the Government, priorities or allocations, act of the Buyer, fire, flood, strike, sabotage, or other causes beyond Seller's control, the time of completion shall be extended a period of time equal to the period of such delay if the Seller gives the Buyer notice in writing of the cause of any such delay within a reasonable time after the beginning thereof"; (3) plan for the effect of defective performances, e.g., "The buyer, without waiving any other legal rights, reserves the right to cancel without charge or to postpone deliveries of any of the articles covered by this order which are not shipped in time reasonably to meet said agreed dates"; (4) plan for a legal sanction, e.g., the clause "without waiving any other legal rights," in the example just given.

In larger firms such "boiler plate" provisions are drafted by the house counsel or the firm's outside lawyer. In smaller firms such provisions may be drafted by the industry trade association, may be copied from a competitor, or may be found on forms purchased from a printer. In any event, salesmen and purchasing agents, the operating personnel, typically are unaware of what is said in the fine print on the back of the forms they use. Yet often the normal business patterns will give effect to this standardized planning. For example, purchasing agents may have to use a purchase order form so that all transactions receive a number under the firm's accounting system. Thus, the required accounting record will carry the necessary planning of the

exchange relationship printed on its reverse side. If the seller does not object to this planning and accepts the order, the buyer's "fine print" will control. If the seller does object, differences can be settled by negotiation.

This type of standardized planning is very common. Requests for copies of the business documents used in buying and selling were sent to approximately 6,000 manufacturing firms which do business in Wisconsin. Approximately 1,200 replies were received and 850 companies used some type of standardized planning. With only a few exceptions, the firms that did not reply and the 350 that indicated they did not use standardized planning were very small manufacturers such as local bakeries, soft drink bottlers and sausage makers.

While businessmen can and often do carefully and completely plan, it is clear that not all exchanges are neatly rationalized. Although most businessmen think that a clear description of both the seller's and buyer's performances is obvious common sense, they do not always live up to this ideal. The house counsel and the purchasing agent of a medium size manufacturer of automobile parts reported that several times their engineers had committed the company to buy expensive machines without adequate specifications. The engineers had drawn careful specifications as to the type of machine and how it was to be made but had neglected to require that the machine produce specified results. An attorney and an auditor both stated that most contract disputes arise because of ambiguity in the specifications.

Businessmen often prefer to rely on "a man's word" in a brief letter, a handshake, or "common honesty and decency"—even when the transaction involves exposure to serious risks. Seven lawyers from law firms with business practices were interviewed. Five thought that businessmen often entered contracts with only a minimal degree of advance planning. They complained that businessmen desire to "keep it simple and avoid red tape" even where large amounts of money and significant risks are involved. One stated that he was "sick of being told, 'We can trust old Max,' when the problem is not one of honesty but one of reaching

NON-CONTRACTUAL RELATIONS IN BUSINESS   59

an agreement that both sides understand." Another said that businessmen when bargaining often talk only in pleasant generalities, think they have a contract, but fail to reach agreement on any of the hard, unpleasant questions until forced to do so by a lawyer. Two outside lawyers had different views. One thought that large firms usually planned important exchanges, although he conceded that occasionally matters might be left in a fairly vague state. The other dissenter represents a large utility that commonly buys heavy equipment and buildings. The supplier's employees come on the utility's property to install the equipment or construct the buildings, and they may be injured while there. The utility has been sued by such employees so often that it carefully plans purchases with the assistance of a lawyer so that suppliers take this burden.

Moreover, standardized planning can break down. In the example of such planning previously given, it was assumed that the purchasing agent would use his company's form with its 24 paragraphs printed on the back and that the seller would accept this or object to any provisions he did not like. However, the seller may fail to read the buyer's 24 paragraphs of fine print and may accept the buyer's order on the seller's own acknowledgment-of-order form. Typically this form will have ten to 50 paragraphs favoring the seller, and these provisions are likely to be different from or inconsistent with the buyer's provisions. The seller's acknowledgment form may be received by the buyer and checked by a clerk. She will read the *face* of the acknowledgment but not the fine print on the back of it because she has neither the time nor ability to analyze the small print on the 100 to 500 forms she must review each day. The face of the acknowledgment—where the goods and the price are specified—is likely to correspond with the face of the purchase order. If it does, the two forms are filed away. At this point, both buyer and seller are likely to assume they have planned an exchange and made a contract. Yet they have done neither, as they are in disagreement about all that appears on the back of their forms. This practice is common enough to have a name. Law teachers call it "the battle of the forms."

Ten of the 12 purchasing agents interviewed said that frequently the provisions on the back of their purchase order and those on the back of a supplier's acknowledgment would differ or be inconsistent. Yet they would assume that the purchase was complete without further action unless one of the supplier's provisions was really objectionable. Moreover, only occasionally would they bother to read the fine print on the back of suppliers' forms. On the other hand, one purchasing agent insists that agreement be reached on the fine print provisions, but he represents the utility whose lawyer reported that it exercises great care in planning. The other purchasing agent who said that his company did not face a battle of the forms problem, works for a division of one of the largest manufacturing corporations in the United States. Yet the company may have such a problem without recognizing it. The purchasing agent regularly sends a supplier both a purchase order and another form which the supplier is asked to sign and return. The second form states that the supplier accepts the buyer's terms and conditions. The company has sufficient bargaining power to force suppliers to sign and return the form, and the purchasing agent must show one of his firm's auditors such a signed form for every purchase order issued. Yet suppliers frequently return this buyer's form *plus* their own acknowledgment form which has conflicting provisions. The purchasing agent throws away the supplier's form and files his own. Of course, in such a case the supplier has not acquiesced to the buyer's provisions. There is no agreement and no contract.

Sixteen sales managers were asked about the battle of the forms. Nine said that frequently no agreement was reached on which set of fine print was to govern, while seven said that there was no problem. Four of the seven worked for companies whose major customers are the large automobile companies or the large manufacturers of paper products. These customers demand that their terms and conditions govern any purchase, are careful generally to see that suppliers acquiesce, and have the bargaining power to have their way. The other three of the seven sales managers who have no battle of the forms problem, work for manufacturers of special industrial machines. Their firms are careful to reach complete agreement with their customers. Two of these men stressed that they could take no chances because such a large part of their firm's capital is tied up in making any one machine. The other sales manager had been influenced by a law suit against one of his competitors for over a half million dollars. The suit was brought by a customer when the competitor had been unable to deliver a machine and put it in operation on time. The sales manager interviewed said his firm could not guarantee that its machines would work perfectly by a specified time because they are designed to fit the customer's requirements, which may present difficult engineering problems. As a result, contracts are carefully negotiated.

A large manufacturer of packaging materials audited its records to determine how often it had failed to agree on terms and conditions with its customers or had failed to create legally binding contracts. Such failures cause a risk of loss to this firm since the packaging is printed with the customer's design and cannot be salvaged once this is done. The orders for five days in four different years were reviewed. The percentages of orders where no agreement on terms and conditions was reached or no contract was formed were as follows:

1953............75.0%
1954............69.4%
1955............71.5%
1956............59.5%

It is likely that businessmen pay more attention to describing the performances in an exchange than to planning for contingencies or defective performances or to obtaining legal enforceability of their contracts. Even when a purchase order and acknowledgment have conflicting provisions printed on the back, almost always the buyer and seller will be in agreement on what is to be sold and how much is to be paid for it. The lawyers who said businessmen often commit their firms to significant exchanges too casually, stated that the performances would be defined in the brief letter or telephone call; the lawyers objected that nothing else would be covered. Moreover, it is likely that businessmen are

least concerned about planning their transactions so that they are legally enforceable contracts.[5] For example, in Wisconsin requirements contracts—contracts to supply a firm's requirements of an item rather than a definite quantity—probably are not legally enforceable. Seven people interviewed reported that their firms regularly used requirements contracts in dealings in Wisconsin. None thought that the lack of legal sanction made any difference. Three of these people were house counsel who knew the Wisconsin law before being interviewed. Another example of a lack of desire for legal sanctions is found in the relationship between automobile manufacturers and their suppliers of parts. The manufacturers draft a carefully planned agreement, but one which is so designed that the supplier will have only minimal, if any, legal rights against the manufacturers. The standard contract used by manufacturers of paper to sell to magazine publishers has a pricing clause which is probably sufficiently vague to make the contract legally unenforceable. The house counsel of one of the largest paper producers said that everyone in the industry is aware of this because of a leading New York case concerning the contract, but that no one cares. Finally, it seems likely that planning for contingencies and defective performances are in-between cases —more likely to occur than planning for a legal sanction, but less likely than a description of performance.

Thus one can conclude that (1) many business exchanges reflect a high degree of planning about the four categories—description, contingencies, defective performances and legal sanction—but (2) many, if not most, exchanges reflect no planning, or only a minimal amount of it, especially concerning legal sanctions and the effect of defective performances. As a result, the opportunity for good faith disputes during the life of the exchange relationship often is present.

The adjustment of exchange relationships and the settling of disputes. While a

---

[5] Compare the findings of an empirical study of Connecticut business practices in Comment, "The Statute of Frauds and the Business Community: A Re-Appraisal in Light of Prevailing Practices," *Yale Law Journal*, 66 (1957), pp. 1038–1071.

NON-CONTRACTUAL RELATIONS IN BUSINESS 61

significant amount of creating business exchanges is done on a fairly noncontractual basis, the creation of exchanges usually is far more contractual than the adjustment of such relationships and the settlement of disputes. Exchanges are adjusted when the obligations of one or both parties are modified by agreement during the life of the relationship. For example, the buyer may be allowed to cancel all or part of the goods he has ordered because he no longer needs them; the seller may be paid more than the contract price by the buyer because of unusual changed circumstances. Dispute settlement involves determining whether or not a party has performed as agreed and, if he has not, doing something about it. For example, a court may have to interpret the meaning of a contract, determine what the alleged defaulting party has done and determine what, if any, remedy the aggrieved party is entitled to. Or one party may assert that the other is in default, refuse to proceed with performing the contract and refuse to deal ever again with the alleged defaulter. If the alleged defaulter, who in fact may not be in default, takes no action, the dispute is then "settled."

Business exchanges in non-speculative areas are usually adjusted without dispute. Under the law of contracts, if B orders 1,000 widgets from S at $1.00 each, B must take all 1,000 widgets or be in breach of contract and liable to pay S his expenses up to the time of the breach plus his lost anticipated profit. Yet all ten of the purchasing agents asked about cancellation of orders once placed indicated that they expected to be able to cancel orders freely subject to only an obligation to pay for the seller's major expenses such as scrapped steel.[6] All 17 sales personnel asked reported that they often had to accept cancellation. One said, "You can't ask a man to eat paper [the firm's product] when he has no use for it." A lawyer with many large industrial clients said,

> Often businessmen do not feel they have "a contract"—rather they have "an order." They speak of "cancelling the order" rather than "breaching our contract." When I began

[6] See the case studies on cancellation of contracts in *Harvard Business Review*, 2 (1923–24), pages 238–40, 367–70, 496–502.

practice I referred to order cancellations as breaches of contract, but my clients objected since they do not think of cancellation as wrong. Most clients, in heavy industry at least, believe that there is a right to cancel as part of the buyer-seller relationship. There is a widespread attitude that one can back out of any deal within some very vague limits. Lawyers are often surprised by this attitude.

Disputes are frequently settled without reference to the contract or potential or actual legal sanctions. There is a hesitancy to speak of legal rights or to threaten to sue in these negotiations. Even where the parties have a detailed and carefully planned agreement which indicates what is to happen if, say, the seller fails to deliver on time, often they will never refer to the agreement but will negotiate a solution when the problem arises apparently as if there had never been any original contract. One purchasing agent expressed a common business attitude when he said,

> if something comes up, you get the other man on the telephone and deal with the problem. You don't read legalistic contract clauses at each other if you ever want to do business again. One doesn't run to lawyers if he wants to stay in business because one must behave decently.

Or as one businessman put it, "You can settle any dispute if you keep the lawyers and accountants out of it. They just do not understand the give-and-take needed in business." All of the house counsel interviewed indicated that they are called into the dispute settlement process only after the businessmen have failed to settle matters in their own way. Two indicated that after being called in house counsel at first will only advise the purchasing agent, sales manager or other official involved; not even the house counsel's letterhead is used on communications with the other side until all hope for a peaceful resolution is gone.

Law suits for breach of contract appear to be rare. Only five of the 12 purchasing agents had ever been involved in even a negotiation concerning a contract dispute where both sides were represented by lawyers; only two of ten sales managers had ever gone this far. None had been involved in a case that went through trial. A law firm with more than 40 lawyers and a large commercial practice handles in a year only about six trials concerned with contract problems. Less than 10 per cent of the time of this office is devoted to any type of work related to contracts disputes. Corporations big enough to do business in more than one state tend to sue and be sued in the federal courts. Yet only 2,779 out of 58,293 civil actions filed in the United States District Courts in fiscal year 1961 involved private contracts.[7] During the same period only 3,447 of the 61,138 civil cases filed in the principal trial courts of New York State involved private contracts.[8] The same picture emerges from a review of appellate cases.[9] Mentschikoff has suggested that commercial cases are not brought to the courts either in periods of business prosperity (because buyers unjustifiably reject goods only when prices drop and they can get similar goods elsewhere at less than the contract price) or in periods of deep depression (because people are unable to come to court or have insufficient assets to satisfy any judgment that might be obtained). Apparently, she adds, it is necessary to have "a kind of middle-sized depression" to bring large numbers of commercial cases to the courts. However, there is little evidence that in even "a kind of middle-sized depression" today's businessmen would use the courts to settle disputes.[10]

At times relatively contractual methods are used to make adjustments in ongoing transactions and to settle disputes. Demands of one side which are deemed unreasonable by the other occasionally are

blocked by reference to the terms of the agreement between the parties. The legal position of the parties can influence negotiations even though legal rights or litigation are never mentioned in their discussions; it makes a difference if one is demanding what both concede to be a right or begging for a favor. Now and then a firm may threaten to turn matters over to its attorneys, threaten to sue, commence a suit or even litigate and carry an appeal to the highest court which will hear the matter. Thus, legal sanctions, while not an everyday affair, are not unknown in business.

One can conclude that while detailed planning and legal sanctions play a significant role in some exchanges between businesses, in many business exchanges their role is small.

TENTATIVE EXPLANATIONS

Two questions need to be answered: (A) How can business successfully operate exchange relationships with relatively so little attention to detailed planning or to legal sanctions, and (B) Why does business ever use contract in light of its success without it?

Why are relatively non-contractual practices so common? In most situations contract is not needed.[11] Often its functions are served by other devices. Most problems are avoided without resort to detailed planning or legal sanctions because usually there is little room for honest misunderstandings or good faith differences of opinion about the nature and quality of a seller's performance. Although the parties fail to cover all foreseeable contingencies, they will exercise care to see that both understand the primary obligation on each side. Either products are standardized with an accepted description or specifications are written calling for production to certain tolerances or results. Those who write and read specifications are experienced professionals who will know the customs of their industry and those of the industries with

---

[7] *Annual Report of the Director of the Administrative Office of the United States Courts*, 1961, p. 238.

[8] State of New York, The Judicial Conference, Sixth Annual Report, 1961, pp. 209–11.

[9] My colleague Lawrence M. Friedman has studied the work of the Supreme Court of Wisconsin in contracts cases. He has found that contracts cases reaching that court tend to involve economically-marginal-business and family-economic disputes rather than important commercial transactions. This has been the situation since about the turn of the century. Only during the Civil War period did the court deal with significant numbers of important contracts cases, but this happened against the background of a much simpler and different economic system.

[10] New York Law Revision Commission, *Hearings on the Uniform Code Commercial Code*, 2 (1954), p. 1391.

[11] The explanation that follows emphasizes a *considered* choice not to plan in detail for all contingencies. However, at times it is clear that businessmen fail to plan because of a lack of sophistication; they simply do not appreciate the risk they are running or they merely follow patterns established in their firm years ago without reexamining these practices in light of current conditions.

NON-CONTRACTUAL RELATIONS IN BUSINESS   63

which they deal. Consequently, these customs can fill gaps in the express agreements of the parties. Finally, most products can be tested to see if they are what was ordered; typically in manufacturing industry we are not dealing with questions of taste or judgment where people can differ in good faith.

When defaults occur they are not likely to be disastrous because of techniques of risk avoidance or risk spreading. One can deal with firms of good reputation or he may be able to get some form of security to guarantee performance. One can insure against many breaches of contract where the risks justify the costs. Sellers set up reserves for bad debts on their books and can sell some of their accounts receivable. Buyers can place orders with two or more suppliers of the same item so that a default by one will not stop the buyer's assembly lines.

Moreover, contract and contract law are often thought unnecessary because there are many effective non-legal sanctions. Two norms are widely accepted. (1) Commitments are to be honored in almost all situations; one does not welsh on a deal. (2) One ought to produce a good product and stand behind it. Then, too, business units are organized to perform commitments, and internal sanctions will induce performance. For example, sales personnel must face angry customers when there has been a late or defective performance. The salesmen do not enjoy this and will put pressure on the production personnel responsible for the default. If the production personnel default too often, they will be fired. At all levels of the two business units personal relationships across the boundaries of the two organizations exert pressures for conformity to expectations. Salesmen often know purchasing agents well. The same two individuals occupying these roles may have dealt with each other from five to 25 years. Each has something to give the other. Salesmen have gossip about competitors, shortages and price increases to give purchasing agents who treat them well. Salesmen take purchasing agents to dinner, and they give purchasing agents Christmas gifts hoping to improve the chances of making sale. The buyer's engineering staff may work with the seller's engineering staff to solve problems jointly. The seller's engineers may render great assistance, and the buyer's

engineers may desire to return the favor by drafting specifications which only the seller can meet. The top executives of the two firms may know each other. They may sit together on government or trade committees. They may know each other socially and even belong to the same country club. The inter-relationships may be more formal. Sellers may hold stock in corporations which are important customers; buyers may hold stock in important suppliers. Both buyer and seller may share common directors on their boards. They may share a common financial institution which has financed both units.

The final type of non-legal sanction is the most obvious. Both business units involved in the exchange desire to continue successfully in business and will avoid conduct which might interfere with attaining this goal. One is concerned with both the reaction of the other party in the particular exchange and with his own general business reputation. Obviously, the buyer gains sanctions insofar as the seller wants the particular exchange to be completed. Buyers can withhold part or all of their payments until sellers have performed to their satisfaction. If a seller has a great deal of money tied up in his performance which he must recover quickly, he will go a long way to please the buyer in order to be paid. Moreover, buyers who are dissatisfied may cancel and cause sellers to lose the cost of what they have done up to cancellation. Furthermore, sellers hope for repeat for orders, and one gets few of these from unhappy customers. Some industrial buyers go so far as to formalize this sanction by issuing "report cards" rating the performance of each supplier. The supplier rating goes to the top management of the seller organization, and these men can apply internal sanctions to salesmen, production supervisors or product designers if there are too many "D's" or "F's" on the report card.

While it is generally assumed that the customer is always right, the seller may have some counterbalancing sanctions against the buyer. The seller may have obtained a large downpayment from the buyer which he will want to protect. The seller may have an exclusive process which the buyer needs. The seller may be one of the few firms which has the skill to make the item to the tolerances set by the buyer's engineers and within the

64 AMERICAN SOCIOLOGICAL REVIEW

time available. There are costs and delays involved in turning from a supplier one has dealt with in the past to a new supplier. Then, too, market conditions can change so that a buyer is faced with shortages of critical items. The most extreme example is the post World War II gray market conditions when sellers were rationing goods rather than selling them. Buyers must build up some reserve of good will with suppliers if they face the risk of such shortage and desire good treatment when they occur. Finally, there is reciprocity in buying and selling. A buyer cannot push a supplier too far if that supplier also buys significant quantities of the product made by the buyer.

Not only do the particular business units in a given exchange want to deal with each other again, they also want to deal with other business units in the future. And the way one behaves in a particular transaction, or a series of transactions, will color his general business reputation. Blacklisting can be formal or informal. Buyers who fail to pay their bills on time risk a bad report in credit rating services such as Dun and Bradstreet. Sellers who do not satisfy their customers become the subject of discussion in the gossip exchanged by purchasing agents and salesmen, at meetings of purchasing agents' associations and trade associations, or even at country clubs or social gatherings where members of top management meet. The American male's habit of debating the merits of new cars carries over to industrial items. Obviously, a poor reputation does not help a firm make sales and may force it to offer great price discounts or added services to remain in business. Furthermore, the habits of unusually demanding buyers become known, and they tend to get no more than they can coerce out of suppliers who choose to deal with them. Thus often contract is not needed as there are alternatives.

Not only are contract and contract law not needed in many situations, their use may have, or may be thought to have, undesirable consequences. Detailed negotiated contracts can get in the way of creating good exchange relationships between business units. If one side insists on a detailed plan, there will be delay while letters are exchanged as the parties try to agree on what should happen if a remote and unlikely contingency occurs.

In some cases they may not be able to agree at all on such matters and as a result a sale may be lost to the seller and the buyer may have to search elsewhere for an acceptable supplier. Many businessmen would react by thinking that had no one raised the series of remote and unlikely contingencies all this wasted effort could have been avoided.

Even where agreement can be reached at the negotiation stage, carefully planned arrangements may create undesirable exchange relationships between business units. Some businessmen object that in such a carefully worked out relationship one gets performance only to the letter of the contract. Such planning indicates a lack of trust and blunts the demands of friendship, turning a cooperative venture into an antagonistic horse trade. Yet the greater danger perceived by some businessmen is that one would have to perform his side of the bargain to its letter and thus lose what is called "flexibility." Businessmen may welcome a measure of vagueness in the obligations they assume so that they may negotiate matters in light of the actual circumstances.

Adjustment of exchange relationships and dispute settlement by litigation or the threat of it also has many costs. The gain anticipated from using this form of coercion often fails to outweigh these costs, which are both monetary and non-monetary. Threatening to turn matters over to an attorney may cost no more money than postage or a telephone call; yet few are so skilled in making such a threat that it will not cost some deterioration of the relationship between the firms. One businessman said that customers had better not rely on legal rights or threaten to bring a breach of contract law suit against him since he "would not be treated like a criminal" and would fight back with every means available. Clearly actual litigation is even more costly than making threats. Lawyers demand substantial fees from larger business units. A firm's executives often will have to be transported and maintained in another city during the proceedings if, as often is the case, the trial must be held away from the home office. Top management does not travel by Greyhound and stay at the Y.M.C.A. Moreover, there will be the cost of diverting top management, engineers, and others in the organization

NON-CONTRACTUAL RELATIONS IN BUSINESS 65

from their normal activities. The firm may lose many days work from several key people. The non-monetary costs may be large too. A breach of contract law suit may settle a particular dispute, but such an action often results in a "divorce" ending the "marriage" between the two businesses, since a contract action is likely to carry charges with at least overtones of bad faith. Many executives, moreover, dislike the prospect of being cross-examined in public. Some executives may dislike losing control of a situation by turning the decision-making power over to lawyers. Finally, the law of contract damages may not provide an adequate remedy even if the firm wins the suit; one may get vindication but not much money.

Why do relatively contractual practices ever exist? Although contract is not needed and actually may have negative consequences, businessmen do make some carefully planned contracts, negotiate settlements influenced by their legal rights and commence and defend some breach of contract law suits or arbitration proceedings. In view of the findings and explanation presented to this point, one may ask why. Exchanges are carefully planned when it is thought that planning and a potential legal sanction will have more advantages than disadvantages. Such a judgment may be reached when contract planning serves the internal needs of an organization involved in a business exchange. For example, a fairly detailed contract can serve as a communication device within a large corporation. While the corporation's sales manager and house counsel may work out all the provisions with the customer, its production manger will have to make the product. He must be told what to do and how to handle at least the most obvious contingencies. Moreover, the sales manager may want to remove certain issues from future negotiation by his subordinates. If he puts the matter in the written contract, he may be able to keep his salesmen from making concessions to the customer without first consulting the sales manager. Then the sales manager may be aided in his battles with his firm's financial or engineering departments if the contract calls for certain practices which the sales manager advocates but which the other departments resist. Now the corporation is obligated to a customer

to do what the sales manager wants to do; how can the financial or engineering departments insist on anything else?

Also one tends to find a judgment that the gains of contract outweigh the costs where there is a likelihood that significant problems will arise.[12] One factor leading to this conclusion is complexity of the agreed performance over a long period. Another factor is whether or not the degree of injury in case of default is thought to be potentially great. This factor cuts two ways. First, a buyer may want to commit a seller to a detailed and legally binding contract, where the consequences of a default by the seller would seriously injure the buyer. For example, the airlines are subject to law suits from the survivors of passengers and to great adverse publicity as a result of crashes. One would expect the airlines to bargain for carefully defined and legally enforceable obligations on the part of the airframe manufacturers when they purchase aircraft. Second, a seller may want to limit his liability for a buyer's damages by a provision in their contract. For example, a manufacturer of air conditioning may deal with motels in the South and Southwest. If this equipment fails in the hot summer months, a motel may lose a great deal of business. The manufacturer may wish to avoid any liability for this type of injury to his customers and may want a contract with a clear disclaimer clause.

Similarly, one uses or threatens to use legal sanctions to settle disputes when other devices will not work and when the gains are thought to outweigh the costs. For example, perhaps the most common type of business contracts case fought all the way through to the appellate courts today is an action for an alleged wrongful termination of a dealer's franchise by a manufacturer. Since the franchise has been terminated, factors such as personal relationships and the desire for future business will have little effect; the cancellation of the franchise indicates they

---

12 Even where there is little chance that problems will arise, some businessmen insist that their lawyer review or draft an agreement as a delaying tactic. This gives the businessman time to think about making a commitment if he has doubts about the matter or to look elsewhere for a better deal while still keeping the particular negotiations alive.

have already failed to maintain the relationship. Nor will a complaining dealer worry about creating a hostile relationship between himself and the manufacturer. Often the dealer has suffered a great financial loss both as to his investment in building and equipment and as to his anticipated future profits. A cancelled automobile dealer's lease on his showroom and shop will continue to run, and his tools for servicing, say, Plymouths cannot be used to service other makes of cars. Moreover, he will have no more new Plymouths to sell. Today there is some chance of winning a law suit for terminating a franchise in bad faith in many states and in the federal courts. Thus, often the dealer chooses to risk the cost of a lawyer's fee because of the chance that he may recover some compensation for his losses.

An "irrational" factor may exert some influence on the decision to use legal sanctions. The man who controls a firm may feel that he or his organization has been made to appear foolish or has been the victim of fraud or bad faith. The law suit may be seen as a vehicle "to get even" although the potential gains, as viewed by an objective observer, are outweighed by the potential costs.

The decision whether or not to use contract—whether the gain exceeds the costs—will be made by the person within the business unit with the power to make it, and it tends to make a difference who he is. People in a sales department oppose contract. Contractual negotiations are just one more hurdle in the way of a sale. Holding a customer to the letter of a contract is bad for "customer relations." Suing a customer who is not bankrupt and might order again is poor strategy. Purchasing agents and their buyers are less hostile to contracts but regard attention devoted to such matters as a waste of time. In contrast, the financial control department—the treasurer, controller or or auditor—leans toward more contractual dealings. Contract is viewed by these people as an organizing tool to control operations in a large organization. It tends to define precisely and to minimize the risks to which the firm is exposed. Outside lawyers—those with many clients—may share this enthusiasm for a more contractual method of dealing. These lawyers are concerned with

preventive law—avoiding any possible legal difficulty. They see many unstable and unsuccessful exchange transactions, and so they are aware of, and perhaps overly concerned with, all of the things which can go wrong. Moreover, their job of settling disputes with legal sanctions is much easier if their client has not been overly casual about transaction planning. The inside lawyer, or house counsel, is harder to classify. He is likely to have some sympathy with a more contractual method of dealing. He shares the outside lawyer's "craft urge" to see exchange transactions neat and tidy from a legal standpoint. Since he is more concerned with avoiding and settling disputes than selling goods, he is likely to be less willing to rely on a man's word as the sole sanction than is a salesman. Yet the house counsel is more a part of the organization and more aware of its goals and subject to its internal sanctions. If the potential risks are not too great, he may hesitate to suggest a more contractual procedure to the sales department. He must sell his services to the operating departments, and he must hoard what power he has, expending it on only what he sees as significant issues.

The power to decide that a more contractual method of creating relationships and settling disputes shall be used will be held by different people at different times in different organizations. In most firms the sales department and the purchasing department have a great deal of power to resist contractual procedures or to ignore them if they are formally adopted and to handle disputes their own way. Yet in larger organizations the treasurer and the controller have increasing power to demand both systems and compliance. Occasionally, the house counsel must arbitrate the conflicting positions of these departments; in giving "legal advice" he may make the business judgment necessary regarding the use of contract. At times he may ask for an opinion from an outside law firm to reinforce his own position with the outside firm's prestige.

Obviously, there are other significant variables which influence the degree that contract is used. One is the relative bargaining power or skill of the two business units. Even if the controller of a small supplier succeeds within the firm and creates a contractual system of dealing, there will be no

COMMENT ON MACAULAY

contract if the firm's large customer prefers not to be bound to anything. Firms that supply General Motors deal as General Motors wants to do business, for the most part. Yet bargaining power is not size or share of the market alone. Even a General Motors may need a particular supplier, at least temporarily. Furthermore, bargaining power may shift as an exchange relationship is first created and then continues. Even a giant firm can find itself bound to a small supplier once production of an essential item begins for there may not be time to turn to another supplier. Also, all of the factors discussed in this paper can be viewed as *components* of bargaining power—for example, the personal relationship between the presidents of the buyer and the seller firms may give a sales manager great power over a purchasing agent who has been instructed to give the seller "every consideration." Another variable relevant to the use of contract is the influence of third parties. The federal government, or a lender of money, may insist that a contract be made in a particular transaction or may influence the decision to assert one's legal rights under a contract.

Contract, then, often plays an important role in business, but other factors are significant. To understand the functions of contract the whole system of conducting exchanges must be explored fully. More types of business communities must be studied, contract litigation must be analyzed to see why the nonlegal sanctions fail to prevent the use of legal sanctions and all of the variables suggested in this paper must be classified more systematically.

[19]

SOCIAL FACTORS IN THE DEVELOPMENT OF LEGAL CONTROL: A CASE STUDY OF TWO ISRAELI SETTLEMENTS

RICHARD D. SCHWARTZ†

"The substance of every attempt to state the fundamental principles of the sociology of law [is that] the center of gravity of legal development lies not in legislation, nor in juristic science, nor in judicial decisions, but in society itself."

EHRLICH, FUNDAMENTAL PRINCIPLES
OF THE SOCIOLOGY OF LAW xv (1936)

LEGAL control is not exercised against all disturbing behavior. Sometimes, such behavior never reaches the courts.[1] At other times, it is not sanctioned by the courts because, we are told, it should be left to "the *interior* forum, as the tribunal of conscience has been aptly called."[2] The effects of non-legal or informal control, whether or not adequately described in terms of "conscience," seem to be an important factor in a court's decision to withhold sanction.

The relationship between legal and informal controls can be theoretically stated and empirically described. The cultures of two Israeli communities were compared in an effort to determine the social effects of economic collectivism.[3] One of the differences noted was that the collective community, or *kvutza*,[4] had no distinctly legal institution, whereas the

---

†Instructor in Sociology, Yale College; Research Fellow in Behavior Science, Institute of Human Relations, Yale University.

1. Professor Karl Llewellyn characterizes law as being concerned only with disputes "not otherwise settled." Llewellyn, *Legal Tradition and Social Science Method—A Realist's Critique* in Essays on Research in the Social Sciences 89, 91 (Brookings Institute 1931).

2. Mills v. Wyman, 20 Mass. 225, 3 Pick. 207 (1825).
   "Without doubt there are great interests in society which justify withholding the coercive arm of the law from these duties of imperfect obligation, as they are called; imperfect, not because they are less binding upon the conscience than those which are called perfect, but because the wisdom of the social law does not impose sanctions upon them." *Id.* at 228, 3 Pick. at 210-11.

3. This work was carried out in 1949-50 with the aid of a Research Training Fellowship from the Social Science Research Council and a Sterling Predoctoral Fellowship from Yale University. A full ethnographic report is presented in the author's INSTITUTIONAL CONSISTENCY IN A COLLECTIVE SOCIETY (unpublished thesis in Sterling Memorial Library, 1951).

4. For useful materials in English on Israel's collective communities, see MALETZ, YOUNG HEARTS (1950) (an account of a member's experience in a collective); BARATZ, DEGANIA (1943) (description of the formative years of Israel's first kvutza) ben Yissakhar, *The Kibbutz at the Crossroads* 2 ZIONIST NEWSLETTER (Nos. 6-13, 1949-50).

moshav,[5] a semi-private property settlement, did. Speculation on the reasons for the difference led to the formulation of a theory of legal control. The theory cannot be presented in detail in this article,[6] but it will be used as a framework for the organization of the empirical data. While the data do not constitute empirical verification of the theory,[7] it is hoped that the theory will help to explain the data, and the data serve to illustrate the theory.

In attempting to ascertain whether or not a social group has legal controls and, if it does, why these controls are applied to some but not to other forms of behavior, this article rests upon several assumptions:

1. For a given individual at a given time, some states of affairs are more satisfying [8] than others.

2. A *gain* in satisfaction is defined as transition from a less to a more satisfying state of affairs; a *loss* of satisfaction is the reverse; an *indifferent* experience as no change in satisfaction.

3. The frequency, vigor, and speed with which an action is performed in a given situation is an *increasing function* [9] of the degree (frequency, magnitude, and immediacy) to which similar behavior has previously been followed by gain, and of the extent of similarity perceived by the present actor between the present behavior and behavior previously followed by gain. Conversely, the frequency, vigor, and speed with which an action is performed in a given situation is a *decreasing function* of the degree of gain following competing (alternative and incompatible) behavior, and of the extent of similarity perceived by the present actor between present competing behavior and similar behavior previously followed by gain.

These postulates are stated in general terms because it is purposed to apply them to the behavior of all participants in the process of social control. Social control involves *interaction, i.e.*, behavior on the part of one actor which affects the behavior of another. Control is distinguished from other forms of interaction in that it includes *sanction, i.e.*, the administration of gain or loss to an

---

5. For some of the few English sources available on the moshav, see DAYAN, MOSHAV OVDIM (1947); MESSINGER, KVUTZAH MOSHAV KIBBUTZ (1949).

6. The detailed theory, on file in the Institute of Human Relations, Yale University, was developed in connection with the Institute's Postdoctoral Program in Behavior Science, under the directorship of Mark A. May. See HULL, ESSENTIALS OF BEHAVIOR (1951), for the postulates which provided the starting point for this theory.

7. For verification, this theory should be tested against data which did not contribute to its formulation, and which are more extensive than those presented here.

8. Many methods have been proposed for the measurement of relative satisfaction, among them verbal reports, decisions of experts, and physiological indices. We would prefer to let the definition rest ultimately on choice behavior. When an individual is given the choice between two states of affairs after having fully experienced both, the one which he selects is defined as more satisfying for him. If verbal or other measures are found to be correlated with such choices under certain circumstances, they may be substituted for purposes of convenience.

9. For "X is an increasing function of Y," read, "Other factors equal, as Y increases, X increases."

actor. Sanction is *positive* when it results in gain for the sanctionee, and *negative* when it results in loss.

From our assumptions it can be deduced that a sanctioner tends to employ positive sanctions following any behavior (x) which is typically gainful to him. If positive sanction occurs after x, the likelihood is increased that under similar circumstances x will be repeated vigorously and speedily. If x continues to be gainful to the sanctioner, his tendency to respond to it with positive sanction is reinforced.

In the same way it follows that negative sanction tends to be employed following behavior (y) which typically results in loss for the sanctioner. Imposition of negative sanction following the performance of y decreases the gain which its performer may have obtained by it and increases the likelihood that he will gain by switching from it to some incompatible behavior. If, as a result, the actor performs y less often and less vigorously, the sanctioner experiences a gain because there is a transition from a less to a more satisfying state of affairs. Therefore his tendency to respond to y with negative sanction is increased.

Other factors also affect the likelihood that a given sanction will recur. The impact of a sanction may be supplemented or reduced by collateral gains and losses experienced by the sanction*ee*. Even if, as a result of all these influences, sanctionee's behavior is modified in a way gainful to the sanctioner, the gainful effect need not reinforce the sanction; it can be offset by collateral losses experienced by the sanction*er*. Important among these are any experiences which have strengthened the tendency of the potential sanctioner to respond in a competing way either by employing a different sanction or by exerting no sanction at all. The greater the tendency to perform such competing reactions, the less is the likelihood that the given sanction will be employed.

In the interactive aggregates of individuals which we call *social groups*, two main forms of control may be distinguished: that which is carried out by specialized functionaries who are socially delegated the task of intra-group control, and that which is not so delegated. These will be respectively designated *legal* and *informal* controls. When, as is often the case, these two forms of control are in competition, the likelihood of legal control arising at all in a given sphere is a decreasing function of the effectiveness of informal controls. It is the thesis of this article that the presence of legal controls in the moshav, the semi-private property settlement, but not in the kvutza, the collective settlement, is to be understood primarily in terms of the fact that informal controls did not operate as effectively in the moshav as in the kvutza.

CONTROL SYSTEMS IN THE KVUTZA AND MOSHAV

In most of their superficial characteristics, the two settlements are essentially similar. Both were founded at the same time, 1921, by young settlers who had come from Eastern Europe "to build a new life." Though the kvutza was smaller at first, it has grown to a population (just under 500 persons) which is almost identical in size with that of the moshav. Both are located on a slope of the Jezreel Valley where they have to deal with the same climate and similar topography. Both have about two thousand acres of land, which supports a mixed farming economy. Both populations have rejected many of the East-European Jewish customs, including traditional religious practices. Though many other Israeli collectives are left-wing socialist, the members of the kvutza under consideration resemble those of the moshav in adhering to the social-democratic political philosophy represented by the *Mapai* party.

Despite these similarities, the two communties have differed from the outset in their members' ideas about economic organization. In the kvutza, members felt they could implement the program, "from each according to his abilities, to each according to his need," as the way to create a "just society." Moshav members, many of whom had spent a few years in collectives, decided that the family should be the unit of production and distribution, and that thus a class of small independent farmers could be developed in the moshav which would provide a strong agricultural base for the country.

As far as could be ascertained, there were no initial differences in specific ideas concerning legal control. Legal jurisdiction over crimes and civil wrongs is recognized by all to reside in the State of Israel, but very few cases involving members of these settlements have been brought before the State's courts or, earlier, before the courts of the British Mandate. The minimal role of these courts has resulted from an absence of serious crime; the shielding of fellow members from British (and now to a lesser extent even Israeli) "outsiders"; and internal controls which effectively handle existing disturbances. In both settlements, the power to exercise these internal controls stems from the General Assembly, a regularly held meeting of all members in which each one present casts a single vote. This form of government works effectively in both communities, perhaps because they are small enough for everyone to be heard and homogeneous enough so that there is basic agreement on means and ends. While the kvutza meetings are more frequent and cover a broader range of issues, moshav sessions are held at least bi-weekly and are generally well attended.

In both settlements, the General Assembly delegates responsibility for certain activities to committees whose membership it approves. Committees are, if anything, more active in the kvutza, which has separate permanent groups to deal with questions of economic coordination, work assignment, education, social affairs, ceremonies, housing, community planning, and health. The moshav also has its committees, but most of these deal with agricultural matters, particularly the dissemination to individual farmers of the kind of scientific information which is handled by managers in the kvutza.

The moshav's Judicial Committee, however, is a specialized agency for which no counterpart is found in the kvutza. This Committee consists of a panel of seven members elected annually by the General Assembly for the purpose of dealing with internal disputes. Complaints by members against members are brought before the Committee either directly or by referral from the General Assembly. A hearing of the complaint is then conducted by a panel of three drawn from the larger Committee. After investigating the circumstances and hearing the direct testimony of both sides, a panel decides whether and how the defendant should bear responsibility. Fines and damages, the major types of punishment, are usually paid upon imposition, but if not, they are enforceable by the secretary of the moshav. Though these panels follow simple procedures, there can be no doubt that they have acted as an agency of legal control in the moshav.

An example will illustrate the operation of this moshav system of legal control. A fifteen-year-old boy took a neighbor's jeep without permission, picked up some of his friends, and went for a joyride outside the village. During the ride, he crashed into a tree and damaged the fender and door of the vehicle. The owner brought a complaint against him which was heard by the panel. When the boy admitted his actions, he was charged for the full cost of repairs. The debt was subsequently discharged by the boy's parents, and the case was considered closed.

By contrast, the kvutza has not delegated sanctioning responsibility to any special unit. Even when administrative or legislative action results in gain or loss to an individual, this is not its primary purpose. In the event of a dispute between workers, for example, the Work Assignment Committee or the Economic Council may decide that the interests of production would be better served if one or both of the workers were transferred. But the objective of such action is not punitive; rather it is to ensure the smooth functioning of the economy, and the decision is made in much the same manner as any decision relating to production.

In the course of its legislative work, the General Assembly of the kvutza also makes decisions which modify the gains and losses of members. Many of these are policy decisions which apply to classes of members, but sometimes an individual's behavior provides the occasion for a policy debate in the Assembly. One young member, for example, received an electric teakettle as a gift from his sister in the city. Though small gifts could be retained as personal property, the kettle represented a substantial item, and one which would draw upon the limited supply of electricity available to the entire settlement. Moreover, the kvutza had already decided against supplying each room with a kettle on the grounds that this would be expensive and would encourage socially divisive private get-togethers. By retaining the kettle, therefore, the young man was threatening the principles of material equality and social solidarity on which the kvutza is believed to rest. This at any rate was the decision of the Assembly majority following three meetings during which the issue was debated. Confronted with this decision, the owner bowed to the general will by turning his teakettle over to the infirmary where it would be used by those presumed to be in greatest need of it. No organized enforcement of the decision was threatened, but had he disregarded the expressed will of the community, his life in the kvutza would have been made intolerable by the antagonism of public opinion.

As will become apparent, it is the powerful force of public opinion which is the major sanction of the entire kvutza control system. It may be focused, as in the case of the electric teakettle, by an Assembly decision, or it may, as occurs more commonly, be aroused directly by the behavior it sanctions. In either case, it is an instrument of control which is employed not by any specialized functionaries but by the community as a whole. Since public opinion is the sanction for the entire kvutza control system, that system must be considered informal rather than legal. We turn now to a more detailed consideration of the factors which have made this system of control so much more effective in the kvutza than in the moshav.

SANCTION IMPACT

From our assumptions, we may deduce that the extent to which a sanction, legal or informal, modifies the tendency of given behavior is a function of the frequency, magnitude, and immediacy with which it follows the sanctioned behavior. Frequency of sanction depends on the number of times the behavior is performed, the proportion of times its performance is observed by potential sanctioners, the proportion of observations which evoke a reaction, and the proportion of reactions which actually have a sanctioning effect. For any given instance of sanction, magnitude of sanction depends on the vigor of reaction, the extent to which the reaction is implemented, and the average gain or loss to the sanctionee per unit of experienced sanction. For example, magnitude of sanction resulting from a fine would depend on how many dollars were demanded (vigor), how many of these were collected (implementation), and how great a loss each dollar constituted for the payer. Immediacy of sanction is a function of how soon after its performance the pertinent behavior is perceived by the sanctioner, how speedily he reacts to it, and how quickly the reaction is experienced by the sanctionee. It follows from all this that *sanction impact* is an increasing function of the numbers of potential sanctioners who perceive or are informed of the pertinent behavior, and of the accuracy, frequency, and speed with which this *information* is obtained; an increasing function of the capacity of informed would-be sanctioners to *implement* their reactions; an increasing function of the *magnitude* of gain or loss which that reaction, once implemented, imposes on the sanctionee; and an increasing function of the extent to which potential sanctionees perceive and therefore *vicariously* learn from the experience of sanctionees.

Information:

For the control of any behavior which would, if known, be effectively sanctioned, it is important that potential sanctioners know accurately and quickly of its occurrence. Accuracy implies that the behavior comes to the attention of the reactors as often as possible and that they know who has done what, under which conditions. Each time such behavior is known to have occurred, reactors gain an opportunity to increase the frequency of sanction.

The more quickly this information is obtained, the greater is the immediacy with which sanction can be administered.

Accuracy and speed of perception tend to be high in what Cooley has described as the "primary group," characterized by "intimate face-to-face association and cooperation."[10] Though such groups are typically small in size, we shall see that under certain conditions a high frequency of face-to-face association or interaction can occur in groups as large as the kvutza. Cooley goes on to hypothesize of primary groups that they are "fundamental in forming the social nature and ideals of the individual," which is close to saying that they are characterized by effective systems of control.[11] Though there is little trustworthy evidence on this point,[12] it seems plausible in light of the propositions that accurate information is a prerequisite to control and that the face-to-face intimacy of the primary group makes such information possible.

The kvutza is in effect a large primary group whose members engage in continuous face-to-face interaction. Each able-bodied member works eight to ten hours a day, six days a week, at a job which is usually performed wholly or partially in the presence of others. The results of his efforts become known to his associates, the work manager, and the top officials who coordinate the economy. All three meals are eaten in a collective dining hall usually in the company of five other residents who happen to have arrived at the same time. Members of each sex share common washing and shower facilities, and these are used by most members at the same time, during the limited period when hot water is available. Housing is concentrated in one area of the kvutza and consists of rows of long houses, each partitioned to make six rooms, with a married couple or two roommates occupying each room. Because most rooms are surrounded by other dwellings, it is easily possible for neighbors to observe entrances and exits and even some behavior within. Child rearing is the primary responsibility of special nurses and teachers, but parents spend about two hours with their children on work days and usually more than this on their days of rest. Much of this relationship is subject to public view as parents and children stroll around the kvutza, eat together occasionally in the dining hall, or play in front of their rooms. Other leisure activities are also subject to public observation: participating in Assembly and Committee meetings, celebrating kvutza holidays, attending lectures and films, perusing news-

---

10. COOLEY, SOCIAL ORGANIZATION 23 (1909). See also Clow, Cooley's Doctrine of Primary Groups, 25 AM. J. Soc. 326 (1919). For a recent discussion, see Shils, The Study of the Primary Group in THE POLICY SCIENCES 23-31 (Lerner & Lasswell eds. 1951). Shils prefers to base his definition on characteristics of group culture rather than on more easily described characteristics such as size.

11. COOLEY, SOCIAL ORGANIZATION 23 (1909).

12. Psychoanalytically oriented studies, e.g., KARDINER, THE PSYCHOLOGICAL FRONTIERS OF SOCIETY (1945), and "folk society" research, e.g., REDFIELD, THE FOLK CULTURE OF YUCATAN (1941), introduce variables, respectively, of primacy of training and rapidity of cultural change which, for our purposes, are extraneous. For a representative experimental study of small group controls, see Asch, Effects of Group Pressure on the Modification and Distortion of Judgments in GROUPS, LEADERSHIP AND MEN (Guetzkow ed. 1951).

papers and periodicals in the kvutza reading room, or taking a vacation tour of the country. Even sexual relations, particularly if they are illicit, can become the subject of general public knowledge, although this was the one type of activity excepted by a member when he said, "amongst us, all things except one are done together."

The same conditions of continuous interaction also make it possible to circulate information throughout the entire community. Mealtime and showering are two informal occasions when large numbers of people forgather and find opportunity for conversation. The shower in particular is a forum for the transmission of information where one can hear about anything from fractured ankles to broken hearts. Though "I heard it in the shower" is a kvutza equivalent for "take this with a grain of salt," much genuine news is disseminated there. Compared with these informal techniques, the weekly news bulletin and the Assembly meetings run slow supplementary seconds.

Moshav conditions do not permit as great a degree of public observation. Work is typically conducted alone, with other members of the family, or occasionally with the voluntary aid of a friend. As long as the moshav farmer maintains a solvent establishment and discharges such community obligations as payment of taxes and correct use of cooperative facilities, he is free to manage his farm as he sees fit. Meals consisting largely of produce from the farmstead are prepared by the housewife and eaten in a family dining room which occupies a central place in the home. Houses are small bungalows ranging from three to six rooms, separated from neighboring dwellings by a hundred yards or more, and screened by hedges and fruit trees. Many activities which are publicly performed in the kvutza can be, and usually are, carried out in the privacy of the moshav home, among them economic husbandry, care of clothing, showering, washing, child rearing, and such recreation as visiting, reading, and listening to the radio. There are, to be sure, places where members come into contact, such as the produce depots, cooperative store, Assembly and committee meetings, and cinema. Though such contacts provide some opportunities for the circulation of information, they are fewer and the information circulated is less complete than in the kvutza.

At least partially as a result of these differences, kvutza members do in fact learn more about the activities of more of their members than is known in the moshav. Less than a week of residence was necessary in the kvutza before virtually everyone knew the ostensible purpose of the writer's stay, whereas similar knowledge was not diffused as widely (or accurately) during two months in the moshav. Information thus transmitted is not confined to work performance and consumption, though these are of great interest, but range over such details as mail received, visitors contacted, time spent with children, and even style of underclothes worn. As a result, it becomes possible to control types of behavior in the kvutza which never become public knowledge in the moshav.

Since we are primarily interested in the effects of such factors as information status on the development of legal controls, it is unnecessary for our purposes to analyze in detail the reasons for these differences. It should be noted, however, that kvutza intimacy was not solely the result of conscious planning concerning social relations. Though the desire for intimacy was a factor, it was strongly supplemented by other pressures, such as those arising as unanticipated by-products of the need for economic efficiency in a collective economy.

Implementation:

If it is important for effective control that the behavior in question be perceived by reactors, it is at least as necessary that their sanctions be perceived by sanctionees. Though a reactor may behave in a way which tends to exert sanction, this reaction cannot achieve maximum control over behavior unless it is experienced by someone who could be sanctioned by it. Uncollected damages and unserved jail sentences are presumably not as effective in controlling negligent or criminal behavior as are implemented judgments. Similarly, in the operation of informal control, the failure of sanction implementation constitutes a major reason for the apparently deviant behavior of such transient individuals as traveling salesmen, hoboes, railroad workers, and hotel guests.[13]

Conditions necessary for the implementation of a sanction depend on the nature of the sanction. The implementation of public opinion—major informal sanction in the Israeli settlements—requires that public approval or disapproval be accurately and speedily communicated to sanctionees. This is accomplished in the kvutza by essentially the same conditions as made the perception of behavior so readily possible, namely, the continuous interaction characteristic of the primary group. In the case of implementation, the interactive process is simply reversed, with sanctioners providing the action which is then perceived by sanctionees.

Public opinion can be manifested often, swiftly, subtly, and with varying degrees of intensity in the kvutza. In the course of a day's continual interaction, positive or negative opinion may be communicated by the ways in which members glance at an individual, speak to him, pass him a requested work implement or dish of food, assign him work, give him instructions, sit next to him, and listen to his comments. To an experienced member, these small signs serve to predict more intense reactions of public acclaim or social isolation. They therefore acquire sanctioning power in and of themselves and become able to control the behavior in question before extremes are reached. In the moshav, by contrast, there are fewer opportunities to convey public opinion quickly and accurately because there is so much less contact between members in the course of the daily regime. This is an important limitation in the use of public opinion as a means of control in the moshav.

13. Some evidence on these points will be found in Burgess & Cottrell, Predicting Successs and Failure in Marriage (1939); Anderson, The Hobo (1923) and Men on the Move (1940); Cottrell, The Railroader (1940); and Hayner, *Hotel Life and Personality*, 33 Am. J. Soc. 784 (1928).

Magnitude of gain or loss:

In order for public opinion to be effective, it is important not only that changes in it be perceived but that these be capable of providing gain or loss to the sanctionee. If he is indifferent to public opinion, his behavior will not be directly changed by such sanction. If, on the other hand, he is "other-directed," so that modification in public attitude involves relatively greater loss or gain to him, we would expect him to be effectively sanctioned by public opinion.[14] As a whole, the population of the kvutza is far more concerned with public opinion than is that of the moshav. Several factors appear to have contributed to this characteristic, among them differences in immigration, emigration, child training and adult experience.

Since these settlements were studied thirty years after they were founded, it is difficult to know whether immigrants were different at the outset. It is possible that people to whom public opinion was important may have gravitated to the collective type of community, or at least that those who stayed were particularly responsive to it. Looking back at their primary reasons for coming, almost three out of four present kvutza members refer to socially oriented motives, *e.g.*, social solidarity, building a just society, changing human nature. Such motives were said to be primary by only one-third of the present moshav members. Many of the moshav members emphasized economically oriented motives, *e.g.*, strengthening the country as a whole or their own economic position in particular.

The effect of this self-selection process may have been aided to some extent by a kvutza policy of admitting to permanent membership those candidates who receive a majority vote after a trial period ranging from six months to a year. In the early years particularly, potential members were carefully scrutinized for the characteristics which were thought to make good kvutza material. For a new person to appear to be a good worker and a harmonious comrade, it was necessary that he respond to public opinion. This ability is still tested in many subtle ways. Candidates for membership are not explicitly told all the ways of the kvutza and must learn many of them through the informal control system. In the dining hall, for example, new residents are not instructed in the complicated standards governing substitution of desired food for allotted dishes. They must learn, mainly by observing others, which kinds of foods can or cannot be taken from the waiter's cart in exchange for a dish which has already been served. Speed of learning is noted by the old-timers, and failure to learn over an extended period contributes to a negative impression of the candidate. Oftentimes individuals who fail to meet such tests are subjected to social disapproval which is sufficiently unpleasant to cause their emigration from the settlement. In general the emigration rate has been higher from the kvutza than from the moshav, and it is presumed that those who have left have been less able to conform to public opinion than those who have remained.

14. Stemming from Freud through Fromm, this distinction has been given recent expression in RIESMAN, THE LONELY CROWD (1950).

By contrast, no such elaborate procedures are used to determine fitness for moshav members. Most of the available farmsteads were taken years ago by the families which still occupy them. Emigration is based primarily on inability to make a success of farming, but it is doubtful whether sensitivity to public opinion enhances or decreases the chances of success. Since a farming tradition has not yet been established, success often comes to the very individual who flouts public opinion and proceeds in accordance with his own notions. New families are accepted primarily on the basis of their promise as successful farmers and secondarily on their apparent conformity to social requirements.

Far less wasteful for the kvutza than a continuous circulation of personnel would be a system of training to increase responsiveness to public opinion. Kvutza child training practices seem to produce this effect. Children are raised from infancy in the constant company of other children of their own age with whom they sleep, eat, bathe, dress, play, and later attend school. Though control is at first the task of the nurses, it is increasingly taken over by the children themselves. Their community is organized politically in a manner similar to the adult kvutza, with children's public opinion playing a corresponding part. When one child was caught stealing bananas reserved for the babies, the Children's Assembly decided to punish the culprit by abrogating *their own* movie privileges. Though this was explained to the adults on the grounds that all were involved in the guilt of one, a reason of at least equal importance was the children's expectation that this reaction would provide such a loss to all the children that a potential wrongdoer would repeat the precipitating action at his peril. At any rate, the practice of stealing was greatly reduced following this reaction.

During their years of training, the kvutza children become very alert to their peers' opinions, on which they are dependent for virtually all their satisfactions. While they are growing up, this force is used to ensure conformity to the standards of the children's community. These standards may conflict with those of the adult community, resulting in behavior which seems wild and capricious to the adults. But adult members remark repeatedly on the suddenness with which, following their accession to formal membership at eighteen, children of the kvutza "mature," *i.e.*, learn to conform to adult standards. This is in contrast to the moshav where adolescence is a period of great stress extending over several years. Moshav children, brought up in the close-knit farm family under their parents' control, never seem to develop the great respect for public opinion characteristic of the kvutza.[15]

Supplementing migration and socialization practices are the day-to-day experiences of adult kvutza members. Quick and accurate response to public opinion enables the member to align his behavior with community standards, and thus to enhance his chances of attaining the acceptance and prestige which

---

15. For a detailed comparison of socialization practices in these types of settlements, see EISENSTADT, AGE GROUPS AND SOCIAL STRUCTURE (mimeographed in Jerusalem, 1951).

are needed for even small advantages. In the kvutza environment, one is re-warded for responding to the unfavorable reaction of his comrades when he talks too long in the Assembly, does not volunteer for emergency work service, wears inappropriate clothes, or debunks a kvutza celebration. Failure to respond has been known to result in serious difficulties, such as that ex-perienced by a teacher who so antagonized public opininon by declining to dig trenches during Israel's War of Independence that he was denied a requested change of job a full year later.

In the moshav, this kind of pressure is exerted less frequently and effective-ly, if for no other reason than that there are fewer gains for which the indi-vidual is dependent on the community. Near self-sufficiency in economic affairs makes it difficult for the moshav to exert informal control. Primary reliance is placed on sanctions such as fines or, in a few cases of economic failure, ex-pulsion from the settlement.

Thus several factors appear to contribute to the relatively greater power exercised by public opinion in the kvutza. It is difficult to estimate the effects of each of these in the absence of accurate knowledge concerning the values of immigrants and emigrants, as well as changes in the values of present residents since their time of settlement. Nevertheless, processes of selection, child training and adult experience were at work which might well be expected to result in kvutza members being more sensitive to public opinion than were moshav members.

This expectation is confirmed in the verbal reports of the members them-selves. A sample of adult members in both settlements were asked whether in the event of clash between their own views and the demands of public opinion they behaved in accordance with the former or the latter. Only one-third of the kvutza respondents said they would follow their own inclina-tions in such a case, while almost three-fifths of the moshav members said they would. Such a difference would have occurred by chance so infrequently that we are justified in considering it statistically significant.[16] These quanti-tative data provide confirmation of differences which had already been ob-served by ethnographic methods.

16.   Behavior in the Event of Conflict

	Kvutza		Moshav	
	N	%	N	%
Follow own inclinations	36	33	87	57
Follow public opinion	74	67	65	43
Total	110	100	152	100

$X^2 = 15.32$ $P < .001$

Four questions were asked, comprising a "Guttman scale." For a detailed description of this method see MEASUREMENT AND PREDICTION (Stouffer, ed. 1950). The writer had the benefit of Dr. Guttman's advice in the construction, pretesting, and administration of this scale. A ninety percent sample was obtained of the adult members, but only three-fourths of these answered all the questions on this scale. Though some sample bias may have resulted from these opinions, it would have to be extreme in order to invalidate these results.

Vicarious Learning:

If the effects of sanction were confined to the behavior of sanctionees, social control would be very difficult. Because people are able to learn from the experience of others, however, the control process is greatly facilitated. Such experience has been discussed in several disciplines, ranging from psychoanalytic theories on "identification" to jurisprudential discussions of deterrence. A definitive answer has yet to be found to the very important question as to *who* vicariously learns *what* from the observed experience of *whom.*

Our theoretical orientation suggests that vicarious learning depends on the extent to which an observer perceives himself similar to an observed actor. As perceived similarity increases, so also does the likelihood that the observer will have his tendencies increased for behavior which the actor has gainfully performed. At least two factors would thus appear requisite to vicarious learning: the observer must know of the behavior of another and its consequences, and he must perceive that actor as somewhat similar to himself.

In the kvutza, both of these conditions for vicarious learning are fulfilled to a very great degree within the informal control system. Intimacy in the kvutza, as noted, permits extensive observation of other members' experiences. Moreover, there is considerable evidence that kvutza members perceive themselves as "comrades" in a homogeneous group. Their perception of similarity may well be enhanced by the mere physical resemblance among members. Men are issued the same kind of clothes, and women wear rather similar ones; even their haircuts are given without much variation by one barber who visits the kvutza. But such factors only supplement the more basic similarities of life conditions, including work schedule, consumption, and leisure activities. In all of these, members are subject to fairly uniform controls, so that they experience gain when they consider themselves similar enough to their fellow members to learn from their experiences. These factors contribute to a strong "we" feeling, one of whose effects may well be to heighten vicarious learning in the kvutza. This feeling is not challenged, as in the moshav, by the distinctive customs of individual families.

The difference between the two settlements is reflected in the responses of the members when asked to construe the phrase "amongst us."[17] Ninety-five percent of the responding kvutza members stated that they referred to their entire community when they used this term. By contrast, more than half of all moshav respondents used the term in application to their families and fewer than a third used it to refer to the entire settlement. The kvutza thus appears to provide more of a "reference group"[18] for its members than does the moshav.[19]

---

17. Ninety percent of the adult members of both communities were sampled, and over eighty percent of the polled members responded to this question.

18. See the discussion of this concept by Merton & Kitt in CONTINUITIES IN SOCIAL RESEARCH, I: STUDIES IN THE SCOPE AND METHOD OF "THE AMERICAN SOLDIER" 40 (Merton & Lazarsfeld eds. 1950).

19. Of 124 kvutza respondents, 118 used the term to refer to the entire community.

This orientation sets kvutza members apart from the outside world, even from members of other collective settlements. This was reflected by the children of the settlement in holding themselves aloof from the children of other collectives, reminding each other, "We are from 'Orah.' "[20] In general, the attitude toward outsiders is one of sharper differentiation than is found in the moshav. This was manifested in the carefully correct or even suspicious manner in which kvutza members reacted to strangers, especially foreigners and Arabs, as against the tendency of moshav members to invite such persons into their homes.

NORMS

Every system of control consists of more than the simple ability to apply sanctions. In order to maximize their gain, reactors must know whether and how to react to different behaviors. By denoting given behavior as similar to a class of behaviors, reactors tend to evoke from themselves and from others the same reaction to the particular behavior as has been learned to the class.[21] Such a classification will tend to result in gain if the reaction to the class results in maximal gain, *and* if the particular behavior resembles the class in its social consequences (*i.e.*, both cause gain or both cause loss), *and* if the learned reaction to the class affects the tendency of the given behavior as it does the class.

The effectiveness of kvutza informal controls is enhanced by a system of norms classifying all behavior with reference to desirability. This system is detailed, generally unambiguous, applicable to wide, clearly defined segments of the population, and well known to the members. As a result it provides consistent guides for the application of sanction and at the same time forewarns potential sanctionees of the consequences of their acts. Such norms, found in every sphere of kvutza life, are particularly striking in economic matters.

Work activities in the kvutza are directed toward maximizing the production of agricultural goods and the performance of domestic services. Each able-bodied adult resident is expected to work in some unit, either an agricultural branch (*e.g.*, orchard, poultry, or sheep) or a domestic service (*e.g.*, kitchen, laundry, or school). Labor allocations are made by a Work Assignment Committee on the basis of economic requirements of each unit, ability of workers to meet those requirements, and lastly the preferences of each worker. Workers learn of their assignments either orally or by notice posted on the bulletin board. This assignment is understood to mean, unless otherwise specified, that the worker will report to the manager of the given unit

---

Only 49 of 157 moshav respondents used it in this way. $X^2 = 117.49$; $P < .001$. These differences would have occurred by chance less than one time in a thousand.

20. "Orah" is a fictitious name which has been substituted for the real name of the kvutza studied in order to preserve the anonymity of the members.

21. See the discussion of legal "reasoning by example" in LEVI, AN INTRODUCTION TO LEGAL REASONING (1949).

within a reasonable time (about fifteen minutes) after the morning bell has rung, and work there. except for breakfast, lunch, and siesta, until the evening bell signals the end of the working day. Some assignments (*e.g.*, nursery, dairy, trucking, and night watch) require special hours, but these are explicitly stated and the kvutza assigns a functionary to rouse such workers and notify them of the start of their workday. Illness constitutes the major reason for exemption from this norm, and all sick persons are expected to consult the resident community physician who decides whether and for how long the patient is to abstain from work.

Each worker is expected to cooperate with the individual recognized by all as the coordinator or manager of his unit. Usually such recognition is relatively spontaneous, based upon superior knowledge, skill, leadership ability, and seniority. When no single individual is clearly superior in these regards, the Economic Council recommends reassignments which bring about this result. As a consequence, the worker typically has someone to whom he turns for guidance whenever he is uncertain as to the correct course of action. On their part, managers, though exercising considerable discretion, are expected to turn to the Economic Council for guidance in significant decisions. Ultimately, the Council itself is responsible to the General Assembly. All kvutza members are expected to perform their various activities to the best of their individual abilities. These abilities are recognized to vary widely, but kvutza members maintain that a certain level of performance exists for each worker in a given kind of job. Though a worker's prestige varies with the height of this level, he may be well esteemed if he consistently meets even a low standard of performance. Since the level of performance is set by the worker's *better* performances, he is likely to be considered a violator of this very significant norm if he is erratic and frequently falls below his standard. In an economy which has abolished wages and private profit, these work norms are of great importance in maintaining production.

Consumption activities in the kvutza are also controlled with the aid of explicit general norms. Objectives which these are supposed to serve include distribution according to need, frugality, solidarity, and of course adequate sustenance of the population. Since differential need is very difficult to ascertain, the kvutza tendency has been to distribute scarce items equally, on the assumption that need is generally equal. Exceptions are made in instances where this is obviously not the case, for example, when youth, age, illness, or pregnancy furnishes grounds for special diet, housing, or medical care. Aside from these, however, consumption of scarce goods is supposed to be as nearly equal as possible. Adults are expected to eat together in the common dining hall at specified times. There they are served meals which are planned by the dietician with an eye toward fitting the budget adopted by the General Assembly. Crops drawn directly from the land are usually sufficiently abundant to permit unrestricted consumption, but other foods such as margarine, fish, meat, hard cheese, and eggs are distributed in limited equal quantities. Though the norms governing such consumption may be a mystery to new arrivals, members are fully aware of them. Occasionally questions arise as to the kinds of dishes for which a given serving may be exchanged, but these are authoritatively settled by the dietician. Similarly, clothes are expected to be issued equally except for differences of sex and size. Women are permitted a small degree of discretion in the selection of materials, but no one may exceed the ration and standard for a given sex, of such items as work shirts, work shoes, and sweaters. In housing, correct behavior is even less complicated: one is expected to live in the room assigned by the Housing Committee, whose discretion is limited by policies established in the General Assembly. Explicit general norms also cover such matters as participation in kvutza festivals, visiting of children by parents, and preservation of a minimal privacy in rooms.

Such a pervasive set of general norms may be of great aid for a system of social control. Its contribution to the system's effectiveness is dependent, however, on the uniformity of the effect of a given behavior, no matter who performs it, and on the uniformity with which a sanction tends to deter or encourage it. Kvutza goals and conditions result in a high degree of both kinds of uniformity in regard to the norms mentioned. Since the uniform effectiveness of kvutza public opinion as a sanction has already been discussed, our discussion will now concentrate on uniformity of effect of a given behavior.

Kvutza members want their society to survive and be productive. They have set up an economic system which requires diligent and cooperative work by all if it is to succeed. Any behavior which is deemed non-diligent and which does not appear to contribute to the required coordination of effort will be viewed as threatening loss to kvutza productivity. Such behavior would include failure to work at one's top ability and to comply with one's work assignment; failure in these respects would be interpreted as causing loss to the kvutza. Similarly, anyone who receives more than an equal share in food, clothes, or housing is threatening the goal of a "just society" and subjecting the other members to "relative deprivation."[22] While variations in the other direction—too much work or substandard consumption—are less of a cause for concern, they also seem to be a source of disturbance, perhaps because vicarious experience makes such behavior unpleasant to those who observe it. Whatever the reasons, strict compliance with these norms is generally considered desirable, while violation of them is typically viewed as a loss to the members as a whole.

One of the greatest weaknesses of kvutza controls arises from failure to specify the identity and special privileges of the high-prestige members.[23] Managers and old-timers are distinguished in fact from the ordinary workers

---

22. For development and use of this concept, see 1, 2 THE AMERICAN SOLDIER (Stouffer, ed. 1949).

23. See the discussion of this stratum in Rosenfeld, *Social Stratification in a "Classless" Society*, 16 AM. SOC. REV. 766 (1951). The picture given there is very similar to that observed in the kvutza studied, except for Rosenfeld's observations on the attitudes of the different strata toward institutional change.

and "simpletons" in the deference shown them and, within narrow limits, in the preference they may receive in housing, furniture, travel, and education for their children. Deviations from the general norms by the "important" people are less disturbing than if performed by ordinary members, since kvutza public opinion recognizes their special worth and power. But difficulties sometimes arise from uncertainty as to how important a given individual is and what privileges, if any, are due him.

Such problems tend to be minimized by a denial that important people are treated differently in any way, or that there is in fact a special managerial status. That an equalitarian society should be unwilling to recognize such privileges is not surprising. Material advantages given the important people are rationalized in terms of the norms and their accepted exceptions. For example, new housing units, built by the kvutza to accommodate an increased population, were made more elaborate than earlier ones by the inclusion of shower and toilet facilities. These units were designated from the first as "old-timers' housing," and it was explained that the increased age of this group made it difficult for them to use the central facilities. On closer questioning, however, it was revealed that these rooms were not intended for other inhabitants who were also advancing in years, namely, a few recent immigrants of middle-age and several resident parents of members. Though the physical need of such persons was at least as great as that of the old-timers, no one even considered the possibility that they should be given modern accommodations as permanent quarters. Actually the reason was a feeling of injustice that so much be given to people who had done so little for the kvutza, but this was never publicly articulated and the fiction prevailed that the distribution met the requirement of "equal or according to need." Accordingly, the behavior, which was in fact a non-disturbing deviation from the general norm, was classified as acceptable behavior and was not negatively sanctioned as were other deviations from the norm.

In most areas, however, norms have been developed which clearly distinguish acceptable from disturbing behavior in a given situation for a clearly delimited category of persons. Ambiguities which arise are usually brought before the General Assembly and are conclusively resolved by its decision. Sometimes the kvutza reaches a consensus informally. The resultant norms are applied with a high degree of certainty. Though for our purposes the reasons need not be spelled out, it would appear that kvutza norms can be unambiguous and simple because behavioral alternatives and variations are sharply limited and because a homogenous population is in general agreement in distinguishing desirable from undesirable behavior among these clear and limited alternatives.

Moshav norms, by contrast, are far less explicit, uniformly applied, or generally agreed upon. While it is important that a farmer manage his own holdings effectively and be a good neighbor, the exact pattern of actions by which this can be accomplished has never been authoritatively laid down. In most

areas, the individual is likely to have his own ideas about the proper behavior in a given circumstance. On particular occasions involving the duty
to aid one's sick neighbor, cooperation in the use of machinery, and a member's
violation of State ration controls, widespread difference of opinion was discerned among moshav members. This difference was partly attributed to the
influence on each member of such factors as the effect of the particular behavior on his own economic interest; his relations with the actor in question;
and his conception of the responsibility owed to the moshav by its members.

Such crucial questions as property relations in the family and between
neighbors are still being deliberated and moshav members vary widely in their
views on such matters. The problem of succession is just beginning to arise
with regularity, and its importance and difficulty for a village with limited,
indivisible and inalienable farmsteads may hardly be over-estimated. Perhaps
a uniform set of norms will be evolved over a period of time to deal with
such problems, or perhaps the problems, especially concerning property, defy
informal concensus. At any rate, for the present, there is little agreement.
It is small wonder, then, that the moshav system of informal controls has
been supplemented by a specialized group of deliberators able to make norms
and to ensure their sanction by legal means.

THE EFFECTS OF PRIOR EXPERIENCE

Those who perceive pertinent behavior and are able to apply effective
sanctions must do so frequently, vigorously, and speedily. The likelihood that
they will is dependent on *past* experiences with these and alternative reactions. A given sanction is likely to be so applied at a given time if it has
previously been followed by gain and if competing reactions have not. The
relative gain which has previously followed a given sanction is a function, at
that earlier time, of the optimality of norms [24] and the capacity of the
sanction to impose the impact needed. Sanction impact, in turn, depends on
information, implementation, magnitude of gain or loss, and vicarious learning
at that earlier time, and on the then extant reaction tendencies. Reaction
tendencies depend in turn on preceding experience and therefore on all the
other factors mentioned as they existed at a still earlier period. Thus, the impact of a given sanction is dependent on its previous impact, in a way which
renders the entire history of that sanction significant for the understanding
of a current control system. To summarize this formally: the impact of a
particular sanction, being affected by frequency, vigor, and speed with which
it is applied, is an increasing function of the reactors' previous experiences of
gain following the use of this sanction in similar situations, and a decreasing
function of the reactors' previous experiences of gain following the use of
competing reactions in similar situations.

---

24. An optimal norm is defined as one which produces the maximum reduction of
disturbance.

Tendency toward Informal Sanction:

As far as could be ascertained, the conditions which promoted effective informal control existed from the first or arose early in the history of the kvutza. Since it started out as a small settlement with a homogeneous population, it was, if anything, ever more of a primary group during its formative years than at present. There is sufficient evidence in reports of old-timers to indicate that pertinent behavior was readily perceived, that public opinion was an easily implemented and effective sanction, and that unambiguous norms defined the circumstances under which such sanctions should be employed. There were, to be sure, instances where these controls failed to work, as for example in regard to the use of spending money. An early norm permitted each member to take as much money from a common fund as he felt he needed for personal expenses. In practice this is said to have resulted in low expenditures by the "idealistic" members and disproportionately high ones by those with a weaker sense of social responsibility. When public opinion proved incapable of controlling this socially disturbing behavior, the General Assembly modified the norm to stipulate a yearly amount for each member's personal use. Clarification of the distinction between acceptable and disturbing behavior in this area permitted the effective application of negative sanction to the latter, with the result that few members exceeded their allotted amount thereafter. The desired result was achieved by changes which increased the effectiveness of informal sanction rather than substituting legal controls for them.

Because effective informal control was achieved in the kvutza, the tendency for its subsequent use was increased. That this tendency was high is indicated not only by the many successful instances of its use, but perhaps even more by the persistence with which it was employed on the rare occasions when it failed. Most striking among the illustrations of this is the case of a woman who was considered by the entire kvutza to be anti-social. Soon after her arrival she began to behave very aggressively, quarreling with all her fellow workers in the kitchen and even striking them. Though the use of violence against a fellow member was shocking to the other members, only the usual mild sanctions were at first applied. For some reason, however, social disapproval failed to deter the woman. She continued the same course of behavior through seven years, during which she was subjected to more vigorous informal controls and was at the same time denied formal membership. But she was never subjected to force, expulsion, or even to material disadvantage. Only during her eighth year in the kvutza was a different type of sanction directed against her: she was given no work assignment and was deprived of the opportunity to work for the kvutza. After a year in which her isolation was thus increased, she bowed to the pressure and left the kvutza. Whether the new sanction be designated informal or legal, it is clear that it was an alternative to the traditional informal sanctions of public opinion. That it was employed only after seven years of persistent exercise of the traditional sanctions is striking indication of the firmness with which the latter were established.

In the moshav, the tendency to exercise informal controls seems much less powerful. This is not surprising in view of previously described conditions which would minimize the effectiveness of such sanctions. Though these conditions are described as existing at the time of the study, they are traceable to the economic structure of the moshav, and thus it is reasonable to assume that they also existed at the inauguration of the community. If so, they preceded the rise of legal controls which evolved gradually during the first twenty years of the settlement's history. During this period and subsequently, informal controls have regularly been tried, but have been ineffective, presumably because of inadequate information, implementation, sanction magnitude, and norms. In the course of time, members have learned that informal controls are ineffective; the resultant lowered tendency to invoke these controls, resulting in even less frequent and less vigorous attempts to use them, has further diminished their effectiveness.[25] This attitude toward informal controls was exemplified by moshav reaction to the prank of a group of adolescents who raided a melon patch and openly ate the stolen melons. Indignation ran high because the melons had been specially cultivated for the wedding feast to be given in honor of the marriage of the farmer's daughter. Failing action by the Judiciary Committee, the feeling prevailed that there was "nothing at all to do" about it. Said one member, "If you scold those fellows, they laugh at you." So on the informal level, no serious attempt was undertaken to exert effective control.

Competing Reaction Tendencies:

Infrequent and non-vigorous exertion of informal sanctions in the moshav may result in part from the competition of legal controls as an effective alternative. It is, of course, impossible to explain the original occurrence of legal controls in these terms, but once they had become established, their success as a competing reaction could have been expected to reduce the impact of informal sanctions. Within the kvutza, there was no comparable history of legal controls which might have constituted a competing alternative to the prevailing system. Free from such competition,[26] the impact of informal sanctions could have been expected to continue without abatement.

---

25. This appears to be an instance of what has been described as the "self-fulfilling prophecy," MERTON, SOCIAL THEORY AND SOCIAL STRUCTURE 179-95 (1949), although the "prophecy" is here taken not as the independent variable, but simply as a reflection of previous failure and low tendency.

26. Another type of competition comes from other reactions which typically exert neither legal nor informal controls and may therefore be designated non-control reactions. Amongst these, two of particular interest are withdrawal from interaction and modification of values. In the kvutza, withdrawal from interaction is very difficult except through emigration. As we have seen, this occurs more frequently in the kvutza than in the moshav. If anything, by removing those individuals who were disposed toward non-control reactions, informal controls were strengthened and not weakened. On the other hand, kvutza members often meet disturbance by a modification of values. Some behavior which is initially thought likely to cause social loss—*e.g.*, demand for individual radios—not

Conclusion

Several factors have been discussed with reference to their effect on social control. The kvutza was characterized by a number of conditions which, our theory suggests, engender a more effective informal control system. Presence of these factors, and the effective controls which they produced, was interpreted as a partial explanation for the failure of the kvutza to develop a legal control system. By contrast, the moshav did not possess these characteristics to the same degree as did the kvutza and accordingly failed to develop an effective informal control system. The development of legal institutions in the moshav is partially explicable in these terms. Law has thus been seen to develop where disturbing behavior occurred which was not as adequately controlled informally as it could be with the aid of legal controls. If a similar process exists in the United States, its accurate description should contribute to the prediction and evaluation of our own legislative and judicial decisions.

---

infrequently comes to be accepted as socially gainful. In any event, since they are usually in competition with both informal and legal controls, the strength of such non-control reactions as modification of values and withdrawal from interaction generally fails to explain the form of control in a given community.

[20]

THE OVEN BIRD'S SONG: INSIDERS, OUTSIDERS, AND PERSONAL INJURIES IN AN AMERICAN COMMUNITY*

DAVID M. ENGEL**

In "Sander County" Illinois, concerns about litigiousness in the local population tended to focus on personal injury suits, although such cases were very rarely brought. This article explores the roots of these concerns in the ideology of the rural community and in the reactions of many residents to social, cultural, and economic changes that created a pervasive sense of social disintegration and loss. Personal injury claims are contrasted with contract actions, which were far more numerous yet were generally viewed with approval and did not give rise to perceptions of litigiousness or greed. The distinction is explained in terms of changing conceptions of the community itself and in terms of the problematic relationships between "insiders" and "outsiders" in Sander County.

I. INTRODUCTION

Although it is generally acknowledged that law is a vital part of culture and of the social order, there are times when

---

* The title refers to Robert Frost's poem "The Oven Bird," which describes a response to the perception of disintegration and decay not unlike the response that is the subject of this paper:

There is a singer everyone has heard,
Loud, a mid-summer and a mid-wood bird,
Who makes the solid tree trunks sound again.
He says that leaves are old and that for flowers
Mid-summer is to spring as one to ten.
He says the early petal-fall is past
When pear and cherry bloom went down in showers
On sunny days a moment overcast;
And comes that other fall we name the fall.
He says the highway dust is over all.
The bird would cease and be as other birds
But that he knows in singing not to sing.
The question that he frames in all but words
Is what to make of a diminished thing.

From *The Poetry of Robert Frost*, edited by Edward Connery Lathem. Copyright 1916, © 1969 by Holt, Rinehart and Winston. Copyright 1944 by Robert Frost. Reprinted by permission of Holt, Rinehart and Winston, Publishers.

** I am deeply grateful to the residents of "Sander County" for their generous participation in this study. I would also like to thank the following

552   THE OVEN BIRD'S SONG

the invocation of formal law is viewed as an *anti*-social act and as a contravention of established cultural norms. Criticism of what is seen as an overuse of law and legal institutions often reveals less about the quantity of litigation at any given time than about the interests being asserted or protected through litigation and the kinds of individuals or groups involved in cases that the courts are asked to resolve. Periodic concerns over litigation as a "problem" in particular societies or historical eras can thus draw our attention to important underlying conflicts in cultural values and changes or tensions in the structure of social relationships.

In our own society at present, perhaps no category of litigation has produced greater public criticism than personal injuries. The popular culture is full of tales of feigned or exaggerated physical harms, of spurious whiplash suits, ambulance-chasing lawyers, and exorbitant claims for compensation. Scholars, journalists, and legal professionals, voicing concern with crowded dockets and rising insurance costs, have often shared the perception that personal injury litigation is a field dominated by overly litigious plaintiffs and by trigger-happy attorneys interested only in their fee (Seymour, 1973: 177; Tondel, 1976: 547; Perham, 1977; Rosenberg, 1977: 154; Taylor, 1981; Gest *et al.*, 1982; Greene, 1983).

To the mind agitated by such concerns, Sander County (a pseudonym) appears to offer a quiet refuge. In this small, predominantly rural county in Illinois, personal injury litigation rates were low in comparison to other major categories of litigation[1] and were apparently somewhat lower

friends and colleagues who read and commented on this article at one stage or another in its development: Richard L. Abel, James B. Atleson, Guyora Binder, Donald Black, Marc Galanter, Fred Konefsky, Virginia Leary, Richard O. Lempert, Felice J. Levine, John Henry Schlegel, Eric H. Steele, Robert J. Steinfeld, and Barbara Yngvesson. I am also grateful to Linda Kosinski for her skill and patience in typing and retyping the manuscript.

The research on which this article is based was supported by the National Science Foundation under Grant No. SOC 77-11654 and by the American Bar Foundation. Opinions, findings, and conclusions are those of the author and not of the supporting organizations.

    [1] By "litigation" I mean simply the filing of a formal complaint in the civil trial court, even if no further adversarial processes occur. The annual litigation rate for personal injuries was 1.45 cases filed per 1,000 population as compared to 13.7 contract cases (mostly collection matters), 3.62 property-related cases (mostly landlord-tenant matters), and 11.74 family-related cases (mostly divorces). All litigation rates are based on the combined civil filings for 1975 and 1976 in the Sander County Court. Population figures are based on the 1970 census and are therefore somewhat understated. That is, the actual litigation rates for 1975-1976 are probably lower than those given here.

than the personal injury rates in other locations as well.[2] Yet Sander County residents displayed a deep concern with and an aversion toward this particular form of "litigious behavior" despite its rarity in their community.[3]

Those who sought to enforce personal injury claims in Sander County were characterized by their fellow residents as "very greedy," as "quick to sue," as "people looking for the easy buck," and as those who just "naturally sue and try to get something [for] . . . life's little accidents." One minister describing the local scene told me, "Everybody's going to court. That's the thing to do, because a lot of people see a chance to make money." A social worker, speaking of local perceptions of personal injury litigation, particularly among the older residents of Sander County, observed: "Someone sues every time you turn around. Sue happy, you hear them say. Sue happy." Personal injury plaintiffs were viewed in Sander County as people who made waves and as troublemakers. Even members of the community who occupied positions of prestige or respect could not escape criticism if they brought personal

---

[2] McIntosh reports a rate of approximately 6 tort actions per 1,000 population in the St. Louis Circuit Court in 1970. He does not state what proportion of these involved personal injuries (McIntosh, 1980-81: 832). Friedman and Percival (1976: 281-82) report 2.80 and 1.87 cases filed per 1,000 population in the Alameda and San Benito Superior Courts (respectively) in 1970 under the combined categories of "auto accidents" and "other personal injuries." The two California courts had original jurisdiction only for claims of $5,000 or more, however, while the Sander County figures include personal injury claims of all amounts. Friedman and Percival do not indicate what proportion of the auto accident cases involved personal injuries as opposed to property damage only. Statewide data for California and New York, compiled by the National Center for State Courts (1979: 49, 51) for tort cases filed in 1975, also tend to indicate litigation rates higher than Sander County's. However, these aggregate litigation rates are understated in that they exclude filings from smaller courts of limited jurisdiction in both states and are overstated in that they fail to separate personal injury cases from other tort actions. Litigation rates for tort cases filed per 1,000 population in 1975 are: California, 3.55; and New York, 2.21 (but in 1977, when additional lower court dockets were included in the survey of tort cases filed, the rate reported for New York more than doubled to 4.47; see National Center for State Courts, 1982: 61). In comparing the Sander County litigation rates to those in other cities or states, it should also be remembered that, because Sander County was quite small, the *absolute number* of personal injury actions filed in the county court was also very small compared to more urban areas.

[3] I use the term "community" somewhat loosely in this discussion to mean the county seat of Sander County and the surrounding farmlands. Since Sander County is rather small, this takes in most of the county. There are a handful of very small towns elsewhere in the county. Although they are not far from the county seat and are linked to it in many ways, it is probably stretching things to consider them part of a single "community." I should add that the problem of defining the term "community" as a subject of empirical study has vexed social scientists for many years, and I aspired to no conceptual breakthrough in this regard. My interest was in finding a research site where the jurisdiction of the court was roughly congruent with a social unit comprising a set of meaningful interactions and relationships.

554   THE OVEN BIRD'S SONG

injury cases to court. When a minister filed a personal injury
suit in Sander County after having slipped and fallen at a
school, there were, in the words of one local observer:

> [A] lot of people who are resentful for it, because . . .
> he chose to sue. There's been, you know, not hard
> feelings, just some strange intangible things. . . .

How can one explain these troubled perceptions of
personal injury litigation in a community where personal injury
actions were in fact so seldom brought? The answer lies partly
in culturally-conditioned ideas of what constitutes an injury
and how conflicts over injuries should be handled. The answer
is also found in changes that were occurring in the social
structure of Sander County at the time of this study and in
challenges to the traditional order that were being raised by
newly arrived "outsiders." The local trial court was potentially
an important battleground in the clash of cultures, for it could
be called on to recognize claims that traditional norms
stigmatized in the strongest possible terms.[4]

II. SOCIAL CHANGES AND THE SENSE OF COMMUNITY

Sander County in the late 1970s was a society that was
strongly rooted in its rural past yet undergoing economic and
social changes of major proportions. It was a small county
(between 20,000 and 30,000 population in the 1970s), with more
than half its population concentrated in its county seat and the
rest in several much smaller towns and rural areas.
Agriculture was still central to county life. Sander County had
10 percent more of its land in farms in the mid-1970s than did
the state of Illinois as a whole, but the number of farms in
Sander County had decreased by more than one-third over the
preceding twenty years while their average size had grown by
almost half. Rising costs, land values, and taxes had been
accompanied by an increase in the mechanization of agriculture
in Sander County, and the older, smaller farming operations
were being rapidly transformed. At the same time, a few large
manufacturing plants had brought blue collar employees from
other areas to work (but not always to live) in Sander County.
Also, a local canning plant had for many years employed
seasonal migrant workers, many of whom were Latinos. In

---

4 Hostility towards personal injury litigation as a form of "hyperlexis"
may also have been influenced in Sander County by mass media treatment of
this form of legal claim. Yet the attitudes and antagonisms I describe had deep
roots in the culture of Sander County itself as well as in the popular culture of
the country as a whole. A critical appraisal of the hyperlexis literature, which
parallels this discussion in some respects, is found in Galanter (1983).

recent years, however, a variety of "outsiders" had come to stay permanently in Sander County, and the face of the local society was gradually changing.

To some extent these changes had been deliberately planned by local leaders, for it was thought that the large manufacturing plants would revitalize the local economy. Yet from the beginning there had also been a sense of foreboding. In the words of one older farmer:

> A guy that I used to do business with told me when he saw this plant coming in down here that he felt real bad for the community. He said, that's gonna be the end of your community, he said, because you get too many people in that don't have roots in anything. And I didn't think too much about it at the time, but I can understand what he was talking about now. I know that to some extent, at least, this is true. Not that there haven't been some real good people come in, I don't mean that. But I think you get quite a number of a certain element that you've never had before.

Others were more blunt about the "certain element" that had entered Sander County: union members, southerners and southwesterners, blacks, and Latinos. One long-time rural resident told us, "I think there's too many Commies around. I think this country takes too many people in, don't you? . . . That's why this country's going to the dogs." Many Sander County residents referred nostalgically to the days when they could walk down Main Street and see none but familiar faces. Now there were many strangers. An elderly woman from a farming family, who was struggling to preserve her farm in the face of rising taxes and operating costs, spoke in troubled tones of going into the post office and seeing Spanish-speaking workers mailing locally-earned money to families outside the country. "This," she said, "I don't like." Another woman, also a long-time resident, spoke of the changing appearance of the town:

> [It was] lots different than it is right now. For one thing, I think we knew everybody in town. If you walked uptown you could speak to every single person on the street. It just wasn't at all like it is today. Another thing, the stores were different. We have so many places now that are foreign, Mexican, and health spas, which we're not very happy about, most of us. My mother was going uptown here a year ago and didn't feel very well when she got up to State Street. But she just kept going, and I thought it was terrible because the whole north side of town was the kind of place that you wouldn't want to go into for information

or for help. Mostly because we've not grown up with
an area where there were any foreign people at all.

There was also in the late 1970s a pervasive sense of a
breakdown in the traditional relationships and reciprocities
that had characterized life in Sander County. As one elderly
farmer told me:

> It used to be I could tell you any place in Sander
> County where it was, but I can't now because I don't
> know who lives on them. . . . And as I say in the last
> 20 years people don't change work like they used to—
> or in the last 30 years. Everybody's got big equipment,
> they do all their own work so they don't have to
> change labor. Like years ago . . . why you had about
> 15 or 20 farmers together doing the exchange and all.

Many Sander County residents with farming backgrounds had
warm memories of the harvest season, when groups of
neighbors got together to share work and food:

> When we had the threshing run, the dining room table
> it stretched a full 17 feet of the dining room, and guys
> would come in like hungry wolves, you know, at
> dinner time and supper again the same thing. . . .
> And they'd fire the engine up and have it ready to
> start running by 7:00. . . . You know, it was quite a
> sight to see that old steam engine coming down the
> road. I don't know, while I never want to be doing it
> again, I still gotta get kind of a kick out of watching a
> steam engine operate.

And all could remember socializing with other farming families
on Saturday evenings during the summertime. In the words of
two long-time farmers:

> A: Well, on Saturday night they used to come into
>   town, and the farmers would be lined up along the
>   sidewalk with an ice cream cone or maybe a glass
>   of beer or something. . . .
> B: If you met one to three people, you'd get all the
>   news in the neighborhood. . . .
> A: If you go downtown now, anytime, I doubt if you'll
>   see half a dozen people that you know. I mean to
>   what you say sit down and really, really know
>   them.
> B: You practically knew everybody.
> A. That's right, but you don't now.
> B: No, no, no. If you go down Saturday night . . .
> A: Everything is dead.

III. THE STUDY

I shall argue in this article that perceptions of personal
injury claims in Sander County were strongly influenced by

these social changes as local residents experienced them and by the sense that traditional relationships and exchanges in the community were gradually disintegrating.[5] I cannot say that the frequent condemnation of personal injury litigation elsewhere in the United States is linked to a similar set of social processes, but investigation in other settings may disclose some parallels. The sense of community can take many forms in American society, and when members of a community feel threatened by change, their response may be broadly similar to the kind of response I describe here.

My discussion is based on fieldwork conducted from 1978 to 1980. Besides doing background research and immersing myself in the community and in the workings of the Sander County Court, I collected data for the study in three ways: (1) A sample of civil case files opened in 1975 and 1976 was drawn and analyzed.[6] (2) Plaintiffs and defendants in a subsample of these civil cases were contacted and interviewed in broad-ranging, semi-structured conversations.[7] (3) Strategically placed "community observers" were identified and interviewed at length. These were individuals who had particular insights into different groups, settings, occupations, or activities in the community.[8] Discussions with them touched on various aspects of the community, including the ways in which the relationships, situations, and problems that might give rise to litigated cases were handled when the court was not used. The insights derived from the community observer

---

[5] The sense of social change and disintegration in Sander County helped crystallize a set of values opposed to personal injury litigation. These values were almost certainly rooted in long established norms, but the targets of their expression and the intensity with which they were asserted may have been new. This article focuses on how and why such values came to be expressed and acutely felt in the late 1970s by many Sander County residents. See note 19 *infra*.

[6] A 20% sample was taken for the years 1975-1976 within each of 12 civil categories mandated by the Administrative Office of the Illinois Courts: (1) Law (claim over $15,000), (2) Law (claim $15,000 or less), (3) Chancery, (4) Miscellaneous Remedies, (5) Eminent Domain, (6) Estates, (7) Tax, (8) Municipal Corporations, (9) Mental Health, (10) Divorce, (11) Family, (12) Small Claims. After the sample was drawn, the cases were reclassified into the substantive categories referred to throughout this article.

[7] Parties in 66 cases were interviewed. Wherever possible, all parties to each case were included. Particular attention was given to the individuals themselves, the relationship between them, and to the origin, development, and outcome of each case.

[8] Among the 71 community observers were judges, lawyers, teachers, ministers, farmers, a beautician, a barber, city and county officials, a funeral parlor operator, youth workers, social service workers, various "ordinary citizens" from different segments of the community, a union steward, a management representative, agricultural extension workers, doctors, a newspaper reporter, the members of a rescue squad, and others.

interviews thus provided a broader social and cultural context for the insights derived from the court-based research.

Personal injuries were one of four major substantive topics selected to receive special attention in this study.[9] It soon became apparent, however, that personal injuries were viewed quite differently from the other topics, and the differences appeared to be related to the fundamental social changes that were taking place in Sander County. Focusing on personal injuries in this article makes it possible to examine the role played by formal law in mediating relationships between different groups in a changing society and to consider why the rare use of formal legal institutions for certain purposes can evoke strong concern and reaction in a community. The answer, I shall suggest, lies in the ideological responses of long-time residents of Sander County whose values and assumptions were subjected to profound challenges by what they saw as the intrusion of newcomers into their close-knit society.

IV. INJURIES AND INDIVIDUALISM

For many of the residents of Sander County, exposure to the risk of physical injury was simply an accepted part of life. In a primarily agricultural community, which depended on hard physical work and the use of dangerous implements and machinery, such risks were unavoidable. Farmers in Sander County told many stories of terrible injuries caused by hazardous farming equipment, vehicles of different kinds, and other dangers that were associated with their means of obtaining a livelihood. There was a feeling among many in Sander County—particularly among those from a farming background—that injuries were an ever-present possibility, although prudent persons could protect themselves much of the time by taking proper precautions.

It would be accurate to characterize the traditional values associated with personal injuries in Sander County as individualistic, but individualism may be of at least two types. A rights-oriented individualism is consistent with an aggressive demand for compensation (or other remedies) when important interests are perceived to have been violated. By contrast, an individualism emphasizing self-sufficiency and personal responsibility rather than rights is consistent with the expectation that people should ordinarily provide their own

---

[9] The other three substantive areas were injuries to reputation, contracts, and marital problems.

protection against injuries and should personally absorb the consequences of harms they fail to ward off.[10]

It is not clear why the brand of individualism that developed over the years in Sander County emphasized self-sufficiency rather than rights and remedies, but with respect to personal injuries at least, there can be no doubt that this had occurred. If the values associated with this form of individualism originated in an earlier face-to-face community dominated by economically self-sufficient farmers and merchants, they remained vitally important to many of the long-time Sander County residents even at the time of this study. For them, injuries were viewed in relation to the victims, their fate, and their ability to protect themselves. Injuries were not viewed in terms of conflict or potential conflict between victims and other persons, nor was there much sympathy for those who sought to characterize the situation in such terms. To the traditional individualists of Sander County, transforming a personal injury into a claim against someone else was an attempt to escape responsibility for one's own actions. The psychology of contributory negligence and assumption of risk had deep roots in the local culture. The critical fact of personal injuries in most cases was that the victims probably could have prevented them if they had been more careful, even if others were to some degree at fault. This fact alone is an important reason why it was considered inappropriate for injured persons to attempt to transform their misfortune into a demand for compensation or to view it as an occasion for interpersonal conflict.

Attitudes toward money also help explain the feelings of long-time residents of Sander County toward personal injury claimants. While there might be sympathy for those who suffered such injuries, it was considered highly improper to try to "cash in" on them through claims for damages. Money was viewed as something one acquired through long hours of hard work, not by exhibiting one's misfortunes to a judge or jury or other third party, even when the injuries were clearly caused by the wrongful behavior of another. Such attitudes were reinforced by the pervasive sense of living in what had long been a small and close-knit community. In such a community, potential plaintiffs and defendants are likely to know each other, at least by reputation, or to have acquaintances in

---

[10] This distinction between the two types of individualism emerged from an ongoing dialogue with Fred Konefsky, whose contribution to this conceptualization I gratefully acknowledge.

common. It is probable that they will interact in the future, if not directly then through friends and relatives. In these circumstances it is, at best, awkward to sue or otherwise assert a claim. In addition, in a small community one cannot hide the fact of a suit for damages, and the disapproving attitudes of others are likely to be keenly felt. Thus, I was frequently assured that local residents who were mindful of community pressures generally reacted to cases of personal injury, even those that might give rise to liability in tort, in a "level-headed" and "realistic" way. By this it was meant that they would not sue or even, in most cases, demand compensation extrajudicially from anyone except, perhaps, their own insurance companies.[11]

Given the negative views that local juries adopted toward personal injury cases, terms such as "realistic" for those who avoided litigation were indeed well chosen. Judges, lawyers, and laypersons all told me that civil trial juries in the county reflected—and thus reinforced—the most conservative values and attitudes toward personal injury litigation. Awards were very low and suspicion of personal injury plaintiffs was very high. A local insurance adjuster told me:

> [T]he jury will be people from right around here that are, a good share of them will be farmers, and they've been out there slaving away for every penny they've got and they aren't about to just give it away to make that free gift to anybody.

And one of the leading local trial lawyers observed:

> [T]here's a natural feeling, what's this son of a bitch doing here? Why is he taking our time? Why is he

---

[11] I heard of only a few cases where injured persons negotiated compensatory payments from the liability insurance of the party responsible for their harm. In these cases expectations (or demands) appeared to be modest. One involved a woman who lived on a farm. When visiting a neighbor's house, she fell down the basement stairs because of a negligently installed door, fractured her skull, was unconscious for three days, and was in intensive care for five days. As a result of the accident she suffered a permanent loss of her sense of smell and a substantial (almost total) impairment of her sense of taste. Her husband, a successful young farmer, told me that their own insurance did not cover the injury. Their neighbor had liability insurance, which paid only $1000 (the hospital bills alone were approximately $2500). Nevertheless, they never considered seeking greater compensation from their neighbor or the neighbor's insurance company:

> We were thankful that she recovered as well as she did. . . . We never considered a lawsuit there at all. I don't know what other people would have done in the case. Possibly that insurance company would have paid the total medical if we would have just, well, I have a brother who is an attorney, could have just wrote them a letter maybe. But, I don't know, we just didn't do it, that's all.

Further discussion of the role of insurance in the handling of personal injuries in Sander County appears in the next section.

trying to look for something for nothing? . . . So I've got to overcome that. That's a natural prejudice in a small [community], they don't have that natural prejudice in Cook County. But you do have it out here. So first I've got to sell the jury on the fact that this man's tried every way or this woman's tried every way to get justice and she couldn't. And they now come to you for their big day. . . . And then you try like hell to show that they're one of you, they've lived here and this and that.

The prospects for trying a personal injury case before a local jury, he concluded, were so discouraging that, "If I can figure out a way not to try a case in [this] county for injury, I try to."

Where there was no alternative as to venue, potential plaintiffs typically resigned themselves to nonjudicial settlements without any thought of litigation. And, as I have already suggested, for many in the community the possibility of litigation was not considered in any case. One woman I spoke with had lost her child in an automobile accident. She settled the case for $12,000 without filing a claim, yet she was sure that this amount was much less than she could have obtained through a lawsuit. She told me that since she and her family knew they were going to stay permanently in the community, the pressure of the local value system foreclosed the possibility of taking the matter to court:

> One of the reasons that I was extremely hesitant to sue was because of the community pressure. . . . Local people in this community are not impressed when you tell them that you're involved in a lawsuit. . . . That really turns them off. . . . They're not impressed with people who don't earn their own way. And that's taking money that they're not sure that you deserve.

Others had so internalized this value system that they followed its dictates even when community pressures did not exist. A doctor told me that one of his patients was seriously burned during a trip out of state when an airline stewardess spilled hot coffee on her legs, causing permanent discoloration of her skin. This woman refused to contact a lawyer and instead settled directly with the airline for medical expenses and the cost of the one-week vacation she had missed. Regarding the possibility of taking formal legal action to seek a more substantial award, she said simply, "We don't do that." This same attitude may help to explain the apparent reluctance of local residents to assert claims against other potential defendants from outside Sander County, such as negligent drivers or businesses or manufacturers.

Thus, if we consider the range of traditional responses to
personal injuries in Sander County, we find, first of all, a great
deal of self-reliant behavior. Injured persons typically
responded to injuries without taking any overt action, either
because they did not view the problem in terms of a claim
against or conflict with another person or because membership
in a small, close-knit community inhibited them from asserting
a claim that would be socially disapproved. Some sought
compensation through direct discussions with the other party,
but such behavior was considered atypical. When sympathy or
advice was sought, many turned to friends, neighbors, relatives,
and physicians. The County Health Department, the mayor,
and city council representatives also reported that injured
persons occasionally sought them out, particularly when the
injuries were caused by hazards that might endanger others. In
such cases, the goal was generally to see the hazard removed
for the benefit of the public rather than to seek compensation
or otherwise advance personal interests.

V. INSURING AGAINST INJURIES

Persons who had been injured often sought compensation
from their own health and accident insurance without even
considering the possibility of a claim against another party or
another insurance company. As a local insurance adjuster told
me:

> We have some people that have had their kid injured
> on our insured's property, and they were not our
> insured. And we call up and offer to pay their bills,
> because our insured has called and said my kid Tommy
> cracked that kid over the head with a shovel and they
> hauled him off to the hospital. And I called the people
> and say we have medical coverage and they are
> absolutely floored, some of them, that it never even
> crossed their minds. They were just going to turn it in
> to their own little insurance, their health insurance,
> and not do anything about it whatsoever, especially if
> [Tommy's parents] are close friends. . . .

By moving quickly to pay compensation in such cases before
claims could arise, this adjuster believed that she prevented
disputes and litigation. It helped, too, that the adjuster and the
parties to an accident, even an automobile accident, usually
knew each other:

> In Chicago, all those people don't know the guy next
> door to them, much less the guy they had the wreck
> with. And right here in town, if you don't know the
> people, you probably know their neighbor or some of

> their family or you can find out real quick who they
> are or where they are.

The contrast between injuries in a face-to-face community and
in a metropolis like Chicago was drawn in explicit terms:

> I think things are pretty calm and peaceful as, say,
> compared to Chicago. Now I have talked to some of
> the adjusters in that area from time to time and I
> know, well, and we have our own insureds that go in
> there and get in an accident in Chicago, and we'll have
> a lawsuit or at least have an attorney . . . on the claim
> within a day or maybe two days of the accident even
> happening. Sometimes our insured has not any more
> than called back and said I've had a wreck but I don't
> even know who it was with. And before you can do
> anything, even get a police report or anything, why
> you'll get a letter from the attorney. And that would
> never, that rarely ever happens around here.

This adjuster estimated that over the past 15 years, her
office had been involved in no more than 10 automobile-related
lawsuits, an extraordinarily low number compared to the
frequency of such cases in other jurisdictions.[12] Of course, once
an insurance company has paid compensation to its insured, it
may exercise its right of subrogation against the party that
caused the accident, and one might expect insurance companies
to be unaffected by local values opposing the assertion or
litigation of injury claims. It is not entirely clear why
insurance companies, like individuals, seldom brought personal
injury actions in Sander County, but there are some clues. This
particular adjuster, who had grown up in Sander County,
shared the local value system. Although she did not decide
whether to bring suit as a subrogee, she may well have affected
the decisions of her central office by her own perceptions and
by her handling of the people and documents in particular
cases. Furthermore, her insurance company was connected to
the Farm Bureau, a membership organization to which most
local farmers belonged. The evident popularity of this
insurance carrier in Sander County (over 75 percent of the
eligible farm families were estimated to be members of the
Farm Bureau; it is not known how many members carried the

---

12 In Sander County as a whole, the litigation rate for automobile-related
personal injury cases in 1975-76 was 0.88 cases each year per 1,000 population.
For *all* automobile-related tort actions, including those where there was no
personal injury claim, the litigation rate was 1.87 cases per 1,000 population.
In the absence of reliable or meaningful comparative data, it is difficult to say
how low or high these county-wide rates are; but my hunch is that these are
rather low for a jurisdiction in which no-fault approaches were *not* used for
motor vehicle cases.

Law and Society

insurance, but the percentage was apparently high) meant that
injuries in many cases may have involved two parties covered
by the same insurance company.

Occasionally, an insurance company did bring suit in the
name of its insured, but given the unsympathetic attitudes of
local juries, such lawsuits seldom met with success in Sander
County.   The adjuster mentioned above told me of a farm
worker from Oklahoma who was harvesting peas for a local
cannery. He stopped to lie down and rest in the high grass near
the road and was run over by her insured, who was driving a
pick-up truck and had swerved slightly off the road to avoid a
large combine. When the fieldworker's insurance carrier
sought compensation, the local adjuster refused, claiming that
the injured man should not have been lying in the grass near
the road and could not have been seen by her insured, who, she
insisted, was driving carefully. The case went to trial and a
jury composed largely of local farmers was drawn:

> I was not even in there because our lawyers that
> represent us said, how many of those people do you
> know out there? And I said, I can give you the first
> name of everybody on the jury. He said, you stay over
> there in the library . . . don't let them see you. . . .
> So I stayed out in my little corner and listened to what
> went on and we won, we didn't pay 5 cents on it.

Thus, even a lawsuit involving insurance companies on both
sides was ultimately resolved in a manner that accorded with
traditional values. The insurance companies' knowledge of jury
attitudes in Sander County undoubtedly affected their handling
of most injury cases.

VI. LAWYERS AND LOCAL VALUES

Sander County attorneys reported that personal injury
cases came to them with some regularity, although they also
felt that many injury victims never consulted an attorney but
settled directly with insurance companies for less than they
should have received. When these attorneys were consulted, it
was by people who, in the opinion of the attorneys, had real,
nonfrivolous grievances, but the result was seldom formal legal
action. Most personal injury cases were resolved, as they are
elsewhere (Ross, 1970), through informal negotiation. Formal
judicial procedures were initiated primarily to prod the other
side to negotiate seriously or when it became necessary to
preserve a claim before it would be barred by the statute of
limitations. The negotiating process was, of course, strongly
influenced by the parties' shared knowledge of likely juror

reaction if the case actually went to trial. Thus, plaintiffs found negotiated settlements relatively attractive even when the terms were not particularly favorable.

But expectations regarding the outcome of litigation were probably not the only reason that members of the local bar so seldom filed personal injury cases. To some extent Sander County lawyers, many of whom were born and raised in the area, shared the local tendency to censure those who aggressively asserted personal injury claims. One attorney, for example, described client attitudes toward injury claims in the following terms: "A lot of people are more conducive to settlement here just because they're attempting to be fair as opposed to making a fast buck." Yet this same attorney admitted that informal settlements were often for small amounts of money and were usually limited to medical expenses, without any "general" damages whatever.[13]   His characterization of such outcomes as "fair" suggests an internalization of local values even on the part of those whose professional role it was to assert claims on behalf of tort plaintiffs.

The local bar was widely perceived as inhospitable to personal injury claimants, not only because there were few tort specialists but because Sander County lawyers were seen as closely linked to the kinds of individuals and businesses against whom tort actions were typically brought. Although plaintiffs hired Sander County attorneys in 72.5 percent of all non-tort actions filed locally in which plaintiffs were represented by counsel, they did so in only 12.5 percent of the tort cases.[14] One lawyer, who was frequently consulted by potential tort plaintiffs, lived across the county line in a small town outside of Sander County. He told me, "I get a lot of cases where people just don't want to be involved with the, they perceive it to be

---

[13] This is particularly striking since Laurence Ross' observation of insurance company settlement practices in automobile accident cases suggests that general damages are a standard part of the settlement "package" and are rather routinely calculated "for the most part . . . [by] multiplying the medical bills by a tacitly but generally accepted arbitrary constant" (Ross, 1970: 239).

[14] These figures are from a sample of cases for the years 1975-1976. See note 6 *supra*. From these data alone one cannot conclude that Sander County attorneys were less often *approached* by potential personal injury plaintiffs, since the data consist only of cases that were filed and tell us nothing about cases brought to an attorney but not filed. We know that Sander County attorneys were sometimes reluctant to bring such actions even when approached by prospective plaintiffs. Attorneys elsewhere, particularly those who were tort specialists, may not have shared this reluctance and may have filed a higher proportion of the Sander County claims that were brought to them.

the hierarchy of Sander County. . . . I'm not part of the establishment."

Thus, even from the perspective of insurance company personnel and attorneys, who were most likely to witness the entry of personal injury cases into the formal legal system in Sander County, it is clear that the local culture tended in many ways to deter litigation. And when personal injury cases were formally filed, it usually was no more than another step in an ongoing negotiation process.

Why was the litigation of personal injury cases in Sander County subjected to disapproval so pervasive that it inhibited the assertion of claims at all stages, from the moment injuries occurred and were perceived to the time parties stood at the very threshold of the formal legal system? The answer, I shall argue, lies partly in the role of the Sander County Court in a changing social system and partly in the nature of the personal injury claim itself.

VII. THE USE OF THE COURT

In the recent literature on dispute processing and conflict resolution, various typologies of conflict-handling forums and procedures have been proposed. Such typologies usually include courts, arbitrators, mediators, and ombudsmen, as well as two-party and one-party procedures such as negotiation, self-help, avoidance, and "lumping it" (see, e.g., typologies in Abel, 1973; Felstiner, 1974; Steele, 1975; Nader and Todd, 1978; Black and Baumgartner, 1983; Galanter, 1983). Analyses of these alternative approaches incorporate a number of variables that critically affect the ways in which conflict is handled and transformed. Such variables include, among others, procedural formality, the power and authority of the intervenor, the coerciveness of the proceedings, the range and severity of outcomes, role differentiation and specialization of third parties and advocates, cost factors, time required, the scope of the inquiry, language specialization, and the quality of the evidence that will be heard. When variables such as these are used to analyze various approaches to conflict resolution, the result is typically a continuum ranging from the most formal, specialized, functionally differentiated, and costly approaches to the most informal, accessible, undifferentiated, and inexpensive. The court as a forum for dispute processing and conflict resolution is typically placed at the costly, formalistic end of such continua.

Yet common sense and empirical investigations consistently remind us that trial courts rarely employ the adjudicative procedures that make them a symbol of extreme formalism. Very few of the complaints filed in courts are tried and adjudicated. Most are settled through bilateral negotiations of the parties or, occasionally, through the efforts of a judge who encourages the parties to reach an agreement without going to trial. This was true of the Sander County Court, as it is of courts elsewhere, and it applied with particular force to the relatively infrequent personal injury complaints that were filed in Sander County. Adjudication on the merits was extremely rare. In my sample only one of fifteen personal injury cases went to trial, and the judges and lawyers to whom I talked confirmed the generality of this pattern. Yet the court did play a crucial role in the handling of personal injury conflicts. It did so by providing what was perhaps the only setting in which meaningful and effective procedures of any kind could be applied. To understand why this was so, we must examine some distinctive characteristics of the relationships between the parties in the personal injury cases that were litigated in Sander County.

Among the relative handful of personal injury cases filed in the Sander County Court, almost all shared a common feature: the parties were separated by either geographic or social "distance" that could not be bridged by any conflict resolution process short of litigation.[15] In at least half of the fifteen personal injury cases in the sample, the plaintiff and the defendant resided in different counties or states. These cases were evenly split between instances in which the plaintiff, on the one hand, and the defendant, on the other hand, was a local resident. In either situation, geographic distance meant that the parties almost certainly belonged to different communities and different social networks. Informal responses by the injured party, whether they involved attempts to negotiate, to mediate, or even to retaliate by gossip, were likely to be frustrated since channels for communication and shared value systems and acquaintance networks were unlikely to exist. This is reflected in the disproportionate presence of parties from outside the county on the personal injury docket.[16]

---

[15] In this discussion of geographic and social distance and their impact on patterns of legal behavior, I draw upon a body of theory that has been developed in several earlier studies. See Black (1976); Perin (1977); Engel (1978); Todd (1978); Greenhouse (1982).

[16] The disproportionate number of cases involving geographically distant adversaries is especially striking when one considers the relative infrequency

568   THE OVEN BIRD'S SONG

A more elusive but no less significant form of distance was suggested by interviews with the parties as well as by the court documents in several personal injury cases. In these cases, it became apparent that "social distance," which was less tangible but just as hard to bridge as geographic distance, separated the parties even when they were neighbors.

Social distance could take many forms in Sander County. In one personal injury case, the plaintiff, who lived in one of the outlying towns in Sander County, described himself as an outsider to the community although he had lived there almost all his life. He was a Democrat in a conservative Republican town; he was of German extraction in a community where persons of Norwegian descent were extremely clannish and exclusive; he was a part-time tavernkeeper in a locality where taverns were popular but their owners were not socially esteemed; the opposing party was a "higher up" in the organization for which they both worked, and there was a long history of "bad blood" between them.

In a second personal injury case, a Mexican immigrant and his family sued a tavernkeeper under the Illinois Dram Shop Act for injuries he had suffered as a bystander in a barroom scuffle. Latino immigration into the community had, as we have seen, increased greatly in recent years to the displeasure of many local residents. Cultural misunderstandings and prejudice ran high, and little sympathy could be expected for a Latino who was injured in the course of a barroom fight. Thus, the plaintiff's wife was quite worried about bringing the lawsuit. She feared that they would create more trouble for themselves and told me, "I was afraid that maybe they'd say our kind of people are just trying to get their hands on money any way we could . . ." The decision to sue was made because they believed that people behind the bar had contributed to the injury by passing a weapon to the man who had struck the plaintiff (although, under the Dram Shop Act, the tavern could have been found liable without fault), and because they saw no other way to recover the income they had lost when the plaintiff's injury had kept him from working.

The tavernkeeper, who considered herself a member of the social underclass (although in a different sense from the

_____

of interaction between persons living in separate counties and states as compared to persons living in the same county or town. In absolute terms, injurious interactions must have occurred far more frequently between neighbors than between distant strangers, yet injurious interactions between distant strangers ended up in the Sander County Court about as often as those involving local residents (compare Engel, 1978: 142-44).

Mexican immigrants), was bitter about the case and about the Dram Shop Act. When I asked her how the plaintiffs had known that she was liable under the Act, she answered, "I haven't any idea. How do they know about a lot of things is beyond me. They know how to come here without papers and get a job or go on welfare. They are not too dumb, I guess."

In this case, then, the two parties were separated from each other and from the community by a great chasm of social distance.   One person was set apart from the general community by ethnicity and was well aware that his injuries were unlikely to be regarded with sympathy. The other party was also, by self-description, a "second class citizen." As a tavernkeeper, she told me, "you come up against many obstacles, prejudices, and hard times, you wouldn't believe." Both descriptions of social alienation were accurate. Yet the defendant had an established place in the traditional social order. She owned a small business in a town dominated by the ethos of individual enterprise. Her line of work was widely recognized and accepted, although not accorded great prestige, in a community where taverns were among the most important social centers. Her acquisition of Dram Shop insurance made her a "deep pocket" comparable to other local business enterprises that might provide substantial compensation in appropriate cases to injured persons. The plaintiffs in this case, far more than the defendant, were truly social "outsiders" in Sander County. For them, nonjudicial approaches appeared hopeless, and passively absorbing the injury was too costly. Only formal legal action provided a channel for communication between the two parties, and this ultimately led, despite the defendant's reluctance, to settlement.

Social distance also played a part in an action brought by a woman on behalf of her five-year-old daughter, who had suffered internal injuries when a large trash container fell on her. The little girl had been climbing on the trash container, which was located in back of an automobile showroom. The plaintiff and her husband were described by their adversaries as the kind of people who were constantly in financial trouble and always trying to live off somebody else's money. The plaintiff herself stated frankly that they were outsiders in the community, ignored or avoided even by their next-door neighbors. As she put it, "Everybody in this town seems to know everybody else's business . . . but they don't know you."

Her socially marginal status in the community precluded any significant form of nonjudicial conflict resolution with the

auto dealer or the disposal company, and the matter went to
the Sander County Court, where the $150,000 lawsuit was
eventually settled for $3,000. Since initiating the lawsuit, the
plaintiff had become a born-again Christian and, from her new
perspective on life, came to regret her decision to litigate. The
little money they had obtained simply caused her to fight with
her husband, who sometimes beat her. She came to believe
that she should not have sued, although she did feel that her
lawsuit had done some good. After it was concluded, she
observed, signs were posted near all such trash containers
warning that children should not play on them.

In my interviews with local residents, officials, community
leaders, and legal professionals, I presented the fact situation
from this last case (in a slightly different form, to protect the
privacy and identity of the original participants) and asked
them how similar cases were handled in the segments of the
community with which they were familiar. From our
discussion of this matter there emerged two distinct patterns of
behavior which, the interviewees suggested, turned on the
extent to which the aggrieved party was integrated into the
community. If the parents of the injured child were long-time
residents who were a part of the local society and shared its
prevailing value system, the consensus was that they would
typically take little or no action of any sort. Injuries, as we
have seen, were common in a rural community, and the parents
would tend to blame themselves for not watching the child
more carefully or, as one interviewee put it, would "figure that
the kid ought to be sharp enough to stay away" from the
hazard. On the other hand, if the parents of the injured child
were newcomers to the community, and especially if they were
factory workers employed in the area's newly established
industrial plants, it was suggested that their behavior would be
quite different. One union steward assured me that the
workers he knew typically viewed such situations in terms of a
potential lawsuit and, at the least, would aggressively seek to
have the auto dealer and the disposal company assume
responsibility for the damages. Others described a kind of
"fight-flight" reaction on the part of newcomers and industrial
blue collar workers. One particularly perceptive minister said,
"Those . . . that feel put down perceive everything in the light
of another putdown and I think they would perceive this as a
putdown. See, nobody really cares about us, they're just
pushing us around again. And so we'll push back." He also
noted, however, that it was equally likely that aggrieved

individuals in this situation would simply move out of the community—the "flight" response.

There was, then, some agreement that responses involving the aggressive assertion of rights, if they occurred at all, would typically be initiated by newcomers to the community or by people who otherwise lacked a recognized place in the status hierarchy of Sander County. Such persons, in the words of a local schoolteacher, would regard the use of the court as a "leveler" that could mitigate the effects of social distance between themselves and the other side. Persons who were better integrated into the community, on the other hand, could rely on their established place in the social order to communicate grievances, stigmatize what they viewed as deviant behavior, press claims informally, or, because they felt comfortable enough psychologically and financially, to simply absorb the injury without any overt response whatever.

Interestingly, this was precisely the picture drawn for me by the evangelical minister who had converted the mother of the five-year-old girl to born-again Christianity. Lifelong residents of the community, he told me, reacted to stressful situations with more stability and less emotion than newcomers to the community who were less rooted and whose lives were filled with pressures and problems and what he called, "groping, searching, grasping." For this minister, born-again Christianity offered socially marginal people a form of contentment and stability that was denied them by their lack of a recognized position in the local society. He argued that external problems such as personal injuries were secondary to primary questions of religious faith. He told me, "[I]f we first of all get first things straightened out and that is our relationship with God and is our help from God, all of these other things will fall into order." This was precisely the message that the plaintiff in this case—and many other socially marginal people in the community like her—had come to accept. On this basis, many social outsiders in Sander County could rationalize passivity in the face of personal injuries, passivity that was at least outwardly similar to the typical responses of Sander County's long-time residents.

The picture of the Sander County Court that emerges from this brief overview of personal injury cases differs substantially from that which might be suggested by conventional typologies of conflict resolution alternatives. In processual terms litigation, although rare, was not strikingly different from its nonjudicial alternatives. It was characterized by informal negotiation, bargaining, and settlement in all but the extremely infrequent cases that actually went to trial. Yet these processes occurred only as a result of the filing of a formal legal action. Because of the distance separating the parties, nonjudicial approaches, even with the participation of lawyers, sometimes failed to resolve the conflict. Resorting to the Sander County Court could vest socially marginal persons with additional weight and stature because it offered them access to the levers of judicial compulsion. The very act of filing a civil complaint, without much more, made them persons whom the other side must recognize, whose words the other side must hear, and whose claims the other side must consider. The civil trial court, by virtue of its legal authority over all persons within its jurisdiction, was able to bridge procedurally the gaps that separated people and social groups. In a pluralistic social setting, the court could provide, in the cases that reached it, a forum where communication between disparate people and groups could take place. In so doing, it substituted for conflict-handling mechanisms which served the well-integrated dominant group but which became ineffective for persons who were beyond the boundaries of the traditional community.

The communication that the court facilitated could, however, give rise to anger and frustration. Plaintiffs often viewed the process negatively, because even when they went to court they could not escape the rigid constraints imposed by a community unsympathetic to claims for damages in personal injury cases. Thus, the plaintiff whom I have described as a Democrat in a Republican town told me that the experience of filing and settling a personal injury claim was "disgusting . . . a lot of wasted time." Low pretrial settlements were, not surprisingly, the rule.

Defendants viewed the process negatively because they were accustomed to a system of conflict resolution that screened out personal injury cases long before they reached the courthouse. Even though settlements might turn out to be low, defendants resented the fact that personal injuries had in the first place been viewed as an occasion to assert a claim against them, much less a formal lawsuit. Being forced to respond in court was particularly galling when the claimant turned out to be a person whom the core members of the community viewed with dislike or disdain.

In short, the Sander County Court was able to bridge gaps between parties to personal injury cases and to promote communication between those separated by social or geographic distance. It did so, however, by coercion, and its outcomes (particularly when both parties resided in the community) tended to exacerbate rather than ameliorate social conflict. In the court's very success as a mechanism for conflict resolution we may, therefore, find a partial explanation for the stigmatization of personal injury litigation in Sander County.

VIII. THE PRESERVATION AND DESTRUCTION OF A COMMUNITY

In rural and archaic Japan . . . people used to believe that calamity that attacked the community had its origin in an alien factor inside the community as well as outside it. The malevolent factor accumulated in the community. It was related also to the sins committed wittingly or unwittingly by members of the community. In order to avoid the disastrous influence of the polluted element, it was necessary for the community to give the element form and to send it away beyond the limits of the village. However, the introduction of the alien element, which could turn into calamity at any time, was absolutely necessary for the growth of the crops. Thus the need for the alien factor had two facets which appear contradictory to each other on the surface: that is, the introduction of the negative element of expiation as well as the positive element of crop fertility (Yamaguchi, 1977: 154).

The social and economic life of Sander County had undergone major changes in the years preceding this study, and the impact of those changes on the world view of local residents and on the normative structure of the community as a whole was profound. Small single family farms were gradually giving way to larger consolidated agricultural operations owned by distant and anonymous persons or corporations. The new and sizeable manufacturing plants, together with some of the older local industries, now figured importantly in the economic life of Sander County and were the primary reasons why the population had become more heterogeneous and mobile.

These changes had important implications for traditional concepts of individualism and for the traditional relationships and reciprocities that had characterized the rural community. Self-sufficiency was less possible than before. Control over local lives was increasingly exercised by organizations based in other cities or states (there were even rumors that local farmlands were being purchased by unnamed foreign interests). Images of individual autonomy and community solidarity were

challenged by the realities of externally-based economic and
political power. Traditional forms of exchange could not be
preserved where individuals no longer knew their neighbors'
names, much less their backgrounds and their values. Local
people tended to resent and perhaps to fear these changes in
the local economic structure, but for the most part they
believed that they were essential for the survival of the
community. Some of the most critical changes had been the
product of decisions made only after extensive deliberations by
Sander County's elite. The infusion of new blood into the
community—persons of diverse racial, ethnic, and cultural
backgrounds—was a direct result of these decisions. The new
residents were, in the eyes of many old-timers, an "alien
element" whose introduction was, as in rural Japan, grudgingly
recognized as "absolutely necessary" to preserve the well-being
of the community.

The gradual decay of the old social order and the
emergence of a plurality of cultures and races in Sander
County produced a confusion of norms and of mechanisms for
resolving conflict.   New churches were established with
congregations made up primarily of newcomers. Labor unions
appeared on the scene, to the dismay and disgust of many of the
old-timers. New taverns and other social centers catered to the
newer arrivals. Governmental welfare and job training
programs focused heavily (but not exclusively) on the
newcomers. Newcomers frequently found themselves grouped
in separate neighborhoods or apartment complexes and, in the
case of blacks, there were reported attempts to exclude them
from the community altogether. The newcomers brought to
Sander County a social and cultural heterogeneity that it had
not known before. Equally important, their very presence
constituted a challenge to the older structure of norms and
values generated by face-to-face relationships within the
community.

IX. PERCEPTIONS OF CONTRACT AND PERSONAL
INJURY CLAIMS

The reaction of the local community to the assertion of
different types of legal claims was profoundly affected by this
proliferation of social, cultural, and normative systems. The
contrast between reactions to claims based on breaches of
contract and those based on personal injuries is especially
striking. Contract actions in the Sander County Court were

nearly ten times as numerous as personal injury actions.[17] They involved, for the most part, efforts to collect payment for sales, services, and loans. One might expect that concerns about litigiousness in the community would focus upon this category of cases, which was known to be a frequent source of court filings. Yet I heard no complaints about contract plaintiffs being "greedy" or "sue happy" or "looking for the easy buck." Such criticisms were reserved exclusively for injured persons who made the relatively rare decision to press their claims in court.

In both tort and contract actions, claimants assert that a loss has been caused by the conduct of another. In contractual breaches, the defendant's alleged fault is usually a failure to conform to a standard agreed upon by the parties.[18] In personal injury suits, the alleged fault is behavior that falls below a general societal standard applicable even in the absence of any prior agreement. Both are, of course, long-recognized types of actions. Both are "legitimate" in any formal sense of the word. Why is it, then, that actions to recover one type of loss were viewed with approval in Sander County, while far less frequent actions to recover the other type of loss were seen as symptomatic of a socially destructive trend toward the overuse of courts by greedy individuals and troublemakers? The answer appears to lie in the nature of the parties, in the social meanings of the underlying transactions, and in the symbolism of individuals and injuries in the changing social order.

Most of the contract litigation in Sander County involved debts to businesses for goods and services. Typically, the contracts that underlie such debts are quite different from the classic model of carefully considered offers and acceptances and freely negotiated exchanges. Yet many townspeople and farmers in the community saw such obligations as extremely important (Engel, 1980). They were associated in the popular mind with binding but informal kinds of indebtedness and with the sanctity of the promise. Long-time Sander County residents viewed their society as one that had traditionally been based on interdependencies and reciprocal exchanges among fellow residents. Reliance upon promises, including promises to pay for goods and services, was essential to the maintenance

---

[17] Four percent of my case sample were personal injury cases and 37.5% were contract cases.

[18] On many occasions, of course, courts import external standards into contracts and impose them on the parties regardless of their agreement or disagreement with such terms.

of this kind of social system. One farmer expressed this core value succinctly: "Generally speaking, a farmer's word is good between farmers." Another farmer, who occasionally sold meat to neighbors and friends in his small town, told me:

> We've done this for 20 years, and I have never lost one dime. I have never had one person not pay me, and I've had several of them went bankrupt, and so on and so forth. I really don't pay any attention to bookkeeping or what. I mean, if someone owes me, they owe me. And you know, I've never sent anybody a bill or anything. I mean, sooner or later they all pay.

In these interpersonal exchanges involving people well known to one another there was, it appears, some flexibility and allowance for hard times and other contingencies. On the other hand, there was a mutual recognition that debts must ultimately be paid. When I asked a number of people in the community about a case in which an individual failed to pay in full for construction of a fence, the typical reaction among long-time residents was that such a breach would simply not occur. Of course, breaches or perceptions of breaches did occur in Sander County and the result could be, in the words of one farmer, "fireworks." I was told stories of violent efforts at self-help by some aggrieved creditors, and it was clear that such efforts were not necessarily condemned in the community (Engel, 1980: 439-40). A member of the county sheriff's department observed that small unpaid debts of this kind were often viewed as matters for the police:

> We see that quite a bit. They want us to go out and get the money. He owes it, there's an agreement, he violated the law. . . . You see, they feel that they shouldn't have to hire an attorney for something that's an agreement. It's a law, it should be acted upon. Therefore, we should go out and arrest the man and either have him arrested or by our mere presence, by the sheriff's department, a uniformed police officer, somebody with authority going out there and say, hey, you know, you should know that automatically these people give the money and that would be it. So therefore they wouldn't have to go to an attorney. Boy, a lot of people feel that.

Other creditors, particularly local merchants, doctors, and the telephone company, brought their claims not to the police but to the Sander County Court. In some cases, contract plaintiffs (many of whom were long-time residents) appeared to litigate specifically to enforce deeply felt values concerning debt and obligation. As one small businessman explained:

I'm the type of a person that can get personally involved and a little hostile if somebody tries to put the screws to me. . . . I had it happen once for $5 and I had it happen once for $12. . . . I explained to them carefully to please believe me that it wasn't the money, because it would cost me more to collect it than it'd be worth. but because of the principle of it that I would definitely go to whatever means necessary, moneywise or whatever, to get it collected. And which I did.

Even those creditors for whom litigation was commonplace, such as the head of the local collection agency and an official of the telephone company, shared the perception that contract breaches were morally offensive. This view appeared to apply to transactions that were routinized and impersonal as well as to the more traditional exchanges between individuals who knew each other well. As the head of the collection agency said, "When you get to sitting here and you look at the thousands of dollars that you're trying to effect collection on and you know that there's a great percentage of them you'll never get and no one will get, it's gotta bother you. It's gotta bother you." Certainly, business creditors felt none of the hesitancy of potential tort plaintiffs about asserting claims and resorting to litigation if necessary. Equally important, the community approved the enforcement of such obligations as strongly as it condemned efforts to enforce tort claims. Contract litigation, even when it involved "routine" debt collection, differed from tort litigation in that it was seen as enforcing a core value of the traditional culture of Sander County: that promises should be kept and people should be held responsible when they broke their word.

X. CONCLUSION

In Sander County, the philosophy of individualism worked itself out quite differently in the areas of tort and contract. If personal injuries evoked values emphasizing self-sufficiency, contractual breaches evoked values emphasizing rights and remedies. Duties generated by contractual agreement were seen as sacrosanct and vital to the maintenance of the social order. Duties generated by socially imposed obligations to guard against injuring other people were seen as intrusions upon existing relationships, as pretexts for forced exchanges, as inappropriate attempts to redistribute wealth, and as limitations upon individual freedom.

These contrasting views of contract and tort-based claims took on special significance as a result of the fundamental social changes that Sander County had experienced. The newcomers brought with them conceptions of injuries, rights, and obligations that were quite different from those that had long prevailed. The traditional norms had no doubt played an important role in maintaining the customary social order by reinforcing longstanding patterns of behavior consistent with a parochial world view dominated by devotion to agriculture and small business. But the newcomers had no reason to share this world view or the normative structure associated with it. Indeed, as we shall see, they had good reason to reject it.[19] Although they arrived on the scene, in a sense, to preserve the community and to save it from economic misfortune, the terms on which they were brought into Sander County—as migrant or industrial workers—had little to do with the customary forms of interaction and reciprocation that had given rise to the traditional normative order. The older norms concerning such matters as individual self-sufficiency, personal injuries, and contractual breaches had no special relevance or meaning given the interests of the newcomers. Although these norms impinged on the consciousness and behavior of the newcomers, they did so through the coercive forces and social sanctions that backed them up and not because the newcomers had accepted and internalized local values and attitudes.

Indeed, it was clear that in the changing society of Sander County, the older norms tended to operate to the distinct disadvantage of social outsiders and for the benefit of the insiders. Contract actions, premised on the traditional value that a person's word should be kept, tended to involve collection efforts by established persons or institutions[20] against newcomers and socially marginal individuals. Such actions, as

---

[19] Were personal injury lawsuits in the late 1970s, although relatively infrequent, more common than they had been before the recent influx of social "outsiders" in Sander County? Because of the unavailability of reliable historical data, it is impossible to say, nor is the answer central to the analysis presented here. It is true that recent social changes in Sander County had brought striking juxtapositions of insiders and outsiders, and some increase in the frequency of tort claims may have resulted; but in earlier periods there may have been other kinds of outsiders as well, and some of them may have brought personal injury actions. In this article, I am interested in the past primarily as it existed in the minds of Sander County's citizens at the time of my study. It is clear that current perceptions of Sander County's history and traditions, whether accurate or not, played a crucial role in constructing and justifying responses to the problems that now faced the community, and such perceptions were often invoked to support the assertion of "traditional values" in opposition to behavior that provoked long-time residents.

[20] Frequent plaintiffs in collection cases were doctors, hospitals, merchants, collection agencies, and the telephone company. Cases of this type constituted 76.5% of all contract actions. The remaining 23.5% of contract cases involved actions based on construction contracts, promissory notes,

we have seen, were generally approved by the majority of
Sander County residents and occurred with great frequency.
Personal injury actions, on the other hand, were rooted in no
such traditional value and, although such claims were
infrequent, they were usually instituted by plaintiffs who were
outsiders to the community against defendants who occupied
symbolically important positions in Sander County society.
Thus, a typical contract action involved a member of "the
establishment" collecting a debt, while the typical personal
injury action was an assault by an outsider upon the
establishment at a point where a sufficient aggregation of
capital existed to pay for an injury. This distinction helps to
explain the stigmatization of personal injury litigation in
Sander County as well as its infrequency and its
ineffectiveness.[21]

Yet personal injury litigation in Sander County was not
entirely dysfunctional for the traditional social order. The
intrusion of "the stranger" into an enclosed system of
customary law can serve to crystallize the awareness of norms
that formerly existed in a preconscious or inarticulate state
(See Fuller, 1969: 9-10 and Simmel, 1908/1971). Norms and
values that once patterned behavior unthinkingly or intuitively
must now be articulated, explained, and defended against the
contrary values and expectations of the stranger to the
community.

In Sander County, the entry of the stranger produced a
new awareness (or perhaps a reconstruction) of the traditional
normative order at the very moment when that order was
subjected to its strongest and most devastating challenges. This
process triggered a complex response by the community—a
nostalgic yearning for the older world view now shattered
beyond repair, a rearguard attempt to shore up the boundaries

---

wholesale transactions, and other less frequent kinds of contractual
transactions.

[21] Sander County tort and contract cases are not unique, of course, in
these basic structural differences. In other localities one might also expect to
find that the majority of tort plaintiffs are individuals asserting claims against
"deep pocket" defendants, while the majority of contract plaintiffs are
business organizations attempting to collect debts from individuals. See, for
example, Galanter (1974) and Yngvesson and Hennessey (1975). It is possible
that outside of Sander County perceptions of the legitimacy and illegitimacy of
contract and tort actions are also influenced by these basic structural
differences. In Sander County, however, this set of distinctions between the
parties to tort and contract actions combined with local reactions to recent
societal changes to produce a powerful symbolism of insiders and outsiders
and of injuries and individualism. The extent to which a similar symbolism
may be found in other localities is a subject for further investigation.

of the community against alien persons and ideas (compare Erikson, 1966), and a bitter acceptance of the fact that the "stranger" was in reality no longer outside the community but a necessary element brought in to preserve the community, and therefore a part of it.

Local responses to personal injury claims reflected these complexities. In part, local residents, by stigmatizing such claims, were merely defending the establishment from a relatively rare form of economic attack by social outsiders. In part, stigmatization branded the claimants as deviants from the community norms and therefore helped mark the social boundaries between old-timers and newcomers. Because the maintenance of such boundaries was increasingly difficult, however, and because the "alien element" had been deliberately imported into the community as a societal act of self-preservation, the stigmatization of such claims was also part of a broader and more subtle process of expiation (to borrow Yamaguchi's [1977] term), a process reminiscent of rituals and other procedures used in many societies to deal with problems of pollution associated with socially marginal persons in the community (Douglas, 1966; Turner, 1969; Perin, 1977: 110-15).

Local residents who denounced the assertion of personal injury claims and somewhat irrationally lamented the rise in "litigiousness" of personal injury plaintiffs were, in this sense, participating in a more broadly based ceremony of regret that the realities of contemporary American society could no longer be averted from their community if it were to survive. Their denunciations bore little relationship to the frequency with which personal injury lawsuits were actually filed, for the local ecology of conflict resolution still suppressed most such cases long before they got to court, and personal injury litigation remained rare and aberrational. Rather, the denunciation of personal injury litigation in Sander County was significant mainly as one aspect of a symbolic effort by members of the community to preserve a sense of meaning and coherence in the face of social changes that they found threatening and confusing. It was in this sense a solution—albeit a partial and unsatisfying one—to a problem basic to the human condition, the problem of living in a world that has lost the simplicity and innocence it is thought once to have had. The outcry against personal injury litigation was part of a broader effort by some residents of Sander County to exclude from their moral universe what they could not exclude from the physical boundaries of their community and to recall and reaffirm an untainted world that existed nowhere but in their imaginations.

REFERENCES

ABEL, Richard L. (1973) "A Comparative Theory of Dispute Institutions in Society," 8 *Law & Society Review* 217.

AUBERT, Vilhelm (1963) "Competition and Dissensus: Two Types of Conflict and of Conflict Resolution," 7 *Journal of Conflict Resolution* 26.

BLACK, Donald (1976) *The Behavior of Law*. New York: Academic Press.

BLACK, Donald and M.P. BAUMGARTNER (1983) "Toward a Theory of the Third Party," in K. Boyum and L. Mather (eds.), *Empirical Theories About Courts*. New York: Longman.

DOUGLAS, Mary (1966) *Purity and Danger*. London: Routledge & Kegan Paul, Limited.

ENGEL, David M. (1978) *Code and Custom in a Thai Provincial Court*. Tucson: University of Arizona Press.

—— (1980) "Legal Pluralism in an American Community: Perspectives on a Civil Trial Court," 1980 *American Bar Foundation Research Journal* 425.

ERIKSON, Kai T. (1966) *Wayward Puritans*. New York: John Wiley & Sons.

FELSTINER, William L.F. (1974) "Influences of Social Organization on Dispute Processing," 9 *Law & Society Review* 63.

FRIEDMAN, Lawrence M. and Robert V. PERCIVAL (1976) "A Tale of Two Courts: Litigation in Alameda and San Benito Counties," 10 *Law & Society Review* 267.

FULLER, Lon L. (1969) "Human Interaction and the Law," 14 *American Journal of Jurisprudence* 1.

GALANTER, Marc (1974) "Why the 'Haves' Come Out Ahead: Speculations on the Limits of Legal Change," 9 *Law & Society Review* 95.

—— (1983) "Reading the Landscape of Disputes: What We Know and Don't Know (And Think We Know) About Our Allegedly Contentious and Litigious Society," 31 *UCLA Law Review* 4.

GEST, Ted, Lucia SOLORZANO, Joseph P. SHAPIRO and Michael DOAN (1982) "See You in Court," 93 *U.S. News & World Report* 58 (December 20).

GREENE, Richard (1983) "Caught in the Better Mousetrap," 132 *Forbes* 66 (October 24).

GREENHOUSE, Carol J. (1982) "Nature is to Culture as Praying is to Suing: Legal Pluralism in an American Suburb," 20 *Journal of Legal Pluralism* 17.

McINTOSH, Wayne (1980-81) "150 Years of Litigation and Dispute Settlement: A Court Tale," 15 *Law & Society Review* 823.

NADER, Laura and Harry F. TODD, Jr. (1978) "Introduction: The Dispute Process—Law in Ten Societies," in L. Nader and H. Todd, Jr. (eds.), *The Disputing Process—Law in Ten Societies*. New York: Columbia University Press.

NATIONAL CENTER FOR STATE COURTS (1979) *State Court Caseload Statistics: Annual Report, 1975*.

—— (1982) *State Court Caseload Statistics: Annual Report, 1977*.

PERHAM, John (1977) "The Dilemma in Product Liability," 109 *Dun's Review* 48 (January).

PERIN, Constance (1977) *Everything in Its Place*. Princeton: Princeton University Press.

ROSENBERG, Maurice (1977) "Contemporary Litigation in the United States," in H. Jones (ed.), *Legal Institutions Today: English and American Approaches Compared*. Chicago: American Bar Association.

ROSS, H. Laurence (1970) *Settled Out of Court*. Chicago: Aldine Publishing Co.

SEYMOUR, Whitney North, Jr. (1973) *Why Justice Fails*. New York: William Morrow & Co.

582   THE OVEN BIRD'S SONG

SIMMEL, Georg (1908/1971) "The Stranger," in D. Levine (ed.), *On Individuality and Social Forms: Selected Writings*. Chicago: University of Chicago Press.

STEELE, Eric H. (1975) "Fraud, Dispute and the Consumer: Responding to Consumer Complaints," 123 *University of Pennsylvania Law Review* 1107.

TAYLOR, Stuart, Jr. (1981) "On the Evidence, Americans Would Rather Sue Than Settle," *New York Times* (July 5) Section 4, 8.

TODD, Harry F., Jr. (1978) "Litigious Marginals: Character and Disputing in a Bavarian Village," in L. Nader and H. Todd (eds.), *The Disputing Process—Law in Ten Societies*. New York: Columbia University Press.

TONDEL, Lyman M., Jr. (1976) "The Work of the American Bar Association Commission on Medical Professional Liability," 43 *Insurance Counsel Journal* 545.

TURNER, Victor W. (1969) *The Ritual Process*. Chicago: Aldine Publishing Co.

YAMAGUCHI, Masao (1977) "Kingship, Theatricality, and Marginal Reality in Japan," in R. Jain (ed.), *Text and Context: The Social Anthropology of Tradition*. Philadelphia: Institute for the Study of Human Issues.

YNGVESSON, Barbara and Patricia HENNESSEY (1975) "Small Claims, Complex Disputes: A Review of the Small Claims Literature," 9 *Law & Society Review* 219.

[21]

NATURE IS TO CULTURE AS PRAYING IS TO SUING:
LEGAL PLURALISM IN AN AMERICAN SUBURB[1]

Carol J. Greenhouse

I. INTRODUCTION

Social scientists interested in the question of disputants'
remedial choice-making, and, specifically, their decisions to
litigate, often treat the question as a dichotomous one: Do
they sue, or don't they? In some contexts, the question is
dichotomous in just this way. For example, judicial administrators concerned with heavy docket loads are interested primarily
in who is and who is not using the court. Judicial reformers
interested in increasing the public's access to the courts are,
similarly, concerned with the treshold between litigation and
non-litigation.

In terms of the cultural choices involved, court use is
not a simple matter of alternatives. Before a person can sue,
he must have not only a legally justiciable issue and a legal
forum, but also a personal conceptualization of conflict that
is adversarial in structure and remedial in orientation. This
article focuses on an ideology of conflict that renders all
conflict "non-justiciable," i.e., on a group that does not
permit its members any overt remedial actions. but which nevertheless manages to survive in secular society. The ethnographic
data derive from a suburban community in the United States. The
people who are the focus of the study reported here do not consider that they lack access to justice, but their concept of
justice specifically excludes recourse to law. In the conclusion, the implications of the findings for the study of litigation and non-litigation in their social-cultural contexts are
explored.

II. CULTURE AND COURT USE

Anthropological studies of litigation divide into three major
clusters, which consider: (1) the social relationships between

Law and Society

the disputing parties; (2) litigants as constituents of the
courts; and (3) court use as a prerogative of an elite.

The relational distance hypothesis proposes that "the
greater the relational distance between the parties to a dispute, the more likely is law to be used to settle the dispute"
(Black, 1973:134). Ample ethnographic evidence exists to support this hypothesis, and the concept of relational distance can
be operationalized in a variety of ways. For instance, a relationship may be measured in terms of residence (Koch, 1974),
kinship (Gulliver, 1963), multiplexity (Gluckman, 1955), or the
social costs of rupturing it (Felstiner, 1974). In closed, kin-
based corporate communities, these four factors merge, but in
other contexts they are analytically distinguishable. The usual
explanation for the effect of relational distance is in terms
of the disruptive or terminal effect of litigation on social
relationships (Krige, 1974; Kawashima, 1969:65; Gibbs, 1967:
289).[2]

Nader and Todd (1978:17-18) criticize the relational distance hypothesis by suggesting that it is incomplete by itself:

> . . . continuing relationships are but part of the
> picture. It is not enough to state that because
> litigants wish to continue their relation they will
> seek negotiated or mediated settlements with com-
> promise outcomes.

While the relational distance hypothesis is intuitively acceptable in many situations, its emphasis on the relationship between the disputants implies some preconditions in the legal
and political context in which disputes occur. For example,
the relationship of both parties to the court must be relatively
equal in terms of access, power, and the justiciability of
claims (see Galanter, 1974). A second precondition is equal
knowledge and acceptance of the law. These conditions of social
and cultural homogeneity certainly can be found, e.g., among
businessmen, rival elite groups, and families, and it is precisely such groups who have contributed importantly to the
literature on relational distance and avoidance of the law (see
Macaulay, 1963).[3] The community discussed in part III is
homogeneous in ways that allow the relational distance hypothesis
to operate, along with other factors.

While the relational distance hypothesis manipulates the
variable of the relationship between the disputants (and their
normative understandings), other approaches to court use focus
on the relationship of the plaintiff to the court, and in broader

terms, to the state. They treat disputants as actual or potential constituents of the courts' authority to implement social
change (either proactively or reactively) and/or to facilitate
existing relationships. Anthropologists and others who view
the court this way divide over the court's role: in some studies,
courts appear as the protectors of the disenfranchised, in
others, as the arms of the dominant elite. Both views are
relevant in the community described below.

When courts are protective, they legitimize the complaint
of otherwise powerless people, and allow them to be heard and
resolved. Vines' (1966) discussion of the United States Federal
Courts in the South during the 1950s and early 1960s shows that
American blacks had no access to effective power except through
the courts, and that the courts' legitimation of their grievances
made social change possible. Todd's (1978:119) analysis of cases
filed by "marginals" in a Bavarian village is parallel:

> . . . the case for the litigious marginal is clear.
> If he is to achieve satisfaction, the social struc-
> ture of the community effectively forces him to es-
> calate his grievances and conflicts into disputes,
> and requires him then to take these disputes outside
> the village.

Collier (1974) and Starr (1978) also show that less powerful disputants sometimes seek the aid of the court in legitimizing their
complaints, thus establishing a new basis for their private relationships within their families and communities.

To some extent, the idea of "litigious marginals" is the
corollary to that of relational distance: if litigation is large
ly obviated by the informal resolution of grievances within their
community, litigants will be people for whom the social community
has failed in that regard. Access to the court is of crucial
importance, since, if socially marginal plaintiffs are barred
from the court, they are without recourse except for some form
of avoidance (Galanter, 1976 and Felstiner, 1974) or self-help
(Merry, 1980). Specific conditions enable "marginals" to litigate. First, the political system must be such that low social
status does not compromise an individual's access to the services
of the court. Second, the court must be physically accessible
(some marginal populations are geographically remote from courtrooms). Third, potential plaintiffs must have knowledge of both
substantive and procedural aspects of the law, and the material
means to initiate (if not win) a lawsuit. Thus, while marginal
plaintiffs may be relatively for even relatively severely) disadvantaged in material and other respects, it is unlikely that

they constitute the bottom stratum of a society's economic
scale.[4] Since all of these conditions are satisfied in the
case of the American non-litigants discussed in part III, their
failure to litigate must be sought elsewhere.

A more common theme in anthropology is of court use by an
elite group that dominates the judicial institutions. A classic
case of elite domination of a court system is described by Davis,
Gardner, and Gardner (1941), who studied the situation of black
tenant farmers in the U.S. South during the Depression (an interesting contrast to Vines, who wrote in a later period). They
report that southern landowners used the courts effectively as
a means of guaranteeing their labor supply: landowners and
local retailers effectively prosecuted tenants' defaults on debts
with the aim of restricting their mobility. An earlier American
example is Baumgartner's (1978) account of law in colonial New
Haven (1639-1665) which concludes more broadly that "law varied
with social status": "the most frequent complaint involved a
high-status complainant and a low-status defendant; the least
frequent was the reverse" (172). Baumgartner says that high-
status litigants were "socially closer" to the magistrates (164),
although she does not link that finding causally to the fate of
low-status defendants. This situation has parallels in the
modern colonial context, especially where the dominant political
group is also culturally dominant.

Historically, the population of the town described in
part III was more sharply stratified than it now is; class lines
and religious lines appear to have coincided, for reasons that
are somewhat obscure. Class differences have been largely ef-
faced over the course of this century, but the religious and
ideological differences remain. Thus, the view of litigation
that focuses on elites and dominanted groups is relevant, but
only in a vestigial sense.

In summary, a review of the anthropological literature
that considers the question of litigation and access to law
through the courts suggests the following themes: First, remedial
strategies differ by degree, not by type. For example, the
intimacy of the disputants, the authority of the third party,
the formality of the process, the accessibility of the forum
(and so forth) can be understood as ranging from low to high,
with predictable (see Black, 1976) consequences for disputants'
remedial choices. Second, all disputants are potential litigants.
And third, litigation and remedial choice-making in general are
structually and functionally congruent cross-culturally. The
situation discussed in this paper suggests that in some circumstances the choice between litigation and non-litigation can be

a discontinuous one, that litigation and non-litigation are not
necessarily complements, and that several cultural conceptions
of law can operate simultaneously within a single community so
that patterns of law use are not always structurally and functionally congruent.

III. HISTORY, IDEOLOGY, AND COURT USE IN AN AMERICAN TOWN

The town which this paper considers is slightly over two square
miles in area, with a population of 4,000 (U.S. Census, 1970) in
a county whose residents number about 100,000. The population
of the town is exceptionally homogeneous: it is white (98 percent in 1970), educated, earning an average yearly family income
of over $12,000, and living in privately owned housing. The
city was founded in the early 1840s (the exact date is disputed)
and named for the surveyor who routed the railroad down its main
street. The fact that the town was a railroad stop made it a
regional commercial center of some importance during its early
history, especially when the nearby metropolis--Atlanta--was
still a minor city with few services. The county was rural until
well after World War II, when Atlanta's booming growth finally
spilled into its periphery. Two-thirds of the local work force
now commutes to the city. In 1970, an interstate highway cut
through one edge of the county, repeating the effect of the railroad a century before: it brought a wave of businesses and, this
time, several tens of thousands of residents. Although the
"downtown" retains its rural look, primarily because its main
business district is preserved as a national historic landmark,
its residential areas are typical of many new American suburbs
in appearance. The old residents and the new live intermingled
in the new subdivisions. The community is not divided along any
visible lines except a racial one: the town's few blacks live
primarily in an old section close to the center of town.

     The county court sits in the center of town in a Victorian
courthouse on Main Street. It is divided into an inferior court
and a superior court, each of which handles both civil and
criminal complaints. A retired judge sits once a week in special
sessions to hear divorce cases. All other cases are heard by
one of two other judges. The county has several justices of the
peace, who invariably refer their cases to the inferior court
after an initial hearing and a processing fee. The court personnel are well-known and well-liked among the long-term residents; the courthouse is centrally located and is frequently
visited for conversation in addition to official business. The
court clerks are members of old families, and the judges' families, although considered "newcomers" by the long-term residents.

have lived in the town for about sixty years.

The general pattern of court use in this town appears to
be simple enough. Virtually no one who is part of the established population (four or more generations of residence) uses the
courts. The civil court is, however, crowded with cases, primarily involving businesses and/or individual "newcomers."[5]
This general pattern is not surprising in and of itself, since
many Americans never consult a lawyer during their lives (Curran
and Spalding, 1974:79), let alone litigate. Whatever interest
there is in this pattern is in the fact that it is the newcomers
who are the constituents of the court, and not the long-term
established residents. The relational distance hypothesis would
suggest that people who are involved in face-to-face relationships of some depth and extent prefer and have available less
formal, more private, and more perfect remedies than the court
offers. Newcomers, having fewer inhibitions or alternatives
deriving from their social ties, use the court more freely.

But a single hypothesis cannot account for the two types
of non-litigants in the town. These subgroups' membership overlap only marginally: (1) The first group uses the court as an
integral part of its adversarial strategies, which take place
outside the courts. These people are not court-users, but they
are certainly law-users, threatening litigation as a prod toward
compliance. This group consists of a network of long-term
residents and/or prominent local businessmen and their families.
(2) The second group uses neither the court nor the law. It
consists of devout Baptists, who comprise the town's oldest
Baptist congregation, a group of about 1,500. In demographic
and socio-economic terms, the two groups are very similar. In
terms of their legal ideologies, they are not. In terms of
legal ideology, the first group of non-litigants is continuous
with litigants, but the Baptists are discontinuous with both of
the other two groups. For the non-Baptists, access to justice
means access to lawyers. They express both a preference for
"getting along" and distaste for the loss of privacy that a
lawsuit represents to them. Their view of the court <u>as an in-
stitution</u> is not a negative one; they <u>prefer</u> other remedies when
circumstances permit, which they usually do. For the Baptists,
on the other hand, access to justice means access to God.

As the town's Baptists explained their faith to me, their
ideology proscribes litigation and, in fact, any attempts at
redress apart from unilateral forgiveness or prayer. They cite
the New Testament: Romans 13:18-19 exhorts Christians to "avenge
not yourselves. . . : for it is written vengeance is mine, I will
repay, saith the Lord." The town's Baptists interpret this

passage as prohibiting remedial initiatives involving any third
party but Jesus. To act otherwise is sacrilege, a failure of
faith. Furthermore, the Bible preaches forgiveness, sacrifice,
and a community built on love. By these things, Christians can
distinguish themselves from non-Christians: ". . . Love one another: . . . By this shall all men know that ye are my disciples"
(John 13:34-35). Finally, the Baptists' concern with spreading
their faith ("witnessing") to non-Baptists inspires them to lead
"lives of good witness," i.e., exemplary lives that will attract
non-Baptists to the church. These three factors: proscription of
secular justice, the ideal of Christian community, and evangelism,
justify avoidance of the courts and all other agents of secular
law, e.g., lawyers, for purposes of interpersonal disputing.
Baptists view the court itself as a profane institution, needed
only by non-believers and the unfaithful. Their rejection of the
court applies equally to the roles of plaintiff and defendant.
They explain that the Bible is quite explicit on the matter of
threatened lawsuits (Matthew 6:40): "And if any man will sue thee
at the law, and take away thy coat, let him have thy cloak also."
Thus, in the local ideology, a devout Baptist settles out of court
quickly and fully any demands made against him.

The local Baptists' view of the court does not preclude their
suffering from grievances, only from resolving them at law. They
do not segregate themselves from the non-Baptist community, and
their range of problems is no different from that of other groups.
They live in town, and many of them commute daily to jobs in
Atlanta. The potential for victimization is obvious; the town's
Baptists often refer to themselves as persecuted--but they also
note that the moral triumph is theirs.

The remedies that the Baptists do allow themselves are of
three sorts: 1) unilateral (avoidance and prayer), 2) bilateral
(apology, joking, and prayer with another person), and 3) trilateral (gossip, counseling, and mediation). These three categories apply to distinct social fields within the town. The
Baptist concept of community precludes avoidance within the church
congregation; avoidance applies only to outsiders. Avoidance is
generally glossed as unilateral forgiveness, but such forgiveness
does not take place face-to-face. Bilateral and trilateral remedies apply within the church and to an intermediate group known
as "prospects," that is, candidates for conversion. The distinction between insiders (including prospects) and outsiders is, for
local Baptists, an absolute one. Acceptance of Christ is the
crucial index of the Baptists' world: it separates Baptists from
the secular and (therefore) profane world. Local Baptists do not
accept other Christian sects as authentic; to be a non-Baptist is
to be a non-Christian.

Importantly, then, Baptist Christianity implies a social
organization of conflict resolution. Because non-Baptists do not
belong to the community of God, Baptists believe them to be dangerous, unpredictable, moved by self-interest--in general, only
partly socialized. Although actual relations between Baptists
and non-Baptists are routine and cordial, they are constrained
by distrust on the part of the Baptists. Baptists expect conflict
from non-Baptists, and so seek to avoid them. In practice, they
cannot avoid them entirely, since, as I have said, they live lives
that are thoroughly enmeshed in the non-Baptists' world. Their
avoidance is mental only, i.e., an inner aversion. What is important is that Baptists define non-Baptists as the source and
embodiment of conflict. By corollary, within their church community, Baptists exclude the possibility of conflict. Disputes
are quickly and generally interpreted as a spiritual lapse: the
offender is redefined as an outsider to the church social community by virtue of his having caused trouble. Troublemakers are
by definition (or by redefinition) outsiders, and vice versa.
Disagreements and minor disputes are handled verbally and, significantly, are not defined as conflict by the participants. Within
the church community, harmony exists by definition, and verbal
remedies (gossip, prayer, joking, and so forth) are referred to
simply as "speech." So, conflict and Christianity follow the
same boundary, Christians on the one side, conflict on the other.

Because Baptists locate their expectation of conflict not in
situations, or in rules of behavior, but in social structure
(Baptists/non-Baptists), their concept of conflict is not defined
in terms of time and space. Baptists do not conceptualize or
discuss conflict in terms of cases, but in terms of salvation,
i.e., acceptance of and by Christ. Harmony and love are immanent
in Christians; conflict is immanent in non-Christians. Cases and
the adversary model of conflict are entirely extraneous to their
concept of conflict. Since the distinction between conflict and
harmony does not pertain to behavioral rules, but to professed
identification with a sacred ideology, the secular courts and the
law in general are completely irrelevant as remedial tools. The
only remedy for conflict, in the Baptists' eyes, is salvation.

Several questions emerge out of this discussion: First, are
there no circumstances under which Baptists use the legal apparatus
of the town; i.e., how well does their ideology account for their
actual behavior? Second, why is the Baptist/non-Baptist distinction so salient in this community? Third, why is the boundary
between the different groups in the town conceptualized by the
Baptists in terms of use of law? Finally, does any of this matter
to the other people of the town? The answers to these questions
are interrelated.

First, to my knowledge, Baptists do not use legal agencies
to press personal claims in the context of disputes, although,
as noted above, this absence of litigation is difficult to evaluate given the general American pattern of court use. Baptists do
pay taxes, write wills, own real estate, call the police to investigate burglaries, register their marriages with the state,
and so on. I have no contemporary evidence that would suggest
that Baptists' aversion to the law extends beyond trouble in
interpersonal relationships. Thus, in their own dealings with
Baptists, non-Baptists do encounter them in the legal settings
that are associated with the life cycle and to some extent with
business. They are less likely to enter into the Baptists' circle
of social relations from which adversarial conflict and the law
are excluded. Non-Baptists, therefore, are unlikely to find the
Baptists' professed law-aversion credible, since they do not
appreciate what the differences between these two settings mean
in Baptist terms.

This raises the second question, i.e., why the Baptist/non-
Baptist distinction is so salient in this community. It is certainly an important distinction to the people themselves. The
local Baptists, for example, lump non-Baptists together as unsaved, and use an array of metaphors for them that merges non-
believers with "city folk," businessmen, the wealthy, newcomers,
and the power elite, although these groups are in actuality not
coterminous, nor even exclusively non-Baptist. For non-Baptists,
religious identity has less importance than it does among the
Baptists, but the Baptists are referred to as a conspicuous social
group in terms ranging from jokingly derisive to overtly hostile.
It is clear from conversations, public prayer, and church services,
that local Baptists believe themselves to be victims of social
prejudice. And although so far as I could observe this is not
the case, their belief is important in itself. Finally, this
group of Baptists, unlike the South's Baptists in general, do not
participate in civic affairs, except, I believe, by voting.
They do not run for office nor publicly support political candidates. The local Baptists, then, do not match the image of
Southern Baptists in general: they do not enjoy the same cultural
hegemony by any means. Why not?

Genealogies, old maps, lists of deacons, church registries,
diaries, letters, land records, and other sources suggest that
the Baptists' sense of isolation has to do with the history of
the town at least as much as with contemporary religious values.
The town's first settlers were Baptists, establishing a church
only three years after the territory was ceded by the Indians in
1821. The early settlers were poor farmers sparsely scattered
over what was to become the town and then the county in the 1840s.

By then, the town was encircled by two "rings" of farms: the
more central consisted of large plantations, and the more peripheral of small farms and small manufacturers, e.g., of jugs and
millstones. In 1849, the Methodists established a church, and
it quickly became the church of the gentry: county officeholders,
doctors, lawyers, merchants, bankers, and the wealthiest farmers
all appear on its first registry. The Presbyterians were a small
minority on the outskirts of town, dominated by one large and
solidary landowning family.

The history of local Baptists, then, is, to some extent, the
history of the local small farmers. The small farmers of the
county rose and fell twice before the ultimate collapse of small
farming in the 1950s and 1960s. During the period just after the
Civil War, farmers with small holdings were relatively advantaged
in comparison with the large plantation owners, since land lost
much of its value, while manufacturing provided a cushion against
loss. Land sales records for this period suggest that farmers on
the periphery were able to buy portions of the former plantations,
improving their economic condition, if not their social position,
considerably. During the Depression of the 1930s, small farmers
again were able to hold onto their land, and as the suburbs and,
later the highway, extended to this area after World War II, their
less profitable farms were the first to be sold for development
as real estate.

Even so, while this brief glimpse of their history helps account for the composition of the membership of the Baptist church,
their conviction that they are disadvantaged, and even their somewhat ascetic values, it does not explain why the Baptists' ideology
of law does not extend to reject other institutions associated with
the power elite--their business, their credit, and their fashions.
Put another way, why is it that the court and the law, for local
Baptists, are the relevant emblems of religious identity and tradition? Why not, as among the Amish, for example, agriculture
and, negatively, television, current dress styles, and business
(Hostetler, 1968)?

Some further history helps answer the last question. At the
period when the county was being formed, two major conflicts divided the Baptist church in the United States and the South. The
first was the issue of slavery: the Southern Baptists formed a
separate convention in 1845 over the slavery question. Soon afterward, the Southern Baptists divided over the issue of missions
(essentially a question of church expenditures for benevolent
associations). The Southern Baptists were officially pro-mission,
but a sizable minority--fearing that some "benevolent associations"
might be abolitionist groups--was vehemently opposed, and seceded

from the Southern Baptist Convention. These national and regional issues had a major impact on local Baptists. By their sect's identification with slavery, the Baptist church became identified with the state's aristocratic planters, but the aristocrats were only a small minority in this county. Most of the county's voters were in what was then the Clarke party--a populist coalition that was the eager mouthpiece of Andrew Jackson.[6] The county voted for secession in 1861 (fifteen years after the period we are discussing), but on states' rights grounds, not slavery. So, on the slavery question, the local Baptist church became isolated by the contradiction between its sectarian aristocratic associations and its local small-farmer constituency.

Simultaneously, the missions question divided the local church so severely that by 1847 few members remained. During the decade before secession, the church had to rebuild itself or fail. It managed to revive in this era of intense political strife by preaching against politics altogether. Withdrawal from politics and from political institutions was a strategy for religious institutional survival and credibility. Why withdraw from the courts? The judgeships were the first "plums" of any new administration--they were the most important of a new governor's political appointments. The anti-politics strategy was successful in the mid-1800s during the county's early years of strife and it remains effective today, when other conflicts (integration, zoning, and planning, for example) threaten the community. The church today is burgeoning with over 2,300 members, and a growing budget and physical plant.

Few townpeople I met were aware of the early history of the Baptist church in the town, and none--even at the Baptist church-- had any interest in such things, except as odd bits of unrelated knowledge. For the Baptists, scripture is an adequate idiom in which to express their position in the town and their behavior in relation to the court and to conflict. The modern Baptists in town merge city people with newcomers, the rich, the wealthy, and the damned because these are all symbols of the profane world in which Baptists refuse to participate and by opposition to which they define themselves. The histories of the Methodist and Presbyterian churches--whose members today comprise the group of non-litigants who are not law-averse--did not take the same course as that of the Baptists. These churches were never so deeply threatened by political conflict. Thus, the answer to the third question--why legal ideology follows religious lines--lies in the relationship of this particular community to the local, regional, and national issues that have shaped its history.

The final question was whether and why the situation of

legal pluralism in this town matters to the people who live there.
Clearly, it matters to the Baptists. A person's orientation toward conflict and the law is determined by his orientation toward
God, and to a believer this makes all other considerations redun-
dant. To the non-Baptists, though, whose preference for out-of-
court settlements is entirely secular, legal pluralism has a
different significance. While they know of the Baptists' aversion
to using the courts and lawyers, they do not accept the Baptists'
explanation of it because it is in terms of a conception of order
that non-Baptists do not share. Where Baptists see the world as
divided into the saved and the unsaved, non-Baptists see multiple
competing social groups. Where Baptists see Jesus as replacing
the secular system, the other groups see Jesus as validating the
secular system. Where the Baptists see contradiction between
heaven and earth, the non-Baptists see authentication. Where the
Baptists withdraw to pray, the non-Baptists assume they are forming a cabal. The role of the "moral majority" in the last presidential election was repugnant to the local Baptists as the very
antithesis of their ethic; to the non-Baptists, the activities of
the moral majority merely confirmed their suspicions that Baptists
use their religion to suit their own political ends. When local
Baptists and non-Baptists happen to differ over public matters,
as in a particularly bitter recent episode involving the destruction of historic buildings to expand the church's parking facilities, factions divide along religious lines that reiterate end-
lessly. The non-Baptists' consciousness of legal pluralism in
their community is in terms of the competition that they feel
divides their community. They perceive the Baptists as a large
anti-progressive group, held in thrall by a spellbinding preacher
(he is in fact effective, but not the hypnotic hellfire sort),
which, as the church grows, threatens to obstruct the development
of the county. For the non-Baptists, this last is the central
political preoccupation.

IV. CONCLUSIONS

The Baptists in the community described above adhere to an ideology which in three major respects differs from the assumptions of
the anthropological literature on dispute settlement and law
generally, discussed at the beginning of this paper. First,
their ideology cuts them off from all judicial resources, and
they are also precluded from all forms of overt disputing. This
is a double problem of containment and effacement of conflict.
In effect, Baptists limit their definition of their jural community to a domain in which conflict is not acceptable. God
solves this problem for them, in that he is believed to create
and fill a normative vacuum simultaneously.

Second, Baptists do not conceptualize conflict in terms of
cases, but in terms of social structure. Conflict is not a question of rules or interests but entirely a question of an individual's spiritual state. Adversarial modes of processing conflict,
then, are not appropriate, nor is a remedial system that is oriented towards redress. The local Baptists classify the components
of their community's social structure in a way that draws the
limits of culture short of the limits of society. Their perception of the unsaved as unsocialized refers specifically to what
Baptists see as their untamed individuality, untrammeled self-
interest, and senseless passion for material things. The Baptists'
view of human nature is just that: natural, with precisely the
connotation that opposes it to culture. Jesus not only saves,
he civilizes. Without Jesus, human law is doomed to fail; with
Jesus, human law is superfluous.

Third, Baptists do not accept that human authority has any
place in private relationships. They resist both human judges
and any secularly-based differentiation of their congregation.
Wealth, education, power--none of these matter. Authoritative
resolution of disputes is rejected so as to protect relationships
from the extension of authority into the relationships themselves.
Disputing creates winners and losers, and that is intolerable to
a group committed to the equality of its members.

These data suggest several conclusions: First, non-litigants
are not all alike. There are conditions under which some non-
litigants will become litigants, and the fact that this group
includes the town's lawyers and judges probably facilitates their
out-of-court effectiveness. For the Baptists, on the other hand,
there are no conditions under which they can become litigants
without leaving the church.

Second, synchronic and diachronic approaches differ considerably in what they reveal about court use as a cultural question. Taken alone, a synchronic approach (religious ideology)
at first appears to be sufficient as an explanation of the
Baptists' withdrawal from the courts, although the distinctive
features of the local ideology remain perplexing. The Baptists
themselves examine their attitudes toward the law in purely
religious terms. But an historical investigation shows other
dynamics at work. The town's Baptists became "more" religious
as they became more threatened by the conflicts of their community. Their sense of isolation as a group and their real
isolation from the courts are products of the particular cross-
currents that shaped the history of the town, the state, and
nation.

Third, as the Baptist example shows, court use may be pre-cluded by an ideology of conflict that is averse to the law and its presuppositions about the nature and meaning of conflict. Specifically, the case underscores three cultural prerequisites of litigation and law use in general:

(a) The law is limited to a domain conceived of as cultural. When social classification limits the cultural domain to some social groups and not others, then we can expect that the ideology of law will see the limits of law in the limits of culture, how-ever culture is conceived. This statement might sound ridiculous or obvious, until we remember that children and the insane are for many purposes outside the bounds of ordinary legal rules and that "natural" relationships such as marriage are also excluded from the law for many purposes (e.g. conjugal privilege, intra-family immunity, the law of rape).

In larger social fields, for example, the absence of overt disputes between American blacks and whites in plantation society (see, again, Davis, Gardner, and Gardner, 1941) or between Indians and Ladinos in Zinacantec (see Collier, 1973) does not mean that conflict does not exist between them, but the opposite. In these cases, the conflict is so profound that it is expressed in an imagery that naturalizes the outsiders, placing them beyond the limits of the cultural (and, hence, remedial) system.

(b) The law requires conceptual links between conflict and self-interest, and between self-interest and redress. This re-quirement is by no means universally met, since concepts of the self, and of interest (a combination of social structural ques-tions and questions about time) vary widely. Litigation in the West implies a concept of time that is linear and infinite: that is the only cosmological framework in which the rewards of liti-gation are relevant. The Baptists have a linear concept of time, but a finite one. Time ends on Judgment Day. They believe that there are no legitimate human interests, only divine interests, and that earthly remedies are mere conceits.

(c) The law gives authority a place in private relation-ships and establishes linkages between individual disputants and their wider society. Social groups who refuse or prefer not to litigate are not only making a statement about the way they value their horizontal relationships, but also about the extent to which they accept the vertical relationships their society offers them. When a disputant ultimately decides to sue, his decision may signify a change in his acceptance of authority more than one in his assessment of his relationship with his codisputant.

At the end of The Ages of American Law, Gilmore (1977:111)
concludes with the following passage: "In Heaven there will be
no law, and the lion will lie down with the lamb. . . . In Hell
there will be nothing but law, and due process will be meticulously observed." Gilmore captures here both ends of a continuum of
legal culture that anthropologists have made familiar over the
forty years since The Cheyenne Way (Llewellyn and Hoebel, 1941).
He also, perhaps unwittingly, reveals much of the romance that
westerners from self-proclaimed litigious societies bring to the
study of order in other places. The implication of Gilmore's
statement--which represents a popular view among both the public
and social scientists--is that law use varies inversely with
social harmony. The case of the Baptists would at first seem to
confirm this view: we might easily conclude that they care so
deeply about their relationships with each other that the very
idea of law is anathema. More accurately, however, the Baptists
reject law first because they reject the intervention of human
authority in their affairs. Their ideology of law does not specify alternatives to litigation and law use, but it is very specific in its proscription of third parties in dispute settlements.
The absence of legal disputes within the group does not necessarily mean that all among them is harmonious and trouble-free;
further, their rejection of law bespeaks cleavage between them
and what they see as their community and state.

Given the cultural prerequisites of law, it is possible to
imagine circumstances under which rising rates of litigation would
indicate the increasing integration of society, not the reverse.
When law-aversion stems from a rejection of judicial institutions
and the state that they represent, rising law use may signal a
positive accommodation to or acceptance of the social system.
The law is a basis and means of social participation, quite apart
from its potential effect of permanently damaging private relationships. When law aversion stems from a negative attitude toward social groups that places them outside the cultural order,
then rising litigation and law use might signal a new acceptance
of groups formerly thought to be alien. Even if we choose to
imagine heaven without law, we cannot conclude that an absence
of law brings heaven to earth.

32   20 JOURNAL OF LEGAL PLURALISM/1982

                            NOTES

[1]The ethnographic research that is the basis of part III of
this article began in 1973 and ended in 1975, with a brief visit
of a few weeks in 1980. With one exception which is noted in
the text, the town reported is that of 1973-1975.

Field work was funded by a training grant from the National
Institute of Mental Health to Harvard University's Department of
Anthropology.

An earlier and partial version of this paper was presented
as "History, Ideology and Court Use in an American Town" at the
annual meeting of the American Anthropological Association in
1978. Other versions were presented to the Law and Society Colloquium at the University of Wisconsin Law School, the Anthropology Colloquium at the University of Rochester, and the Law and
Society Association annual meeting in 1981.

I am grateful to Jane Collier, John Griffiths, the late
Klaus-Friedrich Koch, George Marcus, Dennis McGilvray, and Marie
Provine for extremely helpful readings of early drafts.

[2]Some ethnographers report that tribunals are sensitive to
disputants' needs for enduring instrumental relationships (Nader,
1969; Gluckman, 1955; van Velsen, 1964), and others report no
divisive after effects (see text for examples).

[3]Under other circumstances, intimate relations give rise to
considerable court action. Collier (1974) shows that women in
Zinacantan frequently bring complaints against their husbands in
court as a way of adjusting their rights within their husbands'
families; Zinacantec siblings litigate, especially over inherited
land (Collier, 1973:ch. 8). Starr (1978) also shows that intra-
family disputes are a major source of litigated disputes in a
Turkish village.

Another element implicit in the relational distance hypothesis is the concept of the jural community. A jural community
(by definition) shares a single set of jural institutions, and
presumably shares a high degree of normative consensus. Within a
jural community, then, one would expect low levels of disagreement
over norms. In Aubert's (1963) terms, jural communities exhibit
competition rather than disagreement over norms. Conflicts of interest can be resolved without adjudication through the services
of mediators or through negotiation (Eckhoff, 1966:160)--i.e.,
litigation rates within jural communities can be expected to be

low. Conflicts over norms, on the other hand, require an affirmative and authoritative, binding decision whose substance does
not depend on the consent of the disputing parties (Koch. 1974:
27-29; Nader and Todd, 1978:11). Following this reasoning, intra-
community disputes--that is, disputes among people within a jural
community, who are intimates in the terms expressed above--are
less likely to end in litigation than inter-community disputes.
In other words, the idea of a jural community stresses the "distance" in relational distance. The concept of a jural community
also underscores the necessity any community has for identifying
and resolving conflicts of interest. The community described in
part III accomplishes this in various ways. One group uses the
court as a threat, to expedite compliance. The other--the Bap-
tists--redefine private interests so that they, and the disputes
they engender, are eliminated from their midst.

[4]A population may be marginal in its own view, or in the view
of another group, or both; or it may be marginal in the analysis
of social scientists. In both Todd's and Vines' cases, marginality is probably relative to the views of the "insiders" (Todd
is quite clear on this). Importantly, neither group of marginals
was so peripheral that it was outside the legal systems for practical purposes, nor outside the domain of knowledge and resources
requisite for litigation. Both groups were able to take advantage
of their own consciousness of the law to find protection in the
legitimacy of the court. Both were able to conceptualize and
express their conflict in terms that were justiciable by the legal
system.

[5]The term "newcomer" might mean anyone whose family settled
in town in this century. One judge is considered a newcomer, although his parents moved to town just after the first World War.
Currently, most judicial personnel are well-respected newcomers.

[6]For a complete discussion of Georgia politics in this
period, see Phillips (1967).

[7]Increasing religious participation is not in competition
with secular society, but is a function and facilitator of it,
now as then. In the same way that the church destructures (or
restructures) conflict, it depoliticites secular life for its
congregants by encouraging a devaluation of earthly rewards.
Thus, if Baptist workers are upwardly mobile, they express their
success in terms of a widening opportunity for service, not in
terms of effective competition or increased personal income.

BIBLIOGRAPHY

AUBERT, Vilhelm (1963). "Competition and Dissensus: Two Types of Conflict and of Conflict Resolution." Journal of Conflict Resolution 26.

BAUMGARTNER, Mary P. (1978). "Law and Social Status in Colonial New Haven, 1639-1665." In Research in Law and Sociology, edited by R. Simon. Greenwich: JAI Press, Inc.

BLACK, Donald J. (1973). "The Mobilization of Law." 2 Journal of Legal Studies 125.

_____ (1976). The Behavior of Law. New York: Academic Press.

COLLIER, Jane F. (1973). Law and Social Change in Zinacantan. Stanford: Stanford University Press.

_____ (1974). "Women in Politics." In Woman, Culture and Society, edited by M. Rosaldo and L. Lamphere. Stanford: Stanford University Press.

CURRAN, Barbara A., and SPALDING, Francis O. (1974). The Legal Needs of the Public. Chicago: American Bar Foundation.

DAVIS, Allison; GARDNER, Burleigh B.; and GARDNER, Mary R. (1941). Deep South. Chicago: University of Chicago Press.

ECKHOFF, Torstein (1966). "The Mediator, the Judge and the Administrator in Conflict-Resolution." 1-2 Acta Sociologica 148.

FELSTINER, William L. F. (1974). "Influences of Social Organization on Dispute Processing." Law and Society Review 9(1): 63-94.

GALANTER, Marc (1974). "Why the 'Haves' Come Out Ahead." Law and Society Review 9(1):39-62.

GIBBS, James L. (1963). "The Kpelle Moot: A Therapeutic Model for the Informal Settlement of Disputes." 33 Africa 1.

GILMORE, Grant (1977). The Ages of American Law. New Haven and London: Yale University Press.

GLUCKMAN, Max (1955). The Judicial Process among the Barotse of Northern Rhodesia. Manchester: Manchester University Press.

GULLIVER, Phillip H. (1963). Social Control in an African
    Society. Boston: Boston University Press.

KAWASHIMA, Takeyoshi (1973). "Dispute Settlement in Japan." In
    Social Organization of Law, edited by D. Black and M. Mikeski.
    New York and London: Seminar Press.

KOCH, Klaus-Friedrich (1974). War and Peace in Jalémó. Cambridge:
    Harvard University Press.

KRIGE, J. D. (1947). "The Social Functions of Witchcraft."
    Theoria 8:1.

MACAULAY, Stewart (1963). "Non-Contractual Relations in Business:
    A Preliminary Study." American Sociological Review 28:55.

MERRY, Sally E. (1979). "Going to Court: Strategies of Dispute
    Management in an American Urban Neighborhood." Law and
    Society Review 13(4):891-925.

NADER, Laura (1969). "Styles of Court Procedure: To Make the
    Balance." In Law in Culture and Society, edited by L. Nader.
    Chicago: Aldine Publishing Company.

NADER, Laura, and TODD, Harry F., Jr. (1978). The Disputing
    Process--Law in Ten Societies. New York: Columbia Univer-
    sity Press.

PHILLIPS, Ulrich B. (1968). Georgia and State Rights. The
    Antioch Press.

STARR, June (1978). Dispute and Settlement in Rural Turkey.
    Leiden: E. J. Brill.

TODD, Harry L. (1978). "Litigious Marginals: Character and
    Disputing in a Bavarian Village." In The Disputing Process--
    Law in Ten Societies, edited by L. Nader and H. Todd, Jr.
    New York: Columbia University Press.

VINES, Kenneth N. (1966). "Courts and Political Change in the
    South." The Journal of Social Issues 22(1):59-72.

[22]

everyday understandings of the law in working-class America

SALLY ENGLE MERRY—*Wellesley College*

introduction

In America, working-class and poor citizens with relatively little formal education often take private and personal disputes with neighbors, friends, and relatives to court. Their recourse to the law seems to contradict arguments about the opacity and inaccessibility of the legal process to untrained outsiders (cf. Danzig 1973; Cappelletti 1978–79). To understand why people bring their interpersonal problems to court, I observed citizens in a northeastern city who were using the lower criminal and civil courts to deal with a wide variety of family, neighbor, romantic, and business problems. I wanted to know how they understood the legal system and how that understanding changed as a result of their experiences in court. These litigants were primarily white and working class. They turned to the courts believing that the law was awesome and powerful, capable of uncovering the truth, applying laws firmly, and providing some kind of justice. Their ideas reflected the dominant legal ideology of American society. They emerged from their encounters with the law with a more complex understanding, having experienced the dual legal ideologies embedded within the American lower courts. One of these ideologies expresses the dominant American vision of justice provided by the rule of law, the other a situationally based, lenient, and personalistic vision of justice produced within the local setting.

Ideology, as I am using the term, describes an aspect or slice of culture located within a particular institutional arena. An ideology is a set of categories by which people interpret and make events meaningful. It includes both explicit rules and implicit schemes. As Bourdieu points out, implicit principles or schemes enable actors to generate a wide variety of practices in response to an infinite array of changing situations without these schemes being constituted as explicit principles (1977:16).[1] The categories, rules, and schemes that constitute an ideology are typically organized into a consistent structure.

Anthropologists have long used the concept of ideology to describe systems of meaning and belief. Here, I wish to join the anthropological view of ideology as an aspect of culture with the Marxist view of ideology as a way of maintaining relations of power and dominance. Thinking of ideology as culture highlights questions of harmony, integration, and consensus, while think-

An ethnographic examination of the way working-class Americans who use courts to manage their family and neighborhood disputes think about and use the law suggests that they share beliefs in legal rights and the legal ordering of society characteristic of American society in general. However, when they encounter the courts they develop a more complex understanding that incorporates the plural legal ideologies found within the courthouse. The process of constructing local as well as dominant ideologies has implications for understanding the role of ideology in the maintenance of social order and for analyzing the hegemonic function of law. [legal anthropology, ideology, dispute processing, social control, theory of the state]

ing of ideology in terms of power and dominance highlights questions of conflict, control, and hegemony.

Traditional Marxist views of ideology tend to see ideas as delusions or screens concealing reality rather than as categories for creating social reality as Geertz describes (1973).[2] However, recent work in the Marxist tradition, particularly in the theory of practice, is developing a view of ideology that avoids the proposition that ideology is false consciousness. Instead of viewing ideas and action as analytically distinct, the goal is to develop a way of understanding the social world that bridges these categories (for example, Bourdieu 1977; Sumner 1979; Ortner 1984; Hunt 1985; Silbey 1985). Ideology is not viewed as separate from action but as integral to all social practices (Sumner 1979:ix). Ideology is constitutive, in that ideas about an event or relationship define that activity, much as the rules about a game define a move or a victory in that game (see Martin 1982). In chess, for example, a checkmate is defined by the rules of the game and only exists if the players have followed the rules about how the pieces can move. Ideology contains categories that define experiences and social relationships. It does not conceal reality but constructs it. There is no social world except as it is lived and experienced, and events become socially meaningful only when they are interpreted.

The ability to interpret or apply meaning to an event confers power. Ideology, as a slice of culture, controls by constraining thought. As Ortner points out in her discussion of practice theory,

> Although constraints of material and political sorts, including force, are fully acknowledged, there seems to be general agreement that action is constrained most deeply and systematically by the ways in which culture controls the definitions of the world for actors, limits their conceptual tools, and restricts their emotional repertoires. Culture becomes part of the self" [1984:153].

Mather and Yngvesson point to the power exercised by a third party or audience in a conflict situation who is able to define and transform a dispute (1980). In Turkish courts, judges have considerable power to gather evidence and construct accounts, which is central to their ability to settle cases (Starr 1985). Transactional analysis has explored the implications for control inherent in the creation of meaning (for example, Kapferer 1976; Bailey 1983).

legal ideology and hegemony

Legal ideology, neo-Marxist scholarship suggests, plays a critical role in strengthening the hegemony of ruling groups (see, for example, Cain and Hunt 1979; Sumner 1979; Abel 1982; Genovese 1982). Gramsci's concept of hegemony points to the constraining role of culture:

> By hegemony Gramsci meant the permeation throughout civil society—including a whole range of structures and activities like trade unions, schools, the churches, and the family—of an entire system of values, attitudes, beliefs, morality, etc. that is in one way or another supportive of the established order and the classes' interests that dominate it. . . . To the extent that this prevailing consciousness is internalized by the broad masses, it becomes part of "common sense". . . . In short, hegemony worked in many ways to induce the oppressed to accept or "consent" to their own exploitation and daily misery [Boggs, quoted in Greer 1982:305].

In one of the important currents in recent critical work on law, the Critical Legal Studies Movement, scholars argue that legal doctrine reflects not a systematic and coherent process of legal reasoning but structures of political and economic power (Kairys 1982; Beirne and Quinney 1982). Law plays a critical role in justifying and legitimizing the social order by inducing citizens to perceive the power of ruling groups as fair and acceptable. It confers legitimacy on the rule of dominant groups by mystifying real power relationships, making them appear to the mass of the population as reasonable and just. As Trubek argues,

> Critical scholars see social order as maintained by mutually reinforcing systems of belief and organization. But these beliefs are not in any sense "true." Quite the contrary, the belief systems which structure action and maintain order in capitalist societies present as eternal and necessary what is only the tran-

sitory and arbitrary interest of a dominant elite whose unequal and unjust power is justified by what appear to be a commonly acceptable body of ideas. Thus, systems of ideas are *reifications*, presenting as essential, necessary, and objective what is contingent, arbitrary, and subjective. Furthermore, they are *hegemonic*, that is, they serve to legitimate interests of the dominant class and it alone [1983:41].

However, we have little empirical evidence about the extent to which legal doctrine is known to people in subordinate positions or the implications of this knowledge for their ideas about the legitimacy and justice of the social system. The method of doctrinal legal analysis adopted by critical legal scholars has focused on the explication of elite legal ideology, not on the nature of working-class ideas about law or the implications of this ideology for their acceptance of the existing order (Munger and Seron 1984). Citizens' acceptance of subordinate positions does not necessarily mean they view these positions as legitimate or just; they may simply see no realistic alternative (Mann 1970). As yet, the role of legal ideology in preserving or changing existing power relations has not typically been addressed by anthropologists studying law, although it offers a promising way to move beyond the study of disputes (Collier 1982).[1]

dominant and local ideologies

The traditional Marxist analysis of ideology assumed that its production was a top-down process in which ruling groups imposed ideas onto subordinate groups that absorbed them. This model did not describe the complex meaning systems of the local social systems I observed nor the creative, constructive role of local actors. The view of the law held by these working-class individuals is hardly a simple reflection of the legal ideology produced by a dominant elite. It is a negotiated, constructed reality developed in local social settings through repeated interactions, not a faithful replica of the dominant ideology

I suggest that we need to talk about at least two different kinds of ideology: a top-down, elite-produced and disseminated ideology, and a bottom-up, locally constructed one. Top-down and bottom-up ideologies can coexist within the same social setting, as they did in the lower court I observed. This creates a situation of ideological pluralism. Ideologies can be plural in the same way as subcultures are plural in complex societies. As Hannerz argues, people living in cities often know something and have opinions about many alternative modes of thought and action shared by other social groups, producing a kind of metacultural knowledge or awareness of other modes of thought (1984:4). Plural ideologies can coexist because they contain rules or principles about which ideological frame applies under what circumstances and for which audiences.

In the bottom-up production of ideology, some aspects of the ideology of the dominant society are incorporated and others are not. The top-down ideology is both a resource and a constraint. The important questions concern the limits within which these local ideologies are constructed and the implications of these constructions for maintenance or change in the existing social order.

The legal ideology of the American working-class plaintiffs I observed incorporated conceptions of rights and obligations inherent in social relationships coupled with expectations about the way these rights are enforced. Since legal rights and duties are by definition those the state deems worthy of protection through its coercive powers, the practices by which they are enforced are intrinsic to their definitions. Enforcement of rights may occur in many ways besides bringing a defendant to trial and imposing a penalty on him or her, such as threatening to take action if the offense recurs or requiring social services.

Through the ethnographic study of the plural legal ideologies of an American courthouse, I will explore the extent to which legal ideology, as a system of categories and rules embodied within legal institutions, constrains and controls social action as well as the limitations on the control exercised by dominant ideologies springing from the creative ability of actors to construct their own definitions of social reality and to change and restructure the elements of the larger ideology (see also Nader 1984).

the research and the setting

This paper draws on several years of ethnographic research on the ways working-class and poor Americans in the northeastern United States think about and use the law in interpersonal disputes. From 1975 to 1976, I examined processes of social control and use of the courts in a multiethnic, low-income urban neighborhood (1979, 1981). From 1980 to 1983, Susan Silbey and I observed the ways family, neighbor, and small-claims disputes were handled in courts and in two types of mediation program, an alternative to the court. The study included extensive ethnographic observation of the mediation programs themselves, the courts, and the communities within which the disputes arose.[4] Most of the people in this study were working-class whites; a few were poor blacks and whites and a few middle-class whites (Merry and Silbey 1984). From 1982 to 1984, I examined the way status offender cases involving rebellious, truant, or runaway juveniles were handled in juvenile court and in a mediation alternative, also in a white, working-class population (Merry and Rocheleau 1985).[5]

The working-class people I observed turned to the court for help in dealing with a wide variety of interpersonal disputes. The cases concerned arguments about the duties, obligations, and rights of social relationships. Typical disputes concerned violence or harassment between spouses, lovers, and neighbors, fights over barking dogs, noisy children, and parking spaces within a neighborhood, debts between roommates or landlords and tenants, disagreements over money or how to raise children within a family, and arguments about chores and curfews between parents and adolescent children. Plaintiffs were usually seeking protection, more control in a relationship, or separation. Most said that they wanted a problem to stop or to be left alone.

I observed three channels through which interpersonal disputes arrived in the court system. Some came to the lower criminal courts as charges of harassment, assault, threats, or domestic violence. Some arrived in small claims court as demands for money or return of property in ongoing relationships between merchants and customers, landlords and tenants, employers and employees, roommates, friends, and family members. Complaints by parents about their teenagers' rebellious or truant behavior appeared in the juvenile court. In almost all cases, the conflicts discussed in this paper arrived in court because of citizen initiative. Once in court, a substantial proportion were referred to one of three different mediation programs. In mediation, the parties to the dispute spend between 2 and 4 hours discussing their differences in an informal setting under the supervision of a mediator—a neutral third party. The mediator's role is to help the parties arrive at some written agreement which they sign and carry out themselves.

All these cases share an important characteristic: they present the courts with problems for which their traditional remedies of incarceration, fines, monetary damages, restitution, or removing a child from its parents' custody are usually not helpful. For the legal system, these interpersonal disputes are often unresolvable cases, because the help that the plaintiff is seeking is outside the realm of solutions the courts can provide.

The people who appeared in court as plaintiffs and as defendants can be described as working class. They are not the welfare poor, but hourly wage workers. They often work overtime or at two jobs since they can increase their incomes primarily by working more hours. Most have a high school education or less. The men are typically factory workers, low-level salesmen or managers, truck drivers, maintenance workers, or food service employees, while the women are usually clerical or service workers, homemakers, or factory workers. A few are on welfare, but most support themselves through their own or their spouse's labor.

the legal ideology of the working class

When the working-class court user crosses the threshold into the lower court, he or she unwittingly enters an ideologically complex world. This world can be roughly divided into two ideologies. One, an ideology of formal justice, springs from the dominant political ideology of American society and is expressed to outsiders, particularly representatives of the legal elite. This is a top-down ideology. The second, an ideology of situational justice, also provides categories for interpretation and action but is a bottom-up ideology, locally constructed and situationally determined. Both contain explicit rules and implicit principles of practice, but the first is more extensively constituted by explicit principles and the second by implicit principles.*

the ideology of formal justice   Working-class court users typically see themselves endowed with a broad set of legal rights, loosely defined, which shade into moral rights. These rights are part of the symbolic system by which obligations between neighbors, friends, and family members are understood. Legal rights fall into two general categories: property and personal. Property rights are broad rights to use and retain possessions, including rights to control who comes into one's house and land and what he or she does there. Personal rights are the rights to freedom from insult, harassment, threats, or violence without provocation. All persons have equal rights to property, to privacy, and to a certain level of respect as a person. These rights are routinely enforced by the state through a system of police and courts that are accessible to all. The state takes infractions of the legal rights of its citizens seriously. To be accused of a violation of the law is a serious and frightening event, and to make accusations of others is to invoke a powerful weapon. The court itself is regarded with awe and fear and a court appearance is a scary experience. In this ideology, persons are legally defined as equals and enforcement is predictable and firm.

The ideology of formal justice is the articulated, dominant model of American society. The ideas come from the general political theory underlying the liberal state. According to Ashcraft, liberal political theory views all men as equal and independent individuals with no ties of social dependence (1984:653). It claims that all citizens are entitled to natural rights, toleration, and equality. This political theory emerged at the end of the Middle Ages from artisans, tradesmen, merchants, and small landed gentry who were displaced from control of the means of production (Ashcraft 1984:653–654). It was, Ashcraft argues, a theory proposed by people who did not hold social and political power in their own society, so imagined themselves living in a "natural community" in which they could exercise such power.

These ideas are as appealing to working-class Americans as they were to their original proponents. Their ideas about the law and its role in society grow out of this general political understanding of legal rights rather than accurate knowledge of the rights articulated by law. For example, although in law property owners are obligated to keep their property free from hazards that could harm trespassers, to these working-class court users, rights to determine the actions of others on their property are absolute and unqualified. Further, they seek legal relief when someone has been calling them insulting names and making faces repeatedly, even though the legal codes provide little protection from insult and carefully define the kinds of assault that warrant legal action.

I observed one case in which a tenant moved out of his apartment 10 days after the beginning of the month and failed to pay the entire month's rent. The landlord, assuming that the tenant was legally obligated for the whole amount, made no effort to rent the apartment until the end of the month. Meanwhile, he took the tenant to small claims court. The landlord did not realize that he was legally obligated to diminish his own loss by trying to rent the apartment. Unaware of this duty to mitigate, he was furious when the judge did not award him the entire amount. The legal ideas of these working-class litigants are not linked to concepts and categories within the body of the law, such as assumption of risk, comparative negligence, or duty to mitigate, but are reflections of a more general political consciousness of rights possessed by individuals and protected by the state (Hunt 1985).

the ideology of situational justice   A second set of ideas about the nature of legal rights and the processes by which they are enforced can be described as an ideology of situational justice. In this view, enforcement of laws is not automatic; it must be triggered by complaints. Furthermore, all cases with the same label—harassment, assault—are not viewed as equally serious. Seriousness, and therefore the odds that the court will do anything, such as imposing a penalty, depends on several things. First, it depends on who you are: whether or not you have a job, money, and a reputation for being in trouble with the law in the past. A person who appears in court again and again loses credibility with the court personnel. Those who can claim that they are working and supporting their families will be treated more leniently than those who are not. Second, seriousness depends on the situation surrounding the specific incident, not simply the legal definition of the charge—the relationship between the parties, the mutuality of the conflict, the intent of the offender, the extent of the injury, the past history of the problem. Fights between relatives or neighbors, even when these involve serious injury or personal loss, are not considered real crimes.

In this ideology, interpersonal cases are not generally considered worthy of a full trial. They should be handled earlier and more informally by negotiations and discussions with a clerk, prosecutor, or mediation program. There is constant pressure on the parties by court officials at each level to discuss the problem and settle it themselves, often beginning with the first contact with the police. Severe penalties, even when they are specified by the statutes, are rarely applied to problems that are not viewed as serious. The court typically provides warnings, continuances, alternative social services, and threats that if further problems erupt, it will act firmly. As Feeley observes in his study of a similar court, the process is often more costly and severe in its penalties than the punishment that is ultimately imposed (1979). The court is seen to operate to some extent according to familiar principles of social life rather than abstract legal categories and complex procedures. Situational justice is closer to the clients' commonsense understandings of justice, in that rights are viewed as embedded in social relationships and situations rather than as abstracted from them.[7]

Situational justice differs from the ideology of formal justice in two central points. The first concerns the definition of the person. In the ideology of formal justice, the person is the bearer of rights proffered by the state to all citizens equally. In the ideology of situational justice, the person is socially constructed by his or her history, character, rank, and social or ethnic identity. Behavior is judged in terms of customary standards presumed to exist for such persons. Although the notion of persons as differentially endowed with rights depending on their social position contradicts the provisions of the legal system of most Western states, it is commonly found among nonstate societies in which offenses such as murder are recompensed differently depending on the social status of the victim (see, for example, Evans-Pritchard 1940; Saler 1984; Bentley 1984b).

The second difference between this ideology and the ideology of formal justice concerns the nature of enforcement. Instead of flowing inevitably from a violation of the law, enforcement is viewed as dependent on the social identities of the parties and their relationship. The law is a set of rules that are enforced partially and only when someone complains. Interpersonal disputes are not seen as real "crimes" but as less important, "garbage" cases because of their social context. Enforcement can be manipulated depending on how the problem is presented.[8]

the dual ideologies of the courthouse   One ideology is not more "true" than the other; both reflect a kind of truth about the way the system works. Court officials—judges, prosecutors, defense attorneys, clerks, and probation officers—work within a cultural world constituted by these dual understandings of the law and the tension between them. One does not drive out the other. They coexist as alternative sources of discourse and argument for court officials. Court officials often move back and forth between the two depending on their objectives. A person pressing charges in an interpersonal dispute may be warned of the seriousness of the penalties and be urged to drop the charges while court officials comment privately to each other that nothing will be done about the case. Formal threats to defendants about the seriousness of their offenses and the penalties for them are often coupled with backstage discussions between judges and attorneys about the futility of imposing any penalties on the defendant.

The practice embodied in the ideology of situational justice is typically unarticulated and informal. Since it violates the standards of the dominant ideology, it is often the subject of criticism and demands for reform. It represents the informal rules of the courtroom workgroup (Eisenstein and Jacob 1977; Feeley 1979; Lipetz 1983) but is often not acknowledged to outsiders, particularly those who represent the legal elite. For example, after hearing court officials talk about "garbage" cases on several occasions, I began asking if anyone knew what the term meant. Some denied having ever heard it but could imagine what it referred to, while others claimed that although they had heard the term, they never used it. In another example, a local defense attorney engaged in a trial in criminal court was opposed by a visiting prosecuting attorney from the downtown attorney general's office. As the prosecutor attempted to block his introduction of evidence on procedural technicalities, the local attorney complained angrily, "We're just here to try a case, we're not here to practice law."

An understanding of how situational justice operates and the assumptions on which it is based can be acquired through experience with the court either as a litigant or as a practitioner—a judge, lawyer, probation officer, prosecutor, and so forth. But the ideology of situational justice is largely unarticulated. It is the ideology of formal justice that provides the language of argument and justification within the courthouse.

Lawyers play a critical role in informing their clients about situational justice ideology. Plaintiffs who consulted a lawyer were typically advised not to press their case, that "the court would laugh at it" and that the outcome was very unpredictable, while defendants who turned to a lawyer were assured that, in general, penalties are very light in interpersonal cases. Lawyers provide some map of the way the courts will view each case and some ideas about what the courts will do to their clients, although the pressures of time and disinterest mean that lawyers do not always do so (cf. Sarat and Felstiner 1984).

Although court reformers frequently identify situational justice practices as a failure of due process, they are in fact ways of tailoring the formal law to citizen demands (Silbey 1981). As Silbey argues, the lower courts are caught in the tension between formal legal rationality and substantive justice. As courts become more routinized and oriented to due process, they need to develop more informal procedures to provide a more individualized, situational, and responsive process. Situational justice is the result of the efforts of judges, probation officers, and prosecutors to provide justice within a legal context that does not really fit the problems at hand (Silbey 1981). Yet, because the ideology of formal justice confers legitimacy on their activities, the court officials cannot abandon it (see Lipetz 1983).[9]

the case of the ball-playing ordinance   One neighborhood dispute that was taken to court and referred to mediation illustrates clearly the two ideologies. During the 3-hour discussion, both sides presented their positions to one another and, in private, to the mediators. The description of the dispute is primarily based on the discussion in the mediation session, but it also draws on interviews with some of the participants a few months after the mediation session.

The dispute erupted between neighbors who lived very close together on a small back street with no sidewalks. The complaining side consisted of three families, two of whom owned their small houses and the third of whom was a tenant, and the defendant side, an older couple, whom I will call Mr. and Mrs. Brown, who lived across the street. Their one son was grown and away from the home; the other families had several small children ranging in age from 2 to 13. The Browns were very unhappy about the number and noise of children playing in the street in front of their house and about the cars parked in front of their house. They often called the police to complain. The Browns had discovered that there was an ordinance in the town prohibiting ball-playing and snowball-throwing in the streets. They went to the mayor and the alderman, and were told that this was a city ordinance and must be obeyed. Consequently, they called the police whenever the children came out to play ball, sometimes as often as five times a day.

The families with children were very unhappy about the number of visits from the police, and the police themselves grew tired of coming. They apparently told the families that they come only when someone makes a complaint, and urged them to take the Browns to court for harassment. When the Browns heard that the police were claiming that the law is enforced only when someone complains, they went to the chief of police, who assured them that his officers would never say such a thing. They reported that he said, "If something is against the law, that is all there is to it." The Browns denied responsibility for the frequent appearance of the police because, they said, "The police are simply enforcing the law."

In the mediation session, they complained bitterly: "Your children have not respected any of our rights." The families retorted that the law is old and outdated, that the police enforce it only when someone complains, and that their children's activities were normal play. As one mother said,

> The kids are just playing ball. This is an innocent thing to do, it is not as if they were harassing or bothering the Browns, breaking windows, or causing harm. The way kids act these days, playing ball is very innocent.

The Browns said that the children were breaking the law, while their parents defined their actions as normal play. Six months after this mediation session, in the dead of the northeast winter, the three families reported no further problems with the Browns, said that the calls to the police had stopped, and that they had not gone back to court, but expressed concern about what the summer would bring.

In this dispute, the two sides differed not only in their preferences about when and where children should play, but also in their legal ideologies. They have developed different interpretations of the situation, each side finding justification for its interpretation within the dual legal ideologies of legal officials. Mr. and Mrs. Brown claimed that since there is an ordinance against ball-playing on the streets, they need take no responsibility for having the law enforced. Law, they argue, is absolute: it commands behavior and everyone must follow. They describe their calls to the police as making something happen that is inevitable. They have been supported in this view by the mayor, the aldermen, and the police chief, who provided them with an interpretation based on the ideology of formal justice. On the other hand, the three families see the law as discretionary and situational; incompletely enforced, possibly irrelevant or outdated, and activated only by individual complaints. The police officers appear to have supported this perspective by telling these families that the law is an old, 19th-century statute imposed only when someone complains, interpreting the situation in terms of situational justice.

The law is hardly irrelevant here: in fact it provides symbolic and material resources for the dispute and establishes the boundaries of the settlement. The fact that ball-playing is against the ordinance does make a difference; the dispute concerns what kinds of difference it makes. The parties differ in their ideologies of the law, a difference found within the legal system itself.[10]

encounters with legal practice

Most of the working-class court users I talked to began their encounters with the legal system naively, interpreting it according to an ideology of formal justice. However, after extensive contact with the police and the courts, some became experienced users and acquired both ideologies, together with a theory that explains when one applies and when the other applies.[11] Defendants and plaintiffs who recognize the duality of ideologies in the court and the nature of the linkage between them can become as sophisticated as court officials in the courthouse game. They become increasingly effective in harnessing and using the power of the law for their own purposes. The model of dual ideologies explains the way encounters with the legal system shape ideas about the law and transform attitudes toward law and the legitimacy of the social order. It suggests that the court is indeed a strange, remote, and incomprehensible institution until citizens begin to use it. Then they still see it as unpredictable, but less so because they recognize its implicit principles as well as its explicit rules. The ritual of the court loses its awe and power as the process reveals itself to be informal, negotiated, and flexible.

the case of the estranged lovers   Court personnel sometimes use litigants' ideology of formal justice to induce plaintiffs to drop charges or to frighten defendants into complying with the wishes of the court. The following case provides an example of the way court officials handle an interpersonal case and manipulate these dual understandings of the law. It describes the attitudes of an experienced court user (the 28-year-old defendant) and his far more naive ex-girlfriend, a 26-year-old woman. She had been to court only once before in a dispute with the same boyfriends, but had quickly dropped the charges.

In this case, the young woman charged her former boyfriend with assault and trespass and with intimidating a witness. At a hearing before a clerk on the intimidation charge (after the assault and trespass charges had already been issued), the clerk announced to the defendant that this was a serious case and that there were serious charges against him. The clerk concluded, "I shouldn't do this, but I will give you another chance. I will send this back to mediation." The clerk then issued the complaint on the charge of intimidating a witness. As the young woman was waiting to have the form typed up, however, the police prosecutor, a veteran of many years in the court, tried to persuade her to drop this charge. He pointed out that the penalty was 5 years in prison and said, "Do you really want him to do time? Maybe you should drop it. You have plenty of others against him, and it just makes work for the court." He also told her that, "If you keep coming back to court, filing complaints when things are going badly in a relationship and then dismissing them, it looks bad to the court." The plaintiff was afraid of sending him to jail, both because she thought he needed psychiatric help rather than jail and because his friends had threatened to beat her up if he went to jail. She agreed to tear up the charge. As she left the court, the police prosecutor advised her to stay away from the ex-boyfriend.

However, in a subsequent private conversation with me, the police prosecutor said that although the charge is a felony and would be heard in the higher court, nothing would happen in this case. The charge is serious, he said, only if there is a real threat and the parties are strangers; when there has been a past relationship and the parties know one another, the judge does not take it seriously. Even though the prosecutor recognized that the court would do little on this charge, he used the formal sentence to persuade the plaintiff not to press the charge.

The defense attorney appointed by the state to represent the young man expressed a similar view to me: she said that these people are just "flakes," that if they weren't going to court against each other they would be doing it with someone else, and that this is just the way they live. There was, in her view, no point in doing anything about the case. She felt that if the defendant did not have a prior record, the court would continue the case without a finding and leave it at that. She urged the parties to settle, to try mediation, and advised the defendant to stay away from the woman. She thus provided a more situational justice perspective of the case to the defendant than the court officials did, but could not eliminate entirely the formal justice definition of the seriousness of the charge.

The prosecutor handling the case told me that he also hoped they could settle elsewhere because he did not want to try it. He, too, tried to send it back to the mediation program. When the case came to court for a pretrial conference, the judge warned the defendant to stay away from the girl, and the police prosecutor again urged the parties to settle on their own. The case was sent to mediation for the third time. This time the defendant did appear, but only because the mediation session was held in the courthouse on the day he had to appear for other charges against him.

When the case came to court for trial after a mediation session that had produced an agreement, the attorneys told the parties that the case would be continued for 2 months and would be dismissed if the defendant followed the mediation agreement. The agreement contained essentially the same terms that the attorneys expected the court to impose. The defendant agreed to seek counseling and both agreed to act amicably to one another if they met and to avoid making comments about each other's friends. Two months later, the case was dismissed. The two parties came to court together and acted in a friendly manner. They were not living with each other, but the plaintiff wanted the case dropped. The case had been in court for 4 months.

During the whole court process, the central issue was whether or not this was a "serious" case. Its identification as serious or trivial depended on whether it was judged in its social context—according to the categories of formal or situational justice. The defendant did not think the charges were serious, nor did he anticipate receiving a jail sentence. He was an experienced court user, frequently in court for charges of assault, threats, drunk driving, and driving without a license. He knew his way around the court. His cavalier attitude in failing to appear for two mediation sessions, which would have allowed him to settle the case outside the criminal process, underscored his lack of concern about serious penalties. He was fairly sure that his previous record did not include offenses that would be taken seriously. However, the suspended sentence hanging over his head from a previous charge of trespass, threats, and assault against his former wife was a minor source of concern. He felt he would not receive a serious penalty from the present charge, but he was not certain. He was not entirely sure which of the outcomes his offense merited under the two legal ideologies the court would apply: a stiff prison sentence or a warning to stay away from the woman for 2 months with a threat to take action if he did not.

The more naive ex-girlfriend was afraid that the case was serious, however. She was always willing to try mediation and to drop some charges because she was afraid the defendant would be sent to jail. She was clear that she did not want him to go to jail, only to stop hitting her and to get psychiatric help. The prosecutor, the police prosecutor, and the clerk had all told her that his previous record made this case more serious. She thought that the sentence for her charge was 2 years in prison.

The defense attorney, the prosecutor, and the police prosecutor all told me that this was not a serious case nor one for which there would be penalties. It was not serious because of the relationship between the parties and the fact that they thought the parties were using the court to manage their relationship. They felt that "this is just the way these people live." No one disputed that the defendant had indeed hit and injured the plaintiff. On the other hand, the court officials emphasized to the parties the seriousness of the charges and the power of the legal weapons they were wielding. They repeatedly pressed the parties to settle, to stay away from each other, and to try mediation, using statements about the seriousness of the charges to persuade the plaintiff to drop them and to encourage the defendant to stay away from her.

One implication of ideological pluralism is that it provides flexibility and room to maneuver since either ideology can be applied. The result is some uncertainty about the legal outcome and about the process itself. The experienced court user learns that, in general, interpersonal cases are judged in terms of situation and context rather than the requirements of the formal law. He or she sees that through a series of backstage, informal adjustments, the law is tailored to handle the problem in its social context. Nevertheless, since the dominant ideology is still the explicit principle of operation in the court, there is no guarantee that a case will be handled situationally rather than formally. Understanding this ideological pluralism explains some of the unpredictability of the legal process.

the case of the unacceptable lover   Another case further illustrates the duality in the criminal court's response to an interpersonal conflict. A young man was very interested in a 14-year-old girl whose father heartily disapproved of the match. He tried to persuade the young man to stay away from his daughter, but when this failed, he began to use the court to separate the couple. He charged the young man with assault and trespass and finally with threats against his son.

When this third charge arrived in the court, the judge listened to the claim of the court-appointed defense attorney that the charge should be dropped because the application for complaint contained an error. The description of the incident referred to a threat to punch, while the charge was threat to murder. The judge then called the prosecutor, the defense attorney, and the probation officer to his chambers for a private discussion. Here he asked, "What is going on? What can we do?" The prosecutor and the probation officer, both of whom had seen this case in various guises over the years, explained that it was not simply a case of threats, but a dispute between a stubborn and persistent father and a stubborn and persistent young man who loved the daughter, that they lived close together, and that previous efforts to resolve the problem had failed. They recommended a continuation of probation contingent upon his staying away from the girl. The defense attorney quickly agreed to the extension of probation, apologizing that he was new and did not know the history of the problem. The fact that the application was legally invalid was passed over. The judge agreed to extend probation until the winter months in the hope that the chill temperatures would cool the young man's ardor. When the prosecutor asked the judge to do something to appease the father, who frequently called the prosecutor demanding help from the court, the judge agreed to give a stern lecture in the courtroom.

Returning to the courtroom, the judge was disappointed to see that the father had left, but with a formal manner and legalistic language, he announced his imposition of an extension of probation to the young man and his assembled friends. He emphasized the serious consequences of violating this probation. The young man, an experienced court user, told me that he had no intention of staying away from his girlfriend this time, just as he had ignored the previous threats of the court.

The judge defined the case in its social context and decided upon a course of action appropriate to that definition, despite the fact that within formal justice ideology he should have dismissed the flawed charge. Recognizing the insoluble nature of the social problem, the attorneys acquiesced. Their concerns were to provide justice and respond to the needs of the community they served, not to adhere to an ideology of formal justice that imposes rules predictably. They combined a backstage negotiation of situational justice with a frontstage performance couched in the language and ritual of formal justice.

the juvenile court   A similar pattern can be found in the juvenile court. Judges in juvenile court sometimes use a defendant's naive views of the law to persuade him or her to comply with their demands. Juveniles who fail to attend school or who run away from home or whose parents find they are rebellious can be charged by parents, police, or school officials as status offenders. In the state in which I studied this phenomenon, the court has the power to declare these adolescents "children in need of services" and to assign custody to the social services department. Ultimately, a child can be removed from the home and placed in a group home, foster care setting, or a residential treatment facility. Placements of this kind occur very rarely, however. Of 125 adolescents handled in two local courts over a 2-year period, only 22 percent were placed. Furthermore, a judge cannot place a child, but only assign custody to the state's Department of Social Services (Merry and Rocheleau 1985).

Yet, the threat of placement is one of the most powerful tools that a judge has at his disposal. Consequently, judges frequently threaten placement or removal from the home, particularly in follow-up hearings when a teenager has demonstrated his unwillingness to attend school or counseling despite the court's recommendation. On the other hand, when parents arrive in the court requesting that their children be placed, which they do occasionally, the judge takes a very different approach. At this point, judges typically say that children are very rarely placed and it is difficult to arrange. Thus, the judge presents the child with the penalties inscribed in formal justice and the parents with the penalties applied in situational justice in order to frighten the child into changing while discouraging the parent from pursuing the charge, thereby reducing the likelihood that the child will be expensively placed.

In this example, as in the previous one, court personnel maneuver within their ideological pluralism, depending on their objectives and audiences. As citizens also learn these plural ideologies, however, these threats and maneuvers are less effective. The experienced court user comes to see that his or her interpersonal case is not considered serious or worthy of a serious penalty, despite the provisions of the formal law. Probation officers, clerks, judges, and prosecutors recognize that once defendants have learned that not much happens to them in court, they need not take charges seriously. As one probation officer said, "After a while, they begin to think that the court is a joke."[12]

the plaintiff's response

Some plaintiffs with interpersonal disputes get what they want from the lower courts, but many emerge from their legal encounters bitter and disappointed. Yet, they often return because they think they have no place else to go. Most of the parents who took their children to court as status offenders, for example, did it as a last resort. Of the mothers—the typical plaintiffs—48 percent said that they were satisfied with the court but only 25 percent said that they got what they expected from the court. Eighty-four percent of the mothers and 88 percent of the children said they understood what went on in court (Merry and Rocheleau 1985).

Some individuals who went to criminal court or small claims court were frustrated that the court would not act more firmly. One woman who had been taken to the police, court, Board of Health, and other town agencies by a persistent neighbor with complaints about her dog and about construction on her house finally decided to sell the small house she and her husband had spent a year and a great deal of money fixing up. She took the neighbor to criminal court on a charge of assault, but the charge was dismissed. This woman said in a later interview:

> I don't believe in law or judges or courts any more. I was raised to believe in them, but I am not going to raise my daughter that way. They are just geared to helping who they want and they didn't do anything to help me. They couldn't stop those people from driving me out of my house.

On the other hand, when the neighbor filed a complaint of threats against her, the court dismissed that charge as well.

Another woman, who took her neighbor in a public housing project to criminal court charging that her daughter had attempted to strangle her son, had to make three separate trips to the courthouse, each costing time and carfare. The first two times the other woman did not appear. The complaint was issued, and the third visit was for the arraignment. She said of the court:

> I didn't like the court because they didn't talk to me—they were too busy. I just had to stand there and wait. The judge seemed OK, reasonably fair, but I didn't talk to him at all. The court is too busy dealing with important legal problems, and I shouldn't really have taken my case there, but there was no place else to go. I know it doesn't belong there. I did go to the manager of the project first, but I got nowhere.

A young man who charged his ex-girlfriend with malicious damage to get her to move out of his house also commented that the court treated this as a small problem, although it was a big problem to him.

These plaintiffs typically experience difficulty in getting the court to provide the relief they are seeking. For example, a small landlord who tried to evict a tenant for nonpayment of rent found that, despite a judgment in her favor, the process had taken her a year and meant repeated appearances in court as well as costs, including $280 she had to pay the constable to move the tenant's furniture out. When the next tenant failed to pay rent, this woman was eager for a new process, and tried mediation. When this failed to get the tenant to pay her rent or move out, she again went to court.

Users frequently complain that they are treated routinely, as if they were a category rather than a person. For example, in a landlord/tenant case in which the tenant had gone to small claims court to sue for return of his security deposit, the court awarded him one-third of the money he felt he was owed. The tenant, a college student, said that he had only one minute to give the facts before the judge cut him off. The student had looked up the relevant law on security deposits and attempted to read it to the judge, but said the judge was not pleased by this and interrupted him:

> He made the decision on the basis of stereotypes, because he said, "This sounds like a young bachelor apartment case." There was little discussion of the law. The judge was not interested in the law at all, but only in the details of the situation.

The small landlord in this case also complained that there were no laws cited and that there was no chance to ask questions, no give and take. He felt a little intimidated by small claims court:

> I feel like they are in a hurry to get you through, that your case isn't that important. The decision is just based on who the judge finds more believable.

In the case described earlier, the landlord who had failed to rent his apartment because he was ignorant of the duty to mitigate was also angry and frustrated. He said:

> I used to think there is justice in court, but not now. People are not going to court today—there is no justice. People are going to start taking things into their own hands.

legal ideologies and court use

Despite these dissatisfactions, however, some plaintiffs return to court, frequently saying that the court is a last resort and they have nowhere else to go. As they come to understand the situational as well as the formal character of justice, they continue to use the court, but with more limited expectations. Many disputants who went through mediation and then confronted further problems with the same person or a new problem returned to the court, not to mediation. A significant proportion of plaintiffs who came to mediation with interpersonal problems had a history of turning to the court, the police, and city agencies for other problems in the past.

The same pattern appears in an examination of who uses the clerk's office. In this state, every citizen-initiated charge must have a hearing before a court clerk to determine whether there is sufficient evidence to issue a complaint. Yngvesson's study of two clerk's offices in this state indicates that they generally fail to issue complaints in about two-thirds of citizen-initiated cases (1985:74–75). In one of the courts I studied, 41 percent of non-issued citizen-complaint applications for one year involved interpersonal relationships.[13] Twelve percent of the non-issued citizen-complaint applications involved people who had appeared more than once in the clerk's office that year. Almost all of these were interpersonal cases. In contrast, only 2 percent of the non-issued cases with institutional plaintiffs handled by the clerk's office in 1981—primarily concerning bad checks, welfare, or Board of Health disputes—involved repeat defendants. Many of the institutions were frequent users of the court. Eighteen interpersonal disputes generated 19 percent (42) of the 220 interpersonal case filings, accounting for 66 percent of all repeat cases. Of the 556 cases involving interpersonal relationships handled in the mediation program or the clerk's office in 1980 and 1981, 29 percent involved one or more parties who had had previous contact with the court or mediation in 1980 or 1981.[14]

These data only describe people who return to court within 2 years. Yet, even within this short time period, a small number of individuals use the court repeatedly. They return despite the fact that for most, their case has not gone to trial and no penalties have been imposed. They have received only the court processing itself, including mediation. These increasingly experienced court users have not given up even though they no longer believe that the system operates according to principles of formal justice. Interviews with experienced court users suggest that they have come to see the law as a potentially powerful but unreliable tool that must be applied with persistence and finesse. As one of the plaintiffs against Mrs. Brown observed, "The squeaky wheel gets what she wants." They continue to believe in legal rights and to see these rights as constitutive of their social relationships. But, the meaning of rights shifts as the understanding of legal action changes.'' Rights become resources, not guarantees. They become opportunities for action depending on the social context and history of the problem and the plaintiff's skill in navigating the complicated waters of the ideologically plural legal arena.

conclusions

Sarat's review of survey evidence about American legal culture indicates that those with firsthand contact with the legal system are less satisfied than those without contact (1977:441). He reports that

> most people seem satisfied with the overall performance of the police, the legal profession, and the courts. Disapproval of particular actions or aspects of legal institutions, or of the behavior of legal officials, has not produced deep-seated and widespread alienation from the legal system. People seem to be dissatisfied without being detached (1977:441).

Although the survey data does not explain how people can feel dissatisfied but not detached, I suggest that this dissatisfaction occurs as court users discover situational as well as formal justice. Getting something from the legal system turns out to be a time-consuming, complicated, and uncertain process. Although the dual ideologies allow court officials room to maneuver, they contribute to the inexperienced litigant's sense that the court is unpredictable, confusing, and arbitrary: he or she is lost because he or she does not yet understand the game. But, as we have seen, litigants often try again.

What effect does the existence of plural legal ideologies have on working-class Americans' ideas about the legitimacy of the legal system and the justice of the social order? What does this analysis suggest about the hegemonic function of law? That ideas of legality persist despite disappointment with the legal system shows how enduring and powerful they are. These litigants continue to think about and treat their social relationships in terms of legal rights. Yet, they do not simply absorb the ideology of formal justice, even though it is the dominant formulation in American society. The ideology of formal justice is controlling, but not absolutely controlling. A distinct, local system emerges within the courthouse that combines the ideology of the national system with local, contextual considerations and definitions of justice. With experience, the working-class litigant learns both ideologies. The ideology of formal justice exercises some control over the interpretation of events and the generation of social practices, but it is not passively received and absorbed either by the officials in the lower court or the working-class clients of the court. Definitions of legal rights in social relationships are constructed by litigants and court officials as they deal with day-to-day problems in the court. Since the law includes competing categories and definitions of justice, it cannot perform the simple hegemonic function postulated by critical legal scholars; this hegemony is limited insofar as it is locally constructed and ideologically plural.

The analysis of local as well as dominant ideologies suggests a useful way of thinking about the question of hegemony in more general terms. The extent to which a local ideology is controlled or constrained by a dominant ideology and an institutional structure is an empirical question, central to understanding the ways ideology serves as a means of maintaining power relationships. In different social situations, the relationship between local and dominant ideologies may be quite different. It seems likely that in societies with important ethnic, linguistic, or cultural gaps between rich and poor, or in which the state is perceived as oppressive and foreign rather than friendly and helpful, the ideological difference could be much greater. Empirical work could specify the conditions under which local ideologies are more or less vulnerable to manipulation and control from the center as well as the processes by which local ideologies develop and change. Further, it could specify the kinds of meta-discourses or meta-ideologies that connect these ideologies and allow them to coexist, both in the court and in other social settings. Just's recent description (1986) of the way the Dou Donggo construct a sociological truth or an account of a dispute at variance with the phenomenal truth of what really happened—producing an outcome that both follows the rules and provides justice as the community defines it—is a fascinating parallel to the process I observed in American lower courts. In both situations we see processes for ensuring flexibility and local justice within a framework of formal rules and procedures. There may be similarities in the ways local groups in other societies find ways of providing justice within a framework of formal rules and dominant ideologies.

notes

Acknowledgments. I am grateful for helpful comments on earlier drafts from Lance Bennett, John Brigham, Christine Harrington, Laura Nader, Austin Sarat, Susan Silbey, June Starr, and Barbara Yngvesson. The primary research described in this paper was supported by the National Science Foundation and the National Institute of Justice. Additional research was supported by the W. T. Grant Foundation.

[1]For example, in assessing how serious a theft is among the Kabyle people, a judge will consider a small number of schemes generally applied, such as the distinction between a house or other place, night and day, and feast days and ordinary days. These schemes are applicable in a wide range of other offenses as well, such as brawls. They are so generally and automatically applied that it is only when they are overridden because of the severity of the offense that they are made explicit; in such a case a penalty is fixed regardless of whether the theft was by day or night, from inside or outside the house, or whether the animals belong to the owner or someone else. Bourdieu suggests that if one could spell out the basic, implicit propositions operating in a society, plus the principles by which they are combined, one could reproduce the judgments that make up that society's "sense of justice" (1977:16–17).

[2]As Ortner says of the structural Marxists of the 1970s,

although structural Marxists offered a way of mediating the material and ideological "levels," they did not actually challenge the notion that such levels are analytically distinguishable in the first place. Thus, despite criticizing the Durkheimian (and Parsonian) notion of "the social" as the "base" of the system, they merely offered a deeper and allegedly more real and objective "base" [1984:141].

[3]The "processual" approach within legal anthropology is developing a way of understanding the flexibility of the process of invoking rules and norms in conflict situations that promises to provide the analytical basis for dealing with the relationship between legal ideas and systems of power, as is true of other legal anthropologists who are looking at the implications of systems of meaning for legal behavior (see, for example, Moore 1978; Comaroff and Roberts 1981; Greenhouse 1982, 1985; Engel and Yngvesson 1984; Bentley 1984a; Arno 1985; Starr 1985; Yngvesson 1985; Just 1986).

[4]We observed 118 disputes handled by the mediation programs and followed about 30 that returned to court for further handling. We interviewed 124 litigants who had been in mediation about their views of mediation and court, most of whom had initially taken their problem to court.

[5]This study focused on 51 cases and included similar interviews with 114 parents and children.

[6]One of the *American Ethnologist* anonymous reviewers suggested that this distinction does not reflect two distinct ideologies, but is a manifestation of conflicting ideas within the dominant tradition of America itself. Americans favor the rule of law, yet view the use of law in private disputes as litigious, as an inappropriate invocation of the law. American ideas are derived from a commitment to individual liberty and

limited government (Greenhouse 1985; see also Engel and Yngvesson 1984). There is considerable strength to this suggestion. Litigants bringing interpersonal disputes to court often commented that they thought that their disputes did not belong in court. However, the advantage of an analytic framework that views these variations as distinct ideologies rather than internal contradictions within a single culture or ideology is that it highlights the struggle over meaning, including definitions of justice, between local and national groups. Moreover, the differences between the two ideologies I have described extend beyond views about the propriety of invoking law for interpersonal disputes. They also incorporate different ideas about what rights are, how they are enforced, and how much of a dispute's social context the court considers. In either analytic frame, the hegemonic functions of law are more limited than the critical legal studies writers postulate.

[7] In her research on a clerk's office in this kind of court, Yngvesson argues persuasively that the local culture penetrates the official ideology of the court (1985).

[8] These two ideologies as I have described them are similar to two theoretical perspectives on the law, legal formalism, and legal realism (Mensch 1982). Sarat and Felstiner describe the formalist image of the law as a formally rational legal order which is rule-governed, impersonal, impartial, predictable, and error-free, and the realist view of the law as a system in which rules are of limited relevance, decisions are made in terms of community interests, errors are frequent, and routinization provides the only predictability (1984:7). I am suggesting that these two perspectives may be coexisting ideologies within a local courthouse.

[9] For example, a study of the processing of nonstranger violence cases in three lower courts suggests that these plaintiffs are not looking for punishment or rule enforcement, but for a symbolic statement that their problems are serious, and for protection and control (Smith 1983).

[10] As Silbey points out, legal practices, although influenced by politics, are not simply the exercise of power and interest; the law itself constrains that exercise (1985).

[11] The distinction between naive and experienced court users has been developed in collaboration with Susan Silbey.

[12] In a study of the court handling of nonstranger violence in three jurisdictions, half the cases were dismissed; a third were given prison sentences—mostly very short (under 30 days), and primarily to defendants who were already incarcerated (Smith 1983) Yet, the victims in the study reported that, especially for first-time offenders, the prospect of prosecution was sometimes sufficiently frightening to get them to change their behavior, especially when the judge warned them about it (1983:96).

[13] The clerk's office heard 533 cases in which no complaint was issued during 1981. Forty-one percent (220) of these case filings involved interpersonal relationships. Twelve percent (64) of the 533 cases involved people who had appeared in complaints in the clerk's office in some other capacity that same year. I was only able to gain access to records on non-issued complaints, so that this information is clearly partial. It probably exaggerates the proportion of repeat users since the clerk is less likely to issue complaints in interpersonal cases.

[14] My records included cases that appeared in the clerk's office for which a complaint did not issue in 1981 and all cases referred to mediation by the clerk's office, the prosecutor, or the judge in 1980 and 1981. A substantial proportion of all interpersonal cases are referred to mediation at some point in the court process, although I did not collect quantitative data that would permit me to specify what proportion of all interpersonal cases in court are included in the mediation referrals. These figures are therefore likely to underrepresent rather than overrepresent repeaters.

[15] I am indebted to Austin Sarat for this formulation.

references cited

Abel, Richard, ed.
  1982   The Politics of Informal Justice. Vols. I and II. New York: Academic Press.
Ahern, Emily Martin
  1982   Rules in Oracles and Games. Man 17:302–312.
Arno, Andrew
  1985   Structural Communication and Control Communication: An Interactionist Perspective on Legal and Customary Procedures for Conflict Management. American Anthropologist 87:40–55.
Ashcraft, Richard
  1984   Marx and Political Theory. Comparative Studies in Society and History 26:637–671.
Bailey, F. G.
  1983   The Tactical Uses of Passion. Ithaca, NY: Cornell University Press.
Beirne, Piers, and Richard Quinney, eds.
  1982   Marxism and Law. New York: John Wiley.
Bentley, G. Carter
  1984a   Hermeneutics and World Construction in Maranao Disputing. American Ethnologist 11:642–655.
  1984b   Locating Conflicts in the World: Verbal Structure and Contextualization in Maranao Disputing. Paper presented at the Annual Meetings of the American Anthropological Association, Denver, Colorado.

Bourdieu, Pierre
1977 Outline of a Theory of Practice. Richard Nice, transl. Cambridge: Cambridge University Press.
Cain, Maureen, and Alan Hunt
1979 Marx and Engels on Law. New York: Academic Press.
Cappalletti, M., ed.
1978–79 Access to Justice. 4 volumes. Milan: Guiffre; Alphen aan den Rijn: Sijthoff and Noordhoff.
Collier, Jane F.
1982 Review of The Politics of Informal Justice. Richard. Abel, ed. Newsletter of the Association for Political and Legal Anthropology 6:11–13.
Comaroff, John L., and Simon Roberts
1981 Rules and Processes: The Cultural Logic of Dispute in an African Context. Chicago: University of Chicago Press.
Danzig, Richard
1973 Towards the Creation of a Complementary, Decentralized System of Criminal Justice. Stanford Law Review 26:1–54.
Eisenstein, James, and Herbert Jacob
1977 Felony Justice: An Organizational Analysis of Criminal Courts. Boston: Little, Brown.
Engel, David, and Barbara Yngvesson
1984 Mapping Difficult Terrain: "Legal Culture," "Legal Consciousness," and Other Hazards for the Intrepid Explorer. Law and Policy 6:299–307.
Evans-Pritchard, E. E.
1940 The Nuer. London: Oxford University Press.
Feeley, Malcolm
1979 The Process is the Punishment: Handling Cases in a Lower Criminal Court. New York: Russell Sage.
Geertz, Clifford
1973 The Interpretation of Cultures: Selected Essays. New York: Basic Books.
Genovese, Eugene
1982 The Hegemonic Function of Law. In Marxism and Law. Piers Bierne and Richard Quinney, eds. New York: Wiley.
Greenhouse, Carol J.
1982 Looking at Culture, Looking for Rules. Man 17:58–73.
1985 Interpreting American Litigiousness. Paper presented at the Law and Society Meetings, San Diego, California.
Greer, Edward
1982 Antonio Gramsci and Legal Hegemony. In The Politics of Law: A Progressive Critique. David Kairys, ed. New York: Pantheon.
Hannerz, Ulf
1984 Taking Diversity Seriously: The Study of Complex Cultures. Paper presented at the Annual Meetings of the American Anthropological Association, Denver, Colorado.
Hunt, Alan
1985 The Ideology of Law: Advances and Problems in Recent Applications of the Concept of Ideology to the Analysis of Law. Law and Society Review 19:11–38.
Just, Peter
1986 Let the Evidence Fit the Crime: Evidence, Law, and "Sociological Truth" Among the Dou Donggo. American Ethnologist 13(1):43–61.
Kairys, David, ed.
1982 The Politics of Law: A Progressive Critique. New York: Pantheon.
Kapferer, Bruce, ed.
1976 Transaction and Meaning: Directions in the Anthropology of Exchange and Symbolic Behavior. Philadelphia, PA: Institute for the Study of Human Issues.
Lipetz, Marcia
1983 Routine Justice. New Brunswick, NJ: Transaction Books.
Mann, Michael
1970 The Social Cohesion of Liberal Democracy. American Sociological Review 35:423–439.
Mather, Lynn, and Barbara Yngvesson
1980 Language, Audience and the Transformation of Disputes. Law and Society Review 15:775–823.
Mensch, Elizabeth
1982 The History of Mainstream Legal Thought. In The Politics of Law: A Progressive Critique. David Kairys, ed. New York: Pantheon.
Merry, Sally Engle
1979 Going to Court: Strategies of Dispute Management in an American Urban Neighborhood. Law and Society Review 13:891–927.
1981 Urban Danger: Life in a Neighborhood of Strangers. Philadelphia, PA: Temple University Press.
Merry, Sally Engle, and Susan S. Silbey
1984 What do Plaintiffs Want? Reexamining the Concept of Dispute. Justice System Journal 9:151–179.

Merry, Sally Engle, and Ann Marie Rocheleau
  1985   Mediation in Families: A Study of The Children's Hearings Project. Cambridge, MA: Children's
    Hearings Project.
Moore, Sally Falk
  1978   Law as Process: An Anthropological Approach. London: Routledge & Kegan Paul.
Munger, Frank and Carroll Seron
  1984   Critical Legal Studies Versus Critical Legal Theory: A Comment on Method. Law and Policy
    6:257.
Nader, Laura
  1984   A User Theory of Law. Southwestern Law Journal 38:951–963.
Ortner, Sherry B.
  1984   Theory in Anthropology Since the Sixties. Comparative Studies in Society and History 26:126–
    166.
Saler, Benson
  1984   Guajiro Compensation Principles. Paper presented at the Annual Meetings of the American An-
    thropological Association, Denver, Colorado.
Sarat, Austin
  1977   Studying American Legal Culture: An Assessment of Survey Evidence. Law and Society Review
    11:427–498.
Sarat, Austin, and William L. F. Felstiner
  1984   The Ideology of Divorce: Law in the Lawyer's Office. Paper presented at a workshop on the Study
    of Interactions between Lawyers and Clients at Rijksuniversiteit, Groningen, The Netherlands.
Silbey, Susan S.
  1981   Making Sense of the Lower Courts. Justice System Journal 6:13–27.
  1985   Ideals and Practices in the Study of Law. Legal Studies Forum 9:7–23.
Smith, Barbara
  1983   Non-Stranger Violence: The Criminal Court's Response. Washington, DC: National Institute of
    Justice, U.S. Department of Justice.
Starr, June
  1985   Telling the Truth in Turkish Trial Courts. Paper presented at the Law and Society Association
    Meetings, San Diego, California.
Sumner, Colin
  1979   Reading Ideologies: An Investigation into the Marxist Theory of Ideology and Law. London: Ac-
    ademic Press.
Trubek, David
  1983   Where the Action Is: Critical Legal Studies and Empiricism. Disputes Processing Research Pro-
    gram Working Paper No. 1983–10. Madison, WI: University of Wisconsin Law School.
Yngvesson, Barbara
  1983   Legal Ideology and Community Justice in the Clerk's Office. Legal Studies Forum 9:71–89.

Submitted 15 March 1985
Revised version submitted 12 August 1985
Accepted 14 January 1986
Final revisions received 22 January 1986

[23]

JOURNAL OF LAW AND SOCIETY
VOLUME 16, NUMBER 1, SPRING 1989
0263-323X $3.00

'Consensual Authoritarianism' and Criminal Justice in Thatcher's Britain

ALAN NORRIE* AND SAMMY ADELMAN*

INTRODUCTION

The impact of Thatcherism on the criminal justice system may be understood in terms of two apparent paradoxes. The first is that of continuity and change, so that while there have been significant developments in the direction of authoritarian forms of rule under Thatcherism these developments cannot be viewed in isolation from previous periods of British history. Thus, while Thatcherism is authoritarian, it is inaccurate to identify authoritarianism with Thatcherism as a wholly new departure.

The second apparent paradox is that of consensus and conflict. We argue that a central feature of Thatcherism is its ability to draw upon and renovate consensus through conflict. Taking as our particular focus the development of popular perceptions of and relations with the police from the mid-nineteenth century, we argue that a consistent feature of class relations in Britain has been that the criminalization process has operated with the consent of significant sections of the working class as well as the middle class. We then argue that while Thatcherism involves more authoritarian modes of criminalization, it has been able to draw upon a relative consensus across class lines in order to successfully operate a more conflictual criminal justice system.

This essay contributes to a debate about the specific nature of authoritarianism under the Thatcher Government which owes most to the work of Hall and his use of the term 'authoritarian populism'. We discuss this concept in the fourth section of this paper. More recently, Scraton has edited a series of essays entitled *Law, Order and the Authoritarian State* which draws upon Hall's perspective and seeks to apply it through very thorough empirical analyses of different aspects of the criminal justice system. We have drawn on the essays in this book as a resource for writing this paper, but we feel that it lacks a coherent theoretical framework partly because it follows Hall's analysis. Our argument is that the utility of the term 'authoritarian populism' is limited by its derivation from a mode of analysis that unduly privileges ideological and political factors in opposition to the structural and economic conditions within which ideologies and politics operate.

*School of Law, University of Warwick, Coventry, West Midlands CV4 7AL, England.

We therefore use the term 'consensual authoritarianism' provisionally to denote the need to look at the historical material basis of a relative consensus incorporating important sections of the working class and the need to comprehend the contradictory fusion of authoritarianism and consent so characteristic of the Thatcherite project. In making this argument it is important to realize that we are drawing a distinction between those periods of consent (or, indeed, conflict) which manifest themselves in particular historical conjunctures, and a more fundamental and structural level of consent within British society which has existed for over a hundred years and which has its roots in the division of interests within the working class between, very broadly, its better and worse-off sections. While recognizing the need for historical specification of the meaning of the term in different periods, this division within the working class can be designated as one between a labour aristocracy and other, poorer, less privileged sections of the class.[1] Our argument will be that it is this structural division within the working class, allowing for a consensual alliance across the classes and aligning the better-off workers' interests with those of capital, which forms the historical basis for particular historical periods of consent and, to the extent that it is able, defines the limits of conflict within British society. This alliance on the part of the workers assumes different forms in different historical periods, ranging from resistance within limits to overt collaboration. When we talk of issues such as 'policing with consent' or the fashioning of consensus under Thatcherism, we are thinking of a historically identifiable conjuncture of consent which is based upon (and drawn from) a fundamental division within the working class and the historical cross-class consensus to which it has given rise.

CONTINUITY AND CHANGE

The immediate impression one has of the criminal justice system after nearly ten years of Thatcherism is that which Hall identified as a drift into an authoritarian law and order society.[2] This drift – or perhaps development, for there is nothing to suggest that many of the changes have not been deliberate – towards more authoritarian methods of criminalization has occurred throughout the system, taking in the police, the courts, the prisons, and subsidiary parts of the system such as the various branches of the social services through the use of the concept of 'community policing' or 'multi-agency policing'.[3]

While space precludes a detailed catalogue of all these developments, certain key developments may be briefly mentioned.[4] First, in relation to the police, there has been a move towards a more centralized and militarized form of policing in which technologies and organization have been developed, having as their primary aim the containment and suppression of public disorder. Policing for public order, as one police chief has quite candidly admitted,[5] has become the first priority, with the prevention and detection of individual crimes a secondary and subsidiary motivation.[6] As a result of this declared change in police activity, we have also witnessed the more overt politicization of the police as they have become publicly identified with the successive policies of the Thatcher Government, particularly with regard to notions of what is normal, acceptable, rightful conduct and what is abnormal and alien – descriptions which are constructed in terms of class, race, and respectability, an area of ideological conflict in which the impact of Thatcherism has been particularly significant.[7]

Elsewhere within the system, important developments have occurred concerning the processing of defendants brought before the courts as well as the character of the prison system. We have witnessed a tendency for courts at all levels to be seen more clearly as arms of government rather than in their primary ideological role as independent forums for the just resolution of cases. Magistrates' courts, for example, have used their power to grant bail conditions as an auxiliary form of social control in connection with the miners' strike and the peace convoys in the West Country, and have, on various occasions, effectively connived at 'preventive detention' by the police of such groups through their unquestioning acceptance of police remand recommendations.[8] In the higher courts the decisions to prosecute Sarah Tisdall and Clive Ponting,[9] and the willingness of the courts to accept the Government's arguments concerning 'national security' in the Spycatcher case[10] are manifestations not only of the 'identification' of important elements of the judiciary with the policies and ideologies of Thatcherism, but are also the most overt signs of the drift towards authoritarianism in the protection of state secrets, and towards censorship and creeping erosion of civil liberties in this area.[11] The dubious circumstances surrounding trials arising out of the Broadwater Farm riot in 1985;[12] the decision based on grounds of 'national security' not to prosecute police officers in Northern Ireland 'shoot to kill' cases – despite the recognition that there was a case to answer, together with the suppression of Stalker's inquiry;[13] and the recent rejection by the Court of Appeal of the appeal of the 'Birmingham Six',[14] have all raised questions about the administration of justice in Britain in the 1980s. So, too, have the acquittal of police officers on charges arising from the death of John Shorthouse and the serious injuries to Steven Waldorf and Cherry Groce.[15] The period since 1979 has also been noticeable for persistent attacks on the tradition of trial by jury, ranging from the removal of peremptory challenges to more recent indications of a desire to further restrict the choice of a trial by jury for those charged in magistrates' courts.[16]

As regards the prisons, the rise in the prison population (itself arguably an indirect outcome of Conservative social and economic policies);[17] the Government's prison building programme; the changes in the parole rules for violent offenders and drug traffickers serving over five years as well as for certain categories of those serving life for murder; the failure to provide decent regimes within the prisons; the increased emphasis on security within the system;[18] and the heightened repression of increasing protest against prison regimes[19] have all augmented the authoritarian character of the system.

114

It must also be noted that accompanying these events, trends, and developments there have been substantial changes in the legal frameworks within which the criminalization process occurs. The passing of the Police and Criminal Evidence Act 1984 and the Public Order Act 1986 have both increased the discretion available to police officers in the conduct of their activities in relation to individuals and social groups. The former in particular has extended police powers of detention, stop and search, search of premises, and the creation of roadblocks according to very loosely defined criteria.[20] Justified as involving a balance between police powers and individual rights, this legislation was seen to fail in regard to the latter at its first serious test.[21] As for the Public Order Act 1986, this gives unprecedented powers to the police to ban and impose conditions on marches and to restrict demonstrations and pickets.[22] In addition, under the 'new, improved' Prevention of Terrorism (Temporary Provisions) Act 1984 the original legislation is extended to include within its potential ambit the members and supporters of any organization in the world which uses 'violence for political ends'; in addition, the legislation is made semi-permanent. This means that as well as the political control exercised over Irish politics in Britain,[23] any liberation movement in the world conducting armed struggle, together with its supporters, is potentially affected. Lastly, on the heels of all these other developments, we have the recent announcement that a cornerstone of the trial process, the 300-year-old right to silence, has been abolished in Northern Ireland and will soon be ended in England and Wales.[24]

There is, then, a substantial empirical basis for the claim that the British State has developed an authoritarian mode in the 1980s – that is, a relatively naked emphasis within the criminal justice system upon criminalization and the suppression of resistance, and a relative de-emphasizing of the formal norms and values of individual justice. However, it is important not to oversimplify this development for two reasons. First, it must be noted that while the 1980s mark important changes, there are also substantial continuities between this and previous periods, both recent and not so recent. Thus, we should note that many of the developments of the 1980s are extensions of what had occurred in the 1970s. When Hall wrote about the drift into a law and order society, he was referring as much to the historical period that had immediately passed as to the period that was to come,[25] and the outlines of what Ackroyd and her collaborators called the 'strong state' in Britain were already quite visible in the mid-1970s.[26] Similarly, Poulantzas, in an influential work, identified the phenomenon of 'authoritarian statism', in which the balance between coercion and consent was shifted towards the authoritarian side of the spectrum in this period.[27]

Looking back to the period of the 1970s in Britain, it is possible to view many of the present developments as building upon what happened then, in a different socio-political context. As regards the police, for example, the system of national organization which was so important during the miners' strike was set up in the earlier period in large measure as a response to the successes of the National Union of Mineworkers in the 1974 strike,[28] and the creation of a quasi-military 'third force' of riot-trained police again emanates from the 1970s.[29] Similarly, allegations of police racism, which have been a major cause of riotous resistance to the police throughout the 1980s (and particularly in 1980, 1981, and 1985) were common currency in the 1970s and earlier.[30]

As regards the courts, the consistent and structured injustice confronting working-class people in magistrates' courts was a persistent theme of the 1970s.[31] The recent appeal of the Birmingham Six, together with the cases of the Maguires and the Guildford Four in turn remind us that all of these people were convicted in the earlier period.[32] As far as prisons are concerned, the resistance to jail conditions and maltreatment in the 1980s are no more than the latest chapter in a story that includes, for example, Hull in 1976.[33] It was also in the 1970s that the militarization of prison control began with the institution of Minimum Use of Force Tactical Intervention (MUFTI) squads.[34]

More could be said, but the point has been made: while there are significant differences and changes in the criminalization process in the 1980s, there are also continuities and similarities between the 1980s and developments in the different political conditions of the earlier period. We stress this point because it is important to show that an easy identification of the empirical developments within the criminalization process in the 1980s and the Thatcherite project is not possible. From this it follows that it is not only necessary to be careful in characterizing policies as peculiarly Thatcherite, but it is also important to situate changes that have occurred in the 1980s within a broader historical perspective. Finally, if the reader still requires some persuasion as to the need to confront the continuity between past and present, we cite one historical description of an anti-police riot and its aftermath:

> That evening the Riot Act was read several times and the police and specials paraded the town dispersing enclaves of citizens. Between 10 and 11 p.m. a large crowd rallied at a newly erected church east of Colne, armed themselves with long spear-like iron palisades left over from the construction of the church railings, and entered Colne from Keighley Road. The battle was joined. . . . In the struggle, Joseph Halstead, a special constable and local mill owner, was struck in the head with an iron palisade and killed. Yet again, the police were swept from Colne. . . . The chief defendant in the murder of Halstead was a twenty year old weaver, Richard Boothman. Boothman was tried at the assizes and sentenced to death in March 1841. His sentence was later commuted to transportation. . . . Boothman maintained to the end that he did not murder Halstead. He claimed he had never been a part of the crowd that night, had been arrested after just returning from a neighbouring local feast and that he had been a victim of a case of mistaken identity.[35]

If the events of Broadwater Farm in September 1985 and the subsequent police siege of the estate – involving hundreds of arrests, the disregarding of legal procedures, and the trial and conviction of defendants on the flimsiest of grounds[36] – have a quintessentially '80s' feel about them and therefore symbolize more broadly the nature of the criminalization process under Thatcherism, we should invest Storch's description of events almost 150 years ago with some significance, for it turns the question around: from asking what is distinctive about the 1980s, we should perhaps ask, why does it appear distinctive; for, as we can see, a historical perspective makes easy characterization impossible.[37]

116

Our second concern with the 'authoritarianism thesis' focuses on the extent to which the development of the 'strong state' has been accompanied not by conflict but by consensus in British society. The 'strong state' involves, by definition, a repressive strategy; it is at the heart of a social order which has become more coercive and conflictual. That this is so is clear to see, whether in the form of anti-police resistance in inner cities, in mining communities, or in republican areas of Northern Ireland. At the same time, however, the development of the 'strong state' has taken place with the acquiescence, at least, and often the substantial support of significant sections of the British population. Police attempts, for example, to establish community partnerships through such initiatives as neighbourhood watch schemes have not, it appears, been wholly unsuccessful, at the very least in their ability to generate the support necessary to the very acts of establishing the schemes.[38] Nor have oppressive police tactics such as those used in the miners' strike or in the quelling of inner city disturbances been met with wholesale condemnation. On the contrary, important sections of the working class in addition to the middle class have been drawn into supporting police actions. Politically, this is most clearly evidenced by the programmes of the Labour Party, whose pro-police pronouncements on law and order issues in particular are designed to win the middle ground of middle-class *and* affluent working-class support.[39] In part, what we have seen in the 1980s has been a successful 'divide and rule' strategy in which divisions between black and white, north and south, rich and poor, employed and unemployed have been exacerbated and manipulated to generate *consent behind the state* amongst certain relatively privileged sections of the middle and working classes for control through conflict *against* other less privileged sections of the working class (the unemployed, blacks and Asians, and workers in struggle) as well as *déclassé* groups such as travellers, students, and peace protesters.

The 'authoritarian state' thesis with which we started thus requires modification in two extremely important ways if we are to understand the criminalization process under the Thatcher Government. On the one hand, it is not nearly so distinctive as the impact of immediate events upon the senses suggests. If Thatcherism entails authoritarianism, so too did 1970s Labourism and the very creation of the bourgeois state. So a simple identification between Thatcherism and authoritarianism will not do. On the other hand, if authoritarianism is to be identified as an important feature of Thatcherism, it is authoritarianism *against* some *with* the consent of others. This 'consensual authoritarianism' clearly requires further consideration.

In the next two sections we will argue that the key to understanding these two problems is to be found within the historical development of British class relations and in the context of imperialism. It is only in this broader context that we can appreciate the specificity of Thatcherite criminal justice.

117

CONFLICT AND CONSENSUS

If we are to situate the present period historically, we must be able to get a 'fix' on the developments that have occurred in criminal justice in previous decades, and, more importantly, the social, political, and economic developments that underpin them. Clearly, in the space of a short article we cannot write a complete history of the criminal justice system of this kind. We want instead to focus on one particular institution, the police, and the historical development in the class basis of modern British society which underlies it. In the process we will clear up some confusion in recent writing about the immediate post-war period.

There is an academic consensus that underlies conservative, liberal, and Left Realist accounts of the historical development of policing in the post-war period. It essentially takes the form of a claim, suitably qualified, that in the immediate post-war period there was a substantial measure of consensus in British society about policing, so that the period can accordingly be seen as a benchmark against which contemporary developments in the direction of conflict can be measured.[40] This view of a 'golden age' of policing has recently been attacked on an empirical basis by Gilroy and Sim,[41] who show that the period in question was, like most of the history of British policing, characterized by conflict.

While there is much substance in this criticism, we feel that it misses two important points – one implicitly, the other explicitly. First, it is the case that the history of policing in Britain reveals not only consistent conflict, but also, after the initial period of imposition, consistent *consensus* among significant sections of the working class, and that *both* conflict and consensus relate to historical developments within the British working class. Secondly, it is the case that while the 'golden age' theorists perhaps overstate their claim, there was a real sense in which the immediate post-war period was one of relative consensus across the classes. What is really wrong with the liberal and Left Realist 'golden age' claim is not that it identifies consensus but that it dehistoricizes a period of *relative* consensus by abstracting it from the economic, political, and ideological conditions upon which it was based. In doing so, it turns a historical moment into a normative ideal which then becomes the basis for a particular political stance.

The post-war consensus, with which we shall deal below, is an important part of the story of modern policing but it must not be allowed to obscure an earlier and more fundamental consensus at the heart of British social relations which occurred as much as a century earlier. It is well known that around 1850 the fear of the 'dangerous classes' as a turbulent mob incorporating *all* elements of the working class gave way to a differentiated awareness of the sectional nature of working-class criminality. Observers began to be concerned with 'diffuse criminality' rather than the 'dangerous classes' so that 'contemporary writing in mid-century London exhibits a sense of relief and victory over the forces of mass violence'.[42] What lay behind this change?

Law and Society

Foster's seminal account of social relations in the first sixty years of the nineteenth century is occasionally referred to by police historians for his vivid and detailed discussions of struggles over control of the police in Oldham in the 1830s and 1840s.[43] What these historians usually ignore is Foster's analysis of why such struggles – often of a violent and bloody kind – abated from 1850 onwards. Partly it was a matter of simple economic recovery, but more importantly it was the product of emerging economic, social, and political divisions within the working class itself. The class became politically and ideologically split by the development of a layer whose position as taskmasters and pacemakers placed them above and in opposition to the mass of workers. This newly developed layer – a 'labour aristocracy' – surrounded itself with a 'cocoon of formal institutions' emphasizing respectable behavioural norms so as to insulate itself from 'the constant ridicule reserved for bosses' men'.[44] As for the mass of ordinary unprivileged workers, Foster describes their position thus:

> ... the essence of the non-aristocrats' culture was a rejection of everything associated with their work-time taskmasters: discipline, subservience, abstinence. Its most characteristic expression was the public house – where no free born Englishman need call any man his master. And protected by dialect, a defence the labour-aristocrat had to do without, it needed no formal institutions beyond the friendly society to handle the most unavoidable contacts with the authorities.[45]

The contrast between 'labour aristocratic' respectability and the non-aristocratic culture of dialect and the public house perhaps suggests the roots of that well-known policing distinction between 'roughs' and 'respectables'[46] refined though it must have been down the years. The quotation also indicates that when Storch's 'domestic missionaries'[47] set about their crusades against pub culture, it was only *one* section of the working class (albeit the larger one) that they directed their energies against and from whom they received continuing opposition.

Foster's work is important because it underlines the material basis for a phenomenon that is recognized by many writers, but whose significance is rarely grasped.[48] That phenomenon is the continuous division in working-class attitudes to criminality and the police. A *consensual* history of policing can be traced from Weinberger's observation that anti-police violence in the 1870s came from only 'a section of the working class' who were opposed to 'police action in connection with licensing laws and with Poor Law policing',[49] through Bailey's observation that in the 1886-7 Trafalgar Square clashes between the police and the poor, the 'respectable' working class were conspicuous by their absence,[50] to Cohen's discussion of the expansion of notions of respectability and public propriety amongst increasing sections of the working class in the wake of New Unionism and the success of Labour politics.[51] Respectability and respect (albeit grudging) for the police were real phenomena having a real material basis in economic and social developments.

The significance to the twentieth century of this nineteenth-century development becomes apparent when one considers the relationship between 'respectable' trade unionism, 'respectable' Labourism, and respect for the 'fine traditions' of British policing. This is not a phenomenon that simply appeared during the 1984-5 miners' strike, it is one firmly grounded in historically developed realities. Thus, Geary identifies the commencement of peaceful policing of trade disputes from 1946 but the peaceful *running* of such disputes by workers to the period prior to the First World War, and he relates this latter development to the influence of trades unions and their relationships with the emerging Labour Party – often in the face of great provocation from police and troops.[52] And Weinberger, in an important recent article, shows that in the inter-war period both employed and unemployed workers' organizations were more prone to attack by the police if they could be branded with an unrespectable non-Labourist label such as 'communist'. She writes that police violence 'seemed to have occurred most readily in areas . . . [*inter alia*] where the local labour movement positively rejected all support for the activities of the organized unemployed' and where 'local strikers or the unemployed were regarded as acting under Communist influence'.[53] Such a prejudice, she notes, was as prevalent in the 'respectable' labour movement as it was among Conservatives. In other words, there existed a *de facto* alliance between the police, the Conservatives, and the 'respectable' labour movement by means of which the National Unemployed Workers Movement and sections of the miners' union were isolated and exposed to attack. Empirical similarities between this period and the 1980s may be noted,[54] but the important point here is the underlying material basis not just of class conflict, but of continuing sectional class division, consensus, and collaboration which can be gleaned from the historical perspective. It is within that context that one can understand both the way in which a period of collaboration across the classes – as in the post-war period – can generate a relative consensus in respect of policing, and begin to see the ways in which particular political, ideological, and economic projects such as those of Thatcherism can take root in a soil already prepared for them. We now turn to consider this latter issue in detail.

THE SPECIFICITY OF THATCHER'S CRIMINAL JUSTICE

We began with two apparent paradoxes between continuity and change, consensus and conflict. We argued that the key to understanding these paradoxes was to be found within the historical development of British class relations. The criminal justice system has always been able to rely on support across the classes, most importantly from sections of the working class who, for real material reasons, see themselves as having a stake in the capitalist system. This is borne out by a historical perspective on the history of policing and is given a clear political expression in the view and stances adopted by the Labour Party when it has been in government and in opposition.[55] We agree with Sim, Scraton, and Gordon when they write against 'the romanticized versions of a united homogeneous working class' of:

> . . . the significance and depth of the political and ideological differences within working-class experiences. The fractures and divisions in neighbourhood and workplaces have as

120

much to do with the ideas and politics of patriotism and race, of masculinity and gender, of jobs and materialism, as they have to do with the objective location of paid work, domestic labour or unemployment within the economy.[56]

Unlike these writers, however, we stress the implications of this view for identifying the securing of consent within the working class for state actions. Thus, we do not agree completely that 'an understanding of the processes of criminalization' involves examining how 'consensus is forced rather than forged'[57] because that is only a partial explanation. The key to understanding our two paradoxes resides in the collaboration between significant sections of the working class and the state both at the level of social relations themselves (in particular, the police/public relationship) and at the level of the state (the political role of the Labour Party in and out of government). Herein lies the source of continuity behind the change, of consensus behind the conflict.

Thus far, however, we have not properly addressed the important question of the specific nature of the influence of Thatcherism on the criminal justice system. In this final section, we seek an answer through our use of the concept of 'consensual authoritarianism', and by discussion of Hall's 'authoritarian populism' and the debate it has engendered.[58] Our point of departure takes the form of agreement with Jessop et al. that Hall's 'authoritarian populism' is essentially 'ideologist' in conception. In responding to this criticism Hall characterized authoritarian populism as 'a movement towards a dominative and "authoritarian" form of democratic class politics – paradoxically, apparently rooted in ... populist discontents',[59] and he located its importance in 'the one dimension which above all others, has defeated the left, politically, and Marxist analysis theoretically, in every advanced capitalist democracy since the First World War':

> ... namely, the ways in which popular consent can be so constructed, by an historical bloc seeking hegemony, as to harness to its support some popular discontents, neutralise the opposing forces, disaggregate the opposition and really incorporate *some* strategic elements of popular opinion into its own hegemonic project.[60]

Hall accepts that in taking this stance he 'deliberately and self-consciously *foregrounds* the political-ideological dimension' and he recognizes the limited nature of concepts such as 'hegemony' and 'authoritarian populism'. They do not operate at a level of abstraction sufficient to generalize the entire condition of a particular period. They are 'more specific, time-bound, concrete in their reference' so that authoritarian populism can only be 'a partial explanation of Thatcherism':

> It was an attempt to characterize certain strategic shifts in the political/ideological conjuncture. Essentially, it refers to changes in the 'balance of forces'. It refers directly to the modalities of political and ideological relationships between the ruling blocs, the state and the dominated classes. It attempts to expand on and to begin to periodize the internal composition of hegemonic strategies in the politics of class democracies. ... *It references, but could neither characterize nor explain, changes in the more structural aspects of capitalist social formations.*[61]

It should be noted that there is a crucial difference between this explanation of authoritarian populism as a *descriptive* concept located purely at the level of the *categorization of ideologies* (and thereby conceding that the term 'authoritarian populism' *is* 'ideologist') and the other statement we quoted above. There authoritarian populism was more than just a categorization of ideology, it was a tool for seeing the way *in which popular consent was constructed historically by means of an ideological project*. Hall's claim, then, concerns the real effects of hegemonic projects on class relations, not simply the description of the 'modalities' or the 'internal composition' of particular ideologies. This is a big difference, which brings us onto the principal complaint of Jessop et al. about authoritarian populism: that in considering why a hegemonic project is successful, it is necessary to consider that project in the context of its reception by particular classes and class sections. 'Popular discontents' and 'popular opinion' are not abstractions, they correspond to the views and sentiments of particular sections of the population:

> In emphasizing the specific discursive strategies involved in Thatcherism, authoritarian populism risks ignoring other elements. In particular, it could neglect the structural underpinnings of Thatcherism in the economic and state systems and its specific economic and political basis of support among both people and power bloc.[62]

In contrast with Hall, it is that material basis for the acceptance of authoritarianism that we attempt to incorporate in our term 'consensual authoritarianism'. We do not deny the importance of the ideological forms that authoritarian populism takes, far from it. We do argue that those forms have to be understood within the wider context. For that reason, we do not deny that authoritarian populism has its uses as an analytical tool. But we do assert that it is of limited use in considering the ways in which Thatcherism has achieved the consensus of comparatively broad sections of the British people around its authoritarianism.

We can pursue this line by following Jessop et al. in their argument. We agree with them that there is nothing new in a British national-popular project as such. The British working class has for a long time, as Engels put it, been prepared to '[discredit] itself terribly' by siding with its ruling class. Jessop et al. point out that the Conservative Party has been able to mobilize both the deferential and the self-seeking working class, and that Thatcherism has been extremely successful in harnessing these elements. The success of the Thatcherite ideological project must be seen in the context of pragmatic and extremely real 'interests in lower direct taxation, council house sales, rising living standards for those still in private sector employment, lower inflation, and so forth'.[63] It is amongst those who snap at the bait of private interest and wealth that we should seek the material basis of the acceptance of 'authoritarian populist' ideologies.

We now come to the issue of authoritarianism itself as the other side of the consensus coin, the constructing of support for Thatcher's economic and political strategies against those sections of society who are losers, not winners. We agree with Jessop et al. that the creation of a 'Two Nations' Toryism has had real effects in terms of dividing the working class so that the support of the well-off can be drawn upon while those who experience unemployment and poverty, who are prepared to fight for their jobs and communities, are suppressed under the ideological banners of authoritarian populism. Thatcherism's economic strategy of dismantling the Welfare State in favour of privatization, popular capitalism, and the enterprise culture deliberately unleashes the effects of economic crisis upon those who were at least better able to survive under the old order. Thatcherism seeks not to integrate the poor and underprivileged but to manage their protest. As the effects of other economic policies have taken hold, controls have increased along with protest. The demand for 'law and order' is not a simple paroxysm of popular discontent opportunistically harnessed by Thatcherism. It is a real class response to the management of social conflicts arising from economic policies which have the support, more or less passive, more or less active, of significant sections of the working class.[64] Thatcherite authoritarianism is a product of Thatcherite 'Two Nations' politics and economics.[65]

We can see this if we compare the history of the present period of Thatcherism with the earlier period from 1945-79. Without wishing to endorse any idea of a 'golden age', we can see now with the benefit of hindsight that the earlier period was one of relative consensus. Politically this was formalized in the post-war settlement which established the Welfare State and was run by both 'One Nation' Toryism and the Labour Party on a relatively stable basis. This political consensus overlaid and drew upon the underlying social consensus we have identified at the heart of modern British class relations, symbolically and accurately referred to at the time as 'Butskellism'. This political consensus sought to unify the nation across class lines by providing the promise at least of a measure of support for those who in one way or another became casualties of the system. It was in this context that the immediate post-war period yielded a relative consensus in relation to criminal justice issues amongst others. While the period has been afforded a moral and political significance it by no means deserves, the image of consensus was not a complete illusion. 'Dixon of Dock Green' may be a fiction in both senses of the word, but it was not without a basis in real social developments.

The story of the breakdown of the political consensus (and also to some extent its relationship to the underlying social consent that we have discussed) has been told at length by Hall with his collaborators in his earlier work.[66] *Policing the Crisis* was written before Hall had moved theoretically into the explanation of 'authoritarian populism'. Perhaps for that reason, *Policing the Crisis* appears to us to be a much more rounded analysis of the location of politics and ideology, of a 'crisis of hegemony' within an overall economic context. The 1970s witnessed the failure of Labour's corporatist solution to economic crisis. Its populist 'law and order' slogans, together with moral panics around issues such as mugging, ideologically signalled that failure and provided important legitimations for the move, begun under Labour, towards authoritarianism.[67]

Like the Conservatives, Labour offered a solution to the economic and political crises of British capitalism. But it offered a solution that in the second half of the 1970s was increasingly discredited in practice. Labour offered corporatist consensus which drifted into authoritarianism at the same time as

123

its support for the Welfare State drifted into public spending cuts, the abandonment of a political commitment to full employment policies, and the prioritizing of the fight against inflation.[68] In other words, Labour gradually moved towards the policies which Thatcherism wholeheartedly adopted. Here lies the specificity of Thatcherism as economics, politics, and ideology. It proposes a radical economic solution designed to dismantle the Welfare State, privatize and restructure the economy. It presents this solution under the ideological labels of 'the individual', 'the family', 'the nation', 'law and order', 'the enemy within', and so on. It uses these labels politically to force through its policies, to divide society into 'us' and 'them', the 'productive' and the 'parasitic',[69] rich and poor, employed and unemployed, black and white, male and female, and it is this political/ideological brew, designed as part of a project to set British capitalism to rights economically that lies behind the authoritarian state. It is the radicalism and ruthlessness of the political, economic, and ideological projects of Thatcherism that accounts for the developments in authoritarianism that we have witnessed in the last ten years. There was authoritarianism before Thatcher so that what we experience is importantly a matter of degree. But the ratchet has been turned more than one notch in the process. That Thatcherism has achieved and continues to achieve this scaling up of the authoritarian nature of the state is in part due to Thatcher's ability ideologically to articulate authoritarian ideas in a popular way, but more importantly is due to the fertile social ground upon which these ideological seeds have been scattered. Behind the authoritarian populist ideologies there lie the real material possibilities for consensual authoritarianism within the British class structure.

NOTES AND REFERENCES

1 See footnotes 48 and 64 below.
2 S. Hall, *Drifting into a Law and Order Society* (1980).
3 P. Gordon, 'Community Policing: Towards the Local Police State' in *Law, Order and the Authoritarian State*, ed. P. Scraton (1987).
4 For fuller discussion, see the various contributions to Scraton, op. cit., n. 3, and P. Hillyard and J. Percy-Smith, *The Coercive State* (1988).
5 Geoffrey Dear, Chief Constable of the West Midlands Police (see Scraton, op. cit., n. 3, p. 49).
6 Compare P. Gilroy and J. Sim, 'Law, Order and the State of the Left' (1985) 25 *Capital and Class* 15; also in Scraton, op. cit., n. 3.
7 We have in mind here explicit economic policies to restructure the economy in relation to the newspaper industry (Eddie Shah and the *Stockport Messenger* dispute of 1983-4, Rupert Murdoch and News International in 1986-7) and the mining industry (the miners' strike in 1984-5) which led to overt stances being taken by the police in favour of minorities, sometimes individuals, wishing to return to work, together with the more general notions of normal and abnormal implicit in the identification of inner city areas as being populated by those who are 'different from the rest of society' (Scraton, op. cit., n. 3, pp. 56 and 100), and the marginalization of travellers (the Peace Convoys in 1985-6), peace and anti-apartheid campaigners, and students who by dress and conduct are cast 'beyond the pale'. Compare P. Scraton, 'Unreasonable Force: Policing, Punishment and Marginalization' in Scraton, op. cit., n. 3; N. Davies, 'Inquest on a Rural Riot' *Observer*, 9 June 1985.
8 Hillyard and Percy-Smith, op. cit., n. 3, pp. 295-9.

9 C. Ponting, *The Right to Know: The Inside Story of the Belgrano Affair* (1985).

10 *Attorney-General* v. *Guardian, Times and Observer* [1987] 1 WLR 1250. It appears from newspaper reports that the recent final decision of the House of Lords to accept the newspapers' case was not founded on the belief that the public interest demands publication so much as on the view that since the information concerned is in the public domain anyway, further barring would be ineffectual. For analysis, see G. Robertson, *Guardian*, 14 October 1988.

11 Recent proposals in June 1988 by the Home Secretary, Douglas Hurd MP, to amend the Official Secrets Act (see *The Times*, 30 June 1988) indicate the extent of authoritarian control desired by the Thatcher Government. This legal onslaught is matched by the continuous attempts to undermine the BBC across a range of issues, including the reporting of the air raid on Libya by the United States of America and the showing of programmes such as 'Real Lives' and 'Secret Society'.

12 Amnesty International, *United Kingdom: Alleged Forced Admission During Incommunicado Detention* (1988).

13 Statement by Sir Patrick Mayhew MP, Solicitor General, *H.C. Debs.*, (25 January 1988) and in *Guardian*, 26 January 1988; J. Stalker, *Stalker* (1987).

14 C. Mullin, *Error of Judgement* (1987); *Guardian*, 29 January 1988; *Observer*, 31 January 1988.

15 On the Waldorf shooting, see M. Benn and K. Worpole, *Death in the City* (1986) 55-61.

16 Criminal Justice Act 1988 s. 118; M. Zander, 'Surprising New Moves to Restrict Trial by Jury' *Guardian*, 5 August 1988; see in general Hillyard and Percy-Smith, op. cit., n. 4, pp. 155-60.

17 S. Box, *Recession, Crime and Punishment* (1987).

18 Hillyard and Percy-Smith, op. cit., n. 4, pp. 299-312; J. Sim, 'Working for the Clampdown' in Scraton, op. cit., n. 3.

19 Sim, op. cit., n. 18. In Scotland, the SAS have been used at Edinburgh and Peterhead prisons, and 'élite' riot squads trained to SAS standards have been established. This has occurred on the basis of a conspiracy theory that 'drugs barons' are seeking to destroy Peterhead prison (see *The Scotsman*, 8-11 August 1988). For a more realistic account, see P. Scraton, J. Sim, and P. Skidmore, 'Through the Barricades: Prisoner Protest and Penal Policy in Scotland' (1988) 15 *J. of Law and Society* 247.

20 Such as 'reasonable suspicion' and 'serious arrestable offence'. For discussion, see H. Bevan and K. Lidstone, *A Guide to the Police and Criminal Evidence Act* (1985); for a useful summary, see Hillyard and Percy-Smith, op. cit., n. 4; see L. Bridges and T. Bunyan, 'Britain's New Urban Policing Strategy – The Police and Criminal Evidence Bill in Context' (1983) 10 *J. of Law and Society* 85 for what proved a good prognosis of the likely effects of the legal categories.

21 See above, n. 12.

22 R. Card, *Public Order: The New Law* (1987) ch. 4. See Hillyard and Percy-Smith, op. cit., n. 4, pp. 259-62 for useful summary.

23 C. Scorer et al., *The New Prevention of Terrorism Act: The Case for Repeal* (1985).

24 *Guardian*, 20-21 October 1988. In one dramatic week the Government removed the right of silence, sacked workers at the Government Communications Headquarters (GCHQ) for belonging to a trade union, and banned television interviews with members of legal political organizations such as Sinn Fein. While this article's focus is upon criminal justice, it would be quite wrong to decontextualize the criminal justice issue from the broader developments implicit in these other moves.

25 Hall, op. cit., n. 2. See also S. Hall et al., *Policing the Crisis* (1978).

26 C. Ackroyd et al., *The Technology of Political Control* (1977).

27 N. Poulantzas, *State, Power and Socialism* (1978). Poulantzas's use of the concept 'authoritarian statism' proved influential for Hall's later work on 'authoritarian populism'. We discuss this in the fourth section below.

28 M. Kettle, 'The National Reporting Centre and the 1984 Miners' Strike' in *Policing the Miners' Strike*, eds. B. Fine and R. Millar (1985).

29 C. Lloyd, 'A National Riot Police: Britain's Third Force?' in Fine and Millar, op. cit., n. 28. As the recent substantial *ex gratia* payment by the Metropolitan Police to the family of Blair

Peach reminds us, nine years after his death at the hands of the police during an anti-fascist demonstration in Southall in 1979 (*Guardian*, 8 July 1988). The police continue to maintain their lack of responsibility despite the payment, and no police officer has ever been charged.

30 D. Humphrey, *Police Power and Black People* (1972); M. Cain, *Society and the Policeman's Role* (1973); Institute of Race Relations, *Police Against Black People* (1978); A. Sivanandan, *A Different Hunger* (1982).

31 P. Carlen, *Magistrates' Justice* (1976); A. Bottoms and J. McLean, *Defendants in the Penal Process* (1976); D. McBarnet, *Conviction: Law, the State and the Construction of Justice* (1981) ch. 7.

32 R. Kee, *Trial and Error: The Maguires, the Guildford Pub Bombings and British Justice* (1986); C. Mullin, op. cit., n. 14. For a good review of these and other works in the area, see J. Sim, (1987) 15 *Int. J. Sociology of Law* 225.

33 M. Fitzgerald, *Prisoners in Revolt* (1977); J. Thomas and M. Pooley, *The Exploding Prison* (1980).

34 Sim, op. cit., n. 18; Hillyard and Percy-Smith, op. cit., n. 4, pp. 306-12. It is worth noting that the single really progressive development in recent decades, the Special Unit at Barlinnie prison, was begun in the early 1970s under the Conservative Government, and then undermined by the ensuing Labour Government (see J. Boyle, *The Pain of Confinement* (1984)).

35 R. Storch, 'The Plague of Blue Locusts' (1975) *Int. J. of Social History* 83.

36 See above n. 12.

37 This discussion does not include one of the most important continuities between past and present, the role of the British state in Northern Ireland. The main plank of the state's criminalization strategy remains the Diplock Courts (established in the mid-1970s) and allegations of a shoot-to-kill policy occurred in the 1970s also: see K. Boyle, T. Hadden, and P. Hillyard, *Ten Years on in Northern Ireland* (1980) 27-9. For the interconnection between colony and mainland, see P. Hillyard, 'The Normalization of Special Powers: From Northern Ireland to Britain' in Scraton, op. cit., n. 3. And for an important historical perspective, see M. Brogden, 'An Act to Colonize the Internal Lands of the Island: Empire and the Origins of the Professional Police' (1987) 15 *Int. J. Sociology of Law* 179.

38 P. Gordon, 'Community Policing: Towards the Local Police State?' in Scraton, op. cit., n. 3.

39 P. Gilroy and J. Sim, op. cit., n. 6.

40 T. Critchley, *A History of Police in England and Wales* (2nd ed. 1978); J. Benyon and C. Bourne, *The Police: Powers, Procedures and Proprieties* (1986) ch. 1; I. Taylor, *Law and Order: Arguments for Socialism* (1981).

41 Scraton, op. cit., n. 3, pp. 74-9.

42 A. Silver, 'The Demand for Order in Civil Society' in *The Police: Six Sociological Essays*, ed. D. Bordua (1968).

43 J. Foster, *Class Struggle and the Industrial Revolution* (1974). For critical comment, see G. Stedman Jones, 'Class Struggle and the Industrial Revolution' (1975) 90 *New Left Rev.* 35.

44 J. Foster, op. cit., n. 43, pp. 237-8.

45 id.

46 M. Cain, op. cit., n. 30. See also D. Garland, *Punishment and Welfare: A History of Penal Strategies* (1985) 37-40.

47 R. Storch, 'The Police as Domestic Missionary' (1976) 9 *J. of Social History* 481. For a thorough analysis of the divisions in the working class emerging around the issues of crime and disrespectability in a Welsh town, see D. Jones, *Crime, Protest, Community and Police in Nineteenth-Century Britain* (1982) ch. 4.

48 The exception being P. Cohen, 'Policing the Working Class City' in B. Fine et al., *Capitalism and the Rule of Law* (1979). For a recent analysis of divisions within the working class which returns to the concept of a labour aristocracy, see M. Spence, 'Imperialism and Decline: Britain in the 1980s' (1985) 25 *Capital and Class* 128. The classical reference is to V. Lenin, *Imperialism: The Highest Stage of Capitalism* (1917) especially the Preface to the French and German editions (1920). In arguing for the significance of this distinction, we are not

claiming that those sections of the class which constitute the labour aristocracy always remain the same – plainly that would be absurd in an economic world that has changed dramatically over time. We assert the continued importance of relatively privileged layers within the working class who more easily identify their interests with capitalism and imperialism than the badly paid, the unemployed, those who constitute a 'reserve army of labour'. Nor do we deny the development of new sections of the workforce in the twentieth century such as the 'new middle class' emerging out of the post-war Welfare State. We see these developments, however, as contributing to the strengthening of the divisions first created in the mid-nineteenth century. Compare E. Hobsbawm, *Labouring Men* (1964) 300-3; R. Gray, *The Labour Aristocracy in Victorian Edinburgh* (1976) ch. 10, and *The Aristocracy of Labour in Nineteenth Century Britain* (1983) ch. 8.

49 It was the poorest sections of the class, in particular the youth and the Irish, who opposed the police. Weinberger notes that police assaults were carried out by all classes of labourers but that the semi-skilled were over-represented. She also notes the divisions between the more and less respectable trades, the latter uniting with casual labour in disrespectability and police opposition: B. Weinberger, 'The Police and the Public in Mid Nineteenth Century Warwickshire' in *Policing and Punishment in Nineteenth Century Britain*, ed. V. Bailey (1981) (quotations from pp. 65 and 67). See also the important essay by J. Davis, 'The London Garotting Panic of 1862: A Moral Panic and the Creation of a Criminal Class in Mid Victorian England' in *Crime and the Law in Western Societies: Historical Essays*, ed. V. Gattrell et al. (1980).

50 'The social distinction which had been forged in the mid-Victorian years between the "dangerous" and the "respectable" classes was not thawed by the economic and social crisis of the 1880s.' (See 'The Metropolitan Police, the Home Office and the Threat of Outcast London' in Bailey, op. cit., n. 49, pp. 94-5.)

51 P. Cohen, op. cit., n. 48.

52 R. Geary, *Policing Industrial Disputes 1893-1985* (1985) chs. 3-5.

53 B. Weinberger, 'Police Perceptions of Labour in the Inter-War Period: The Case of the Unemployed and of Miners on Strike' in *Labour, Law and Crime*, eds. F. Snyder and D. Hay (1986) 174.

54 D. Howell, ' "Where's Ramsay MacKinnock?": Labour Leadership and the Miners' in *Digging Deeper: Issues in the Miners' Strike*, ed. H. Benyon (1985).

55 J. Sim, P. Scraton, and P. Gordon, 'Introduction: Crime, the State and Critical Analysis' in Scraton, op. cit., n. 3, pp. 50-9; Gilroy and Sim, op. cit., n. 6.

56 Sim, Scraton, and Gordon in Scraton, op. cit., n. 3, p. 61.

57 id., p. 63.

58 B. Jessop et al., 'Authoritarian Populism, Two Nations and Thatcherism' (1984) 147 *New Left Rev.* 32; S. Hall, 'Authoritarian Populism: A Reply to Jessop et al.' (1985) 152 *New Left Rev.* 115.

59 Hall, op. cit., n. 58, p. 118.

60 id., pp. 117-18.

61 id., p. 119, emphasis added.

62 Jessop et al., op. cit., n. 58, p. 37.

63 id., p. 42. See also p. 49.

64 We refer here to the view of Jessop et al. that 'Thatcherism involves a passive revolution rather than mass mobilization' (op. cit., n. 58, p. 43), a conception that they contrast with the activism that would be present if the Conservatives had 'organize[d] the working class politically'. This seems to us a rather 'politicist' view of the relationship between politics and society. Thatcherism can rely to an extent on a support that may not be politically organized in its favour but which perceives interest in common with its projects. This may be characterized as 'more or less active or passive' – the terms are not wholly satisfactory. Compare Spence, op. cit., n. 48, for whom a modern labour aristocracy has 'the most immediate material interests in upholding existing industrial priorities, financial priorities, and a continuing commitment to the world imperialist system' (p. 134). The recognition of an identity of economic interests transforms the way in which one understands the character of

political organization and its articulation with social forces.

65 Compare Jessop et al., op. cit., n. 58, p. 52: 'There is an authoritarian element in the Thatcherite programme. But it is much better interpreted in terms of the problems of economic and political *crisis-management*, than in terms of a generalized authoritarian populism.'

66 Hall et al., op. cit., n. 25. Hall summarizes his early position in his reply to Jessop et al., op. cit., n. 58, p. 116.

67 id. Described by Hall as a 'pragmatic and creeping authoritarianism': see Jessop et al., op. cit., n. 58, p. 35.

68 Jessop et al., op. cit., n. 58, p. 40.

69 id., p. 50.

Name Index